Re-imagine!

Re-imagine!

Tom Peters

"Uncertainty is the only thing to be sure of."
—Anthony Muh, Citigroup, head of investment in Asia

"If you don't like change, you're going to like irrelevance even less."
—General Eric Shinseki, Chief of Staff, U.S. Army (Secretary of Veteran Affairs as of 2009)

LONDON, NEW YORK, MUNICH, MELBOURNE, AND DELHI

For Susan

Editor **Michael Slind**
Designer **Jason Godfrey at Godfrey Design**

Project Editor **Laura Palosuo**
Project Designer **Katherine Raj**
Managing Editor **Adèle Hayward**
Managing Art Editor **Kat Mead**
Production Editor **Ben Marcus**
Production Controller **Alexandra Mew**
Creative Technical Support **Sonia Charbonnier**
Publisher **Stephanie Jackson**
Art Director **Peter Luff**

First published in Great Britain in 2003
by Dorling Kindersley Limited,
80 Strand, London WC2R 0RL

This edition published in Great Britain in 2009

A Penguin Company 2 4 6 8 10 9 7 5 3 1

A CIP catalog record for this book is available from the British Library.

ISBN: 978-1-4053-4509-5

Printed and bound in Great Britain by Clays Ltd, St Ives plc

See our complete catalogue at
www.dk.com

Reader's Guide ...

1. ORGANIZATION OF THE BOOK ... The book is divided into what we call Main Text and Footnotes. The Main Text is the logical nub of our argument in each chapter. The Footnotes provide examples and pointed observations that flesh out the Main Text. Dive into them as you wish. (Hint: I like the Footnotes better than the Main Text ... but, then, I'm a non-linear guy.)

2. ICONS ... You'll notice icons beside many of the Footnotes. See right for a brief guide to these icons.

3. BEYOND THIS TEXT ... The times are crazy. And with this book we've tried to provoke re-imaginings. We've pushed as hard as we can, and then some. The book is definitely not the last word, and we hope you'll be engaged enough, perhaps enraged enough, to react. To ... JOIN IN A DIALOGUE.

Our device:

tompeters.com

Please get in touch and stay in touch! Please rant. (Or rave.) Please share your victories and defeats. In short, we are going to discuss—no holds barred—every damn topic in this book.

4. FOR THE CURIOUS ...
Also at tompeters.com you'll find detailed source notes (tompeters.com/reimagine/notes) on the stories and data in this book. And at the site's Cool Friends (tompeters.com/coolfriends) board you'll encounter in-depth interviews with many of the people I quote in the book. To keep abreast of my latest ramblings and re-imaginings, you can review or download the PowerPoint slides I post (tompeters.com/slides) immediately following each of the 80 or so speeches I give every year.

Exclamation mark: Generally a brief story that supports and often adds to a point in the Main Text. Other times it's a stand alone example of the chapter argument.

Quotation marks: A cool quote from someone in the world of business—or elsewhere!

Book: Buy the book! Read it! It has influenced me; it might influence you.

Left-pointing bracket: Reminder of a point previously discussed.

Right-pointing bracket: Preview of a point to be discussed later at more length

Brackets pointing both ways: We've placed this icon at the top of short summaries. The text beside it is a recap of what has gone on earlier; it also serves as a departure point for what lies ahead.

Contents

FOREWORD 2009

Does any of what follows, in a book published in 2003, make sense if, or as, the world wrestles with financial and economic madness and malfeasance? That's the obvious, and only, way to start a foreword in early 2009.

The answer, of course, is "Yes"—and "no."

Re-imagine! describes a brave new intertwined world of commerce, organizational formats, and career strategies in which many or even most of the old rules have been broken, then shredded. While the economic scene is dramatically altered in 2009, and will surely be altered more in 2010 and perhaps beyond, the old rules that *were* broken that animated *Re-imagine!* in the first place are *still* broken; much of the work to be done in 2009, beyond dealing with day-to-day survival issues, comes from the worklist we laid out in 2003—there is far more unfinished than finished business when it comes to readiness for unrelenting, global, speed-of-light, twenty-first-century marketplace competition.

Boundaries *are* disappearing—and, altered circumstances or not, neo-protectionism or not, we live in a global village; mindblowing new technologies are announced, it seems, by the day, from Apple's latest to the consequences of fullblown genetic mapping; and muscular new members of the Vital Economy Club only accelerate the emergence of a new reality. Most any task can be done anywhere. Alliances of every imaginable flavor are created, do their thing, and evaporate. Radical tools such as "crowdsourcing" change dynamics of work and human communication that are thousands of years old—and such tools continue, regardless of macro-economic circumstances, to arrive on the scene and grow like Topsy with startling regularity. And hence the race to add value to keep one's job, or to keep lots of jobs at home by re-imagining an entire economy (I leave for Korea a week after writing this to talk about such large-scale renovation), or to enable a going concern, even a small one, continues to intensify.

Hierarchies are dying, at least in larger firms; and the troubled economic situation accelerates that—lard in the superstructure is first on the chopping block, and not just at GM and Citi. We do most of our work via project teams that involve members from hither, thither and yon; and that exist for a year—or just a week. Order shouting is out. These disparate team members from disparate places, tasked to concoct new stuff, based on combining ideas of every description, can only be motivated by persuasion and passion and the promise of personal growth, not the rattling of the hierarchical saber. "Who's in charge" varies by the day; Cisco Systems, the communication equipment giant, weathering the current storm by re-inventing itself once again, calls it an organization based on "emergent leadership"—the de facto leader of a critical team can emerge electronically in a literal flash from three levels down in the organization, by dint of her stellar electronic contributions made from a cramped cubicle or her bedroom at home at 3 a.m.

Those of us in the high wage nations, economic uncertainty, even chaos, notwithstanding, will only survive by scrambling way up the same "value-added" ladder described in the 2003 edition of this book—and by being prepared, also as specified in 2003, for more or less constant re-invention. In fact, our new powerhouse competitors, China for one, are already beginning their own trek up that ladder—and are hardly content, in China's case, to remain "the world's workshop."

Indeed, the rise of the likes of China and India and Brazil proceeds apace—and said pace, even with current hiccups, or the flu, is nothing short of breathtaking (look at Shanghai's skyline!)—and will be more so if your time horizon moves out to, say, 15 years, a near certainty, professionally, for readers under 40 or so. "Yesterday is over" is the ultimate truism, but at the moment more true, if possible, than at any time in the last 100 years.

There is a finance tsunami.
There is a generic economics tsunami.
There is a technology tsunami, just gathering a head of steam.
There is a geo-political tsunami, just gathering a head of steam.
There is a work-structuring tsunami.
There is an organization effectiveness tsunami.
There is a careers tsunami.

And they play out differently and in different combinations every day.

So does this brief recitation of forces at work now, most of which were at work then, in 2003, suggest that "I wouldn't change a word"?

Of course not.
I'd change a lot.
But probably in a direction you'd not expect.

Oddly, I'd look back, not forward, mostly, if I made major modifications. As on Wall Street, I'd pay attention, lots more attention, to the bedrock.
In fact, I beat myself up daily for not having done so before.
(Frankly, I'm irritated with anyone who isn't beating themselves up.)
Oddly on yet another dimension, my re-assessment began a year or so before the fissures in the financial system's understructure began to be visible.
I can in fact even put an exact date on the start of my re-assessment.

April 14, 2006.

There were some very modest signs of Winter reluctantly giving way to Spring at home in Vermont. But my view that April 14th was 100 percent ice and snow as Air Siberia approached Novosibirsk, Siberia.

I was in Novosibirsk to lead a one-day seminar. I had been invited as even this outpost was beginning to integrate into the global economy, and local leaders were keen to hear new views of enterprise management in a universally competitive environment. Others may have been asked before me, but I was the first of my sort to make the journey to what was the most forbidden part of the world when I was a boy.

I thought, if the landscape didn't send a loud enough signal, "This is different, and requires a different approach." Not condescending—this city of scientists could turn out more IQ points in a room than any, short of Cambridge, MA or Palo Alto, CA. Yet as I pondered my approach, my mind wandered back to 1982 and *In Search of Excellence*, and the parallels to the changing scenery, economic and intellectual, from which the book emerged.

"Search," as my pals and I call it, was squarely aimed at a specific pair of challenges—a formidable U.S. competitor for the first time since the end of World War II, namely Japan; and a whopper of a recession that brought double-digit unemployment, soaring inflation and sky-high interest rates to my country. But the book that was born, oddly and in many ways, was a "back to the future" tome.

From the late sixties, "strategy" and "the quantification of positively everything" were the king and crown prince at the B-schools, in the consultancies (such as my employer, prestigious McKinsey & Co.), and in the corporations themselves. This was pre-Jack Welch and his merciless focus on operational excellence at GE; the company's Giant Headquarters Strategy Corps of detached thinkers and modelers, circa 1975, was home to the best and the brightest—their "brilliant" visions were thought to be enough to keep GE on top of its game.

"Get the strategy right, and the rest will take care of itself." In effect, that was the mantra—and the quantification of positively everything was the animating force; if it couldn't be reduced to and expressed in numbers, it wasn't worthy of consideration.

(Sound familiar, circa 2008–2009? More later.)

McKinsey's new boss, Ron Daniel, was troubled as he assessed the Firm's work product. He fretted about the almost total absence of emphasis on implementation, and asked me, a fresh-caught Stanford Ph.D. who'd worked on organizational effectiveness for the past five years, to "take a look around"—I was shortly joined by my colleague Bob Waterman.

Fast forward a few months, and following a series of visits I made in the U.S. and Europe looking for those new ideas about the practice of management, and you'll find Bob and me on a road trip—black-suited McKinsey consultants to the core, quantitative credentials to die for (in my last normal assignment, I'd been working on oil-discovery simulation models, doing the Fortran programming myself). We left our San Francisco office one Spring morning in 1978 and journeyed a short 30 miles "down the Peninsula," to Palo Alto. We met there with Hewlett-Packard president John Young.

The "Holy Smokes" came fast, before we officially started for that matter. The president of a billion dollar or so company, characterized by its total commitment to sustaining innovativeness, shared a half-wall cubicle, about 8 feet by 8 feet, or 9 by 9, with his secretary. It was a long, long way, figuratively as well as literally, from the 15-

foot (!) high doors at the entrance to the secretary's office guarding the CEO's office one floor up from us in the San Francisco tower where we worked for McKinsey. Said doors, fifty floors up, belonged to the Big Boss of ... the Bank of America.[1]

As the interview subsequently unspooled, John introduced Bob and me to a four-letter term that remains to this day the centerpiece of my work and philosophy.

Namely: MBWA.
Managing By Wandering Around.

It means what it sounds like—getting out and about, literally wandering around. But I've come to appreciate how much more it means than that, especially and ironically, given new communication tools, in 2009. MBWA is in its largest meaning a metaphor about being in touch and staying in touch with reality. Being in touch with the car you make—not just the numbers that surround making it.[2] Being in touch with the people who do the work where the rubber meets the road.[3] Being in intimate touch with "the little things" ("little," my a**) that make a product better or get in the way of fast approvals of this or that—the "real stuff" that determines success or failure, a job done or just talked about, excellence or mediocrity.

I thought a lot about MBWA as the sub-prime crisis escalated into global economic implosion, fully 30 years after the research for *In Search of Excellence* began. There's a lot to the current sorry story, to be sure, but I remembered with laserlike clarity a long ago comment from a seminar participant, Chairman of a mid-sized regional bank:

"Tom, let me tell you the definition of a good lending officer. After church on Sunday, on the way home with his family, he takes a little detour to drive by the factory he just lent money to. Doesn't go in or any such thing, just drives by and takes a look."

"Just drives by"—needs to take a look. At the tidiness, the orderliness. To see if anyone's in, beavering away after hours. Just to sniff, really, to "blink," in the language

---

[1] Some things never change, eh? B of A, on the dole, seeking more dole, implodes—at the same time in early 2009 HP announces far better than expected quarterly earnings.

[2] The founder-CEO of a giant retailer told me about sitting next to Henry Ford at a White House dinner 20-odd years ago. He was, he said, "intimidated" by Ford's recounting tale after tale of visits with kings and presidents and prime ministers. He laughed as he said, "I woke up with a start in the middle of the night and thought, 'I sat next to Henry Ford for three hours, and he never once mentioned cars.'" To my mind, alas, decades later, that goes a long way toward explaining why the Ford I rented in New Zealand in late February 2009 was so obviously inferior to the Kia I rented for two weeks earlier in the month.

[3] I read another MBWA story recently, about U.S. Army General David Petraeus, as he attempted to clean up the mess in Iraq. On the wall of his office in the so-called "Green Zone" was a hand-done poster on which he'd lettered the cornerstones of his philosophy. At the top of the very short list was, in exceptionally large letters, "WALK." Get out of the compound, get out of the vehicle, get close to the neighborhoods you are trying to stabilize. "WALK!" It has become the foundation and metaphor for a surprisingly successful turn-around in this insanely difficult situation.

of Malcolm Gladwell. To, yes, tacitly stay in touch.

So MBWA is the opposite of abstractions and "models," the opposite of "by the numbers" management, the opposite of "strategy as the alpha *and* the omega." (And numbers can indeed lie, maybe even most of the time, as we learned from Enron and Worldcom and are in the seemingly endless process of relearning, painfully, from virtually all of our big banks and, of course, dear old Bernie Madoff.)

Time passed, and with a hundred or more interviews and a hundred or more presentations to test our findings under our belts, Bob and I and Harper & Row birthed *In Search of Excellence* in 1982. Yup, back to the future. Stuff your grandfather the shopkeeper knew:

> *People matter most.*
> *Give people ample room to experiment and encourage them to grow.*
> *Honor the front-line worker over the MBA. (Whoops, Bob and I were both Stanford MBAs.)*
> *Listen until your ears turn red to your customers—and love 'em up day in and day out, from pre-dawn to the black of the night.*
> *Try stuff in a flash, instead of talking and talking and talking it to death.*
> *Don't let screw-ups ruffle you, just try again—and skip the soul-sapping, time-devouring blame game.*
> *Keep it simple, fight for simple—declare total war on your own bureaucracy, and put your best general in charge.*
> *Lay out your guiding values, like Johnson & Johnson's fabled "Credo," values that'll make your employees and children and neighbors proud—and stick to them.*
> *Walk. Walk the talk. Stay in touch. Practice MBWA Monday through the Sunday "drive by."*
> *And aim for Excellence in everything you do.*[4]

Now, as I prepared for my day-in-Siberia, all the above, except the sub-prime bits that were 18 months in the offing, came back with a rush. Was I going to give my standard, hard-hitting, take-no-prisoners speech about embracing the speed-of-light global village which now included Novosibirsk? Or was I going "back to the future"?

I did both. But I leaned toward the latter. Jeff Skilling (former Enron CEO) was a colleague for a while in my McKinsey days—and as I recall he reported to jail to begin serving a, gulp, 25-year sentence, at about the time I landed in Siberia. Jeff was bright as hell and then some, but got totally caught up in the numbers game and obviously went to any lengths to make the numbers dance to his tune. And the "any lengths" made a Godawful mess of maybe millions of lives—e.g., as million-dollar pension nest eggs, earned with 30 years' work, literally evaporated to absolute zero. He epitomized the extreme end of the scale of those who lived by the numbers, for the numbers, and of the numbers—and wouldn't have known MBWA if he/they tripped over it. He and his pals didn't see the real people, one-at-a-time, screwed by Enron's playing with the California electricity market. Jeff, in short, was the enemy and villain to all that Bob Waterman and I espoused.[5]

---

[4] Yup, it all could have been written 200 or 500 years earlier. I don't deny it.

With all this churning through my mind, I labored over the approach to my Siberian seminar. To set the tone, I resorted uncharacteristically to abstract language. But I wanted to lay down the gauntlet about the bedrock of organizational life and purpose and responsibility—and set the hurdle high. Here's what the keyboard produced, almost without my intervention. I've used it probably 100 times since April 2006:

Enterprise at its best is ... an emotional, vital, innovative, joyful, creative, entrepreneurial endeavor that elicits maximum concerted human potential in pursuit of Excellence and the wholehearted provision of service to others.

I throw today and threw in Siberia that gauntlet down and, while admitting that this state is hardly the norm, asked-ask:

What could possibly be the point of organized human endeavors if not something more or less like this?[6]

Perhaps surprisingly, most in my seminars, in Amsterdam or Abu Dhabi, eventually admit, many with delight, that this *is*, almost obviously, the ultimate aspiration of any organized activity. From this heavenly aspiration and unstinting endorsement of human growth, excellence and service, I move/moved to the achievement thereof, offering advice consistent with the logic and tools from the first edition to this book—but never, and this is the key, and the centerpiece of my work in 2009, allowing us (me, participants) to stray for a moment from the deeper purpose of "OHB" (organized human behavior).[7]

I could almost, with a straight face, call the Siberian experience an "epiphany."

---

[5]Mea culpa: Bob and I could have written more about integrity and character than we did. My lame excuse is that our parents did a pretty good job, and we took it for granted. My mea culpa is that we should have known better and sounded off—it might not have helped, but it wouldn't have hurt. B-schools' deafening silence on this issue, until long after the cat had escaped the bag, is shameful at the very least—a criminal act in its own way.

[6]Fact is, we spend the majority of our adult waking hours as members of organizations. Hence, if said organizations shortchange us on growth opportunities (the majority do in fact shortchange their members) then we are in deep trouble—as individuals and as a nation. You might well say that National Excellence is a direct product of the collective growth opportunities offered by organizations to their workforce. This is especially true in a global economy where national growth is measured in terms of collective adult individual growth.

[7]My friend and colleague Jim Collins coined the term "BHAG"—Big Hairy Audacious Goal. I love it! One of my clients was proud of his BHAG, about transforming an industry; it was indeed a stretch, and a big and bold one. But as we talked through "the Siberia message" about higher organization purpose, he literally scuttled the old BHAG. He in fact kept the industry goal intact, but the BHAG now focused on the "total commitment to extreme human growth" within his firm that would necessarily precede marketplace success.

Confronted by the strangest environment I've ever encountered, I revived my rusting clarion call for Excellence, even took it up a notch or two or three from its 1982 incarnation—and insisted on nothing less than a Jeffersonian goal for any and all organizations and units within. And furthermore insisted that any lesser aspiration was almost shameful!

(Okay, drop the "... almost" from the prior sentence. Make it "... was shameful.")

But there was another epiphany of sorts to come.

Oddly, it was the Australian Institute of Management, in September 2007, which decided to present the first major tribute to the life's work of the late and great Peter Drucker—with the likes of Doris Drucker, 90-odd and easily as spry as someone 25 years younger, in attendance. I was asked to keynote an event featuring many of the luminaries in the field of management studies.

I was honored. And nonplussed.

As I carefully re-read Drucker's work, I was struck anew, in fact for the first time, by his deeply held beliefs about the power of superior management to transform all of society for the better. Hence once again I was wont to dig more deeply than my norm. The conclusion, stealing in part from, not Drucker, but Robert Greenleaf, creator of the Servant Leader "movement," was:

> **"Organizations exist to serve. Period.**
> **"Leaders live to serve. Period."**

And once more, as in Siberia and to my surprise, that deep digging and Mr. Greenleaf, led me to observe my keyboard, almost without my assistance, arguing that organizations, *all* organizations, should be ...:

"Passionate servant leaders, determined to create a legacy of earthshaking transformation in their domain (a 600 square-foot retail space, a four-person training department, an urban school, a rural school, a city, a nation), create/must <u>necessarily</u> create organizations which are no less than <u>Cathedrals</u> in which the Full and Awesome Power of the Imagination and Spirit and Native Entrepreneurial Flair[8] of diverse individuals[9] is unleashed in passionate pursuit of jointly perceived Soaring Purpose (= win a Nobel peace prize like Yunus, or at least do something worthy of bragging about 25 years from now to your grandkids) and Personal and Community and Client Service Excellence."

I'll admit that it's a prize-grabber when it comes to the run-on-sentence category, but I am not willing to edit it—tested as it is now in over 100 presentations from Baltimore to Bucharest to Bologna. And, once again, I argue to my seminar participants, be they Canadian grocers or corporate security chiefs or Silicon Valley techies: *"If not this, what?"*

---

[8] We are all entrepreneurs—Muhammad Yunus, father of micro-lending and 2006 Nobel peace prize winner.

[9] 100% Creative Talent—from checkout to lab, from Apple to Wegmans, the regional grocer judged to be America's '#1 Place to Work' in 2004, to Jane's one-person accountancy in Invercargill, NZ.

In fact, as time passes I find myself less and less taken aback for arguing "no less than Cathedrals in which the Full and Awesome Power of the Imagination and Spirit and Native Entrepreneurial Flair of diverse individuals." The idea in my mind is not in the least religious, despite my use of the word "cathedral."

The idea is that the first order of business is developing people—who will in turn go all out for our customers. Frankly, I'm doing no more than stealing from Hal Rosenbluth and Dave Liniger. Hal took Rosenbluth International from local travel agency (Philadelphia) to global travel services giant, which he subsequently sold to American Express; his winning philosophy, based entirely on maximizing internal human development, was perfectly captured by his book *The Customer Comes Second*—put your people first, and you'll end up giving the best service possible to your clients. Dave has made miracles for decades at RE/MAX—and calls his firm "a life success company"; make your agents successful and they'll, in turn, go all hell bent for leather for their customers.

I also was inspired by one of what I call "the parable books," which usually leave me (very) cold. Against my better judgment I ended up forking over a few bucks at O'Hare for Matthew Kelly's *The Dream Manager*. The title bugs me too—too soft for an old engineer like me. But Mr Kelly captured me in a flash with a simple but profoundly important observation: *We all have dreams!*

The next step of Kelly's is insisting that if we devote ourselves, in an open and deliberate fashion, to helping people—e.g., the single mother trying to raise two kids on a receptionist salary—achieve their dreams—she'd die for a community college degree—we will turn them into inspired employees. Kelly summarizes:

"A company's purpose is to become the-best-version-of-itself. The question is: What is an employee's purpose? Most would say, 'to help the company achieve its purpose'— but they would be wrong. That is certainly part of the employee's role, but an employee's primary purpose is to become the-best-version-of-himself or -herself. ... When a company forgets that it exists to serve customers, it quickly goes out of business. Our employees are our first customers, and our most important customers."

(Re-read slowly, please).

So in a thoroughly revised edition of this book, there would be a long section, like the one that appeared at the start of *In Search of Excellence*, that dealt with the basics of the purpose of enterprise, and the duties and obligations of managers. The Great Recession of 2008–2XXX has, one hopes, taught us (taught me!) not to take the bedrock for granted. I didn't in 1982; I did, like so many others, in 2003.

In the October 2008 *Harvard Business Review*, Rakesh Khurana and Nitin Nohria offered us "It's Time to Make Management a True Profession." At one point the authors write, "Managers have lost legitimacy over the past decade in the face of a widespread institutional breakdown of trust and self-policing in business. To regain society's trust, we believe that business leaders must embrace a way of looking at their role that goes beyond their responsibility to the shareholder to include a civic and personal commitment to their duty as institutional custodians. In other words, it is time that management finally became a profession."

I agree—and even the ultra-reserved Peter Drucker would, I suspect, have smiled at that formulation.

One book I've read during these troubled times has influenced me far more than any other. It's by Vanguard Mutual Fund Group founder John Bogle. His extraordinary and lasting success as an investor has flowed from always attending to the bedrock of an enterprise he chooses to support. He recently penned *Enough: True Measures of Money, Business, and Life*. I will simply share a sample of his chapter titles:

"Too Much Cost, Not Enough Value" ... *"Too Much Speculation, Not Enough Investment"* ... *"Too Much Complexity, Not Enough Simplicity"* ... *"Too Much Counting, Not Enough Trust"* ... *"Too Much Business Conduct, Not Enough Professional Conduct"* ... *"Too Much Salesmanship, Not Enough Stewardship"* ... *"Too Much Focus on Things, Not Enough Focus on Commitment"* ... *"Too Many Twenty-First-Century Values, Not Enough Eighteenth-Century Values"* ... *"Too Much 'Success,' Not Enough Character."*

I can do no more than say "Amen."

So there's the story, in shorthand form, of my journey from 2003 to 2009. Except for one final thing that I've implied throughout this Foreword but not been explicit enough about to this point. In a major revision of *Re-imagine!* I would resurrect Excellence. Beginning in Siberia (14 April 2006, remember), I fell in love all over again with the idea and ideal of Excellence. To be quite honest, Excellence wore me out in the mid-eighties. (I'm not complaining!) But I have returned to the fold with a Vengeance.

Most of my presentations these days, and since mid-2006, are titled:
EXCELLENCE. ALWAYS.

And they invariably end with a slide that reads:
IF NOT EXCELLENCE, WHAT?
IF NOT EXCELLENCE NOW, WHEN?

In a recent exercise anticipating a presentation in New Zealand, my keyboard play resulted in a list that I called "The '19Es' of Excellence." Here they are:
Enthusiasm. (Be an irresistible force of nature!)
Energy. (Be fire! Light fires!)
Exuberance. (Vibrate—cause earthquakes!)
Execution. (Do it! Now! Get it done! Barriers are baloney! Excuses are for wimps! Accountability is gospel! Per American professional football coach Bill Parcells: "Blame nobody! Expect nothing! Do something!")
Empowerment. (Respect and appreciation! Always ask, "What do you think?" Then: Listen! Liberate! Celebrate! 100% innovators or bust!)
Edginess. (Perpetually dancing at the frontier, and a little or a lot beyond.)
Enraged. (Determined to challenge & change the status quo!)
Engaged. (Addicted to MBWA/Managing By Wandering Around. In touch. Always.)
Electronic. (Partners with the world 60/60/24/7 via electronic community building and entanglement of every sort. Crowdsourcing power rules!)
Encompassing. (Relentlessly pursue diverse opinions—the more diversity the merrier! Diversity per se "works"!)
Emotion. (The alpha. The omega. The essence of leadership. The essence of sales. The essence of marketing. The essence. Period. Acknowledge it.)
Empathy. (Connect, connect, connect with others' reality and aspirations! "Walk in

the other person's shoes"—until the soles have holes!)

Experience. (Life is theater! Make every activity-contact, inside the firm or out, memorable! Standard: "Insanely Great"/Steve Jobs; "Radically Thrilling"/BMW.)

Eliminate. (Keep it simple!)

Errorprone. (Ready! Fire! Aim! Try a lot of stuff and make a lot of booboos. Then try some more stuff and make some more booboos—all of it at the speed of light!)

Evenhanded. (Straight as an arrow! Fair to a fault! Honest as Abe!)

Expectations. (Michelangelo: "The greatest danger for most of us is not that our aim is too high and we miss it, but that it is too low and we reach it." Amen!)

Eudaimonia. (Pursue the highest of human moral purpose—the core of Aristotle's philosophy. Be of service. Always.)

Excellence. (The only standard! Never an exception! Start now! No excuses! If not Excellence, what? If not Excellence now, when?)

The story goes that Tom Watson, de facto founder of IBM, was once asked how long it takes to become excellent. He is said to have replied (three decades before the one-minute manager rode onto the scene), "a minute." Asked to explain, Watson apparently said, "It's simple. Make yourself a promise that starting right now you will not do anything in other than an excellent fashion."

As we deal with every variety of turbulence, the search for bedrock has never been so important. Make this your minute to declare for Excellence in all you do. I hope the following pages and ideas will help. And remember that it is the tough times, not the easy ones, which define a person professionally and personally. What better time for Excellence as a guiding star.

Tom Peters
Golden Bay
South Island
New Zealand

....

THE MISSING LINK/S:
GIVING GOOD TEA AND SMILES THAT SAVE MILLIONS OF LIVES

It's those damnable basics! Ignored by Citicorp and AIG—and me, in the glory days of 2003. In a fullscale rewrite, what follows are a couple of the full sections I'd add, starting with an essay that reminds us of the reality, seldom sexy, of "getting things done." It starts with tea-in-the-salons-of Paris. In 1776.

VICTORY AT TEA
The ragtag and victory-less Continental Army was retreating, George Washington's generalship notwithstanding. For the Americans, finding an ally was a life-or-death proposition. Short, fat, old Benjamin Franklin was our man in Paris. Short, fat and old though he may have been, he was a Charmer. (And if ever the word deserved a capital "C," this is the occasion.) He won the hearts and devotion of the ladies of high society with his Mastery of Tea & Flattery. In a July 4 story (2008), "In Paris, Taking the Salons By Storm: How the Canny Ben Franklin Talked the French into

a Crucial Alliance," *U.S. News & World Report* described it thusly: "The enduring image of Franklin in Paris tends to be that of a flirtatious old man, too busy visiting the city's fashionable salons to pursue affairs of state as rigorously as John Adams. When Adams joined Franklin in Paris in 1779, he was scandalized by the late hours and French lifestyle his colleague had adopted, says [Stacy Schiff, in *A Great Improvisation*]. Adams was clueless that it was through the dropped hints and seemingly offhand remarks at these salons that so much of French diplomacy was conducted. ... Like the Beatles arriving in America, [Franklin] aroused a fervor ... his face appeared on prints, teacups and chamber pots. ... The extraordinary popularity served Franklin's diplomatic purposes splendidly. Not even King Louis XVI could ignore the enthusiasm that had won over both the nobility and the bourgeoisie. ..."

Yes, it was indeed victory at tea—in a situation which did no less than change the world.

A NICE FACE AND A GRIN THAT WAS TO BECOME FAMOUS

In a Borders at Boston's Logan Airport, I picked up a copy of the magazine *Armchair General*, and happened across this quote from General Dwight David Eisenhower, which the article's author claimed was the Key to Ike's success in the D-Day landings: "Allied commands depend on mutual confidence and this confidence is gained, above all through the development of friendships." The author went on to note that this was a lifelong Eisenhower trait: "Perhaps his most outstanding ability [at West Point] was the ease with which he made friends and earned the trust of fellow cadets who came from widely varied backgrounds; it was this quality that would pay great dividends during his future coalition command."

The *Armchair General* article in turn led me to grab Michael Korda's *Ike: An American Hero*, from which I grabbed these gems, among others:

"infectious grin and great charm" ... "nice face" ... "grin that was to become so famous" ... "got along famously" ... "goodwill was spontaneous and easily recognizable" ... "good impression that Ike had made in six weeks" [newcomer junior general to supreme commander of D-Day] ... "least rank-conscious of generals" ... "Men were happy to serve under Ike, even British admirals and generals who might easily have raised objections. His sincerity ... and lack of ceremony made it difficult, even impossible, to refuse him, and enabled him to assemble very rapidly a team" ... "Ike was gregarious, seldom had anything bad to say about anyone, and, on the surface at least, was relaxed and good-natured."

"The Allies had generals with, perhaps, a sharper strategic and political vision than Ike. ... There were also generals who were more experienced at 'fighting a battle.' ... But there was nobody who had anything like Ike's record of leading an alliance—always the most difficult feat in warfare. ... What is more, Ike somehow inspired people: civilians and ordinary soldiers of both nations, even cynical political figures and the always troublesome French. Something about his big grin; his long-limbed, loose American way of walking (the Kansas farm boy grown to a man); his easy, familiar way of speaking to everybody from King George VI down to privates in both armies; his lack of pretension; his evident sincerity ... They were willing to be led by him. They were willing to have him command their sons and husbands in battle. They trusted him. They were willing to die for him."

These descriptions of Ike rang a loud bell: Just as Franklin was dismissed by many at the time as a frivolous sipper of tea with the ladies, Eisenhower was dismissed as a man who during war enjoyed his time on the golf course a bit too much.

STUDENT OF THE WHITE MAN'S GAME

Next, and finally (for now), consider these excerpts from John Carlin's *Playing the Enemy: Nelson Mandela and the Game That Made a Nation*. Newly elected President Nelson Mandela used the Rugby World Cup final match, in Johannesburg in 1995, to bring black and white together as never before. The book, though, delves into Mandela's Franklin-like and Eisenhower-like interpersonal skills:

"Prison was a political stage. ... He honed his natural ability for theater toward the achievement of his political ends, rehearsing his role among his jailers. ... taught himself their language ... set about understanding the Afrikaner mentality ..."

Mandela, on his jailers: "The key to it ... was respect, ordinary respect." ... During a visit to jail by Mandela's lawyer, George Bizos: "George, I'm sorry, I have not introduced you to my guard of honor [prison guards]." "Mandela identified each of the [eight] officers to Bizos by name. The guards were so stunned 'that [per Bizos] they actually behaved like a true guard of honor, each respectfully shaking my hand.'"

Major Van Sittert, brute prison commanding officer, heretofore immune to Mandela's charm: "Mandela thought hard ... probing for weaknesses. And ... he found one. Sittert was a rugby nut. So Mandela, who had no special interest in rugby [the quintessential white man's sport], set about zealously learning about the game in preparation for the major's monthly visit." Christo Brand, guard, on a subsequent meeting between Mandela and Warden Sittert: "Mandela was very polite, as usual. He greeted [Sittert] with a big smile and then immediately started talking rugby. ...Once the major got over his own amazement, he became quite animated, agreeing with Mandela on almost every point he made. 'You could see all those doubts of the major's just melting away.'"

Mandela meets surreptitiously with apartheid justice minister after decades in prison—and turns on the charm: "Mandela, a model host [in his prison hospital room, after surgery] smiling grandly, put [Justice Minister Kobie] Coetsee at his ease, and almost immediately, to their quietly contained surprise, prisoner and jailer found themselves chatting amiably. ... [It had mostly] to do with body language, with the impact Mandela's manner had on people he met. First there was his erect posture. Then there was the way he shook hands ... the effect was both regal and intimidating ... were it not for Mandela's warm gaze and his big, easy smile. ... Coetsee was surprised by Mandela's willingness to talk in Afrikaans, his knowledge of Afrikaans history." Coetsee: "He was a born leader. And he was affable. He was obviously well liked by the hospital staff and yet he was respected, even though they knew that he was a prisoner."

100 PERCENT TIMELESS

For me, it's more "back to the future." I used to collect stories like these (Franklin, Eisenhower, Mandela), lost the strand, and have begun to pick it up again. The challenges laid down in *Re-imagine!* circa 2003 were enormous—and the current economic terrain has made the task of re-imagining both far more difficult and far more urgent. The "secrets" of success in implementing great change, however, are—and this is inarguable as far as I'm concerned—timeless.

One-hundred percent timeless.

A thoroughly revised *Re-imagine!* could hardly be expanded to 1,000 pages, but I would, on the other hand, clearly and regardless of any editor's or publisher's pushback, add three or four chapters on the "timeless arts of getting [big] things done." The likes of "giving good tea" and "the power of affability and a great smile" would feature prominently.

As to the current times and challenges, Johns Hopkins psychiatrist Kay Redfield Jamison, in *Exuberance: The Passion for Life*, writes of Franklin Roosevelt, the American president who, along with Lincoln, faced the sternest challenges in our history. FDR's "secret," if you must call it that, was captured by two great admirers:

"To meet Roosevelt, said [Winston] Churchill, 'with all his buoyant sparkle, his iridescence,' was like 'opening a bottle of champagne.' Churchill, who knew both champagne and human nature, recognized ebullient leadership when he saw it."

The philosopher Isaiah Berlin on FDR: "'At a time of weakness and mounting despair in the democratic world,' Roosevelt stood out 'by his astonishing appetite for life and by his apparently complete freedom from fear of the future; as a man who welcomed the future eagerly as such, and conveyed the feeling that whatever the times might bring, all would be grist to his mill, nothing would be too formidable or crushing to be subdued.' He had unheard-of energy and gusto ... and was 'a spontaneous, optimistic, pleasure-loving ruler' with an 'unparalleled capacity for creating confidence.'"

Give good tea to the ladies of the Paris salons.
An infectious grin.
Affability.
Sincerity.
A smile that lights up a room—perhaps the whole world.
Empathy for thine enemies.
A great student of others' personalities.
Sparkle.
Iridescence.
Ebullience.
Gusto.

The tasks may be mighty, the consequences measured in the lives, or deaths, of millions, but the "tools" that determine victory or fiasco, that translate strategic ambition into success borne by and on the shoulders of the multitudes are intensely human and intimate.

And they belong in a book like this.

....

MISSING: JIM, LARRY & THE "REAL WORLD"

I'm pissed off. Pissed off at 30 years of neglect on my part. And while I can hardly atone for my absurd neglect "of almost everything" in a paragraph or two—at least I can acknowledge my sins. Someday...

Jim's Antennas • Jim's Bookkeeping • Jim's Building Maintenance • Jim's Carpet Cleaning
Jim's Car Cleaning • Jim's Computer Services • Jim's Dog Wash • Jim's Driving School • Jim's Fencing • Jim's Floors • Jim's Painting • Jim's Paving • Jim's Pergolas [gazebos] • Jim's Pool Care • Jim's Pressure Cleaning • Jim's Roofing • Jim's Security Doors • Jim's Trees • Jim's Window Cleaning • Jim's Windscreens

Australian Jim Penman was pursuing a degree in cross-cultural anthropology—and was more or less broke, as most Ph.D. students are. (Take it from me.) He had a need for bucks and a knack for mowing lawns, and started Jim's Mowing in 1984.

Segue a quarter century, and you find an award-winning (top franchise business, etc., etc.) operation—Jim's Group—with over 2,500 franchises in Australia, New Zealand, the UK, and Canada. Product: Doing ... stuff. (See the list above, a small sample.) Doing stuff that others, especially two-professional families, numbering in the tens of millions these days, don't have time to do. Yup, like washing—or even walking—the dog.

Want to learn more? Download, free, Jim Penman's book: *What Will They Franchise Next? The Story of Jim's Group.*

(There is indeed a lot more to the story—great people practices, etc. Do, indeed, download the book if you've any interest at all.)

Segue 10,000 miles or so to Seymour, CT. Meet Larry Janesky.

If you have a basement (I do) it's probably damp, moldy, hence unhealthy and mostly useless—the complete collection of World War II *Life* magazines my Dad bequeathed me died in my damp moldy basement—both damp *and* moldy.

The folks at Larry Janesky's Basement Systems Inc. franchises and dealers know just what to do. They can prove it. The business, started in 1990, performs basement rejuvenation miracles and now has revenue of over sixty million dollars a year—and was growing at 20 percent a year through 2007. Larry's got a book, too. *Dry Basement Science* has, I believe, sold about as many copies as *Re-imagine!*

In Search of Excellence, and my subsequent books, through *Re-imagine!*, didn't, to be brutally honest, bother much (if at all!) with the likes of Jim and Larry—though I'm delighted to say that many Jims and Larrys bought my books, and seemed to get more from them than the Big Company readers. That is, my books, and the books of virtually all of the so-called "gurus," focus on (1) big (2) publicly traded companies (3) doing "sexy" (Google-, Genentech-like) things.

Well, me-we blew it!
Big time!

The heart of any economy, including gross GDP numbers, are small-to-medium sized private companies doing decidedly "unsexy" things. And the pick of that huge litter are in turn the Jims and Larrys who have made the clearly unsexy decidedly sexy! And profitable! And employers of literally millions of us!

I, of course, knew about, but had mostly skipped past, Thomas Stanley's and William Danko's wildly popular *The Millionaire Next Door*. While I don't know Jim P's or Larry J's personal stories, Stanley and Danko tell us in general about the economy's real superstars, the millionaires-superemployers next door. E.g.:
• Lived in same town all adult life.
• First generation that's wealthy/no parental support for starting the business.
• "They don't look like millionaires, they don't dress like millionaires, they don't eat like millionaires, they don't act like millionaires."
• "Many of the types of businesses [they] are in could be classified as dull-normal. [They] are welding contractors, auctioneers," scrap-metal dealers, lessors of portable toilets, dry cleaners, re-builders of diesel engines, "paving contractors. ..."

Great!
On all counts!

So in that in-my-mind-to-be (GREATLY) expanded version of *Re-imagine!* there will be another (BIG) section, this one on the Jims and Larrys—who are peerless when it comes to defining and exemplifying both Excellence and Re-imagining.

Think about Ben Franklin.
Think about D.D. Eisenhower.
Think about Nelson Mandela.
Think about Jim Penman.
Think about Larry Janesky.
And ponder "Excellence."
Please.
Please.
Please.
Excellence. Always.
If not Excellence, what? If not Excellence now, when?

NB: The main body of the book begins with the Iraq War. There is reason to cut the old intro—but it is, I believe, almost immoral to do so. So here we go, as was in 2003!

FOREWORD
I'm Mad as Hell

The Dean's Dissembling

In 2002, I tried (without success) to induce Stanford University to retract my MBA.

Here's why: The dean of the business school when I got my degree there was Robert Jaedicke. He was also an accounting professor, and I took his advanced accounting course while I was a student. I last saw Jaedicke, 30 years later, on TV. He was testifying about his involvement in the Enron fiasco. Not only was he an Enron board member—he was chairman of the board's Audit Committee. Yet he claimed he had no clue about the truckload of peculiar transactions that brought the company down!

When a guy who served as Enron's *audit* boss ... the last bastion of bean counting ... invokes the "clueless" defense, it makes you wonder: Did he have any clue as to the usefulness of the curriculum at the school where he'd been a dean? Did he have any clue as to what lessons I'd extract from his "advanced" accounting course?

Needless to say, my view of MBAs and of traditional business education soured even more than it already had. (Which is saying a lot.) The same goes for my view of "accepted business practices" in general.

You see, this is personal to me. But, then, business is personal ... not an abstraction.

THAT'S THE WHOLE POINT OF THIS BOOK!

I'm Mad as Hell!

I'm 60 years old as I write. I've been doing my "thing" for well over a quarter of a century. I've achieved some degree of acclaim. At this point, I don't have to write a book. My speaking and consulting gigs keep me busy to the breaking point and beyond. So why am I sitting inside, scrunched over a makeshift writing desk ... on a gorgeous July day on Martha's Vineyard ... cranking out Book Number 11?

Because I'm pissed off.

I happen to believe that all innovation comes, not from market research or carefully crafted focus groups, but from pissed-off people. People who just can't stand the opacity of current financial reports. People who are enraged when the CIA database doesn't connect to the FBI database. People who throw their hands up in frustration at the little slips of paper that fall out of their hymnals (and who thence proceed to invent Post-it Notes).

My old friend Bob Waterman, co-author of *In Search of Excellence*, once told a reporter, "Tom's not happy unless he's madder than hell about something."

True enough. And right now I am precisely that—madder than hell. I'm mad that I (and a lot of people far more clever than I) have been screaming and yelling and shouting about bankrupt business practices for 25 or 30 years ... mostly to no avail.

Every chapter in this book starts off with a "Rant."

My overall rant, in brief: People ... *in enterprise, in government ... are by and large well-intentioned. They'd like to get things done. To be of service to others. But they're thwarted ...at every step of the way ... by absurd organizational barriers ... and by the egos of petty tyrants (be they corporate middle managers, or army colonels, or school superintendents).*

An eloquent expression of that message appears in *Zero Space: Moving Beyond Organizational Limits*, by Frank Lekanne Deprez & René Tissen:

"The organizations we created have become tyrants. They have taken control, holding us fettered, creating barriers that hinder rather than help our businesses. The lines that we drew on our neat organizational diagrams have turned into walls that no one can scale or penetrate or even peer over."

Yes. Walls. Barriers. Tyrants.

Can we regain control ... ?

But I (We) Don't Have to Take It Anymore

A lot of yogurt has hit the fan. Security concerns (global terrorism, including the potential use of weapons of mass destruction) unsettle us all. Globalization has turned out to be a mixed blessing—a worthy end point, but messy and uneven to the extreme in its immediate impact. Tsunamis of technology change engulf us—and confuse us. CEOs are falling like flies—not because of lousy strategic plans, but because of malfeasance. A lot of people have gotten screwed, including, to cite one particularly nasty example, thousands who trusted the company's board and had Enron "assets" locked into their 401K pension plans.

And yet there *is* a New Economy.

Would you change places with your grandfather? Would you want to work 11 brutal hours a day ... in yesterday's Bethlehem Steel mill, a Ford Motor Company factory circa 1935? Not me. Nor would I change places with my father ... who labored in a white-collar sweatshop, at the same company, in the same building, for 41 l-o-n-g years.

A workplace revolution is under way. No sensible person expects to spend a lifetime in a single corporation anymore. Some call this shift the "end of corporate responsibility." I call it ... the Beginning of Renewed Individual Responsibility. An extraordinary opportunity to take charge of our own lives.

We need radically different public policies to make this new opportunity viable. For example, healthcare benefits that are universal and not attached to the company. Hearty and perpetual retraining opportunities, supported in part by the government. Pensions that are self-managed and independent of one's employer.

But most of all, we need the will and the passion and the know-how to take on the responsibility that is falling to us—whether we welcome it or not.

Put me in charge! Make me Chairman & CEO & President & COO of Tom Inc. That's what I ask! (Beg, in fact.)

I *love* business at its best. When it aims to foster growth and deliver exciting services to its clients and exciting opportunities to its employees. I especially love business at this moment of flux. This truly magical, albeit in many ways terrifying, moment.

Cool Business: Not Optional

I'm no Pollyanna. I've been around. (And then around.) The rose-colored glasses were long ago ground to powder by brutal reality.

Yet I am hopeful. Not hopeful that human beings will become more benign ... or that evil will evaporate ... or that greed will be regulated out of existence. But I am hopeful that in the New Economy people will see the power that comes from taking responsibility for their professional lives. I am hopeful that they also will find pleasure in unleashing their instinctive curiosity and creativity that has been so effectively quashed by schools and corporations alike.

The harsh news: **This is Not Optional**. The microchip will colonize all rote activities. And we will have to scramble to reinvent ourselves—as we did when we came off the farm and went into the factory, and then as we were ejected from the factory and delivered to the white-collar towers.

The exciting news (as I see it, anyway): **This is Not Optional**. The reinvented *you* and the reinvented *me* will have no choice but to scramble and add value in some meaningful way.

Every chapter in this book follows the opening "Rant" with a "Vision."

My overall vision, in brief: *Business is cool. It's about Creativity and Invention and Growth and Service. It's about Adam Smith's "hidden hand." And Nobel* laureate Frederich Hayek's "spontaneous discovery process." And economist Joseph Schumpeter's "gales of creative destruction." At its best, it's about building things that make life less burdensome than it was in medieval times. About getting us beyond—far, far, far beyond—the quasi-slavery of the Middle Ages, the indentured servitude of the first 150 years of the Industrial Revolution, and the cubicle slavery of the last three-quarters of a century.

Yes, business is cool.

(Or at least it can be.)

Colors of the Rainbow: Pity the Poor Brown

Winston Churchill had a thing about brown. Me, too. "I cannot pretend," the Savior of Western Civilization once said, "to be impartial about colours. I rejoice with the brilliant ones and am genuinely sorry for the poor brown."

Amen.

I like Color by Technicolor. I rejoice in Bright Red in particular. My company logo, two years in the making, is a bright red exclamation mark. Pantone PMS 032.

I also rejoice in Technicolor Language.

Yet my "thing" is cold logic, not personal prejudice.

Cold Logic:

1. These *are* Technicolor Times. (Without doubt.) Thence ...

2. They *demand* Technicolor Words and Technicolor Ideas and Technicolor Actions.

3. Q.E.D.

"Initiatives" Are for Wimps

I will write about women—as a woefully untapped source of effective leaders; and selling to women as Market Opportunity No. 1. I will *not* suggest a "Women's Initiative." I *will* suggest you turn your whole-damn-enterprise Upside Down—Right Now!—to embrace the Staggeringly High-Potential Women's Thing.

You see, I don't believe in "initiatives." (Color*less*.) I believe in Full-Scale Assaults ... on Enormous Opportunities. (Color*ful*.)

Jack Welch led GE ... brilliantly ... for two full decades. He changed the rules. You can mark his 20 years at the top by Epochs: e.g., destroy bureaucracy, go after quality, embrace the Internet, and so on. But these, I contend, were *not* "initiatives." They were ... Major Technicolor Assaults on Huge Opportunities.

So if you don't cotton to Technicolor ... well ... you picked the wrong author, the wrong publisher, the wrong book.

Be prepared!

Have fun!

Pity the poor brown!

The Book: Not Optional, Either

At age 60, I'm making a new start. My first totally new start, as I see it, since *In Search of Excellence*, published in 1982. I'm working with a new publisher ... a design-driven, in-your-face publisher ... Dorling Kindersley. Together we aim to "reinvent the business book."

Audacious? Yes.

Egocentric? That, too.

Absurd? We'll see.

But that's exactly what we intend to do.

In the 20-plus years since Bob Waterman and I wrote *In Search of Excellence*, the world has indeed "come a long way, baby." But it has a much, much longer way to go. And as new technologies begin (yes, "begin"!) to reveal their incredible potential, we learn every day that we have only begun (yes, "begun"!) to re-invent those tried-and-true rules of management that a number of us started to question in about 1980.

I honestly believe you'd have to be an outright fool not to see that we're in the midst of something big ... VERY BIG. And, to reinforce the obvious: Very Big Problems ... call for ... Very Big Solutions.

Very Big Solutions: At the level of the individual. At the level of the organizational unit. At the level of the small business. At the level of the large enterprise. At the level of the school. At the level of the hospital. At every level of government.

And ... at the humble level of the business book. Hence the not-so-humble tome that you hold in your hand. I didn't have to write this book. And yet ... I *had* to write this book. (Remember: Mad as hell. Not going to take it anymore.)

Writing this book was ... Not Optional.

Why "Business" Books Matter

The American armed forces performed brilliantly in Iraq in 2003. But ... trust me ... it didn't hurt that we spend $400 billion a year on defense ... and the sanction-starved Iraqis were spending $1 billion a year.

The Yanks tipped the balance in World War II. "Greatest Generation"? Perhaps. (I'd personally choose George Washington's way-under-funded Revolutionaries.) But ... Greatest Weapon Producers ... via Greatest Economy?

Yup.

Fact: Rosie-the-Riveter may merit more "victory points" than Paul-the-Private in the U.S. Army.

Business matters!

Economics matters!

The Brits ruled the world, from a wee island, for hundreds of years. While I, an old Navy guy, admire the Royal Navy, I more admire the Entrepreneurial British Trading Companies ... that made it all possible ... and funded the Royal Navy's ships.

Our nuclear subs were priceless defenders against the Soviets for almost a half-century. Yet it was ... The Economy, Stupid ... that brought Gorbachev & Co. to its knees, when Ronald Reagan promised to spend them into the ground with Star Wars. The jig was up. The Sovs didn't have the bucks to play on our turf.

Business books are good ... and bad. (Of course.)

But the idea of Enterprise Excellence is ... matchless. Fact: Whoever has the ... Best Business Practices ... and the Most Competitive Markets ... Rules.

Don't believe me?

Just ask the Dutch, the British, and the Americans ... who have effectively "overseen" the last half-millennium of history.

Forget Neutrality

I don't expect you'll agree with everything that I say here. But I hope that when you disagree ... you will disagree *angrily*. That you will be so pissed off that you'll ... Do Something.

DOING SOMETHING. That's the essential idea, isn't it? (Pity the poor brown.) (Technicolor reigns.) The punch line to my story ... the story of "Why this book" ... is a tombstone. (Punch line, tombstone—an odd juxtaposition, maybe; but you think about such stuff when you get to be 60.) It's a tombstone that bears the epitaph I most hope to avoid. To wit:

Thomas J. Peters
1942–2003
He would have done
some really cool stuff,
but his boss wouldn't let him

Oh, Lord, don't give me that one! (And please, kindly erase the "2003" while you're at it.)

On the other hand, I know exactly how I do want my tombstone to read:

Thomas J. Peters
1942–Whenever
He was a player

Not "He got rich." Not "He became famous." Not even "He got things right." Rather: "He was a player." In other words: He did not sit on the sidelines ... and watch the world go by ... as it was undergoing the most profound shift of basic premises in the last several hundred years (if not the last thousand or so years).

Agree or disagree with me on anything else, but if you have a grain of integrity or spirit or spunk or verve or nerve, you must agree on this: Getting off the sidelines—being a player— is Not Optional.

INTRODUCTION
New War
New Business

The Attack

On September 11, 2001, a tiny band of Internet-savvy fundamentalists humbled the world's only superpower. It turned out that the FBI, the CIA, a kiloton of tanks, and an ocean of aircraft carriers and nuclear subs were no match for passionate focus, coordinated communication, and a few $3.19 box cutters.

The terrorists conceived the ultimate "virtual organization"—fast, wily, flexible, determined. And then, despite numerous slip-ups, said terrorists trumped the bureaucratic behemoths lined up against them. As the *Boston Globe* put it a few days after the attack, "In an era when terrorists use satellite phones and encrypted e-mail, U.S. gatekeepers stand armed against them with pencils and paperwork, and archaic computer systems that don't talk to each other."

In fact, in my native Maryland, a state trooper had stopped one of the 19 terrorists—on September 9. But the trooper's database wasn't connected to the CIA database, which would have informed the cop that the fellow he stopped for a minor traffic violation was apparently on the agency's terrorist watch list. But who's surprised? Not me! The CIA doesn't talk to the FBI. And nobody in the prissy federal agencies would deign to speak to a local yokel in Maryland.

The Context

This is not a book about the war on terror. But it *is* a book about the war on terror. It is about the failure of organizations invented for another era. "Our military structure today," wrote Admiral Bill Owens, former Vice Chairman of the Joint Chiefs of Staff, "is essentially one developed and designed by Napoleon." The same principle applies to most of our business organizations—with exceptions like Dell and Wal*Mart proving the rule.

In the case of the military, we have the perfect structure for dealing with the (former) Soviet Union ... and a lousy structure for dealing with al Qaeda. Likewise, Sears was brilliantly equipped to deal with Montgomery Ward ... and totally unprepared for Wal*Mart. IBM nailed Control Data's scalp to the wall, but was flummoxed by the new kid on the block, geeky Bill Gates. Merrill Lynch rode the Bull to the top of the hill, only to take a hit when Charles Schwab came along and changed all the rules in the brokerage business.

(And on and on it goes.)

The concept of the "virtual organization" is essential to understanding how new business works. And I repeat: The New Terrorists have proven to be masters of that concept. How we will deal with terrorist "associations" is more than a little relevant to ... how business must deal with new forms of competition.

"Virtual organization" was the worst sort of consultant-speak on 10 September 2001, especially with the ruins of dot-coms littering the landscape. By late morning, 11 September 2001, "virtual organization" was the new, dominant reality.

The Challenge

"It may someday be said that the 21st century began on Sept. 11, 2001 ...

"Al-Qaeda ... represents a new and profoundly dangerous kind of organization—one that might be called a 'virtual state.' ... On Sept. 11, a virtual state proved that modern societies are vulnerable as never before. ...

"We are entering a period in which a small number of people, operating without overt state sponsorship but using the enormous power of modern computers, biogenetic pathogens, air transport and even small nuclear weapons, will be able to exploit the tremendous vulnerabilities of contemporary open societies."—*Time*, 9 September 2002

"The deadliest strength of America's new adversaries is their very fluidity, Defense Secretary Donald H. Rumsfeld believes. Terrorist networks, unburdened by fixed borders, headquarters or conventional forces, are free to study the way this nation responds to threats and adapt themselves to prepare for what Mr. Rumsfeld is certain will be another attack. ...

"Al Qaeda ... has leaders and budgets and command-and-control and has proved it can inflict terrible damage, yet it cannot be attacked in a traditional battle.

"Mr. Rumsfeld, inside a Pentagon built of bricks and mortar and, now, bomb-resistant, shatterproof glass, focuses on maneuvering a steel-and-circuitry military so its forces can better fight a 'virtual enemy.'

"'Business as usual won't do it,' he said. His answer is to develop swifter, more lethal ways to fight. ... 'Big institutions aren't swift on their feet' in adapting but rather 'ponderous and clumsy and slow.' In terrorist networks, on the other hand, 'changes can be cheaper, quicker, and for a period—a longer period than in our case—but for a period, invisible.'"—*New York Times*, 3 September 2002

"The Industrial Revolution was about scale: vast factory complexes, skyscrapers, and railway grids concentrating power in the hands of rulers of large territories: not only responsible rulers such as Bismarck and Disraeli, but Hitler and Stalin, too. ... But the post-Industrial Revolution empowers anyone with a cellular phone and a bag of explosives. America's military superiority guarantees that such new adversaries will not fight according to our notions of fairness: they will come at us by surprise, asymmetrically, at our weakest points." —Robert Kaplan, *Warrior Politics*

The Response

Eric Shinseki was hell-bent on revolution. On preparing his organization to compete within a radically new environment.

The task of military transformation is daunting. Called RMA—Revolution in Military Affairs—it began long before 9/11. But until that day, the impetus for change

... let alone "revolution" ... was more or less tepid. Now the pressure for almost total overhaul is irresistible.

I, too, am hell-bent on revolution. And because the military is traditionally loath to change ... and because it faces a completely new (and completely deadly) kind of threat ... I find the Shinseki story to be compelling. Very compelling.

Shinseki's bid to transform the way the Army does its business maps perfectly the kind of change that private enterprise (along with education, and healthcare, and civil government, and so on) must undertake ... lest it be routed by what military tacticians call "facts on the ground."

Consider these elements of the Shinseki change program, mainly as outlined by Peter Boyer in his masterful *New Yorker* article "A Different War." (And for "basic training" in military transformation, see the "Contrasts" chart at the end of this Introduction.)

1. New Strategy. The military—like all enterprises—is best fit to fight the last opponent. Until quite recently, it was perfectly designed to deal with the Cold War. The basic strategy was this: Our Heavy Stuff versus the Soviets' Heavy Stuff. And our Heavy Stuff was Heavier and Better!

Everything changed on 9/11.

That day brought home the fact that the next war would not involve a definitive battle against another great war machine. Instead, a long-into-the-future series of "skirmishes" with exceptionally elusive enemies would be our new fate. We used to know exactly where the Bad Guys were. And exactly how Big their Bazookas were. (Big mattered most.) Now we didn't know *where* they were ... or *who* they were ... or *what* they were armed with. (Box cutters as Weapons of Mass Destruction?) All we knew was their motive. A motive defined, unlike the motives of the Soviet Union throughout most of the Cold War, by fanaticism. (Lenin may have been a fanatic. But remember Leonid Brezhnev and Yuri Andropov? Not exactly fanatics! Phenomenally Old Guys, more conservative than *our* Phenomenally Old Guys. Praise be.)

2. New Tactics. In the "old days," military confrontation was all about head-to-head encounters. Now ... we are shifting from a "direct" to an "indirect" model. Hence, for one thing, the Army's new Stryker Brigade. Heavy armor to light armor. Stealth. Avoidance of direct contact. In Boyer's words: "Choose your moment ... depend heavily on information technology, and enhanced intelligence, surveillance, and reconnaissance capabilities."

There's even talk of "virtual tanks." (Shades of Silicon Valley, eh?) A virtual tank would involve multiple discrete parts—one bit with sensors, another bit with weaponry.

Far-fetched? Hardly. I recently saw a photo of a soldier holding the New Military equivalent of a Game Controller. Like the teenager he recently was, Private Modern was guiding a remote robotic vehicle into a potentially lethal cave in Afghanistan.

The military has understood the need for this change ... a combination of greater battlefield flexibility and greater information intensity ... for quite a while. But implementing the change has been excruciatingly difficult ... for "cultural" reasons rather than technological reasons.

My suggested New Motto for the U.S. Army ... courtesy of Muhammad Ali:

"Float like a butterfly, *sting like a bee.*"

3. New Soldier. The Army has changed its slogan from "Be All You Can Be" to "I Am an Army of One." And indeed, in the Afghanistan conflict, U.S. "ground troop" action hardly resembled the insane moments of World War I's trench warfare or the bloody World War II assault on the likes of Iwo Jima. In fact, it never amounted to more than a handful of individuals in any given operation.

Truly: Armies of One.

"Substituting information for armor is a discomfiting notion to a tank soldier," one general told Mr. Boyer. "Soldiers will learn that battlefield awareness can be as comforting as armor."

What a shift! Yes, what a "culture change"! (Can they use that term in the Army?) Being armed with a computer and an array of sensors is very different from being armed with the Biggest Tank in the Neighborhood. (Against the New Enemy, the Biggest Tank doesn't do you much good. Ditto the Biggest Aircraft Carrier or the Biggest Nuclear Sub.)

4. New Weapons. Army talk used to be about "tanks" and "artillery." Now the Army talks about "Future Combat Systems." (Systems = Big word. Much more later.)

Lumpy object (tank) vs. "System" (software)? Semantic quibble? Or profound Shift in Point of View? I think the latter.

In the private sector, UPS ads say "Let Brown Do It." That is, UPS provides Logistics Systems Services ... of which Ye Lumpy Olde Brown Truck is but one (diminishing) part. The "brown truck" is to UPS as the rifle is (or soon will be) to the Army. Likewise, GE's old circuit-breaker division has become GE Industrial Systems. What used to be an Old Economy manufacturing operation now peddles information-intensive solutions to major customer needs ... and tosses in some Chinese-manufactured circuit breakers on the side.

In short, the system(s) is (are) the solution, and software rules. For UPS. For GE. For Eric Shinseki and the U.S. Army.

5. New Command-and-Control Model. Against the New Enemy, our No. 1 vulnerability is lousy cross-functional communication. Between the Army and the Navy and the Air Force. Between the CIA and the FBI and Customs. And every combination thereof.

How will we know when we have solved that problem?
The answer is crystal clear to me: When a fresh-caught, 26-year-old, front-line CIA operative is able to communicate with her counterpart, a fresh-caught, 26-year-old, front-line FBI agent ... through the latest technology ... and without needing to wade through four (five?) (six?) levels of supervisors in each organization.

We're still far, far away from that goal—again, not for reasons of technology, but for reasons of "corporate culture" (in the Army, it's called "tradition") and "internal politics."

6. New Enemy. For years, parochial political issues—for example, Congressional support for Ever Bigger Versions of Yesterday's Weapons with Contracts in My District—sidetracked the Revolution in Military Affairs. Everyone knew that, in theory, the military needed to be agile—because the Soviet threat was no longer the most important one. But, practically speaking, we hadn't yet focused on any particular new threat. The morning of 9/11 changed all that. Now we knew the genotype of the New Enemy: fanatical, elusive, virtual.

> ## Ah, the "joys" of competition! FedEx is as good as it is, to a large extent, because UPS (and DHL and Ryder System, and so forth) are as good as they are. The same goes for the U.S. military in its fight against al Qaeda.

The Stakes

We know pretty much what the New Military should look like. The question is: Can we get from here to (distant) there ... before catastrophe envelops us? Can we undo the bureaucratic stickiness that keeps us from ... Doing the Things That Need to Be Done ... or will we get stuck in trying to "manage" change when we need to be leading it?

As bold as he is, General Shinseki learned the perils of not being bold enough. Also hell-bent on revolution is his boss ... Secretary of Defense Donald Rumsfeld ... who decided that Shinseki was too much a creature of the regnant bureaucracy, and who thence undercut him.

The general, explains Peter Boyer, "tried to harness the military revolution and to apply it in measures that his reluctant organization might accept; it was too much for the old order, not enough for the revolutionaries. The defense analyst Loren Thompson compares Shinseki's role to that of Aleksandr Kerensky, the Russian Revolutionary who was undone by the Bolsheviks. 'Shinseki represented a change over what came before, but the world wanted more change than he was able to deliver in the time frame that he had,' Thompson says. 'He was prepared to make changes that, within the context of Army tradition, were significant. But, by the standards of the outside world, not party to those institutional rhythms, it seems very incremental and conservative.'"

That's what change is like. In the New War on Terror. In the New World of Business.

The totally new challenges the military faces are exact analogs to the challenges that established global corporations face. To be sure, the stakes are higher in the military than they are in, say, retailing, but the issues and the models, the friends and the foes, that are in play in each situation are exactly (EXACTLY!) alike in character.

And in one very personal sense, at least, the stakes are equally high. Recall the epigraph in which I quote General Shinseki:

"If you don't like change, you're going to like irrelevance even less."

! Contrasts

WAS	IS
"Old Economy" Army	"New Economy" Army
Steep, bureaucratic, with lots of "brass"	Flat, decentralized, with little "brass"
Slow but sure	Fast and sure
Heavy and thus lethal	Light but no less lethal
Overwhelming force, difficult to maneuver	Precision munitions, able to "turn on a dime"
Biggest Guns in Town	Smartest Systems on Earth
Soldiers in massed formation, riding in tanks and towing heavy artillery	Units of five or ten "Army of One" soldiers, "armed" mostly with technology and capable of calling remotely upon an array of armaments
Firepower-intense	Information-intense
Hierarchical, with independent units that relate via top-down command-and-control operations	Network-centric, with interdependent groups that engage in ad-hoc operational planning
Lots of friction, low coordination especially with other armed services and with government agencies	Friction-free, open communication—both within units and across organizational divisions
Very "real"	Very "virtual"

We are in a brawl with no rules!

new bus!ness
new context

In ancient times, cartographers would label uncharted waters with "Here be dragons." In 1991, with the Cold War ended and capitalism unfurling its banner around the globe, it appeared that the dragons had all been slain.

Little did we know ...

The polarity has reversed in a scant decade. Dragons are all about; and there is much to be frightened about. In fact, the *unknown* has always been frightening.

The *unknown* today and tomorrow ... meaning the basis for the creation of Economic Value. The *unknown* ... meaning the essential idea of "life forms" in the age of human cloning and genetic engineering. The *unknown* ... meaning the definition of a job where software enhanced by Artificial Intelligence is brainier than you or I. The *unknown*... meaning who is the enemy, where is the enemy, how do we find the enemy, how do we punish the enemy before the other shoe drops.

On the other hand ... yes, there is an "other hand" ... the "unknown" provides matchless opportunity ... for today's Captain Cooks and Amelia Earharts ... those bold enough and determined enough to take advantage of it. It is an age that begs for those who break the rules, who imagine the heretofore impossible.

And stride forth ...

RE-IMAGINING THE WORLD: ALL BETS ARE OFF

! Technicolor Rules ...

- Old rules? Going ... going ... gone.
- It's a fluid, fluid world.
- "Value," "assets"—it (it? what? where?) is all up for grabs.
- Mess is the message.
- Foraging amid the mess alone yields ... Stunning Breakthroughs.
- Static planning exercises are virtually useless!
- Enjoy the Fray!
- "Fail faster. Succeed sooner."

! RANT

We are not prepared ...

We act as if the dot-com crash signaled the end of the New Economy. But we are, in fact, on the verge of the biggest and most profound wave of economic change in a thousand years.

We avoid failure at all costs, and cling to ideals like "order" and "efficiency." But we must embrace failure; we must glory in the very murk and muck and mess that yield true innovation.

! VISION

I imagine ...

A New Brand of Employee. Dancing from (Cool) Project to (Cool) Project. Making "it" (her "career") up as she goes along. Her appetite for change? High! Higher! Highest!

A New Breed of Enterprise. Reducing its bureaucracy to almost nothing. Making the "empowerment" movement of the '80s and '90s look like Small Beer. Agile. Innovative. Entrepreneurial.

A New Social Contract. Societies that educate their young to break the rules and invent vivid new futures. That encourage labor mobility through policies that support the entrepreneurial instinct. That embrace the idea of global village and change, rather than close their minds and borders to change.

NEW BUSINESS ! ● NEW CONTEXT

Easy Come, Easy Go

Years ago, I interviewed the late Bill McGowan, founder of MCI. He didn't live long enough to see his company go through its full life cycle, but he had a prescient grasp of how the world had changed. (After all, he'd done a lot to change it!) "Tom," he said, "the chump-to-champ-to-chump cycle used to be three generations. Now it's about five years."

(Okay, it took 20 in his case.)

MCI took on AT&T ... and won. Bernie Ebbers bought MCI ... and folded it into WorldCom. WorldCom got caught in a web of accounting scandals ... and declared bankruptcy. Now WorldCom is attempting to rise from the ashes, and trying to make us forget WorldCom by renaming itself ... MCI. Go figure.

Meanwhile, as telecom consumers, you and I have benefited beyond our wildest dreams from the unleashing of competitive forces in the industry.

MCI: Born yesterday. Changed the world. Got swallowed up. Died. Perhaps born again, at least for a while.

It is *not* ... your father's world.

"Paving the Cow Paths"

Item: Wal*Mart flummoxes Sears. Bumpkins from Bentonville (Arkansas) take on the heroes of retailing ... and end up the Brightest Star in one of the most extraordinary chapters of productivity growth in American history.

Item: Microsoft trumps IBM. A bunch of unkempt geeks cause decades of havoc for what was arguably the world's greatest company ... and quickly come to dominate the world's most pivotal industry.

Item: Charles Schwab throws the Fear of God into Merrill Lynch. An upstart from San Francisco brings the word "discount" into the staid world of cigars and booze and clubs and stocks and bonds ... and rocks Wall Street.

Was IBM napping? Was Sears napping? Was Merrill Lynch napping?

No. No. And no.

But ... each was fighting ... *the last war*! IBM was guarding its flank against Fujitsu and Siemens. Sears was still fighting Montgomery Ward. Merrill Lynch was tussling

---

ALL INDUSTRIES ARE ... "OFF"

Change doesn't affect every industry equally, right?

Wrong! *All* bets are off.

Just go down the list ...

Financial Services: From "gentlemanly relationships" to ... cutthroat competition.

Manufacturing: From clumsy Ford & GM & U.S.Steel to ... hyper-fast, hyper-efficient Dell and Cisco.

Energy: From market dominance and stability to ... the constant threat of wholesale supply interruption in the Middle East, Latin America, and elsewhere. Plus: a world where (outside the U.S.) Green Rules.

Telecoms: From monopolies that offer incremental "improvements" to ... upstarts that drive basic innovation. (And, sure, sometimes go broke.)

Healthcare: From markets built around employers that foot the (whole) bill and pricey blockbuster drugs that guarantee extraordinary cash flow for Big Pharma to ... employer revolt and technological upheaval and consumer dominance.

An "oasis of calm"? I can't find one.

with the ghost of J.P. Morgan. And they were caught ... not napping but *looking the other way*! Caught ... nabbed ... nailed ... embarrassed ... by those who were "born only yesterday" and who naively used New Tools and New Technologies and New Ideas better ... faster ... more thoroughly.

No, don't blame Sears. (Or IBM. Or Merrill Lynch.) Sears wrote the book on retail ... *in* a different era ... *for* a different era. Wal*Mart was lucky. It was born at the right moment, and it entered its growth spurt at the right moment, too. In the early 1980s, just as the computer became ready for prime (retail) time, so did Wal*Mart. (The pattern repeats itself with Microsoft. And with Schwab.)

Michael Hammer, reengineering guru, distilled this phenomenon in a 1990 article in the *Harvard Business Review*. The first three decades of the computer revolution, he wrote, were all about "paving the cow paths." (Love that!) That is, we spent 30 years automating ... *yesterday's procedures*.

What's more ... the "cow paths" often didn't lead to where we needed to go. They were the codification of yesterday's maps. **(Wrong dragons!)**

Consider the U.S. government. Its appetite for information technology is immense. But its acquisition processes are hopelessly clunky. The big issue is not the $$$ but the sense: The expensive and extensive CIA IT system ... refuses to consort with the expensive and extensive DEA IT system ... which can't connect with the Customs IT system ...which won't deal with the FBI system ... etc. ... etc.

Sane People, Insane Statements

"There's going to be a fundamental change in the global economy unlike anything we've had since cavemen began bartering," says Arnold Baker, chief economist of the Sandia National Laboratories.

"I genuinely believe that we are living through the greatest intellectual moment in history," writes Matt Ridley in his book *Genome*.

"In 25 years, you'll probably be able to get the sum total of all human knowledge on a personal device," asserts Greg Blonder, venture capitalist and former chief technical advisor for corporate strategy at AT&T.

Quotes like those—and I've got dozens more of them—are part of a set I call

---

LOOK, MA, NO PILOT!
Headline from the *Economist*, December 2002: "Help! There's nobody in the cockpit. In the future, will airliners no longer need pilots?" Upshot: A Grumman Global Hawk prototype flew non-stop from Edwards Air Force Base in California to South Australia ... without a pilot.

HAVE A BRAWL!
"We're in a brawl with no rules." So says Paul Allaire, former CEO of Xerox.

That was one alternative title that I considered for this book. In the end it seemed a little over the top for a book title. But my heart lies with that wonderful, pull-no-punches phrase. As we attempt to navigate individual careers, corporate strategies, war and statecraft, we find ourselves caught in ... brawls with no rules.

Practical Implications: Enormous! If there are no rules, then we draw our paycheck—admiral or middle manager—for making it up on the fly. (As opposed to the past, when "rule-followers" thrived, and impresarios got their hands slapped, or worse.)

"insane statements by very sane people." That is, a large number of people with their feet planted ... Very Firmly on the Ground ... are beginning to say that they feel ... the ground shifting beneath their feet.

Shifting now.

Shifting fast.

My hero-in-chief in all this is Ray Kurzweil, computer guru and pragmatic futurist with numerous patents and a hatful of start-ups to his name. Applying the tools of mathematical modeling to all of human history, Kurzweil persuasively argues that fundamental change is happening at an ever-faster rate. Before about 1000 A.D., he avers, a major shift in the way that people thought about things—a "paradigm shift"—typically took thousands of years to unfold. (Remember all that stuff you learned in the fifth grade: Iron Age, Bronze Age, and so on.) By 1000, a paradigm shift was taking place about every 100 years. The rate of change kept accelerating: In the 1800s alone, there was more change than there had been during the previous 900 years; then, in the first fifth of the 20th century, there was more change than there had been even during the "mad" 1800s. And by the year 2000, a massive paradigm shift was occurring *every decade.*

Looking ahead, Kurzweil predicts that there will be *one thousand times* more technological change in the 21st century than there was in the 20th century. Exhibit A in support of that claim is "singularity"—the "merger between humans and computers that is so rapid and profound it represents a rupture in the fabric of human history."

Two-Way Risk Watch

The statisticians insist there's a huge difference between "uncertainty" and "ambiguity."

Uncertainty: You work in the exploration department at ExxonMobil. You punch a hole in the floor of the Gulf of Mexico. Knowing what you know about geology and geophysics, you can predict that the odds of finding hydrocarbons where you drill that hole are between (say) 57.5 percent and 64.5 percent. (Or some such.)

That's uncertainty. You don't know everything, but you know something, and you know how what you do know relates to what you *don't* know.

Ambiguity: You find yourself asking ...

Where's the Gulf of Mexico? What's a hydrocarbon? Who cares?

That's ambiguity.

You don't know enough even to know if you're asking the right questions.

And that's where we are now.

All bets are off.

THE CASE FOR CONFUSION

"There is probably going to be more confusion in the business world in the next decade than there has been in any decade, maybe, in history ... and the pace of change is only going to accelerate," said former AOL Time Warner Chairman Steve Case (who has seen more than his share of confusion over the past few years).

I believe it. But I like Case's comment for a special reason—the word "confusion." It's a pretty good synonym for "ambiguity," and it's actually not so ambiguous. It captures the anxiety and the excitement that characterize our current age.

Losing Bet I: Systematic Planning Rituals

When my business career effectively began, in the mid-1970s, the once "invincible" United States was being economically humbled by a new breed of competitor ... and, in particular, by Japan. All things Japanese were "good"—that was the conventional wisdom. In response, the best minds in business offered their best ideas on how to survive in the new competitive environment. These were the big strategic "bets" of the late 20th century.

First, there was *The Strategic Planning Bet*. People believed in five-year plans. Ten-year plans. A strategy "guru," completely cowed by Japan's industrial success, claimed that one Japanese company (I think it was Canon) actually had a 500-year plan. Those of us enslaved by Wall Street's crazy quarterly-earnings requirements wept openly. Imagine, we intoned as one ... a 500-year perspective!

Ah, those were the days.

Meg Whitman has seen the faith in long-term strategy[1] come and go. She's CEO of the insanely successful eBay ... and a survivor of the dot-com conniptions. In the old days, she says, enterprise "strategy meetings" were held "once or twice a year." Now, in eBay World, "strategy sessions" are "needed several times a *week*."

Forget the 500-year plan: You're lucky if you can write a five-*week* plan that makes any sense ... yes ... after five weeks.

Losing Bet II: The Quality Thing

Next, there was *The Quality Thing Bet*. Call it TQM. Call it Six Sigma. Call it (as the Japanese mostly did) Kaizen ... that is, "continuous improvement." Or just call it tinkering. The Japanese took the ideas of industrial precision to the Ultimate Heights. They taught us a lot about high-class tinkering. Nothing wrong with that—we learned an incredible amount from them. I would not want to turn back the clock; I would not want to forget those harsh and valuable lessons. Nonetheless, those lessons represented the Last Scene of the Old Economy. The Japanese are now floundering, after more than a decade's worth of ever-deepening trouble. It appears as though, in the '60s and '70s and '80s, they were simply polishing the last patch of skin on the Industrial Revolution's souring apple.

Now we need something Dramatically Different from "getting better"—from even getting "a whole lot better"—at what we did for a couple of hundred years. Now we need to train ourselves to play an Entirely New Game[2]... a game called Re-imagine, in which the rules that define "better" no longer apply.

"PLAN" TO BUY THIS BOOK
[1]My favorite management book in the last 25 years?
No contest. *The Rise and Fall of Strategic Planning*, by Henry Mintzberg.

HIGH STAKES
[2]**Perfecting the procedures on our aircraft carriers will not prevent the next set of 19 terrorists from causing havoc—perhaps on a scale that makes 9/11 look like petty vandalism.**
New Game. New (Super-High) Stakes.
Needed: New Tools. New Rules. And (Organizational Commandment No. 1): A new agility.

Losing Bet III: Sustainable Competitive Advantage

And then, there was *The Sustainable Competitive Advantage Bet*. To put it simply: Figure out the one or two things you can do better than anybody else ... and keep doing the hell out of them. (Did I put it too simply? Barely.) And how did this "bet" go wrong? I can't put it better than my friend Rich D'Aveni did in his book *Hypercompetition: Managing the Dynamics of Strategic Maneuvering*. D'Aveni, a professor of strategic management at Dartmouth, argues thus:

"Chivalry is dead. The new code of conduct is an active strategy of disrupting the status quo to create an unsustainable series of competitive advantages. ... This is not the age of defensive castles, moats, and armor. It is rather an age of cunning, speed, and surprise. It may be hard for some to hang up the chain mail of sustainable advantage after so many battles. But hypercompetition, a state in which sustainable advantages are no longer possible, is now the only level of competition."

Dealing with hyper competition? Agility redux. Eh?

Re-Defining Moment

Business has been through a nasty period. First there was dot-com mania ... then the dot-com bust. Then Enron. Then Andersen. Then Merrill Lynch. Then WorldCom. Then ImClone. Not to mention al Qaeda.

And on and on it goes. Some of this mess was an outgrowth of the garden-variety business cycle. Expansion, followed by contraction. A time when "anything is possible" ... followed by a time when some go too far in pursuit of "limitless opportunities."

But the key to grasping the situation, as I see it, is something altogether different. Yes, a lot of people broke the law. And yes, a lot of egos pursued outlandish excesses. And all of those miscreants should suffer the full consequences, legal as well as financial, of their grievous misdoings. Even so ... there is something far, far bigger going on.

FUNDAMENTAL IDEA: We are in the midst of redefining our basic ideas about what enterprise and organization and even being human is ... and about how value is created and "careers" are pursued. All of our heated discussions about business "malfeasance" boil down to debates not just over how to deal with "assets" and "expenses," but over how to define those things. And the seemingly simple matter of defining basic terms is getting even murkier, not more transparent, SEC rulings and Sarbanes-Oxley flavors of "accountability" legislation notwithstanding.

For What It's Worth

Until very recently, we lived in a world where "assets" were "things you could touch." A smokestack. A conveyor belt. A bricks-and-mortar store. Then, quite suddenly, we entered a world where the assets of, say, Martha Stewart Omnimedia were things like ... "Perception of Martha." Thus:

Ubiquitous Martha = Billions in Market Capitalization.

DON'T BE A DEFENSIVE DRIVER
From *BusinessWeek*:

"Gone are the days when a company such as Chrysler could ride a single hit product such as the mini-van straight to the bank. 'In this kind of industry, you have a mindset to defend your core segment,' says Wolfgang Bernhard, Chrysler's chief operating officer. 'But if everybody is playing offense and you're playing defense, you lose.'"

Martha-as-Indicted-Insider-Stock-Trader = Far (Far!) Less.

Duration of Transformation: Days.

Consider Harley-Davidson. A "motorcycle manufacturer." Right? Well, that's what federal statisticians think. (Stuff rules!) But that is not what former Harley CEO Rich Teerlink thinks. Teerlink spent years sparring verbally with Wall Street's wizards over the very definition of his company. "I pushed at them over and over again," he told me, "to understand that we were a 'lifestyle company,' not a 'vehicle manufacturer.'" (Image rules!) Teerlink prevailed. And Harley's market valuation soared by billion$$$ as a result.

"Vehicle manufacturer." "Lifestyle company." A semantic quibble? If so, it's a quibble that's collectively worth Trillion$$$ ... a "quibble" that lies at the Very Heart of our Enormous Economic Conundrum.

Welcome to a world where "value" (damn near *all* value!) is based on *intangibles*... not lumpy objects, but weightless figments[3] of the ... Economic Imagination.

None of this excuses phony accounting or document shredding or lying to investors. But it does "excuse" the confusion that all of us have over: What *matters*? What's *real*? What *is* value?

Relish the Mess! (That's All There Is)

Life is messy. *Very* messy. (That's why I read fiction for instruction, not management books. Most management books provide "answers." Great fiction raises great questions.) (P.S.: I hope we raise more questions than we answer. See Chapter 25: Most important phrase in leader's lexicon: "I don't know." It is the phrase-mantra that launches Explorer-employees on Great & Cool Quests.)

Richard Farson (a Big Hero of mine) and Ralph Keyes, in their fabulous book *Whoever Makes the Most Mistakes Wins*, offer a lovely vignette. It seems that a fellow of some renown was drafting a blurb about his life for his alumni annual. He started out by sketching an extraordinary story of moving from success to (ever greater) success. Fair enough. He was very successful. The accomplishments were real. But then he caught himself... and produced this revisionist screed:

"Because I didn't receive a single 'A' in college, I couldn't get into medical school ... . I worked as a lifeguard, but got fired at the end of the summer. My next job, selling

NEW BUSINESS ● NEW CONTEXT

LETTING THE GENES OUT OF THE BOTTLE

Wired writer David Ewing Duncan offered his body as guinea pig to start-up Sequenom. From his report:

"Sequenom [has] industrialized the SNP [single nucleotide polymorphisms] identification process.

"This, I'm told, is the first time a healthy human has ever been screened for the full gamut of genetic-disease markers.

"On the horizon: multi-disease gene kits, available at Wal*Mart, as easy to use as home pregnancy tests."

I'M SHOCKED, SHOCKED

[3] Are there no limits?

Apparently not. One day after our troops entered Iraq on 21 March 2003, Sony applied to trademark "Shock and Awe"—for a future video game. After public outcry, Sony retracted. Nonetheless, the application is New Economy to the Hilt!

advertising in the Yellow Pages, was interrupted by breaking my leg ... while skiing. This gave me three months to think about what to do with my life. Since I'd enjoyed my psychology courses in college, I thought I might try to become a school psychologist. So, I enrolled at UCLA to pick up psychology and education courses, but got kicked out of student teaching because I couldn't get along with my supervisor. Back to lifeguarding. Then I noticed that a prominent psychologist was giving a summer seminar at my alma mater, so I quit my job and enrolled. This experience was electrifying. The psychologist invited me to study with him at the University of Chicago. I was so intimidated by that most serious academic institution, however, that I put off going there for a year. Just before receiving my Ph.D. from Chicago, I was given a one-year fellowship on the Harvard Business School faculty. I left there at the end of the year with almost everyone mad at me."

Of course, he had still accomplished all those ... Grand Things ... he had reprised in the first version of his blurb. But the trajectory of his ascent to such heights had been anything but smooth ... or predictable.

Beware the champions of order.

Beware those who prescribe "rules" for Righteous Living—rules that will (supposedly) vault you into the ... Pantheon of the Gods.

Hey, it doesn't work that way! Get a life! Enjoy the mess! With a bit of luck, you just might rise from the Ruins of a Failed Career ... as a Lifeguard ... to Change the World!

I cherish ... life-as-it-is-served-up.

Hence I ...

Revel in the Mess!

Because ...

The Mess has a Message!

Pursue Failure (Damn It!)

Consider this exchange between Regis McKenna, Silicon Valley's premier marketing guru, and the late Robert Noyce, co-inventor of the integrated circuit, co-founder of Intel,

---

AN ARMY MARCHES ON ITS ... DATA

The *New York Times* reports that the U.S. Army's new Infantry Battalion will have just 270 soldiers—one-third of the normal complement.

Soldiers? Guns?

"Every soldier is [an] IT-enhanced sensor," the *Times* stated. These "sensors" (um, soldiers) will be aided by 140 off-road robotic armored trucks.

and a Silicon Valley legend:

McKenna: "A lot of companies in the Valley fail."

Noyce: "Maybe not enough fail."

McKenna: "What do you mean by that?"

Noyce: "Whenever you fail, it means you're trying new things."

Or, as futurist Paul Saffo puts it: "The Silicon Valley of today is built less atop the spires of earlier triumphs than upon the rubble of earlier debacles."

Kevin Kelly, author of *Out of Control*, makes the point this way: "The secret of fast progress is inefficiency, fast and furious and numerous failures."

If nothing goes awry, then nothing new can emerge. That is an Iron Law of Nature.

The secret to Success is ... Failure.

The secret to Fast Success is ... Fast Failure.

The secret to Big Success is ... Big Failure.

It is failure, not success, that makes the world go around. Because failure typically means that someone has stretched beyond the comfort zone and tried something new ... and screwed it up ... and learned something valuable along the way.

A few years ago, the *Economist* published a feature on the success secrets of Silicon Valley. Topping the magazine's list of traits that distinguish The Valley: "pursuit of risk." To illustrate the point, the *Economist* described the outcome set from a portfolio of 20 investments ("bets") that a typical venture capitalist might make:

Four would go broke.

Six would lose money.

Six would do "okay."

Three would do well.

One would "hit the jackpot."

Such a record ... effectively, a success rate of 1 in 20 ... would be deemed "brilliant." (Okay, I exaggerate. Add in the "do well" bets, and the success rate jumps to 4 in 20.)

At too many companies, and in too many hapless "careers," the No. 1 imperative is to ... Avoid Failure & Embarrassment Associated Therewith at All Costs.

My take: "Failure" (supported by wildly imaginative hypotheses and incredibly hard work!) is something that companies and individuals must ... embrace. Frankly, at all costs. Unless you're stretching ... wildly! ... you're not going to reach that Brass Ring Called ... Hyper-Success amidst a Brawl with No Rules.

NEW BUSINESS ● NEW CONTEXT

SHELF LIFE SUPPORT

From *Investor's Business Daily*, 26 July 2002: "'Historically, Williams-Sonoma would introduce a floor set at the beginning of a shopping season, then leave things pretty much the same until the next one came along,' says analyst Joan Bogucki-Storms of Wedbush Morgan Securities. 'And if the merchandise wasn't in sync with the big fashion or trend, [it would] just mark everything down at the end of the season,' she said. The problem was, customers got bored before the season ended. So Williams-Sonoma changed its tack. It began introducing new goods every couple of weeks. Stuff that wasn't selling was marked down more quickly to move it off the floor. 'You have to train your customers that you have a new and ever-changing assortment,' Bogucki-Storms said. The strategy worked. Customers started to come in more frequently to see what was new, and Williams-Sonoma has the results to prove it."

"Play" Is the Thing

In his book *Serious Play*, innovation guru Michael Schrage makes a simple (but profound) argument: Those who are willing to invest in and test unproven ideas, based on a hunch or a gut reaction, are likely to find their noses bloodied ... routinely. But by the ... Very Act of Entering the Fray With Vigor ... they increase the odds ... DRAMATICALLY ... of joining the small set of True World-beaters Who Shape Tomorrow's Extraordinary Contours.

And those who hunker down? Who practice disciplines of the '80s and '90s, such as Kaizen? Who try to make their product or service "a little bit better than it was yesterday"? Well, to be frank, I think they are *doomed*. Too much is happening too quickly for the tinkerer to succeed. Only those who play hard—who try any damned thing that comes to mind, as long as it's crazy enough to possibly change the world— are likely to survive. Many (most!) such risk takers will indeed be consumed by the flame. On the other hand, the handful who persevere will be those who lead us into an ... Age of True Re-imagination.

THE MESSIER THE BETTER

Thomas Middelhoff, *ex*-CEO of Bertelsmann. Jean-Marie Messier, *ex*-CEO of Vivendi. Ron Sommers, *ex*-CEO of Deutsche Telekom.

All three of those gentlemen (who are not so *gentle* men) are Europeans. Europe Needs Entrepreneurs! Europe needs more ... Middelhoffs, Messiers, and Sommerses.

Lesson: Bold Visions that run amok, assuming integrity, may be more important than so-called "successes."

BOYD GENIUS

Thirty-six hours before the Official Establishment of the Department of Homeland Security (27 February 2003), I'm in Washington, D.C., lecturing to many of the leaders of the DHS.

My mantra to those assembled:

RAISE THE "100% AGAINST ZERO DEFECTS" FLAG. FLY IT PROUDLY.

That flag, which flies at Eglin Air Force Base, traces its roots to Colonel John Boyd, the revolutionary military strategist, called by some the most original strategic mind in a thousand years. The same Boyd who once told a general he wasn't killing enough pilots in training. The same Boyd whose own pilots beat an enemy with far better equipment in the Korean War.

"Zero Defects" is great ... in a known environment. But it is Death Itself ... in Ambiguous Surroundings.

So join me. Raise the Flag. 100% Against Zero Defects.

! Contrasts

WAS	IS
A job for life (key word: "career")	A life full of jobs (key word: "project")
Clunky bureaucracies, plodding toward success	Agile alliances, failing their way to success
Accountants rule	Innovators rule
Tangible assets	Intangible assets
Success-to-failure cycles last decades	Success-to-failure cycles last months
Technology supports change	Technology drives change
Upstarts disrupt ... occasionally	Upstarts disrupt ... constantly
Industry rules: etched in stone	Industry definitions: scribbled in quicksand
By-the-book management	Rewrite-the-eBook improvisation

NEW BUSINESS ❗ ● NEW CONTEXT

2 CONTROL ALT DELETE: THE DESTRUCTION IMPERATIVE

! Technicolor Rules ...

- Destruction Rules!
- Destruction is Natural. (In nature.)
- Big acquisitions are stupid.
- (Dummy + Dummy = Big Dummy.)
- "In perpetuity" is an Obscene Phrase.
- The time for mellow prescriptions is gone.
- Time to take charge. Time to destroy.
- "Change the rules before somebody else does."
- "Organize" for performance and customer satisfaction.
- "Disorganize" for ... renewal and innovation.

! RANT

We are not prepared ...

We pursue preservation. But the old order is doomed.

We value permanence. But "permanence" is the last refuge of those with shriveled imaginations.

We practice change. But "change" is not enough. (Not nearly.)

! VISION

I imagine ...

A World Where the Idea of Corporations That Exist in Perpetuity is considered ... So Much Nonsense.

A World Where the Urge to Merge is buried beneath ... the Drive to Self-Destruct (and to Re-imagine).

A World Where the Timid Goal of "Improvement" (and the Tendency to Tinker) has given way to ... an Unabashed Commitment to Destruction.

A Word About a Word

"Destruction" (along with its verb-cousin "destroy") is a harsh word. And yet I firmly believe—I insist—that it is the right word for our time.

We must "destroy," in effect, the military and domestic-security structures of yesteryear ... structures that have proven inflexible in the face of new and hyper-flexible enemies.

We must *destroy* the timid cubicle slave within ... the one whose life is "celebrated" (or should I say "decried"?) by Scott Adams in *Dilbert*.

We must *destroy* the barriers that keep us (with rare exceptions, such as Dell and eBay) from taking but the slightest advantage of the new technologies available to us.

And so on. Yes ... and so on. We must destroy barriers everywhere. In schools. In hospitals. In the Armed Forces. In the CIA. In the big banks. In the big auto companies.

Destruction. Try swallowing that word. See how it tastes. It won't digest *comfortably* (key word). Not at first.

More Insane Statements by Very Sane People

Change-watcher Kevin Kelly told me it's "much easier to kill an organization than change it substantially." And I agree. That outrageous statement should send a Loud & Clear Message to all of us ... and to all of our organizations. That is: If it's truly easier to live without us ... if it's easier to create a Wal*Mart than to change a Sears ... or to hire an Internet-savvy 26-year-old than to "retool" a Web-wary 52-year-old ... then the ante is indeed Sky High. The need to embrace "change" (in fact, to go beyond "change" ... way beyond change) is imperative.

ENEMY OF THE ... STATIS

Virginia Postrel, writing in her book *The Future and Its Enemies:* "How we feel about the evolving future tells us who we are as individuals and as a civilization: Do we search for stasis—a regulated, engineered world? Or do we embrace dynamism—a world of constant creation, discovery, and competition? Do we value stability and control, or evolution and learning? ... Do we think that progress requires a central blueprint, or do we see it as a decentralized, evolutionary process? Do we consider mistakes permanent disasters, or the correctable by-products of experimentation? Do we crave predictability, or relish surprise? These two poles, stasis and dynamism, increasingly define our political, intellectual, and cultural landscape."

Jack Welch had a remarkable tenure as CEO of General Electric. Remarkable, of course, in terms of value created for the shareholders of that proud, legendary, but (in 1980) sluggish enterprise. But it was no less remarkable for the way that he just kept changing ... himself and the company ... up to the end of his tenure. Although he was in his 60s when the Internet arrived full-bore, Jack embraced it with childlike vigor.

As the Net gathered momentum, Jack asserted that there would be a New GE Way. He named it ... DYB.com. With DYB standing for "Destroy Your Business." That is: Blow the damn thing up ... *before* the competition does.

Peter Drucker has a nasty habit of getting things right. Very right. About 20 years before the rest of us. (Me included.) And I believe he was right when he said recently: "The corporation as we know it, which is now 120 years old, is not likely to survive the next 25 years. Legally and financially yes, but not structurally and economically."

Kevin Kelly is a visionary ... but he's no wild-eyed radical. And neither, of course, are Jack Welch and Peter Drucker. These men are sages, all of them. And yet they are *comfortable* (there's that word again) with terms like "easier to kill," "destroy your business," and "not likely to survive the next 25 years."

What does it mean when nonradicals use radical language?

It means ... it's time to take charge. Time to destroy.[1]

The Myth of Perpetuity

Just about the first thing you learn in Accounting 101 is the "fact" (the purely contrived "fact") that the corporation exists "in perpetuity."

I find the notion of "in perpetuity" ... arrogant.

In 2003, I find it *unspeakably* arrogant.

One of the biggest business best-sellers of the past 20 years is *Built to Last*, by Jim Collins and Jerry Porras.

I find the idea of "built to last" ... offensive.

In 2003, I think it's ... embarrassingly bad.

I've known both Jim and Jerry for a long time. I admire them. I admire their research. But to say that Jim and Jerry and I are not joined at the hip is understatement.

The editors of *Fast Company*, in a comment on a cover story by Collins that appeared in their magazine, made the case against the Collins View of the World as well as anyone could. "The problem with Built to Last," they wrote, "is that it's a romantic notion. Large companies are incapable of ongoing innovation, of ongoing flexibility. Increasingly, successful businesses will be ephemeral.[2] ... They will be built to yield something of value—and once that value has been exhausted, they will vanish."

TIME TO TAKE CHARGE

[1]"I groove on destruction." That's easy for me to say, right? But what about those who are just starting out—or simply trying to get by?

This book is not in fact aimed at chief executive officers of enormous public or private enterprises. It is aimed at "chief executive officers" of five-person project teams and heads of 30-person IS or HR departments. As I will subsequently suggest ("harangue" is more like it), each of us is now the Big Boss of our own enterprise (Me Inc.).

I sincerely believe that in turbulent times bosses at all levels and at all ages ultimately earn their keep by Blowing Things Up and Inventing a New Way ... not by preserving and (merely) Making Better the Old Way.

So yes ... take charge.

In any job.

At any age.

DYB.COM ... rules.

JUST BROWSING

[2]My favorite (recent) company is Netscape. Or I should say: My favorite (recent) company *was* Netscape.

Netscape: Born ... Changed the world ... Died.

All in about five years.

Makes sense to me.

What's true of companies is also true of individual careers:[3] A truly Big Impact often comes in a remarkably small amount of time. Swedish professors Kjell Nordström and Jonas Ridderstråle get at that point in their marvelous book *Funky Business*: "Greatness is fleeting and, for corporations, it will become ever more fleeting. The ultimate aim of a business organization, an artist, an athlete or a stockbroker may be to explode in the dramatic frenzy of value creation during a short space of time, rather than to live forever."

And here's Warren Bennis and Patricia Ward Biederman, offering a typically trenchant observation in their book *Organizing Genius*: Great Groups don't "last very long." (Bennis and Biederman know what they're talking about. They base that generalization on a close study of the Best of the Great Groups, as they label them: The Manhattan Project. Disney's first animation lab. Xerox PARC. And several more.)

Great Groups. Careers. Companies. Everywhere you look, the model of greatness comes down to this ... Make a Big Impact ... and then a Quick Exit. You even see it in nature. The most beautiful flowers (e.g., tulips) don't bloom very long. (Geraniums bloom forever. Enough said.)

(Sometimes the Public abets the process: Britain's two most potent 20th Century leaders—Churchill and Thatcher—were unceremoniously dumped when the citizenry judged that they'd done their thing. Transforming Leaders ... tend eventually to wear their followers out.)

Orson Welles, as Harry Lime in *The Third Man*, made the same point ... and put it in a grand historical context: "In Italy for 30 years under the Borgias they had warfare, terror, murder, bloodshed—and produced Michelangelo, Leonardo Da Vinci, and the Renaissance. In Switzerland they had brotherly love, 500 years of democracy and peace—and what did they produce? The cuckoo clock."

Of course, that's unfair.

(Or is it?)

Built to ... Deflate

The first of the major "biggest"/"best" lists that business magazines love to publish was the Forbes 100, which greeted us in 1917. Seventy years later, in an anniversary issue, *Forbes* surveyed the subsequent performance of those Rushmorian Leaders of our Nation's Peerless Economy. McKinsey senior officer Dick Foster and his colleague Sarah Kaplan analyzed all of that data and put it into context. The title of their brilliant book on this subject says it all ... *Creative Destruction: Why Companies That Are Built to Last Underperform the Market.*

Reading their findings, I recall Brando in *Apocalypse Now*: "The horror. The horror."

Net result: Of the 100 Sure Things of 1917, 70 years later, 61 were ... dead. (Thirty-nine were alive.) Of the 39 survivors, only 18 still numbered among the 100 biggest companies of 1987. Furthermore, those 18 "survivors" had underperformed the stock

---

IT'S IN THE HOLE

[3]Tiger Woods is the best player in the history of golf (so far, that is). Twenty years from now, he will be on the Senior Tour.

Tiger Woods: Born ... Changed the world of golf irrevocably (and for the better) ... Teed off into his sunset years.

Again: Makes sense to me.

market by 20 percent between 1917 and 1987. Just two (that is, 2 percent!)—GE and Kodak—had actually outperformed the market over that 70-year period. And now, 16 years later, you can kiss Kodak good-bye, too.

Foster and Kaplan then move to the Standard & Poor's 500, a list of top companies that S&P inaugurated in 1957. A scant 40 years later, only 74 of the initial 500 companies were still alive, which means that 426—*more than 80 percent*—were K.I.A. And of the remnant 74, just 12 (or 2.4 percent of the total) had outperformed the market during that 40-year period.

Foster and his team added their own analysis, even more damning. Consider this summary from the *Financial Times* in November 2002: "Mr. Foster and his McKinsey colleagues collected detailed performance data stretching back 40 years for 1,000 U.S. companies. They found that none of the long-term survivors ... managed to outperform the market. *Worse, the longer companies had been in the database, the worse they did.*"

Foster's conclusion: "It's just a fact: Survivors underperform."[4]

Wow! (Or, rather: Ouch!)

What the hell is going on here?

Answer (in part): Even before our own insane era, Big Guys had an inevitable tendency to get sluggish ... Very Sluggish. And if they didn't disappear, they performed in a way that can only be described as ... pitiful.

Beware ... Good Management

So did all the superstars of 1917 just get tired? Did their managers ... numbed by their own success ... forget how to manage? If only it were that simple! Harvard Business School professor Clayton Christensen gets at the heart of the issue in his best-selling book *The Innovator's Dilemma*. Read his analysis ... and then read my version of it:

"*Good management was the most powerful reason [leading firms] failed to stay atop*

MOZART MAKES ME WEEP ...
Because he created such beautiful music. Because he died at age 35.
Consider this (hypothetical) tombstone:

W.A. Mozart
1756–1791
He changed the world.
He enriched humanity.
He was only around for 35 years.

Think about it.

FLUX TIME
[4]In *The Company*, John Micklethwait and Adrian Wooldridge report that the rate of companies dropping out of the Fortune 500 increased *fourfold* between1970 and 1990. "Far from being a source of comfort," they write, "bigness became a code for inflexibility."

their industries. Precisely because these firms listened to their customers,[5] invested aggressively in technologies that would provide their customers more and better products of the sort they wanted, and because they carefully studied market trends and systematically allocated investment capital to innovations that promised the best returns, they lost their positions of leadership."

Again: Wow! (Or: ye gads!)

Now, let's rewrite that paragraph just a bit. I give you my word that the editorial additions (*in italics*) are true to the extensive research presented in the book:

"Good management *was* the most powerful reason leading firms failed to stay atop their industries. Precisely because these *giant, bureaucratic firms* listened to their *giant, bureaucratic, largest* customers, invested aggressively in *marginally innovative* technologies that would provide their *giant, bureaucratic* customers more and better products of the sort that they *already had and therefore* wanted more of, and because they carefully studied market trends, *which always say 'Do more of what you're already doing with a micro-twist or two,'* and systematically allocated investment capital to innovations that promised the best returns, *which are always the most conservative innovations,* they lost their positions of leadership."

Am I being unfair? I don't think so. Or if so, not by much.

Old Technology = New Trap

Working just downriver from Christensen in Cambridge, Massachusetts, is Jim Utterback, a stellar professor at MIT and the author of *Mastering the Dynamics of Innovation.* Jim's book—the pick of the litter in this arena—rips apart the brain-dead way that most companies respond to traumatic change:

"A pattern emphasized in the cases in this study [the typewriter, the DC-3, etc.] is the degree to which *powerful competitors not only resist innovative threats, but actually resist all efforts to understand them, preferring to further entrench their positions in the older products.* This results in a surge of productivity and performance that may take the old technology to unheard-of heights. But in most cases this is a sign of impending death."

Utterback offers, among others, the example of the electric-lighting industry, which arrived on the scene a hundred years ago and threatened to overwhelm the sleepy gas-lighting industry. But faced with such a grave threat, the gas-lighting people woke up from their long snooze, got on their horses—and quickly improved productivity. They were so effective in getting their act together that—in the short term!—they drove many of the electric-lighting pioneers out of business. Needless to say, today our cities are lighted by electricity. (Does this help clarify why I shiver at the idea of "continuous improvement" in a time of discontinuous change?)

THE CUSTOMER *ISN'T* ALWAYS RIGHT

[5] Good management is about giving our best customers what they want ... right?

Right. And that's the problem. Again, here's Clayton Christensen from *The Innovator's Dilemma*: "The highest-performing companies ... have well-developed systems for killing ideas that their customers don't want. As a result, these companies find it very difficult to invest adequate resources in disruptive technologies—lower-margin opportunities that their customers don't want—until [those same customers decide that they] want them. And by then it is too late."

Do the big guys ever learn this lesson? Don't bet on it! Consider this comment about today's (wealthy) pharmaceutical industry from the *Wall Street Journal*:

"Most drugs don't work well for about half the patients for whom they are prescribed, and experts believe genetic differences are part of the reason. The technology for such genetic testing is now in use ... . But the technique threatens to be so disruptive to the business of big drug companies—it could limit the market for some of their blockbuster products—that many of them are resisting its widespread use."

A fair assessment? I don't know. But given what I do know about the big drug companies, with their penchant for hyper-complexity and increasing addiction to conglomeration ... and to those blockbuster drugs ... I suspect that it's quite fair.

Not the Answer: Gigantism

If you acknowledge that "good management" is the bane of sustained success, that doesn't leave you with much, right? Well, I don't know what's "right." (I'm not that arrogant.) But I am convinced that I know what's wrong. (I *am* that arrogant.)

What's wrong? Above all, this is what's wrong: In an age that demands agility and flexibility, to go in the opposite direction ... to bulk up, to conglomerate, is ... STUPID.

In theory, companies opt for conglomeration in the name of "efficiency" (i.e., slash unnecessary administrative jobs) and "synergy" (i.e., combine the assets of different companies to create new value). There's not a damn thing wrong ... with the ... *theory*.

It's the practice that doesn't add up.

Every major merger creates a "conglomerate"—and the more loudly the conglomerators deny that point, the more likely it is to be true. And they deny it for very good reason. In the blunt and brutal words of *New Yorker* economics specialist James Surowiecki, "*Conglomerates don't work.*"[6]

There's now a ton of research on the M&A phenomenon. And the upshot of it is crystal clear: Most big mergers don't pan out. They *don't* achieve those promised "efficiencies." They *don't* create those celebrated "synergies." Some studies say that 50 percent of them don't work. Some studies say that 80 percent, or even 90 percent,

---

BLANK SLATE

[6]From *The Synergy Trap*, by Mark Sirower, a senior Boston Consulting Group professional and a strategy professor at New York University: "When asked to name just one big merger that has lived up to expectations, Leon Cooperman, the former co-chairman of Goldman Sachs's investment policy committee, answered, 'I'm sure there are success stories out there, but at this moment I draw a blank.'" Please re-read that. And weep.

BEES DO IT ...

Maybe the urge to *de*-merge is at least as "natural" as the urge to merge. That's the argument pressed by David Lascelles, co-director of the UK-based Centre for the Study of Financial Innovation:

"Since merger mania is now the rage ... what lessons can the bees teach us ... ? A simple one: merging is not in nature. [Nature's] process is the exact opposite: one of growth, fragmentation and dispersal. ... There is no megalomania, no merging for merging's sake. The point is that, unlike corporations, which just get bigger ... bee colonies know when the moment has come to split up into smaller colonies which can grow value faster. ... What the bees are telling us is that the corporate world has got it all wrong."

NEW BUSINESS ! NEW CONTEXT

don't work out. The most recent major analysis I came across, from *Business Week* in 2002, pegged the merger failure rate ("destroyed shareholder wealth") at precisely 61 percent. No study that I've come across argues that more than half of them actually are effective.

Do the Math (1+1=0)

The table below summarizes the financial impact of the 10 biggest mergers of the 1998–2002 period.

Recent Merger (Year)	Value Created (+) or Destroyed (–) Since Acquisition*
AOL/Time Warner (2001)	–$148 billion
Vodafone/Mannesmann (2000)	–$299 billion
Pfizer/Warner-Lambert (2000)	–$78 billion
Glaxo/SmithKline (2000)	–$40 billion
Chase/J.P. Morgan (2000)	–$26 billion
Exxon/Mobil (1999)	+$8 billion
SBC/Ameritech (1999)	–$68 billion
WorldCom/MCI (1998)	–$94 billion
Travelers/CitiCorp (1998)	+$109 billion
Daimler/Chrysler (1998)	–$36 billion

*As of 1 July 2002. From "Size Is Not a Strategy," *Fast Company*, September 2002.

Think about *that*.

But today, in 2003, you don't really have to think that hard. Just read the newspaper. In the first quarter of 2002 alone, new accounting rules required companies to write down one trillion dollars (*yes, trillion!*) in value from recent acquisitions.

Holy smoke.

Partial Answer: Disorganize

Am I saying that bigness never works ... that all conglomerates are doomed to fail? Not quite. Recall the Foster-Kaplan analysis. The one Forbes 100 company that beat the market over an 86-year period was GE, and GE turns out to be one of the biggest, most acquisition-friendly companies that ever was.

But here's the irony: GE is also arguably the ... Most Disorganized ... of our Giant Companies. Not undisciplined. *But* disorganized. GE was founded in the Entrepreneurial Edisonian Spirit. And it has somehow managed to retain that spirit.

Jack Welch had a lot to do with that in recent times. But he didn't do it alone. He inherited a Great and Obstreperous Institution. Some act as if GE, pre-Welch, was a basket-case. Not so! True, in 1981, when Welch began his long and illustrious tenure at the top, there was way too much bureaucracy at GE. Yet lots of innovative people in the company were happily ... and productively ... beyond the reach of that bureaucracy.

I should know. I consulted to GE back then ... in the boondocks. Louisville, Kentucky. Pittsfield, Massachusetts. Rutland, Vermont. And out there, GE bosses may have genuflected to HQ as required ... but only so that they could then go their ... Own Merry Way. In the hinterland, the hallmark of operations was ... disrespect.

In short, GE is a *self-destructing* company. It's always been that way. And the genius of Welch lay in taking it further in that direction. (Recall: DestroyYourBusiness.com.)

As I see it, the few "conglomerates" that have lasted are ... yes ... those that are best at ... Self-Destruction.

Partial Answers (Plural): The World According to Hamel

Strategy maven Gary Hamel has developed a riff on the secrets to enterprise vitality that echoes my own view of how organizations change. Here are three of his "secrets":

1. Use a "sell by" date. Every business unit should have a date by which it must either prove its value or close up shop.

2. "Spin in." Buy young firms to bring aboard excellent innovators. (Cisco. GE.)

3. "Spin out." Let the entrepreneurial types in your company take flight under your wing. Fund and support them in their start-up efforts. If one of these start-ups works ... buy it back (and damn the premium)!

Great stuff! And we've only begun.

(See "20 Ways to Self-Destruct", page 62.)

Partial Answer: Merge Smart

This is not a time for building defensive castles and moats ... and that's what "conglomeration" amounts to. It *is* a time for creation. "Acquisitions," said former Reuters CEO Peter Job, "are about buying market share. Our challenge is to create markets. There is a difference."

Fabulous.

In fact I acknowledge that acquisitions *can* have a role to play. But acquisitions, arguably, should follow the pattern set by John Chambers at Cisco Systems. By Jack Welch at GE. Or by John Wren at the advertising super-agency Omnicom. That is: Not

NEW BUSINESS **❗ •** NEW CONTEXT

> **CAPSIZING OF INDUSTRIES**
> It didn't happen overnight. It took 20 or 30 or 40 years. But in industry after industry, once-mighty empires have hit rough waters and begun to founder.
> *Cars.* America's Big Three were indomitable. And along came Honda and Hyundai.
> Oops.
> *Computers.* IBM rules, and Peters and Waterman certified it. And along came Microsoft and Intel. And. And.
> Oops.
> *Television.* NBC, ABC, CBS ... is all you need. And along came cable.
> Oops.
> *Pharma.* Big Pharma = Invincible. And along came new science ... and a dozen dozen dozen bio-techs.
> Oops.
> *Retail.* Sears! Macy's! Kmart! (And then The Gap ... Wal*Mart ... Home Depot.)
> Oops.
> *Finance.* Wells. Chase. Citi. And then Schwab, Fidelity, and dozens of others.
> Oops.

20 Ways to Self-Destruct

Allow me to pick up where Gary Hamel leaves off ... with an even score of ideas for turning your company into a self-destruction (read: reinvention) machine.

1. Establish a "sell-by" date for every business unit.

2. "Buy" R & D (the Cisco–Omnicom Acquisition Model). Pay so much money that you're forced to make the most of the acquisition!

3. Recruit World's Best ... and pay World's Best Compensation.

4. Change Top Execs' assignments every 36 months.

5. Start a HUGE Venture Capital fund. (Example: Intel.)

6. Encourage every Business Unit ... to Start Skunkworks ... staffed only with Premier Performers ... and Misfits.

7. Make sure that your Board is ... Sufficiently Weird. (Dull Board = Dull Co.)

8. Pepper all training programs with Freak Instructors.

9. Install (and instill) an "Up or Out" Philosophy.

10. Religiously seek out ... Strange Customers & Strange Suppliers.

11. Foster tension ... not "consensus."

12. Replace yourself with your Opposite.

13. Honor results ... not Great PowerPoint Presentations.

14. Constantly bring Proven Outsiders into the Top 100. Many should be from (way) outside the industry.

15. Diversity! (Diversity = Creativity.) (Period.)

16. Sell a minority interest in several key divisions to outsiders!

17. Move Key Divisions to ... New & Energetic locations.

18. Make sure the leadership team is heavily international, if you are a global firm.

19. Reduce middle management by 90 percent.

20. Charter a New Wholly Owned Subsidiary (and then another.)

acquisitions that involve One Sluggish Giant acquiring Another Sluggish Giant—but rather acquisitions that are about *purchasing innovation*. Not "bulk acquisitions"—but, rather, moderate size, on-the-rise "specialist acquisitions."[7]

Of course, incorporating a specialist company into a large entity is not easy. No acquisition is. Often the acquirer inadvertently stomps on the toes (and hearts) of the purchased company's feisty stars; and they leave. But a few companies, such as Cisco,

INABILITY TO CONCENTRATE

In a March 2003 article for the *Financial Times* called "Survival of the Fittest Not the Fattest," John Kay wrote: "I have heard it from people who make pharmaceuticals and from people who make defence equipment. From executives in utilities and executives in advertising. Among banks and law firms. ... They all expect their industry to develop the way the car industry has. In an increasingly globalized marketplace, maturing industries will become steadily more concentrated. Only a small number of big companies will survive.

"There is one problem with these analogies. What is said about the motor industry is not true. The peak of concentration in the automobile industry was reached in the early 1950s and since then there has been a substantial decline. ... However you look at it, small carmakers have been steadily gaining market share at the expense of large ones. Back in the 1960s, the 10 largest carmakers had a market share of 85 per cent; today it is about 75 per cent. ... Concentration has fallen, even though weak firms have repeatedly been absorbed through mergers.

"As markets evolve, differentiation becomes steadily more important. ... Success in the motor industry comes not from size and scale but from developing competitive advantages in operations and marketing these advantages internationally. The same is true in pharmaceuticals and defence equipment, utilities and banking, telecommunications and media."

SPECIALISTS OF THE HOUSE?

[7]GE under Welch acquired well over one thousand companies. Can you name any of them? My answer, just one: namely RCA, which brought NBC into the fold. The point then: The rest were no-name acquisitions, at the likes of GE Capital, in particular, that were best-in-brand, modest-sized specialists.

SEVEN "BIG" IDEAS

My guidelines for thinking about "consolidation":

    1. Big + Big = Disaster. (Statistically.) (There are exceptions: e.g., Citigroup.)

    2. Odds on achieving "projected synergies" among Mixed Big "cultures": 10 percent.

    3. Big (GE, Cisco, Omnicom) acquires Cool Specialist = Good. If you are willing to do "whatever it takes" to retain ... Top Talent.

    4. Max Scale Advantages can be achieved at a much smaller size than imagined. (Research is clear on this.)

    5. Common sin: Attacked by Big, Mediocre Medium marries Mediocre Medium to "bulk up." Result: Big Mediocrity ... or worse. (Retailers and distribution companies fall into this trap time and again.)

    6. Any size—if Great & Focused—can win, locally or globally.

    7. Increasingly, alliances deliver more value than mergers—and clearly abet flexibility. (Caveat: You have to be damn good at the ... Strategic Art of Alliance Management.)

NEW BUSINESS ! ● NEW CONTEXT

have mostly figured out how to stop the brain hemorrhage, and how to channel the creative spark of the specialist not only into the broader marketplace ... but also into the acquirer's own far more broad customer base.

Another way to merge smart is to merge ... virtually. The Internet changes everything! (As usual!) (See Chapter 4.) "Virtualization," writes Richard Rosecrance in his brilliant *The Rise of the Virtual State*, "is the recognition that territorial size does not solve economic problems. ... Economic access must become the substitute for increasing domain." In other words, size—"old" size, at least—may no longer be necessary. Companies are increasingly able to achieve the benefits of size—i.e., a larger scope for action—by means other than ownership. Simply put, a one-person enterprise, working out of a spare bedroom, can be in direct contact with the entire world and can have incredible scope and scale—all without owning a damn thing.

Bottom line: Bulk is not the same thing as breadth. Access and connection ... may well beat ownership.

Not the Answer: Incrementalism

Here's one item you won't find in Hamel's riff ... or in any other reasonably perceptive analysis: "Slow and steady wins the race, take one sensible step at a time."

"Sensible" baby steps won't cut it, I'm afraid. No, the CEO challenge today calls for broad leaps ... big plans ... staggering risks.

Everybody is wrestling with that challenge ... a challenge that will literally determine the fate of nations. In December 2000, Xavier Comtesse, former head of Swiss House for Advanced Research & Education, offered this blunt assessment of his countrymen: "You never hear a Swiss say, 'I want to change the world.' ... We need to take more risks."

And the Japanese are belatedly starting to question the merits of their deeply embedded don't-rock-the-boat culture. Hideki Shirakawa, a chemist who is one of Japan's (*very*) (surprisingly) few Nobel Laureates, says that his country faces a giant "science gap." He attributes the problem to the gène-deep rice-farming culture, in which "uniqueness [is] suppressed." Japanese scientists receive promotion on the basis of seniority. They believe in consensus and frown on debate—unlike their U.S. counterparts, who can be pals in private life, but "mortal enemies" when it comes to a scientific debate, Shirakawa says. The bias for Kaizen ("continuous improvement") in Japanese automobile and steel manufacturing equally affects Japanese science. Shirakawa similarly cites a lack of competition and critical evaluation—which is in sharp contrast to the brutally unvarnished "peer review" process that marks U.S. science. Syukuro Manabe, a fellow Japanese scientist, puts it this way: "What we [Japanese] need to

WANNA BET ...?
How the mighty do fall! But you can't imagine the toppling of Wal*Mart. Or Dell. Right?
    Hey, that's the way it feels to me. But ... recall that 1917 list: Who in 1917 would have imagined the death of Big Steel? The crumbling of Sears?
    To my 30-year-old readers: I hereby wager that when you're my age, Wal*Mart and Dell will be either dead or irrelevant.

ROSY SCENARIO
From Kaizen to "Cut, then": Turn to page 70 for more on the virtues of wise pruning.

create is job insecurity rather than security to make people compete more."

Switzerland and Japan. Two very different countries. One very powerful diagnosis: In a time of discontinuous change, incrementalism is *the* enemy.

But maybe calling incrementalism "the enemy" isn't strong enough. How about "the worst enemy"? Don't take my word for it. I cribbed that designation from MIT Media Lab boss Nicholas Negroponte: *"Incrementalism is innovation's worst enemy."* Sad fact: Big organizations ... by their very nature ... are addicted to incrementalism. No matter how well intentioned or how well led, they seldom make the changes that are necessary to deal with a truly discontinuous environment.

Thus ... Wal*Mart comes along. All the rules are changed. Some competing retail giants are unable to cope at all. Kmart. Montgomery Ward. Bradlees. And some, such as Sears, do a dramatic about-face ... and avoid the guillotine. (At least for a while.)

But face it: Most Big Enterprises that survive a challenge from an upstart do so as shadows of their former selves. Still alive. Still big. But no longer the pathfinders.

Some big-company types do get it. In 2001, I listened to an address by the CEO of one of the world's largest financial-services firms. After talking about the revolutionary developments now taking place in his industry and his planned response, he told his assembled troops, "I don't intend to sit quietly and be known as the 'King of the Tinkerers.'"

Nice. But all-too-rare.

There usually isn't time to "improve things." Take your pick. "Improve" ... or "Destroy and Rebuild." The Siren Call of 2003 is almost inevitably the latter.

More Than a Partial Answer: Destroy, Destroy, Destroy

"Destroy and Rebuild" ... that has been the hallmark of (for example ... and it is a *huge* example) the Great American Jobs Miracle.

Consider the following analysis of the U.S. economy. Between 1980 and 1998, we managed to create an amazing *29,000,000* net new jobs. About two-thirds of those jobs were high paying, and most of them were in industries that didn't exist prior to 1980. (We're a long way from Lee Iacocca's noxious prediction in the early 1980s that all new jobs would come courtesy of the likes of Wendy's.) During the same period, the European Union, which is one-third larger than the U.S. in population terms, managed

---

ASK YOURSELF ...

Hey, you ... yes, you ... the 42-year-old Process Manager who's leading a logistics overhaul for a 200-person division.

Ask yourself: Will you "improve the system" to "take advantage of the Web"? Or will you invent a mini-Dell ... a Novel & Revolutionary Supply-Chain Model ... that scares the pee out of people with its brashness?

It's your choice.
(Damn it.)
Think about it.
(Hard.)

ANOTHER GREAT WORD

Among my heroes is the Austrian economist Joseph Schumpeter, who famously argued that economic success derives from "gales of creative destruction."

"Gale" (like "destruction") (like "creative"): the perfect word to convey a perfectly necessary concept.

to add but 4,000,000 net new jobs.

What's the difference between +29,000,000 and +4,000,000—beyond the obvious "25,000,000"? Much of the answer can be seen in two simple equations (though the issue is anything but simple):

$$+29M = -44M + 73M$$
$$+4M = +4M - 0M$$

The Americans got to +29,000,000 by having the nerve ... often without grace ... to destroy 44,000,000 jobs. At General Motors. At Ford. At Sears. At Chrysler. At AT&T. At IBM. Then we offset those lost jobs with 73,000,000 new jobs. At Microsoft. At Dell. At CNN. At Genentech. At Amgen. At Fidelity. At Charles Schwab. The European Union got to the rather paltry sum of +4,000,000 by destroying nothing and created 4,000,000 new slots ... in the public sector. (Some interpretations are worse, suggesting that millions of private sector jobs were eliminated in order to keep feeding the government sector's employees.) (Does Europe, heaven forbid, need Newt Gingrich?)

Message (BIG): If you don't have the nerve to destroy (jobs), then you will never create (jobs) on a large scale.

Which is one (big) reason ... I AM A DESTRUCTION FANATIC.

America = Re-imaginings

But then ... America is all about destruction, all about restlessness, all about reinvention, and re-imaginings. That's why, about 400 years ago, we got "out of town"—that is, England—and set off for an unknown continent. (Here Be Dragons.) That's why, about 200 years ago, we again got "out of town"—that is, *New* England—and headed West. (Here be Mountain Passes.) Americanism = Restlessness.

And that's why so many of us feel a similar restless urge today. An urge to destroy the identities of the past, to put on the proverbial coonskin hat, and to become ... once

---

HATS OFF!
Charles Schwab!

They change their "fundamental strategy" every year or two. They disinherit their own (glorious) past. They love the New Technologies. They ... Groove On Change.

Schwab wins. For its ... Inconstancy. Its ... Utter willingness to go 89.5 degrees in a New Direction ... at the Drop of a Hat. If Necessary. (And it's often necessary.) (About every 24 months.)

COLOR COMMENTARY
I'm trained as an engineer. Trained to think in logical terms: "It's black. It's white."

But, as I've learned over the years, the real world doesn't work that way. In the real world, there's no relief from the fundamental tension between conservation and change. Between order and freedom. Between organization and disorganization.

Does that mean we're cursed to live in a world that's neither black nor white, but rather one shade or another of drab, dreary gray?

No! The alternative to black/white is not gray but ... Technicolor! Let a hundred colors bloom!

again ... explorers. To rip away the shackles of cubicle slavery. To take charge of our lives. To reinvent. And Re-imagine.

It won't be easy, just as it wasn't easy for those brave families in their Conestoga wagons, heading across the dusty and dry plains, and then on to the virtually impenetrable Rockies and Sierras. But if there wasn't always gold at the end of the rainbow (or, to be precise, in Northern California), there was—almost always—an opportunity for reinvention. A new start.[8] A new you.[9]

Consider the U.S.A.:

Government: 13 obstreperous colonies became 50 obstreperous states. Federalism (the devolution of power to states and localities) is alive and well in the U.S.—to a degree virtually unknown in the rest of the world.

Religion: We have more vigorously competing sects and congregations than any other nation. Because we compete in re ... EVERYTHING. Business. Sports. Even Matters of the Spirit.

Business (but not just business): We reserve our highest esteem for the Upstarts— the nonestablishment sorts who knock the Establishmentarians off their pedestals. And then, as soon as those upstarts become established, we work like hell to knock *them* off. (Knock *her* off: Martha Stewart.)

In short ... We are always "mixing it up." We Revel in the Fray Per Se.

The Changing Political Economy of Organizations

When you really get down to it, that Fray—the Key Issue throughout American history— is a matter of *governance*. Who rules? And how? And how much? Order vs. Freedom.

The same questions apply to companies. After all, every organization is more or less a nation unto itself. Some organizations are the economic equivalent of China (Wal*Mart); others are the economic equivalent of Monaco (Tom Peters Company). Either way, these "nutty" times demand a different set of organizational skills and strategies from those that won the day in quieter times ... back when most industries consisted of a small set of known competitors. Those days, the Era of Tidy Oligopolies, are over.

As I see it, the oligopolists of yesteryear were the Socialists of their time. By contrast, new times require much friskier enterprises, the exemplars of which I call Free Market Democrats ("Democrats," meaning believers in Open Democracy, not members

---

GOING WEST, AS A YOUNG MAN

[8] I followed the well-worn wagon tracks myself, in 1966, when I left my East Coast home to go on active duty in the Navy in Port Hueneme, about 65 miles north of Los Angeles. I ended up staying in California for 35 years, 8 months, and 21 days. When I finally came back East, I didn't have any trouble giving up California sprawl or California smog. But I had a lot of trouble giving up the *idea* of Tom-in-California. The idea of having made a new start, of having made myself up as I went along.

THE NEW (E)ME

[9] Turns out, away from the spotlight, that this Re-invention Proclivity is pretty universal.

For one (not so small) thing, just look at the way kids—*and adults!*—from *all* cultures have taken to assumed names and assumed roles on the Internet. This "trivial," child-like phenomenon is actually of great consequence: Playing with new identities has never before been so readily possible.

of a particular political party). *Only* Free Market Democrats, I believe, will survive in these perilous times.

(See, on the page opposite, a bonus list of "Contrasts" ... which I offer to illustrate the shift from the old to the new Political Economy of Organizations.)

The Eternal "Governing" Tension

As I was working on this treatise about destroying and then re-imagining business, I happened upon two books that made me think anew about the whole issue of governance.

First, there was David McCullough's splendid biography of John Adams—the story of Adams and his colleagues wrestling with the nature of humankind and the governance thereof. The key actors had differing points of view. (To put it mildly.) Hamilton wanted centralization, standardization, a solid and stable currency. Jefferson, decentralization, grassroots democracy, a commitment to the agrarian, entrepreneurial ideal. The Hamiltonians and Jeffersonians have battled ever since! (FYI: Hamilton died in a duel.)

Second, there was Garry Wills' *A Necessary Evil: A History of American Distrust of Government.* Wills covers a lot of the same ground as McCullough, and begins by describing the basic American attitude toward institutions of state:

"Government is accepted as, at best, a necessary evil, one we must put up with while resenting the necessity. We want as little of it as possible, since anything beyond that necessary minimum instantly cancels one or another liberty."

My attitude, exactly!

Battling over the essentials of governance is actually what this and every other management book is all about! For a nation. *Or* ... for a seven-person project team that is crafting a business-process change. Do we listen to some Hamiltonian type, who wants to take the process that we've got now, erase the worst of its inefficiencies, and make it "more efficient" and more "under control"? Or do we seek out some zany Jeffersonian spirit who will say that the whole thing "is bullshit," that we ought to be thinking on an entirely different plane, that we ought to be reinventing the world, not just making some "efficiency" changes?

That's the eternal tug-of-war—the dramatic push and pull, the essential and never-ending tension—between conservation and change. Which side will ultimately win? There is no answer. Or rather, the answer is to realize that ... there is no answer.

SAD FACT (ENHANCED)

Big organizations mean well. It's their baggage that weighs them down. In early 2003, I attended a top management retreat of a big company ... facing big problems.

The top tier is as smart as it comes. And they know the score. (And know that their options are underwater—buried at the bottom of the Marianas Trench.) Yet the language of change was tepid. A host of new "programs"—but each one buried in complex algorithms and encumbered with "We tried that in 19XX and it didn't work." I've seldom viewed the Perils of Being the Establishment so clearly.

Good luck!

! Contrasts

"OLD ECONOMY" SOCIALISTS	"NEW ECONOMY" FREE MARKET DEMOCRATS
Conserve	Destroy
Promote from within	Welcome "foreigners"
Nepotistic hiring	Creative recruitment
Restrict speech	Honor free speech
"Political correctness" prevails	Dissent flourishes
Legislators-for-life	Term limits
Tortoises	Hares
Seniority	Meritocracy
"Wait your turn"	"Up or out"
Centralize	Decentralize
HQ planners rule	Divisions ("States") rule
(1 government = 1 way)	(50 states = 50 labs)
Preserve the Establishment	Topple the Establishment
Respect the administrators	Honor the entrepreneurs
Retrench	Reinvent
Defense	Offense
Fat HQ	Lean HQ
The center rules	The periphery rules
Equal pay	Merit pay
Calibrate pay scales carefully	Reward top performers abundantly
Marginalize misfits	Lionize misfits
"Bigger is better"	"Better is better"
Pessimism	Optimism
Hobbes	Locke
Sadism	Masochism
Fear	Greed
Avoid defeat	Obsess about victory
Strive for uniformity	Strive for excellence
Best practices	New practices
Monochromatic thinking	Technicolor dreaming
"Works well"	"Knocks your socks off"
Calm. Quiet. Stability.	Frenzy. Noise. Churn.
Police	Lawyers
Brahms	Dylan
William Henry Harrison	TR (Teddy Roosevelt)
Honor the old!	Welcome the new!
Plans	Action
Ready. Aim. Fire.	Ready. Fire! Aim.
Order & Obedience	Disorder & Disobedience
Batten down the hatches	Fling open the windows to "Gales of Creative Destruction"

NEW BUSINESS **!** • NEW CONTEXT

MORE COLLINS, MORE CLAPTRAP

In Jim Collins' latest, *Good to Great*, the author celebrates "self-effacing, quiet, reserved, even shy" leaders who bring about the big transformations. Examples included.

Fine, Jim.

Psychologist-management expert Michael Maccoby and I have frequently clashed. Not this time.

Michael recently wrote of "larger than life leaders" ... e.g.: "egoists, charmers, risktakers with big visions." Exemplars he cites: Carnegie. Rockefeller. Edison. Ford. Welch. Jobs. Gates. He, of course, could have added Messier and Middelhoff and Ebbers and Lay. Nonetheless, I'll still take Michael's list over Jim's.

While flying across the U.S. a while back, I got so agitated about "quiet" and "even shy" that I started scribbling madly on the inside back cover of the spy novel I was reading. Here's what I was able to subsequently decipher from my hen scratches:

T. Paine/P. Henry/A. Hamilton/B. Franklin/A. Lincoln/U. S. Grant/W. T. Sherman/M. L. King, Jr./M. Gandhi/G. Steinem/W. S. Churchill/M. Thatcher/Picasso/Mozart/Copernicus/ Newton/J. Welch/L. Gerstner/L. Ellison/B. Gates/S. Ballmer/S. Jobs/S. McNealy.

Quiet. Stoic. Hardly! Made the World Wobble on its Axis? Amen..

The Promise of a Rose Garden

Change is inevitable. Destruction is the order of the day.

Yes, I *groove* on destruction.

(Are you getting comfortable with that word yet?)

Still ... the essential, unsolvable dilemma remains:[10] Organization versus Disorganization. Order versus Disorder (aka Chaos, aka Freedom). Even as we move aggressively toward one end of that spectrum, we must negotiate the complex ways in which Order and Disorder (and so on) coexist.

To consider all this, let's shift from Matters of High Statecraft to ... the humble rose garden. Arie de Geus, who pioneered scenario planning at Royal Dutch/Shell, offers the following horticultural analogy in his book *The Living Company*:

"Rose gardeners ... face a choice every spring: how to prune our roses. ... The long-term fate of a rose garden depends on this decision. ... If you want to have the largest and most glorious roses of the neighborhood, you will prune hard. You will reduce each rose plant to a maximum of three stems. ... This represents a policy of low tolerance and tight control. You force the plant to make the maximum use of its available resources, by putting them into the rose's 'core business.' However, if this is an unlucky year [late frost, deer, green-fly invasion] you may lose the main stems or the whole plant! Pruning hard is a dangerous policy in an unpredictable environment. Thus, if you [are] in a spot where nature may play tricks on you ... you may opt for a policy of high

---

PARADOX FOUND

[10]To deal with terrorism we must question some of the very freedoms that we are defending in the war on terror. Talk about paradox! And talk about high stakes!

ONE PERCENT SOLUTION

Only 1 of the 100 "best" companies of 1917 did better than average over the course of the following 86 years. Not exactly impressive.

tolerance. You will leave more stems on the plant. ... You will never have the biggest roses ... but you have a much enhanced chance of having roses every year. You also achieve a gradual renewal of the plant. ... In short ... tolerant pruning ... achieves two ends: (1) It makes it easier to cope with unexpected environmental changes. (2) It leads to a continuous ... restructuring of the plant. The policy of tolerance admittedly wastes resources ... the extra buds drain away nutrients ... from the main stem. ... But in an unpredictable environment,[11] this policy of tolerance makes the rose healthier. ... Tolerance of internal weakness, ironically, allows the rose to be stronger in the long run."

I'm not a rose gardener. Yet I find this passage—at least upon third or fourth or fifth or sixth or seventh reading—to be one of the most profound Strategic Organizational Messages I have come across in 35 years of worrying about such issues.

Driven to ... Destruction

Remember the Big Idea put forth by Clayton Christensen: "Good management" is the No. 1 (!) (Ace of Hearts) reason that big firms fail. Because, all too often, "good management" means big, bureaucratic blobs ... peopled by big, bureaucratic, blobby employees ... paying attention to big, bureaucratic, blobby customers ... supplied by big, bureaucratic, blobby suppliers.

It's time to change all of that. Dramatically.

Time to destroy what we are. (New technology ... and new threats ... are helping us along mightily!)

Time to build anew.

A frightening time. A fun time. Both, in equal measure. It is always so at moments of dramatic change.

My goal in this chapter: To get you to feel my frustration ... to *feel* my anger with the Forces of Order that continue to hold sway in a *Dis*orderly Time. And then to make you *comfortable*, both in word and in deed, with ... DESTRUCTION!

Mantra: Cherish IMPERMANENCE ... Cherish UPSTARTS ... Cherish ... DISRESPECTFUL COLLEAGUES (and customers, suppliers, employees) ... Cherish DESTRUCTION.

Message: Destruction rules! Destroy to create. Learn to *love* the word ... DESTRUCTION. Or Else. (Else = Irrelevance.)

TO BE ... (DIS)CONTINUED

[11]From Dick Foster and Sarah Kaplan's *Creative Destruction*: "The difficulties ... arise from the inherent conflict between the need ... to control existing operations and the need to create the kind of environment that will permit new ideas to flourish—and old ones to die a timely death. ... *We believe that most corporations will find it impossible to match or outperform the market without abandoning the assumption of continuity.*"

! Contrasts

WAS		IS
Servants of stability triumph	–	Masters of instability rule
Honor (and preserve) the ones that brung you	–	Blow up (or sell) the ones that brung you
Bulk Up!	–	Be Agile!
Achieve dominance through (permanent) acquisitions	–	Achieve reach through (temporary) alliances
Acquire ... BIG THINGS	–	Acquire ... COOL THINGS* (*Hint: Cool Things are usually small)
Learn ... Remember ...	–	Unlearn ... Forget ...
Honor ... Cherish	–	Dishonor ... Reinvent

The impact of the New Technologies...
changes everything. Yes ... everything!

new bus!ness
new technology

The modern computer has been with us for more than half a century. But it was arguably a member of the supporting cast, not a prime determinant of enterprise strategy, until the early- or mid-1990s. Then the emergence of the Internet and the wild growth in telecommunications technology together changed everything. Virtually overnight.

Fact is, despite sectoral turmoil and disappointments of the last two or three years, we are merely in the baby stages of the infotech revolution. Established organizations do not exactly shine in discontinuous times. Neither do successful 40-year-old middle managers. On the contrary, orgs and hierarchs tend to hunker down, to guard their turf ferociously—and to pray that "This, too, shall pass."

Well it won't ...

IN THE CROSSHAIRS:
WHITE-COLLAR CATACLYSM

! Technicolor Rules ...

- White-collar employment as we've known it is dead.
- The time frame for total reinvention of your job is 15 years (if you're lucky).
- "Old" bureaucracy (read: tall towers full of bureaucrats) is over.
- New white-collar software systems = forklifts for the mind.
- "A bureaucrat is an expensive microchip."
- "Don't own nothin' if you can help it."
- The unthinkable is thinkable. No: likely.

 ## ! RANT

We are not prepared ...

We aim to "improve white-collar productivity" ... here and there. Instead, we must destroy bureaucratic processes and bureaucratic structures—and build anew, from a new base.

We scurry to shore up the last bastions of "job security." Instead, we must recognize that single-employer "job security" is over.

We focus on developing "marketable skills." Instead, we must cultivate the only quality that matters—a Deep Understanding That Anything Is Possible.

 ## ! VISION

I imagine ...

The Demise of the Cubicle Slave—and of his or her numbing, unsatisfactory work.

An average career that consists of 10 different jobs ... in 5 different companies ... from 3 different industries.

Jobs that grant Extraordinary Leeway to those with the Vigor and the Moxie to Invent New Futures.

A return to Self-Reliance: I AM IN CHARGE HERE!

The 98.5 Percent Factor

An old man who had been a union organizer on the London docks told my colleague Richard King that when a timber ship pulled into those docks in 1970, it took 108 guys some five days to unload it.

That's **540 man days** (Grueling man days.)

At about that time, something happened ... something called "*containerization*."

Thirty years later, at the turn of the century (and of the millennium), when a timber ship pulled into the same docks in the same city, our Grand Old Man told Richard it took eight guys one day to unload it.

That's **8 man days** (Moreover: Those "blue-collar" guys are now mostly doing "white-collar" work with computerized controllers.)

Net result: a **98.5%** reduction in the blue-collar manpower requirement for an essential task.

When I recount those statistics, whether in land-locked Omaha, Nebraska, or at the Port of Dubai in the United Arab Emirates, no one gasps. Everyone is well aware of what containerization has done to the docks ... just as they understand what the forklift has done to the distribution center ... or what robotics[1] has done to the automobile factory.

Welcome to the Blue-Collar Revolution.

Been there. Done that. Right?

"EXTREME"? ME?

The 98.5 Percent Factor! Do I really believe this stuff (you might well ask), or am I just trying to scare the hell out of you?

Answer: I really believe it. And I am trying to scare the hell out of you.

I do not resort to hyperbole. When I make an extreme statement ... it's because I've come across an extreme example. And when I come across such an example ... I ask: WHY NOT? I always argue from data—extreme data, to be sure—but accurate extreme data.

"Extremism" is the standard, in my view. (Hey, these are extreme times.)

SHORT CIRCUIT

[1]The automation juggernaut just keeps gathering speed. Consider this description, from the *New York Times*, of a recently inaugurated IBM chip factory: "Throughout the 500 processing steps, which typically last 20 days, the wafers are not touched by human hands. The circuits etched into the chips are less than one-thousandth the width of a human hair. Human operators are there to monitor the systems, catch errors and fine-tune production processes for greatest efficiency."

White-Collar Blues

In one sense, Blue-Collar World doesn't really matter that much. Damn few of us—at least in the fully developed countries—even work there anymore. In the United States, about three-quarters of us work in the service sector. But that figure is misleading, because well over 80 percent (perhaps 90 percent) of people who work in "manufacturing" don't do any manufacturing: They're accountants and lawyers and engineers and purchasing officers and finance professionals and human-resources people. Work as an accountant at Caterpillar, and the labor statisticians say that you're in "manufacturing." Do the same thing for Airborne Express or DHL, and you're a member of the "service sector." Only the statisticians seem to think the difference is worth noting.

Truth is, we fretted about blue-collar productivity for more than a century—at least since the days of Frederick Winslow Taylor, whose time-and-motion studies helped launch a necessary revolution in blue-collar efficiency. Another blue-collar productivity frenzy began around 1980, when we Americans started to realize that the Japanese were hammering us—in ship building, in steel making, in automobile manufacturing, even in semiconductor production.

The 100-Square-Foot Factor

Take three paces and a skip-step. That's about 10 feet. Turn 90 degrees. Take another three+ paces. That's another 10 feet. Repeat twice more. You've just circumscribed an area consisting of 100 square feet ... an area smaller than the average spare bedroom!

One hundred square feet. That's roughly the total amount of space required for spare-parts storage at Dell Computer's new OptiPlex facility, a manufacturing operation that turns out 80,000 custom-engineered computers ... per day.

One hundred square feet ... I just can't deal with it.

Years ago, as an MBA student at Stanford, I learned how to compute EOQ (Economic Order Quantity); that is, how to calculate the amount of inventory required to deal with a certain level of sales and inherent organizational stickiness. (Bottom line: Crappy processes = Lots of required inventory.)

One hundred square feet ... makes a mockery of EOQ.

The real meaning of the "100-Square-Foot Factor": *Every iota's worth of Bureaucratic Bullshit has been drained from Dell's Extended Supply Chain Family.*

100SQFT

Meanwhile—from Omaha to Dubai—we paid the scantest attention to white-collar productivity. And in that sense, Blue-Collar World does matter. Because the revolution that happened in Blue-Collar World is coming soon in a slightly different costume to a white-collar profession near you.

The spotlight is now clearly on White-Collar World. That's the true nature of the New Software Revolution. The revolution is not about sexy websites (successful or failed); it is about the thoroughgoing, thoroughly unsexy reconception and automation of white-collar business processes within the firm and among its connected partners.

Yank Your Supply Chain

A colleague of mine once asked me: "Hey, Tom, what's the true definition of a middle manager?" Me: "Don't have a clue." My friend: "A middle manager is a person whose power can be measured by his or her ability *not* to sign something."

That is, we say: "Wow, that Dick Jones is one powerful guy. My project proposal has been on his desk for two weeks now, and he hasn't done a thing with it."

Amusing? Maybe.

Tragic? I think so.

True? Without a doubt.[2]

And that's where the "100-Square-Foot Factor" gets its bite. In DellWorld, scraps of paper cannot sit on Dick Jones' or anybody else's desk for two *seconds* ... or two minutes, or two hours, or two days. Let alone two weeks. In DellWorld, strategic and tactical decisions involving the whole extended family of partners happen at the Speed of Light.

Here's an example of how things work at Dell: You order a thousand terminals from Dell, specifying that you want them ASAP. But then a dust storm somewhere in northern Mexico causes a shipping delay. Dell's master "supply chain" computer system surveys the inventory of those terminal-makers that operate within your delivery radius. The system discovers that although no terminals of the model you ordered are currently in stock, some larger terminals are available—but they cost about $100 more apiece. The Dell system gets back to you instantaneously, tells you about the availability of the larger monitors, and offers a $50 per-item discount (plus on-time delivery) if you will accept those monitors in fulfillment of your order.

IN THE CROSSHAIRS

[2] *Critical point: This is not Tom Peters, self-appointed expert, lecturing to the unwashed masses. This is Tom Peters, first and foremost, lecturing to himself.*

The days of the "talking head" management lecturer, giving seminars in hotel ballrooms, are numbered.

I am in the white-collar crosshairs as much as any of you are.

Proof? Consider IBM. Among many profound changes, Big Blue has recently moved most of its training activities out of the classroom and onto the desktop. As a result, the company has saved around a quarter-billion dollars in annual costs. More important: Employees who receive training via desktop computer report higher customer satisfaction scores than do those who get their training in a classroom setting. That's particularly big deal, since classroom training is one area where IBM has consistently been the best of the best. Moreover, today's training software is primitive compared to where it will be in a scant five years, let alone 10 years—when the "Gameboy Generation" starts their professional careers.

The point? In the dreary old days of (say) 1998, that process would have required "strategic pricing decisions" involving three or four levels of middle management. Now microprocessors "handle" such "strategic decision making" ... and do so in nanoseconds.

The result? Happy customers! Incredible business efficiencies! And the elimination of almost all mid-level "white-collar" jobs—clerical and managerial—throughout the Dell Supply Chain! (Which is the primary reason that Dell has given companies like IBM, the *former* Compaq, and Hewlett-Packard such fits over the last decade or so.)

Forklifts for the Mind

Grunge. That's the term used by technology guru Michael Schrage to describe all the "business process" stuff—all the wasted motion—that defines White-Collar World. Says Schrage: "The coefficient of friction associated with the grunge of business is amazing!"

That's the verbal version. You'll find the pictorial version in Scott Adams' *Dilbert* cartoon strip, the most popular business "writing" in decades. *Dilbert* lets us know that, even in 2003, virtually all "business processes" consist mostly of grunge ... i.e., bullshit heaped upon bullshit.

But we are suddenly training all of our artillery on that grunge!

And our weapons stride forth in a phalanx of acronyms. E.g.: ERP. (Enterprise Resource Planning.) ASPs. (Application Service Providers.) Whatever. The point is clear: The new white-collar software systems are nothing more (and nothing less!) than ... *forklifts for the mind.* The goal of this new software is to take that grunge[3] out of business processes ... to take that grunge out of the lives of *Dilbert*'s Cubicle Slaves. All of it. Using the latest technology, Wal*Mart launched a white-collar productivity barrage that, according to some research, accounted directly and indirectly for as much as one-third of America's total productivity increase during the 1990s.

Not so incidentally, when you scour all the grunge from the systems, you've done far more than "increase productivity," even dramatically. Instead you have re-imagined the fundamental terms of reference for the industry, and for all the industries with which it is connected. No, this is not a dramatic "improvement" story—it's a True Saga of Connected Re-imaginings.

LET THE CHIPS FALL
Dan Sullivan, consultant and executive coach, frames the White-Collar Cataclysm this way: "A bureaucrat is an expensive microchip." The late Bill McGowan, CEO of MCI during its years of extraordinary growth, likewise said, "A middle manager is a human message switch."

FINNISH LINE: STAY "ON"!
[3]Attention, grunge-encrusted bosses: If you don't watch out, technology will leap right over you.

Consider this comment from Risto Linturi, a Finnish m(mobile)-guru: "Managers in Finnish companies always keep their phones on. Customers expect fast reactions. ... [And] if you can't reach a superior, you make many decisions yourself. Managers who want to influence decisions of subordinates must keep their phones open."

For more on how InfoTech is helping people eliminate grunge (and bosses?), read *Smart Mobs*, a brilliant book by Howard Rheingold.

eLIZA and Co.

Think about the White-Collar Revolution, as I call it, and typically you think about a microchip replacing a $35,000-a-year staffer who does mundane paper-processing chores in the back office of a bank or an insurance company. But recent developments suggest that the $239 microprocessor is taking dead aim at the $150,000-a-year manager whom that $35K staffer used to report to.

Recent developments like ... Project eLIZA.

Project eLIZA, the biggest research project under way at IBM, focuses on what are called "artlects" ... artificial intellects. The products of eLIZA aim to repair busted computer systems by creating wholly new solutions ... solutions that had never been imagined before. Much more than Deep Blue, IBM's computerized chess maestro, eLIZA constitutes a true ... Next Generation Thinking Machine.

I'm no expert on all of this. But I know enough as a lay observer to claim confidently that when it comes to artificial intelligence, eLIZA and its ilk are increasingly (and finally) ... The Real Thing.

The next 25 years are going to bring *astounding* advances in artificial intelligence[4] and related branches of information technology.

Implications for the individual?

Astounding.

Implications for the organization?

Astounding.

THE HEART OF THE MATTER

[4]Consider the practice of reading an ECG to figure out whether a patient has had a heart attack. To see whether a computer was up to that task, Swedish scientist Lars Edenbrandt created some relatively primitive AI software, and then compared the success of this software in reading ECGs with that of seasoned doctors. For example, he asked Hans Öhlin, the chief of coronary care at the University of Lund Hospital, to examine 2,240 ECGs, half of which represented patients who were known to have suffered heart attacks. After taking as much time as he needed with all 2,240 read-outs, Öhlin correctly identified 620 of the 1,120 heart attacks. And Lars Edenbrandt's software? It easily trumped Dr. Öhlin, identifying 738 of the 1,120 cardiac arrests correctly.

Dr. Atul Gawande, who cites the Edenbrandt study in his book *Complications*, also discusses a research review that examined 100 studies of artificial intelligence (And recall: Most AI technology is still fairly primitive.) The conclusion of that review: "In virtually all cases, statistical thinking equaled or surpassed human judgment."

Message: Your doctor can be replaced by a microprocessor. And if she can be replaced ... so can you and I!

It's Later Than You Think

Allow me to offer a prediction: *At least 80 percent of white-collar jobs, as we know them today, will either disappear entirely or be reconfigured beyond recognition ... in just the next 15 years.*

That is, the employment world of the 35-year-old in 2003 will bear no resemblance to the employment world of that same person, age 50, in 2018.

Easy for me to say, right? I'm just one of those management gurus who hustles books by uttering extreme statements—but faces no real consequences for getting it wrong.

Well, maybe. But you can't say the same about Jeff Immelt, CEO of GE. Wall Street analysts slice and dice every word he utters, and so he utters them ... very carefully. In an interview in early 2002, Jeff said that 75 percent of GE's administrative and back-office jobs would be "digitized" (accomplished by microprocessors and computer-telecom networks) within ... 3 years.

(Holy smoke!)

I say "15 years." GE's No. 1 says "3 years."

Recall the "98.5 Percent Factor." I see no reason to believe that the 98.5 percent man-hour reduction in Blue-Collar World won't be repeated—to the last man hour—in White-Collar World.

That's my world ... and yours.

For Export: Your Job

The microprocessor and the densely networked computer will supplant many of us. (Maybe even me.) But that's not the only force now at work. We in the developed world have spent the last two decades shipping blue-collar jobs offshore. First those jobs left countries such as the United States and went to the likes of Korea. From Korea, they went to Taiwan. Then, from Taiwan they departed for Mainland China, Indonesia, and India.

And ... now ... we're doing ... precisely the same thing ... down to the dotting of longitudes and the crossing of latitudes ... with white-collar jobs.

Computer guru Michael Dertouzos said in 1999 that India would add $1 *trillion* to its GDP in short order, by insourcing 50 *million* white-collar jobs at $20,000 each. That's not hyperbole. Already, airlines and banks and insurers, among many others, are zapping great gobs of work ... everything from routine "back room" activities to advanced software-design tasks ... off to places like Bangalore and Hyderabad, an area that some already consider to be the second-largest software center on earth, currently behind only Silicon Valley. A network of satellites makes Bangalore and Hyderabad as "close" to me as the guy in the building next door ... in downtown Chicago or Miami.

And that's just the first step. Indian wages are rising (just as the wages of Korean manufacturing workers rose 20 years ago), and the next phase of white-collar export has already begun. Not long ago, for example, Aetna began doing sizeable amounts of back-office chores in ... Ghana. That is, Ghana is now to India, in the white-collar job-outsourcing cascade, as Indonesia was to Korea, in the progressive shift of blue-collar labor from one developing country to another.

Buckle Up—We're In for a Bumpy Ride

White-collar employment as we've known it is dead. The transformation may be Ugly. And Painful. But it's on ... with Unimaginable Fury.

All of our organizations will be reinvented—*completely*—in the next 25 years. All of our careers will be reinvented—*completely*—in the next 25 years. All job security, as we have known it over the past three or four generations, is over. Over and gone.

Now, I say good riddance to most of the above. But I do so acknowledging how unnerving all of these changes may seem. Particularly if you're over about 35 years of age, and if you weren't born with a joystick or a mouse in your hand. But terrifying or not ... here we go.

Remember: *There's no opt-out button*.

Flat Org Society

The company org chart isn't the only place where you can see the White-Collar Revolution making an impact. Just look at the places where we do our work.

Only a century or so ago, most Americans lived on farms. Over the short space of the following half-century, more and more Americans moved toward the city ... and began working in factories. Then, over the past half-century, we deserted the factories and found work in White-Collar Towers.

Now, at the start of the 21st century, the Age of White-Collar Towers is coming to a close. Consider Silicon Valley. Land of the Low-Rise—flat buildings[5] put together fast. And home to flat, relatively nonbureaucratic organizations.

Remember Sears-versus-Wal*Mart? Want to visualize it? Consider these two "snapshots".

Snapshot No. 1: The Sears Tower, alongside Lake Michigan in Chicago. Until recently, this hundred-story behemoth was the headquarters of Sears. And a perfect picture of Sears, one might say: about a hundred levels of Formidable Bureaucrats ... stacked one on top of the other.

Snapshot No. 2: A *non*descript *non*tower in Bentonville, Arkansas. This building ... flat as a pancake, relatively speaking ... is where Wal*Mart runs its empire.

The Sears Tower looks like old Sears: hierarchical, bureaucratic, sluggish, bound by Ancient Procedures. The Wal*Mart nontower looks like Wal*Mart: Flat. Fast. Agile. No baloney. No grunge.

Bottom line: The Tall Tower ... and with it the Old White-Collar Job ... are D.O.A.

WHITE-COLLAR GROUND ZERO?

[5] I would argue ... and I know this may seem a little outrageous ... that the destruction of the World Trade Center on 11 September 2001 had a symbolic impact that goes far beyond the heinous act of terrorism that caused it. That is: The Age of Large Numbers of Human Beings Crammed into Tall Towers is over. Finito. History.

People still work in Tall Towers. But we'll never be able to look at that work, or at those towers, in the same way again.

The Disembodied Enterprise

The organization (rock solid, by tradition) is becoming disembodied.[6] That $239 microchip is taking over many jobs. The Indians and Ghanaians are taking over many more jobs. Anything and everything is being outsourced: Pharmaceutical research. Customer service. HR. Finance. Logistics. And ...

"We own all the intellectual property," said Jim McDonnell, a Vice President of HP. "We farm out all the direct labor."

Just how disembodied can an enterprise get? I have only the slightest difficulty imagining, in 2020, a $10 billion global enterprise ... with seven full-time employees. Admittedly, that seems far-fetched. But I find it increasingly easy to imagine the unimaginable. No thought is too outrageous!

Nothing is unimaginable! Imagine that!

Just a few years ago, who would have supposed that 157,000,000 people would be using the Web ... in the United States alone ... by late March 2002?

Yes, anything is possible. In fact, the nuttier the supposition, the more likely it is to come true. (Again: Who would have guessed that 19 terrorists, using the Internet and armed with box cutters, could bring the United States effectively to its knees?)

Anything is possible.[7]

Anything is *likely*.

Are you ready?

SHOE TIME

[6]Forrest Gump, that great unsung management guru, anticipated the advent of the disembodied enterprise: "Don't own nothin' if you can help it. If you can, even rent your shoes."

A BRIEF HISTORY OF ... YOUR JOB?

[7]Don't believe me? Believe Stephen Hawking, whom some have called the smartest person on earth. In an interview with the German magazine *Focus*, he said: "Unless mankind redesigns itself by changing our DNA through altering our genetic makeup, computer-generated robots will take over the world."

Yikes! I'm just talking about robots taking over your job. He's talking about robots taking over the *world*.

NEW BUSINESS ●!● NEW TECHNOLOGY

Change is coming, and coming fast.

One question confronts every institution and every individual: Fight the change ... or grab hold and enjoy the ride?[8]

I say: Enjoy yourself!

It's later than you think!

! Contrasts

WAS	IS
Tall towers	Low-rises
Paper	Silicone
Meetings ad nauseam	Groups as needed
Planning, planning, planning	Doing. Testing. Adjusting. Fast.
We worship Stability	We groove on Wild & Wacky
"Mind my rank"	"Mind my ability to contribute"
Ninety percent of all work is drudge work	Microprocessors do most drudge work
Workin' with the "same old gang"	Constantly expanding one's network of teammates
Well-defined organizational borders	Shifting organizational alliances
Products last for years	Products last for weeks
Accounting	Innovation
Employees	Talent

THE WAGES OF CHANGE

[8]Not all changes in White-Collar World are terrifying. Some of them are just ... complicated.

Example: At one point early in 2002, according to *BusinessWeek*, U.S. unemployment was two percentage points above its level at the height of the boom. Normally, such slack would lead wages to head abruptly downward. Not this time! Real-wage growth was at its highest since the 1960s. The White-Collar Revolution is upon us. Companies use recessionary pressures as an excuse to lay off "marginal" workers—even as they view their core personnel as more valuable than ever.

4 INFOTECH CHANGES EVERYTHING: "ON THE BUS" OR ... "OFF THE BUS"?

! Technicolor Rules ...

- The Web changes everything. (Everything = Everything.) Embrace it. Totally. Or else. (There's no "sorta" solution.)
- Message: On the bus or off the bus. No halfway. Take advantage of idiots! If your competition cuts IS/IT projects, re-double your efforts! (And your budget!)
- eCommerce is not a "technology play." It's a people play, a power play, a political play.
- It's the politics, stupid!
- "Hyperlinks subvert hierarchy!"
- The Internet allows us to dream dreams we could never have dreamed before!

⚡ ! RANT

We are not prepared ...

We chop IS/IT budgets and defer "big projects" when the economy softens. But the only way forward, and out of the economic doldrums, is by Total Commitment to IS/IT.

We talk about the "Tech Boom" (and the concomitant "Tech Bust") as if the promise of technology were a thing of the past. BUT THE STUPENDOUS IS/IT ADVENTURE IS ONLY BEGINNING!

We aim to "take advantage" of the Web in our "proven" "business model." Instead, we must re-imagine that business model so that it is driven—internally and externally—by the Web and the power of Total Connectivity.

👁 ! VISION

I imagine ...

The triumphant rise of a marketing-services company, circa 2005: It's an "organization" of 300 people. Six are permanent staff: the CEO, the CFO, the Exec VP of Alliances, and three Super Project coordinators. The other 294 are independent contractors. One contractor is 19 years old, and on his first gig with the company. Another is 42, and making her 9th appearance. The company has no "headquarters." Its people, starting with the six "permanent" employees, are all m-powered (wireless, mobile) to the nth degree.

The Web: All—or Nothing at All

I'm not an expert. (Sorry.) I'm not a true believer. (Too jaded.) I don't wear rose-colored glasses. (Too old.) And yet I *do* believe this: *WebWorld = Everything.*

Prior to presenting a keynote address to a techie conference, I concocted a single PowerPoint slide that laid out my encompassing beliefs about the Web:

Web as a way to run ... ALL ... your business's innards.

Web as connector for your ... ENTIRE ... supply-demand chain.

Web as "spider's Web" which re-conceives the ... VERY DEFINITION OF THE INDUSTRY ... in which you participate.

Web/B2B as ULTIMATE WAKE-UP CALL to "commodity producers."

Web as the ... SCOURGE OF SLACK, INEFFICIENCY, SLOTH, BUREAUCRACY, MISSING OR INCOMPLETE CUSTOMER DATA.

Web as an ... ENCOMPASSING WAY OF LIFE.

Web = EVERYTHING (from product development to after-sales service).

Web forces you to ... FOCUS ON WHAT YOU DO BEST ... and dump the rest.

Web is entrée, for anybody, at any size, to the World's Best at Everything as ... NEXT DOOR ENTERPRISE NEIGHBOR AND ALLIANCE PARTNER.

That *is* the potential. And *if* somebody in your neck of the woods gets there first, then you're likely to be toast ... far more quickly than you'd imagine.

The Web: Found in Translation

For the same speech, I offered the following translation of some of the wretched but (alas) necessary jargon phrases that people have used to describe WebWorld:

Bureaucracy free = Flat organization, absolutely no BS or grunge (recall the "100-square-foot factor").

Systemically integrated = Entire Supply & Demand Chain (supplier's supplier to customer's customer), tightly wired, friction free.

Internet-intense = Do everything via the Web!

Knowledge Based = Open access ... to Everything ... by Everybody ... from Individual Employee ... to all members of the supply and demand chain. (The new I-net equivalent of "by the people, for the people ...")

Time and Location free = Do whatever, whenever, wherever ... at the speed of light and convenience of each and every player.

Instantly responsive = Speed demons!

Customer-centric = Customer calls the shots! Customer is in charge! Cus-tom-er cus-tom-izes ... everything.

Mass-customization enabled = Every product and service is rapidly tailored to the client's particular and peculiar and immediate requirements.

That's still quite jargony, even with the "translation." But it does compactly

---

KNIGHT MOVES

Consider this remark, from *Business 2.0*: "Imagine a chess game in which, after every half-dozen moves, the arrangement of the pieces on the board stays the same but the capabilities of the pieces randomly change: Knights now move like bishops, bishops like rooks. ... Technology does that. It rubs out boundaries that separate industries. Suddenly competitors with new capabilities will come at you from new directions. Lowly truckers in brown vans become geeky logistics experts."

represent the overarching notion of Web potential:

Web = Everything. (Or else.)

Power Point

A couple of years ago, I was keynote speaker at a giant eCommerce shindig. I was nervous. I had to set the tone—and I was confronting several thousand people, all of whom knew more about the topic than I did. I decided to begin by startling them, as best I could.

I strode in confidently and began, "Each of you is working on a project of great strategic importance to your enterprise. It is my guess that 75 percent of you will fail, fail miserably, make a mess of your careers as a result thereof, and that the project will fall short of its potential."

Hey, I did grab their attention. I expressed my concerns on two PowerPoint slides.

Slide No. 1: eCommerce is *not* a technology play! It *is* a relationship, partnership, an organizational and communications play, made possible by new technologies.

Slide No. 2: There is no such thing as an effective B2B or Internet-supply chain strategy in a low-trust, bottlenecked-communication, six-layer organization.

In other words ... *It's the politics, stupid!* Make no mistake: This whole tale is a pot-boiler about power. About the raw, naked redistribution of power.

Paradise Postponed: Who Do You Trust?

Consider this vision ofWeb nirvana offered by *Red Herring* magazine: "When Joe Employee at Company X launches his browser, he's taken to Company X's personalized home page. He can interact with the entire scope of Company X's world—customers, other employees, distributors, suppliers, manufacturers, consultants. The browser—that is, the portal—resembles a MyYahoo for Company X and hooks into every network associated with Company X. ... The real trick is that Joe Employee, business partners, and customers don't have to be in the office. They can log on from their own cell phone, Palm Pilot, pager, or home office system."

I love that. Alas, it's so very far from the space that most traditional companies occupy. In fact, many companies are re-trenching at exactly the moment when they should be stealing the march on their more timid competitors. The prime stumbling block: The *Red Herring* vision demands that we *trust* Joe Employee with access to the Information Assets of the entire "supply chain." In short, we don't trust Ole Joe in 9.95 cases out of 10; hence, all the above is a sick joke.

"Baron" Wasteland: Enemies at the Top

A colleague spent three years attempting to implement SAP's most sophisticated software throughout the European retail operations of a British multinational. He

---

2 OUT OF 10 AIN'T GOOD

In an interview, I was asked to rate how well big companies had done in their implementation of "enterprise computing."

My answer: On a scale of 1 to 10, big companies earn ... about a 2. Many of them are using the new tools. But few of them have taken a genuine blank-sheet-of-paper approach to re-imagining their operations from the ground up, based on an Entirely New Friction-Free Way of Communicating and Deciding and Acting.

worked hard. He contracted with the best consultants. (Damn good.) But, alas, progress was spotty.

The problem? It's all about the sticky superstructure of the enterprise. Implement SAP R/3 correctly ... and little scraps of paper can't languish on middle managers' desks for hours or days or weeks or months, waiting to be initialed. In this case, the infestation goes higher up the chain: Implement SAP R/3 correctly ... and you chop away at the traditional power bases of "the barons": Mr. Italy, Mr. Germany, Mr. UK, Mr. Switzerland, et al. And those barons weren't about to ride off quietly into the night.

It's ironic. When we implemented containerization dockside (remember: 108 x 5 to 8 x 1), there were tooth-and-nail rearguard skirmishes ... with the Unions. That is, the "bottom" of the organization revolted. This time, the "top," the VPs and their immediate henchmen, are in jeopardy from the New Technology. Fighting SAP R/3 turns the Apex of The Hierarchy into the Arch Enemies of Wholesale Change.

So what do you do about all this? Essential answer: Take the ... political part ... seriously. Very seriously. This is not primarily a "technology play." It is a people play, a power play, a political play.[1] Technology allows it to happen. But it is not about technology. Second-rate technology with first-rate implementation beats by far first-rate technology with second-rate implementation.

Alternative: Delete "Control"

Yes, the Internet's promise depends on the raw redistribution of political power. Overall, however, it is about a Whole New Way of Life. The authors of *The Cluetrain Manifesto* summarize it this way: "Hyperlinks subvert hierarchy!"

Fact: You simply can't (CANNOT ... PERIOD) have a hierarchical organization where people wait for orders and those damnable papers gather dust on desks and a totally Web-based enterprise. Of course, this is also the source of the tenacious resistance thereto. As our *Cluetrain Manifesto* friends add about such resistance to the new technologies: "It all goes back to fear of losing control."

"Fear of losing control"? Try: *Reality of losing control.* By those old (hierarchical) standards, the Internet-driven company ... in which everybody openly talks to everybody else "24/7" ... is an organization that is "out of control." The animals run the zoo![2]

POLITICAL SCIENCE
[1]Here's a thought: Maybe all of those project teams trying to implement Internet-based business processes should hire fewer "techie consultants"—and more sociologists and anthropologists or even former politicians. Fewer people who talk about "powering the Net"—and more people who are masters of the "power nexus" of corporate life.

ORACULAR WISDOM
[2]It isn't just young mavericks who are making this point. According to *Business 2.0*, Ray Lane, formerly president of Oracle and now a partner at the venture-capital firm Kleiner Perkins, was drawing on deep experience when he said: E-business is about "rebuilding the organization from the ground up. Most companies today are not built to exploit the Internet. Their business processes, their approvals, their hierarchies ... the number of people they employ ... . All of that is wrong for running an e-business."
Re-read, please. Slowly.

WebWorld Without Baedecker

Internet guru David Weinberger recently authored a lovely book called *Small Pieces Loosely Joined.* He captures the spirit I'm trying to convey here:

"Suppose—just suppose—that the Web is a new world we're just beginning to inhabit. We're like the earlier European settlers in the United States, living on the edge of the forest. We don't know what's there and we don't know exactly what we need to do to find out: do we pack mountain climbing gear, desert wear, canoes, or all three? Of course, while the settlers may not have known what the geography of the New World was going to be, they at least knew that there was a geography. The Web, on the other hand, has no geography, no landscape. It has no distance. It has nothing natural in it. It has few rules of behavior and fewer lines of authority. Common sense doesn't hold there, and uncommon sense hasn't yet emerged."

Fabulous!

Weinberger speaks poetically—and poetry is vitally important—about the limitless possibilities the Web writ very large serves up. New ways to structure organizations. New ways to interact with our fellow human beings. New ways to "do" commerce. New ways to do politics. (E.g., to bring vast and instant pressure to bear on the powers that be—see Howard Rheingold's extraordinary *Smart Mobs*, referred to earlier.) New ways to educate. (Why shouldn't most nine-year-olds' pen pals on a research project be cohorts 6,000 miles away, or better yet, 10,000 miles away?) New ways to "do" healthcare. (Welcome to the Age of the Feisty Informed Patient ... uncowed by the M.D.'s white coat.) New ways to wage war. (It's the terrorists, unfortunately, who were the first to inform us of the new order of battle.)

Go Ask Alice

"There's no use trying," said Alice. "One can't believe impossible things."

"I daresay you haven't had much practice," said the Queen. "When I was your age, I always did it for half an hour a day. Why, sometimes I've believed as many as six impossible things before breakfast."

I love those words from Lewis Carroll's *Through the Looking Glass.* They lead me to the central point of this chapter.

Yes, I've just screamed as loudly as I can (in print): In IT, politics rules! The dirty, grubby, raw redistribution of power is the Full Name of the Big Tech Revolution Game!

But now I want to address the other side of the coin. Yes, the Tech Revolution is about politics. Yes, it's about sophisticated technology. Yes, it's about spending (gobs of) money on that very same technology.

But it's about something else—which actually is bigger.

In short: *The Internet allows us to dream previously undreamed-of dreams!*

Dreams. Yes, dreams. Plastic. Dissolving. Evolving. Fantastic. Ridiculous. Profound. A dream called Microsoft. A dream called Dell. A dream called eBay. A dream called ...

NEW BUSINESS ● NEW TECHNOLOGY

DREAMING OF

... Incredible Operational Efficiency

CISCO

The fact is, Cisco Systems does 90 percent of its $19 billion in annual business over the Web. That is, about $50 million dollars in Web sales ... per day.

I'm particularly enamored with the Cisco example because Cisco sells sophisticated, highly integrated *systems*—the components of which come from factories all over the world owned by all sorts of folks other than Cisco. That is, the whole process of custom-specifying, producing, and delivering at Cisco is as complicated as it gets. And yet the company is able to do virtually everything ... over the Web. And it scores higher satisfaction marks from customers who do business exclusively over the Web than from those who don't.

Bottom line: Cisco estimated that in 2000, the savings in service and tech support from customer self-management came to more than *one-half billion* dollars.

ORACLE

Speaking of half-billion dollar savings ... that's what Oracle got (times two!) in a little over a year after making the dramatic decision to rapidly shift every business process in the company (TAKING ITS OWN MEDICINE) ... to the Web. A technically intense service call, according to Oracle VP Ralph Seferian, which cost Oracle $300 in 1998 was completed for $1.50 just 18 months later.

Yeow.

IBM

Big Blue embraced the Web with incredible vigor. Consider purchasing practices. "We've put out the word to all our suppliers," said Chief Purchasing Officer John Paterson in 2000. "By the end of the year we'll only do purchasing over the Internet." That "purchasing" amounts to $50 billion ... from 18 thousand suppliers around the world, from tiny to large. In fact, the *Industry Standard* reported in 2000 that IBM was doing some 42 million transactions online ... and saving close to $1 billion in the process.

GE

During his last four years at the helm, Jack Welch cozied up to the Web. Some statistical implications follow.

Purchasing on the Web at GE in 2000: $6 billion. In 2001: $15 billion.

Sales on the Web at GE in 1999: $1 billion. In 2000: $7 billion. In 2001: $20 billion.

Step down a level from Corporate: GE's PartsEdge, a component of GE Power Systems, reduced the two weeks it typically took to analyze a major generator problem ... to one day. (Once more: Do you understand why I routinely use Extreme Language? Two weeks. One day. Extreme? No?) At GE Appliances, the cost of a Web-based service call versus a call to a Service Rep amounted to $0.20 versus $5.00 pre-Web (a big deal, given that GE gets some 20 *million* calls like this per year).

... Speed, Speed, Speed

PROGRESSIVE INSURANCE

Peter Lewis is a radical. "Radical" is not a term normally associated with an "insurance guy." Lewis, CEO of Progressive, said recently, "We don't sell insurance any more. We sell speed." When a member's property-damage automobile accident takes place, it's not unusual for a Progressive van to arrive at the scene of the mishap within minutes of being called. Using the latest in wireless technology, and astonishingly sophisticated computer databases, the Progressive claims adjustor may well assess the nature of the damage ... and issue the *final* settlement check ... on the spot ... within 20 minutes of the time that tin whacks tin. As I see it, that's probably half a year ahead of the industry norm. (If not half a year, awfully close.)

When you produce that kind of speed ... you've fundamentally ... reinvented an industry. And "it" can happen ... *anywhere*.

NEW BUSINESS ! • NEW TECHNOLOGY

... *Huge Customer Savings*

AUTOBYTEL.COM

In 2001 a potential automobile buyer who "qualified" his or her $20,000 deal via Autobytel.com saved, on average, $400. Why is this a big deal? Obvious answer: $400 is a lot of money. Slightly less obvious answer: The average dealer margin on a new car runs a couple of hundred bucks. Within such a context, $400 is a *lot* of money.

WAL*MART

Consider this study of Wal*Mart's indirect as well as direct power. Take a Wal*Mart, draw a circle around it that compasses its effective trading range. Look at prices—of *every damn* thing—within that trading range. *BusinessWeek* reports that if you're within a Wal*Mart "zone" /circle-of-influence, retail prices on average are 13 percent less than if you are outside the Wal*Mart "zone." Thus the impact of Wal*Mart's simply "being there" runs about five *times* the average retailer's margin!

... *Entire New Communities*

TOWTRUCKNET.COM

TowTruckNet.com. I love TowTruckNet.com. In many ways, more than Dell or Cisco or IBM or GE. I believe TowTruckNet.com represents the true, long-term Power and Ubiquity of the Web. Take TowTruckNet.com ... *and multiply it by a million ... and then perhaps another million* ... and you begin to "get" the Web's ability to intrude into every nook and cranny of the world ... and change ... *everything*.

So, who the hell are they? TowTruckNet.com is, in part, a little eBay and then some ... for tow trucks. News about tow trucks. *Tools* to help you buy and sell tow trucks. *Communities* of people who are Deeply Interested in Tow Trucks.

Truthfully, I'm not slightly interested in tow trucks. (Except when stuck in the mud in Vermont in the Spring.) But I'm wildly interested in TowTruckNet.com. Because this "community"—*information, advice, friendship, economic trading*—is a "mini mart" and "knowledge affinity community" that is the essence of the Web. (Again: x 1,000,000. Or more.)

... Seamless Transactions

ELLIE MAE

At first blush the mortgage business sounds pretty simple. Realtors work with third-party lending organizations—typically small, entrepreneurial shops. These "originators" broker/sell the loan to huge lenders such as Countrywide, Washington Mutual, and Wells Fargo. The giant retail lenders in turn bundle their loans and sell them again, this time to the likes of Fannie Mae and Freddie Mac.

As I said ... sounds simple. But then the "grunge factor" (incompatible information systems and the like) messes things up. The "system" is so fuzzy that the average loan is handled by 61 people, and requires 45 days from application to funding.

Enter Ellie Mae!

Ellie Mae is a four-year-old company, a dot-com survivor, and part of a growing breed I call the "fixers" or the "enablers." The losing breed of dot-coms primarily focused on the visible front end of business life: e.g., peddling us groceries or pet supplies. But winners like Ellie Mae focus on the invisible back end—and aim to revamp grunge-clad processes like those that mark the mortgage banking industry.

Ellie Mae is the brainchild of longtime industry veteran Sig Anderman. He "retired" to Sonoma County, California, in 1997 and started "messing around with the Internet," *Mortgage Banking* reports. Two years later Ellie Mae was born, along with its primary product, ePASS Business Center. It's an Internet-based platform, or "universal credit switch" (as Sig described it to me), that allows all the players to communicate with one another instantly and seamlessly. In March 2003 alone, Ellie Mae facilitated 700,000 transactions, Anderman reports, "saving the industry over 100,000 hours of wasted work." Growth is running 10 percent per month. No wonder co-founder Scott Cooley claims that "Ellie Mae can do more for American forests than Greenpeace can"—through the elimination of unnecessary, confusing, and expensive paperwork.

Sometimes appetites are so big, even on the back end, that they lead to failure. (Prime example: The bid by legendary Silicon Valley entrepreneur Jim Clark to clear the grunge out of healthcare through the founding of Healtheon, now WebMD.) We're still a ways short of having One Universal Cleansing Agent. But this new and mostly unsung breed of Web Draino-meisters is ... changing the world as it removes detritus from system after system and industry after industry.

GROWTH IS RUNNING 10 PERCENT PER MONTH

NEW BUSINESS ! NEW TECHNOLOGY

... A Logistics Revolution

CEMEX

Mexico's biggest cement company. Making noticeable inroads into the United States. What's the secret? In part, it's an improbable alliance between a Mexican cement company (Cemex) and an American logistics-management company (FDX—parent of FedEx).

It turns out that about 50 percent of cement truckloads are dumped. Lost because, for some reason or other, the building site is not ready to receive this very perishable product. But in a number of metropolitan areas, Cemex and FDX have gone a long way toward fixing that. The Cemex truck pulls up to the job site. And discovers no one is ready to receive the load. The driver quickly turns to his in-truck computer system—and launches a very quick, eBay-like auction for his cement, to anybody in need within the perishability radius of the truck. As a result of these micro, hyper-rapid auctions, Cemex has reduced its lost truck share from 50 percent to just 15 percent.

Construction is a multi-trillion dollar industry, marked by minuscule investments in R&D. While the Cemex saga is the tiniest part of it, it nonetheless reveals the power of the Web to change—dramatically!—the way this enormous industry operates. Resulting in more rapid construction. Resulting in more construction efficiencies.

50%-15% WASTE

A Declaration of ... Interdependence

Richard Rosecrance is an academic who wrote a very practical (from a dreamer's perspective!) book: *The Rise of the Virtual State: Wealth and Power in the Coming Century*. In this new, Internet-based century, the prototype for Rosecrance is ... Hong Kong. *Eighty-three* percent of Hong Kong's revenue comes from services. *Eight* percent comes from manufacturing. Such stats would have been unthinkable only a few years ago—even in Hong Kong. Now it's very thinkable in every Major Urban Center in the world, almost regardless of how far up the development ladder the host nation is.

Furthermore, in a world where the motto is quickly becoming "Don't own nothin' if you can help it. If you can, even rent your shoes," there is an Entirely New Form of Interdependence. Or "new dependence," per Rosecrance. "The new dependence on productive assets located within someone else's state," he writes, "represents an unprecedented trust in the integrity and peacefulness of strangers. ... In its pure form—an ideal model toward which many states are tending—the virtual state carries with it the possibility of an entirely new system of world politics."

How will it all work out? What will the New Politics look like? What will the New Forms of Interaction be? Must we have more trust? *Will* we have more trust? Can it all happen if there is heightened suspicion based on new kinds of (terrorist-driven) warfare?

Ours is a time of Vast Confusion.

It's history's oldest story: Vast confusion = Vast opportunity. For "Good guys." (Silicon Valley, Singapore, Bangalore.) For "bad guys." (Al Qaeda.)

Recall what David Weinberger said: There are no road maps. We don't even know what a road is. All we know is that "it" is undefined by yesterday's standards.

"Paradise" Realized

Miracles do happen. Consider this story, from *Business 2.0*:

"Dawn Meyerreicks, CTO of the Defense Information Systems Agency, made one of the most fateful military calls of the 21st century. After 9/11 ... her office quickly leased all the available transponders ... covering Central Asia. ... The implications should change everything about U.S. military thinking in the years ahead.

"The U.S. Air Force had kicked off its fight against the Taliban with an ineffective bombing campaign, and Washington was anguishing over whether to send in a few Army divisions. ... Donald Rumsfeld told Gen. Tommy Franks to give the initiative to 250 Special Forces already on the ground. They used satellite phones, Predator surveillance drones, and GPS and laser-based targeting systems to make the air strikes brutally effective. In effect, they 'Napsterized' the battlefield by cutting out the middlemen (much of the military's command and control) and working directly with the real players. ... The data came so fast that headquarters revised operating procedures to allow intelligence analysts and attack planners to work together simultaneously. ... Their favorite tool, by the way, was instant messaging over a secure network."

This is the most heartening news item I've read in years. (Decades.) And it comes from about the least likely setting for such a success.

The Bad Guys ... with no effective hierarchies ... used the Web masterfully. Perhaps there's hope that the Good Guys can as well.

Overarching message? Consider this *New York Times* headline about the 2002 Consumer Electronics Association's annual trade show: "At Big Consumer Electronics

Show, the Buzz Is All About Connections."

My re-write: *The New Web Order Is All About Unfettered Connections.*

That's the dream: unfettered connections.

Here and there ... it is a reality.[3]

Due to Control Beyond Our Circumstances

The IS guru Don Tapscott is a dreamer. He dreams those beloved Impossible Dreams. Which are no longer impossible. "Imagine a world," he writes, "where a citizen could search the globe to assemble 'my government,' the ultimate in customized, customer-centric services. Healthcare from the Netherlands, business incorporation in Malaysia."

Nothing is impossible to imagine! (Almost) nothing is impossible to bring to fruition! (And, in a few years, that "almost" will most certainly disappear.)

The rapidity with which people have embraced the Internet should come as little surprise to anyone who is even the most casual student of psychology. The psychologists agree on very little. (Understatement.) But they do agree on One Primary Thing: The strongest force on earth, bar none, is ... *my need to be in perceived control of my universe!*

And that's exactly what the Internet gives us. Maybe not the reality of total control. But surely the Perception of Total Control.

Smart businesspeople understand this. "Changes in business processes will emphasize self-service," said Ray Lane, when he was president of Oracle. "Your costs as a business go down and the perceived service goes up because customers are conducting it themselves."

Tough Customers? You Ain't Seen Nothing Yet

The experts agree ...

Anne Busquet, of American Express, said that this is not, in fact, the "Age of the Internet." Try, instead, the "Age of the Customer."

Regis McKenna, the Silicon Valley marketing guru, wrote an entire book on the topic. I love the title (as well as the innards): *The Age of the Never Satisfied Customer*.

Swedish business professors Kjell Nordström and Jonas Ridderstråle, in *Funky*

A VITAL SIGN

[3]Studies repeatedly show that lousy practices in U.S. hospitals lead to as many as 50,000 to 100,000 unnecessary deaths per year. (And perhaps another one or two million patients are injured.) These horrors are mainly a result of clunky, manual processes and an unwillingness to embrace procedures, such as bar-coded patient wristbands, that would help nurses confirm appropriate doses of meds.

But there are signs of hope! People are making ... connections.

Here's David Veillette, CEO of the Indiana Heart Hospital, quoted in *HealthLeaders*: "Our entire facility is digital. No paper, no film, no medical records. Nothing. And it's all integrated—from the lab to X-ray to records to physician order entry. ... Patients don't have to wait for anything. The information from the physician's office is in registration and vice versa. The referring physician is immediately sent an email telling him his patient has shown up. ... It's wireless in-house. We have 800 notebook computers that are wireless. ... Physicians can walk around with a notebook that's pre-programmed. If the physician wants, we'll go out and wire their house so they can sit on the couch and connect to the network. They can review a chart from 100 miles away."

Business, write: "IT enables total transparency. People with access to relevant information are beginning to challenge any type of authority. The stupid, loyal and humble customer, employee, and citizen is dead."

Michael Lewis, author of *Next*, chimes in: "Parents, bosses, stockbrokers, even military leaders are starting to lose the authority they once had. ... There are all these roles that are premised on access to privileged information. What we are witnessing is a collapse of that advantage, prestige and authority."

And Deloitte Research, in "Winning the Loyalty of the eHealth Consumer," concludes: "A seismic shift is underway in healthcare. The Internet is delivering vast knowledge and new choices to consumers—raising their expectations and, in many cases, handing them the controls. [Healthcare] consumers are driving radical, fundamental change."

Relationship Talk

CRM. Customer Relationship Management. That's a jargony term. Translation: The new technologies give us an opportunity to be more entwined with our customers than ever. To manipulate them, to be sure. But also to be their Intimate & Useful & Responsive Pals ... if done right.

Consider this, from a 2001 *New York Times* piece: There are now six *million* E-ZPasses in New England alone. These get us through the tollbooths faster.

Brilliant.

Now the E-ZPass folks are doing tests with McDonald's, gas stations, and parking lots. That is, the E-ZPass will let us do more ... a lot more ... than ever imagined.

Likewise, GM now has two million members in OnStar. Offering more and more services with the passing of every day. (Perhaps OnStar will be the tail that wags the dog? Some in GM think so.)

Again: Brilliant.

Beyond "Service with a Smile"

But if CRM is so brilliant, why is it also the case, as the Butler Group, a UK-based consultancy, claims, that "CRM has, almost universally, failed to live up to expectations"?

RING THE BELL (CURVE)
A quick word about the examples that I use ...

I am not a "hype-meister." I am a truth-meister. It's just that the truths I "tout" are not truths that are widely emulated. Yet.

I don't believe there's a requirement to "think" about all this. I believe there's a requirement to "find." To find, in 2003, the people who are already living the e-world of 2013. (Progressive. Cemex. Ellie Mae. And so on.)

It's the ancient "Law of Large Numbers." The Ironclad Logic of the Normal Distribution/Bell-Shaped Curve. Find the "four-sigma" (one in 10,000) person ... who, in 2003, is already "doing" 2013.

That's the end of the Bell Curve ... where I "do my thing."

I have a hunch about the answer.

Dare I say it, the *Financial Times* (of London) got it all wrong when they commented in a special section on CRM: "The aim is to make customers feel as they did in the pre-electronic age when service was more personal."

I don't think that's true. I don't want more "personal" service. I want the ability to do things that have previously been unimaginable: To research a disease. To send a book posthaste via Amazon to a pal, while I'm traveling in Southeast Asia. I don't even think it's the *perception* of "personal." I don't *want* Amazon to offer smiling faces when I place an order! I want to ... take charge ... do things as *I* wish them done, when I wish them done.

Paul Cole heads Cap Gemini Ernst & Young's CRM practice. He says the problem is that we haven't thought broadly enough.

I say: "Amen." (Shades of Alice and the Queen.)

Cole's thinking dovetails with mine. The idea, he insists, is not "a pleasant transaction." And, it is *not* a "better job of doing what we're doing today." Instead he demands thinking in terms of "systemic opportunities" ... a "rethink of overall enterprise strategy."

That is, it's not about "pleasantness" or that better job at what we did yesterday. It's about having an in-depth, seamless, highly integrated relationship—that lets me be in charge and do the things I want to do as and when I want to do them.

Cole establishes a very high hurdle. And he admits as much. The ability to offer his "systemic opportunity" which allows the customer, in her own fashion, to tap into the full set of resources of the service/product-providing firm and its supply chain requires nothing short of ... Total Enterprise Reinvention.

All Aboard! (The Bus Is Leaving *Now*)

Oops! There I go again!

I began with a section and chapter on "Destruction." The reason: *Destruction is required!* That's right ... required! You can't deliver a "synergistic" (as much as I blanch when I see the word) and/or "systemic" (as much as I blanch at *that* word) "opportunity" unless *all* the damned internal barriers go. Completely.

Unless we (the enterprise) can bring to bear on Customer Tom Peters *all* the resources of the ... Entire Damn Supply Chain. From the damn supplier's supplier's supplier's supplier ... to the damn customer's customer's customer.

All of it!

No friction!

I want that damn book!

I want it now! I want to be able to send it to my best friend!

Now!

I want that drug!

I want it delivered today!

I want to be informed about the side effects!

Totally!

I don't want to be treated like a child!

I want total knowledge!

I want absolute convenience!

I want the ability to get what I want![4]

Now!

"Petulant little brat," you say. "Exactly," I reply. The Web allows me to be just that: a petulant little have-it-my-way-now brat.

How cool.

How weird.

How unsettling.

How revolutionary.

NEW BUSINESS ! NEW TECHNOLOGY

THE NEW FARMERS' MARKET

[4]The perception of control is increasingly reality. From my farm in ever-so-tiny West Tinmouth, Vermont, I can immediately:

- Shop for $1 million homes or $1.95 office supplies.
- Manage all my financial dealings—from the trivial to the grand.
- Work with my doctor, or the world's best medical experts, or humble support groups, on any health issue imaginable.
- Recruit talent ... from all over the world ... to help me with any project.
- Develop documents, collaboratively, with anyone from anywhere at any time.
- Share (Blog!) my quirky ideas with the world.
- Chat with anyone, anywhere, any time.
- Research anything. (And very quickly become ... to some extent ... more expert than the "experts.")
- Take a course on any topic, from the intricacies of sushi cooking to advanced software design.
- Stay in touch with my 94-year-old mom. (Or my three-year-old nephew.)
- Play a gazillion games to while away the time.

So, in that context, what is the traditional, charts-and-boxes "organization" for?
Damned if I know.
You figure it out.[5]

Are you up for it? Are you able to dream? Do you have the guts to deal with the power issues associated therewith?

WebWorld is cool. That is, if you're not paralyzed by fear. If you are imaginative. If you are inventive. If you can imagine a world turned upside down. If you can just ... Get on the Bus.

FAR TO GO? NOT AT WELLS FARGO

[5]Some (big) companies are starting to Figure It Out. Example: Wells Fargo. One-third of its retail customers (about three million folks) bank online. The stats, as reported in the *Wall Street Journal*, are ... staggering:

- There's a 50 percent lower attrition rate among the on-line group.
- The on-line group sports a growth rate in account balances 50 percent above the Off-Line Luddites.
- The on-line group is more likely to cross-purchase.
- The on-line group, the *Journal* reports, is "happier and stays with the bank much longer."

ON THE BUS ... GRUDGINGLY?

I am a bit offended by the message of this chapter. I am offended because it attacks one of my sacred principles: Namely, that the way forward is to try something new, see if it works, try a little more of it if it does work ... and slow down a little if it doesn't. And yet the Web Game doesn't seem to be played that way.

    Not at Dell.
    Not at Oracle.
    Not at Cisco.
    Not at Schwab.
    Not at Fidelity.
    Either "Buy the act"—and get wholly on board—or don't bother. There is no such thing as "sorta" in WebWorld.

! Contrasts

WAS	IS
Technology helps link parts of an organization	– The Network Is the Organization
Every department uses IS/IT	– Every department lives on the Web
Department = Compartment	– Access = Success
Everyone labors under strict "need to know" rules	– Every employee has access to everything
Project teams have regular phone conferences	– Project teams "meet" 365/24/60/60
We favor independence	– We savor interdependence
We are proud of being "close to our customer"	– We are proudly "at one" with our customer
We sell rigorously engineered "great product"	– We sell information-enabled "awesome experiences"
Here today ... here tomorrow	– Here today ... reconfigured tomorrow
Men in suits	– Women in charge

NEW BUSINESS **!** • NEW TECHNOLOGY

The entire basis for creating value is up for grabs!

new bus!ness
new value

It's simple. We need a New Business Model to deal with a
Crazy New Economy. I'd dearly love to avoid that term ...
"business model." And yet we do need something like it ...
some New & Radical & Profound Idea for Creating Value in
an Intangibles/Intellectual-Capital/Creativity-Driven/Rapidly-
Gyrating/Technologically-Insane Economy.

(Gulp.)

Building off Part II, I believe the journey must begin with a
straightforward first step: re-assessment of the fundamental
nature of what "work" can—and must—become in an epoch
when friction-free organizations, and entire value chains, are
the norm; and where excellent quality and timely service,
powered by ubiquitous computing and communications
devices, are commonplace. That is, what does "special" look
like when "runs like clockwork"—Dell-, Amazon-, Ellie Mae- or
Wal*Mart-style—becomes merely the price of entry?

FROM "COST CENTER" TO STARDOM: THE PSF/PROFESSIONAL SERVICE FIRM TRANSFORMATION

! Technicolor Rules ...

● Every job (every!) done in White-Collar World is also done "outside" ... for profit! By: Professional Service Firms.

● A PSF adds value through one ... and only one ... thing: the accumulation and application of ... Creative Intellectual Capital.

● Turn every task into a "product." Put everything on the Web. Export your "non-great" stuff to those who are great at that stuff. And hold onto the Little Bit that is Worth a Lot.

● The way to become a PSF is to drop the word "improve," adopt the word "transform" ... and become a PSF. Now.

! RANT

We are not prepared ...

We aim to improve "departmental" "efficiency" and "effectiveness." But "improvement," no matter how dramatic, misses the point. In fact, it is deeply misleading. We must *destroy* "departments"—and create aggressive, imaginative, entrepreneurial Professional Service Firms (PSFs) in their stead. We must embrace PSFs as the Primary Engines for Creative Work ... and thus of virtually all Enterprise Value Added.

! VISION

I imagine ...

"Exciting" Finance Departments ... selling their creative services far beyond the company's border.

A "McKinsey Attitude," an "IDEO Attitude," in Every "Department" in the Organization. ("We're the Movie Stars of the Business World," my first McKinsey partner-boss declared; and I gleefully bought the act.)

Bold, brash, diverse, creative "talent" in each of these internal departments-turned-PSFs (Professional Service Firms) ... "doing" WOW Projects. (Use the damn word: "WOW!" Damn it!). Projects that ... put a Dent in the Universe (in the immortal words of Apple's Steve Jobs).

"Overhead" Is Dead

You work 50-hour weeks. Bust your back. Put up with a bunch of Dilbertian BS. And what do "they" call you? "They" call you a ... "cost center." "They" call you "overhead." Frankly, they call you much worse. ("Oh shit, here comes the HR guy.")

Who *are* you? You're part of the 90 percent. The 90 percent who work in ... purchasing ... logistics ... finance ... human resources ... information systems ... engineering.

Must you be "overhead"? Is it your lot in life to be a "cost center"?[1]

I think not!

In fact I *know* not—and I *think* I can prove it.

I boldly asserted in Chapter 3 that 80 percent or more of white-collar jobs, as we know them today, will disappear or be reconfigured beyond recognition in the space of the next 15 years at most. (GE's boss, recall, says 3 years.) All the rote work—the heavy lifting, as it were—of White-Collar World will be taken over by Indians, Ghanaians, and $239 microchips. (That goes all the way to reading ECGs!)

So, with fewer and fewer employees, what will the enterprise actually amount to? Perhaps not much.

And what will be left for us to do?

Perhaps not much.[2]

But perhaps ...

Rockin' Hard in the Big Easy

I went to New Orleans. To speak to NAPM—the National Association of Purchasing Management (now the Institute for Supply Management).

I looked out at the sea of several thousand faces. Mostly middle aged. Mostly white. Purchasing "professionals."

I looked out at this group. And in my loudest voice (a glass-breaker), I shouted: *"When I look at you, I see the Rock Stars of the B2B Age!"*

They thought I was crazy.

Funny thing: I meant it.

I was Dead Serious.

As I indicated in the last couple of chapters, I believe in the Encompassing Power

---

WHAT DOES *YOUR* DADDY DO?

[1]Sara loves her Daddy. Her Daddy is a damned hard worker. Hence the tragedy of this hypothetical exchange:

Sara (eyes wide with curiosity): Daddy, what is it that you actually do?

Daddy (chest filled with pride): I run a "cost center," honey. I'm in charge of what's called "overhead." I'm boss to 20 marvelous "obfuscating bureaucrats." Our internal "clients" refer to us as "those bastards in finance." Whenever they want something we make them fill out innumerable forms—and then in the end, after insufferable delays, we tell them they can't have what they want anyway.

FORREST GUMP, CEO?

[2]*Recall: "Don't own nothin' if you can help it. If you can, even rent your shoes."*

Once, at a company's annual "strategy" meeting, I heard an obviously frustrated CEO say something that turned every face in the room ashen. "I can fix this 'profit problem' in 15 minutes," he snapped. "Fire everybody. Then re-hire the best as independent contractors." Um ....

of the eCommerce Revolution. (Remember: "On the bus. Off the bus." No "sorta.")
Furthermore, I believe that the Internal eCommerce Revolution (REVOLUTION ... Damn
It) ought to be led by a cabal that includes the purchasing folks, the logistics folks, the
IS folks, the finance folks.

That is, I fervently believe those "purchasing professionals" I was talking to should
see themselves as Rock Stars ... Revolutionaries ... Champions of Bold Change ...
Supporters of Disruptive Technologies ... Re-inventors of Enterprise.

Cool Dudes. Cool Dudettes.

Re-imagineers.

That's the way I looked at them.

Damn it.

... And in the Windy City

On to Chicago. A speech to HRMAC—the Human Resources Management Association
of Chicago. Several hundred people in the audience.

Again ... I must admit ... I screamed: *"Aren't you tired of being a 'support function'?
A 'cost center'? 'Bureaucratic drag'? When I look at you, here's what I see: Rock Stars
of the Age of Talent."*

It was the same logic as with my Purchasing Pals. (Oops: Rock-Star-eWorld-
Revolutionaries.) HR people are a classic example of "staffers" who are looked upon
with suspicion ... as the ultimate paper-pushing, form-demanding, "just say no"
bureaucrats.

Maybe they've earned that reputation. Maybe they have mostly behaved
bureaucratically. But that's ancient history. (I pray.) We acknowledge (right!?) that this is
an age where Value will be created on the basis of Intellectual Capital. And if that is duly
acknowledged, then we must also (obviously) acknowledge that it is an ... Unadulterated
Age of Talent. And to continue this incredibly pedestrian logical chain ... if it is an
Unadulterated Age of Talent ... WHO IN THE HELL OUGHT TO BE LEADING THE
PARADE, ENERGIZING THE ENTIRE VALUE-CREATION PROCESS?

The HR people.

(Duh.)

If they conceive their jobs correctly. If they understand the monumental nature of
their opportunity.

ROOM SERVICE? THE ROOM *IS* A SERVICE

Starwood's Sheraton Hotels is a hotel chain, right? And a hotel is the ultimate lump,
right? Well, sorta. In the case of the Sheraton Princeville on Kaua'i, Hawaii, Starwood
"owns": the brand, some customer data, a process for creating Memorable Guest
Experiences, a management contract. And that's it. (Non-management employees are
not even on the payroll.) Starwood owns hardly any real estate. Have *you* checked into
a Sheraton PSF (um, hotel) lately?

If ... If ... **If** ...

The PSF Solution: Hidden in Plain Sight

If what?

Maybe we've had "the answer" all along! Sitting right under our collective noses! And we've paid no attention. None! (Literally.)

There now exists a set of organizations that operate "virtually" ... and solely "by their wits" ... a set of organizations that add value through one ... and only one ... thing: the accumulation and application of Creative Intellectual Capital.

Call them PSFs.

Professional Service Firms.

Perhaps this is their hour.

I think it is.

The Professional Service Firm can be a 100,000-plus-person entity, such as Accenture or EDS. Or it can be a one-woman accountancy, staffed by a 46-year-old former Xerox accountant, laid off in the latest wave of downsizing; and now, out of a spare bedroom, say, providing strategic small-business financial assistance throughout the Rochester, New York, environs.

(Or perhaps the one-person accountancy is offering unique services throughout the world ... thanks to the Internet. That spare bedroom, 10 x 13, is a garden-variety Global Headquarters for a Professional Service Firm ... if you're good enough/special enough at what you do.)

Firm Offerings

Professional Service Firms ...

- ... Provide security. (Kroll.) (Guardsmark.)
- ... Conduct clinical trials for pharmaceutical companies. (Radiant Research.) (nTouch Research.)
- ... Conduct research for pharmaceutical companies. (Health Decisions.) (Covance.)
- ... Build prototypes for auto companies. (ESG Automotive.)
- ... Maintain office equipment of all shapes and sizes. (OfficeZone.)
- ... Manage call centers. (Tel*Assist.) (Convergys.)

{ } **LOGIC SO FAR**
1. **White-Collar Jobs are ... EVAPORATING.**
2. **Indians, Ghanaians, and $239 microprocessors will take over rote work.**
3. **Staff "Departments" are viewed as "overhead."**
4. **Departments must re-invent themselves.**
5. **Ultimate re-invention: Become rock stars!**
6. **Such "rock stars" already exist in ... Professional Service Firms (PSFs).**
7. **PSFs do "staff work" on the outside and for "profit."**

... Perform all travel services for Big Co. (Rosenbluth.)

... Run schools. (Edison Schools.) (Mosaica.) And jails. (Correctional Systems Inc.)

... Hire CEOs. And provide temp CEOs. (Heidrick & Struggles.) (Executive Interim Management.)

... Provide turnkey logistic services. (Ryder.) (UPS.) (FDX.)

... Manage employee benefits. (Accord Human Management.) (Back Office Solutions.)

... Run training activities. (Forum Corporation.)

... Operate Customer Relations Management activities. (Accenture.)

... Manage entire facilities. (Accenture ... redux.)

... Run entire information-technology operations. (EDS.)

Key point: Every (e-v-e-r-y) job done in the White-Collar World (90 percent of jobs, remember) is done ... on the *outside* ... for *profit*. (By a ... "PSF.")

Black Hole

Professional Service Firms. Nobody takes them seriously. They do "sissy work" ... compared to "real men" who toil in "steel mills." (Oops, the latter are about gone.) Almost nobody studies PSFs. Find me a book on the topic. Fact: There are a few. Damn few. (Almost none.)[3]

Go to Borders. Go to Barnes & Noble. Wander the business section. Twenty or 30 books on Total Quality Management. Another dozen on "installing self-managing work teams"—for the auto factory or pulp mill.

But not one single, solitary book on creating a ... Way Cool Accounting Department ... a Supercalifragilisticexpialidocious Human Resources Department. Nary a title, astoundingly, on Building a Remarkable Research & Development Operation.

Why? Why? Why?

I'm quite sure that for every person who works on the line in a U.S. auto plant, there are 50, if not 150, who toil as Cubicle Slaves in Accounting Departments.

And yet ... nary a word.

(Am I the only one who's noticed this?)

MY BACK PAGES

[3]Okay, there is one book about the PSF phenomenon that I'm keen on.

And I wrote it, back in 1999. It's called *The Professional Service Firm50: Fifty Ways to Transform Your "Department" into a Professional Service Firm Whose Trademarks Are Passion and Innovation!*

Feel free to buy a copy. (Along with anything David Maister has written on the topic, such as *Managing the Professional Service Firm.*)

NEW BUSINESS ! NEW VALUE

On the Road Again

In 2001, I spoke to IHRIM—the International Association for Human Resource Information Management. In preparing for my presentation, I came across a superb article by John Sullivan in the association's journal. Title: "E-HR: A Walk Through a 21st Century HR Department."

The basic idea is straightforward. The "HR Department" will become "eHR." That is, a Web-based department in which every HR activity takes place online ... and is thus available to every employee (remember "Joe Employee") ... who can pursue, mostly, self-management of all the many aspects of his or her job, from guiding the evaluation process to training to selecting a benefits portfolio.

Since we have automated HR's drudge-rote work, what's left? Very simple, Mr. Sullivan concludes: The HR Department becomes a "PCC" ... a Productivity Consulting Center. And HR types become Seriously Cool Value-Added Members of a Rockin' PSF. (Perhaps the ... Troubadours of Talent?)[4]

Training Wheels: A Job Makeover

Okay, Janice Nelson-Smith, you're sitting in a comfy chair. You pull your wallet from your briefcase, extract one of your business cards. You've been promoted three or four times. The card reads, *Janice Nelson-Smith, Director of Training, Widgets Division, XYZ Corp.*

Here's what I want you to do, Janice: Get up. Go over to the fireplace. (A roaring fire awaits, I trust.) Take that business card. Toss it into the fire. Watch it burn.

Tomorrow ... I want you to go to the local stationer's shop. And get new cards. You can keep the first line, the one with your name on it. But now your card will read: *Janice Nelson-Smith, Managing Partner, Rock Star Training, Inc.*

(RSTI is a wholly owned subsidiary of the Widgets Division of XYZ Corp.)

Janice, you're a Managing Partner now!

("Mommy, what's 'overhead'?" That's no longer you.)

HR = "HARD ROCK"?

[4]GE grooves on talent development. Bob Nardelli trained at GE. Then he became CEO of Home Depot. He immediately tapped, for an EVP slot, Dennis Donovan, his former HR exec at GE. According to the *Economist*, Donovan pocketed $21 million in 2001.

> That's Rock Star pay!
> HR World is Rock Star World at Home Depot!
> And at your place?

THE PSF MODEL: KEEP IT SIMPLE, MAKE IT GREAT

With John Sullivan's "eHR" construct in mind, I concocted the following Generic PSF Model. The idea holds equally for a finance department, an IS department, a logistics department, an engineering department ... and an HR department. There are four basic building blocks.

Product-ize it

Translate every "departmental" activity into a discrete WWPF (Work Worth Paying For) "product." "Product-ize" is an ugly word, jargony as the dickens. But it has its value. **Bottom line:** If you can't envision what you are doing ... right now ... as a "product" that ... SOMEBODY WILL PAY FOR ... then bloody well quit damn doing it. (Okay?)

Web-ify it

That is: All of it. Put 100 percent of your "stuff" (products!) on the Web. Recruiting. Training. Benefits. Policies. Processes. (100 percent = 100 percent.)

If it ain't great, outsource it

Look at every activity or "product" that your PSF is responsible for: training, benefits management, recruiting, evaluation, whatever. If you're not Demonstrably Great at it ... hand it off to somebody outside who *is* Demonstrably Great at it. This will end up encompassing 75 percent to 95 percent of what you now do. No bull. (Oops. It could end up 100 percent. No more you.)

If it is great, celebrate it

Whatever remains becomes a "Center of Global Excellence." Leverage it to the hilt! Simple Message: Hold on dearly to what you are good at. (Damn good at.) (Notably damn good at.) ("World class" good at.) Turn it into stuff that can be sold ... for a pretty penny ... to others. (Even to your competitors!) The stuff that is ... SERIOUSLY COOL.

The above adds up to a "simple model." But it's a model that is, alas, profoundly different from the way we do things now. (Recall: "Cost center," "overhead.") Reprise: Everything becomes a "product." One hundred percent goes on the Web. Non-great stuff gets shipped out to those who are great at that stuff. And we hold onto a little bit ... which is worth a lot ... A HELL OF A LOT.

NEW BUSINESS ● **NEW VALUE**

THE PSF: THE SHORT COURSE

So what are the contours of the Professional Service Firm Model—this landmark element of the New Economy landscape? Here are my "front nine" principles:

1. HVA Projects

One hundred percent (no rounding error!) of the work we do becomes HVA (High Value-Added) projects. All work = Scintillating Project Work. Message: Value-Added Projects. Period. (Or else.) (Or ... Control Alt Delete.)

2. Pioneer Clients

Achieve "departmental" "revolution" by seeking out Pioneer Clients. As an "internal service provider" you have to answer the phone from all the units you serve. Fair enough. But you don't have to give them all equal attention. Fact is, you're an idiot if you do. The unvarnished truth: You want to devote the very best people, and create the very best projects, with the 10 percent of your internal clientele who are appropriately classified as "freaks," "weirdos," "revolutionaries," "pioneers." Mantra: We will be known by the quality of our work for pioneering clients! (Believe me—more later. Much, much more.)

3. WOW Work Only

Work that WOWs! And that's all! That damn $239 microchip reads the ECG better than you do, Doc—so what the hell are you up to? Answer: Doing Seriously Cool Stuff, or going out of "business." Rigorously apply the Quantitative WOW Test to all "work" (see Chapter 15).

4. Hot Talent

It's all about ... TALENT. That's the whole idea behind adding (serious) value. Whether you're a baseball team, a symphony, a theater company ... or a logistics department (now Rockin' PSF!).

Pursue Great Talent!
Hire Great Talent!

Give Great Talent wide-open spaces in which to roam! Promote Great Talent! Pay Great Talent! (Also see Chapter 20, for an in-depth analysis of "all this"— i.e., the "talent thing.")

5. Adventurous culture

I'm sick and tired—fed up!—with the notion of "dreary accounting department." Or ... whatever. If it's a "*dreary* accounting department," that's because the accountant-in-charge is ... uh ... dreary. Adventurous ... Finance Department! (Yes!) Adventurous ... Logistics Department! (Yes!) Adventurous ... Purchasing Department! (Yes!) If (lotsa) (cool) value is going to be added through the accumulation and application of Intellectual Capital and Creativity ... then these (previous) "cost centers"/accumulators of "overhead" had better damn well become ... fabulously, awesomely *"exciting."* WHY NOT? (If you think I'm going too far ... explain yourself. I am right about this. And if you don't agree ... well ... you're wrong. AND DOOMED.) (Sorry, I feel exactly that strongly.)

6. Proprietary Point of View/Proprietary Methodology

There is an "EDS Way" of getting things done. A "McKinsey Way" of getting things done. Such proprietary methodologies, in the true professional service firms, can be worth billion$$$ of dollar$$$. So ... what is the "Proprietary" "Point of View"/"Methodology" that marks your finance, logistics, IS, HR, training "department"?

What's (v-e-r-y) special about you?

So special that no one else has it? (No one else ... on earth.) (I hope you've got a good answer to this.) (Few "internal" departments do. Alas.)

7. WWPF/Work Worth Paying For

All worthy work is worthy of an invoice! And a stiff one at that! If nobody will foot the (hefty) bill for the work you do ... then the work you do wasn't worth doing in the first place. (Don't "trust me" on this—but do "think about it.") Great lawyers routinely bill out at $500/hour. Or more. Why not the World's Greatest Logistician ... in your "Department"-Turned-Scintillating-PSF?

8. Outside Clients

Outsiders must account for at least 25 percent of what we do. All PSFs must pass the ... Market Test. WILL AN "OUTSIDER" PAY FOR IT? PAY A BUNDLE FOR IT?

9. When: Now!

Maybe you feel you can't go the whole nine yards with this idea of "PSF-ing." Your corporation isn't ready. But you surely can go the whole nine yards ... *emotionally.* Immediately. This "idea" (the Internal PSF) is a matter of attitude (90 percent) and contractual details (10 percent).

Financial Independence: Job Makeover Redux

Suppose, David Yang, you're the Director of Finance for a 2,000-person division. Sixty-eight people report to you.

Here's my fundamental belief: *I see no difference ... none, whatsoever ... between you and the head of the 68-person Deloitte & Touche office down the street from you.*

Well, I've lied.

I do see a difference.

And a big one at that.

At the end of the month, the Managing Partner of that D&T office sends invoices to her clients. And they pay. Because she provided services of value.

Hey, David, what would happen if *you* sent "invoices" to your internal clients? How do you suppose they'd respond? I suspect they would laugh themselves silly ... or go into cardiac arrest.

That's sad, isn't it?

You trained like hell.

You're damn good at what you do.

You were promoted several times.

You provide services of value.

Why isn't that recognized? Why, David, do they continue to call you "overhead"? Why, David, do they continue to label you a "cost center"?

Let's cut the crap, Dave. Let's get on with doing Work of Value. Let's promote you to Managing Partner. Hey, if you don't ... that inexpensive microprocessor is going to take over your job anyway. (Yours and your friendly cardiologist's, too, recall.)

GM + VC = PSF Leader

Congratulations, Janice and David. Each of you is now a Managing Partner!

Just what does that mean?

THE NEW PONY EXPRESS
Frank Eichorn is Director of the Credit Risk Management Data Group at Wells Fargo Home Mortgage.

Ho-hum?

No!

Here's how Eichorn describes the transformation of his "overhead"/"cost center" department: "Typically in a mortgage company or financial services company, 'risk management' is an overhead, not a revenue center. We've become more than that. We pay for ourselves, and we actually make money for the company." He did it with the help of SAS, a brilliant software company whose sophisticated statistical packages allow departments to leverage-to-the-hilt what they do.

Way to go, SAS!

Way to go, Frank Eichorn!

Way to go, Wells Fargo!

OPERATION "PSF"
Recall the news footage from the Allied Command Center in Qatar during the Iraq War in 2003.

Guys with guns? Hardly!

Rather: guys and gals, by the dozen, all hunched over computer terminals. If that Command Center didn't resemble a PSF, I don't know what would!

I see you as embodying two very specific "types":

Type I: *Professional Sports Franchise GM (General Manager)*. What does a professional sports franchise GM do? One and only one thing: *recruiting and developing the Top Talent in the World*. That is, putting together the Very Best Roster Imaginable.

Type II: *Venture Capitalist*. What does a Venture Capitalist do? Two and only two things: "Bets" on "talent." "Bets" on "projects." (Ideas.) That is, the venture capitalist also has a "roster"—it's called a "portfolio." Some pieces are conservative. Fair enough. Some pieces are radical—they will fail miserably, or succeed wildly.

Again: A Managing Partner (formerly an insipid "department head") is two—*and only two*—things:

General manager ... Developer of Awesome Talent.

Venture capitalist ... Developer of a Portfolio of Awesome Projects.

This is the department head's role!

This is the department head's life!

This is the department head's future!

What you are *not*, Janice and David, is ... Ms. or Mr. Overhead.

Damn it.

You are (simultaneously) the GM of an Awesome Franchise ... and a VC putting together an Awesome Portfolio.

Attitude Adjustment

How long does it take to bring about this "profound change" from "department"/ "overhead"/"cost center" to full-fledged "PSF"?

Years and years, right?

How does **"one minute"** sound?

GRIDIRON GAMBIT

An NFL franchise—that is, the "skill package" of 48 active-duty players—is easily worth $500M. That's one valuable PSF!

I see no difference (NONE ... ZIP) between a 48-player professional football team ... and a 48-person Logistics Department/PSF.

On that football team, even the bit players are B.I.P. (Best in Planet) at what they do. Why not the same standard at Logistics Inc.?

AND WRITE WHEN YOU FIND WORK ...

Designworks/USA is BMW's U.S. design operation. The powers that be at BMW HQ in Munich have decreed that 50 percent of the unit's activities must be revenue-producing stuff ... done for outside clients (including near competitors).

The idea goes like this: If you are creating fabulous chairs for Steelcase ... then that creativity will eventually work its way into the interiors you design for BMW's next new model. And if you can't make it in the "real world" with "outside clients" ... then you shouldn't be in business.

Plus: The more interesting the work you do, the better the people you'll be able to attract to your team.

Put aside the "full-fledged" part of the equation for now. And consider the "profound change" part, which is 99 percent ... attitude. And I think the key to the "attitude bit" is ... One Minute Excellence.

For 10 years I wrote a weekly syndicated column, thence some 520-odd pieces. A half dozen of that lot drew particularly strong responses. One of them had the following absurd title: "One Minute Excellence!"[5]

The problem is ... I wrote it ... *and* I believed it.

The whole idea is personal commitment. A "simple" but determined commitment that one will never again, under any circumstances, do anything that is less than totally excellent.

Forget the legalities. Forget whether or not your "department" officially becomes Training Inc., a wholly owned subsidiary of the Widgets Division of the XYZ Corporation.

Instead, ask yourself: How do you achieve the "PSF Attitude"?

Here are my guidelines:

Culture Change is not "Corporate."

Culture Change is not a "Program."

Culture Change does not take "Years."

Culture Change does not start "Today."

Culture Change starts *Right Now!*

Culture Change *Lives in the Moment.*

Culture Change is *Entirely in Your Hands!*

The way to become a PSF is ... to ... become a PSF.

Now.

Try this Mantra:

We will ... *Survive.*

We will ... *Thrive.*

We will ... do *WOW Work.*

THINK ...

[5]Fact is, I stole this idea from legendary IBM boss Thomas Watson. Somebody apparently asked him, "How long does it take to become excellent?" "A minute," he replied.

NO MORE MR. NICE GUY

As I wrote this chapter, I got ... angrier and angrier. I've been writing and jawing about "all this" for five years. For the first 4.9 of those 5.0 years I pulled my verbal punches. I said that the Professional Service Firm Model was a "pretty good idea."

Well, I don't believe that anymore. I believe that it's a ... GREAT IDEA.

I believe that I'm right.

I believe that the microprocessor—or the folks in India and Ghana—will replace 80 percent of white-collar jobs. I believe that the United States can't make it as a manufacturing nation. I believe that our value added will come from intellectual capital. From awesome "talent" pursuing awesome "projects."

My tolerance has evaporated! I won't accept the notion that the PSF model is a "pretty good idea." There are many twists and turns, life is subtle ... but this is ... THE RIGHT IDEA.

(Okay, perhaps I'm wrong. But read the above. What if ... I am right? What if my arrogance relative to this idea is appropriate? Do me one favor only: THINK ABOUT IT. SERIOUSLY.)

We will ... seek out *Pioneering Clients.*
We will ... *fully automate the grunge that* Dilbert *so perceptively maligns.*
We will ... *focus on the things that make us special and distinct.*
We will ... *push to the hilt the things at which we are ... BIP (Best in Planet).*
We will ... *start NOW!*
This ... *minute.*

The PSF Way: 5 Easy Pieces

It all comes down to this ... a simple 5-step program. (Hey, that's 7 steps fewer than Alcoholics Anonymous!)

❶ TAKE PROFESSIONAL SERVICE FIRMS SERIOUSLY. *VERY* SERIOUSLY.

❷ LEARN FROM THEM.

❸ TURN EVERY PART OF YOUR ENTERPRISE INTO A SCINTILLATING "PROFESSIONAL SERVICE FIRM." ("Scintillating" = Good Word, Big Word.)

❹ TOLERATE NOTHING LESS THAN "DEPARTMENTAL" "EXCELLENCE" & "COOLNESS."

❺ DUMP ... WITHOUT CEREMONY ... ANYONE IN YOUR DEPARTMENT (PSF!) WHO DOESN'T "GET IT."

! Contrasts

WAS		IS
Cost Center	–	Profit Center
Procedure-centric	–	Client-centric
Minimizes expenses	–	Maximizes value added
Totally bounded by the company's walls	–	Totally liberated to work for outsiders
Minimizes payroll ... and hires accordingly	–	Hires superstars ... and pays accordingly
Passive: Performs "tasks," as requested	–	Active: Creates WOW projects, as inspired
Improves "enterprise efficiency"	–	Spurs "enterprise transformation"
Cubicle Slaves	–	Proud Professionals
Conservation	–	Creation

NEW BUSINESS ❗ ● NEW VALUE

6 PSFs MEAN BUSINESS: THE SOLUTIONS IMPERATIVE

! Technicolor Rules ...

- "These days, building the best server isn't enough. That's the price of entry."
- "Customers will try 'low-cost providers,' because the majors have not given them any clear reason not to."
- Copying—with excellence—has become the norm.
- We are afloat, awash, adrift in a Sea of Sameness.
- The only way to make a difference is to ... Make a Difference.
- "You are headed for commodity hell if you don't have services."
- "Customer satisfaction" is out. "Customer success" is in.

 ! RANT

We are not prepared ...

We believe that offering an excellent product or an excellent service is enough. Instead, we must understand that a "product" or "service"—even an "excellent" one—is but the "price of entry," the bare-bones beginning. The systematic application of new technologies, rock-bottom international wages, and a wildly successful 25-year global campaign to improve quality and customer satisfaction are devastating every kind of commodity producer.

 ! VISION

I imagine ...

A world where companies provide sophisticated "turnkey" "solutions" and awesome/memorable/scintillating/cool "experiences" to "never-satisfied customers." (Okay. Lots of jargon.) (Evidence to follow.)

A "Model 2005" economy in which this is the governing formula for success: Dell ("Cut all the crap") + IBM ("Add overwhelming soft-service value") + Harley-Davidson ("It's the experience, stupid") = Magic.

A time when everyone finally recognizes the Professional Service Firm idea as ... the Fundamental Basis for Value Added in the Enterprise ... and the Foremost Intellectual-Capital-Added Device known to humankind!

(At least for the next several years.) (Until it all changes again.)

Big Day

That's what I call it: THE BIG DAY. Ironically, it occurred one year—to the day—before the horrific terrorist attacks on Lower Manhattan and Northern Virginia. I surely recall 9/11—11 September 2001. But I also vividly recall logging onto Yahoo! around noon ... on 11 September 2000.

I've been around the block a couple of times. Very little in the world of enterprise surprises me. But I was in for a shock that day.

The headline says it all: *Hewlett-Packard Bids $18 Billion for Pricewaterhouse-Coopers' Consulting Business!*

HP: One of the Tippy Top ... manufacturing companies ... on earth. HP: One of the Tippy Top ... engineering companies ... on earth. This *brilliant* engineering and manufacturing firm—quality-conscious to a fault, innovation-obsessed—was saying, in effect: "*We can't make it engineering-manufacturing.*"[1]

But why?

Ann Livermore, who heads the services organization at HP, stated the case starkly: "These days, building the best server isn't enough. That's the price of entry."

The price of entry!

She might as well have said this: "*We need to leap (not merely climb) up the value-added chain—to add Integrated Consulting Services. We will offer Strategic Consulting for IS-Enterprise Transformation, Organizational Re-design, and Total Implementation. And hey ... perhaps we'll throw in an HP server or 10 for the hell of it.*"

That's not exactly what HP was saying—but it's e-x-a-c-t-l-y implicit in what the company was planning to do.

I found it a stunning announcement[2] for several reasons. For one thing, it surely suggested that "PSFs" can be worth a buck or two. (Eighteen *billion* dollars is a fair chunk of change!) But on a larger canvas, HP's move brought many chickens—many full chicken coops, for that matter—home to roost. And I also realized I was beginning to hear versions of that same story, from every point on the corporate compass.

JILTED AT THE ALTAR

[1]Footnote: The HP-PwC deal fell through, for a number of reasons. A year or so later, HP acquired Compaq. And a bit after that, IBM ended up acquiring Pricewaterhouse-Coopers! Thirty-one *thousand* consultants. The tech market by then was a shambles, and IBM parted with a mere $3.5 billion. More on IBM anon.

ANOTHER SUITOR IN THE WINGS

[2]Just before the HP announcement, I had spoken to the leaders of Sun Microsystems' services division. They had accounted for just a few percent of Sun's revenue a half-dozen years before. Now, as I recall, the share was moving toward 20 percent. And their new boss imagined that the percentage could be doubled, perhaps tripled, in fairly short order.

"How the hell do you do that?" I asked. "Simple," he replied. "We buy Pricewater-houseCoopers consultants for a few hundred thousand dollars per head."

I suspect that, in making a bid for PwC, HP CEO Carly Fiorina aimed, in part, to take those PwC consultants off the playing board—that is, keep 'em away from the likes of Sun (and IBM ...).

Big Problem: No "Clear Reason Not To"

I get ahead of myself ...

Not so long ago, I attended a leadership meeting at one of the world's top insurance companies. It is squarely in the "value-added" pool. (According to its marketing spin.) A prominent industry analyst addressed the meeting immediately before I did. I scribbled down his comment: "*Customers will try 'low-cost providers,' because the majors have not given them any clear reason not to.*"

Profound indictment, that! I.e.: Offerings from the likes of Progressive and GEICO are fine and dandy, because the "value-added leaders" just ain't addin' that much value.

The same goes for the commercial airline industry, a business that is (seemingly) far removed from insurance. All the airlines, bitching and moaning aside, work pretty well. Flights pretty much leave on time. Pretty much arrive on time. Baggage handling is actually pretty miraculous. And safety is ... stunning.

But none of them any longer rank "special" on the service side. That is, the "majors" have given us no "clear reason not to" fly (say) Southwest. Why pay hundreds of dollars for a lunchless ticket on USAir to Anywhere, USA, when you can get to the same place ... with the same growling stomach ... for $70 via SWA?

Big Trap: A Sea of Sameness

Bottom line: We (in the rich, expensive, high-wage, developed world) simply can't make it as manufacturers. It's no coincidence that damn near everything you and I buy seems to have a label in it that reads "Made in China." Now that includes airplane wings ... as well as baseball caps.

Instant knock-offs—with excellence—have become the norm. From sweaters to computers to restaurants. The quality of damn near everything is terrific. Things that work are not unusual. Things that don't work *are* unusual.

We are afloat, awash, adrift in a ... Sea of Sameness. High-quality sameness ... but sameness nonetheless.

An idea that has legs ... lasts only a few weeks, a few months at best. Then the sequel. And the sequel that follows the sequel. And so on.

Big Idea: The 10X/10X Phenomenon

We race around. Follow each other's tails. From Hollywood to Silicon Valley to Madison Avenue. As Swedish business professors Kjell Nordström and Jonas Ridderstråle put it in *Funky Business*: "The surplus society has a surplus of similar companies, employing similar people, with similar educational backgrounds ... coming up with similar ideas, producing similar things, with similar prices ... and [similar] qualities."[3]

Ouch.

I call all this "the 10X/10X phenomenon":

10 times better.

10 times less different.

Cars start at -20°F in Vermont in February. All of them. Starting at -20°F in Vermont

PRACTICE MAKES (ALL TOO) PERFECT

[3] Jesper Kunde, the Danish marketing phenom, makes the same point: "Companies have defined so much best practice that they are now more or less identical."

NEW BUSINESS **!** NEW VALUE

in February is no longer special.

In *Funky Business*, Nordström and Ridderstråle stoop to the vernacular to describe it all: "To succeed we must stop being so goddamn normal. In a winner-takes-all world, Normal = Nothing."

Ouch. (Again.)

Paul Goldberger, in the keynote story ("The Sameness of Things") on retail in a special edition of the *New York Times Magazine*, wrote, "While everything may be better, it is also increasingly the same."

Basic Idea: "Good stuff" has become commonplace. "Normal = Nothing." It's no longer exceptional for stuff (anything, everything) to work. Which means that the bar for "standing out" has risen ... dramatically.

Dreaming Big

Back to insurance: My first speech in 2002 took me to the annual agency-heads gathering of the Farmers Group. Marty Feinstein, the CEO, is well aware of the GEICO-Progressive challenge. "No longer are we only an insurance provider," he says. "Today, we also offer our customers the products and services that help them achieve their dreams, whether it's financial security, buying a car, paying for home repairs, or even taking a dream vacation."

Typically, language like "help them achieve their dreams" makes you want to check your wallet to be sure that it's still where it belongs. But there's more going on at Farmers Group than a flowery marketing ploy. Feinstein, for example, has several thousand of his agents taking the NASD exams, so that they can sell stocks. Thousands more are becoming licensed financial planners. That is, his minions are aggressively adding to their tool kits ... so that they can become Full-Service Client Financial Advisors and Dream-Fulfillment Providers ... who will toss in a couple of insurance policies on the side.[4]

GET OUT OF THE (HP) WAY

"We make over three new product announcements a day," said Hewlett-Packard CEO Carly Fiorina upon taking up the HP helm. **"Can you remember them? Our customers can't!"**

HP has dramatically shortened time to market for new products in the last ten years.

Even so, Fiorina is moved to say, **"Our customers can't remember HP products."** Again: Ouch!

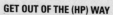

INSURING SUCCESS

[4]In other words: The only way to make a difference is to ... Make a Difference.

If you're an "insurance company," then offering insurance (once upon a time, your very reason for being!) is just ... the price of entry.

Again: Normal = Nothing!

Support for the potency of this idea: Northwestern Mutual, a proud *insurance* company, recently and portentously changed the moniker of its field sales force to NMFN ... Northwestern Mutual Financial *Network*. (The italics are mine.) Translation: more service offerings. (Or: more "dream fulfillment"?)

Standing out in a world where most everything works is stupefyingly difficult. And yet some companies are making a go of it.

Something *is* happening.

Something big.

THE BIG DITTO: TOURING THE PSF+ ECONOMY

You see it throughout the world of enterprise: Where "products" and "services" once were, now "solutions" will be. Just connect the dots ...

IBM. IBM. In early 2002 Lou Gerstner retired after an exceptional nine-year run as Big Boss of IBM. The company grew by about $20 billion in sales during his reign. How much of that was due to the "M" in IBM, more and better "machine" (computer) manufacturing? The answer is simple:

None. Zip. Nada. Zero. Z-e-r-o.

IBM still makes, in its own shops, chips and memory. But it does not "make" computers anymore.

Virtually all of IBM's hearty growth ... perhaps more than "all" ... came from IBM Global Services. That entity grew during the Gerstner reign from a near afterthought (real men don't do services ... or some such) to a whopping ... $35 billion ... in revenue.

What is IBM Global Services? Simple: THE BIGGEST "PSF" IN THE WORLD.[5] WHEN GERSTNER ARRIVED, IT WAS A FRACTION OF THE SIZE OF EDS. WHEN HE LEFT, IT WAS ONE AND A HALF TIMES AS LARGE AS EDS.

As *BusinessWeek* put it, IBM's goal under Gerstner was to become the "systems integrator of choice." Gerstner got his training at McKinsey & Company ... the preeminent PSF. And at IBM, he more or less built the Mother of All PSFs! The logic that Gerstner offered for this strategy bears stating in bold, italic type: ***"You are headed for commodity hell if you don't have services."***

And, indeed, IBM did have services when Gerstner left—to the tune of those tens of billions of bucks. That's how much money the company pocketed in the name of "Integrated Strategic Consultative Services." (Sure, I hate the term "Integrated Strategic Consultative Services." Jargony as hell. But that is exactly what IBM has created!)

Incidentally (I), Gerstner gets my vote as "top turnaround exec" of recent times.

Incidentally (II), it wasn't easy. Gerstner was a "strategy guy"—and as such got by admirably in top positions at American Express and RJR Nabisco. But performing his "consulting services transformation miracle" at IBM took something more. "I came to see in

GO BIG BLUE
[5]As noted, within months of Gerstner's departure, new CEO Sam Palmisano bought PricewaterhouseCoopers.

Arguably, it was IBM's brilliant success with Global Services that forced Hewlett-Packard first to go after PwC and then, failing that, to grab hold of Compaq ... all in a frenzied effort to remain a big-time IT "solutions" player.

my time at IBM," he later reflected, "that 'culture' isn't just one aspect of the game—it *is* the game." That kind of switcheroo[6] is no cakewalk.

AT&T. AT&T has been through at least nine lives (and, it often seems, deaths) in the 15 or so years since the Big Bell Breakup. Now, under President David Dorman, it's aiming for yet another lease on life. On the one hand, that "new" life might seem a little old-hat, coming as it does under the banner "back to long distance." On the other hand, the new strategy is, in fact, anything but "back to." It involves selling … ahem … "bundles of lucrative corporate services," as *BusinessWeek* put it; that is, a lot of software and a lot of consulting to giant corporations like Merrill Lynch, MasterCard, and Hyatt. And perhaps a little long distance "capacity" will be tossed in on the side.

But that's only the mellow start of the Big Story. IBM scuttled the stuff that didn't work. (By the bushel.) So, too, AT&T. One estimate suggests that Mr. Dorman will dump fully 50 percent of AT&T's current L.D. subscribers (that's 25 million customers!) in order to focus on those high-end, high-value-added subscribers who need those "integrated consultative services."

ERICSSON. Ericsson, AT&T's hurtin' Swedish rival, apparently unearthed the same musical score. The "product manufacturer" has shipped over 50 percent of its manufacturing to premier outsourcers Solectron and Flextronics, and a substantial share of its R&D to India. Instead? Welcome to … Services World! There's a spanking new division for licensing technology, and one observer concludes the company aims to become "a wireless specialist that depends on services more than manufacturing, on knowhow more than metal."

GE POWER SYSTEMS. In 2000 I visited Bob Nardelli, then the big boss at GE Power Systems … a $20+ billion outfit that lies in the Old Economy heartland of GE. (It was headquartered in Schenectady, New York.) (Now Atlanta. Message there too, eh?) The transformer dudes. The gas-turbine dudes.

BIG-IRON LADS.

As I prepared to speak to Nardelli's execs, I discovered to my surprise that his patch of Planet GE was the company's most profitable bit. More profitable than GE's broadcast division. Or its aircraft-engine division. Or its medical-devices division. Or even GE Capital.

That didn't compute, and I asked Nardelli (now chairman and CEO of Home Depot) how he and his team did it. "It's the execution of our vision," he said. "We want to be the air-traffic controllers of electrons." That is, GE PowerSystems didn't want simply to be a

---

PROMISE KEEPERS

[6]There are twists upon twists in the IBM story. For example, in 1999, Gerstner insisted that his top executives sign a pledge to provide IBM's customers with the best device or software available in a particular arena, even if it wasn't made by IBM.

To show their seriousness, Gerstner and company dropped lots of in-house programs and projects in order to focus on outside strategic partners. Siebel, for example, became IBM's partner of choice in the CRM arena, supplanting a major in-house IBM effort, which was subsequently scrapped.

provider of "manufactured boxes" ... a commodity (an excellent commodity, to be sure). GE Power Systems aimed to provide ... Systems & Services ... to get a little piece of the action whenever a switch was turned on or off, from the Arctic to the Antarctic. Successful?[7] In short order Power Systems' "services bit" marched from peanuts to the $10 *billion*-in-revenues mark.

Nardelli added that the most verboten words in his lexicon were "customer satisfaction." Instead, he and his team aimed to provide "customer *success*."

Call that a semantic quibble,[8] if you wish. I don't. I call it a distinction that cuts to the very heart of this encompassing discussion.

Power Systems is "getting better at [Six Sigma Quality] every day," Nardelli added, "but we really need to think about ... the customer's profitability. *Are customers' bottom lines really benefiting from what we provide them?*"

It *is* important that the GE "blackbox" works. And it *is* important that it arrives on time. But that's not enough. Not nearly enough. Such performance, once again, is merely the "price of entry." The real question: Does the power-generation-plant customer make more money (bottom line!) because he purchased an encompassing products and services "package" from GE rather than, say, Siemens? Does the "Turnkey GE Experience" provide the customer with measurable "success" ... something far more significant than (mere) "satisfaction."

Happiness is one thing. ("Nice doin' business with you, Bob.") Getting *rich* from one's purchasing decision to "go with GE" is another thing ... entirely. ("Bob, you are The Man!")

GE INDUSTRIAL SYSTEMS. GE Redux. Once upon a time, there was a big division in GE called ... Bunch of Real Guys Who Make Circuit Breakers Division. Well, okay, not really. But that's what it was, in effect. A bunch of guys ... who manufactured circuit breakers. Well, it doesn't get much more commodity-ish than the circuit breaker.

Today, that division is a $10 billion business called ... GE Industrial *Systems*. Over the last few years, GE Industrial *Systems* has been on an acquisition binge ... buying all sorts of systems and software companies. And now the division is able to sell (yup!) "integrated facility services" ... and then throw in a few circuit breakers, more or less for the hell of it.

FROM MODEL T TO MODEL PSF
In *The Company*, John Micklethwait and Adrian Wooldridge report that Ford aims to become a "vehicle brand owner." The venerable "manufacturer" would "design, engineer, and market" automobiles—but not "actually make them." (!)

JUST ADD ETHICS
[7]For what it's worth, such an idea was near the core of the Enron strategy as well ("clunky pipelines" to "market makers")—although GE Power Systems executed its strategy with a smidgen or two more integrity!

DISTINCTIVE TERMINOLOGY
[8]Keep that distinction in mind (we'll come back to it later): CUSTOMER SATISFACTION versus CUSTOMER SUCCESS. It's a big deal. Arguably, The Big Deal. New Business Distinction No. 1.

SIEMENS. Nobody prides itself on manufacturing excellence more than the Germans. No German company has more pride in engineering excellence than venerable Siemens. Thus you can imagine my surprise at this report from *Forbes*: "A little-known fact: Siemens is now the world's largest application service provider to the health business. Digitally stored x-rays, recordkeeping, the cameras that guide surgeons in the operating theater—all run on Siemens software." For example, *Forbes* adds, Siemens is "giving HealthSouth an all-digital 'hospital of the future.'"

And on it goes. And goes ...

UPS. "UPS wants to take over the sweet spot in the endless loop of goods, information, and capital that all those packages [it moves] represent," one reporter has written. To my mind, "sweet spot in the endless loop of goods, information and capital" sounds an awful lot like ... "air-traffic controllers of electrons." UPS is, effectively, betting its future on its UPS logistics "systems" operation.

In fact, UPS is betting the whole bag of marbles on its huge "What Can Brown Do for You?" marketing and re-branding campaign, which aims to re-position the boxy-brown-truck outfit into ... um... a Turnkey Systems & Solutions Supplier, an IBM Global Systems look-alike for logistics. Among many other things, necessary financial services, such as insurance and certain sorts of financing associated with "supply chain" activities, are part of "Brown's"[9] offering.

UTC. I visited with the R&D leadership at United Technologies Corporation. The elevator folks, at UTC's Otis division, told me that the path to their future success was clear. Get beyond "selling boxes" (elevators) and instead peddle "integrated building systems." (Been in an elevator that displays stock quotes, sports scores, weather, etc., as you shoot from the 7th to the 37th floor? That's the least of it, but the idea. Also, re maintenance, the elevators now talk directly—without prompting—to UTC's maintenance facilities, as needed.)

The AC folks, at UTC's Carrier division, were also on hand. And what's their "strategic" plan? Get beyond "selling boxes" (air conditioners) and instead peddle (yup!) "integrated building systems." In fact, Carrier often *leases* air-conditioning systems—and sells units of "coolness," or "Coolth." Instead of those oh-so-passé "boxes."

{ **WHERE IT STOPS, NOBODY KNOWS**
Holy smoke!
> *My advice: Pause just a bit to ponder these examples.*
> *The HP story is the IBM story! Which is the AT&T story! Which is the Ericsson story! Which is the GE Power Systems story! Which is the GE Industrial Systems story! Which is ...*
> *Okay. You can continue reading now.*

! **VALET PARKING, ON A GRAND SCALE**
[9]Among its other operations, UPS Logistics manages the integrated logistics activities associated with managing the movement of 4.5 million Ford vehicles from 21 manufacturing sites to 6,000 North American dealers.
(Hey, they don't arrive in boxy brown trucks!)

HOME DEPOT. Perhaps one can readily imagine adding "integrated consultative turnkey services" at HP, Sun, IBM, AT&T, Ericsson, or even at capital-intense GE Power Systems or GE Industrial Systems. Or Siemens. But retail? Get real.

Well, that's not the way our colleague Bob Nardelli sees it. Having lost out on the chance to succeed Jack Welch as CEO of GE, Bob settled for the Top Spot at Home Depot, the $58 billion DIY colossus. His goal for the company is staggering: Double revenues ... to $100 billion ... by 2005.

How does he propose to do it?

By opening stores? Sure.

By going international? Sure.

But the heart of the answer is ... you guessed it (by now) ... Integrated Services. One analyst reports that Nardelli's main aim is to move Home Depot "beyond selling just goods to selling home services. He wants to capture home improvement dollars wherever and however they're spent." Case in point: Nardelli has started something called At-Home Service. This DIY "house calls"[10] business aims for ... *$10 billion* in revenue ... just by 2005.

As one Home Depot exec notes, the home-services business is exceptionally fragmented. Using the power of its "Orange Box" logo, the company could become the one-stop shop for lawn care, pool care, house cleaning, home-electronics and entertainment installation and maintenance, home-security systems, and, of course, home-remodeling projects. And what an appeal that combination would have to harried, two-worker families! Not so incidentally, each of these elements encompasses tens upon tens of billions of dollars in potential sales.

Just a (not-so-errant) thought: Just as Wal*Mart rules the discount "product" world, so Home Depot rules the "home services" world?[11]

HOME IS WHERE THE PROFITS ARE
[10]More examples from Nardelli:

To develop "a deeper selling relationship" with his retail clients, he has created Project Management System—a "home project management" software and service business.

And to go after the building professional, he has created Pro Set, a "pro shop" service that operates within Home Depot.

DEERE ME
[11]Bob Nardelli isn't alone. At least one Big Competitor has an eye on part of this space: Deere & Co.

"While green industry pros are all potential buyers of Deere's equipment," write Adrian Slywotzky and colleagues in *How to Grow When Markets Don't*, "they also need huge amounts of plants and planting materials, consumables such as fertilizer, mulch, plant food and pesticides, irrigation gear, lawn maintenance supplies, and other products. All in all the 'green market' amounts to $100 billion per year."

Hence the birth of ... JDL. John Deere Landscapes. The internal entrepreneurs championing the cause were initially the targets of much derision. But a new CEO said, in effect, "Get over it. This is our future."

NEW BUSINESS ● NEW VALUE

ARCHITECTURAL FIRMS. Yet another stop on my speaking tour in 2001 brought me before members of SMPS, the Society for Marketing Professional Services. Members are concentrated in the architecture, engineering, and construction business.

What did I hear?

THE SAME DAMN STORY. DOWN TO THE DOTTING OF THE "I"s AND THE CROSSING OF THE "T"s.

"Architecture is becoming a commodity," an SMPS executive told me. "Winners will increasingly become 'turnkey facilities[12] management' providers." They won't provide just "drawings," or "oversight of the construction process." They will provide all that … plus every iota of the "service package" that could take the entire "facilities headache" out of the client's hands. In fact, my short SMPS riff leads to a pop quiz: Who was the number-one employer of architecture-school graduates in the U.S. in 2000?

Tick. Tick. Tick.

Your time is running out.

And the answer is, according to my SMPS colleagues: Accenture. "PSF" Accenture wants to do for "turnkey facilities management" what EDS did for "turnkey IS management."

SPRINGS. Springs Industries makes towels, sheets, and pillowcases. Sounds like a commodity business to me! But Springs Industries, one of our most fully modernized textile "manufacturing" companies, is playing the New Game for keeps.

Springs used to serve customers of every size and shape … including very small sizes and very small shapes. Now they're focusing virtually all their activities on the giants. Target. Wal*Mart. A few others.

Does Springs simply lob truckloads of "low cost" sheets and pillowcases at Wal*Mart? Hardly. Instead, it does some market research on its own and discovers (say) that you can sell a lot more beach towels from an end-cap display at Wal*Mart if you include beach umbrellas and picnic baskets as part of the tableau. Problem: Springs doesn't make beach umbrellas or picnic baskets. So does it approach Wal*Mart with its data and say, "Buy some picnic baskets, fellas"? Hardly.

Springs itself sources the picnic baskets. (China?) Sources the beach umbrellas. (Thailand?) Puts the Entire Tableau together into a "collection" (read: "system"). Merchandises it. Creates promotional material surrounding it. And actually does significant site management for those zillion end caps in those zillion Wal*Mart stores.

Old Springs: a "box-of-sheets provider." New Springs: a Turnkey Integrated Systems.

BACK TO THE DRAWING BOARD
[12]Some months after the SMPS gig, I keynoted the American Institute of Architects annual convention. My theme: EAT OR BE EATEN.

In other words: Either Accenture will hire architects (to do the "design bit"), or AIA members will hire accountants and administrators, so that their firms can be Lead Dog in the IFMS (Integrated Facilities Management Systems) business.

Is there no end to all this?

Apparently not.

Marketing Management Company ... that throws in a few sheets and towels, more or less for the hell of it.

EQUITY OFFICE PROPERTIES. Speaking of developers ... let's stick with the real estate game. "Location, location, location"? The sine qua non! Nobody does commercial real estate better than Sam Zell, whose Equity Office Properties owns more office buildings than any other company around. Sam, however, is revising his fundamental "product"/"service" offering.

Here's how a *New York Times* report from late 2001 summed up the matter: "Sam Zell is not a man plagued by self-doubt. ... Mr. Zell controls public companies that own nearly 700 office buildings in the United States. ... Now, Mr. Zell says, he will transform the real estate market by turning those REITs (Real Estate Investment Trusts) ... into national brands. Mr. Zell believes [clients] will start to view those offices as something more than a commodity[13] chosen chiefly by price and location."

RCI. In mid-2002, I stumbled across an absolutely marvelous company, Resort Condominiums International. RCI (as it's best known) is part of the Cendant Corporation, and it is the premier company involved in market-making for time-share—which is evolving into a monster industry. (Talk about "dream merchants"!)

RCI World 2002: 3,700 resorts in "the system." Some 2.8 million members. In 100 countries. And 2,000,000 exchanges in 1999. Basic idea: You "buy" two weeks of a condo in Jackson Hole. But via RCI, you need not go there 20 consecutive winters-summers. RCI allows you to spend your weeks, via a point system, with any of its participating members, in return for offering up your condo to someone else.

RCI has about 70 percent of the market in traded timeshare transactions. But that's not enough. (As they see it.) Consider the precise nature of this language, courtesy RCI boss Ken May: "*Our mission is to go from being the world's premier timeshare—which is a large idea in a small industry—to being what we call the market makers for global travel and leisure. We need to enable developers to be involved in more travel and leisure markets, rather than just the timeshare side.*"

Today, RCI has two principal customers: the owner of the timeshare, and the developer who is creating the destination that involves the timeshare locations. But RCI is now heading up that value-added chain ... and into the quarterback's role in every nook and cranny of the travel and leisure world! (Air traffic controllers of Travel & Leisure?)

BEYOND "CALL THE SUPER"

[13]"In fact, last I heard, EOP was negotiating with my training company to provide management training for professional service firms that lease space in Zell's buildings. That is, Zell's EOP would be providing "turnkey professional services" to its rental clients ... not just clean bathrooms, bright lights, and a decent location.

OMNICOM. How silly I am! I thought "advertising" agencies made "ads." That is, I thought so until I had the opportunity to talk to the spirited leaders of Omnicom, a $7-billion giant in what used to be known as "the ad business."

I kept getting correspondence on letterhead that read DAS. Turns out that DAS stands for Diversified Agency Services. Turns out, moreover, that those "mere" "services" account for over half of Omnicom's revenue.

What's the point?

Same-same.

Ditto.

Omnicom is now in the ... you've probably guessed it by this point ... Integrated Marketing Services ... business. A GM division, say, may soon be "farming out" *all* of its marketing activities to an outfit like Omnicom or WPP, which will also provide a few ads ... just for the hell of it.

THE U.S. ARMY. The Army? Yes. Decidedly. "War" is no longer a matter of "gun" versus "gun." (Or about whose guns are bigger.) The apparent enemy for the foreseeable future is a highly motivated, elusive, nation-less "virtual enterprise."

Thus, the New Army must draw upon the "integrated resources" of the other armed services, the intelligence agencies, and so forth. Its "core competence" and "competitive advantage" correspond to the degree of "integrated" "systemic" "information intensity" that it possesses. (As well as agility/shape-shifting skills.) That's exactly parallel to what I've been discussing in this chapter.

ONCE MORE FROM THE TOP

I'm hitting you over the head with examples, because I want to suggest just how encompassing this trend is.

Think back to our look at the insurance industry. The major insurers are getting beaten up because "low-cost providers" are offering damn fine services ... at, well, a damn low cost. To which Marty Feinstein, CEO of Farmers Group, responded by announcing: "No longer are we only an insurance provider. Today, we also offer our customers the products and services that help them achieve their dreams, whether it's financial security, buying a car, paying for home repairs, or even taking a dream vacation."

Sorry for the repeat. It's important.

PASSING LANE TO INDIA

In Chapter 3, I talked about the migration of white-collar jobs to India. But the "solutions" card trumps the India card, right?

Not so fast ...

Consider this from a 2003 *Economist* Special Report: "The leading Indian [software] outsourcers reckon that the key to their long-term prosperity is bagging ever larger deals and moving ever higher up the value chain."

Are you a betting sort? I lay 5:6 odds that the next "Value-Added Services" Superstar will be ... India.

(Really) Big Idea: Turnkey Nation

In this tour d'horizon, I have compassed the entire economy. That is: A surprising number of industry leaders are heading in the same direction ... away from the *excellent* "commodity" service/product ... and toward the turnkey provision of, to use Nardelli's words, "customer *success*." Just go down our list:

Hewlett-Packard ... Computers & IS/IT Integrated Services.
Sun Microsystems ... Computers & IS/IT Integrated Services.
Farmers Group ... Insurance & Financial Services.
Northwestern Mutual Financial Network ... Insurance & Financial Services.
IBM ... Computers & Integrated IS/IT Services.
AT&T ... Telecommunications & Communication Systems.
Ericsson ... Ditto AT&T.
GE Power Systems ... Utility Systems.
GE Industrial Systems ... Building Subsystems.
Ford ... Vehicle Brand Owner.
Siemens ... Health Services.
Home Depot ... DIY & Integrated Home Services.
Deere & Co ... Green Systems.
UTC Otis ... Building Subsystems.
UTC Carrier ... Building Subsystems.
UPS ... Logistics Systems & Services.
Springs Industries ... Textiles & Integrated Marketing Services.
RCI ... Timeshare & Travel-Leisure Transactions & Services.
Equity Office Properties ... Space & Integrated Office Services.
Architectural firms ... Design & Turnkey Facilities Services.
Omnicom ... Ads & Integrated Marketing Services.
The U.S. Army ... Guns & Applied Information-centric Systems Power.
India ... Global Systems redux.

Now, for the sake of argument, I offer "Model 2005." Namely:

Dell + IBM + Harley-Davidson = Magic:

FEES HIGH: HO HUM?

In mid-2003 concern about deflation made headlines. Fair enough. But a look beneath the surface provides powerful evidence in support for this chapter's argument. Consider this price data from the *Wall Street Journal* (changes in price for 2002):

Televisions (-12%)	**Cable TV service (+5%)**
Toys (-10%)	**Child care (+5%)**
Photo equipment (-7%)	**Photographer's fees (+3%)**
Sports equipment (-2%)	**Sports-event admission (+3%)**
New car (-2%)	**Car repair (+3%)**
Dishes and flatware (-1%)	**Eating out (+2%).**

I guess I need not explain the "trend" revealed by this compelling data. Oh well, I will: Bye-bye "commodity" manufacturing. Hello services.

Dell = Cut all the bullshit. (100 square feet.)

IBM = Add lots (and lots!) of "soft"/"integrative"/"turnkey"/"success" value.

Harley-Davidson = A Seriously Cool Experience.

Cut the crap. Add soft-service value. Make it memorable. That's the story that seems to be unfolding—and will continue to unfold in the next two chapters.

Is my ad giant pal right? And what about that computer-equipment CEO? Is the plot-line I've hawked in the last several pages incorrect?

No.

Or, at least, not entirely so.

There are several ways to skin this cat. And you damn well better pay attention to all of them. (Virtually impossible. Oh well.)

This "integrated systems"/"integrated solutions" "stuff" makes a lot of sense to me. But it only makes sense if the ... Original Product (that is, the "price of entry") ... is great. Not "good," but "great."

I don't believe in the tooth fairy. If your focus is on Product Innovation ... to the point where you create Major Revolutions in Your Space ... then you're probably not focusing as much on the "integrated services" stuff. And if you are focusing on (say) "integrated marketing services," then, yes, your "product" may well suffer.

What's the answer?

Very simple: There is none.

Well, there is *one*.

That is ... forget the tooth fairy.[14]

Being "great at everything" just isn't on.

Trust me. (Please.)

Big Recap: One Hell of a Trip

Let's briefly review the bidding from the last several chapters.

1. *108 x 5 to 8 x 1/eLIZA/100 SF.* It used to take 108 people five days to unload a timber ship. Now it takes eight people one day. A 98.5 percent reduction in blue-collar labor. IBM's Project eLIZA aims, through the advanced application of artificial intelligence, to use microprocessors to supplant $100,000-a-year jobs. Dell Computer requires only 100 square feet of spare parts storage to support a plant that churns out 80,000 custom-engineered computers per day. Bottom line: The Grunge Removal Team is on the job.

2. *Department to PSF/WWPF.* We used to have "departments" that were called "overhead"/"cost centers." Now we have exciting "PSFs"/Professional Service Firms that conduct only Work Worth Paying For.

SYSTEMS OVERRIDE?

[14]A computer-equipment executive read me the riot act. And, frankly, I think I deserved it. "Not all of us," he said "buy this 'integrated solutions' routine. I don't, for one. I freely admit that I'm betting this company on truly innovative products—and only secondarily on the systems and services that surround them." An advertising-industry guru made an eerily similar comment to me: "But what about 'great ads,' Tom?" To which my response at the time was: "Um. Uh."

Nice job, Tom.

But read on.

3. *Enterprise Value Added comes via PSFs and "Solutions"/"Customer Success" provision.* The Professional Service Firm is unleashed to join seamlessly with its peers and provide value added through the provision of "integrated services" ... which, essentially, become the Core of the Company's Business Model ... whether the company's world consists of Real Estate, Insurance, Timeshare, Computers, Transformers, Elevators, Air Conditioners, War-fighting, or ... Whatever.

THAT'S IT.

! Contrasts

WAS	IS
"Product" & "Services"	– "Experiences" & "Solutions"
A Great Widget, mass-produced on a "you can have any color you want, as long as it's black" basis	– A Fabulous Turnkey Experience, tailor-made for each customer and supported by an array of Great Widgets from all over the globe
Manufacturing Rules!	– All the strengths of an extended supply chain are seamlessly brought to bear on a particular customer
Staunchly inflexible. We (producers) rule!	– Infinitely flexible. They (customers) rule!
"Lump"-intense	– Information- & Packaging-intense

NEW BUSINESS **!** ● NEW VALUE

HEY, KIDS, LET'S PUT ON A SHOW
I love playing with words. How about: From **Product Provider** *to* **Solutions Impresario.** *First I made you a rock star. Now I want you to be the late Bill Graham, or even Don King.* **Rodale's Synonym Finder** *offers these words for impresario: director, producer, maestro, choirmaster, precentor, coryphaeus. It all sounds great—except for "coryphaeus," whatever that may be.*

7 WELCOME TO XF/CROSS-FUNCTIONAL WORLD: THE SOLUTIONS50

! Technicolor Rules ...

● **Rules? I've got 50, wrapped in a nice, neat package.**

 ! RANT

We are not prepared ...

We say that we will provide high-level "integrated solutions" and promote "customer success" embodied by the Professional Service Firm Model. But we must go beyond this "vision" and ... Cut the Crap. We (especially those at the top of the enterprise) must become deeply immersed in the minutiae of insuring that the Warring Princes and Princesses disassemble their functional towers, grass over their moats ... and start sashaying with one another.

We say that we will create "great customer experiences" that bring to bear the full resources of the enterprise on any transaction. But we must move a Giant Step further—and acknowledge that removing/trashing/obliterating any and all barriers to cross-functional communication is nothing short of our ... Single Highest Strategic Priority.

Single.
Highest.
Strategic.
Priority.

We say that new technology is the prescription that we need to open the lines of organizational communication. But we must realize that this issue is about the nature of Human Nature. We must demand total ... and detailed ... concentration by the management team on the everyday human interactions that make up ... and discombobulate ... the most scintillating business processes ... because God *is* in and of the details on this one!

⊙ ! VISION

I imagine ...

Something that I despair of ever seeing: A time when Historically Warring Tribes will truly start ... conversing with one another. A time when the walls that separate departments will finally ... come tumbling down. A time when ...

(But enough: "Vision" is mostly beside the point here. It's those damnable details. See "Rant," above.)

"Only an Engineer ...

"Engineers are such idiots. (I should know ... I am one.)

I attended a top management "retreat" for a large aerospace company. The firm was up to its eyeballs in doggy doo-doo. At the end of two days, about a dozen pressing issues had emerged, and it was time to assign responsibility for "ameliorative initiatives."

The Biggest Cheese, an engineer himself, allowed as how "the fix" should be "pretty straightforward." After all, he added nonchalantly, all these problems were "simple communications issues." (I kid you not.)

"Only an engineer could say that," I muttered to myself. Well, not quite to myself. The HR Vice President[1] sitting beside me looked at me, and couldn't suppress a grin.

The Israelis and the Palestinians. "Only a communications issue."

NYC's Fire Department and Police Department. "Only a communications issue."

Finance and Marketing. "Only a communications issue."

Mom and Dad in divorce court. "Only a communications issue."

This issue is *the* issue. On the one hand, of course, it's eternal. (Or even genetic ...) On the other hand, this "eternal" issue is now, if possible, more pressing than ever, and slightly more amenable to fixing thanks to the new enabling technologies. (Thumb Texting Rules! Or just might.)

Walls! Damn Walls!

All of this "integrated solutions"/"customer success" stuff I yapped about in the last chapter is ... so much crap. Mostly. And mostly, because to deliver "integrated solutions" (yadda, yadda) or "customer success" (yadda, yadda) requires that every Bit & Piece of an enterprise—in fact, its entire supply & demand chain—work together in a harmonious, boundary-less fashion.

Good luck, amigo! (Yadda, yadda.)

A good friend had been a solo practitioner for years. She'd been doing great design work. Selling it successfully. Practicing, virtually alone, from her studio. Subsequently, she got into the licensing business. And began to work with giant companies. She, for the first time, at age 50, "discovered" the innards of giant corporations.

And what she discovered was ... walls ... walls ... impenetrable walls. "Obvious stuff" that should have taken hours ... taking weeks, sometimes months. Left Hands (in the client org) that had to be introduced to Right Hands (in the client org) ... by her. Etc.

It was fascinating ... and perhaps more than a little depressing ... to observe *my* professional and jaded world through her *virgin* eyes.

This *is* ... The Mother of All Issues. Our failure to deal with it ... and our habit of treating it as "only a communications issue" ... makes a joke of any talk about "synergy."

Message 2003: Clunky doesn't cut it!

ALWAYS A WOMAN

[1] Um, that VP of Human Resources was the only woman among the 25 or so top corporate officers who were at this retreat.

Coincidence? Hardly.

More—much more!—on the women's issue later. See Chapters 13 and 21.

Whose Side Are They On?

What's the biggest problem in the world of national security today?

Simple. The CIA won't talk to the FBI ... who won't talk to Customs ... who won't talk to the INS ... who won't talk to the Air Force ... who won't talk to the Army ... who won't talk to the Navy. (And the few who do choose to talk across walls are seen as "disloyal" to, say, "200 proud years" of Army or Navy tradition.) And so on.

Fighting "virtual states," like al Qaeda, demands *seamless* (Big, Big Word) integration of our domestic and international security forces. In fact, integration of the civilized world's domestic and international security assets.

How to do it? That is not the "64-dollar question." That is the 64-*trillion*-dollar question. *The* question in the New Wars of Terror ... *the* life and death issue.[2]

Can We Talk?

The same phenomenon cripples enterprise relative to communications between logistics and engineering ... and purchasing and finance and HR and customer service ... and so on ... and so on. (Not to mention the whole supply and demand chain that girdles the globe in both directions, far beyond the legal enterprise boundaries.)

Case in point: A style-driven apparel maker wishes to present an exciting, integrated "collection" to its customers. It will include, say, shirts and pants and sweaters and socks and shoes. (Or whatever.) But the whole damn thing looks like a mess when it's presented. It doesn't cohere. It doesn't make a "story."

Why? Simple. The shirt people don't talk to the pants people ... who don't talk to the sweater people ... who don't talk to the sock people ... who don't talk to the shoe people. And so it goes. ("Cozy up to *shoe* people," the sweater buyer says, oozing contempt from every pore.)

So there we are: The CIA won't talk to the FBI. And the shirt people won't talk to the pants people. What's new? Nothing![3]

Message: This issue must become our Top Priority. Everywhere. From the White House Situation Room ... to the Corporate Boardroom.

CAN CITY HALL FIGHT THIS?

[2]From the front page of the *New York Times* (20 August 2002): "MAYOR PROMISING BETTER RESPONSE TO CATASTROPHES: Bloomberg Wants Police and Fire Officials to Cooperate."

Mayor Michael Bloomberg wants emergency-response agencies to talk to one another. It won't be easy. "At the [Bloomberg] plan's core," the *Times* reports, "is an ambitious goal: a profound change in the culture of the Police and Fire Departments, two agencies with a long history of rivalry."

Good luck, Mr. Mayor: You may be a billionaire—but that doesn't make you a match for the police and fire bosses, whose "friction at emergency scenes is legendary," notes the *Times*.

OH, THE HUMANITY!

[3]Can the Internet "solve" the communication issue? In your dreams! The new technology is just that: technology ... a tool.

Human nature rules. And human nature tends to support ... "stovepipes" & "silos."

There's no "solution" to human nature. But we can start by being honest. And by not trying to engineer it away.

NEW BUSINESS ● NEW VALUE

Executive Suite Confidential: The Heart of Dullness

I just returned from a three-hour meeting in Chicago with a (very) senior executive of a Giant Company. One of the top 50 American companies (as measured by revenue). Call it an engineering company. In other words: a company driven by its confident belief in and reliance on the excellence of its logical engineering skills.

But competitors have effectively matched those once towering skills. And now, said corporation is looking to differentiate itself, to get closer to the marketplace. It's considering ideas such as a wholesale commitment to branding. And adding more of those integrated services I'm so keen on.

My senior exec acquaintance recounted the gory (to me, not to him) details of a recent top management meeting. Lots and lots of analysis had been done in preparation. Presentation after presentation spewed forth. The meeting, typical of giant corporations, was really a meeting … to prepare for a meeting[4] … to prepare for a Big Meeting. That is, a meeting of the top 20 people in his huge unit, to prepare for a round table of the top five people … who in turn would report their results to the Really Big Guy.

Many of the presentations were apparently scintillating. Rather radical change was proposed. And "proposed" is the operative word.

When the time came to prepare the Semi-Big Guys for the Meeting about the Meeting with the Really Big Guy … almost all the radicalism evaporated.

The issue, said one executive, was "cultural." That is, a shift toward a "demand-side," customer-driven, brand-centric enterprise. As opposed to a down-the-line "supply-side," engineering-driven approach/"culture." But, one of the Semi-Big Guys patiently explained, the Really Big Guy "won't tolerate the word 'culture.' He thinks it's bullshit."

The Really Big Guy is apparently happiest with charts and graphs and sterile analysis. God help the presenter who strays into the "softer side of things."

And on it went.[5] Every radical proposal had to be translated into the ABL … Acceptable Bland Language … favored at the Tippy Tippy Top of Giant Corp.

Executive Suite Confidential: Bland Man's Bluff

The acquaintance who reported to me is a VPP … Very Powerful Person … by any normal standard. Salary. Org Chart. Intelligence. Political savvy.

MEETING MANIA
[4]Such meetings to prepare for meetings … to prepare for more meetings (which end up sapping everyone's vital juices) are commonplace as hell. You see that going on at the FBI, the CIA, and the DEA. You see it in the Navy, the Army, and the Air Force.

And, alas, you see it among the leadership cadre of America's top companies.

PROZAC MOMENT
[5]*When I left that meeting with my pal, I was utterly depressed. Indeed, I saw no reason, whatsoever, to continue writing this book.*

What's the point … when every Seriously Cool Idea evaporates in meetings to prepare for meetings? When "powerful" people turn into gutless people? When nothing happens other than … tiny incremental adjustments at the margin?

And yet, in the end, he is toothless, spineless. He may share my California Wanderlust in theory, but he does not have a "vision" of anything much beyond ... "success at the next meeting." And he's surely not willing to go to the mat for anything that is truly revolutionary. E.g., God help us should we ever utter that word "culture" in front of the ... Really Big Guy.

What bullshit. (Yes, *bullshit*. Sorry.)

One perversely prays that a Wal*Mart look-alike lands in his market space. Somebody who scares the bejesus (shit) out of this Established Enterprise. And forces it to take on the baggage of new words, new ideas, new possibilities.

The final proposal that came from the semi-semi-big guys, forwarded to the semi-big guys (in preparation for the meeting with *the* Really Big Guy), was thought by One and All to be ... Radical.

Problem: I was *not* looking at it from their perspective. I was looking at it from the perspective of somebody who doesn't live in or near their Lake Michigan house. And to an outsider, it was the most insipid damn "PowerPoint Deck," as insiders call it, I've been exposed to in a long time. To them, there was an *adjective* adjusted here, an *adverb* adjusted there ... but it added up to the most trivial nonsense known to humankind.

(Trust me.) (Alas.)

Executive Suite Confidential: Speak Truth to Power

This ... Monster Company ... has problems. Big ones, I perceive. And they don't have the Raw Nerve to confront them. They don't ... and it's one of the Main Messages of this book ... have the nerve to alter the ... Language. To start talking or imagining in different terms, about ... Radically Altered Future States of Being.

Language is ever so powerful! If you can't use the word "culture" ... when a ... Culture Change ... is clearly/desperately needed ... is there any hope ... whatsoever?

Frankly, I don't think so.

But there is another vital point here. Do we really know ... for sure ... that the Really Big Guy *will* "go berserk" if the word "culture" is uttered in His Magisterial Presence? The answer, because my client is very savvy, may well be "yes."

But what if ...

What if ... Mr. Really Big[6] is secretly tired of the incredible layers of insulation that buffer him from the ... Unadorned Truth? What if he longs, desperately, for ... Straightforward Human Interaction ... with someone who will tell him that he's ... Full of Baloney ... and that he perhaps needs to steer the ship 180 degrees (or at least 32.67

A LAUGHING MATTER

[6]I was talking on the phone to another Big (BIG) Guy. I knew him somewhat well, but not intimately. We were chatting about a topic that is very dear to my heart: the need to orient business toward the woman consumer.

I said to this (BIG) guy at one point, "You are so full of shit. You just don't get it. You aren't even close to seriously dealing with this issue."

He could have hung up. Instead, he started laughing.

"Bless you," he said. "If only a few more people would tell me I'm full of shit. Don't get me wrong, I don't think I am. But sometimes I need to be *told* I'm full of shit."

NEW BUSINESS ! • NEW VALUE

degrees) away from where he is now navigating it?

If a few more people could speak a little more frankly, maybe more Necessary Miracles of Dramatic Change would occur.

But when the Group that meets with the Group ... to prepare the Group ... that meets with the Group to meet with the Big (REALLY) (BIG) Guy ... are all worried about nuances piled upon nuances topped by nuances ... and about the Code Words that Cannot Be Uttered in His Presence ... then there's not a snowball's chance in hell of getting Truly Big Things done. (Like changing the ... oops ... c-u-l-t-u-r-e.)

Same Old, Lame Old Story

I'm in despair. Utter despair.

New Economy ... Old Economy. "Services" ... "Solutions." The story, I fear, is always the same. S-A-M-E. "If we could just ['just'!] get folks to talk to one another ..."**7**

What to do?

My advice: Hit 'em over the head with 50 Brickbats.

Subtle I'm not ...

"GULF" CRISIS?
7From *Lifting the Fog of War*, by Admiral Bill Owens: "Once devised in Riyadh [in 1991], the tasking order took hours to get to the Navy's six aircraft carriers—because the Navy had failed years earlier to procure the proper communications gear that would have connected the Navy with its Air Force counterparts. ... To compensate for the lack of communications capability, the Navy was forced to fly a daily cargo mission from the Persian Gulf and Red Sea to Riyadh in order to pick up a computer printout of the air mission tasking order, then fly back to the carriers, run photocopy machines at full tilt, and distribute the document to the air wing squadrons that were planning the next strike."

the solutions50

What follows are 50 Immodest Ideas for trying to sort out what I call "Stovepipe Myopia" ... the unwillingness/inability of people in various parts of an organization to talk to people in other parts of that organization, and in other associated organizations. Here goes:

1. It's the (OUR!) organization, stupid!
Let's begin at the beginning. The "only" thing that lies between us ... and dramatic success is ... *organizational friction*. That is: "stovepipes." It ain't "them"! It ain't the "outside world." We've seen the enemy ... and it is us.

2. Friction-Free!
Back we go to "100 square feet." (See Chapter 3.) *All* the friction must be expunged from the system! *All* the bullshit has got to go! *All* the vice presidents have got to go! *Ninety-five percent* of the middle managers have got to go! Little slips of paper—one more time—can't sit on "power-freak" middle managers' desks. For a week. For an hour. For a second. For a fraction of a second.

3. NO STOVEPIPES!
Turf wars must end. (Boy, is that a helpful comment. It's as if I said, "Change human nature. Now.") (Still, this rant must seek the truth—even if the odds are of the snowball's not melting in Hell.) (Idea for TV series: Cross-functional non-communication as Dante's 10th Ring.)

4. "Stovepiping"/"Silo-ing" Is an A.F.O. (Automatic Firing Offense).
"Stovepipers" are to be tarred. Feathered. Lashed. Unceremoniously dumped overboard. ZERO [Silo-ing] TOLERANCE RULES. Make "it" clear in ... recruiting ... training ... rewarding ... promoting ... and F-I-R-I-N-G.

5. ALL on the Web!
(ALL = ALL) Recall: Hyperlinks do subvert hierarchy. See Chapter 4. These New Tools are powerful. It ain't automatic ... and that's an understatement; but it can/does help. But: ALL = ALL. "All" ... on ... the ... Web.

Yes, hyperlinks ... *do* ... subvert hierarchy.

6. Open access!
Everybody (ALL) must have access to everything. (ALL.)

Recall (sorry for the repeat) this scenario from *Red Herring*: "When Joe Employee at Company X launches his browser, he's taken to Company X's personalized home page. He can interact with the entire scope of Company X's world —customers, other employees, distributors, suppliers, manufacturers, consultants. ...The real trick is that

Joe Employee, business partners, and customers don't have to be in the office. They can log on from their own cell phone, Palm Pilot, pager, or home office system."

Issue: TO DO THIS ... WE MUST TRUST JOE!

7. Project Managers Rule!

Project managers running XF (cross-functional) projects control the ... *purse strings*. Project managers running XF projects control the ... *evaluations*. Project managers running cross-functional teams control ... *everything*.

Again: XF PROJECT MANAGERS RULE ... PERIOD.

8. VALUE ADDED THROUGH INTEGRATED APPLICATION OF RESOURCES RULES!

"Integrated Services" rule. "Experiences rule." (Re-read Chapter 6. Read Chapter 8.) (Act accordingly.) (Damn it!)

9. SOLUTIONS RULE!

"We sell SOLUTIONS." Period. "We sell CUSTOMER PRODUCTIVITY, PROFITABILITY, and SUCCESS." Period.

WHICH MEANS: WE HAVE TO ... TALK TO EACH OTHER ... TALK TO EVERYONE ... BUILD OFF EACH OTHER ... ALL OTHERS. PERIOD.

10. INTEGRATED SOLUTIONS = "Our 'Culture.'"

Solutions R Us. Period.

Hence: Solutions "CULTURE" R Us. Period. (P-E-R-I-O-D.)

11. Partner with B.I.C. (Best-In-Class).

Great partners push us toward ... Greatness. Help us get beyond ... Pettiness/Silo-ing. Great Partners ... Embarrass Us ... When We Are Stupid. Hence: Welcome B.I.C. into our fold. Anywhere. Everywhere. (Hooray.)

12. All Functions Contribute Equally.

IS. HR. Finance. Purchasing. Engineering. Logistics. Sales. Etc. Recall the Basic "PSF Idea." There are no more "support" functions. There are no "poor second cousins." There is no "other side of the railroad tracks." We're all ... ASTONISHINGLY TALENTED AND COMMITTED ... BLOOD KIN ... IN PURSUIT OF INTEGRATED "SOLUTIONS-DELIVERY" EXCELLENCE.

(Sure, the jargon makes my stomach flip, too. But the Big Idea is right, and we must ... Stand & Deliver. Collectively. Eh?) (COLLECTIVELY.)

13. Project Management Can/Will Come from Any Function.

Leadership will change over time ... depending on the situation. A GE exec reports that he used consultation concerning GE's fabled (rightly so) HR practices as the Big Foot-in-the-Door with international CEOs ... in the utility turbines business. Nice! (Sales folks were flabbergasted at HR's moxie—but gladly pocketed their commissions.)

14. WE ARE ALL IN SALES. PERIOD.

Selling "Integrated Solutions" means that we are ... ALL ... front, center, and customer-centric. (See also Chapter 18.)

NEW BUSINESS ! NEW VALUE

Again: No "second-string" players. *And* ... when a True Sales Mentality prevails ... then petty XF non-communication makes one feel truly foolish and petty. (Historic truth: Great salespeople, including Prime Ministers, sleep with the enemy if it abets getting the deal done.)

15. We ... ALL ... Invest in "Wiring" the Customer Organization.

"Integrated solutions" "selling" is a ... pure ... RELATIONSHIP GAME. No embarrassing second cousins redux! Everybody is into everybody else's turf; the magic of oh-so-rare (delivered) "synergy" is a ... Dense XF Network ... of Connections ... four levels down in every involved organization.

16. WE ALL "LIVE THE BRAND."

Brand = Integrated Solutions. (That's the Basic Proposition of this book!)

Brand = Solutions that ... MAKE MONEY FOR OUR CUSTOMER-PARTNER. (That's also the Basic Proposition of this book ... dialed up a notch.)

In the "solutions business" ... THE BRAND ... is ... our ability to bring All Enterprise & Supply & Demand Chain Resources Seamlessly to Bear ... on the ... Customer Opportunity ... Right Now.

17. We Use the Word "PARTNER" Until We Want to Barf!

Words Matter. "Partner" matters. A LOT. A "partnership attitude"[8] lies at the core of the Best PSFs (e.g., McKinsey & Co.). *We honor personal excellence ... but we equally honor those who ... Live the Spirit of Partnership ... with their Internal Colleagues ... and Clients.*

(Back to No. 4 above: And ... we ... FIRE ... CONTROL ALT DELETE ... those who don't "get it.")

18. We Also Use the Word "TEAM" Until We Want to Barf.

Sure, "Go team" is way overused. But it just happens to be right.

Message: DON'T BE AFRAID TO BE CORNY IN PURSUIT OF "TEAM SOLIDARITY IN PURSUIT OF DELIVERED SOLUTIONS EXCELLENCE."

HOWDY, PARTNER

[8]Many moons ago I taught at Stanford's business school. My mentor was deeply involved in the school's governance affairs. Though I was only a transient lecturer, he explained the true nature of the tenure process.

The technical specs were daunting, to say the least. To "pass," you had to be considered one of the three best in the world (!), relative to your specialty, among your age cohort.

Assuming (big assumption) you cleared that formidable hurdle, yet another equally important jump loomed. "We ask," he said, "'Will he be a good colleague?' Despite his towering skills, will he shoulder his share of the mundane chores of university governance? Put in his two years, near the peak of his career, in the Dean's Office? And so on."

Bottom line: The True Partnership Test is every bit as important as the Awesome Competence Test.

New mantra: Get along with a grin ... not a grimace ... to go forward.

19. Buttons & Badges Matter.

Or: Tupperware knows! Do you? "Team" Buttons and Badges & Awards & Certificates are important. (VERY.)

20. Reward Cooperation/Teaming/Partnering.

Yes, fire offenders. (We need exemplars of those who don't get it!) But ... *PROMOTE & REWARD LAVISHLY & PUBLICLY THOSE WHO DO "GET IT"—AT ALL LEVELS.*

"NEW CULTURE" MAVENS = CORDIAL COOPERATORS = OUR P-U-B-L-I-C "HEROES" = $$$ = !!!

21. WE NEVER BLAME ... Other Parts of Our Organization for Screw-ups. NEVER.

"Blaming" = F.O./Firing Offense.

("Firing Offense" ... I apparently toss the term off lightly. I don't at all. Again, this is ... the issue ... thence ... Extreme Sanctions ... are upon occasion merited.)

22. We Believe in "High Tech, High Touch."

No question, technology (Web, wireless, broadband, texting, etc.) is the Great Enabler. But, paradoxically, if the "Solutions Thing" rules ... then the "human bit" is more, not less, important than before.

Which, of course, affects ... ENORMOUSLY ... our "talent acquisition and development process."

Mantra: Invest Lavishly in High Tech. Voraciously Hire & Promote High Touch.

23. Women Rule.

Women are better ... Much Better ... at this "RELATIONSHIP STUFF" than men. One reason: They are far (far!) less ... Power Mad and Barrier Impaired.

The "Integrated Solutions" thing may turn out to be a "Women's Thing." (No small thing.) (A helluva Big Thing.)

(Also see & ingest Chapter 21.)

24. Our XF Team Needs 100 Percent Imaginative Contributors.

Professional sports bosses ... TRULY ... PUT "PEOPLE"/"TALENT" FIRST. ALL THE TIME. (Duh.) A lot of the "petty communications crap" recedes if we have an awesomely talented/motivated ... Winning Team.

For one (BIG) thing, when "winning" and "excellence" are 24/7 passions, there's far less time left for ... Turf Wars. And far less peer patience for Turf Warriors.[9]

THERE'S NO "WHY?" IN "TEAM"

[9]Been on a winning team? Part of a winning theatrical performance? Even the bit players are totally committed. You can smell their ... Search for Excellence. Sure, you want the critics to appreciate your moments in the sun. But you are also aware that to the degree that all shine and achieve excellence means that you will shine, too.

No hierarchy? Nirvana? Hardly! Championship teams only "love one another" after the Super Bowl is won. In the grueling process they push one another to the limits.

Big point: The abiding commitment to individual and group excellence may encompass many testy exchanges—but it also diminishes the tendency to invest in petty turf battles.

25. "XFTs" (Cross-Functional Teams) Are Us.

Simple. Simple. Simple. We do our work ... ALL OUR WORK ... via cross-functional project teams. Thus, *"XF" must be as routine as breathing*.

Moreover, everyone's performance is driven/determined by *XFE* ... Cross-Functional Excellence.

26. WOW Projects Rule!

The "WOW Project" ... the emotional grabber ... the Everest of Cool Challenges ... which brings to bear the resources of all departments ... and indeed the Entire Supply & Demand Chain ... is how we get ... ALL THE WORK DONE. (All = All.) (*Hint:* Please, please use the word "Wow." It matters. Also see Chapter 15.)

(Subtext: Boss Role One becomes turning ... EVERY ... project into a WOW project, respecifying the apparently mundane until it locks in the hearts and minds of would-be participants.) (Which means their Pursuit of Awesome Achievement waxes and their Tolerance of Petty XF baloney wanes.)

27. Open "Talent Market"

"Up" or "Out" is our name. Get with this WOW/"XFT"/Integrated Solutions notion ... or Get Out ... FAST. Like the symphony conductor or football coach, we seek only those who "come to play" at a fever pitch. (And why—again—shouldn't I keep comparing the IS or HR chief to a Big City Symphony Conductor or NFL Football Coach?)[10]

28. "Cause-based" Projects

Strategy guru Gary Hamel says that enterprise survivors in chaotic times will "create a cause, not a business." I imagine our "integrated solutions stuff" as ... Causes Worth Fighting For. I.e.: fight for the "cause," not "turf rights."

Boss job: Create-a-Cause!

(Hint I: All Great Leaders do this as a matter of course.)

(Hint II: No "cause" = No commitment = NO WOW = petty politics fill the void.)

29. FLAT

"This stuff" only works in a v-e-r-y f-l-a-t organization. Period. (PERIOD.) (Flat = Fast.) (Steep = Slow.) (PERIOD.) (Re-read Chapter 3 in its entirety.) (Remove frictioneers ... reduce friction.)

GOAL POST
[10]My goal is to drive you crazy. But if you finish this book and see ... Any Difference ... between a 48-person department-turned-PSF and a 48-person NFL roster ... I will have failed. Totally.

30. Proactively and Systematically and Perpetually Cut the Crap

We are our own worst enemies—via hopelessly complicated systems & procedures. We need ... TOTAL (*ORGANIZED!*) WAR ON OVERCOMPLICATION! (See also Chapter 11 on "Beautiful Systems.") WMDs are justified when over-complication is the enemy.

31. Get Physical!

Co-locating is *the* Unsung Marvel. People who live together ... and share camaraderie-in-pursuit-of-a-cool-cause together ... tend to get beyond Petty Turf Crap. *XFTs (cross-functional teams) ... MUST ... LIVE TOGETHER.*

Better Yet I: They must live together in their own space, away from the Tall Buildings rife with the Turf Kings and Turf Queens.

Better Yet II: They must live in fairly grubby environs that foster Our-Band-Taking-on-the-World-of-the-Fat-Cats. Forget Herman Miller tables. Bring on sheets of plywood on sawhorses!

32. FIRE "TURF KINGS"

It's not enough to oust Petty Silo-ing Politicians. We need ... desperately ... one or two ... PUBLIC HANGINGS[11] ... of VSTWs ...*Very* Senior Turf Warriors. (Oops ... have I said this twice? Good.)

33. H-U-G-E "COOPERATION BONUSES"

If you are King (Queen?!), how about a $1,000,000 bonus ... WITH FANFARE ... to the Top Performer of a Cooperative Strategic Act? I'm told that one Big CEO, tired of all the petty crap, did just that; at an Exec Committee meeting he surprised one and all by handing a Cooperating Baron an unexpected $1,000,000 check.

34. "Dip" Deep

Wanna send a ... BIG MESSAGE ... about ... COOPERATION? "Deep dip" (a military term) 3 or 4 levels ... and make a Bold (Very) Promotion to the (Very) Top Ranks. (OF SOMEBODY WHO "GETS IT.")

35. Musical Chairs

Don't let the (TURF) grass grow ... between toes. DO NOT ... allow people to become wedded to a job/function. Move them into their Arch Enemy's job. (And, of course, vice versa.)

(For years this was a staple of Digital Equipment's superior performance.)

36. It's a Kid's World

"Raw" "Youth," raised on Texting/Instant Messaging (etc.) are far less Turf Conscious than "we" are. (I.e., they literally don't understand it and they simply won't tolerate it.) SUPPORT YOUTH! (RETIRE ANCIENT "TURF KINGS"!)

FIRING LINE
[11]A colleague of mine tells of an aerospace CEO who got serious about "synergy." There was a division manager who ran the most profitable hunk of the enterprise. But this fellow wouldn't sing the "synergy song." He was fired. Publicly. Synergy grew. Immediately.

37. (Very) Early Project Management Experience

There's nothing like XFT (Cross-Functional Team) Project Management R-E-S-P-O-N-S-I-B-I-L-I-T-Y to nurture one's desire to Snuff Turf Tussles. Hence, put Raw Youth ... quickly ... in charge of "mini-XFT-projects" ... within Maxi-projects. Duh: To become XF-conscious, lead XF work. (IMMEDIATELY.) (ALWAYS.)

38. Take "Techies" on Sales calls (Or some such)

Help "functional bigots" understand others' roles ... any way you can.

If you are an MIT-trained techie, "sales" sounds like fluff. If you are confronted with two hours of rigorous "objections" to your fave project, you may respect the struggles of the "mere" salesperson a bit more.

39. Symbolic Stuff Redux (Because it's so damned important)

Symbols *do* matter! XFT badges ... MATTER. Team Photos ... MATTER. CEO "congrats" letters to XFTs ... MATTER. T-shirts matter. *Message from Human Nature 101*: SYMBOLS & AWARDS & CELEBRATIONS ... MATTER.

(Napoleon taught us Ribbon Power: "A man will not sell you his life for the largest fortune, but he will give it to you for a mere scrap of ribbon." Or words to that effect.)

40. Celebrate ... TROJAN HORSES

Stealth ain't all bad.

THE ENEMY: FUNCTIONAL PAROCHIALISM. But *you* ... are not quite ... THE KING OF KINGS. So you install an "innocent" "matrix" organization. The "function" ("staff") dimension still carries clout. But the (integrated) "project dimension" is important, too. Then the Stealth: Over time you ... "increase the weighting" of the "Project Dimension" in evaluations, promotions, etc. Thus: XFTs ... and all they stand for ... Quietly Achieve Pre-eminence.

41. PROMOTION RULES

Promote those at all levels who ... GET IT. Obvious? (Of course.) Honored in the breach? (Mostly.) *Bonus*: Make it Crystal Clear to One & All why "they" were promoted: XFTX. I.e., Cross-Functional Team Excellence.

42. Entry-level Training

The moment to "Teach the New Culture" (would-be XFTs!) is at ... THE INSTANT OF CREATION. Ensure that the "new hire" is ... CRYSTAL CLEAR ... about the Rewards & Penalties of appropriate cross-functional behavior.

43. Outside Hires

Diversity Rules! Diversity = NEW PERSPECTIVES. Shake Up Turf Barons: Bring in ... Weird New Blood. Bring in New Blood that has no investment in the ... Old Culture.

44. Involve the Full Supply & Demand Chain

Getting "Our House" in order is no small thing. (Understatement.) But the Real Bang for the Buck comes, à la Dell, when the Entire Supply & Demand Chain is Intimately Involved.

Message I: "Outsiders" = Insiders. (If "this stuff" is to work.)

NEW BUSINESS ● NEW VALUE

Message II: Thence ALL the above must be applied equally to said "outsiders." (If "this stuff" is to work.)

45. Pick Partners Based on Their "Cooperation Proclivity"

Concerning the so-called "supply chain": Make sure that Vendor Selection is based on much more than price; i.e., based on the vendor's ... Demonstrated Commitment ... to True Partnership.

46. Fire Vendors Who Don't "Get It"

Same as for insiders. Even otherwise "excellent" partners ... Must Go ... if they are not True Partners in providing I-n-t-e-g-r-a-t-e-d Solutions.

47. We Need ... JUDGES

I support the role of XFT Ombudsman. That is, the senior "honest broker" who weighs in on the degree to which Forbidden Turf Protection Covenants are violated. (Or not.) (Judges with a "00" license, eh?)

48. Free Passes to Whistle Blowers

This is ... *not*... "a" Big Deal. THIS ... XF COMMUNICATION ... IS *THE* BIG DEAL. So those who "rat out" Turf Kings ... are ... HEROES. Or HEROINES. (E.g., Sherron S. Watkins of Enron.)

49. Lock "It" in as Tenet No. 1 in the Vision Statement

Sure, there are a ton (literally) of "vision statements" not worth even the recycled paper they're printed on. But some do stick. This ... is ... The Vision. Inscribe the XFT/No Turf Warriors bit in ... New Hampshire Granite.

50. Shout from the rooftops

Jaw, jaw, jaw. Let no opportunity pass to declaim on the centrality of XF Cooperation. Repetition is Virtue One.

FIRE
TURF KINGS

That's All, Folks

Maybe you'll be able to implement one or two of these 50 ideas. Maybe you're the Big Boss. Maybe you'll implement most of them ... and maybe the whole damn thing will work for you.

Or maybe it won't. I'm not so arrogant as to believe that I've offered the ... Key to Changing Human Nature. This is one war that will never be "once and for all" won. What I do think is that by devoting ... A FULL CHAPTER ... to this topic in gory detail I've implied how central it is to all that precedes and all that follows.

I *am* right ... in that I've diagnosed the *problem* correctly.

In previous chapters, I have gone on ... *and on and on and on* ... about "on the bus" Web strategy and the Professional Service Firm "model" and "integrated solutions" ... and all the rest.

But none of that will work ... none of it will work worth a damn ... *UNLESS THE BARRIERS ARE SHATTERED.*

Question: Is that all there is?

Answer: Quite possibly

I had that little exchange (with myself ... uh-oh) after reading an article in *Fast Company* magazine about Roche, the pharmaceutical company. Roche, it was reported, is going to "Unleash an Organizational Revolution."

And the "revolutionary" "secret" ... that will Rock the World of Big Pharma?

Cross-functional teams! People in different functions will ... IMAGINE THIS ... start talking to each other![12]

Is it really that simple? (Is it really that hard?)

It *is* that simple. (It *is* that hard.)

So ... DO SOMETHING. (PLEASE.)

NOW BE SERIOUS
This list could be twice as long. But I'm sure by now you get the idea.
The list is not "right." But it is suggestive. It suggests the enormity of the situation that we face.
Think about it. Discuss it. Steal from it. Re-write it.
But ... ABOVE ALL ... PLEASE ... Take It Seriously.

(EMERGENCY) ROOM FOR IMPROVEMENT
[12]Dr. Ben Honigman, of the University of Colorado Hospital Emergency Room, as quoted in the *Denver Post*: "We've come up with a solution. ...We've begun to create a form of communication that is much better than we had before and that's allowed us to gather better data. We've finally realized that we must have an interplay with other hospitals and with pre-hospital caregivers."

NEW BUSINESS

NEW VALUE

! Contrasts

WAS	IS
"Silos" & "Stovepipes"	One Seamless Enterprise
Fight	Talk
Men lead	Women lead
Competition rewarded	Cooperation rewarded
Hire "competitive" types	Fire noncommunicative types
Everyone knows his/her place	All work is XF (cross-functional) work
Functional purity	Cross-functional unity
Boss as "visionary" who leaves "mere" details to his underlings	Boss as micro-manager of XF processes and incentive systems
Loyalty to the unit	Loyalty to the solution
Career = many tasks within one specialty	Career = a series of cross-over assignments

**The Age of Aesthetics has arrived!
Design rules!**

new bus!ness
new brand

I am convinced that the chain-of-analysis presented in the past
several chapters is constructed of strong links. Bottom line:
Surge up the value-added chain, in the direction of more and
more "intellectual capital" added.

To accomplish such a mission means bringing to bear the
entire resource set of the organization and, indeed, its entire
supply-demand-value chain; which means ... finally & inevitably
... addressing the absurdly difficult (but now patently requisite)
task of destroying/smashing/eliminating all barriers between
and within those pieces of the enterprise that deliver the
"integrated" "solutions" offering.

That said, there can be more still to the "look, feel, taste,
touch" of the "integrated" "solutions" we provide our
customers. That's as true for IBM Global Services as it is for
Starbucks. Hence, this section examines the often-neglected
"aesthetic" dimensions of this "systems"-"solutions"-
"presentation" process. We will pursue the heart of "cool,"
what converts an effective "solution" into one that, yes, chills
and thrills ... and adds enormous value.

BEYOND SOLUTIONS: PROVIDING MEMORABLE "EXPERIENCES"

! Technicolor Rules ...

- The "value added" for most any company, tiny or enormous, comes from the ... Quality of Experience provided.
- An "experience" is holistic, total, encompassing, transforming ... and emotional.
- A "service" is a transaction. An "experience" is an event. (A "happening" ... as that wonderful old hippie Ken Kesey would have had it.) An event-happening with a beginning ... a middle ... and an end. An experience-event-happening leaves an indelible memory.
- This "experience" thing is ... extremist. Not just a dab of "delight" here; not just a pinch of "amusement" there. But ... An Entirely Different Way of Parsing Life.

! RANT

We are not prepared ...

We (still) applaud the ideal of the "satisfied customer." (Little was more important in 1982, when *In Search of Excellence* was written.) Instead, we must focus on creating a scintillating ... encompassing ... dramatic ... novel ... "customer experience."

We continue to talk about "service" and "quality" as the key attributes of Value Added. Instead, we must understand that "experience" is not only a Very Big Word ... with gigantic connotations ... but it is nothing short of the basis for a ... Totally Revised Organizational Life Form. (Truly.)

If we use terms such as "experience," we limit them to the likes of Starbucks or Disney. Instead we must apply them to the IBMs and GE Power Systems, as well as to departmental (PSF!) activities and WOW Projects.

! VISION

I imagine ...

The *Theater* of IBM Global Services. (Or the *Theater* of Starbucks.) The computer is fine. (The coffee is great.) But it's the *Theater* part that I'm really buying ... the *Character* of the *Relationship*. The *Promise* of *Transformation*. IBM provides ... New Org World. (Starbucks provides ... New-Me-for-the-Morning.)

NEW BUSINESS ! NEW BRAND

The Language of ... Experience

The "integrated solutions" idea, painstakingly developed in the last three chapters, takes us only so far, at least as I presented it. It came across (by design, at that stage of my argument) as a rather severe, intellectual concoction.

Yet Moving Up the Value Chain has always meant ... even if circuit breakers are under consideration ... Something More. It has meant emphasizing the ... Soft Attributes (the INTANGIBLES) ... of "Products" or "Services." Attributes such as Convenience, Comfort, Warmth, Companionship, Beauty, Trust, and ... Being Seriously Cool.

There is a Word that sums up what customers get from "all of these" attributes. That not-so-innocent word: *Experience*.

Thus the "integrated solution" from Farmers Group or Springs or GE Power Systems is ... a Full-fledged Experience. Increasingly, the "value added" a company offers ... the "stuff" that can add Billions of Dollars to its market cap ... comes from the ... Quality of the Experience.[1]

The Main Event

One could easily write this entire chapter off as being based on a mere "semantic twist"—the use of "experience" instead of "service." Any service offering *is* an "experience." I wouldn't deny that for a second.

But words are funny things.

They can change everything.

When I think of a "service transaction," my mind is not in the same place as when I think of a trip to Disneyland or Walt Disney World or Circus Circus on the strip in Las Vegas or Super Bowl Week or the legendary Bass Outdoor World store in Springfield, Missouri. A whole different "thing" is conjured up when a Disney ... *experience* ... is under consideration.

I think that difference is critical. And I think it plays directly into the hands of these unique value-adding "things" (experiences?) that I discussed in the last three chapters.

For me, at least, an "experience" is far more "holistic," "total," "encompassing," "emotional," and "transforming" than a mere "service." A service is a transaction. (Good or bad.) An experience is an *Event* ... an Adventure ... a Happening ... a Soul-Jogging,

---

BANK ON IT

[1] Take the example of financial services. If the price of a loan were the only issue, I'd simply go to the cheapest source. But as a small businessman, I care most about the depth, and stability of the "relationship" with my financial services provider. Will she call my loan the minute I hiccup? Or will she get to know me and become my ... "trusted partner"?

Believe me, if my banker is my "trusted partner," then she's welcome to a whole basket of "points"!

THE ULTIMATE FRILL

Southwest Airlines is a "discounter." Yet its success is at the least as much due to the ... Company Character ... as it is to the low fares.

The message: "We're safe." (The best.) "We get there on time." (Usually the best.) "Join us! Come to Camp Southwest! No 'frills.' But darn nice people." (The Ultimate Frill.)

Spirit-Lifting "phenomenon." With a beginning ... a middle ... and an end. An experience leaves an Indelible Memory, adds to my History, provides fodder for a thousand future. Conversations with Old Pals and Grandkids.

Thus we have two discrete conceptions—as different as day and night—of what a company's "offering" does.

Conception I: It pays for itself (Service).

Conception II: It makes the world wobble on its axis a bit (Experience).

As far as I know, Joe Pine and Jim Gilmore are the inventors of this idea, at least in the modern business context. Their book, *The Experience Economy: Work Is Theatre and Every Business a Stage*, is simply brilliant. Their basic hypothesis is easy to state: *"Experiences,"* they write, *"are as distinct from services as services are from goods."*

What's in a Word

Consider ...

1. From *The Random House Dictionary of the English Language*:

experience (ik sper'e ens), n.v., -enced, -encing.

—n.1. a particular instance of personally encountering or undergoing something: *My encounter with the bear in the woods was a frightening experience.* 2. the process or fact of personally observing, encountering, or undergoing something: *business experience.* 3. the observing, encountering, or undergoing of things generally as they occur in the course of time: *to learn from experience; the range of human experience.* 4. knowledge or practical wisdom gained from what one has observed, encountered, or undergone: *a man of experience.* 5. *Philos.* the totality of the cognitions given by perception; all that is perceived, understood, and remembered. —v.t. 6. to have experience of; meet with; undergo; feel: *to experience nausea.* 7. to learn by experience. 8. *experience religion*, to undergo a spiritual conversion by which one gains or regains faith in God. [1350-1400; ME < L *experientia*, equiv. to *experient-* (s. of *experiens*, ptp. of *expiriri* to try, test; see EX-, PERIL) + *-ia* n.suffix; see -ENCE] —*ex pe'ri ence a ble*, adj. —*ex pe'ri ence less*, adj.

—Syn. 6. encounter, know, endure, suffer. EXPERIENCE, UNDERGO refer to encountering situations, conditions, etc., in life, or to having certain sensations or feelings. EXPERIENCE implies being affected by what one meets with: *to experience a change of heart, bitter disappointment.* UNDERGO usually refers to the bearing or enduring of something hard, difficult, disagreeable, or dangerous: *to undergo severe hardships, an operation.*

EXPERIENCE THIS!
I hope, by the way, that this book serves a purpose—that it provides a useful "service." A smidgen of enlightenment or edification about this or that.

But more to the point: I harbor a fond dream that this book's energetic style of verbal presentation will do nothing less than alter your view of the way organizations might work and the benefits they might deliver—that it will be a memorable, maybe transforming "experience."

NEW BUSINESS ! ● NEW BRAND

2. *The Synonym Finder*, by J.I. Rodale:

experience, *n.* 1. affair, episode, ordeal, event, incident, occurrence, happening; encounter, transaction, adventure, *Sl.* trip; circumstance, case. 2. involvement, encountering, meeting, facing; exposure, observing, observation, perceiving, perception, impression; trials, vicissitudes, ups and downs. 3. life, existence, background, lifework; *U.S. Inf.* school of hard knocks. 4. wisdom, common sense; sophistication, enlightenment, knowledge, learning, cognizance, ken; know-how, savoir-faire. —*v.* 5. encounter, meet, face; observe, perceive, apprehend; taste, sample, test, try; sense, feel; undergo, go through, get [s.t.] under one's belt; live through, endure, suffer through. 6. understand, learn about, become knowledgeable about, become familiar with, find out about; realize, discover, become enlightened, appreciate; know, cognize, *Chiefly Scot.* ken; assimilate, absorb, take in.

experienced, *adj.* 1. accomplished, practiced, skillful, polished, proficient, adept, good [at], *Fr. au fait*; knowledgeable, versed, prepared, qualified, well-grounded, trained, primed, ready; competent, fit, fitted, capable, able, efficient, *Sl.* on the ball; veteran, professional, *Inf.* knowing the ropes, *Sl.* savvy; expert, master, masterful, masterly. 2. mature, ripened, seasoned, salted; weathered, hardened, toughened, battle-scarred, *Inf.* through the mill, *Inf.* through the wringer; sophisticated, knowing, *Sl.* in the know, worldly, wordly-wise, *Sl.* wise, *Inf.* been around, initiated. 3. undergone, lived through, gone through, endured, suffered through; contacted, met, faced, observed, perceived; tasted, sampled, tested, tried; sensed, felt.

Keep considering ... these words and phrases from the above entries:

episode happening encounter adventure perception life existence taste sense live through undergo affected by what one meets with spiritual conversion

How often do we use such words and phrases in business?

My answer: *seldom, rarely, never.* And yet, as *the* Value-Added Proposition of Business becomes more and more ... intangible ... such words become more and more ... relevant and practical and valuable.

Rebel Yell

A lot of people work for Harley-Davidson. The good news ... none of them are so silly as to believe that they "make *motorcycles*."

If not "motorcycles," what?

How about "experiences"?

A Harley Big Cheese summed it up this way: *"What we sell is the ability for a 43-year-old accountant to dress in black leather, ride through small towns, and have people be afraid of him."*

Say again?

It's the *experience*, stupid!

In particular, the experience that Harley calls the "Rebel Lifestyle."

A few years ago I ran into former Harley CEO Rich Teerlink, as we raced in opposite directions through the Atlanta airport. In the course of a couple of minutes of chatter, I asked him where he was coming from and/or going to. He replied he was just returning from a several-day training activity at ... Disney University. That's the place where Disney teaches us civilians how to ... Sprinkle Pixie Dust on our Clientele. And Sprinkling Pixie Dust is precisely what Harley does to its Bikes and Bikers ... and what makes the firm ... So Damn Special.

(And don't you find it intriguing that the CEO of a Big *Mfg.* Co. was enrolled as "ordinary student" in a "mere" training program run by an *entertainment* company?)

Harley-Davidson: an "experience," not a "product." So call it a semantic quibble. (If you must.) Yes, call it a semantic quibble. (If you dare.) But Teerlink's eventual success in changing Harley's "persona" added Billions upon Billions of $$$ to his company's stock-market capitalization.

Some quibble!² [2]

"Something More"

More and more companies are following in Harley's tracks.

"Club Med is more than just a resort," writes marketing guru Jean-Marie Dru in his book *Disruption.* *"It's a means of rediscovering oneself, or inventing an entirely new 'me.'"*

Semantic frou-frou redux? Well, again, to the extent that Club Med succeeds in implanting this image (and arguably they've been quite successful), they are able to attract an entirely different clientele to whom they can charge an entirely different price point—leading to an exceptional record of growth and profitability.

"We have identified a 'third place,'" Starbucks district manager Nancy Orsolini told us in a TV interview. *"And I really believe that sets us apart. The third place is that place that's not work or home. It's the place our customers come for refuge."*

I don't know how the hell they do it! (Read founder Howard Schultz's book, *Pour Your Heart into It: How Starbucks Built a Company One Cup at a Time,* to find out the secrets.) But the point is ... they *do* do it. And they have transformed an "innocent cup of java" into a "Starbucks way of life" that, wittingly or not, many of us subscribe to ... whether it's a couple of minutes' break in an airport, or an hour-and-a-half reading the newspaper or editing a chapter of this book at a Starbucks in whatever town I happen to have landed in.

"Guinness as a brand is all about community," comments Ralph Ardill. *"It's about bringing people together and sharing stories."*

NEW BUSINESS ! ● NEW BRAND

Ralph is one of the top bosses at Imagination, a pioneering British design and marketing-services and experiences-creating company. His firm recently finished an eye-popping assignment for Guinness. Called the Guinness Storehouse, it captures, as a sort of home port, the Soul of Guinness.[3]

Think about it. Harley-Davidson does *not* sell motorcycles. Starbucks does *not* sell coffee. Club Med does *not* sell vacations. And Guinness does *not* sell beer.

Have you ever *ridden* on a Harley, *been* to Club Med, *stopped* at a Starbucks, *imbibed* a Guinness? I believe that there is something "more" going on here. And I believe that the "something more" is ... the Fundamental Basis for its Value Added.

What "Experience" Does for "Brown"

I'm rounding on myself here. From "pity the poor brown" to ... wildly turned on by brown and the application of this experience idea by one particular company. That sells neither beer nor coffee. (Stuff.) But business services. (Ephemera.) It's expressed in a new series of advertisements. And expressed in a new company logo. Namely: *WHAT CAN BROWN DO FOR YOU?*

Brown ... of course ... is UPS. How great! Brown is the most dreary of colors. (See above, Churchill on "pity the poor brown.") Almost the anti-color color. And yet those "plain brown trucks" have come to mean an awful lot in our lives.

But now UPS, first mentioned in Chapter 6, is working overtime to get way beyond the "brown trucks" driven by "guys in brown shorts" image. UPS is "repositioning" itself. (Big Time.) It aims to become a Full Scale Partner in Logistics and Supply Chain Excellence.

There is a ... *phenomenon* ... UPS wants to sell you. And what a lovely way to describe it: *BROWN*. It is a phenomenon that has to do with Taking Full Care of a Huge Part of Your Business Life in a Way that Will Allow You to Shed Your Logistics Burdens and simultaneously Add Incredible Value for Your Beloved Customer.

Don't ask me. Call 1-800 PICK-UPS ... and find out precisely what ... BROWN CAN DO FOR YOU!

GET A "LIFE"

[3] Okay, okay. You're skeptical. ("Those Guinness bastards sell beer by the pint, for heaven's sake!") That skepticism is totally appropriate.

Because most companies trying to pull this "experience thing" off will fail miserably. They won't get it. They'll add a touch here. A touch there.

But in the case of Harley-Davidson and Club Med and Starbucks and Guinness, the "experience"—the "way of life"—is the enterprise.

This "experience" thing is ... extremist. Not a dab of "delight" here. Nor a pinch of "amusement" there. But ... An Entirely Different Way of Life.

Harley-Davidson Life.

Starbucks Life.

Club Med Life.

Guinness Life.

I cotton to the UPS saga for another reason. The previous examples come from the world of consumer goods—Harley, Club Med, Starbucks, Guinness. But UPS is in the business of selling ... *professional services*. WHAT CAN BROWN DO FOR YOU?[4] is aimed directly at the business customer.

Plot Power

Freeman Thomas co-designed the new VW Beetle and designed the Audi TT. Now he does his thing for Chrysler. Here he is, speaking of the Plymouth Prowler: "Car designers need to create a story. Every car provides an opportunity to create an adventure. ... The Prowler makes you smile. Why? Because it's focused. It has a plot, a reason for being, a passion."

I'm not much of a car guy, and I'm not particularly interested in the ins and outs of that Prowler. I am interested in ... once again ... words.

Consider these words from Mr. Thomas:

story adventure smile focus plot reason for being passion

I love *all* those words.

Score Tactics: The Plot, Thickened

Soon after reading the Freeman Thomas quote above, I had an opportunity to test the power of this plot. I was working with a mid-size retail enterprise that aimed to dramatically improve its catalog business. The products offered were fine and dandy. The company has an excellent and widely respected history. But it seemed as though "tactical marketing initiative" after "tactical marketing initiative" was falling flat.

I suggested that the executive group look at their catalog ... and think about the "experience"/"plot" it conjured up. I stuck my neck out and provided a personal assessment of a bunch of catalogs that I'd randomly grabbed on the way out the door while heading to the seminar. In fact, I audaciously graded them on a scale of **1 to 10** on "plot." Scoring key: One is ... dreary and pointless; 10 is a plot that ... sizzles!

Williams-Sonoma. **5.** Used to be a clear 10. Williams-Sonoma reinvented the American kitchen—along with Julia Child, and prior to Martha Stewart. The products

---

COLOR ME PROFITABLE

[4]Colors are funny things. Powerful, too.

Coca-Cola "owns" RED. Probably true. And Kodak "owns" (or, alas, "owned") YELLOW.

Likewise, with its new marketing campaign, UPS aims to cement its ownership of ... BROWN.

The same kind of "color theory" is being applied at Home Depot, where boss Bob Nardelli aims to make "The ORANGE Box" synonymous with solutions to all home-care problems.

Then there's BP, which is trying to alter the entire perception of its industry (and itself) by "owning" ... Green.

Hmmm.

Color may just be the ultimate ... experience.

Williams-Sonoma provides today are excellent. (Quality.) But for me the "plot" has lost its edge. "La difference" is missing. I.e.: What's the Point? What's the Plot?

Crate and Barrel. **8.** Crate and Barrel, at least until its recent Marimekko incarnation, wasn't very colorful, which leaves me cool/cold. On the other hand, Crate and Barrel clearly has a ... Distinct Point of View. A plot. They do a damn good job with that "plot," in my opinion.

Smith & Hawken. **8+.** Maybe it's not your bag of mulch. No matter. The product, once again, is fine and dandy. *The story* is *great.* Smith & Hawken sells a certain "lifestyle" "thing."

Sharper Image. **9.** Sometimes I like their stuff. But sometimes I hate their stuff. But I know what the hell the story is going to be—and I can't wait to view the next episode. (That is, the next catalog.)

L.L.Bean. **3.** L.L.Bean probably deserves a higher score. My negativism is partially a nostalgia trip gone sour. Fact: I well remember L.L.Bean when they had one hell of a "plot"! I remember those days, years and years ago, when I simply couldn't wait to get my hands on my Dad's L.L.Bean catalog—even if I was in no position financially to order a damn thing. It was a wild, scintillating, Starbucks-level story and approach to life. The products, no doubt, are still extremely good, still well made. (I have a few. They are.) But the story has lost its edge.

When my clients and I got beyond dry analytics, and started talking "story," "plot," "experience" ... the nature of our discussion changed dramatically from what it had been before. Discussing "brand power" and "strategic coherence" did little or nothing for them. Talking "plot"[5] at Williams-Sonoma almost led to a shouting match in which points of view were offered at machine-gun pace.

ESPRIT DE "CORE"

"Speaking of the limits of traditional marketing, consider this, from *BusinessWorld* of India:

"HAVE MBAs KILLED OFF MARKETING? Prof Rajeev Batra says: 'What these times call for is more creative and breakthrough reengineering of product and service benefits, but we don't train people to act like that.' The way marketing is taught across business schools is far too analytical and data-driven. 'We've taken away the emphasis on creativity and big ideas that characterize real marketing breakthroughs.' In India there is an added problem: most senior marketing jobs have been traditionally dominated by MBAs. Santosh Desai, vice president, McCann Erickson, an MBA himself, believes in India engineer-MBAs, armed with this Lego-like approach, tend to reduce marketing into neat components. 'This reductionist thinking runs counter to the idea that great brands must have a core, unifying idea.'"

THE EXPERIENCE OF ... LANGUAGE

[5]For participants in that seminar, thinking in terms of "plot" was an invaluable exercise ... or should I say "an invaluable *experience*"?

Because language is an experience, too. Words per se ... words like "story," "plot," and, yes, "experience" ... make all the difference. They change the way we respond to a product, a service—or a catalog marketing seminar.

Car Art

Bob Lutz is single-handedly, it seems, changing the look, feel, taste, touch, smell, and (yes) plot of the formerly sluggish industrial giant ... GM. And I think he's doing so precisely along the dimensions described in this chapter.

"I see us as being in the art business," Lutz said at one point. *"Art, entertainment and mobile sculpture, which, coincidentally, also happens to provide transportation."*

This is where the rubber meets the road, literally and figuratively.

Again: You can write off the Lutz statement as so much smoke and marketing mirrors. Or you can say, as I believe, that it's the heart of the apparent re-imagining of General Motors. A focus on the experience. (Not just the low finance charges.) An understanding that one is in the "art, entertainment and mobile sculpture business"—which also provides that basic transportation.

Other car companies, of course, are getting "it"—following two decades of "quality-is-all," foisted and forced on us by the Japanese. We're starting to remember that our car is ... who we are, a keystone of our identity. Sidney Harman is the founder of Harman International, the provider of ultra high-end sound systems. The automobile industry in general, and Lexus in particular, is central to his exceptionally effective strategy. Harman went so far as to say recently, "Lexus sells its cars as containers for our sound system. It's marvelous."

Sounds a bit self-serving. (It is.)

Sounds a bit outrageous. (It is.)

But I'm not sure he's all wet. (He's not.)

Hundreds of billions of dollars are at stake in what is still an enormous industry, and the shift back to "cool cars"[6] (terrific experiences!) is very noticeable.

NEW BUSINESS ! NEW BRAND

AND WHILE WE'RE AT IT, HERE'S AN ENGINE

[6]Sidney Harman and Bob Lutz are defining the front edge of something phenomenal—the biggest auto-industry transformation in decades.

Consider this sizzling headline for a November 2002 *Newsweek* article: "Living Room, To Go: Cars of the future will be sanctuaries, with mood lighting, aromatherapy and massage seats. For long drives: movies and popcorn."

Now, *that's* an experience!

PLOT IT YOURSELF

Pause, just for a second, and think about this "plot" idea ... relative to the training services (experiences!) that you offer, or the accounting services (experiences!) that you offer, or the engineering services (experiences!) that you offer.

Think about your training and accounting and engineering in terms of: *Story. Adventure. Smile. Focus. Plot. Reason for Being. Passion.* See if thinking that way doesn't change the Essential Nature of your own, um, experience.

Have Your Cake—And Experience It, Too

Our tour guides Joe Pine and Jim Gilmore summarize their argument in terms of a value-added "experience ladder." "*Raw materials*" are at the base. Next up ... "*goods*." Then "*services*." Then ... scraping the sky ... "*experiences*."

Let's examine this ever-so-potent notion in a somewhat humble fashion. My friend Tim Sanders is a senior executive at Yahoo! The irrepressible Mr. Sanders (an experience himself) is responsible for the "experience" part of the business. (Which is most of what Yahoo! is about.) Tim loves to describe "all this" in terms of the humble birthday cake.

Think of Cakes Through Four Generations:

1940. The raw-materials economy. Grandma spends about a buck to buy flour, sugar, and other "raw materials." (Okay, flour and sugar are both industrial processed goods—but you know what I mean.) Using those "raw materials," Grandma produces a birthday cake. *($1.)*

1955. The goods economy. Ma goes down to the local supermarket, spends a couple of bucks, and makes the cake from a packaged industrial good ... Betty Crocker cake mix. *($2.)*

1970. The service economy. Bakeries are available to ordinary folks, not just the rich and super-rich. So Mom heads to the bakery at birthday time and shells out $10 for a professionally baked cake. *($10.)*

1990. The experience economy. Dad is in charge of the kid's birthday now. And the kid lays down the law: "I'm having a party, Dad. It's going to be at Chuck E. Cheese, and I'm bringing my pals." Dad obliges, and forks over a C-note ... for the "experience." *($100.)*

A silly example, perhaps. But is it so different from Starbucks? (Or IBM Global Services?) The most interesting part of this example—and you can replay it chapter and verse for Starbucks or Harley-Davidson or IBM—is that the Big Leap takes place when the "experience dimension" enters the mix. In the case of the cake: $1.00 to $2.00, $2.00 to $10.00, $10.00 to $100.00. The Chuck E. Cheese "experience bit" added the last $90!

No Limits I: It's Geek to Me

Joe Pine tells a wonderful story about a next-door neighbor of his in Minneapolis. Robert Stephens owns a small business that installs computer-telecommunications systems. So-called "local area networks," or LANs. The company name was to the point: LAN Installation Company.

Fine. Accurate.

MEASURING UP

Like many others, I believe that "what gets measured gets done." Thus, we need new metrics for a new era.

The Raw Materials Economy: Raw Quantity ... a Practical Measure.

The Goods Economy: Six Sigma ... an Excellent Measure!

The Services Economy: Customer Satisfaction ... a Brilliant Measure!

The Experiences Economy: Customer Success ... the Ultimate Measure!

"Customer success" in "transforming your image" ... following a visit to Club Med. "Customer success" in "organizational transformation" ... following the use of professional help from IBM Global Services.

And so on. And on.

But over the back fence, Joe and his techie neighbor got to talking about the "experience thing." (Quite a push for a "techie.") To make a long story short, LAN Installation Company morphed ... hold onto your hat ... into *The Geek Squad.* That is, the talented techies, who had done good work, now emphasized the fun, energy, excellence, reliability ... *the experience provided* ... behind what they do. To keep on with making this relatively long story very short, their business quickly grew from 2 percent of Minnesota's LAN installations to 30 percent.

Lots of things happened in the process, beyond the scope of this chapter—which is just meant to introduce the "experience" notion and titillate a bit. That is, employees are far more turned on by being a member of the "Geek Squad" than "LAN Installation Company." It's not that they weren't technically competent before—they were and still are. But it is about that self-image, of being ... *flying, roving, awesomely competent problem solvers relative to a set of technology issues.*

No Limits II: (Don't) Leave It to Beaver

I was thinking about "all this" when I happened upon a *Wall Street Journal* article in mid-2002. It turns out that New England has seen an extraordinary share of its previously open grazing land returned to forests. One implication: an explosion of wildlife, which sometimes mixes very uncomfortably with nearby human neighbors.

Beavers, in particular, have become a problem. If you've ever had a farm pond (I have three), you know that, in short order, a beaver can destroy any damn tree-like thing it needs, and then plug up the pond, causing the worst sort of flooding.

People who "deal with beavers" have historically been called "trappers." And there are, indeed, trappers alive and well in New England. In recent times, trappers have netted $20 per trapped beaver's pelt. Transforming "beaver" to "pelt" is the trapper's life. (Call it the "raw materials" economy?)

But along comes a "problem." Too many relatively well-off people living next to too much wildlife. So the wise trapper decides he's no longer a "trapper." Now he becomes a ... *"Wildlife Damage-Control Professional."* (The "experience economy" rules! All!) (Geek Squad to the rescue!) And ... a W.D.C.P. (Wildlife Damage-Control Professional) can charge $150 ... not a mere $20 ... for the "removal of a problem beaver." (Like Carrier selling "Coolth," not "boxes.") ("Removed" beavers, not "dead" beavers. Perhaps.)

SHE'S THE BOSS (OR SHOULD BE)
Just an idea ...

Old Economy = Basic Goods & Services. Dominated by men. By male thinking and male ideas.

New Economy = Solutions & Experiences. Dominated by women. By female thinking and female ideas.

In *EVEolution*, Faith Popcorn and Lys Marigold comment, "Women don't buy brands. They join them."

In other words, the "experience" idea is one that women take to naturally. Men ... not necessarily so.

Thus, promoting more women to leadership positions makes sense. We are, quite possibly, entering into a ... Women's Economy.

Again, just an idea. We'll come back to it. (See Chapters 13 and 21.)

Some *nouveau* residents, however, love their beavers, and wish to keep them around. But they don't want that noxious flooding. Our wily W.D.C.P. (now full-scale member of the PSF/"professional service" fraternity!) charges a full $750 to $1000 for providing flood control piping ... so that the beavers can stay ... and the floods will go away.

Love that.

Welcome to the "experience economy."

Welcome to the "solutions economy."

Welcome to the world of "professional services."

Instead of a Redneck Totin' a Gun who makes 20 bucks a pelt ... we now have a Wildlife Damage Control Professional Services and Solutions Provider who bills out at $1,000 to deliver an "experience."

(Ah, life.)

Let's Get Metaphysical!

Getting started in the "experience business" is (mostly) about frame of mind. The requisite transformation is not easy. "Most managers," writes Danish marketing expert Jesper Kunde, in *Unique Now ... or Never*, "have no idea how to add value in the metaphysical world. But that is what the market will cry out for in the future. There is no lack of [physical] products to choose between."

Kunde's exemplars include Nokia, Nike, LEGO, and Virgin ... all Masters of Experience ... all makers and marketers of physical products that have a metaphysical presence. But how many leaders are taking those examples—and examples of the sort that I provided above—seriously? "Seriously" to the point of fundamentally altering enterprise strategy? How many of the Big Guys (and it's no coincidence that most of them are guys and not gals) are comfortable dealing with Kunde's "metaphysical world"?[7]

{
BIG BLUE MARVEL
[7]One notable exception (call him a Master Metaphysician) was Lou Gerstner at IBM. As I noted in Chapter 6, a great deal of the stunning success IBM has had in its Global Services Division is traceable to Gerstner's former life as a McKinsey & Co. consultant.

At McKinsey, Lou learned the meaning of "professional services" ... and the value of the "professional services experience." The firm's legendary leader, Marvin Bower, was the original PSF Master Metaphysician—and a man who was very aware of the "plot" he painstakingly labored to create.

A REALLY (BIG!) SHOW
In Las Vegas in 2003, I had a free night. I pulled some strings, and went to my first Cirque du Soleil performance.

WOW!

I'll never be the same!

Now I *own* the Gold Standard for Experiences. More than that, I had a practical business *epiphany*. (Not a favorite word of mine, but sometimes it's called for.) I just don't see ... why (say) a business process redesign project shouldn't be held to the Cirque du Soleil Standard.

You, dear reader, are a proud professional, right? So why should your standard for projects—for *experiences*—be less than that of the leaders and cast members of Cirque du Soleil?

Feet, Don't Fail Me Now ...

I got through a Big Retailer's day-long strategy session. I heard a lot of "thrash the competition," "go for the gold." I was impressed by a striking array of merchandising initiatives (almost one per aisle) that would "bring in the quarter." My head reeled from the jargon bath of new programs for this and that and more.

But my foot kept wiggling. Something—what?—felt oddly off. Well, maybe it was just the Thai dinner I'd had the night before.

My day done, I moved on to another city, and then proceeded home. But, at least metaphorically, I couldn't still the wiggling in my foot.

I'd exaggerate if I said it came to me in a flash, but it more or less did. Our retail pals had sliced and diced and talked about everything but "it." It? The whole shebang, the adventure, the story, the plot, the "holistic" experience.

What the hell is it like, from parking lot to checkout, to "imbibe" of a given store? What's the Niketown or Starbucks or Disney equivalent? Where's the pixie dust?

The CEO, trust me, is not a metaphysical sort of guy. But I wrote him an impassioned letter. Call it The Tale of the Wiggling Foot that Would Not Be Stilled.

Who knows, but I think I was on to something. Big. Even enormous.

Are You ... Experienced?

Re-read the last few chapters. They amount to a steady, logical accumulation of ideas. Re-read this chapter in particular. Look at the examples. Think of other examples. Play with this word ... *experience*.

Then what? Should you hire a theater director to join your accounting department? Or your product-development department? Or your marketing department?

Perhaps.

Think experience. *Talk* experience. *Look* at examples of experience. *Analyze* those examples. Then get on with it, and remember:

1. This is not a semantic quibble. It is ... the Essence of Life in the New Economy.

2. Billion$ upon Billion$ upon Billion$ (and then some more Billion$) are at stake for giant companies. And, relatively speaking, the same high stakes apply to the individual accountant ... or to the beaver trapper turned Wildlife Damage Control Professional.

UP CLOSE AND PERSONAL

Experiences. I have seldom, if ever, been so affected by a single word.

I now view ... positively everything ... through a new lens. "What is this experience like?" That's ... so, so ... very, very ... different from "Were you satisfied with the 'service'?"

I lament what may be my inability to transmit my enthusiasm for this idea to you. I dearly want to inflame you about "all this" as much as I have become inflamed. I want you never to view any transaction through any lens other than ... Experience Magnification.

3. THIS IS A BIG DEAL.

! Contrasts

WAS	IS
"Product" or "Service" –	"Experience"
It's good stuff –	It's a kick, a hoot
It works –	It leaves an indelible memory
"I'm glad I bought it" –	"I want more!"
Satisfied customer –	Member of a club
Repeat customer –	Word-of-mouth viral-marketing agent
You get what you pay for –	You're surprised and delighted at every turn
Agrees with your wallet –	Agrees with your psyche
Deals with one of your needs –	Helps define Who You Are

9 EXPERIENCESPLUS: EMBRACING THE "DREAM BUSINESS"

! Technicolor Rules ...

● "A dream is a complete moment in the life of a client. Important experiences that tempt the clients to commit substantial resources. The essence of the desires of the consumer. The opportunity to help clients become what they want to be."

● We shape our words. Thereafter, they shape us.

● GET INTO THE "DREAM BUSINESS" ... THE "INCREDIBLE IMAGININGS" BUSINESS.

! RANT

We are not prepared ...

We are still mired in Old Economy, Old Product Thinking. But we must—all of us!—take pages from the likes of Virgin Group—and come to grips, "strategically," with the fact that Winners will be ... *Masters of the Dream Business.*

! VISION

I imagine ...

Totally "Insane" Schools ... Hospitals ... War-Fighting approaches ... Enterprises. Permutations and combinations providing something so, so far beyond services ("Impossible-Turned-Possible Dreams").

He's Just Dreamy

I love the "experience" idea. (I tried to convey some dimensions of my flagrant love affair in the last chapter.) That idea is a big stretch for many, compared with our normal "business" way of looking at products and services. And yet perhaps we can stretch our minds even further. Much further?

The stakes are high ... billions upon billions of dollars. (Again.)

So ... next vocabulary s-t-r-e-t-c-h: *dreams*.

Now, that word/idea far exceeds this old civil engineer's comfort zone—which was already reeling from our visit to the ethereal-but-hard-dollar realm of "experiences."

The power of the "dream" was revealed to me when I was fortunate enough to sit in on a presentation in Mexico City by former Ferrari North America CEO Gian Luigi Longinotti-Buitoni. Dreams are his shtick.

Dream products.

Dream fulfillment.

Dream marketing.

Dream provision.

Consider ... very carefully ... the following statement by Mr. Longinotti-Buitoni: "A dream is a complete moment in the life of a client. Important experiences that tempt the client to commit substantial resources. The essence of the desires of the consumer. The opportunity to help clients become what they want to be."

What marvelous words![1] "Complete moment." "Tempt." "Commit." "Essence." "Desires." And, summing it all up: "the opportunity to help clients become *what they want to be*."

I'm not sure I fully understand all of those words. But I think I "sort of" "get" them. And I suspect that if I did understand them fully ... I would ... gasp.

Yes, the right word: *gasp!*

TRAGEDY OF THE "COMMON"

Longinotti-Buitoni distinguishes between "common products" and "dream products." To wit:

Common Product ...		Dream Product
Maxwell House ...	*versus* ...	STARBUCKS
BVD ...	*versus* ...	VICTORIA'S SECRET
Payless ...	*versus* ...	FERRAGAMO
Hyundai ...	*versus* ...	FERRARI
Suzuki ...	*versus* ...	HARLEY-DAVIDSON
Atlantic City ...	*versus* ...	ACAPULCO
New Jersey ...	*versus* ...	CALIFORNIA
Carter ...	*versus* ...	KENNEDY
Connors ...	*versus* ...	PELE
CNN ...	*versus* ...	"WHO WANTS TO BE A MILLIONAIRE?"

Nothing necessarily wrong with the first part of each of those pairs. Each offers a solid, workaday response to some need or another. But the second part ... the part after "versus" ... "stuff" that all carries a dreamlike power that goes far, far beyond the realm of mere "need fulfillment."

Adventures in ... "Dreamketing"

Longinotti-Buitoni preaches the "marketing of dreams"—an idea that he compresses into a word of his own coinage: *dreamketing*. It's rather klutzy, especially concerning such an aesthetically rich topic.

Nonetheless, I find myself reeled in by it:

Dreamketing: Touching the client's dreams.

Dreamketing: The art of telling stories and entertaining.

Dreamketing: Promoting the dream, not the product.

Dreamketing: Building the brand around the Main Dream.

Dreamketing: Building "buzz," "hype," a "cult."

Longinotti-Buitoni also provides hard financial data which demonstrate ... clearly ... that what he calls "dream" products provide (along with fulfillment to customers) returns to shareholders that are miles and miles beyond the returns from "common" products.

This is *not* pie in the sky. It's a "business message," delivered by a practical businessman who has created and enhanced some extraordinary franchises. I think he's well worth listening to—especially in light of the fundamental argument I've attempted to develop in this book. The Fundamental Argument about Totally New Sources of Value Added ... in a Totally New Economy.

Project: Dream

I hope to sign you up! I hope that you'll play with (right term) the ideas in this chapter—and consider applying them to your current project.

(In finance.)

(In purchasing.)

(In HR.)

(In engineering.)

(In IS.)

Here are your instructions: RE-IMAGINE THAT PROJECT. DO NOT REST ... UNTIL THAT PROJECT PASSES THE TESTS OF IMAGINATION (OR DREAMKETING) SET FORTH BY GIAN LUIGI LONGINOTTI-BUITONI. UNTIL YOU'VE TURNED THAT "SUZUKI" TRAINING COURSE INTO A "HARLEY-DAVIDSON" TRAINING COURSE, THAT "MAXWELL HOUSE" BUSINESS PROCESS INTO A "STARBUCKS" BUSINESS PROCESS.

Think about a staff department ... now known as a PSF ... in your company. Shouldn't its "training course" Radically Change the Life View of *Every* Participant?

NEW BUSINESS

NEW BRAND

DREAM LANGUAGE

[1]*This is how it is with me: I come across a word. In a speech. In a book or an article. And suddenly ... a great deal of what's been troubling me ... for the last two months (or the last two or twenty-two years) ... gets sorted out. In a flash. In a word. By a word.*

And ... life is never the same again.

Words ensnare me. They cause me to look at everything I do ... in a totally different way.

I'd been pondering the "commodity trap" issue. To little avail. Then I found ... the word. Or, rather, pair of words: experience, dream. And with an Ear-Shattering Thunk ... tectonic plates broke loose ... and a slew of scattered observations snapped into place.

YES. (DAMN IT.)

Shouldn't the next "business process reengineering project" be an ... Exercise in Dream Fulfillment?

YES. (DAMN IT.)

Why bother with a project unless it is a Dreamketing Project ... unless, that is, it will Dramatically Alter the Perspective of both Designer-Provider and User-Client?

Key words:

DRAMATICALLY. ALTER. PERSPECTIVE.

Dream Logic

Mr. Longinotti-Buitoni offers specific advice for those who seek to turn their project team into ... a dream team:

- Maximize your value added by fulfilling the dreams of your clients.
- Only invest in what is valuable for your client.
- Don't let short-term results weaken the long-term value of your brand.
- Balance rigorous control of the financial endeavor with the emotional management.
- Build a financial structure that allows risk-taking: NO RISKS—NO DREAMS.
- Establish long-term "price power" in order to avoid the trap of the commodity product.
- Choose a Creator: the cultural leader who gives the company an aesthetic point of view.
- Hire eclectically: Hire collaborators with different cultures and past histories in order to balance rigor with emotion.
- Lead emotionally: Engender passionate dedication through vision and freedom.
- Build for the long haul: Creativity requires a lifetime commitment.

The "Zero Defect" Defect

Secretary of Defense Don Rumsfeld is determined to remake the U.S. military. He insists that the military needs ... Genuine Revolution ... totally new performance scenarios. In two words: New Dreams.

Alas, he's fighting the biggest City Hall of all: hyper-conservative admirals and generals. "In the modern military," *Newsweek* said in a cover story on Rumsfeld, "risk is anathema to rising stars, who cannot afford any slip-ups on their records. 'Zero defects' and 'zero tolerance' are common bywords."

TRANSFORMATION GUARANTEED!

To guarantee anything in this world gone nuts is ... nuts. But this is one time I'll take the leap.

Dear Ms. Finance Department Head, Mr. Purchasing Director, Ms. Retail Store Owner:

I will guarantee you a new lease on your professional life ... if you do just one thing. You must drop, excise, remove, expunge the terms "product" and "service" from your work-day vocabulary. When either term springs to your lips, substitute "experience" or "dream."

That's all.

And "totally new performance scenarios" ... New Dreams ... are slow to arrive if leaders measure themselves by a "zero defect" standard.

Problem with "zero defect": No "bold" failures, no "grand" successes. PERIOD. THERE IS NO ESCAPING THAT LOGIC. NONE.

Dream Metrics: Beyond (Way Beyond) "Zero Defects"

Our tour guide, Mr. Longinotti-Buitoni, insists that "zero defects" and other such sterile measures of "quality" are but a starting point. His measurements of choice:

"Love at first sight."

"Design for the five senses."

"Development to expand the Main Dream."

"Design so as to seduce through the peripheral senses."

To which I say: YES. YES. YES. And YES.

Do I fully understand all of that? No! On the other hand, I've never created a Starbucks ... or a Victoria's Secret ... or a Ferragamo ... or a Ferrari ... or a Harley-Davidson. (Or an IBM Global Services!) (Or the new found ... BROWN.)

But think about it. Think about an aspect of your business ... a clunky "procedure," say, yearning to become a dream-come-true. Then apply Mr. LB's Measurement No. 1: *"Love at first sight."*

Makes sense to me. For a product or service or (yes) solution. For a business process. (See above.) For a training course. (See above.) As well as for a new product or a new marketing campaign.

Next, rigorously apply Longinotti-Buitoni's other dream metrics ...

Design for the five senses!

Expanding on the Main Dream!

Seduce Through the Peripheral Senses!

NEW BUSINESS ● NEW BRAND

{ **EXTREME DREAM**
Do not forget the context. Go back to Chapter 6. Most everything "works." And damn well at that. So what goes beyond "works well"?
   Excitement. *That's what.*
   Surprise. *That's what.*
   Things not previously thought possible. *That's what.*
   Clients becoming what they want to be. *That's what.*
   My point: to urge you to "raise the bar." WAY UP.
   Say "experiences." (SAY IT.) Say "dreams." (DAMN IT.)
   (Please.)

"DREAM" WEAVING
From *Rodale's The Synonym Finder*: "dream, *n.* 1. vision, nightmare; apparition, will-o'-the-wisp, *ignis fatuus*, chimera, fairy; phantom, shade, specter, ghost, wraith, incubus, succubus, bugbear; fantasy, phantasm, phantasma, *Lit.* fantasia, *Inf.* pipe dream, romance; figment, figment of the imagination, fiction, invention, fabrication; visualization, envisagement, hallucination, mirage, illusion, delusion; shadow, vapor, nothingness."

Once More, with Feeling (Damn It)

One of the most popular measures, in the business world, of Quality or Customer Satisfaction is ... "exceeds expectation."

OH, HOW I DESPISE THAT.

Suppose you attended the seventh game of the Western Conference NBA play-offs in June 2002. You watched the Los Angeles Lakers war with the Sacramento Kings. It was an "exceptional" match. (Or some such.)

Let's say you went with a good pal. On the way out of Arco Arena in Sacramento, you're shaking with the emotional afterglow (win or lose) of the contest. You turn to your best pal of some 25 years, and say: *"My, my, George, that round-ball contest certainly 'exceeded expectations.'"*

OF COURSE YOU DON'T UTTER SILLINESS LIKE THAT.

You scream![2] You shout!

Expletives ignite the air!

Adjectives of the most extraordinary nature rip the sky asunder!

This was an ... Extraordinary Moment. An ... Extraordinary Event. (Dare I say it ... win or lose ... a Dream Come True ... to have attended.)

As I said at the outset, I am an ... unabashed ... Business Lover. I believe that our enterprises, public *and* private, *can* be ... Wildly Creative. I believe that they can provide ... Extraordinary Experiences ... for our Employees ... our Suppliers ... our Customers.

I *believe* that "emotion" is "where it's at."

I *believe* in "experiences."

I *believe* in "dreams."

I *believe* in language. *Extreme* language. *Emotional* language.[3] Language that ... *Engages You*. That makes you ... Take Off.

DOG DAYS

[2]You might think, given my ... language ... that I am always "up." A Walking WOW.

But no: I do have totally crappy days when I can barely get out of bed. On those days I force myself up and go on long rambles with my dogs. For me, the *dog experience* beats even the finest psychopharmaceuticals.

Then ... I get on with it. I force my all-down self back into the fray—not to "finish a project" or "prepare a speech," but to *transform* a project or a speech into a (potentially) transforming experience for someone else.

My greatest fear is that I will not have done stuff that *mattered*. That I won't have made the world ... a little better place.

So, between my dogs and the possibility of producing "experiences that matter" (that scintillate!), I muddle through. And a funny thing happens: When I re-ignite my enthusiasm, other folks invariably respond in kind.

Message: Enthusiasm begets enthusiasm.

WISE TO THE WORD

[3]Winston Churchill said, "We shape our buildings. Thereafter, they shape us." I say: "We shape our words. Thereafter, they shape us."

Something special happens when we talk about "dreams," or "dreamketing," or "experiences." We view the world through a new lens.

True, I speak and write for a living. Words are therefore *everything* to me. But one of my goals in this book—one of my principal goals—is to turn you into the same sort of Certified Word Fanatic I am.

Dreams!, Dreams! Dreams!

Nike. More than high performance gear. Try: The promise of a High Performance Life.

Armani. We wear Armani. We *become* Armani.

Google. It's a ubiquitous search engine. As one commentator put it, "Google is a bit like God."

Intel Centrino. An invisible chip? No! The guarantee of a cutting-edge life enhanced by sexy technology.

Virgin. Use Virgin. Be cool.

Porsche. Tough to drive at times? Yes. But who cares: I AM MY PORSCHE.

NEW BUSINESS ! ● NEW BRAND

The "Feel" of Dreams: If You Build It ...

If you get comfortable (in business ... or the Army) with words like "dream" and "dreamketing" ... then you'll get comfortable with other "un-business" words like ... COURAGE.

The product development and marketing expert Doug Hall provides, in an e-missive he sent me, a brilliant exit to the last two chapters:

"The Internet is the most effective profit-killer on earth. It stimulates a TRUE FREE MARKET [He likes capital letters too!—TP]; and a REAL free market is the most dangerous of marketplaces for companies selling THE SAME OLD STUFF. To those with COURAGE [Dreamketers?—TP], free markets are great—they kill off the deadwood competitors who don't have the Courage to Change—making way for them to LEVERAGE their DRAMATIC DIFFERENCE into profitable growth."

Hats off to ...

SCINTILLATING EXPERIENCES.
DREAMKETING.
DRAMATIC DIFFERENCE.
HOT WORDS.
CAPITAL LETTERS.
COURAGE.
DOUG HALL.

And to hell with "cubicle slavery" and "zero defects"!

Dreams. Entirely new possibilities. Incredible Imaginings.

I DARE YOU ... TO GET INTO THE DREAM BUSINESS ... THE "INCREDIBLE IMAGININGS" BUSINESS.

Will you take me up? Join Dreamers Un-Anonymous? Those Courageous Souls ... willing to Pursue the (Increasingly Possible) Impossible Dream(s)?[4]

! Contrasts

WAS		IS
"Mere" experiences	–	Wild Imaginings
(Good enough for Chapter 8)		... and Dreams Fulfilled
Things done well	–	Things not thought possible
"It's damn good"	–	"You can do that?"
Pleased	–	Elated
Surprised	–	Stunned
Selling to customers	–	Tempting customers
"I'm not sure I need it."	–	"I GOTTA HAVE IT. NOW."

INTO THE VALLEY OF DREAMS

[4]My excuse for falling in love (yes, at first sight) with the notion of "incredible imaginings" and "impossible dreams"? Answer: my 25-plus years in Silicon Valley. Where Davids have again & again humbled Goliaths ... only to become overnight vulnerable Goliaths themselves.

A land of drama. And of dreams (and, yes, nightmares) come true.

In Silicon Valley, I fell in love. With Steve Jobs. Scott McNealy. Larry Ellison. Jim Clark. People who were ... larger than life. People who had ... DREAMS.

DESIGN:
THE "SOUL" OF NEW ENTERPRISE

10

! Technicolor Rules ...

- "Design is the fundamental soul of a man-made creation."
- Design is not a surface thing or a "prettifying" thing.
- "Designers are people who think with their hearts."
- Design is not about "like" or "dislike." It's about passion. Emotion. Attachment.
- Design is about stuff that ... makes me chortle. (And stuff that makes me ... scream.)
- Design is the NO.1 DETERMINANT of whether a product-service-experience stands out—or does not.

! RANT

We are not prepared ...

We consider "design" ... when we consider it at all ... to be about "patina" ... "a little something on top." But we must appreciate that design is the Seat of the Soul ... if one is in the Solutions-Experiences-Dream-Fulfillment Business. (And we *all* must be—from individual contributor to CEO.)

We view design as a "finishing-off process." But we must understand that a thoroughgoing "design sensibility" can effectively drive Enterprise Strategy, as at Sony or Nokia, and cease to be a neglected second cousin.

We think of designers ... when we think of them at all ... as odd ducks who should be confined to their cubes, far away from the strategy "war room." Instead we must invite the designers to sit, like Braun's Dieter Rams, on the CEO's immediate right at the boardroom table.

! VISION

I imagine ...

A Finance "Department" (that is, a Value-Adding PSF!) ... with a Musician, a Poet, an Artist, an Actress, and an Anthropologist. (As well as Some Numbers Dudes.) This "Department" stands for accuracy and integrity. But it is also a ... Scintillating Business Partner. The members of this PSF are not drones. They do not hide behind thick, obscure Excel presentations of arcane figures. They are *exciting* Their ideas are *exciting*. Their presentations are *exciting*. And Clear. And Beautiful. Because these new-breed "finance people" are ... DESIGN DRIVEN.

It's Got Soul

I, not the Greek philosophers, have discovered the "Seat of the Soul."

At least in enterprise.

And it is ... Great Design.

Does saying that make me arrogant?

Yes.

So what?

Hey, I've got Steve Jobs on my side. "In most people's vocabularies, design means veneer," says Jobs, the genius behind Apple, Next, Pixar ... and Apple again. "Nothing could be further from the meaning of design. Design is the fundamental soul of a man-made creation."

Damn few "get it." Most people consider design a surface thing, a "prettifying" thing, an after-the-fact cosmetic-makeover thing. But in Apple-land and Sony-land and Nokia-land it is the antithesis of all that.

Design is about "soul."

Design comes first.

Design's tenets drive and define the enterprise and its fundamental value proposition.

I, alone among the "management gurus," write extensively about design.

Why?

IT TURNS ME ON.

(Right phrase.)

Design Turn-On: Smooth Sailing

I grew up on the water. Sullivan's Cove, on the Severn River, near Annapolis, Maryland.

Rivers are in my blood. (And soul.)

I just returned from a trip. My back aches. (It always does.) Yet my suitcase is three pounds heavier than it needs to be.

Why?

The turnbuckle I carry with me. I got it at Fawcett's, Annapolis' premier yacht supply store. (When I was a kid. And today, when I'm not.)

A turnbuckle tightens rigging. It's an 8-inch-long, $60 piece of chrome sailboat hardware. It's also ... more to the point ... beautiful.

Confession time: *I fondle it as I write.*

{ } **PASSION PLAY**

Consider our Story So Far. (Remember: Stories Rule.)

    1. The end of White-Collar Work as we know it.

    2. The shift to Higher Value Added, Intellectual-Capital-Intensive activities.

    3. The emergence of the Professional Service Firm.

    4. The creation of New Services ("Solutions") to stack on top of "products."

    5. The notion that "services" are not services per se but ... Scintillating Experiences. (Or: Dreams Come True.)

    6. The recognition that "solutions," "experiences," and "dreams" all derive from ... a Passion for Design.

    7. Again (note well): A PASSION FOR DESIGN

Design Turn-Off: Hotel Hell

I'm on the road about 200 nights a year. That's extreme. But a lot of you/us surely score 100 "nights away" a year.

Most of us—I suspect—hit the hotel room, sigh twice, plug in, and get to work on our "second-day-of-work."

Fact is, I arrive in the room ... unzip my rolly bag ... get out my balls of tangled wires ... crawl around on the floor ... plug in ... hook up ... and ... SPEND FOUR TO SIX HOURS OF THE NEXT TEN ... ONLINE OR SCREWING AROUND WITH TOMORROW'S POWERPOINT PRESENTATION.

Problem: *Only one hotel in 10 or 15 "gets it."* I'm *not* talking DSL. I'm talking MAB: My Aching Back. I AM PISSED OFF. (VERY.) I am pissed off at hotels that provide great couches and armoires ... which I *never* use ... but ... offer ... CRAPPY DESKS ... WITH UNBELIEVABLY CRAPPY "DESK CHAIRS" THAT RUIN MY BODY.

(DAMN IT.)

Message to hotel "stylists": YOUR HOTEL ROOM IS MY "OFFICE." (More than my "Official Office.") PLEASE ... RESPECT THAT FACT! PLEASE ... RESPECT MY ACHING BACK! (Do so, and you'll earn my custom. And *affection*.)

"Design" Defined: A PowerPoint Epiphany

Defining "design": It ain't easy; it is important.

In late 2000, I was charged with keynoting a major design conference. I spent an eternity on my presentation. But as dawn of "the day" approached, I still was unhappy. Extremely unhappy. I'd been working at this "damn design thing" for years. And I still hadn't figured out why it had gotten so, so far under my skin.

At about 5 a.m. on the morning the conference opened, I got up, and tapped out simple text for some PowerPoint slides. And said to myself (I'm embarrassed to say, I really did): "Ah-ha."

Here's what erupted onto the slides:

1. *Design "is" ... WHAT & WHY I LOVE. L-O-V-E.*

Design is not about "like." It's not about "dislike." It's about passion[1] ... emotion ... attachment.

At design conferences, I discovered, designers invariably bring along their favorite toys. It took forever for me to figure out what to bring. In the end, all I had to do was

---

PASSION POINT
Design—along with Design Mindfulness (not "prettification"!)—is the Mt. Everest of "intellectual capital."

It is—like Music, like Art—the pinnacle of Human Accomplishment. It involves nothing less than bringing to bear on the task at hand ... what it means to be fully engaged and fully human.

FEELING—GROOVY!
[1]According to a study published in the *Journal of Advertising Research*, emotions are twice as important as "facts" in the process by which people make buying decisions. The study involved more than 23,000 U.S. consumers, exposed these subjects to 240 advertising messages, and covered 13 categories of goods (with emotion trumping "fact" in all 13 categories).

look in my suitcase. And there they were—a couple of boxes of them. *Ziplocs!*

Ziplocs!

Ziplocs!

Ziplocs: Couldn't live without them. If "they" quit making them, I would probably pull the last one over my head—and sign off. "Just" a "plastic bag." But not so! A million uses.

Brilliant.

Spectacular design.[2]

2. Design is ... WHY I GET MAD.

M-A-D.

Design is about stuff that ... makes me chortle. (And stuff that makes me ... scream.)

As I said, I probably spend 200 nights a year in hotels. And I'm not as young as I used to be. I've worn glasses for about 20 years. (Trifocals, these days.) But ... I don't wear glasses when I'm in the ... bathroom. (Who does?) Hence ... nothing ... on earth ... pisses me off more ... than shampoo bottles on which the "shampoo" is in such fine print that you can't read it.

I don't find the experience/problem "unpleasant." It flat out ... *pisses me off.*

SHAMPOO

3. Hypothesis: DESIGN IS THE PRINCIPAL DIFFERENCE BETWEEN ... LOVE AND HATE!

That statement above took fully ten years to get to. It's pretty blunt. But I think it was worth the ten-year wait—because it's precisely what I believe.

It's not about "sorta."

Hence I began my presentation to that boffo Design Conference as follows:

"*I am a design fanatic. Though not 'artistic' I love 'cool stuff.' But it goes [much, much] further, far beyond the personal. 'Design' has become a ... PROFESSIONAL*

! **BEST BED**

[2]And speaking of love ...

I'm hooked ... on the Westin *Heavenly* Bed.

What do you do in a hotel room? You have a full day of meetings. You're zonked. You get to the room. You check your email and work on your next presentation. You go to sleep. You get up. You go to some more meetings. Thus, the "sleeping part" is right at the center of it along with the office-ing bit. And I, for one, don't believe that man or woman was meant to sleep under polyester.

Those Westin beds?

Fabulous!

Westin knows it!

And exploits it!

Great beds!

Great duvets!

Great experience.

Great marketing ploy!

And, via the catalog you find in your room, you can even order a duvet or set of towels for ... your home.

OBSESSION. I SIMPLY BELIEVE THAT DESIGN—per se—IS THE PRINCIPAL REASON FOR EMOTIONAL ATTACHMENT (or detachment) RELATIVE TO A PRODUCT OR SERVICE OR EXPERIENCE. Design, as I see it, is arguably the NO.1 DETERMINANT of whether a product-service-experience stands out—or does not. Furthermore, it's 'one of those things' that damn few enterprises put—consistently—on the Front Burner."

I wish, somehow, I could take you on my adventure. My adventure of "Love" and "Hate" and "Never Neutral." My conclusion: Design is the Heart (SOUL) of the Matter.

The "matter" called ... New Value Proposition.

Design Myths I: What FedEx Knows That You Maybe Don't

Think about design, commonly, and one thinks about a Ferrari. A Rolex. Perhaps an iMAC. That is: lumps, not (mere?) services.

Baloney.

I.D. [International Design] magazine published in 1999 its first, and so far only, list of the 40 "most design-driven companies in America." To be sure, Apple Computer was on the list. As were Caterpillar. Gillette. IBM. New Balance. Patagonia. 3M.

More interesting to me, fully half the companies ... were ... *service* companies.

Amazon.com made the list. So did: Bloomberg. FedEx. CNN. Disney. Martha Stewart. Nickelodeon. The New York Yankees. The Church of Jesus Christ of Latter-day Saints.

Message: *Design is about services as much as it is about lumps.*

Which brings me to you and me. Design is ... damn it ... about the purchasing department. The training department. The finance department.

Presentation of a financial report is as much a "design shtick" as is the creation of a sexy-looking product at John Deere. *(Yup, Deere long ago made "cool" and "farm implement" synonymous. And shareholders clip fat coupons as a result.)*

Big (B-I-G) Message: *We are all (A-L-L) designers.* Each and every one of us gives off dozens—probably hundreds, perhaps more—of "design cues" every day. In the way we present ourselves, our project "output."

So: Design is *not* about lumpy objects. Design is *not* the provenance of the new product or marketing department alone.

Design Myths II: What Tar-zhay Knows That You Maybe Don't

Think again about that Ferrari. That Rolex. Even that iMac. These are iconic triumphs of design, right? And they're not only lumps—they're expensive lumps.

SELF-SERVING PERSONAL EXAMPLE
Since "breaking on to the public scene" (management corner thereof) in 1978, I have given roughly 3,000 speeches and seminars. Some are good, some are bad, some are indifferent. A few are (for me) highs that no drug—and perhaps not even sex—can match.

What's the secret? Not "better data." Not "sounder logic." It's this: All of my senses are perfectly and harmoniously attuned to the audience. An aesthetic bonding occurs. We're "doing theater" together ... the Theater of Cool Business. Taking the potential for such aesthetic bonding seriously is the ... Essence of Design Mindfulness.

Trust me, there is nothing that makes you feel more Fully Alive than being "in the zone" (as athletes call it). Once you've been there, you never want to leave. You become an instant addict ... a Pure Design Addict.

But design is *not* restricted to $79,000 objects. Or even to funky $1,000 computers. If ever we needed evidence of the latter, then the startling ascent—in the face of Wal*Mart's awesome prowess—of *Target/Tar-zhay* is proof positive of design's potentially Transforming Role.

Time magazine called Target "the champion of America's new design democracy." *Advertising Age* awarded Target its coveted "Marketer of the Year" award in the millennium year ... 2000.

I love Target. I love the fact that Target has *not* changed its strategy in the slightest. Target *was* a discounter.[3] Target *is* a discounter. Target *plans to be* a discounter from now until hell freezes over. Nonetheless, Target has gone after design-as-exceptional-differentiator; and in doing so, has proven once and for all (I hope) that "discounter" and "cheap crap" do not have to be synonymous.

Gillette is another leader in demonstrating that Awesome Design can be applied to relatively inexpensive/"common" items. Consider the Sensor. It redefined women's shaving. And when we thought we'd seen the last word for men, the Mach3 turned out to be *very* special, *very* different—and, not so incidentally, cost Gillette about three-quarters of a *billion* dollars to develop. (I didn't say design was a ... Free Good.)

The OralB CrossAction toothbrush ... from Gillette ... is another Prime Time Design Example. It changed the brushing of teeth! It cost $70 million to develop. Intriguing factoid: Gillette took out 23 patents on this "mere" toothbrush—including six patents for the packaging alone. (That sort of thing happens when one gets ... serious about ... Design-as-Strategic-Differentiator.)

I AM MY SKIN

Listerine is the latest in a long, powerful line of ... Strategic Packaging Makeovers. In 1870, oatmeal was eaten by "horses and a few stray Scots." Just 20 years later, in 1890, oatmeal was an established "delicacy for the epicure, a nutritious dainty for the invalid, a delight to the children." The secret to this sudden strategic transformation? A humble box. More precisely, the round and still effective Quaker Oats container.

That's the story according to Thomas Hine, author of *The Total Package: The Secret History and Hidden Meanings of Boxes, Bottles, Cans, and Other Persuasive Containers.* "Packages have personality," Hine writes. "They create confidence and trust. They spark fantasies. They move the goods quickly."

And consider this powerful extension of that idea: It applies not just to goods, but also to ... experiences. Fast-food and motel chains are not *like* packages ... they *are* packages. Packaged experiences.

And as in any experience, seconds count. Hine cites research demonstrating that grocery consumers are aware of 30,000 items in the typical 1,800 seconds they spend walking a store's aisles. Translation: Designers have .06 second (!!) to make a ... Lasting Impression ... on the consumer.

"LUV" STORY

[3] LUV is the stock-ticker symbol for Southwest Airlines. Like Target, SWA is a discounter that revels in the aesthetic of what it produces. The energy and enthusiasm of its ground and in-air staff are a product of ... True Design Mindfulness.

Or: True Design Luv.

Design. About *services* as much as lumps. About the HR and IS departments as much as about new product development. And about *$0.79* items as much as $79,000 items. Those are the Terms-of-Reference with which I approach this Very Big Idea.

Designing Women
And Now for Something Totally Controversial ...

Men *cannot* design
for *women's* needs!
(Gulp.)

Did that ever stir the pot (and bring it to an instant boil) at a design conference I recently addressed.

A woman friend, an architect, told me about a friend of hers (female) who was shopping for a relatively pricey house. One day she looked at half a dozen possibles. Only one had a laundry room on the second floor—where the kids' bedrooms were. Guess what? That anomalous house was the only one of the bunch designed by a woman.

The fact is ... no Guy would ever think ... not in a Million Years ... to put a laundry room on the second floor ... near the kids' bedrooms.

Is a "second-floor laundry room" a Big Deal ... worthy of an Oceanic Generalization? Of course not. But it is ... INDICATIVE. Because ... from the mundane to the profound ... from residential housing to financial services ... when it comes to design, Guys Are Impaired ... Relative to Women. Men lack the ability ... mostly (*very* mostly) ... to deal with women's issues.[4]

TARGET OF OPPORTUNITY
I just couldn't help myself. In a meeting with the senior merchandising staff of a huge discount retailer, I let loose my wrath: "Target has done it. So what's holding you back? You have incredible purchasing might. Flatly demand of your vendors that every product that you put on your shelf, mundane or grand, be a Pure Aesthetic Joy. Why not be as tough on your vendors about design as you are about price?"

Yes, why not? (Damn it.)

FROM "KILLS GERMS" TO KILLER DESIGN
Pfizer develops incredible, *life-saving* drugs. Yet in 2001 my friends at Pfizer were most happy about ... Listerine's PocketPaks.

Who would have thought that such a ... DRAMATIC DIFFERENCE ... could result from changing the presentation form ... for a silly little "breath enhancer"?

(I contend that PocketPaks will single-handedly resurrect the two-Martini lunch.)

A STAR(C)K REALIZATION
[4]It's a woman's world!

"Perhaps the macho look can be interesting," designer Philippe Starck writes in *Harvard Design Magazine*, "if you want to fight dinosaurs. But now to survive you need intelligence, not power and aggression. Modern intelligence means intuition—it's female." (More later.)

Design Voices

Design, I've discovered over the last ten years, is the most devilish of topics to write about. It's Exhibit No. 1 in the "I know it when I see it" school. We know "cool," and we know "uncool." And we don't need a road map. Perhaps the best way that I can define "design" is to steal some others' assessments I've come across. (A big share of what follows comes courtesy of the Design Council in the UK.)

"I wish more money and time was spent on designing an exceptional product, instead of trying to psychologically manipulate perceptions through expensive advertising."— **Phil Kotler, the marketing guru**

"Design is a way of demonstrating how beautiful something can be. It has a very profound quality. Design is a way of changing life and influencing the future."— **Sir Ernest Hall, Dean Clough**

"Every new product or service that Virgin group offers must: (1) Have the best quality, (2) provide great value, (3) be innovative, (4) dramatically challenge existing alternatives, and (5) provide a "sense of fun" or "cheekiness."— **Richard Branson, CEO of Virgin Group**

"It was a revelation to discover how design could change people's behaviour. I learned that simply by altering the graphic content of an exhibit you could double the number of people who visited it."— **Gillian Thomas, formerly of The Science Museum/UK**

"The future will fascinate. A place where experience becomes more important than information, truth more important than technology, and ideas the only global currency."— **Ralph Ardill, Imagination**

"Outstandingly good design in service industries is not an optional extra. It is an essential part of everything a company does, and what it stands for."— **Richard Dykes, Managing Director, Royal Mail**

"Design is one of the few tools that, for every dollar you spend, you actually say something about your business. You have it in your power to use design to further the wealth and prosperity of your business."—**Raymond Turner,[5] BAA/British Airports Authority**

SAY IT LOUD!
[5]"Design" means … *"you actually say something about your business."*
    Nice.
    Profound.

"My favorite word is grace—whether it's amazing grace, saving grace, grace under fire, Grace Kelly. How we live contributes to beauty—whether it's how we treat other people or the environment."— **Celeste Cooper, Designer**

"Lust for beauty and elegance underpinned the most important discoveries in computational history." ... *"The Beauty of a proof or a machine lies in a happy marriage of simplicity and power."* ... *"Beauty is the ultimate defense against complexity."* ... *"A good programmer can be at least 100 times more productive than an average one. The gap has little to do with technical or mathematical or engineering training—and much to do with taste, good judgment, aesthetic gifts."* — **David Gelernter, *Machine Beauty: Elegance and the Heart of Technology*.**

Leave it to the 10- and 11-year-olds polled by the Design Council to "get" the essence of design from the start:

"Designers are people who *THINK WITH THEIR* **hearts."** — *James, age 10*

"If there was **no design** there would be nothing to do, and nothing would progress or get better. **The world would fall apart."**— *Anna, age 11*

"My favourite design is the Nike 'tick' because it makes me feel confident — *even though I am not so good at* sports."— *Raoul, age 11*

NEW BUSINESS ! NEW BRAND

{
WORDS TO DESIGN BY
Consider the *words* that emerge from these "voices":
"Demonstrating how beautiful something can be."
"Changing life and influencing the future."
"Sense of fun or cheekiness."
"Future will fascinate."
"Amazing grace, saving grace, grace under fire."
"Lust for beauty and elegance."
"Happy marriage of simplicity and power."
"Think with their hearts."
These words and phrases that are all too seldom heard in the Sacred Halls of Business. (As Usual.)
WHY NOT? Why not ... add (say) the word "cheekiness" to your business lexicon? To your precious "values statement"? DAMN IT.

17 Habits of Highly Design-Driven Companies

So ... suppose you focused on putting ... DESIGN ... Front and Center in your enterprise. (Incl. "finance department.") What would you do?

Here are some possible starting points. Design-Driven Companies ...

1 Put design per se On The Agenda of every meeting—in Every Department throughout the Enterprise.

2 Have Professional Designers on virtually all project teams.

3 Have physical facilities that Sing and Scintillate, that reflect the SERIOUSLY COOL DESIGN SENSITIVITY of the products and services and experiences that the Enterprise produces.

4 Have internal and external Academy Awards Programs (employees, new products, vendors) that focus on DESIGN ... per se. THESE ARE BIG DEALS.

5 Measure the amount of External Recognition the enterprise gets for its design activities. (Per se.)

6 Make diversity a Top Priority: The essence of Design Excellence is sensitivity to the ... Dramatically Different, often subtle, needs of various members of our internal and external communities.

7 Include Design Sensitivity explicitly in ... ALL training activities ... and in everyone's evaluation. WHAT GETS MEASURED GETS DONE—INCLUDING A FOCUS ON DESIGN.

8 Openly use the Emotional Language of Design. Steve Jobs, Apple founder, talks about "stuff" as being "insanely great." (Or not.) Love that ... Insanely Great. People who are Design Fanatics use such ... Hot Language. And are comfortable with it. (And those who aren't ... DON'T.) (More's the pity.)

9 Use formal "Design Cops" (YES ... COPS!) to ... Stomp Out All Vestiges of Lousy Design, internally within departments as well as externally regarding the business or retail consumer.

10 Have a Formal Design Board that includes external as well as internal members ... which oversees the Strategic Design Sensitivity Program.

11 Talk openly about the Design Mindfulness of our "corporate culture"—and work, systematically and programmatically, to insure that it is fostered.

12 Routinely invite Top Designers to address the company in any number of forums. THE IDEA: KEEP THE HEAT ON—IN PERPETUITY—RELATIVE TO THE "BIG DESIGN IDEA."

13 Have great art on the walls. The late Jay Chiat of Chiat/Day believed that having great art around would inspire Teams to create Great Ads. (Amen.) (And ... again ... why not in the Logistics Department? Please.)

> **(DE)SIGN OF THE TIMES**
> From a July 2002 report in *BusinessWeek*: "After watching consumers flock to striking new foreign models, U.S. automakers have been recruiting hot designers from European rivals and paying fat salaries to design-school graduates. More important, they're giving designers and marketers a stronger voice in developing new models, and they're lifting design bosses higher in the corporate hierarchy. The result: no more sedans shaped like jellybeans. Detroit is turning out head-turners such as the retro Chrysler PT Cruiser, the Euro-styled Ford Focus, and designs that morph into a cargo hauler."

⑭ Support the arts. "Design-centric" enterprises pay attention to Community Activities that emphasize design. "DESIGN IS PART OF OUR CHARACTER"—THAT'S THE MESSAGE HERE.

⑮ Have a strong, formal "design function." DESIGN SHOWS UP ON YOUR COMPANY'S ORGANIZATION CHART ... NEAR THE TOP. (PERIOD.)

⑯ The Chief Designer is a Member of the Board of Directors[6] or, at the very least, a member of the Executive Committee. (RANK ... DOES ... MATTER.)

⑰ Have an annual or biannual ... "Design Audit" ... the results of which The Company publishes in its Annual Report or in a special Annual Design Report.

This is a strong set of "requirements." I don't suspect any innocent enterprise would tackle them all. The point of this "laundry list" is to suggest that this "soft"/"emotional" idea of a "Design-Driven Company" can be translated into ... Hard Practical Actions.

Be Your Own Design Critic

Perhaps you're not artistic. I'm not. (Understatement.) Is there any hope? I have no doubt that there is. And I'm a case in point. I'm no more artistic than I was 30 years ago; I dropped out of architecture school and took up civil engineering, because of my total lack of artistic ability. But I can say, for certain, that I'm a darn sight more "design sensitive" and "design aware" than I was 10 years ago.

My secret: Waking up. Becoming alert.

My personal trick: Create and keep ... a *Design Notebook*. It was a simple item, from a Ryman's in London. On the front cover I wrote ... "COOL." On the back cover I wrote ... "CRAPPY." Then I started recording. Little things. Mostly. Things that pissed me off. Or thrilled me. Shampoo bottles ... where I couldn't read "Shampoo." Signage that misleads. Software commands that were silly. Those were the negatives.

Or the thrill of Ziplocs. Or that Heavenly Bed. (Westin.) None of these examples was necessarily related to what I do for a living—write and give lectures and involve myself with enterprise consulting activities. But the key thing was that the list, per se, made me a lot more ... *sensitive*. Made me aware of all the dozens ... upon dozens ...

FLEX YOUR DESIGN MUSCLE
Here are some design warm-up exercises you might try:

1. Save great—and awful—junk mail. Consider: Why do you love this one? Why do you hate that one?

2. Go on a less-than-$10 shopping spree: Learn that Design comes at $2.95 ... not just at $22,295.

3. Pay especially close attention to signage. And instruction manuals.

4. Compare the order forms or other data fields at various websites. (The Web, after all, is a Pure Design Medium.)

DESIGNER ON BOARD
[6]Dieter Rams ... was Braun's chief designer.
Dieter Rams ... designed Very Cool Stuff.
Dieter Rams ... was on Braun's Board of Directors.
Message: WHEN DESIGN REALLY MATTERS, IT REALLY MATTERS.

upon dozens of ... Design Variables ... that are at play ... when I give a presentation ... or undertake the writing of a book. (This book!)

"Design Rage": Stop Blaming Yourself!

Oh, oh ... and one other ... Command ... courtesy design observer and curmudgeon Donald Norman (author of, among other things, *The Design of Everyday Things*):

STOP BLAMING YOURSELF.

NEW BUSINESS ● NEW BRAND

Norman insists that one of the Primary Problems that we have in ... Paying Attention to Design ... is assuming ... whenever there is a screw-up ... that it's because ... we are such klutzes.

Well, we may or may not be "klutzes," but when you have trouble, again and again, with some computer program ... Blame The Dreadful Designer!

Design (Bad) is what causes those glitches ... because a designer wasn't sensitive to you, a normal, or perhaps novice, user of whatever.

Reporter Susan Casey, writing in *eCompany.com*, said, "I sometimes have episodes of wild fury in rental cars. It's not road rage. It's more like design rage."

Amen, Susan.

I'm not suggesting (I guess) that you shoot designers. Even the lousy ones. I am suggesting that "design rage" is a *brilliant* starting point in raising Design Sensitivity.

Now, of course, we must translate the Design Rage that we have against "others" into our own world, and our department, with our customers, regarding the provision of our "experiences."

What a difference Awful Design makes!

What a difference Brilliant Design makes!

Object of Design

Billions upon billions of dollars are at stake. (Trillion$$$?) Some companies do get it: Sony. Nike. Gillette. Apple. Body Shop. VW. Amazon. Nokia. Target. Bloomberg.

Nothing ... NOTHING ... (!!!) ...

is more important to the executives of these enterprises than unadorned ... unabashed ... *Fanaticism* ... about ... *Design*.

MORTALS WELCOME
I have two degrees in ... ENGINEERING.
I have two degrees in ... BUSINESS.
I do not have ... an ARTISTIC molecule in my body.
I cannot ... draw. (At all.)
But that does not stop me from ... APPRECIATING GREAT DESIGN.
"Appreciate" = BIG WORD. (Meaning "to understand" ... and "to love.")
Aesthetically challenged people may indeed apply. (And succeed.)
This chapter is not about ... "Art." It is about ... APPRECIATION.

Design Voices (Redux)

More words of wisdom on design's large (and potentially enormous) place in the universe.

IN TERMS OF DESIGN

Again: Look closely at the language in these quotes ...

"Tomorrow it's design ..."
"Design is the only thing ..."
"Design is ... religion ..."
"Drop-dead charm ..."
"Object of desire ..."
"Design is my passion."
"Passionate maniacs ..."
"Insanely great ..."

"What's imperative is the creation of a style that becomes a culture linking you to the community. You can only do that through good design."—Anita Roddick, founder and chairwoman of The Body Shop

iPod: another "insanely great" product from Steve Jobs at Apple

The best American product design "comes out of big-idea organizations that don't believe in talking to the customer. [They're] run by passionate maniacs who make everybody's life miserable until they get what they want." — Bran Ferren, Applied Minds (formerly the Chief Imagineer at Disney)

"Design is treated like a religion at BMW."—*Fortune* magazine

"Fifteen years ago companies competed on price. Now it's quality. Tomorrow it's design."—Bob Hayes, professor emeritus at the Harvard Business School

"At Sony, we assume that all products of our competitors have basically the same technology, price, performance and features. Design is the only thing that differentiates one product from another in the marketplace."—Norio Ohga, recently retired chairman of Sony

"Every now and then, a design comes along that radically changes the way we think about a particular object. Case in point: the iMac. Suddenly, a computer is no longer an anonymous box. It is a sculpture, an object of desire, something that you look at."—Katherine McCoy and Michael McCoy, Illinois Institute of Technology

"The new Beetle fails at most categories. The only thing it doesn't fail in is drop-dead charm."—Jerry Hirshberg, Nissan Design International

But most companies (the vast majority!) don't get it. Hence they don't really bother about design. (And it is a bother. It's damned hard work, and it requires constant care and attention and love and affection and ... obsession.) And those that don't bother are, to put it simply ... BLOWING OFF A V-E-R-Y BIG THING.

The (my) language is strong.

BACK TO (B) SCHOOL (UGH!)

Whatever you do, don't direct your Design Rage only against designers.

Other prime targets: businesses. And ... *business schools*.

The esteemed Design Management Institute devoted the Summer 2002 issue of its journal to the connection between design and business education. One article included a survey of "design in core and elective classes" in "top business programs." Here's a selection of the results (sample sizes vary from question to question):

Question	
Design as a core class	NO NO NO NO NO NO NO NO NO NO NO NO NO NO NO NO
Design as an elective class	YES NO NO NO NO NO NO NO NO NO NO NO NO NO NO NO
Creativity as a core class	NO NO NO NO NO NO NO NO NO NO NO NO NO
Creativity as an elective class	YES YES YES YES NO NO NO NO NO NO NO NO NO
Innovation as a core class	NO NO NO NO NO NO NO NO NO NO NO NO NO
Innovation as an elective class	YES YES YES YES YES YES NO NO NO NO NO NO NO

One dean's (VERY REVEALING) explanation for the lack of focus on design, creativity, and innovation at his institution: "Our programs are very quantitatively focused. It's the background of making decisions—the skills and processes to make decisions."

I guess he is content to train future controllers for the likes of Enron, Tyco, and WorldCom. (Now do you better understand my contempt for most business schools? And the insanely high level of my frustration?)

MANQUÉ BUSINESS?

Barry Sternlicht, CEO, Starwood, quoted in *Elite Traveler*: "I am a frustrated artist at heart so I am constantly sketching designs for our new hotels. ... Design is my passion. ... I was recently in the new Prada store in Aspen and I loved the design so much I tracked down the Milan-based designer, Roberto Baciocchi, to do our Milan hotel. That's typical of how we do business around here."

THE EYES HAVE IT

Sometimes I ramble into an art supply store ... and go berserk. To the tune of several hundred dollars.

I write it off as a business expense. "It" refers to an almost random collection of design books.

A recent visit to one store netted: *New Business Card Graphics ... Catalog Graphics ... Ads International ... Graphics Packaging ... The Best of Business Card Design ... Direct Response Graphics ... What Logos Do and How They Do It ... Raymond Loewy and Streamlined Design ... Logo, Identity, Brand, Culture ... and ... Open Here: The Art of Instructional Design.*

What's the point ... given that I'm not a designer? Eyeball Calisthenics!

Great design = Great eye candy = Great inspiration. Fact: My "design muscles" are now tighter than my tummy muscles.

The (my) language is emotional.

But the language is also ... frustrating. It's frustrating because Steve Jobs, my favorite denizen of Silicon Valley, got it *exactly* right when he said, *"Design is the fundamental soul of a man-made creation."* You don't become "design-minded" by opening the checkbook, spending a few hundred thousand dollars on a "great designer"—and then telling him/her to please "do the 'design thing.'"

Design *is* soul deep.

(Again: TRILLIONS ARE AT STAKE. AS WELL AS OUR COLLECTIVE SOULS.)

Design = Soul.
Believe it.

WORK SPACE: THE FINAL FRONTIER

Niels Diffrient, a designer and Fortune 500 consultant, writing in a piece for *Metropolis* magazine called "Re-imagining Work": "My ideal office wouldn't have a chair. You would do two things there: stand up or lie down. These are the body's most natural positions."

Designer Lise Anne Couture says: "I think it's a chicken and egg proposition. Do furniture manufacturers make cubes because of the demand, or is the demand there because it's artificially created by the absence of any real alternatives?"

Both comments resonate with me. Not long ago, I addressed a group of corporate real estate professionals. I talked about the changing nature of work—virtual teams, creativity-as-basis-for value added, and so on. Then I said, almost as an aside, "If you'd 'decorate' your living room with Steelcase' furniture,' then do so with your office. If not ..."

A firestorm followed. (Led by the Steelcase–Herman Miller–Grand Rapids, Michigan contingent.)

Good. (Damn it.)

"Work space" is important. ALL IMPORTANT. I am ... disgusted ... by how "human-unfriendly" 99 percent of work spaces are. (Especially the ones that win awards.)

NEW BUSINESS **!** • NEW BRAND

!Contrasts

WAS	IS
Design-challenged department	Design-driven PSF
Design as cost item	Design as value-driven
Design is an after-the-fact prettifying element	Design is the heart and soul of a dream/solution
Designers labor away in a peripheral department	Designers have influence at the Head Table (Board of Directors)
Design is outsourced to this or that vendor	Design is integral to the entire organization (Design Mindfulness is everywhere)
Drab HQ (Just a place to work: You punch out ASAP)	Cool HQ (A place to create: You come early and stay late)
Boring, "Businesslike"	Exciting, "WOW-like"
Brown* (*Unless you're UPS)	Red
Brooks Brothers	Armani
Frowns	Smiles
Recruit from "Best" schools	Recruit from "Most Interesting" schools

11

DESIGN'S LONG COATTAILS: BEAUTIFUL SYSTEMS

! Technicolor Rules ...

● Over time, even a beautiful system tends to get elaborated and elaborated. We end up "serving the system" rather than having the system serve us.

● The primary reason we've "made it so damn difficult for people to get things done" is ... Ugly Systems.

● We must not shy away from addressing "dreary" systems issues. And the way to address them is through a lens called "beauty."

● Beautiful systems ... reflect and magnify the Basic Brand Proposition.

● Beautiful systems are ... dynamic.

● Beautiful systems ... foster rather than quash innovation.

● Systems are too important to be left to "systems administrators."

⚡ ! RANT

We are not prepared ...

We avoid words like "beauty"—and the concept of beauty—between 9 a.m. and 5 p.m. (Especially if we work in the likes of HR or IS or Logistics.) But as part of the urgent process of re-imagining organizations, we must embrace both the word and the concept—and make beauty the primary attribute not only of *product* design but also of *process* design. In short, we must create an enterprise environment in which enterprise systems are no less than ... Beautiful Systems.

👁 ! VISION

I imagine ...

A Policy Manual ... in HR or IS or Finance ... that is one page long.

A hospital's patient consent form or a title insurance policy written in ... Plain English.

A plane that flies directly from someplace I'm leaving to someplace I'm going ... without going through a "hub."

A website where I can complete a transaction in 90 seconds.

Beauty ...

The Napkin: Today, you'll find a replica of it on a wall at company headquarters in Dallas. (Quite possibly, for the sake of veracity, it's stained with Wild Turkey—the founder's favorite.) On the original napkin, which Herb Kelleher and colleague Rollin King sketched out at a bar in San Antonio in 1966, you'll observe a simple triangle. At the three corners you'll find ... San Antonio ... Houston ... Dallas. And from that *beautiful* triangle has emerged nothing less than Earth's Best Airline. Namely, of course, Southwest.

The absolute, gorgeous simplicity that marked the original napkin sketch-route design has subsequently been applied to every activity Southwest undertakes. The airline's exceptionally low cost structure is, overall, a direct reflection of the approach initiated on that historic napkin.

Herb's napkin was ... beautiful.

And Southwest Airlines is a ... beautiful system.

The Thesis: The paper got a C grade. In 1965, the idea outlined therein seemed silly: You're in a hurry to send a package from Manhattan to Newark. Got to get it there. Absolutely, positively gotta get it there. The obvious solution: Send it via Memphis! In that thesis, which barely earned passing marks for Fred Smith at Yale, lay the origins of Smith's hub-and-spoke concept—a concept that changed package delivery. Indeed, the company that grew out of his thesis has changed life itself, for a lot of us. Namely, of course, Federal Express.

Fred's thesis was ... beautiful.

And Federal Express is a ... beautiful system.

... And the Beast

I'm willing to bet a pretty penny that in the halls of business, when the talk turns to "systems," one seldom hears terms such as "beauty," "aesthetic virtue," "grace," and a dozen other words of that ilk.

When we think about "systems" or "processes," we think about nuts and bolts—the dirty engineering details—that go into creating something that will "get the job done." We think in terms of "efficiency," not "elegance."

And yet most of the trouble businesses get into—in serving their customers and in general getting things done with dispatch—is directly attributable to the *ugliness* of their systems and processes. Over time, even a beautiful system tends to get elaborated and elaborated ... and then more elaborated ... with every change. Each one made, of course, for a "good reason." Until the whole ugly, sloppy, inefficient, demoralizing, dehumanizing mess makes everybody unhappy. We end up "serving the system" rather than having the system serve us.

The Real Obesity Epidemic

Think "systems," and ordinarily what comes to mind is Obese Manuals ... thousands of pages of fine print ... lining the walls of every department in public and private enterprise. Or Obese Files[1] ... paper or electronic ... adding up to thousands upon thousands of reasons not to act ... or to delay action ... on any and every initiative.

Obese Systems are Enemy No. 1 of Change and Agility. And they are Ally No. 1 of Osama bin Laden (in the realm of national security) ... and of upstart commercial rivals (in the realm of business competition).

Hence we must not shy away from addressing "dreary" systems issues. We must understand their strategic significance and confront them squarely if change—nay, revolution—is our goal. And I believe that the best way to confront them is through a lens called "design" ... which is to say, through a lens called "beauty."

More Than Skin-Deep

"Design," I argued in the previous chapter, goes far beyond the beauty of (say) an iMAC. Or the compelling nature of Target's logo—and compellingly designed items found in its stores. (Though, at both Apple and Target, design fanaticism per se has been worth billions of dollars in market capitalization.)

One arena where design matters most—and is least considered—is in the creation of essential enterprise systems. Indeed, systems of all sorts.

The easy way to talk about this issue would be to say that "design" involves how a thing looks, and that "system" pertains to how a thing works. But that misses the point, which is that "design thinking" and "system thinking" are one and the same. Or should be—no, must be, if we are to make a go of it in the "solutions"-"experiences"-"customer successes" business. In great design, form and function come together in a way that appears seamless, and every part contributes to the whole in a way that seems ... inevitable. So, too, in a great system that allows us to proffer a great solution or experience[2] to our clientele. Hence this term that I've coined: *Beautiful Systems*.

Monster Mash

Years ago, as a McKinsey consultant, a colleague and I developed what we called an "anthropological systems analysis."

Systems are typically invented when problems arise. There's a screw-up with a

LIVING OFF THE FAT OF THE LAW

[1]This gradual larding-up of rules and regulations played a big role in the accounting debacles that humbled the business world in 2002.

Here's legendary Citicorp chairman Walter Wriston, writing in a *Wall Street Journal* article titled "The Solution to Scandals? Simpler Rules": "The Financial Accounting Standards Board has, at last count, enshrined generally accepted accounting principles into three volumes comprising some 4,530 pages. Some of the FASB rules run to over 700 pages on how to book a single transaction. It should surprise no one that two skilled accountants, looking at the booking of the same transaction and using their knowledge of the same rules, come out with different results.

"Many years ago, James Madison foresaw the problem and wrote in 'The Federalist Papers': 'It will be of little avail to the people that laws are made by men of their choice, if the laws be so voluminous that they cannot be read, or so incoherent that they cannot be understood ... that no man who knows what the law is today can guess what it will be tomorrow.' It can be argued that we have now arrived at that point in the accounting profession."

BRAND = SYSTEM

[2]I once heard Jesper Kunde, the Danish marketing star, argue that *all* systems *must* be clearly and unequivocally "brand-driven."

That is a stunning insight. Every HR Director, for example, should ask: Are my processes and policies ... Aesthetically Aligned ... with the Corporate Brand Promise?

The Brand Promise defines us. Indeed ... Brand Potency = Alignment between Brand Promise and Enterprise Systems.

For more on Branding, see Chapter 12.

customer's order. We devise a "system" to make sure it doesn't happen again.

Great!

Smart!

Jane Doe was the head of Customer Service when that system was concocted. After three years she was promoted and followed by **Arthur Doe** (no relation). During Arthur's watch, another Bad Problem quickly cropped up.

What did Art do? He added "stuff" to Jane's system. You can guess the rest of the story: Arthur Doe was succeeded by **Cathy Doe** (no relation), who was followed by **Miriam Doe** (no relation), who was followed by **Richard Doe** (no relation).

Each of the Assiduous Does put their Stamp on the System. And, before you could say "John Doe," the system was so elaborated that it (1) required an Army to administer and (2) left no room whatsoever for front-line initiative.

The Does, all well-intentioned ("Fiximus Problemi Daminatus," or "Fix the Damn Problem" is on the ancient family shield), had inadvertently created a monster. A *complex* monster. An *ugly* monster. An ugly *system*. A system that ever-so-effectively saps enterprise vitality and turns front-line operatives into anonymous John Does.

KISS and Tell

"Beautiful systems" are simple. Allow me to illustrate that "simple" point with a story:

The book/booklet came to me with a note asking for a blurb of endorsement. I tossed it aside. (Alas, I often do that.) But it happened that my wife was in the process of starting a business. And she wanted to put together a compelling business plan.

I vaguely remembered the book. Author: Jim Horan. Title: *The One Page Business Plan*. What a silly idea, the engineer-MBA within me thought. What an interesting idea, the design freak within me thought.

So I took a look. And became fascinated. On a single page,[3] Mr. Horan claimed, we could travel all the way from over-arching vision to tactical details of execution.

Again: An absurd idea at face value. (Like Mr. Smith's silly thesis—with Memphis as the Center of the Logistical Universe.)

But, what the hell, why not give it a try?

Trust me ... Mr. Horan was the devil's consultant. Putting together a 70-page business plan—replete with charts and graphs and spreadsheets—is a walk in the park. Getting it all right—exactly right—on a single page. Whoa!

She/we labored and labored ... and labored some more. Days and days went by. And I'm here to testify: It was *damn well worth it!* The results were ... *beautiful.*

TALK ABOUT "BRIEF"!

[3] A little dirty laundry ...

John De Laney is counsel at International Creative Management, the agency that handled negotiations on my contract for this book. At one point in that process, I got very frustrated, and said to my agent, "What's going on here?"

About an hour later, I got a one-third-page email from John, outlining in Plain English the serious issues. As we progressed, I received more communications from him—none of them longer than one-third of a page.

I've worked with a host of lawyers over the years. Trust me, boiling *up* is their hallmark. John was the first Lawyer-as-Boiler-Way-Down I've ever dealt with.

Hence the Law of John D: Anything Truly Important Can Be Summarized and Clarified in One-Third of a Page.

That one-page business plan *idea* is beautiful, too.

It's never too late to learn (or relearn) that old bit of sales-and-marketing wisdom: "Keep it simple, stupid."

Or KISS, for short.

System Overload

The magnitude of potential simplification is ... staggering.

Jim Champy, co-author along with Michael Hammer of the Bible on reengineering (titled *Reengineering the Corporation*), keeps executive audiences enthralled as he recounts tale after tale after horrid tale of critical business processes gone to flab. Consider a process for verifying an insurance claim. It takes 23 *working days*. Yet when Champy looks inside with an electron microscope, he discovers that, literally, 17 *minutes* of actual work are performed. The rest is all about scraps of paper flying (crawling is more like it) from here to there. Sitting on desks. Unnecessary complications[4] to forms to be filled out. And initialed. And initialed some more. And so on. And ... on.

Yes, it is that bad.

23 days.

17 minutes.

Too Many ~~Cooks~~ Engineers

Gordon Bell is, among many other things, the developer of the fabled VAX operating system, which revolutionized the minicomputer industry at Digital Equipment. Several years ago I listened to one of Gordon's presentations, and we chatted afterward. He waxed particularly eloquent about this simplicity business—and the degree to which bureaucracies run amok. "I've never seen a project being worked on by 500 engineers," Bell flatly stated, "that couldn't be done better by 50."

Think about the enormity of that statement. (Beginning with Mr. B's Olympian Credibility.) The idea is not to introduce a "touch of efficiency" (Kaizen rules!)—and shave the 500-person engineering/design team to 462. (No small saving!) The idea Bell, and others like him I've come across, suggests is a 90 percent cut ... from 500 to 50.

Charles Wang, the brilliant and crusty founder of Computer Associates, has always been the software industry's resident contrarian. He and Bell emerged, it would appear, from the same peapod. Wang Reasoning: Is a project team behind schedule? What do you do? Double the amount assets (people)? No, not in the The-World-According-to-Wang. Project team behind schedule? Wang says: Identify the least productive 25

BIG PHARMA'S LITTLE HELPER

[4]Case in point: the pharmaceutical industry.

The requirements for patient safety that are placed upon it are appropriately stringent. Of that I have no doubt. Nonetheless, the "systems" for drug discovery that giant pharma has created are ... wildly over the top. That is: convoluted, sluggish, actually absurd.

And that is one of the main reasons that giant pharma has created so many alliances with relatively small biotech companies. The biotech companies can attract more interesting talent, to be sure. But, far more important, they haven't had time to develop systems that are so elaborated that they make it virtually impossible to get anything done!

percent of the folks on the team ... and eliminate them.

Wang Rule: No job being done sloppily and slowly by 30 people can't be done better by the Best 23. (Gordon B. might well say the Best Three.)

Systems: Can't Live with 'Em, Can't Live Without 'Em

I am *not* an anarchist.

The world is a complicated place. Damn complicated if you're ExxonMobil. And pretty damn complicated if you're running a 26-table Mexican restaurant in El Paso, Texas. Thence, we must have systems. *Must have them.* Period.

But as we must *have* them, we must also hate them.

Systems: Must have. Must hate. Must design. Must un-design.

And that's *the* secret.

There's another secret. The Big One: There is no evil!

That's the problem. (Remember the ubiquitous well-intended Does.)

Help Wanted: EVP (SOUB)

The only answer to The Big Systems Conundrum: MAKE PERPETUAL WAR ON THE VERY (LIFE-SUSTAINING) SYSTEMS THAT WE HAVE CREATED.

I worked with one growth company's management team. Trying (desperately) to stay "entrepreneurial." Trying (desperately) to acknowledge the complexities that attend growth. The upshot of our labors was to add an executive position with an intriguing name. (Their idea, not mine.) Said name: EVP/SOUB.

Figure it out yet? *Executive Vice President/Stomping Out Unnecessary Bullshit.*

I am *not* flipping off the real world. I want a *brilliant* systems designer sitting in Room 103. And right across the hall, in R104, I want his equally powerful peer, the de facto or de jure EVP/SOUB. I want one of them working 19-hours-a-day to deal with problems, to get the system/s "right." And I want the other working 19.1-hours-a-day to unwind the stultifying thing ... just as it's being built!

TAKE A DEEP BREATH

Is the respiratory system central to "effective bodily functioning"?
> Of course!
> > **Is an "organizational system" the enterprise equivalent of a respiratory system?**
> > Of course!
> > **Is the respiratory system worth "getting worked up about"?**
> > Of course!
> > **Is a mere organizational system worth "getting worked up about"?**
> > Of course!
> > Q.E.D.

VOTE OF INCOMPETENCE
[5]A form is never *just* a form.
> Consider the role that form design played in the U.S. presidential-election "system" in 2000. A poorly designed paper ballot in Palm Beach County, Florida, may have cost Al Gore the White House.
> Think about it.

Beautiful Systems:
Been there, Dung that

Garth Thompson, the guide who took my family and me on safari in Zimbabwe in 2001, is one of the world's leading experts on elephants. Through his tutelage I came to revere those extraordinary creatures. Yet it was the ... termites ... that mesmerized me. These talented creatures routinely build mounds 20 or 30 feet high. (That's about 3,000X the termite's height; the tallest man-made structure is about 300X our height—talk about excellence in structural engineering!)

But here's what really got me in a tizzy:

Elephants have inefficient digestive systems. What's perhaps bad news for an elephant is good news for termites. As a result of such digestive failure, elephant dung is loaded with nutritious goodies. And then the story begins.

Let's say a termite construction site (a mound-to-be) is 200 yards from an elephant watering hole, where dung is plentiful. The termites' "GPS" somehow locks on to the dung warehouse, and the creatures then proceed with a precision-guided underground assault. But they don't leave their mound empty-mouthed; each lugs a monstrously large grain or two of sand or soil. Soon our raiders pop up under the dung site and extract succulent morsels that the elephant had grabbed from a tree 25 feet above ground. In place of the extracted food parcel, the termites deposit their grains of soil or sand.

I go to the watering hole and am awestruck by the Termite Skyscraper. Then Garth Thompson orders me to pick up an old piece of elephant "dung." I reluctantly do so—it damn well looks like shit to me—and I'm in for a shock. The "dung" turns out to be 100 percent sand or soil!

Yes, I *was* mesmerized. And, ever unable to put my passion for management aside, I said to no one in particular, "Now *there* is a ... Truly Beautiful System." Beauty ... Clarity ... Grace ... Efficiency ... Elegance ... WOW ... all-in-one. Now if only *our* enterprise systems could match such design excellence!

Beauty Contest

I pray that this brief screed has introduced you to the idea: BEAUTIFUL SYSTEMS. It's an important *strategic* addition to the overall experience-design notion that is central to my Core Argument.

Now I'd like to offer up a tested starting point. Namely: a Beauty Contest! Here's the gorgeous drill:

1. Select a single form[5] or document: invoice, airbill, sick leave policy, customer returns claim form.

2. Rate the selected document on a scale of 1 to 10 [1 = Pitiful. 10 = Work of Art] on four dimensions:

simplicity   clarity   grace   beauty

3. Reinvent the document in the next 15 working days, using the criteria in Step 2.

4. Repeat, with a new selection, once per month. Forever. Why shouldn't an invoice be a ... Work of Art? (After all, it's an important point-of-contact with a customer!)

Why shouldn't a sick-leave policy be a Work of Art? (Given the importance of attracting the Best Talent, one would hope that an HR Manual would be as compelling in its presentation as a fabulous novel, albeit slightly less fictional.)

Four words: Simplicity. Clarity. Grace. Beauty.

Why shouldn't any and all financial documents—any and all policy documents—be judged by that (specific) set of criteria? Why, in short, shouldn't any and all company documents be ... Beautiful?

Final Word: All Systems Go

Ah, words. (Again.) As I see it, enterprise is all too short on *simplicity, clarity, grace,* and *beauty.* And the near-absence of those traits results more or less directly from the near-absence of those words from the language of business.

Here's the lesson I've learned: If you start talking about "beauty"—obsessing on "beauty"—then "beauty" will become a commonplace part of your everyday affairs! So, too, grace. So, too, clarity. So, too, simplicity.

In our "real lives" (as opposed to our "business lives"), we are "out-of-the-closet"

CHAPTER AND VERSE
Poets. Poets. Poets.

That's the meta-message of this chapter: We need fewer techies and more poets in our systems design shop. And more artists ... and more jazz musicians ... and more dancers ...

Period.

(Or, rather, consider that an action item.)

GAMING THE SYSTEM
Years ago, Wal*Mart introduced an employee contest, replete with awards and prizes of all sorts. The idea was that everyone in the company should identify the "stupidest thing we do around here."

Frankly, I think it's better than a "suggestion" system. Suggestion systems usually end up *adding* more stuff ... more grunge. But this program focused on *subtraction.*

Message: *Addition* is the exercise of fools. *Subtraction* is the exercise of genius.

(Not a new idea. The greatest sculptors have hewed to the same path. How do you create a brilliant sculpture of X? You take a gorgeous piece of stone and then remove everything that's not X.)

{ } **SYSTEMS: A SUMMARY**
Systems matter.
Systems grow, essentially untended, like Topsy.
Systems, however well-intentioned, will eventually impede innovation and thwart progress.
Systems are too important to be left to "systems administrators."
Systems must be the concern of CEOs.
Systems can ... FOSTER CHANGE.
Systems can ... FOSTER INNOVATION.
Systems can ... BE CLEAR.
Systems can ... BE SIMPLE.
Systems can ... BE GRACEFUL.
Systems can ... BE BEAUTIFUL.

fans of simplicity, clarity, grace, and beauty. In a work of art. In a Michael Jordan dance down the basketball court. Whatever.

So why not apply the very same criteria to a purchasing procedure? A training course? A recruiting process? An evaluation scheme? And so on. (And so on. And so on.)

Systems ...

Love 'em.

Hate 'em.

Design 'em.

Un-design 'em.

Make 'em simple.

Make 'em clear.

Make 'em graceful.

Make 'em beautiful.

! Contrasts

WAS		IS
More	–	Less
Efficient	–	Elegant
Off-putting	–	Welcoming
Slapped together	–	Organically whole
Impedes communication	–	Spurs communication
Closed	–	Open
"Let the techies handle it"	–	"Bring in design-driven leaders"
Complex	–	Simple
Obscure	–	Clear
Awkward	–	Graceful
Ugly	–	Beautiful

12

THE ULTIMATE VALUE PROPOSITION: THE HEART OF BRANDING

! Technicolor Rules ...

- Branding is so bloody obvious. When one has an "identity" ... life gets a lot simpler.
- *BRANDING IS SIMPLE. BRANDING IS IMPOSSIBLE.*
- "Success means never letting the competition define you. Instead, you have to define yourself based on a point of view you care deeply about."
- "A brand reaches out with a powerful connecting experience. It's an emotional connection point that transcends the product. ... A great brand is a story that's never completely told."
- Branding is ultimately about nothing more (and nothing less) than heart. It's about passion ... what you care about. It's about what's inside—what's inside you, what's inside your company.

! RANT

We are not prepared ...

We acknowledge the unique power and value of "effective branding" in our ever more ethereal economy. And yet it remains the rare institution that truly grasps what it means to be Totally Brand Driven. That must change. Now.

We consider branding as the provenance of giant corporations. Instead we must understand that the branding idea applies as much to the one-person accountancy, or six-person training department, or six-person project team as to Coke or Pepsi. Branding is the hard-earned Certification of True & Cool Distinction within the organization's sphere of influence, enormous or minuscule.

We persist in seeing a "brand" as the "external image" of a company, or of a product or service. Instead, we must learn that branding goes straight to the heart (and comes straight from the heart) of an enterprise. Bottom Line: Effective Branding is in fact more INTERNAL than EXTERNAL.

! VISION

I imagine ...

A 22-person Training "Department" (PSF!) imbedded in a 700-person Division of Big Co. It is known as the Best-in-Industry at Sales Training. This "inconsequential" training department offers courses Globally, via the Web, and becomes a No-bull Profit Center and Source of Corporate Recognition—perhaps even the tail that wags much of the divisional dog. I.e.: "Mere" Department = Potent Brand.

Tea Time!

When it comes to branding, my friends Ron Rubin and Stuart Avery Gold get it! They are the head honchos of the Republic of Tea. In their wonderful book, *success@life*, Ron and Stuart write: "As Ministers of the Republic of Tea, our not-so-covert mission is to carry out a Tea Revolution."

I love that.

Simply love it!

(How great!)

(Don't you wish they were your Big Bosses?)

"Our free and open immigration policies," the R of T duo continue, *"welcome all who wish to flee the tyranny of coffee crazed lives and escape the frazzled fast paced race-to-stay-in-one-place existence that it fuels. In our tiny land, we have come to learn that coffee is about speeding up and losing sight, while tea is about slowing down and taking a look. Because tea is not just a beverage, it is a consciousness altering substance that allows for a way of getting in touch with and taking pleasure from the beauty and the wonder that life has to offer."*

You might find all that to be a wheelbarrow load of crap. (I don't.) (I think instead of wheelbarrows filled with gold.)

My point: "All of that" gets at ... the Heart of Branding. The Essence of the Brand Promise. Something that you ... *Care About*. Something that ... *Matters*. Something that you will ... *Stand For*. Something that, perhaps, *270 people who work for you will care about*. (And wouldn't that be ever-so-delightful?)

Identity Crisis

"The increasing difficulty in differentiating between products and the speed with which competitors take up innovations," write New Zealand marketers Gillian Law and Nick Grant, "will assist in the rise and rise of the brand."

"Products from the major competing companies around the world will become increasingly similar," Wally Olins writes in *Corporate Identity*. "Inevitably, this means that the whole of the company's personality, its identity, will become the most significant factor in making a choice between one company and its products and another."

Yes. Branding is more important than ever. There are "brilliant" product or service offerings in almost any category you can name. But while being brilliant (effective stuff at a competitive price) is incredibly important—it's now a starting point, not the end game.

What's the point?

What's the purpose?

> **BRANSON ON BRANDING**
> Virgin Group Founder and Brand Maestro Extraordinaire Richard Branson: "The idea that business is strictly a numbers affair has always struck me as preposterous. For one thing, I've never been particularly good at numbers, but I think I've done a reasonable job with feelings. And I'm convinced that it is feelings—and feelings alone—that account for the success of the Virgin brand in all of its myriad forms."
>
> (And "myriad" is precisely the right word. In a business world where "conglomerate" has rightfully become a maligned term, Branson has performed his Bright Red Virgin Magic in everything from air travel to financial services to music retailing. An exceptional story. Based on an unadorned love affair with Love & Branding & Red.)

What ... at heart ... are you made of?

That—and that alone—is what Branding is all about. Branding is ... so bloody obvious to me. When one has an "inspiring" "identity" ... life gets a whole lot simpler. The problem is ... an Identity that Inspires ... is insanely hard to inculcate ... and insanely hard to maintain. But the rewards for getting it right—just ask the folks at Nike or Starbucks or Coke or The Body Shop or Virgin or Harley—can be worth billions, if not hundreds of billions, of $$$ in Market Capitalization. Plus the pride of knowing that what you're doing has Meaning & Recognition.

Frequently Un-Asked Questions

Branding. I believe in it.

Insanely.

I believe in "branding"—for myself. As an individual. As a small company owner.

I believe in branding—for you. As a Junior Staffer in the Purchasing Department of Giant Co. Or as a ("mere") waiter in a family-style restaurant ... or as the chief housekeeper in an 800-room hotel.

I'm befuddled by branding. (It's confusing.) I'm impressed by it. (It's powerful.) I'm turned on by it. (It's fun.) Most of all, I care about it. (It ... Matters.)

Branding is simple.

Branding is impossible.

Branding is *not* about marketing tricks. It is about answering a few simple (and yet impossible) questions:

WHO *ARE* YOU?

WHY ARE YOU HERE?

HOW ARE YOU *UNIQUE*?

HOW CAN YOU MAKE A *DRAMATIC DIFFERENCE*?

And ... most important ... WHO *CARES*? (DO *YOU* CARE?) (Starting Point.)

Who *Are* You? (I Really Wanna Know)

The top management of a Giant American Company invited me to speak with them. They had experienced a couple of decades of exceptional growth, and it seemed to be

BRAND VALUE: WHEN IT RAINS, IT POURS
Tom Asacker, marketing guru: "Salt is salt is salt. Right? Not when it comes in a blue box with a picture of a little girl carrying an umbrella. Morton International continues to dominate the U.S. salt market, even though it charges more for a product that is demonstrably the same as many other products on the shelf."

THAT'S THE SPIRIT
This chapter is not a "guide to branding." Others have already done that much better than I could. (See, for example, *A New Brand World*, by Scott Bedbury—mentioned below.)
This chapter is a Screed about the Spirit of Branding. The Heart & Soul of Branding. The Fire-in-the-Belly of Branding. Frankly, I think there are too many "guides" in the ever-expanding world of business books and not enough tracts on ... Matters of Spirit.

NEW BUSINESS ▬ ● NEW BRAND

slowing. Employee morale, surveys showed, was slipping a bit, resulting in higher than usual turnover. Their formerly awesome customer service ratings were a bit wobbly. No, the world hadn't come to an end, but it was suddenly (to them) "uncertain." And talented, brass-knuckled competition with an investment cache to die for made the issue even more worrisome and urgent.

I studied like hell. Talked to customers. Talked to vendors. Talked to front-line employees. I had but three hours to spend with the Top 50, and my pride and professionalism insisted that I make each moment count. The first half was to be a presentation; I'd parade my "insightful" PowerPoint slides for 90 minutes. Then we'd talk for the second half of the "show."

As usual, I was suffering from pre-presentation insomnia. It was 4 a.m. The speech would begin at 7 a.m. And, yes, I had those slides ready ... 127 of them. (Exactly.) I thought. And fretted. And then I did something strange: I deleted 126 of the 127 slides. Just one remained. It read:

"WHO ARE YOU [These Days]?"

The company had made several acquisitions in the last half-dozen years. Though I'm a publicly avowed enemy of most big acquisitions, I had no complaint with what this firm had done; each purchase had filled a gaping hole in its portfolio, relative to its most powerful competitors. But somewhere ... somehow ... the firm's True Identity seemed to have slithered away, deep into the bushes. So I said: "You can have your fee back[1] if you want, but we're going to spend the entire three hours talking about 'WHO ARE YOU?'"

Mission Control: Why Are You Here?

"You can't just go on forever floating on the tide these days," writes Danish marketing expert Jesper Kunde, "monitoring the competition and conducting surveys to find out what your customers want right now. What do you want? *What do you want to tell the world in the future? What does your company have that will enrich the world?* You must believe in that. Believe so strongly enough to be *unique* at what you do."

There's more.

"Some companies," Mr. Kunde adds, "equate branding with marketing. Design a sparkling new logo, run an exciting new marketing campaign, and voilà—you are back on course. They are wrong. The task is bigger, much bigger. It is about the company fulfilling its potential, not about a new logo.

"WHAT IS MY MISSION IN LIFE? WHAT DO I WANT TO CONVEY TO PEOPLE? AND HOW DO I MAKE SURE THAT WHAT I HAVE TO OFFER THE WORLD IS ACTUALLY

THE "COME BACK" KID

[1] By the way, my nervy approach worked out brilliantly. The CEO, whom I know well, told me later that this was perhaps the best morning his management team had spent: "Nobody, Tom, has basically told us that we're full of shit—and don't know who we are. Well done. We might even invite you back."

Postscript: They did.

Post-Postscript: Whew.

(We all survive courtesy repeat business.)

UNIQUE? THE BRAND HAS TO GIVE OF ITSELF, THE COMPANY HAS TO GIVE OF ITSELF, AND MANAGEMENT HAS TO GIVE OF ITSELF. ... TO PUT IT BLUNTLY, IT IS A MATTER OF WHETHER [OR NOT] YOU WANT TO BE UNIQUE NOW."

I think that's brilliant.

Branding: It's about meaning, not marketing ... about deep company logic, not fancy new logos.[2]

The Best—or Bust: How Are You Unique?

UNIQUE. There is no bigger word. None.

Unique means ... SINGULAR. RIGHT? (And ... PERIOD.)

"Success," says Tom Chappell, founder of the personal care products company Tom's of Maine, *"means never letting the competition define you. Instead, you have to define yourself based on a point of view you care deeply about."*

Brilliant.

But even Tom can be upstaged. By ... *the man*... the late Jerry Garcia of the Grateful Dead: *"You do not merely want to be considered the best of the best. You want to be considered the only ones who do what you do."*

And the Grateful Dead were precisely that. They changed the world. (I am a fan, by the way. Not a Deadhead, but a sympathizer ... to be sure.)

If not *unique* ... WHY BOTHER?[3]

It's the Law: How Can You Make a Dramatic Difference?

Doug Hall is an "idea guru." *The* idea guru (according to a 2001 *Inc.* magazine cover story). A former P&G marketer, and now overseer of Eureka Ranch, he has guided big corporation team after big corporation team to stunning new product breakthroughs. Now focused on translating those ideas to the world of small business, Doug has written a wonderful and meticulously researched book, *Jump Start Your Business Brain.* (In a foreword to the book, I called it ... SUPERCALIFRAGILISTICEXPIALIDOCIOUS.

GREEN MEANS (LO)GO

[2]I agree with Jesper Kunde about the limits of logo fixation. And yet ...

In some cases, a New Logo can make a ... Dramatic Difference. I think British Petroleum is one such case.

BP is re-imagining itself, establishing a Dramatic Difference within its industry (and irritating many of its competitors in the process) by Going Green. While many are justifiably skeptical of this move, I believe that this Green Thing is very real, and very potent.

One part of this effort is the introduction of an absolutely stunning new logo. I am struck by how I am struck by the logo as I drive down a street or a highway.

Nice! (And good luck!)

(DON'T) FOLLOW THE MONEY

[3]It's surprisingly easy to move from the world of the Grateful Dead to ... Polly Hill Arboretum on Martha's Vineyard. Stephen Spongberg, who runs this magnificent facility, says, "We're not going to be driven by where we think a funding agency would like to see us go. We're going to build our case about what's important to us ... and then find a funding organization that agrees with us."

What he is saying, in other words, is that he is very ... VERY ... clear that he knows the answer to: HOW ARE YOU UNIQUE?

Reason: It uses a ton of "hard data" to support a slew of brilliant "soft" ideas.)

At the book's heart are three "laws" of "marketing physics."

Law #1: Overt Benefit. What is the product or service's *"One Great Thing"*? (One or two "great things" is far better than three or more "great things." When you get to three or more ... you just confuse the consumer. A ton of hard data support the point.)

Law #2: Real Reason to Believe. Does the organization Really and Consistently Deliver that "One Great Thing"?

Law #3: DRAMATIC DIFFERENCE.

The Hard Data Scream: *Dramatic Difference in a product or service offering makes a very Dramatic Difference in Top- and Bottom-line Success.* Alas, Hall reports, damn few (Very Damn Few!) execs get it.

Consider: A few hundred consumers are asked to evaluate a potential new product or service. They confront two questions: "How likely are you to *purchase* this new product or service?" and "How *unique* is this new product or service?"

The consumers' responses to those questions are intriguing—but not nearly as intriguing as the way the company's top executives then responded to the survey.

Execs—*no exceptions in 20 years, per Mr. Hall!*—give 95 percent to 100 percent weighting to results from the "intent to purchase" question, and a 0 percent to 5 percent weighting to the "uniqueness" consideration.

Fact: THEY GET IT ASS-BACKWARDS.

Trust the data. The predictor of future success, relative to the questions posed, is ... UNIQUENESS. (Or: DRAMATIC DIFFERENCE.) Not "intent." Because ...

UNIQUENESS = THE EMOTIONAL CONNECTION.

Who Cares? (You'd Better Care!)

When Bob Waterman and I penned *In Search of Excellence*, the received dogma of the time had reduced "management" to a dry, by-the-numbers exercise. Bob and I roamed the nation, looking at companies that worked, and we saw something else. What we saw was "soft," by the Harvard Business School standard. It had to do with people & engagement in work & love of quality & entrepreneurial instinct & values worth going to the mat for. *The "surprising" (circa 1982) Waterman-Peters Mantra:*

SOFT IS HARD.
HARD IS SOFT.

In other words: It's the "numbers" stuff that's abstract and lifeless. *(Hard Is Soft.)* It's the "people" and "passion" stuff that moves mountains. *(Soft Is Hard.)*

To our delight (and surprise), the world took note—not because of our scintillating

---

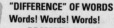

"DIFFERENCE" OF WORDS
Words! Words! Words!
  DRAMATIC DIFFERENCE.
  Add that pair to your "Tom's Word Pile."
  "Dramatic" is a hot word. A ... Big Word. So, too, "Difference."
  (Hey: Tell me about your current project: Is it ... DRAMATICALLY DIFFERENT?)
  (DAMN IT.)

prose, but because the competitive situation demanded it. Our "wild stuff" has now become commonplace:

Engage your folks.

Make things that are cool and that work.

Stick your neck out.

This is all a long-winded way of saying that ... PASSION (aka EMOTION, aka CARING, aka DRAMATIC DIFFERENCE) ... has finally become recognized as *the* Staple of *Successful* Business. Not a poor second cousin to the "quant stuff" that business schools still thrive on. Not an "option."

Verb Power: Go Where the Action Is

TBWA/Chiat/Day CEO Jean-Marie Dru is the most provocative marketer I've run across in recent times. His recent books—*Disruption* and *Beyond Disruption*—are among the best business books I've read in many a year. Jean-Marie makes this extraordinary point:

"Apple opposes, IBM solves, Nike exhorts, Virgin enlightens, Sony dreams, Benetton protests. ... Brands are not nouns but verbs."

I admit it. I'm absolutely enamored of JMD's idea. *It's driving me batty.* I don't know exactly what to do with it. But I know that I need to do ... *something important* ... with it. (Dru's idea, by the way, ties brilliantly into the "experience" stuff and the "dream" stuff I talked about earlier.)

Again, I am trying to provide a *feeling* here. (Beyond "programs" redux. Eh?) The short and simple question: *What is your verb?* What *verb* describes the (Unique/Dramatically Different) "thing" you're doing (verb) in your ... Training Department ... Logistics Department ... Purchasing Department ... Finance Department ... New Product Development Department ... Engineering Department ... IS Department ... 18-table restaurant ... four-person professional financial advisory firm?

To the quantitative bigots, this reeks of fluff. To me (a Reformed Quantitative-ist), it sounds like the Billion-Dollar Question.

A Promise Is ... The Premise

I frequently take my clients through a little drill. I call it the "Brand Promise Exercise." It goes like this:

1. *WHO ARE WE?* (a) Write a two-page Short Story about ... Who We Are. (With a Scintillating Plot Line.) (b) Now boil it down to one page; better yet, capture it as a Poem or Song. (Yes, including the Brand Promise Song of the Finance Department!) (c) Reduce it to 25 words. (Or perhaps 10.) (Or 5.) (Or a verb.)

WORTH THE BOTHER

Jesper Kunde provides this report of an exchange with a client from an ostensibly "mundane" business:

> *Client:* "But we're nothing like Nike! We sell paper clips, notch grinders and 9mm bolts. Who can be bothered?"

> *Jesper Kunde:* "The whole world can be bothered ... if you brand them well. Nike does not actually sell shoes. Nike sells the *experience* of using Nikes, the feeling of being a winner, and they condense the whole message into the three words: *Just Do It!* ... It is a question of being the only one, of offering your market something unique."

2. *THREE WAYS.* List Three Ways in which we are ... UNIQUE to our clients.

3. *DRAMATIC DIFFERENCE.* State ... Precisely ... the ... One Great & Dramatic Thing ... that distinguishes us from our competitors. In 25 words. (Or less.) (Much less.)

4. *WHO ARE "THEY"?* (a) Explain who each Major Competitor is. In 25 powerful, precise, flattering ... and truthful ... words. (Or less.) (b) List Three Extremely Distinct "Us" vs. "Them" differences. (No bull here. No cutting corners.)

5. *TRY IT ON TEAMMATES.* Test the "results" of all this on our teammates. Talk about it. Argue about it. SCREAM ABOUT IT. Seriously. At length.

6. *TRY IT ON CLIENTS.* (a) Test the results on a Friendly Client. (b) Test them on a Skeptical Client.

7. *TRY IT ON ... EVERYONE ELSE.* Try the results on a cross-section of Checkout & Stock Clerks (just for starters).

BRAND CALISTHENICS: MARK MY (AND YOUR) WORDS

There are dozens of ways to improve your branding muscle tone.

Danish marketing phenom Jesper Kunde has the people who work for him write an essay on *"Who we are."*

I like that. (An "essay" goes ... beyond "programs.")

In my case, the *discipline* of branding became real when I decided to write "Bookmarks" for a series of publications I recently produced. I thought it was a great idea. That is, I thought so ... until I sat down to write the copy for these things. I had about 15 words to summarize ... WHO I WAS, AND WHAT I HAD BEEN DOING FOR THE LAST 30 YEARS, AND WHY IT OUGHT TO MATTER TO HUNDREDS OF THOUSANDS OF READERS.

(Gulp!)

Promises to Keep

I spoke at a seminar for a large financial services company. I listened to the CEO give a fine address. (Truly, it was damn good—and I'm a damn good judge by now.) He laid out a Vision. (And don't forget to capitalize that "V" in Vision!) It made sense. But it was a stretch—which is the point. A big stretch, at that. I spoke immediately after the Big Dude had finished. And I warned ... *and challenged* ... the several hundred people in the room.

I said that the Brand Promise (New Vision) was important. And it made all sorts of

---

EMOTION NOTION: "HEART SHARE"

Swedish professors Kjell Nordström and Jonas Ridderstråle, writing in *Funky Business*: "In the funky village, real competition no longer revolves around market share. We are competing for attention—Mind Share and Heart Share."

EMOTION NOTION: ONLY CONNECT

Scott Bedbury, who played a lead role in the branding of both Nike and Starbucks (Wow!), writes in his marvelous book *A New Brand World*: "A Great Brand taps into emotions. Emotions drive most, if not all, of our decisions. ... A brand reaches out with a powerful connecting experience. It's an emotional connection point that transcends the product. ... A great brand is a story that's never completely told. A brand is a metaphorical story that connects with something very deep—a fundamental appreciation of mythology. ... Stories create the emotional context people need to locate themselves in a larger experience."

sense to me. But I added that unless those-in-the-room Totally Bought In ... then the whole exercise was ... a Crock.

"Does this 'Brand Promise' make sense to *you*?" I asked. *"As Individuals? In your Daily Work? With your Clients? Is it a Genuine, Dramatic, Inspiring Departure from the Past? Does the new 'story line' give you, yes, goose bumps?"* And if not, I said to them, "Please ... PLEASE ... Raise Holy & Unmitigated Hell with the CEO ... and tell him why the products and services that you offer do not add up to the Scintillating (Dramatically Different) Brand Promise Story (New Vision) that he has just laid out."

Maybe I won't be invited back. Maybe I pissed him off. "He" had gone on at length about how the "top team" had "worked hard" on the vision. Top team, shlop team. Who the bloody hell cares? "Visions" only matter ... if the PFC (Private First Class) ... Buys In ... and Will Run into Professional Machine-gun Fire because of his Belief in that Vision-Story-Inspired Brand Promise.

Branding is about the logo. The slogan. The marketing campaign. The advertising (and the advertising budget). But, in the end, branding is about ... CREDIBILITY.

Do the 99.99 percent of your people who Work in the Trenches ... Buy the Act? Do they Live It? (With Vigor.) Do they Convey It? (With Passion.)

BRAND CALISTHENICS: ELEVATOR ... GOING UP!

In the Brand You training that my company offers (see Chapter 19), we find that the most useful exercise is having clients concoct a one-eighth-page Yellow Pages ad ... for *themselves*. Many tell us it's the toughest professional task they remember ever doing. ("Essence of Tom" ... in 25 words!)

Likewise, in our WOW Project training (see Chapter 15), the centerpiece is preparing "The Elevator Speech," a 90-second spiel that you might use to get support for your project ... if you found yourself alone with your Big Boss for a 20-floor ride.

These exercises aim for one thing: CAPTURING THE ESSENCE OF THE BRAND PROMISE & ITS DRAMATIC DIFFERENCE & TOTAL COOLNESS IN A VERY SUCCINCT AND VERY COMPELLING FASHION.

Brand Leadership: An Easy Act to Follow

Branding and "Leadership" are Siamese twins. The Brand Promise is a vibrant, living, changing saga called ... Things We Care About. It requires Passion—the variety of

---

BRAND IDENTIFICATION

Great enterprise leaders take on the "role" (read: the "brand") of their company or product. Thus:

> Steve Jobs is ... Apple.
> Bill Gates is ... Microsoft.
> Larry Ellison is ... Oracle.
> Andy Grove is ... Intel.
> Scott McNealy is ... SunMicrosystems.
> Sam Walton is (was) ... Wal*Mart.
> Richard Branson is ... Virgin Group.
> Anita Roddick is (was) ... The Body Shop.
> Giorgio Armani is ... Armani.
> Charles Schwab is ... Charles Schwab.
> Oprah is ... Oprah.

passion that only Inspired Leaders can project.

Franklin Roosevelt, America's Brand Manager of Dignity and Freedom during the Great Depression ("The only thing we have to fear is fear itself") and World War II ("December 7, a date which will live in infamy"), said, "It is necessary for the President to be the nation's number one actor."

In fact, all of leadership *is* an Act! It's an act called conveying the Brand Promise via demonstrated High Conviction in pursuit of Great Purpose.

That Great Purpose can be Democracy, Peace, and Prosperity; or it can be the provision of the finest Cajun cuisine in New Orleans, the coolest business processes in the mortgage-banking industry, or the Best-Ever Employee Memorial Day Picnic.

In any event, to carry it off, leaders of all descriptions must live and even look the part. As John Peers, CEO of Technology Inc., says, "You can't lead a cavalry charge if you think you look funny on a horse." In fact Roosevelt, no horseman as a result of his bout with polio, was careful never to be seen incapacitated; what we did consistently observe was a supreme air of tenacity and confidence (like Churchill's cigar, Roosevelt's cigarette holder was an Oscar-quality prop) during a time of mortal trial.

However the Oscar goes to Mohandas Gandhi, who dressed brilliantly for the part of non-violent nation-builder and chose his main prop, the humble spinning wheel, with care. Mr. G.: "You must be the change you wish to see in the world."

Brand Leadership: A Great Story to Tell

"Leaders achieve their effectiveness chiefly through the stories they relate. ... In addition to communicating stories, leaders embody those stories," writes Harvard leadership guru Howard Gardner in *Leading Minds: An Anatomy of Leadership*. "Stories have identity. [They are] narratives that help individuals think about and feel who they are, where they come from, and where they are headed. [They] constitute the ... *single* most powerful weapon in the leader's arsenal."

Great leadership is ... Great Storytelling. Churchill. De Gaulle. Lincoln. TR. Reagan.

Great Branding is ... a Great Story. The Coca-Cola saga. The UPS saga. The IBM saga. (And the incredible story you tell *all* your friends about a 4-table San Francisco deli.)

Can you, as a Brand Leader (of a 4- or 4,000-person operation), convey Your Story succinctly? Can you convey-animate it in a Powerful Way? Is it Believable? Exciting? Mind-altering? (Literally.) To employees? To vendors? To customers? To the media? (To your banker?)

Thus, we have ... leadership as *Acting* and leadership as *Storytelling*. But Real Leadership—especially inspired Brand Leadership—is about something more. It's about ... well, I'll just say it: "Leadership is all about ... LOVE."

That's not a "soft" statement. IT IS THE "ULTIMATE" HARD STATEMENT. Leadership

---

EMOTION NOTION: STORY TIME

Rolf Jensen, head of the Copenhagen Institute for Future Studies, writes: "We are in the twilight of a society based on data. As information and intelligence become the domain of computers, society will place new value on the one human ability that can't be automated: emotion. Imagination, myth, ritual—the language of emotion—will affect everything from our purchasing decisions to how well we work with others. ... Companies will thrive on the basis of their stories and myths. Companies will need to understand that their products are less important than their stories."

is all about ... *Winston Churchill & Mohandas Gandhi & Albert Einstein & Martin Luther King & Caesar Chavez & Gloria Steinem & Charles de Gaulle & T. Roosevelt & F. Roosevelt & Thomas Jefferson & John Adams & Alexander Hamilton & Susan B. Anthony.* Passion ... Enthusiasm ... Appetite for Life ... Engagement ... Commitment ... Great Causes and Determination to Make a Difference ... Shared Adventures ... Bizarre Failures ... Growth ... Insatiable Appetite for Change.

That's *the* Gandhi "secret." *The* FDR "secret." Every effective leader's "secret." (Alas, it remains, mostly, a "secret.")

BRAND CALISTHENICS: HAIKU = HIGH COUP
Consider taking a course in creative writing. Business writing is typically stilted and insipid. Keep in mind the Rolf Jensen remark about stories and myths: We need training in story, myth, and metaphysics far more than we do ... another accounting course.

Case in point: I recall the story of a brilliant Japanese exec who devoted his long flights around the world not to working through a briefcase full of memos and financial reports, but to constructing haiku—those miraculous 17-syllable poems. Maybe your next "business" course ought to be on haiku?

Where's the Fire?
I had a troubling conversation with a very senior executive. Someone I know reasonably well. We were talking about a Monstrous Strategic Initiative that his firm was launching. It had to do with little less than redefinition of the enterprise. We talked intensely for an hour and a half. Some of the programs that he mentioned were as exciting as the dickens.

But during those 90 minutes, I "heard" (sensed) virtually no emotion. I thought of meetings that I've had with the likes of Scott McNealy (CEO of Sun Microsystems). Steve Jobs (Apple). Anita Roddick (Body Shop). Mickey Drexler (The Gap). Rich Teerlink (Harley-Davidson). Their language—especially the "subtle" (like a freight train!) body language—wouldn't have been the same. At all. When you spend time with them ... you can ... Feel the Fire.

Sure, branding requires those "programs" and "strategic initiatives"—but it comes from the Gut. From the Heart.

In other words: You Gotta Believe! You Gotta Vibrate!

God, this is hard. (This "soft stuff" is always the "hardest.") It is *so* abstract, *so* ephemeral. When you pull this "brand thing" off, there is a level of engagement that is ... Purely Visceral.

DEAR OLD DATA
Nothing I say here should suggest that you shouldn't do a ton of analysis.

I'm a civil Engineer and an MBA. I understand what it takes to build a Tall Building. I understand "just the facts, ma'am" (in the words of the immortal Sergeant Joe Friday). I understand the need to "know your numbers" ... "know your demographics." I always rely on enough data to re-sink the Titanic.

But, well, all of that misses the point ... and the Passion ... of Branding.

Use the data? Yup!

Rely on the data? Never!

(TO DENY IT IS INSANITY.)

Pure ... Raw ... Emotion. Pure ... Raw ... Commitment ... to do "The Thing" ... because ... it's the "Life Transforming Thing to Do."

(BECAUSE IT IS WHY YOU ARE HERE.)

How do we *instill* this? How do we *hire* for it? How do we *promote* it? How do we *get it into* top management? How do we *keep it alive* from generation to generation?

NEW BUSINESS ● NEW BRAND

Attention Must Be Paid: The Heart of Branding

I hate Dilbert.

I *h-a-t-e* Dilbert. I *laugh* at *Dilbert* ... but I *hate* him ... because the strip exudes ... unabashed cynicism. And I *hate* cynicism. I am 60. I don't have all that many years to go. I would like to make those years count.

I care. Passionately.

And people who don't care ... appall me.

In any walk of life. Street sweeper. Top engineer at Cisco Systems.

I care. I hope you care.

I lived in Silicon Valley for over three decades. There is one guy I take a shine to more than anybody else ... who has inhabited and helped form that Valley of Dramatic Dreams. Steve Jobs. Steve is ... The One Who Really Made the Revolution Happen. His company, Apple, was the engine of all else that has followed. Here is my favorite Steve-ism:

"Let's make a dent in the universe." How sweet that is.

Most of us won't "make a dent in the universe." But ... and every one of us has this ability ... we at least can *try.*

It's simple.

It's impossible.

{ } **BRANDING FROM THE HEART**
Let's review. Branding from the heart ... from the top:
> **REAL Branding is ... Personal.**
> **REAL Branding is about ... Integrity.**
> **REAL Branding is ... Consistency and Freshness.**
> **REAL Branding is ... Memorable.**
> **REAL Branding is a ... Great Story.**
> **REAL Branding ... turns on the Checkout Clerk as much as the consumer.**
> **REAL Branding ... Matters. (To employees, customers, suppliers.)**
> **REAL Branding answers ... WHO ARE WE?**
> **REAL Branding is ... Available to One and All ... Large and Small.**
> **REAL Branding centers on ... Uniqueness & Dramatic Difference.**
> **REAL Branding ... Clarifies One Great Thing.**
> **REAL Branding is about ... Passion & Emotion.**
> **REAL Branding is about ... why We Get Out of Bed in the Morning.**
> **REAL Branding ... can't be faked.**
> **REAL Branding is ... Systemic, 24/7, All-departments, All-hands Affair.**

It demands your attention. Your attention to ...

Who are we?

Why are we here?

How are we unique?

How can we make a Dramatic Difference?

Who cares? (Do we care?)

That is the Heart of Branding. Because Branding is ultimately about nothing more (and nothing less) than *Heart*. It's about Passion ... what you Care About. It's about What's Inside ... what's inside you, what's inside your unit, your company.

There's more to it. (Of course.) But if you "get" this part of BRANDING ... then you've got its ... HEART.

!Contrasts

WAS		IS
Good product	–	Great "buzz"
Reliable	–	Unique
Excellent	–	Memorable
Serves a function	–	Tells a story
Satisfies a need	–	Fulfills a dream
What you see is what you get	–	What you imagine is what you get
Customers own it	–	Customers use it to shape their identities
"Damn good food"	–	"Place to be seen"
"Drives smooth"	–	"Makes a statement"
"Processes my data"	–	"Helps me make meaning"

NEW BUSINESS ! • NEW BRAND

Sins of omission? Or commission? We ignore the two biggest market opportunities!

new bus!ness
new markets

So strange.

So very, very strange.

Namely the ... Two Biggest Market Trends ... for reasons I am completely unable to explain ... go virtually unnoticed:

1. *Marketing to Women.* This is ... THE BIGGEST TREND IN THE WORLD ... and it has gone A.W.O.L. (I AM AN UTTER LUNATIC ABOUT THIS. Read on.)

2. *Marketing to the Aging Population.* WE IN THE DEVELOPED WORLD ARE GETTING OLDER ... FAST. Consider: Boomers. Eighty million of them/us in the U.S. Enough money to sink an Armada. And the marketing world completely misses the boat.

Problem (Big): To truly embrace either of these trends ... and tap a substantial share of this potential ... demands ... Total Enterprise Realignment. I.e.: This is a "vision" and "brand promise" discussion, not a "marketing tactics" discussion.

13

TRENDS WORTH TRILLION$$$ I: WOMEN ROAR

! Technicolor Rules ...

● Women are the sole or primary decision makers for just about every kind of purchase, commercial stuff as well as consumer stuff.

● If a Board does not look at all like the market being served ... then something (Big) is (Badly) wrong. (Which means something big is badly wrong.)

● "Men and women don't communicate the same way ... don't buy for the same reasons. He's interested in completing the transaction; she's interested in establishing the relationship. Women make connections everywhere they go."

● "Women don't buy brands. They join them."

● "Women are not a niche. Women *are* the long run!"

⚡ ! RANT

We are not prepared ...

We dice the market into micro-segments and treat women as one "niche" among many. Our organizations, meanwhile, are still overwhelmingly male in the composition of their top management & boards of directors, in their corporate culture, in their approach to product design & marketing. But we must wake up and smell the truth: Women are the primary purchasers of ... *Damn Near Everything*. We must, therefore, strive to achieve nothing less than Total Enterprise Realignment around this awesome, burgeoning, astoundingly untapped market.

👁 ! VISION

I imagine ...

A car dealership ... where sales*people*, both men and women, understand that ... *Women Buy the Cars*; and where the entire approach to marketing and merchandising and sales and service and follow-up caters to ... Women's Way of Being and Buying.

An Investment House ... that builds its business not around the prospect of frequent commissions (a formula that works only if customers are impatient, trigger- and trade-happy men), but around the goals and sensibilities of women.

Break of Day: I Begin to See the Light

18 December 1996.

At around 9 a.m. I enter the Boston HQ of Wordworks, one of America's 10 million women-owned businesses.

Business owner Donna Carpenter and 30 other women are gathered ... *and me*. They own businesses. They've written books. Their combined net worth—including not a penny from trust funds or spouses—runs to the tens of millions of dollars. (At least.)

I am here to ... listen.

I do listen. I am staggered. My life takes if not a 90-degree turn, at least a 65-degree turn. I listen to these ... *Incredibly Powerful Women* ... dispassionately report stories of having been held in contempt. Of having been invisible. Of having been treated as brainless.

By bankers and banks and investment advisors.

By doctors and hospital staffers.

By car salesmen and car dealers.

By clerks and waiters and hotel managers.

By airline staffers and managers.

By auctioneers.

By computer salesmen.

I am a "with-it" guy. I "get it." I marched in the giant pro-choice rally in Washington in 1989. I put the toilet seat down after I pee. I do my own laundry. (I even keep track of the detergent level and buy the refills.)

And yet I learned ... *in three short hours* ... that I just *didn't* get it. I admit it. *Reluctantly. I didn't know what I didn't know. (Didn't have a clue, actually!)* Hence, the last six-plus years have been penance—an effort to "get it" (which I can do pretty well intellectually, but *never* emotionally), and become a ... Noisy Champion.

Not a champion for "women's rights." Many others have done that much better than I ever could. And continue to do so. But a champion for ... OPPORTUNITY. The opportunity[1] that exists ... AMOUNTING TO TRILLIONS OF DOLLARS IN THE U.S. ALONE ... if bankers and carmakers and hoteliers and healthcare providers "got it" ... and started to develop the products that women want, and started to deliver

---

THE APPOSITE SEX

[1] I've also become a champion of another ... Big Opportunity ... that women present. Namely: the opportunity that would ensue ... *if* still male-dominated management took advantage of the ... Leadership Skills ... of under-valued and under-represented women in their ranks.

See Chapter 21 for more on how women are Answer No. 1 to the Talent Problem.

ECONOMICALLY CORRECT

My passion about this "women thing" is not about "political correctness."

It's true: I believe that the advances made not only by women, but also by African-Americans, are the two most important things that have happened in the United States during my 60-plus-year lifetime. These are Moral Achievements of the Highest Order.

However: I am not in any way on a Moral Crusade. I am on a Crusade. But it is a Businessman's Crusade ... against stupidity and lost opportunity ... against the economically shortsighted practices of the male powers-that-be.

I do not believe that most men are ... Sexist Pigs. I do believe that they (we!) are ... Oblivious Idiots.

them and service them in ways that women would appreciate, or at least not be offended by.

Women's Day: I Hear Women Roar!

12 October 2000.

I walk into the Convention Center in Long Beach, California, early in the morning. I notice immediately that most of the men's-room signs are taped over. Now they say "Women." Why? Because I am here attending and co-keynoting the 2000 California Governor's Conference for Women. I was invited by California's First Lady, Sharon Davis. Ten thousand "screaming and shouting and raving women," as a female friend put it, are surging (YES, SURGING) into the hall. (That's why the restroom designations have been changed.) Other men present? The Governor's wife's husband. (Gov. Gray Davis.) A handful of other token males ... all bowing and scraping, and remarking on the matchless energy in the hall. And me.

I had come a long way in four years. Concerning this "women's thing," I'd gathered a ton of stories, a raft of data, and a full front-end loader's worth of conviction. So, scared to death by the enormity of the honor I'd had bestowed, I worked as hard as I've ever worked on my 40-minute speech to ... The Conference. I spent hours, literally, on just the opening PowerPoint slide. I called it "Statement of Philosophy." It read like this:

I am a businessperson. An analyst. A pragmatist. The enormous social good of increased women's power is clear to me; but that is not my shtick. My "business" is haranguing business leaders about my fact-based conviction that women's increasing power—leadership skills and purchasing power—is the Strongest and Most Dynamic Force at Work in the American Economy today. Dare I say it as a long-time resident of Palo Alto and Silicon Valley ... this is even bigger than the Internet!

The theme of the conference was "Celebrate the Past, Create the Future." And yes: Women *have* come a long, long way, baby! As Andrew Sullivan wrote in the *New Republic*, "Greater opportunity for women is probably the most significant gain for human freedom in the last century." So there *was* much to celebrate.

And yet ... there was/is a long, long (LONG) way to go.

The *Real* Chick Lit: Horror Stories

I have collected hundreds of horror stories about women being dismissed or ignored in the marketplace:

CONSTRUCTION CRITICISM

One sign of modest progress: The horror stories occasionally come via men. Once, after an all-day seminar in which (as usual) I addressed the "woman's thing," a fellow approached me. Turns out that he was the most successful shopping-mall developer in the large American urban center where I was presenting that day.

"I must apologize," he began with a chuckle, "I was the one who burst out laughing at one point during your discussion on the women's issue. It got me thinking. I remembered a meeting last week. A bunch of guys—about 15 developers, architects, contractors, engineers, bankers—sitting around designing a shopping center. Every one of us was male! Every one of us! And the 'end users' of the mall will be overwhelmingly women. And it never occurred to us. In retrospect, how bizarre."

Indeed.

• A California State Senator with severe back and neck problems visits a renowned physician, and brings along her husband for moral support. Ten minutes into the conversation with the doc, she is forced to interrupt: "Excuse me, Doctor, but it's my neck that's in pain." (The doc had been talking exclusively to her husband about her problem.)

• A woman who has a bank balance to die for attends a land auction in Kentucky. ("I was probably the only one in the room who could have bought anything that was up for bid by writing out a check on the spot," she tells me later.) Time and again during the initial two-hour session, the auctioneer fails to respond to her standard signals for recognition. At the first break, she approaches him and says, "Start recognizing me, or the next person you'll hear from will be my lawyer. He's very good."

• A woman accosts me after I finish keynoting the First Annual MacDonald Communications Marketing to Women seminar, held in New York in early 1998. It's Kathleen Brown. Former twice-elected Treasurer of the State of California. Former Democratic gubernatorial candidate (she lost a close race against a popular incumbent). Now Ms. Brown's one of the top half-dozen executives at BankAmerica.

"Tom," she says (we know each other from her gubernatorial campaign), "would you do me a favor the next time you're in the Bay Area?"

Me: "If I can, of course."

Kathleen: "I'd like you to have dinner with me and David Coulter." (Coulter was CEO of BankAmerica prior to the NationsBank merger.)

Me: "Sure. Why?"

Kathleen: "I'd like you to tell him what you just told this group."

Me: "Me? You were *Treasurer* of the Earth's Sixth-Largest Economy, and considered by one and almost all to be a brilliant success. You're one of the half-dozen ... Most Powerful Women ... in one of the most powerful single 'nations' on earth, our dearly beloved Great State of California. I'm just a 'consultant.' Why me?"

Kathleen: *"He'll listen to you."*

"Little" vignettes like that one ... drive me batty. No: They ... PISS ME OFF. BIG TIME. And I just keep asking:

WHY? WHY? WHY?

Horrors! Clueless in Carolina

My wife is the CEO and Chief Designer of an extremely successful home-furnishings company, headquartered in Vermont. Twice a year, she makes the pilgrimage to the giant furniture show in High Point, North Carolina. I usually join her for a few days as an accompanying spouse.

The furniture industry is out of it. (Understatement.) Dominated at the cash register

---

MEETING EXPECTATIONS

Talk about "dumb"!

Back in 1970, women constituted only 1 percent of American business travelers. That figure now sits at roughly 50 percent. (Wow!) What's more, many of those women business travelers are big-time "influentials." Women, for example, constitute the majority of CMPs. As in: Certified Meeting Planners. As in: people who book enormous blocks of hotel rooms!

In this area alone ... tens upon tens of billions of dollars are at stake ... each year.

by women, but run almost entirely by old white males with manufacturing backgrounds. ("The future is wood, my boy.") Pathetic. But I hadn't quite got the ... *perfect illustration.*

And then it happened, courtesy of a mere advertisement in an industry magazine that puts out a daily during the show. It was a double-page ad for a seminar that would take place during the High Point show. Title: *"MEET THE EXPERTS! How Have Retailing's Most Successful Stayed That Way."*

Among the presenting "experts," there are 16 ... MEN. I have an engineering degree. I did the math. Women purchase about 94 percent of the product. (WOMEN ... REALLY & TRULY DO RULE ... THIS INDUSTRY.) Thence, if there are 16 men presenting, and if men buy 6 percent of the product, I calculated that there should be ... 272 women "experts" on tap. No problem with that logic, eh?

The reality was slightly different. The actual number of women (of course): ZERO.[2]

Stupid.

Pathetic.

Awful.

Embarrassing.

(Alas, it probably didn't embarrass those "experts" in the least.)

Horrors! Finding "Hostility" in "Hospitality"

Next, from a July 2002 *New York Times* article written by Joe Sharkey titled "One Woman's Account of Two Hotel Experiences" ...

"A female business traveler reports on a two-night trip she made recently to the Phoenix area:

"'I stayed at two hotels, both Hilton properties, that could not have been more different in their accommodation of women,' she wrote in an e-mail message. Her impressions illustrate the challenge hotels confront in marketing to female business travelers, whose ranks are growing rapidly.

"'The first hotel I stayed at was an Embassy Suites in Tempe,' she said. 'I'd reserved online and asked for a quiet room. When I checked in, the young woman at the counter greeted me by name and explained that she had set aside a top-floor room, and that no one was next door to me. She gave me information on the pool, the complimentary

---

"PORN" YESTERDAY?

[2]In my seminars, I often use a slide with a black background and purple letters. It reads: *"WANNA SEE MY PORN COLLECTION?"*

My "porn" consists of photographs ... torn from the back of Fortune 500 company annual reports ... featuring Boards of Directors.

Typically, the board shot features 20 somber faces. Eighteen Very Old White Male countenances. One woman. (HR?) One African-American. (Corporate Communications?)

No, I am not asking to see 51 percent women. I'm actually not "into" quotas in any way, shape, or form.

But I am a ... business pragmatist. And I believe: If a Board does not at all resemble the market being served ... then something (Big) is (Badly) wrong.

(Quota fan or not, I say: Hooray to the Norwegians ... who have proposed legislation that would require the boards of publicly traded companies to be 40 percent female by 2005.)

happy hour and the cooked breakfast in the morning.

"'I went out for meetings. When I got back, the guest services manager had sent up a welcome box with two bottles of water, an apple granola bar, bite-sized cookies and a bag of blue corn chips. The evening happy hour was social, with families as well as groups of businessmen. I wandered in for a draft beer, which I enjoyed by the pool as kids splashed around.

"'The hotel had a Mexican restaurant where I went for dinner. The maitre d' seated me at a booth with no raised eyebrows that I was alone. Later, my room was dead quiet, as promised, and in the morning after an early business meeting, I returned for a cooked breakfast omelet and tea in a cheery café setting with families and other single women travelers, as well as businessmen. It was terrific. I checked out content. The bill was $87.'

"Her other hotel was the Phoenix Airport Hilton.

"'I got lost en route, so I called for directions from my cell phone,' said the woman, who didn't want her name used. 'Reception put me on hold for three minutes and 48 seconds, which I noted only because of the roaming charges. I hung up and had to call back.

"'When I arrived I saw the problem: one clerk at the desk, and 12 customers milling around to check in. When my turn came, there still was a line behind me. 'Okay, you're in room 408,' he announced. Normally they do not publicly announce the room of a single woman, especially in a crowded lobby.

"'My room was near the executive lounge, which was open for drinks and snacks from 5 to 7 p.m. I went in around 6:40 and there were 20 people, and only one other woman. The men were clearly well into their second hour there. A television was blaring and the buffet snacks looked like a three-year-old had crawled across them. Cheese bits were scattered on the counter; tortilla crumbs were everywhere, and there was not a single piece of appetizing food that hadn't been mangled, except a very neat, untouched stack of raw broccoli florets. Let me tell you something: I would rather be in a buffet with a dozen nine-year-olds than with a half-dozen males in their 20s and 30s.

"'The bartender asked me what I wanted. Several people looked. 'Umm,' I said, embarrassed, tired and a little defensive.

"'We don't have Umm,' he said. I flushed and glared. I ordered a Coors Light and fled to my room, where I had a room-service cheeseburger.

"'Bill for the room, with tax and dinner, was $170,' she concluded. Guess which hotel I'm going back to the next time? But let me ask you something: Do hotels really think about these things when they think of female travelers?'"

I've got dozens of stories of women abused by hospitality companies. Arguably only Wyndham, with its program oriented toward women business travelers, does much "strategically" to serve this huge, and hugely lucrative, market.

Note that word: "strategically." The problem is not that my many pals in the hospitality industry deny that there's "an opportunity" here. But they consign that opportunity to "tactical program" out back, and can't imagine it as becoming the basis for ... Wholesale Brand Realignment.

Horrors! Showroom Shenanigans

A smartly turned-out, six-figure-income financial services executive approached me after one of my riffs on women's treatment in the marketplace. During her lunch-hour a few days before, she'd gone to a Mercedes dealership with every intention of buying a car.

NEW BUSINESS !● NEW MARKETS

REALLY, I'D SETTLE FOR JUST A MINT

I was so pissed off.

I was in a well-known London hotel, preparing for a seminar. In the elevator was a picture of a woman guest under a lush duvet. So what's the problem? Don't I believe that hotels should try to cater to women business travelers by featuring them in marketing material?

Well, this woman was no average "woman business traveler." (Average female business traveler: Age 41.6, dog tired, bags under her eyes.) No, the woman in this ad was a gorgeous babe, about 25 years of age. In short, a man's fantasy of the surprise he'd love to find in his room. (I'm being honest here.)

During the seminar, I asked the female segment of my audience if I was wrong to deem that elevator advert blatantly offensive. The gathering of about 600 included over 40 percent women, I'd judge, many staying in the hotel. I could see that lots of the "guys" were taken aback by my ire. But every (EVERY!) (Repeat: EVERY!) woman who had seen the ad thought it was stupid. Alas, most of the women also said, in effect, "But what do you expect?"

Is it any wonder that *91* percent of women say, "advertisers don't understand us"? Or that *58* percent go much farther and claim they are downright "annoyed" by advertising pitches apparently aimed at them?

All three salesmen were in their cubicles, eating sandwiches. (Yes, they were men. Do you even need to ask?) As she prowled the showroom floor, not one of the three bothered to acknowledge her. Finally, some guy finished his lunch and ambled toward her. First words out of his mouth: "Honey, are you sure you have the kind of money to be looking at a car like this?"

Some men who read this story will say, "Bullshit. She's making it up." Or at least, "She's exaggerating."[3] (Admittedly, that would have been my response before that ... Pivotal Day ... back in December 1996.)

FACT: None of the women who read this will have the reaction that some of the men did. None will even find the exchange exceptional. This is something that, after six years of listening and study, I :.. know.

FACT: Yes, I do have a gazillion stories like this. From financial service companies. From hospitals and docs. From hotels. From computer companies. As well as those forever-silly car companies. And when I've told these stories, I've never ... NEVER ... ...NEVER ... among the tens of thousands of people to whom I've told them ... seen one woman's head shake in disagreement.

FACT: It is rare for me to speak on this topic ... and not have at least two or three

COMPANY CAD
[3]True story: The female CEO of a UK financial-services firm goes to a dealership to lease a company car. The saleman greets her by saying, "I didn't know that [company name] was offering company cars to secretaries."

THEY'VE COME A LAWN, LAWN WAY
In 2001, after my first speech of the year, a fellow comes up to me. He'd attended a seminar of mine about three years before, when I was just warming upon this topic. He says that he had dismissed my comments on the women's market, but then had decided to take me somewhat seriously. He had done "a little research." The results astounded him. He reports that 80 percent of the buyers of his primary product are women.

That product? *Riding lawn mowers.*

women wait in line, often expending many minutes of their very precious time, to pass on yet another tawdry tale.

"Tom, here's another one for you ..."

"Tom, you won't believe this one, but ..."

"Funny thing: I DO BELIEVE.

Do the Math: Decisions, Decisions

That women are grossly underserved in the marketplace might make sense ... if it made sense. But it doesn't. It's absolutely insane. Because women are the sole or primary decision makers for just about every kind of purchase. Commercial stuff as well as consumer stuff. Research that I have come across over the years yields the following numbers:

In category after category, women are instigators-in-chief of most consumer purchases. To wit:

- All consumer purchases: **83** percent.
- Home furnishings: **94** percent.
- Vacations: **92** percent.
- New homes: **91** percent.
- DIY ("home projects"): **80** percent.
- Consumer electronics: **51** percent.
- Cars: **60** percent.(And in the latter category, cars, women significantly influence

another **30** percent of purchases, bringing their Power Score to **90** percent.) The same pattern holds in services. To wit:

- New bank accounts: women make the choice **89** percent of the time.
- Healthcare: women make **80** percent of decisions, and are responsible for about

two-thirds of spending.

Do the Math: Buyer, Be ... Woman

And on it goes. Two-thirds of working women in the United States and more than **50** percent of working wives earn more than half of their family's income. American women write **80** percent of all checks, pay **61** percent of all bills, and own **53** percent of all stock. Women fueled the Mutual Fund boom ... almost single-handedly.

American women constitute **43** percent of Americans with a net worth of a half-million dollars or more; said women significantly influence **75** percent of financial decisions, and they make **29** percent of such decisions single-handedly.

More: Between 1970 and 1998, men's median income rose by **0.6** percent, while women's median income[4] rose by **63** percent. (*Holy smoke!*)

RETURN TO SPENDER

A few weeks after one of my talks to Women Future—a favorite group of mine—I received this email from Shelley Rae Norbeck (who had presumably tuned into the event via teleconferencing):

"I make one-third more money than my husband does. I have as much financial 'pull' in the relationship as he does. I'd say this is also true of most of my women friends. Somebody should wake up, smell the coffee, and kiss our asses long enough to sell us something! We have money to spend—and nobody wants it!"

More: As of the first quarter of 2000, more women than men were using the Web; six out of every ten new Web users were women; and among wired women, 83 percent were the primary decision makers on matters of family healthcare, finances, and education. (And yet failed retail dot-coms were invariably headed by swashbuckling guys.)

All the foregoing relates to women's (huge) role as "purchasing officers" for themselves and their families. But women also play a predominant role as professional purchasing officers for corporations and or public agencies. They now constitute more than 50 percent of purchasing managers and purchasing agents. Their "commercial spending power" also encompasses their majority status in HR departments, where they're responsible for (among other things) employee benefits decisions. And they make up more than 50 percent of corporate admin officers, with awesome power when it comes to opening (or not) the commercial purse.

Add up all of the above, and the result is an American women's economy that accounts for more half of U.S. GDP. That is to say: around five trillion dollars. Hence, according to one wag, the world's largest economies could be ranked as follows:

- Earth's third-largest economy: American men.
- Earth's second-largest economy: All of Japan.
- Earth's largest economy: American women.

Do the Math: The 10-Million-Woman March

Want to hear women really roar? After years of mashing their heads against the corporate glass ceiling, they've begun to say ... almost in unison ... GO TO HELL.

Sure there are more highly-sung female Fortune 500 CEOs, such as HP's Carly Fiorina or Xerox's Anne Mulcahy or eBay's Meg Whitman. But the real story is the 10.1 million women-owned businesses in the United States alone. These enterprises employ 27.5 million of us. (In other words: one out of every four American workers.) In fact, women-owned businesses employ more workers *inside the U.S.A.* than the "fabled" Fortune 500 employ *worldwide*.

(Scoreboard: Women, 1; Fortune 500, 0.)

In total, American women-owned businesses at last count tallied about $3.5 trillion in revenue. To put that in proper perspective: The revenue from American women-owned businesses exceeds the GDP of Germany!

(Zounds.)

Start looking at this stuff, as I have been doing now for a half-dozen years, and you'll be stunned. Stunned—and then outraged.

"Outraged" because: Women as purchasers, professionally and privately, are responsible for more than half of all spending in the U.S. economy. And yet:

"HIGHER" MATH

[4]From *BusinessWeek*, 26 May 2003: Women's share of family income rises dramatically with education level. Men still dominate joint earnings in low-education families, but have been eclipsed in families where women have graduate degrees.

What's more: That trend will only accelerate.

Reason: Women are coming to dominate higher education—in both attendance and graduation rates.

Result: Families with highly educated women are ... where the loot is.

Financial services companies ... *don't get it*.
Health services companies ... *don't get it*.
Hospitality services companies ... *don't get it*.
Computer companies ... *don't get it*.
Automobile companies ... *don't get it*.
Home furnishings companies (!) *don't get it*.
NONE OF THEM GET IT. (Or so, alas, it seems.)

His and Hers: Across a Great Divide

I'm an unabashed "difference" feminist. There is no doubt in my mind that men and women are equal. There is also no doubt in my mind that men and women are ... *different*.

And the differences are profound. And relative to my turf, business excellence, those profound differences have profound implications for the way we create and distribute products and services and ... experiences.

Consider Harvard psychologist Carol Gilligan's classic study *In a Different Voice*. To summarize her brilliant and meticulous work:[5]

- *Men* want to get away from authority and family. **Women** want to connect.
- *Men* are self-oriented. **Women** are other-oriented.
- *Men* are rights-oriented. **Women** are responsibility-oriented.

Martha Barletta, in *Marketing to Women*, echoes Gilligan's findings:

- *Men* have an "individual perspective" (The "core unit is 'me.'") **Women** have a "group perspective." (The "core unit is 'we.'")
- *Men* take "pride in self-reliance." **Women** take "pride in team accomplishment."

Barletta reports findings that demonstrate that such differences are wired into us at the deepest level:

- Vision: *Men*, focused. **Women**, peripheral.
- Hearing: **Women's** discomfort level is half that of *men's*.
- Smell: **Women**, sensitive. *Men*, relatively insensitive.
- Touch: The most sensitive *man* is less sensitive to touch than the *least* sensitive **woman**. (No exaggeration.)

PAUSE & PONDER
[5]Please. Don't read these points as "interesting." (Though they are.) Please.
Instead, think about how they (fundamentally) affect—or ought to affect—
e-v-e-r-y aspect of your product development and marketing strategy.

TALK IS DEAR
The novelist and former *New York Times* columnist Anna Quindlen: "I only really understand myself, what I'm really thinking and feeling, when I've talked it over with my circle of female friends. When days go by without that connection, I feel like the radio playing in an empty room."

I've shared that remark with audiences that included tens of thousands of men, and repeatedly asked, "Can you imagine—in any way, shape, or form—any man ever making that remark?"

We all agree: No way!

Message. We are not worse. We are not better. We are different. And the impact on enterprise strategy is enormous. Or ought to be.

- People orientation: By age three days, baby girls exhibit twice as much eye contact as baby boys.

Judy Rosener, in *America's Competitive Secret: Women Managers*, couches these enormous (yes) differences in terms of ... language: "Women speak and hear a language of connection and intimacy, and men speak and hear a language of status and independence. Men communicate to obtain information, establish their status, and show independence. Women communicate to create relationships, encourage interaction, and exchange feelings."

Helen Fisher, in *The First Sex*, intriguingly adds, "The [Hollywood] scripts that men write tend to be direct and linear, while women's compositions have many conflicts, many climaxes, and many endings."

He Said, She ... Listened

I sometimes think: *The two sexes have nothing in common!* Consider the marvelous *Why Men Don't Listen & Women Can't Read Maps*, by Barbara Pease and Allan Pease. This book simply could not have been written 25 years ago, at the time of Gilligan's pioneering research. It's not based on anecdotal evidence, but on the latest findings from neurobiology; that is, the differences come from the hardest of sciences.

Consider: "It is obvious to a woman when another woman is upset ... while a man generally has to physically witness tears or a temper tantrum or be slapped on the face before he even has a clue that anything is going on. Like most female mammals, women are equipped with far more finely tuned sensory skills than men."

More? "A woman knows her children's friends, hopes, dreams, romances, secret fears, what they are thinking, how they are feeling .... . Men are vaguely aware of some short people also living in the house."

Some will find the above amusing. Some will find it threatening, or even offensive. The point: It makes sense ... from the standpoint of biological sciences. We simply haven't advanced since the days in the cave. In that epoch, guys were either "on" or "off." We got up, pre-dawn, and went out on the dangerous hunt; the adrenaline surged; we spent the day pursuing game, came in at dusk ... and promptly fell asleep. Men, the biological research reveals, are either *all the way on* ... or in a "resting" state, 30 percent on. Women, on the other hand, are responsible for defending the cave-community ... 24/7. Thus, women are *never* off: Their "resting" state is 90 percent *on.* Women are always tuned in. Men are tuned in or tuned out ... and seldom in between.

"As a hunter, a man needed vision that would allow him to zero in on ... targets in the distance," the Peases write, "whereas a woman needed eyes to allow a wide arc of vision so that she could monitor any predators sneaking up on the nest. This is why modern men can find their way effortlessly to a distant pub, but can never find things in fridges, cupboards, or drawers."

FLICK CHICK TICKED
Early in 2003, a senior Hollywood producer who is a woman told me this: "Each time a 'women's movie' is a success—like *The First Wives Club*—everybody in the industry is surprised all over again, and nothing much happens. But if some 'action movie' is a hit, it instantly spawns a dozen frenzied knock-offs."

NEW BUSINESS

NEW MARKETS

And: "Female hearing advantage contributes significantly to what is called 'women's intuition' and is one of the reasons why a woman can read between the lines of what people say. Men, however, shouldn't despair. They are excellent at ... imitating animal sounds."

More from the Peases:[6]

- "Women love to talk. *Men talk silently to themselves.*"
- "Women think aloud. Women talk, *men feel nagged.*"
- "Women multitrack."
- "Women are indirect. *Men are direct.*"
- "Women talk emotively, *men are literal. Men listen like statues.*"
- "*Boys like things*, girls like people."
- "*Boys compete*, girls cooperate."
- "*Men hate to be wrong. Men hide their emotions.*"

Concerning that last point, the Peases add: "When a woman is upset, she talks emotionally to her friends; but an upset man rebuilds a motor or fixes a leaking tap."

Why Women Buy

Women ... are different. No surprise, women buy for ... different reasons. And the practical consequences of such differences for product development, positioning, marketing, distribution, and services are worth ... Trillion$$$.

The editorial director of the UK's *Redwood Publications* (which puts out mega-circulation company magazines for the likes of Boots and Volvo) patiently explained to me how to concoct a story that will attract men ... and/or women: The men "need" (NEED!) "tables, comparisons, rankings." Women want "narratives that cohere."

Martha Barletta supports this notion, observing from the research that women are more "contextual" and "holistic." In approaching a story, she notes, "Men start with the headline." ("Just the facts, ma'am.") While "women start with the context." She also reports that during the process of "initiating purchases," men study "facts and figures," whereas women "ask lots of people for input."

Faith Popcorn, the trend-spotting maven, makes a similar point in her book *Clicking*: "Men and women don't communicate the same way, don't buy for the same reasons. ... He simply wants the transaction to take place; she's interested in establishing the relationship. Every place that women go, they make connections."

PAUSE & PONDER
[6]Again: The point of these insights is not to amuse. (Though they are amusing.)
  The point is to say: Just imagine the implications of all this for e-v-e-r-y aspect of how you develop and distribute products!

READING BETWEEN THE (GENDER) LINES
I read far more fiction than nonfiction. Since taking on this topic, I've paid attention to portrayals of women by male and female authors. The language men use to describe women and the language women use to describe women are totally different.
  Women's characterizations of women are subtle and complex. But in 9 out of 10 cases, even among honored authors, male characterizations of women are men's fantasies of women. And when a woman character is an admired professional, she is invariably described in male terms—as "tough," "steely-eyed," and so on.
  It's hilarious (more or, mostly, less.)

There is no more meticulous researcher of purchasing behavior than Paco Underhill. Consider this vignette from his book *Why We Buy*: "Men seem like loose cannons.[7] Men always move faster through a store's aisles. Men spend less time looking. They usually don't like asking where things are. You'll see a man move impatiently through a store to the section he wants, pick something up, and then, almost abruptly, he's ready to buy. ... For a man, ignoring the price tag is almost a sign of virility."

Judith Tingley, in *GenderSell: How to Sell to the Opposite Sex*, offers an overview of women's assessment of male salespeople. Male peddlers are seen as "technically knowledgeable" and "assertive"; they get "straight to the point." They are also seen as "pushy," "condescending," and "insensitive to women's needs." IBM's significant effort to market to women business owners (recall, 10 million of 'em in the U.S. alone) underscores all this.

IBM's Robin Sternbergh, who'd circled the block more than once, found the research data "hard to believe." Women and men, she observes, purchase computer systems based on "different criteria." Men are obsessed with the technical specs; women are more interested in the relationship with the vendor.[8] There's nothing at all "wrong" about guys' approach to shopping. But guys are minority shoppers—and almost all retail spaces are designed by men and, de facto, for men. That includes car dealerships, electronics shops, banks, DIY stores, docs' offices.

Selling the "Setting": My Wife's Tale

My wife, Susan Sargent, licenses a line of branded furniture through Lexington Industries. I was in the North Carolina showroom where her launch took place in April 2002. Were it not for the general backwardness of the furniture industry noted before, the scene would have been hilarious. The male sales reps on the floor pushed technical specs to prospective buyers. The specially hired female docents, meanwhile, talked about "setting," "context," and even "soul."

Here is how Lexington positioned the new Susan Sargent brand, apparently the first "female brand" in the industry, and, more interestingly, the first brand aimed specifically at professional women purchasers:

"The Underserved Susan Sargent Customer:

"Just as a novelist writes a novel with a particular reader in mind, Susan Sargent has a clear idea of her primary consumer. The busy, creative, unfussy, energetic professional woman makes her own choices in her work, her life, and her home. She is confident and unpretentious, eclectic and diverse. She probably makes 90% of all

NEW BUSINESS ● NEW MARKETS

SHOPPING TALK

[7]The *Charleston* [West Virginia] *Gazette* in June 2002 had this headline: "Shopping: A Guy's Nightmare or a Girl's Dream Come True?" For boys, the paper reported, it's "buy it and be gone." For girls, it's "hang out and enjoy the experience." One respondent, Antaun Hughes of Capital High School, put it this way: "Women enjoy going through the actual process of everything, while guys like to get straight to the point."

THE (NEW) SHOE FITS

[8]John Hoke, a designer at Nike, quoted in *Fast Company*: "Women weren't comfortable in our [Niketown] stores. So I figured out where they would be comfortable—most likely their own homes. The [first NIKEgoddess] store has more of a residential feel. I wanted it to have furnishings, not fixtures. Above all, I didn't want it to be girlie."

home-furnishings buying decisions. She has limited time, no patience for design dictators—and wants more accessible, better quality, comfortable, younger and more colorful choices that can be efficiently located and attractively shopped. She is adventurous and eclectic in her tastes. As a primary consumer of home furnishings, there is an obvious, gaping hole in the marketplace: She is underserved.

"The professional woman's home is a work-in-progress. As her career, her personal growth, her family, and her varied interests evolve, her home interior reflects the breadth of her individual style. She is not cookie-cutter. She is creative. She is looking for choices that appeal to that creativity, yet connect in a modern and livable way. While Sargent's look appeals to a wide range of customers, it is with this consumer that she particularly resonates.

"A home is like a garden: We nourish it, we plant it with colorful things, we expect it to evolve with the seasons and the years. With her designs, Sargent provides her customer with the tools to decorate her home landscape in a fun and modern way. Susan establishes a relationship with her customers, inviting them into her particular vision. This modern woman doesn't just buy furniture. She grows her own colorful environment, bit by bit, evolving and comparing notes with Susan Sargent."

Some story. (Yes, of course, I'm prejudiced.) (For more information ...)

Query: Could such language have been produced by men, about men?

Answer: No.

Message: Different language attracts and "speaks to" different purchasers.

The Popcorn Stand: Women Are Joiners

Read this book.[9] Better yet, memorize it. Title: *EVEolution: The Eight Truths of Marketing to Women*.

Authors: my friend, trend spotter Faith Popcorn (she attended the fateful Boston Meeting in 1996), and her creative director, Lys Marigold.

Eight Big Ideas for attracting Eve's custom. I'll briefly examine just one, to give you a flavor of what's included. (Desperately hoping, of course, to pique your interest.)

Truth No. 1: Connecting Your Female Consumers to Each Other Connects Them to Your Brand. "The Connection proclivity in women starts early," Popcorn and Marigold write. "When asked, 'How was school today?' a girl usually tells her mother every detail

---

DUMB MOVE: KING BLOCKS QUEEN

A colleague of mine, Steve Farber, knows well my passion for the Women's Market Opportunity. I got an email from Steve in April 2002. He'd done a Google search, typing in two things: "Customer is King" and "Customer is Queen."

The results:

"Customer is King": 4,440.

"Customer is Queen": 29.

BOOK BLANK

[9]QUESTION. Why are *EVEolution* and Martha Barletta's *Marketing to Women* about the only major books on this subject?

Go to your local Borders or Barnes & Noble. On the burgeoning business shelves, you'll find 25 books—maybe twice that number—on Six Sigma or some other version of the "quality thing." And yet I believe ... with TOTAL CERTAINTY ... that the "marketing to women thing" is FAR BIGGER than the "quality thing."

of what happened, while a boy might grunt, 'Fine.'"

In my seminars, after using a PowerPoint slide that shows that quote about the roots of the Connection Proclivity, I always ask the same question: "Is there anyone in this room who disagrees with that characterization of the difference between boys and girls?" I leave plenty of space for people to object. I have yet to get a *single* objection.

For each of the eight "truths," Popcorn and Marigold proffer advice to would-be clients. Take that Connection Proclivity: "What if ExxonMobil or Shell dipped into their credit card database to help commuting women interview and make a choice of car pool partners?" "What if American Express made a concerted effort to connect up female empty-nesters through on-line and off-line programs, geared to help women re-enter the workforce with today's skills?"

Indeed. What if companies did those sorts of things? More important: WHY THE HELL DON'T THEY? (TRILLION$$$ ARE AT STAKE.)

Bottom line, per Popcorn and Marigold: *"Women don't buy brands. They join them."*[10]

Cases: Faith's Faves ... and a Few of My Own

For years now, people have asked me, Where are the examples of companies that get this right? And for years, the answer was clear: I HAVE NONE.

Well, we do seem to be nearing a *first* threshold. *Some* companies are doing *some* things to address this huge opportunity. It's not enough for me, and it's not the wholesale strategic alignment I deem necessary, but what the hell. I'll take what I can get.

Jiffy Lube. "In the male mold," Popcorn and Marigold write, "Jiffy Lube was going all-out to deliver quick, efficient service. But, in the female mold, women were being turned off by the 'Let's get it fixed fast, no conversation required' experience." The new Jiffy Lube is working ... *strategically* ... to change all that. The premise is, per Popcorn and Marigold: "*Control* over her environment. *Comfort* in the service setting. *Trust* that her car is being serviced properly. *Respect*[11] for her intelligence and ability."

(Note: As of the 2000 publication of *EVEolution*, Jiffy Lube was Faith's favorite example of a firm's pursuing systemic realignment around female customers.)

Lowe's. "War has broken out over your home-improvement dollar," writes Forbes. com, "and Lowe's has superpower Home Depot on the defensive. Its not so secret

---

WORD OF MOUTH? DO THE MATH!

[10]It just could be that branding is ... a woman's thing.

The implications for Total Enterprise Market & Brand Positioning are staggering. One "small" piece of supporting data: A major stockbroker told me he has oriented his practice toward female clients—with great success. A research nut, he reports that his average male client recommends him to 2.6 others. On the other hand, his women clients recommend him to an average of 21 other people. Yes: that's *two-point-six versus twenty-one*.

Holy smoke!

BUY WORDS

[11]These are all key (KEY) words: *Control. Comfort. Trust. Respect.*

Especially the latter. In every conversation I have with women on any related topic ... healthcare, financial services, real estate, car care ... the word "respect" (and, much more often, its opposite) comes up. Again and again.

ploy: Lure Women." (Who'd a thunk!? DIY?!)

"Home Depot," Forbes.com continues, "is still very much a guy's chain. But women, according to Lowe's research, initiate 80 percent of all home-improvement decisions, especially the big-ticket orders like kitchen cabinets, flooring and bathrooms. 'We focused on a customer nobody in home improvement has focused on. Don't get me wrong, but women are far more discriminating .than men,' says [CEO Robert] Tillman, 59, a Lowe's lifer."

Wow! Another icon to men tumbles! The hardware store! Way to go, Lowe's!

Mattel. Headline, *Wall Street Journal*, April 2002: "Mattel Sees Untapped Market for Blocks: Little Girls." "Last year, more than 90 percent of LEGO sets purchased were for boys," the *Journal* writes. "Mattel says Ello—with interconnecting plastic squares, balls, triangles, squiggles, flowers and sticks, in pastel colors and with rounded corners—will go beyond LEGO's linear play patterns."

(So hadn't LEGO, a sophisticated company, figured out that girls weren't buying? I doubt that the LEGO folks were that dense. My hunch: They assumed that LEGO is a "boys' thing"—and just didn't give a damn. Or, to offer a more benign interpretation, they never thought about it at all.)

Tomboy Tools. Tomboy Tools are smaller and lighter in weight than standard (that is, male) tools. Equally important: They are being marketed through a "Tupperware party" model of distribution. (Remember: "Women don't buy brands. They join them.")

Procter & Gamble. Cover story, *Advertising Age*, June 2002: "Crest Spin-off Targets Women." The product: Crest Rejuvenating Effects. The leadership group: Crest's "chicks in charge" team. A $50 million advertising launch took place. The packaging was changed. The taste was changed. The features were changed.

Great stories, all! And yet, to take only that last example: Why, oh why, in 2002, the date of the story, is it "news" that a premier consumer-goods company has done something "special" to appeal to women? I can see why some companies (IBM, say) would be late to this particular party. But *P&G*? P&G, whose products so obviously fall within women's traditional domain. And why just this one initiative? Why doesn't Procter & Gamble ... Totally Reorient Its Enterprise ... to focus on woman-as-consumer? Why?

"Hi, Finance": Gentleman, Meet Your Customers

As noted earlier, women are part of virtually all consumer financial decisions, and make close to a third of those decisions single-handedly.

So ... how do these "flighty" women do? BETTER THAN MEN. CONSISTENTLY BETTER. And in particular ... they are consistently less "flighty" than men.

"Women Beat Men at Art of Investing," reads the headline to an article in the *Miami Herald*. The *Herald* reports on a study by Professors Terrance Odean and Brad Barber, of the University of California at Davis. In the study, women outperformed men as investors. Reason: Men are typically "in and out" of a stock; they love "the game" way too much. Women choose more carefully. They focus on achieving a secure future for their family. And they hold on for the long (or at least longish) haul.

Speaking of holding on, consider this feisty commentary by Jane Bryant Quinn, in *Newsweek*, January 2001: "Why all this focus on women and our supposed lack of investment guts? A far greater problem, it seems to me, is trigger-happy speculation, mostly by men. The kinds of guys whose family savings went south with the dot-coms. Imagine a list of their money mistakes. *1. Shoot from the hip. 2. Overtrade their accounts. 3. Believe they're smarter than the market. 4. Think with their mouse rather than their brain. 5. Praise their own genius when stocks go up ... . 6. Hide their mistakes from their wives."*

The National Association of Investors on investment-club returns in 1997:

- Women-only clubs: 17.9 percent
- Mixed clubs: 17.3 percent
- Men-only clubs: 15.6 percent

In 2000, *Value Line* reported on the top investment clubs in each state. Herewith, the results. (The reason for the total of 49: Vermont and Maine are not included, the District of Columbia is included.)

- All female: 22
- Co-ed: 19
- All male: 8

Message: Women make most of the investment decisions. Women are better investors than men. Q.E.D.

Why, then, are women still treated like s*** by most financial-services providers? (That's not fair. Women are not "treated like s***." They are ... *dismissed.* Treated as ... *brainless.* Treated as ... *gutless.* And frankly, that's worse than being treated like ... shit!)

Cases: Investor Relations As If Women Mattered

Here are a few examples, from a summer 2002 article in the *San Jose Mercury News*, on the efforts of a few financial-services companies to pursue the enormous women's market:

Citigroup. In October 2001, "Citigroup rolled out Women & Co. ... a membership service aimed at women under 55 who have $100,000 in investable assets," the *Mercury News* reports.

Wells Fargo. In June 2002, "Wells Fargo Bank earmarked an extra $5 billion for its Women's Loan Program." That's in addition to $10 billion that Wells previously committed to the program. Wells has, among other things, jointly sponsored events for the National Association for Women Business Owners.

Merrill Lynch. Merrill Lynch has set up "a multi-cultural and diversified business development group this year to target women and ethnic investors. The focus is on forums where female investors can learn and network."

Charles Schwab. Charles Schwab is promoting Women Investing Now. It's a two-year-old educational initiative that "features classes taught by women."

Cents & Sensibility. Financial planners Erin J. Kincheloe and Sharon A. Almeida

NEW BUSINESS ! NEW MARKETS

VICTORY!
Nike is also getting with the (women's) program. From *Fast Company*: "Darcy Winslow is a leading figure in NIKEgoddess, a companywide grassroots team whose goal is a once-and-for-all shift in how a high-testosterone outfit sells to, designs for, and communicates with women."

gave their practice "a face lift in mid-2000 to appeal more to women, who make up three out of every four clients," the *Mercury News* reports. "They started with a new name—Cents & Sensibility, a play on the title of Jane Austen's novel. Other cues run from the magazines in the lobby (The Academy Award issue of *People*, not *Forbes* or *Fortune*) to the office décor (impressionistic paintings, not historical stock-market charts). Most important, they spend more time talking with women about what they want to accomplish with their money—such as saving for college or helping family—rather than how they'll grow it. For example, their sessions for women have 'changed from a pretty analytical male-think type of seminar with all these facts, into something that starts with the heart and ends with the figures,' Kincheloe said."

The good news: These cases actually do exist. Now my litany is not quite so bereft of stories about companies that are "getting it right." Or at least *thinking* about *trying* to get it *somewhat* right.

The bad news: There's not a single case study, other than that of Cents & Sensibility,[12] of a company that has moved purposefully to ... reorient its entire enterprise ... in the direction of serving women.

No More Ms. Niche Gal

To "go after" the woman's market, one does not go down to a party store, buy a thousand balloons, fill them with helium, launch them into the sky, and declare that today marks the beginning of XYZ Corp's "Year of the Woman."

What we're talking about (MAKE NO MISTAKE) is ... Re-imagining the Total Enterprise: Recruiting. Hiring. Promoting. Organizational structure. Business processes. Product development. Marketing. Branding. Strategy. Culture. Leadership. Everything.

Martha Barletta agrees. BIG TIME. In the last chapter of her book *Marketing to Women*, she provides "Notes to the CEO."[13] Herewith, the gist of her argument:

GLOBAL GAL-FEST

Most of my thinking on the Women's Thing, and most of the research I've gathered on the subject, relates to the fully developed Western world.

But I've found that my "women's riff" translates ... remarkably well.

Case in point:

The plane landed in Kuala Lumpur. Eighteen hours before I was to put on an all-day seminar. It was late 1998, and I'd been polishing that women's "riff" for a couple of years.

But now I was in Asia, and in a Muslim-majority nation on top of that. I guessed that only 10 percent or so of the seminar participants would be women.

So, should I respectfully drop the women's chapter?

I decided not to. And I'm very happy about my decision. I did use some sandpaper, and removed some burrs here and there. But otherwise I offered my "straight" pitch.

I was right on one score: The audience was only about 10 percent women. But I have seldom received such a heartfelt response as I did from this vocal minority. Almost every woman approached me, and thanked me for giving them a voice.

Did I change the world that day? No. Or not by much. But I did increase my resolve not to pull my punches—regardless of my map coordinates.

MY TWO CENTS

[12]The Cents & Sensibility example is huge. The company name has been changed. The look has been changed. And the story has changed ... from a focus on numbers, tools, and instant returns ... to a focus on long-term goals.

NOT-SO-EASY TERMS

Rosanna Hertz, Chairwoman of the Women's Studies Program at Wellesley College, on the topic of investment advisors: "I feel like they've never understood me and never will understand me. They talk in a masculine language. It's 'how risk-averse are you?' It's not a language I think in."

1. *Women are not a "niche."* So get this out of the "Specialty Markets" group.

2. *The competition is starting to catch on.* Nike. Nokia. Wachovia. Ford. Harley-Davidson. Jiffy Lube. Charles Schwab. Citigroup. Aetna.

3. *If you "dip your toes in the water," what makes you think you'll get splashy results?*

4. *Bust through the walls of the corporate silos.* One must bring the ... Total Enterprise ... to bear in this enormous opportunity.

5. *Once you get her, don't let her slip away.* Women: Tough to convince, loyal once convinced. (180 degrees from men!)

6. *WOMEN ARE THE LONG RUN!* This is the ... Main Game.

The Guru Gap

I despise the designation "management guru," but if such a designation has any validity, then I guess I am one. There are probably about 20 of us lucky to be in the front ranks. I'm not sure how many there might be in the next tier. But I'm sure of one thing: There are damn few management guru-*esses*. And I'm even more sure of something else: There is not one male management guru other than me who has focused—in any way, shape, or form—on the "women's issue." The point is not that I'm proud of that. (Though, to be perfectly honest, I am proud.) The point is that I'm befuddled by it: WHY HASN'T ANYONE ELSE ... AMONG THIS AWESOMELY SMART BUNCH ... SEEN THIS

TALENT PROSPECT

Note (again): The women-as-primary-market-for-everything issue is only half of this (VERY BIG) story.

See Chapter 21 on the women-as-most-effective-New-Economy-talent side of the equation.

Put the two parts of the story together, and what do you get? Helen Fisher, author of *The First Sex: The Natural Talents of Women and How They Are Changing the World*, sums it up perfectly:

"TOMORROW BELONGS TO WOMEN."

"TURNAROUND TOM"?

[13]I've never wanted to be a CEO. Why? Too damned hard!

But I admit that I have gotten the itch ... as a direct result of getting on this "women's shtick."

I would love (LOVE!) to be CEO of a large financial services corporation ... for exactly 60 months. I would take that enterprise, dig into its every nook and cranny, and redirect its strategy ... by 179.5 degrees ... in the direction of developing products for, marketing them to, and distributing them to women.

For starters: I guarantee that at the end of those 60 months, 11 out of 20 members of my Board, and 13 out of 20 members of my Executive Committee, would be ... women. (Oops! Maybe *I* am into quotas, after all.)

COLORS OF THE RAINBOW

Among huge, under-tapped "segments," women are not alone. While marketers slice and dice demographic data at secondary and tertiary levels, they frequently miss the main game.

I backed into this "women's thing" and was overwhelmed by it. I didn't do a "strategic analysis." I simply acquiesced to Heather Schultz, then president of my training company, and unenthusiastically agreed to go to the fated December 1996 meeting.

It could have been another topic. For example, I could have gotten the bug about the Hispanic market. While the U.S. population as a whole will grow by about 10 percent over the next decade, the Hispanic population will grow by almost 40 percent.

The marketer looks at the data and conceives a program for left-handed Hispanic teenage males, or some such. At some point, such fine-grained differentiation is imperative. But we risk ignoring the bigger question: As part of our Overall Brand Promise, do we give a damn about Hispanics? (The grocery chain Albertsons, for example, is starting an entire new division to serve the Hispanic market. Now that's more like it!)

At any rate, I cannot do it all. In my perfect world I'd have knock-your-socks-off chapters on the Hispanic market, the African-American market (14 percent of Americans), and the Green Products market. But that'll have to wait for another day. Meanwhile, there is one other "demographic" that I'll turn my attention to. See Chapter 14, on the "Boomer Bonanza."

HUGE OPPORTUNITY? (Or even written, literally, a single word about it?)

Why? Why? Why?

Well, *I* am determined. I'm going to push this "women's thing." And I'm going to piss some people off in the process. (I HAVE ALREADY PISSED OFF ... A LOT OF PEOPLE. AND LOST SOME BUSINESS: "FORGET IT, HE'S JUST GOING TO BEAT US OVER THE HEAD ABOUT THAT DAMN 'WOMEN'S STUFF.'") But I'm pushing it ... dear impaired male executive colleagues ... because ... in the words of bank robber Willie Sutton ... *"That's where the money is."* Money that comes from effectively developing products and services and experiences that respect and serve women in every industry: from automobiles to healthcare, from financial services to information technology, from hospitality to ... *riding lawnmowers.*

A PERFECT TEN?

At a recent talk, I shed the last of my engineer's and MBA's reticence and offered a grand finale to my Women's Opportunity riff. My ... Ten Commandments:

1. Men and Women are different.
2. Very different.
3. VERY, VERY DIFFERENT.
4. Women and Men have nothing—absolutely nothing—in common.
5. Women buy lots of stuff.
6. WOMEN BUY ALL THE STUFF.
7. Men are (STILL) in charge.
8. MEN ARE ... TOTALLY, HOPELESSLY CLUELESS ABOUT WOMEN.
9. Women's Market = Opportunity No. 1.
10. NO SHIT.

Going to China; Or, Hear *Me* Roar

Nixon went to China. Only an old Red-baiter could have pulled it off. I'm a junior member of that same league. An Old White Male (OWM). Two tours in Vietnam. Swear like the sailor I once was. A guy's guy. And yet I'm dead square stuck on this ... Women's Thing.

If nothing else, it has led me to some amazing encounters with amazing women.

• Media superstar Linda Ellerbee, one of my all-time heroines, approached me at a reception following the Fifth Worldwide Lessons in Leadership Teleconference, the biggest show of its kind (Management Town Hall) on earth. Linda was the host-referee of the show, which featured three OWMs: Ken Blanchard and Stephen Covey, both over 60, and Youthful Tom Peters, aged 58 at the time. Linda—the Toughest Dudette or Dude in Any Damn Town!—not only gave me a hug, but teared up. WHY? "Thank you, thank you for doing the 'women's thing,'" she said. "Coming from you makes all the difference."

• August 2000. After my speech in Hong Kong to a meeting of top managers from SC Johnson, the giant consumer-goods company, I headed for the streets for some of that city's fabled shopping. (I am the shopper in my family!) As I approached the hotel's front door, an elegantly turned-out professional woman accosted me and thanked me effusively for doing the "women's thing." She said that she was, if I recall correctly, the first working mom ever promoted by her company to corporate VP. And in saying what I had said at that meeting, I'd offered "public confirmation" from a Respected OWM for her achievement.

In short, I've been blown away. By incredible stories. By hard, cold facts. By the immensity of this opportunity. By the degree to which "we" (by which I mean "men") have neglected it. By the extent of the emotional response I have elicited from hard-nosed, successful businesswomen.

Hey, I'm having the time of my life with this issue! I intend to stick the needle in OWMs as often, as deeply, and as painfully as I possibly can! I think it's a hoot to watch

---

RESTROOM BREAK

I had the distinct honor of keynoting the 2002 convention of the American Institute of Architects. And I had the distinct pleasure of giving my audience hell about ... the Women's Issue. In particular, I gave those (males) assembled a piece of very practical advice.

Instructions:

1. Purchase ticket to symphony ... 7:30 p.m. show.
2. Drink three large bottles of water between 5 p.m. and 7 p.m.
3. Cross-dress.
4. At Intermission, wait in queue at the Ladies room.
5. Squirm.
6. And, uh ...
7. Realize what total wretches you are.
8. Return to auditorium, seize the microphone, and apologize ... publicly ... to every woman in the hall.

Go to a symphony. A play. A ballet. Whatever. At Intermission: Men's room: No line, no prob! Women's room: Lines that seem to stretch for half a block.

Will "we" ever learn? Somehow ... I fear not.

them squirm! (And to watch a few of them—Big Wigs, especially—turn beet red with ire.) And I know that ... for those who can stop squirming, for those who can contain their vainglorious anger ... the collective payoff will be in the ... yes ... TRILLION$$$.

! Contrasts

WAS	IS
Transaction	Relationship
"Buying" brands	"Joining" brands
Equality for women: a moral issue	Equality for women: an opportunity!
Condescending to women	Catering to women
Women buy, big-time (and men ignore that fact)	Women buy, big-time (and men embrace that fact)
Women spend men's money	Women spend their own money
Women are a "specialty" market	Women are the market
Women's-market "initiatives"	Women's-market strategy
Men design, unthinkingly, for men	Men and women design— with women in mind
Women hit a "glass ceiling"	Women have corner offices

14 TRENDS WORTH TRILLION$$$ II: BOOMER BONANZA

! Technicolor Rules ...

- Reject "It's 18-44, Stupid!" Embrace "18-44 Is Stupid, Stupid!"
- "This notion of 'impressionable kids' and 'hidebound geezers' is little more than a fairy tale, a Madison Avenue gloss on Hollywood's cult of youth."
- I HAVE NOT YET BEGUN TO SPEND!
- "The mature market is the dominant market in the U.S. economy, making the majority of expenditures in virtually every category."
- Review the numbers: If a group controls the vast majority of wealth and discretionary income, then ... it is the market.

! RANT

We are not prepared ...

We remain caught in the grip of a "youth fetish." We orient most of our enterprise activity ... in marketing, in product development, even in strategy ... toward the over-coveted 18 to 44-year-old demographic set. We assume, wrongly, that older consumers constitute a stagnant, unapproachable market ... and thus we overlook an enormous opportunity. But we must understand that the 50-and-over population is growing immensely in terms of numbers, wealth, and longevity. And to serve that market we must ... *completely reorient our enterprises.*

! VISION

I imagine ...

A stream of new products designed for older consumers who seek not to "give in to" the aging process ... but rather to confront and transcend it.

The development of new marketing approaches by people who don't worship at the Altar of Youth ... approaches that recognize the particular demands and the abundant, fast-growing wealth of 50-and-over Boomers.

The emergence of enterprises that ... *Strategically Realign* ... their entire organization around serving a population whose members are reinventing the very meaning of "old."

An understanding by businesses of all stripes that Boomers are more than a niche. They are a ... Gigantic Vault ... where (damn near all) the loot is.

"Meat Market" Madness

In 2001, I had the privilege of speaking to the International Health, Racquet & Sportsclub Association (IHRSA).

A bit of background: I've been fighting weight problems since I was a kid. And I've been fighting them with (shall we say) very modest success in the last half-dozen years. But there I was in San Francisco, addressing a group of several thousand health-club owners and managers. So lean. So fit. So vibrant. And: So annoying! (Not a male waist bigger than 32 inches ... or so I imagined.)

The moment came in my remarks to IHRSA members when I harangued them about the biggest trend facing their industry. I unveiled a slew of startling statistics (perversely, *their* statistics)[1] on the demographic tsunami bearing down on them. Then the show's lighting director (I had connived with him beforehand) put the spotlight on my none-too-emaciated frame. And I bellowed.

"BEHOLD ... the Body of Your Future. Love me! Love my ... Wallet."

Some laughed. Some scowled. No matter. I WAS RIGHT.

Health- and sports-club types love to serve people with young, trim bodies. And yet, it is people like me—the not-so-young and not-so-trim-but-ever-so-determined— who embody the real growth market for their historically youth-obsessed business.

Despite my advanced age, I am more than willing to look at attractive members of the opposite sex. Nonetheless, I would rather not work out ... in my bumbling, puffing fashion ... in an atmosphere geared toward Lithe Human Machines.

Health clubs are not designed for, or marketed to, people like me.

Why not? Don't they like money?

Marketing Mantra Makeover

America loves youth! More to the point: Marketing types love youth!

Implicitly if not explicitly, they develop and direct almost every product or service you can imagine ... at "grabbing hold of teens and young adults, and keeping those consumers as 'customers for life.'"

Hence the marketing mantra (and I mean *the* Marketing Mantra): "It's 18–44, Stupid!"

What a load of crap!

I have a suggestion. No ... A COMMAND.

Reject: "It's 18–44, Stupid!"

Embrace: "18–44 Is Stupid, Stupid!"

MEMBERSHIP DOOZY

[1]IHRSA sent me a bale of background material. I was surprised ... no, stunned ... by one set of stats in particular.

Between 1987 and 1997, IHRSA club membership among those aged 18 to 34 grew by 27 percent. Among those aged 35 to 54, membership grew by 103 percent.

And what of those aged 54 and above? Membership growth: *123 percent*.

Talk about bulking up!

"We" are getting older. LOTS OF US. Populations in the industrialized world are aging. FAST. And the meaning of "older" and "aging" is changing. RADICALLY.

An overview of my argument in this chapter:

1. The "new mature" are numerous. (In the United States, Boomers—those born between 1946 and 1964—number almost 80 million people.)

2. They (we) are astonishingly wealthy.

3. They (we) have decades of productive, free-spending, "wild" years left.

4. They (we) are accustomed to being well served by commercial enterprise.

5. They (we) are now being ill served by commercial enterprise. (The older they/we get, it seems, the more steadfastly enterprise seeks to avoid their/our custom.)

This trend is big. So must be our response to it.

The Age-Old "Old Age" Taboo

"'Age Power' will rule the 21st century," writes Ken Dychtwald in *Age Power: How the 21st Century Will Be Ruled by the New Old*, "and ... we are woefully unprepared."

"Woefully unprepared": I humbly disagree with that assessment. It is not that we are "unprepared." It is that we ... JUST DON'T SEEM TO GIVE A SHIT.

That's vivid language. But I don't see how the cold, logical facts in the matter could lead to any other conclusion.

I asked Ken why he thought people had paid so little attention to such an enormous issue. His take: We are so youth-obsessed that we remain squeamish, frankly, about the very notion of getting older. Aging, indeed, is frighteningly close to ... a Taboo Subject.

Fine. But ignoring it won't make it go away. And if you're in business today, ignoring the "older" market may well cause you to dodge enormous potential revenues.

To put it bluntly: TRILLION$$$ UPON TRILLION$$$ ... ARE UP FOR GRABS. (In the U.S. alone.)[2]

A "MATURING" THESIS
This Boomer Market trend is big—as big as the Women's Market trend.

However, even though I am a Prime Example of the Boomer Market trend, it didn't really capture my attention until somewhat recently. Hence, this chapter will be quite brief. I have spent more than six years on the "Women's Thing," and I have collected a ton of data and another ton of telling anecdotes about it. (See Chapter 13.) Not so the "Geezer Thing."

But I will attempt to present this ... well ... skimpy chapter with the same degree of PASSION as the previous "Trends Worth Trillion$$$" chapter. The market opportunity here is no less huge.

BELIEVE IT.

GRAY EXPECTATIONS
[2]Compared with other fully developed nations, the U.S. case is far from extreme. Indeed, the "Aging Thing" will be ... more extreme ... in Western Europe and Japan than in the United States.

Italy, for instance, recently passed a first-time-in-human-history threshold: There are more Italians over 60 years of age than there are Italians under age 20.

Overall in the industrialized countries, the over-60 crowd makes up 20 percent of the population, up from 12 percent in 1950. And they are on the way to forming one-third of the population (in Japan, the figure will be *40* percent) by 2050.

Voices: In the Demographic Dogma House

"Advertisers pay more to reach the kid because they think that once someone hits middle age he's too set in his ways to be susceptible to advertising. ... In fact, this notion of impressionable kids and hidebound geezers is little more than a fairy tale, a Madison Avenue gloss on Hollywood's cult of youth." —James Surowiecki, *New Yorker*, April 2002

"Many businesses have not yet shed the outdated view that the mature market is made up of stingy old-timers set in their ways. Unless you are in the business of prescription drugs or retirement homes ... why bother?" —*Economist*, August 2002

"[Marketers' attempts] to reach those over 50 have been miserably unsuccessful. No market's motivations and needs are so poorly understood." —Peter Francese, founding publisher of *American Demographics*

"The mature market ... cannot be dismissed as entrenched in its brand loyalties." — Carol Morgan and Doran Levy, *Marketing to the Mindset of Boomers and Their Elders*

Ms. Morgan and Mr. Levy add: "Focused on assessing the market place based on lifetime value (LTV), marketers may dismiss the mature market as headed to its grave. The reality is that at 60 a person in the U.S. may enjoy 20 or 30 years of life."

Yes!

Do the Math: Attack of the Godzilla Geezer

If you remember nothing else from this chapter, please remember the following set of simple stats. In the United States, between 2002 and 2010 ...

- The number of people between 18 and 44 years of age (remember the overweaning "18–44" mantra) will **DECLINE by 1 percent**.

(DECLINE = -1%.)

- The number of people aged 55 and older will **INCREASE by 21 percent**.

(INCREASE = +21%.)

- In particular ... and here we face ... the Ultimate Marketing Tsunami ... the number of people between 55 and 64 years of age will increase by **... 47 percent**.

(INCREASE = +47%.)

The only proper response to numbers like these:

Holy shit!

Do the Math: Codgers with Cash

Ken Dychtwald is to *aging* ... as Faith Popcorn is to *women*. He has been covering the "aging market" for more than two decades. And, until very recently, he was damn near the only one writing about it.

Here are some figures that Ken adduces regarding people aged 50 and above in the United States alone:

- They control *$7 trillion in wealth*—which is 70 percent of *all* U.S. wealth.

- They bring in *$2 trillion in annual income*, and account for 50 percent of all discretionary spending. (Remember: Their mortgage is paid, the kids are out of school, the pension checks are rolling in ... and so on.)

- 79 percent of them own homes.

- There are *40 million credit-card users* among them.
- They buy *41 percent of new cars and half of all luxury cars*.
- They account for *$610 billion in healthcare spending*, and for *74 percent of prescription-drug spending*.

Which leads Dychtwald to wonder: *Why are they the target of only 5 percent of advertising dollars?*

Why?[3]

The Maturing of the "Mature" Market

In an important sense, the numbers are the least of it. Or, at least, not the most of it. The salient truth about the Boomer Bonanza is this: It represents an *Entirely New Market*. Because Boomers are ... an *Entirely New Group* of aging folks.

I'm 60. My Dad is now dead, but I well remember when he turned 60. The future for him? No particular aspirations. His main idea (as they say in football and basketball): RUN OUT THE CLOCK.

NO MORE!

America's almost 80 million Boomers, whose first cohort turned 57 in 2003, have had a Unique Life History. They have ... AND THEY ARE THE FIRST GENERATION IN HISTORY TO DO SO ... Taken Full Charge of Their Lives.

Their attitude, then and now, as summed up in a few simple phrases:

"I am in charge." "I am active."

"I have a lot left to do. And I can afford to do it."

Voices: The New "Age-Appropriate" Behavior

"From jogging to plastic surgery, from vegetarian diets to Viagra, [aging Boomers] are fighting to preserve their youth and defy the effects of gravity."—M. W. C. Howgill, "Healthcare Consumerism, the Information Revolution, and Branding"

"The Latest Golden-Years Trend: Going Back to College."—Headline, *Newsweek*, June 2002

HEY: BIG SPENDERS!

[3]Carol Morgan and Doran Levy, in their marvelous book *Marketing to the Mindset of Boomers and Their Elders*, offer statistics that are as stunning as Dychtwald's. They choose age 40 as their threshold for measurement. While 40 might seem young to some of you, that's not what marketers think. They shower attention on teens and twenty-somethings—and pay almost as little attention to forty-somethings as they do to members of the 50-plus bunch.

Morgan and Levy write: "Households headed by someone 40 and older enjoy 91 percent [$9.7 trillion] of our population's net worth." And: "The mature market is the dominant market in the U.S. economy, making the majority of expenditures in virtually every category." Please reread that last sentence. Slowly. Then share it with a colleague. Or two or three. (Or 23.) Key words: EVERY. CATEGORY.

"Such a critical mass of older women with a tradition of rebellion and independence and a way of making a living has not occurred before in history."—Gerda Lerner, historian

"NOT ACTING THEIR AGE: As Baby Boomers Zoom into Retirement, Will America Ever Be the Same?"—Cover story, *U.S. News & World Report*, June 2001

The answer to the *U.S. News* query is implicit in the question itself: NO! Boomers are NOT "acting their age" ... and don't intend to.

And America ... along with Western Europe and Japan and the rest of the developed world ... WILL NEVER BE THE SAME.

You're Only As Old as You ... Look!

"Growing old gracefully" used to mean "giving in to nature" ... and thus losing your luster. No more. Older folks are rewriting that old joke "Age before beauty." The new motto: "Age *and* Beauty."

From a late 2002 Associated Press report: "After Hazel York's husband died, she moved into a retirement home, convinced the better part of her life was over. Then she met Damon. She's 81. He's 79. They were married about a year and a half ago at The Village Community Care Retirement Community in Hemet, Calif. She feels she won a second chance at life, so she decided to give her face a second chance, too. York underwent a five-hour face-lift in June in Beverly Hills, Calif., to erase some wrinkles and shave off a few years. Her husband is supportive, but said, 'I love her as is.' She says she did it for herself. 'Don't get me wrong. I don't want to look 16 again,' she said, 'but I also don't want to look like Damon's mother.'

"Experts say thousands of men and women 65 and older are getting plastic surgery. They want to feel young and attractive, and battle age discrimination. Since 1997, the number of cosmetic procedures for those 65 and older jumped from about nearly 121,000 to more than 425,000 last year. Seniors accounted for about 5 percent of 8.5 million surgeries performed in 2001, according to the American Society for Aesthetic Plastic Surgery in Los Alamitos, California."

Dr. Sheldon Sevinor, a plastic surgeon based in Boston, said he had at least 30

GOLDEN YEARS, GOLDEN WORDS
Key terms that define the lifestyle priorities of the "new old," according to Ken Dychtwald, author of *Age Wave:*
"Experiences" ...
"Convenience" ...
"Comfort"...
"Access" ...

"GRAY" UNDER PRESSURE?
Unlike the "Women's Thing," "this "aging thing" hits me personally. Age-wise, I'm traveling north of 60. (Hence, I'm not even officially a Boomer. I've graduated to Geezer.) Will somebody help me—and many, many tens of millions like me—as we continue our "travels"? If you do, we will shower you with riches. And, actuarially speaking, we will do so for many years to come.

Remember the famous clarion call of naval commander John Paul Jones during the American Revolutionary War: "I have not yet begun to fight"? Well ... I HAVE NOT YET BEGUN TO SPEND!

patients last year that are older than 70. 'We're living longer and feeling more vital,' he said. 'Age 40 today is what age 30 used to be like.' He recently performed breast enlargement surgery on an 82-year-old Boston woman, his oldest patient to have the procedure. 'She's healthy, she's spunky and she wanted to look how she felt,' he said.

"Dr. John Grossman, who performed York's surgery and runs cosmetic surgery clinics in Denver and Beverly Hills, Calif., said he has had many patients her age. 'Hazel's a perfect example that chronological age doesn't have to relate to how you feel about yourself. Just because you're 80 doesn't mean you have to look and feel like it,' he said."

Do the Math: Aging Assumptions

More startling stats, courtesy Ms. Morgan and Mr. Levy:

"While the average American aged 12 and older watched at least five movies per year in a theater, those 40 and older were the most frequent moviegoers,[4] viewing 12 or more ..."

(Holy smoke!)

"Women 65 and older spent $14.7 billion on apparel in 1999, almost as much as that spent by 25- to 34-year-olds. While spending by the older women increased from the previous year by 12 percent, that of the younger group increased only 0.1 percent. But who in the fashion industry is currently pursuing this market?"

(Holy smoke!)

Geezer Goods: A Market Comes of Age

What would feeding the Godzilla Geezer market actually look like? The *Economist*, in a rare article on this subject, offers a few glimmerings[5] of what-might-be:

Makeup. In 2001, cosmetics maker L'Oréal signed up then-57-year-old French actress Catherine Deneuve to plug its products. Estée Lauder countered by turning to Karen Graham, a 1970s model.

Margarine. Unilever's margarine category was slumping until it introduced Pro-activ, a spread that lowers cholesterol. Kaboom! An entire division was rejuvenated.

Mineral water. Danone introduced calcium-rich mineral water. Better yet, it created packaging for the product that features large print and an easy-grip cap that aids arthritics.

Telephones. NTT DoCoMo introduced a new cell phone, Raku-Raku ("easy-easy"), with larger buttons and easier-to-read numbers. *(Where can I get one?)* Intriguingly (but perhaps not surprisingly), younger folks loved it, too.

Transit. Paris public transport (RATP) introduced an easy to read, simplified map for the aging population. Acceptance was universal, and the old map was dumped.

"OLD" MOVIES
[4]Hey, I loved *The Royal Tenenbaums*. Watched it twice in theaters, three times in hotels. Made me aware of what's not available on the silver screen.

Psst: Are you paying attention, Hollywood?

GET A GRIP
[5]Serving the "older" market has synergistic effects down the age scale.

A wonderful case in point: OXO-brand kitchen devices, whose arthritic-friendly grips have made them global bestsellers ... among people of all ages.

NEW BUSINESS **!** NEW MARKETS

Cars. From the article in the *Economist*: "To help young designers to understand older users' limitations, Age Concern, a British non-profit organization, has developed a 'through other eyes' training programme for retailers. It tries to simulate the physical limitations that older customers experience when shopping. Ford, a car maker, has come up with something called 'the third-age suit' to help its design engineers—most of whom are under 40—grasp the needs of aging drivers. The outfit adds about 30 years to the wearer's age by stiffening the knees, elbows, ankles, and wrists. It also adds material at the waist—a rotund stomach affects people's ability to sit easily—and it has gloves that reduce the sense of touch. Ford's lucky designers also have to wear yellow scratched goggles to find out what it is like to have cataracts. The exercise has been fruitful. Thanks to the third-age suit, the company's cars are now easier for everyone to get into and out of; their seat belts are more comfortable to wear; glare has been reduced; and the controls are more readable and reachable."

My Target: "Target" Marketing

Those are all great cases. But they are just ... *cases*.[6] Isolated events in a ... Grand Marketing Narrative ... that continues to treat Youth as its hero.

They are a far cry from ... Strategic Realignment. And anything less than Strategic Realignment ... that is, reorienting your enterprise from the ground up to serve the emerging markets ... will leave you in the cramped, low-growth world of "niche" marketing.

Martha Barletta begs CEOs not to consign the "Women's Thing" to a "specialty market group." Women *are* the market, she says. (And I most definitely agree—see Chapter 13.) So, too, the Godzilla Geezer Thing.

Review the numbers: If a group controls the vast majority of wealth and discretionary income, then ... it is the market.

"ZOOM" TIME
[6]Headline from *Advertising Age*: "Take the Road Less Traveled." The story: Sony is belatedly targeting "Zoomers"—the heretofore neglected 34 percent of its customers who are aged 50 and older.

GOING, GOING ... STRATEGIC!
It was a gorgeous, late July morning on Martha's Vineyard. I was at breakfast at the Black Dog Café with a very senior executive from an enormous corporation.

I mentioned my "Trends Worth Trillions" stuff to him: "I see lots of 'initiatives' around. Some bank launches a 'Women's Initiative.' Some health services company starts a program to focus on Boomers. But I don't see anybody ... ANYBODY ... that is 'Going Strategic' around these trends.

"Tell me," I continued, "have I got it wrong?"

"No," he shot back, "you don't have it wrong."

We talked on, and wandered back to the Women's Thing, in particular. "I don't know why it hasn't 'gone strategic,' as you put it," he said. "I think we treat it as an aside. There's no real champion who holistically shoves it down our throats, day in and day out. Want to do that for us?"

I'm not looking for a full-time job. But I am looking to goad people into going beyond the "aside" mentality. So please ... *GO STRATEGIC!*

Which is not to say that my argument here is "about" marketing. Rather: It is about marketing ... *and* product development ... *and* distribution ... *and* branding ... *and* strategy. In conclusion:

Think ... WOMEN. Think ... BOOMERS.
Think ... TRILLION$$$.
Think ... BRAND PROMISE.
Think ... STRATEGIC REALIGNMENT.

! Contrasts

WAS	IS
Gray means "gray"	Gray means green
Retirement	Rejuvenation
"Borrowed time"	"Decades to go"
Old = Decrepit	Old = Active
Marketing mantra: "18 to 44"	Marketing mantra: "50 & up"
"Older people don't switch brands"	"Older people make brands"
Fountain of "youth"	Freedom of "age"
"Maturity"	Longevity
"Running out the clock"	"Revving up the engine"
Lost earning power	New spending power
"I'm starting to clip coupons"	"I have not yet begun to spend!"

NEW BUSINESS **!** • NEW MARKETS

**New Age! New Work! Reward
excellent failures... punish mediocre
successes!**

new bus!ness
new work

There's a funny thing about management books. They talk about "organization structure." About "motivation." About "marketing strategies." And so on.

They talk about damn near everything. Except for ... THE WORK ITSELF.

I don't give two hoots in hell about "theory" or "strategy." I like "doing stuff." And I'm drawn to people who like "doing stuff." That is, I am obsessed about ... THE WORK ITSELF.

Work that ... Matters. Work you can ... Brag About. That's the whole shtick here ... the Whole Shtick and the Only Shtick.

My mantra: It's WOW Projects, stupid. (Or else.)

15 MAKING WORK MATTER: THE WOW PROJECT!

! Technicolor Rules ...

- WOW.
- "Nobody gives you power. You just take it."
- "Obeying the rules is obeying their rules."
- "Don't just express yourself. Invent yourself."
- "Astonish me."
- "Build something great."
- "Make it immortal."

 ! RANT

We are not prepared ...

We too often view ourselves as victims of heartless organizations, as pawns, as hapless and helpless "cubicle slaves." We must remind ourselves that the White-Collar Revolution will erase all that. We must understand that in the New Economy all work is project work—and that every project must be a WOW (special) Project. (Or else.) ("Or else" means "No role whatsoever" ... for cubicle slaves content to perform de facto "rote chores.")

 ! VISION

I imagine ...

A world where ... WORK MATTERS.

A world where ... *Dilbert* Is Denied.

A world where we ... Learn Something New Every Day.

A world where we ... Revel in the Thrill of Changing Times.

A world where we can ... Brag About What We Do. ("Brag" = Big Word.)

WOW—What Is It Good For?

In *The Leader's Voice*, my colleagues Boyd Clarke and Ron Crossland tell a wonderful story about Marilyn Carlson. When Marilyn was a young girl, she told her dad, Kurt Carlson (owner of the Carlson Travel network), that she thought Sunday School was dull. She felt the time had come for her to start going to adult church.

Young Miss C. got an earful from Dear Old Dad. He said it was *not* time to go to adult church. Instead, he told her: "If you don't like Sunday School, change it."

So she did.

That was ... for all intents and purposes ...

Marilyn Carlson's First WOW Project. But hardly her last. She's now Big Boss of the entire Carlson mega-enterprise. Marilyn Carlson learned early on that the road to success was paved with ... WOW Projects. Project: a task that has a beginning and an end, as well as deliverables along the way. WOW Project: one that has "goals and objectives" that inspire. And inspire others.

WOW Projects are ...
- Projects that Matter.
- Projects that Make a Difference.
- Projects that you can Brag About ... forever.
- Projects that Transform the Enterprise.
- Projects that Take Your Breath Away. (Appropriate technical measure.)
- Projects that make you/me/us/"them" Smile.
- Projects that Highlight the Value that You Add ... and Why ... You Are Here on Earth. (Yes. That Big.)
- WOW Projects are ... not hype.
- WOW Projects are ... a necessity. (New necessity.)

The Tao of WOW

The best way to get at the Quintessential Spirit of the WOW Project is to listen to those who "get it."

First up ... Roseanne! *"Nobody gives you power,"* she said. *"You just take it."*

"Obeying the rules," writes Harriet Rubin in *The Princessa: Machiavelli for Women*, *"is obeying their rules. [Women] can never be powerful as long as they try to be in charge the same way men take charge."*

Henry Louis Gates Jr. put it this way in a commencement address at Hamilton College: *"Don't just express yourself. Invent yourself. And don't restrict yourself to off-the-shelf models."*

The great ballet choreographer Sergei Diaghilev routinely begged his prima ballerinas: *"Astonish me!"*

Nintendo's former president Hiroshi Yamauchi, when the company's top game designer once asked what he should do next, responded: *"Build something great!"*

Legendary ad man David Ogilvy told a copywriter who inquired about the desired outcome of a project: *"Make it immortal!"*

The "How" of WOW

How should you evaluate a project? Any project? Every project?

In my book *The Project50*, I urge readers to measure every project they undertake along four dimensions (and to measure each dimension *quantitatively*):

Wow!
Beauty!
Impact!
Raving fans![1]

So what, in particular, do I mean when I refer to measuring the "WOW!" dimension? Consider your current project. Or, if you're the chief, consider your portfolio of departmental projects.

On a scale of 1 to 10, rate each project more or less as follows:

1 "Another day's work. Pays the rent."

4 "We do something 'of value.' "

7 "Pretty damn cool (and definitely subversive)."

10 "WE AIM TO CHANGE THE WORLD."

With every project, you should continually be asking: *Is it ... WOW? Is it ... still WOW? Does it ... "take your breath away"?*

"Take your breath away." In these ... yes ... Breathtaking Times ... shouldn't that be the Goal of Anything that You Do? Isn't that routinely what a ballplayer tries to do during a ball game? Isn't that routinely what a cellist tries to do during a three-minute solo? Why the hell shouldn't that be what you try to do ... in ... Finance ... Engineering ... HR ... IS?

Jim Collins, co-author of *Built to Last*, and I disagree about a lot of things. (See Chapter 2.) But one idea of his that I agree with ... that I LOVE ... is his notion that every

---

RAVING REVIEW

[1] I stole that last "dimension" from Ken Blanchard and Sheldon Bowles, who in their book *Raving Fans* tell readers to ask themselves: Do customers "rave" about what we do?

Rave!
Not: "Are you 'satisfied'?"
Not: "Did we 'exceed expectations'?"
Rave = Very Cool Word.
Rave = Very Big Word.
(Not so incidentally, Mr. Bowles invented this idea while running a string of discount gas stations in the Canadian wilds. Not an arena for "raving fans," you'd think. Think again! No limits.)

project must have a ... BHAG.[2]

BHAG: Big Hairy Audacious Goal.

Awesome term. Awesome ... indeed, audacious ... concept.

Legacy: Leaving WOW in Your Wake

Legacy. L-e-g-a-c-y. It's a Huge word. It asks, "Did I Matter?" (Yikes.) (As in, Yikes.)

Legacy is not, I've concluded, a word that applies only to those who are over age 60. It is a word ... for ... all of us ... all the time.

I had a dispiriting session in Bermuda with several of that country's top CEOs. This was not long after the imposition of the new, restrictive Sarbanes-Oxley financial-services legislation, and these CEOs felt trapped.

I wasn't very helpful.

I said, "Baloney."

"You are ... C-E-Os," I continued. "By mortal standards, that's a ... Big Deal. So the issue—THE ISSUE—is whether you see these new 'restraints' as 'restraining' or as disguised 'opportunities.'"

I was so frustrated by the undercurrent of negativism that I finally said (to these Very Powerful People): "Please leap forward to 2007, then 2012. Write a Brief Business History of Your Post-Bermuda Career. WHAT WILL HAVE BEEN SAID ABOUT ... YOUR COMPANY ... DURING YOUR TENURE AT THE TOP?

"Somehow," I added with perhaps a sniff of sarcasm, "I doubt you'll write, 'I was flummoxed by regulation and really didn't get much done.'"

Distressed by my "CEO Summit," I was very happy the next morning to move on to my meeting with ... Kids!

Hooray!

At a formal session with "Future Leaders of Bermuda" I was bombarded by the ... Toughest Questions ... I've ever faced:

"What's your vision of the future?"

"Do you feel you have an obligation to make the world better?"

"What have you accomplished since your first book 20 years ago?"

WOW!

Talk about stretching!

Why! (Why!) Why ... aren't questions from 50-year-olds as ... Fundamental ... as those from 20-year-olds?

BHAG MAN

[2] A very senior financial services executive I know latched on to Collins' lingo. He started to ask his people where (specifically!) "the BHAG" was in their part of his firm's current strategic plan. In response, he mostly got red faces ... and probably, when he wasn't looking, a few titters.

But that was two years ago. Today, Mr. Big is still singing the BHAG Anthem, and BHAG-ing is in Full Flourish at said (GIANT) firm.

Why?
Legacy?
Did I Matter?

Nothing Succeeds Like ... Failure

Phil Daniels is a successful Australian businessman who attended a seminar I gave in Sydney. Amid an audience of over 1,000 people, he stood up to support a point I'd made. But what he said ended up making me see the world in a different light. His career success, Daniels said, flowed from a "very simple philosophy."

Two sentences. Six words. Namely:

"Reward excellent failures." "Punish mediocre successes."

I love that!

In my master PowerPoint presentation, I have well over 1,000 slides. By definition, one of them must appear first on the Provocative/Important scale. In my mind ... *The Daniels Formula*... occupies that lofty spot.

An "excellent failure": You take a Bold, Brash, Brassy Leap Forward.[3] Oops ... it doesn't work. And you end up on your hindquarters ... bruised *and* battered. Good for you! You went for it! You got a heady whiff of the Land of BHAG! That whiff, despite the subsequent bruises, eggs you on toward your Gold Medal in IS or training.

It's simple (if daunting): No true WOW-BHAG project ever comes into being without ... a willingness to court ... Excellent Failure/s.[4]

In a world where ... confusion reigns ... where we must ... Experiment Our Way into the Future ... the Only Way Forward is to ... Court & Reward Excellent Failures.

NO BULL.

PEAK (AND VALLEY) EXPERIENCES

[3]I spent 30 years living among the "excellent failures" of Silicon Valley. They were the hallmark of Valley Culture, long before Dot-Com Madness came along. Somewhere in Santa Clara County, there is a Business Cemetery of the Mind, where you'll find thousands of unmarked graves of failed computer companies, failed semiconductor companies, failed software companies, failed memory storage companies—and, yes, failed dot-com companies.

Several economists, all of them wiser on this issue than I am, have argued that those Bold Failures are not just a "byproduct" of the Valley's success; they are the Primary Enabler thereof.

JACK, OUT OF THE BOX (AS USUAL)

[4]Jack Welch once made essentially the same point as Phil Daniels. Welch claims that nobody who worked for him ever got in trouble for swinging for the fences and missing. What people got in trouble for was spending two years on a project that—even if it succeeded—wasn't going to make the world wobble on its axis.

That is: Mediocre Success = Big Trouble.

(B-I-G TROUBLE.)

The JAMS Jam

Now to the flip side of the Daniels Formula ... "Punish mediocre successes."

Remember Mr. Kaizen ... aka Continuous Improvement Man? Now's the time to ... just say "No" to Mr. K. To be sure, the work that Mr. K. does is valuable: A bit of improvement here. A touch of change there. In other words, one mediocre success after another. (Incrementalism ad nauseam.)[5]

Problem: "Mediocre successes" may be just fine ... for Mediocre Times. But these are *not* ... mediocre times. These are *not* times that demand "a bit of" this or "a touch of" that. These are times that demand ... Going For It.

WOW or Wuss!
BHAG or Bust!
Excellent or Extinct!
Different or Dead!

So let's make this our motto for the times: *No Damn JAMS.* No more ... "Just Another Mediocre Success." Far too much effort is wasted by far too many intelligent people pursuing ... Just Another Mediocre Success.

NO DAMN JAMS. P-E-R-I-O-D.

I clearly remember when I started airing the Daniels Shtick in my presentations. I was speaking to the top 300 officers of one of our largest financial services companies. The CEO was startlingly silent throughout my remarks, but he approached me afterward.

"You pretty much ruined my day, though I'll pay you for your services," he said with half a laugh, and with more than a little chagrin. "It was that 'mediocre successes' thing. We are dependent upon the quality of our information technology. We launch project after project. Truth be told, spend tens of millions of dollars a year. And the simple fact is, after those projects have been dumbed down and politicized by various factions within the enterprise—well, damn it, virtually all of them end up as 'mediocre successes.' I'm beside myself. Maybe there's some intriguing merit in the other half of your friend's idea: 'Reward excellent failures.' I'm going to think on that."

PRESS "RELEASE!" (PLEASE)
[5] *I pick up the* **Wall Street Journal.** *News flash: A giant company has announced a "major" reorganization. One unit will be hitched to another unit—in order to make doing business somewhat easier.*

Nothing wrong with that.

So why does my stomach turn when I read that story?

The problem: There is nothing right about that, either! *This is a proud company. But it's going nowhere. It's beset with killer problems. And this announcement fails to address the deep "corporate culture" issues that keep it from moving forward.*

In fact, suggesting that the move is "serious" and "strategic" reinforces the sense that leadership is even further out of touch than I'd imagined.

Shifting the boxes on the org chart—that's all that I see here. The word "WOW"? Or "BHAG"? I can't imagine anyone at this company ever using such words. Or any other form of hot language.

The Wasted Life: How *Not* to WOW

In my seminars, I frequently point to a *Fortune* magazine story that compared the most admired corporations in the world to the "also-rans." The losers had in common a tendency to focus on these four goals (LHMGs: "Little Hairless Mediocre Goals"?):

"Minimize risk."

"Respect the chain of command."

"Support the boss."

"Make budget."

Aargh!

What a (timid) way to live!

But often as not, when I cite that report, I'm actively confronted by people who say: "Tom, you just don't get the 'real world.'" (A helluva thing to say to a 60-year-old.) In the real world, they say, respecting the chain of command is "where it's at" ... supporting the boss is "non-negotiable" ... making budget is "critical" ... minimizing risk is "essential."

Then I attack. Savagely.

"Look at a damn history book," I spit. *"Go and get your 10th-grade daughter's text. Pull out 50 names. Drop the jerks (Hitler, Stalin). Then look at the rest. Jefferson. Washington. Hamilton. Steinem. Madame Curie. Einstein. Newton. Picasso. De Gaulle. Churchill. Gandhi. King.*

"Did anyone on that list 'minimize risk'? (Oh, how I can utter that phrase with dripping contempt.) 'Respect the chain of command'? 'Support the boss'? 'Make budget'?"

What I really want to do is to put those "real world" people to ... The Epitaph Test. I wonder ... I really wonder ... whether any of them, down deep, could live with the following epitaphs:[6]

Joe J. Jones

1942–2003

He always made budget

(Or: "He minimized risk")

(Or: "He respected the chain of command")

(Or: "He supported the boss")

Joe J. Jones

1942–2003

CEO, 1993–2003.

He hit quarterly earnings
targets 44 times in a row

NEW BUSINESS → • → NEW WORK

GRAVE THOUGHT

[6]Recall, from the Foreword, my most feared epitaph:

Thomas J. Peters

1942–2003

He would have done some really cool stuff ...

But his boss wouldn't let him

There is nothing wrong with any of the above. The problem: *There is nothing "right" about any of the above ... either.*

WOW Is Me: The Red Exclamation Mark!

For better or for worse, I buy my own act. I shun the ... Mediocre Goals ... of "also-ran" companies. And I believe that the ... Essence of Enterprise Excellence in Disruptive Times ... is ... the ... Relentless Pursuit of WOW.

All of which came to a "point" (you'll see what I mean by "point" in a flash) when I tackled a particular WOW Project of my own. A couple of years ago, I decided to re-brand my company. To give the Tom Peters Company a new look, a new logo. I knew it would be a daunting task. I worked with a designer, Ken Silvia, who is so simpatico with me that we finish each other's sentences.

It took us over a year and a half. (Truly.) And you know what we ended up with as a logo: a red exclamation mark (!).

Yes! One-point-five years to create ... a "simple" red exclamation mark. And I couldn't have been more ecstatic.

Go ahead. Chuckle. But we think it's as powerful ... though not (yet) as valuable ... as the Nike Swoosh.

What do the last 35 years of my professional life add up to?

Simple. **A Red Exclamation Mark.**

Please, do not steal my logo. But please, do steal the Spirit of the Logo.

The Spirit of WOW!

BIG "PHAT" TRUTH

Words, words, words ... again. Why do I use words like WOW! (complete with capital letters and, yes, maybe an exclamation mark)? Let me answer the question this way. An Amazon.com reviewer of my book *The Professional Service Firm50* asked why I would use a word like "phat" in "business writing"—especially given my ... *very advanced* age.

Implicit (or not-so-implicit) message: Grow up!

My response:

1. I do not intend to ... "grow up."
2. I do not like ... "business writing."
3. *I am on a* ... mission. *A mission to Drive Dilbertian Cynicism and Cubicle Slavery and Terminal Insipidity out of the Workplace.*

I am all about: PASSION. COMMITMENT. HUGE RISKS. EXCELLENT FAILURES. WORK THAT MATTERS. WORK THAT MAKES A DIFFERENCE. WORK THAT DEMANDS TO BE PUNCTUATED WITH A ... RED EXCLAMATION MARK.

In a word ... PHAT.

Weekend WOW

Scenes from a trip to New York City ...

Thursday night. The Orchestra of St. Lukes, under Sir Charles Mackerras' inspired direction, performs "A Haydn Miscellany" at Carnegie Hall.

Friday night. The Metropolitan Opera, with Plácido Domingo, presents a stunning *Simon Boccanegra.*

Saturday morning. At Rizzoli's bookstore on 57th, I pick up a copy of Sir Peter Hall's *Cities in Civilization.*

Somewhere along the way, it occurs to me that the production of each of those "events" was a WOW Project ... and thus a long (long) way from a *Dilbert*-style "dreary day at the office." The difference is immense. Think about it.

! Contrasts

WAS	IS
A job	— A performance
Puttin' in time	— Puttin' on the Ritz
"Phoning it in"	— Fully "in the moment"
Forgettable	— Memorable
A bureaucratic task	— A signature piece
Faceless	— Full of "character"
A descent into routine	— A plunge into the unknown
Another day's work	— A product of enormous investment
"Acceptable work"	— Mastery of craft
Numbing	— Exhausting
Hierarchy reigns	— Talent rules
Enervates employees	— Energizes performers
Tepid	— Hot
Pastel	— Technicolor
Predictable	— Quirky
(It's "ho-hum.")	— ("It matters!")
Risk-averse	— Venturesome
Hunkering down	— Reaching Out
"Another day older"	— "A growth experience"
"Colors within the lines"	— "Curious to a fault"
Boss-driven (Suck-up City)	— Project-driven (Teamwork City)
Blah	— WOW!

Reward EXCELLENT Failures!

Punish MEDIOCRE Successes!

16 NO LIMITS: WOW PROJECTS FOR THE "POWERLESS"

! Technicolor Rules ...

- "Getting Things Done" ultimately is not about "power" or "rank." It's about ... PASSION and IMAGINATION and PERSISTENCE.
- The biggest waste of time in the world: trying to sell an idea "up the chain of command."
- A Cool Idea is by definition a ... Direct Frontal Attack ... on the Holy Authority of Today's Bosses.
- The power of the "powerless" lies in "Boss-Free Implementation."
- You don't need an Officially Big Project to attack a Very Big Opportunity.
- Volunteer for Crappy Jobs: crappy jobs that let you take independent charge of things quickly—and early in your tenure.

! RANT

We are not prepared

We labor under the delusion that we must "wait our turn" ... that we must "work our way up the organization ladder." But the decimation of hierarchies, the deconstruction of career ladders, and the re-definition of Work-of-Value make that a false—nay, a *dangerous*—assumption. So we must Grasp the Nettle at the beginning of every job and every assignment. We must appreciate the power that comes with being "powerless" ... and turn every mundane "task" into a Remarkable (WOW!) Project.

! VISION

I imagine ...

A 24-year-old "independent contributor" who gets totally turned-on by ... Wi-Fi. She chats up some Wi-Fi experts. She leverages her growing knowledge—and her boundless enthusiasm—to cadge some bucks from vendors. (Perhaps with minimal "chain of command" approval. Perhaps not.) And she gets a Beachhead Wi-Fi Project going at Enormous Enterprise Inc. Afterward, the world is never the same again at EE Inc. (Or for our 24-year-old.)

Autobiography: "Powerless" Like Me

My seminar had gone on for a couple of hours. It was time for the first break. A relatively young man approached me. A fairly junior staffer in finance, it turns out. He began with flattery: "This is really great stuff." (I beamed. Naturally.)

Then it came ... the phrase that mothballed a thousand ships. "But I'm not a vice president," he said. "I can't implement any of this stuff. I don't have the power."

"I don't have the power."[1]

What do I do? I flip out. Okay, not true. My Mom taught me to be polite, so I'm polite. But inside I'm flipping out.

Can you imagine Martin Luther King, Jr., saying, "Civil Rights is Cool, but I don't have the power"? Can you imagine Gandhi saying, "The Brits stink, but I don't have the power"? Or de Gaulle in Britain following the fall of France in 1940: isolated, a longtime maverick and outcast within the French Army, recently convicted of treason by a kangaroo court in Pétain's France—Can you imagine de Gaulle, at that moment, saying, "Fuhgeddabouditldon'thavethepower"?

Now, intellectually, I know that this young man was making a fair point. "I don't have the power" describes a common (indeed, ubiquitous) state of affairs. Still, talk like that does get my dander up.

I read—and think and speak and write—about many, many things. Major issues in business. And beyond. (That's how I earn my living.) But this issue is different. *It's up-close and personal!* It gets right to the core of how I've lived my life ever since I was a "powerless"[2] junior officer in the U.S. Navy in 1966 ... ever since I was a "powerless" new-kid-on-the-block consultant at McKinsey & Co. in 1974.

In each case, I reveled in my powerlessness. It was precisely the challenge (and cover!) I needed. I urge you to think about your "powerless" situation in the same way.

The Power of "Powerless Thinking"

"Getting Things Done" is not about formal "power" or official "rank." It is ultimately about ... PASSION and IMAGINATION and PERSISTENCE.

Say you've got a Seriously Cool Idea. The very worst thing you can do—*the biggest waste of time in the world*—is to try to "sell" that idea "up the chain of command." Doing so will only remind you of how (officially) "powerless" you are. (De Gaulle didn't stick around and try to talk Pétain out of executing him.)

{

POWER LASS
[1] Remember Roseanne's mantra? (See Chapter 15.)

Granted, "lass" may not be quite the right word to describe Roseanne. But she very much had the right idea when she said, *"Nobody gives you power. You just take it."*

MY "EXCELLENCE" ADVENTURE
[2] I really believe in this "power of the powerless" thing. That's how I approached the research at McKinsey & Co. that led to *In Search of Excellence* (the offspring of which apparently constitute around 50 percent of that firm's business these days).

My secret (and thus my stroke of great good fortune): NOBODY GAVE A DAMN. Hence I could scurry about pretty much as I pleased. I could recruit any Committed Junior Freaks I could find. And I did recruit them. One of them became—well over a decade later, and long after I was "urged to seek other employment"—Managing Director of the Whole Shebang.

The "chain of command": What is that, anyway? It's a bunch of people who have been promoted for skillfully adhering to "the certified-pure way we do things around here." In other words: They are the Designated and Appointed Guardians of Yesterday. For your purposes—as a "powerless" junior type with a Seriously Cool Idea—the "chain of command" might as well be ... a chain gang.

Query: What constitutes a Seriously Cool Idea? Simple. It's something that runs directly counter to ... "the way we do things around here." That is, a Seriously Cool Idea is—by definition—a Direct Frontal Attack on the Holy Authority of Today's Bosses.

Oops!

Hence, as I said, the power of the "powerless" lies in what I call "Boss-Free Implementation." Or: What "they" can't see, "they" can't kill!

What's Wrong with This Picture? Or: Reframe It!

So there you are, low person on the organizational totem pole, "powerless" to create your own WOW Project. But look around. What projects—non-WOW projects, to be sure—are you involved in? Ask yourself: Can I *reframe* one of them in a way that lets me do ... under-the-radar ... Boss-Free Implementation of a Seriously Cool Idea?

My view: The answer is almost invariably "Yes!" Accordingly, I bid you to consider the following Reframers' Rules, as I call them.

Rule #1: *Never accept an assignment as given.*

Only idiots accept assignments as given! Those who will change the world (in the smallest of ways, even) twist any assignment until it can be turned into a ... SeriouslyCool/WOW/BHAG Project.

Rule #2: *You are never so powerful as when you're "powerless."*

When are you truly hemmed in? When everybody is watching! (Welcome to VP World.) Everybody views your slightest twitch through an electron microscope. But when you are Officially Powerless ... you are virtually free to dig into any assignment ... and Raise Hell at Will. "They" are effectively blind to your machinations.

Rule #3: *Every "small" project contains the DNA of the entire enterprise.*

Perhaps this is the "real" secret-of-secrets: Every "small" project is a ... Transparent Window ... on the Soul of the Organization. A far better window than "official policy."

In sum: You don't need an *Officially* Big Project to attack a *Very Big* Real Opportunity.

The Army of WOW Credo: Always Volunteer ...

Opportunities! They are always (ALWAYS!) lying around. More often than not they're lying around in the form of ... Crappy Jobs. Jobs that nobody else wants, seemingly for good reason. But think again ... and follow what I call the VFCJ Strategy. That is:

RULES FOR THE "OVER-RULED"

Early on in the WOW Project training that my company offers—before my own book on the topic was available—we used an unusual text. Title: *Rules for Radicals.* It is over 30 years old, written by the tough Civil Rights and union-organizing militant Saul Alinsky.

The message: Getting Things Done that Fly in the Face of Conventional Wisdom is a Matter of Energetic and Persistent Community Organizing, a Matter of Unearthing and Engaging Passionate Others (who previously viewed *themselves* as ... yes ... "powerless").

Volunteer For Crappy Jobs.

Yes, *volunteer*. In the Army, there used to be a credo: Never Volunteer. Don't step out or stand out. Hide within the infantry ranks, and you'll increase your odds of coming home safely. Well, that was the Old Army. In the New Army, every soldier is ... An Army of One. Likewise, in the New Economy, you must ... Create Your Own Army of WOW. Which means: Volunteer! Even for ... Crappy Jobs. *Especially* for those ... Crappy Jobs. Because ... Crappy Jobs ... let you take independent charge of things quickly and early in your tenure.

The pivotal question: *Is that "unwanted" project a "throw-away task," a distraction to be "gotten out of the way?" Or is it a Seriously Cool Chance to turn a "trivial" problem into a ... Stealth Opportunity ... a chance to address a ... Great Cultural Issue ... that strategically affects the entire organization?*

Let's get down to cases:

Voluntary Contribution #1: A Memorial Day to Remember.

Which is it? The "Oh-Shit-I-Wish-It-Were-Over Memorial Day Picnic"? Or the "First Annual Seriously Cool Celebration of Our Incredible Staff"?

Nobody wants the job. Yes, the job of "boss" of the Memorial Day company picnic. But you say, "Aha! What an opportunity![3] Nobody wants this thing. Everybody hates it. But ain't it true that we do have a ... Seriously Cool Staff ... in our 73-person Telemarketing Department? Doesn't it make sense to Celebrate their Seriously Cool Greatness? And what better opportunity than the dreaded ... Memorial Day Picnic?"

So you cobble together a little band of "powerless" but determined volunteers. You all throw Heart & Soul into what may be on the verge of becoming a ... WOW Project. You find some entertainers on the cheap. You discover untapped skills among staff. Friends of friends provide other resources. For two months, you let your "real work" slip. The powers-that-be think you're nuts ... that you're taking your eye off The Ball. ("The Ball," meaning ... Your Official Career.)

But the Dreaded Picnic becomes ... an Insanely Great Event! There is Buzz. Serious Buzz. "Powerless," you are "on the map." (Your betters were watching!) Plus, you gained the Unstinting Respect of 73 folks in the previously under-appreciated but vitally important telemarketing department. Plus, it was Fun! Plus, you added Members to your Network. ("It's all about The Rolodex, Baby!")

Voluntary Contribution #2: Safety First.

Is it "Wrestle the damn safety manual into line with the nutty new OSHA regs?" *Or:* "Make an Advance in the All-Important War for Talent by figuring out how Safety Matters help to make this an ... Insanely Great Place to Work?"

Once more: Nobody wants the job. (To put it mildly.) But *you* see it as an ...Incredible

---

WOW CHOICE: FROM "CRAPPY" TO "COOL"

[3]Like most things in life, the meaning of a project is all about ... attitude. Is it a *chore*, or is it a *chance*—a chance to do Something Great? How we answer that question says everything about who we are and how we see the world.

The way we respond to a "mere picnic" is a ... *perfect snapshot* ... of the degree to which we give a damn (OR DON'T) about our staff. That "mere" annual "social" event provides a better tip-off of our view of fellow employees than 100 pages of turgid prose in an HR policy manual.

Opportunity ... to Win a Major Battle in the Great War for Incredible Talent.

Voluntary Contribution #3: Process Makes Perfect.

Is it "Fix these bloody customer problems that have dogged the release of the new 2783B machine?" Or: "Work with a hotshot young division boss on using Internet Speed to gather customer input—not just after, but before and during the product-design process?"

Yet again: Nobody wants the job. Except you. Okay, by now you get the idea. Opportunities are where you see them. Power ... not official power, but the power of Initiative and Imagination ... is yours for the taking.

Play Well with Others: The F4 Way

So success with several reframed crappy jobs has earned you Gold Stars ... and a flicker of recognition. But truth be told, you're still preoccupied with your own Seriously Cool Idea—and frankly not much closer to launching it on the world. As a young engineer, your power score is still low, and your discretionary budget is zero.

Is there any hope?

There's more than that: There's a Eureka Moment awaiting you.

Find a playmate! What you need is ... ONE ... *sympathetic, enthusiastic, piratical, conspiratorial* friend. Yes, one. (One is plenty. For now.)

You've done some research on, say, your radical notion of Totally Transforming Project Management. And you've done some serious reading. You've chatted up some people who've tried similar ideas at other places.

Your excitement level rises. So, too, your frustration level. You desperately want to collar your boss and announce ... that you have figured out a way to ... Change the World.

Don't do it!

Resist the temptation!

Instead: Head to a company online chat room. Attend a company meeting. Start cold-calling to set up lunches with interesting people in the company you've gotten rumor of. In short, the time has come to take this Seriously Cool Idea ... and start talking it up with some Would-Be Seriously Cool Allies.

Another name that I like for this "playmate" strategy is ... the F4 Approach: Find a Freaky Friend Faraway.[4]

A (Play) Date with Destiny

An example of the F4 (Find a Freaky Friend Faraway) Approach:

You have a colleague—call her Nancy—who runs a medium-sized engineering unit

---

FREAK OUT: THE OUTSIDE-IN GAMBIT

[4]The Freaky Friend does *not* have to be a colleague from your company. One of the most effective ways to innovate is to turn somebody on in a client organization. (Call it a Cool Customer). Or somebody in a supplier company. (Call it a Vivacious Vendor.)

Again: You have a Seriously Cool Idea. The "cool" part means that the "establishment" ... your company's hyper-conservative Crucial Customers (or Vaunted Vendors) ... won't even consider the idea. So find a small, innovative customer (or vendor) instead—and use that organization as your playpen.

within in a subsidiary of your company. Her office is a few hours' drive[5] from the divisional HQ where you labor away as that Junior Dude on the Engineering Staff.

You already know Nancy slightly. The grapevine says she's aggressive and energetic, and willing to try damn near anything—as long as it's interesting. You drive out to meet her, and the two of you dive into conversation. You talk up your Seriously Cool Idea.

Nancy enthuses over your pitch. Particularly since she's now working on a project that has become stalled—and for which your Seriously Cool (and Potentially Subversive) Idea might be just the thing.

Nancy says that while she's not quite "in love with" your idea (that's *your* job!), she is "very intrigued" by it. She tells you that she'll mull over your approach, sound out some of her staff about it, and look into testing some version of it in her shop.

Eureka! (Redux.) You're closing in on Finding that first Freaky Friend Faraway.

Again: *One* is the critical number. *One* excited recruit at a time, at least in the beginning, at least until Dramatic Demos and Small Wins are in place (see below).

Try, Try Again: The Power of Prototyping

You're junior. You're "powerless." No vice presidential chevrons on your sleeves. But you've got that Seriously Cool Idea. And you've found Nancy—that first Freaky Friend Faraway. Now what you need is ... a track record. A record of events-nuggets-stories that send the signal "something's up."

I believe there is one—and in fact only one—way of getting your Seriously Cool Idea honed and ready for Prime Time. One and only one viable approach to creating a track record. And for that, I turn to innovation expert Michael Schrage.

Michael spent most of the last decade on what may seem like an obscure, dry-as-dust topic: *prototyping*. That is, the process by which enterprises move from abstract concept to concrete working model, and then put that model through its paces ... over and over again.[6] Prototyping has its origins in manufacturing, but the idea goes way, way beyond that.

Schrage goes so far as to claim that excellence in Rapid Prototyping is the *chief* difference between organizations that innovate brilliantly ... and those that don't."

OUT OF SIGHT!

[5]Distance matters. The point is to stay under the "radar screen" until your idea begins to gel. "Out of sight, out of mind" remains a potent axiom even in the Age of the Internet.

Fact: Most world-beating projects were incubated along way from HQ, a place where intriguing ideas invariably get politicized and homogenized into submission. I am convinced that much of the success that Bob Waterman and I had 20-odd years ago stemmed from our being in San Francisco—a full continent away from McKinsey's Corporate Shark Tank in Manhattan.

SERIOUS PLUG

[6]Schrage pressed the prototyping idea to the limits in his book *Serious Play*. In a foreword to the book, I called it the "best book on innovation I've ever read." I meant it.

"You can't be a serious innovator," Schrage begins, "unless you are willing and able to play. 'Serious play' is not an oxymoron; it is the essence of innovation."

(Note how Schrage's language echoes my own emphasis on words like "playmate" and "playpen.")

Effective prototyping," he writes boldly, "may be the most valuable competence an innovative organization can hope to have."

Strong language. The message: *Become a Rapid Prototyping Maniac.*[7]

Big "Wins" Come in Small Packages

Years (and years and years) ago, in my Ph.D. dissertation at the Stanford Business School, I coined another term for what I now call Rapid Prototyping. (Or "Serious Play," to use Schrage's language.) Namely: the "small win." That is, the wee "demo" whose success adds to your track record ... and thus to your credibility.

Yes, that "small win," that "little test," that "successful prototype" shows that your Seriously Cool Idea isn't just fantasy, after all. It shows that your Seriously Cool Idea may well become ... One Very Big Deal. An all-important entry on the credit side of your nascent track record. In fact, a giant and necessary leap from Gleam in Your and Your First Freak's Eyes to Dirt Under Your Fingernails. A matchless tool for attracting future Freaky Friends. A catalyst for buzz that begins to ooze up the chain of command.

Nor does the "small win" even need to be a "win" in the obvious, conventional sense of the word. Sometimes a small win comes in the form of a "quick loss."[8] That's certainly how Thomas Edison saw the matter. The Greatest Inventor of All went through some 9,000 experiments before he finally landed upon the right design for his incandescent bulb. Did he see the first 8,999 experiments as "failures"? Hardly! Each of those earlier "prototypes" was ... a Brilliant and Unequivocal Demonstration of something that didn't work ... in other words, a Clear Victory!

"Ouch," you shout. Save me from "those stories" management gurus love to tell. Who has the time for a 8,999-game losing streak? Fair enough, but the Edisonian "secret" is an Eternal Truth. We only win in the long run by getting out there and bloodied in the short run. As Churchill put it, "Success is the ability to go from one failure to another with no loss of enthusiasm." Not so incidentally, the story of his life prior to the Ultimate Win in 1945. Another platitude? Sure. But ... all of the Truly Great Ones seem to sing from the same page of the same hymnal.

IN THE "MEAN TIME"
[7]Schrage cites an interview with former Sony CEO Nobuyuki Idei, who said that the key to that company's extraordinary record of new product development was this: At Sony, the "Mean Time To Prototype" (the elapsed time between the glimmer of an idea and a one-sixteenth-baked test of that idea) is a scant *five* days.

THE REAL "FAIL-SAFE": FAIL QUICK
[8]Variations on the theme of "quick loss":
   A high-tech executive who attended a seminar of mine shared his philosophy: *Fail. Forward. Fast.*
   IDEO founder and innovation guru David Kelley gives it another twist: *Fail faster. Succeed sooner.*
   Glib? Perhaps.
   Profound? Surely.

Power Suite:
Tools for the Putatively Powerless

To review: You're in love with a Seriously Cool Idea. You want to turn it into a WOW Project. But ... you're a "junior person" and hence "powerless." My advice:

Don't screw around. START NOW. Find an excuse. ANY EXCUSE. Do something. DO ANYTHING. Get going. POSTHASTE.

More specifically ... try taking some version of these steps:

1. You get passionate about a Seriously Cool and Subversive Idea.

2. You successfully resist blubbering to the boss about your idea. (Even if it's your Dad at a family-owned company.) (Especially if it's Dear old Dad.)

3. You express your passion with folks from hither or thither.

4. You find (or trip over) One Freaky Friend ... One Passionate Playmate.

5. With your One Passionate Playmate, you test and modify your idea in her Podunk Playpen.

6. You and your First Faraway Freak scour your networks for "line" folks who might be interested in "playing" with you at the next stage of the game.

7. You concoct a rough Rapid Prototyping schedule.

8. You start prototyping like a fiend.

9. You have a bunch of failures. You have a few successes. You learn ... a lot. You learn ... fast. You begin to accumulate a compelling track record. You sharpen your story.

10. You score some "small wins" and also get some quick learning ("small losses") under your belt.

11. You continue to resist the impulse to tell the boss.

12. A freshly recruited (don't forget those lunches!) Freaky Friend of your First Freaky Friend Faraway (Premier Passionate Playmate) starts the Dance of Prototyping in his little bailiwick.

13. The Friend of the Friend unearths yet another Freaky Friend, maybe not quite so far away now, who wants to play with your now battle-tested idea. And so on ...

14. Meanwhile, you adjust and adjust and adjust. (Remember: Innovation = Reaction to Rapid Prototyping.)

15. You start low-key "buzz building," letting word of Cool Small Wins trickle out—always giving Freaky Friends the credit. (Remember, Nancy's *line* engineering. You're wet-behind-the-ears non-credible division *staff*.)

16. You begin nudging your growing Coven of Cool Converts to initiate a Major Proposal "up the line."

17. Before you know it, you are on the way to Surrounding the (Establishment) Bastards.

18. Now, and only now—flush with compelling data about successful "demos" by real line players—your "pitch" gets made to the Big Boss.

19. Only you don't make the pitch even now! Remember: You are a Junior Staffer. Instead, you get those "real" line people—people who have been working successfully with Your Baby—to make it for you.

PERSUASION: HOW TO BE HEALTHY, STEALTHY, AND WISE

We don't have space here for a full-blown treatise on the Politics of Persuasion. But suffice it to say, in a perfect world, the boss has heard the "trickle up" stories of your prototypes. You "allow" him to assume ownership of your project—and act as if he dreamed the whole damn thing up on his own. Hence he congratulates you on having read his mind. And signs on to a $4 million roll-out plan!

---

20. And so it goes ... *Forever!*

The Dance of Innovation

Rapid Prototyping turns out not to be about discrete "tests." It is ... a Way of Life. Think of it as a *dance*. With a particular series of steps and a particular rhythm. Think of it as ... the Dance of Innovation.[9] It goes like this:

You get an idea. You run a (very) quick and (very) dirty test. That's great. But you've only begun. Now, after that first hair-brained test, you immediately sit down with your co-conspirators, and you ask yourselves: "What happened? What can we learn from that test? What can we do differently next time?" And then you get on with that "next time" ... RIGHT AWAY. And so on. Again and again.

After a while, you get good at it. You develop ... a *rhythm*. And that's when innovation really starts to occur. Yes, your initial idea is Seriously Cool. (Don't let anyone tell you otherwise.) But it's just that—an idea. As yet, it is only *potentially* subversive. As Schrage astutely observes, the Real Work of Innovation consists of ... *the reaction to the prototype*. True innovation is not a cool idea.

True innovation is instead what we learn when we observe what goes down when we actually test a potentially cool idea. The Big-Big idea: We can't innovate until we have something tangible to ... PLAY WITH.

Play! Innovate! Fast!

Thence your goal: rapidly executed prototypes ... prototypes that may succeed or may fail ... but which have Charisma[10] ... and from which we reap Quick Learning and generate Growing Excitement and Growing Credibility. And, yes ... Growing Power.

NEW BUSINESS ! ● NEW WORK

ALL THE WORLD'S A ... PROTOTYPE
[9]The arts have lots to teach us here. Consider theater. We start by reading through the play. (Proto-prototype.) Then we have slow walk throughs. (Prototypes.) Then we do bits and pieces of the prospective performance at full speed. (More prototypes.) Then we practice full scenes. (Yet more prototypes.) Then comes the dress rehearsal. (Mega-prototype.) Then we put on the play for real.

Such "serious play," while common in the arts (and in sports), is highly unusual in business—where we typically plan and plan, and meet and meet, before we ever ... *do* anything.

SAME (NEW) STORY
[10]"Good prototypes have 'charisma,'" Schrage writes. "They create narratives and tell stories."

I love that: *Great Prototype = Cool and Compelling and Charismatic Story!*

Remember: Skillful storytelling is the essence of leadership. The best leaders are the best storytellers ... from Churchill to Roosevelt to Gandhi.

And, to state explicitly the converse, the worst "leaders" are the worst storytellers. They "stick to the facts" and fail to stir the imaginations of would-be followers with compelling tales of Changing the World.

(Hint: This holds as much for the on-the-make 25-year-old as for the leader of a nation.)

! Contrasts

WAS		IS
Know your place	–	Do your thing
Wait	–	Act
Follow "the rules"	–	Make new rules
Accept assignments	–	Remake assignments
Play it as it lays	–	Make it up as you go
Get along to go along	–	Get up and go
Constrained by seniority	–	Amused by "seniority"
(your lack thereof)	–	(pretensions thereof)
Barriers	–	Opportunities
"No power (alas)"	–	"No constraints (yes!)"
Cubicle slave	–	Free agent

17 BOSS WORK: HEROES, DEMOS, STORIES

! Technicolor Rules ...

- "Ordering" systematic change is ... a waste of time.
- You, the boss, must turn your company (or bit thereof) into a Smorgasbord of—Excellence—where Amazing Stuff is *always* being initiated. Most of which you're unaware of.
- "Find Heroes. Do Demos. Tell Stories."
- If you want to "leapfrog" change ... well, then, you need "*lead* frogs."
- A good leader asks one question: *GOT ANY GOOD STORIES?*
- "He who has the best story wins." (What's your story?)
- "Some people look for things that went wrong and try to fix them. I look for things that went right and try to build on them."

 ! RANT

We are not prepared ...

We still think in terms of *planning* and *ordering* change. But there's no longer time for that. We must understand that every boss's top job is not to "make change" but to *find* and *celebrate* change makers—hidden heroes who contribute to a Scintillating Portfolio of WOW Projects, and whose work inspires others-by-the-bushel to step out from hiding and mimic them.

! VISION

I imagine ...

A 123-person IT Department. The department head, Ava Jamison, has five senior project managers, and she treats each of them as a venture capitalist who deals with a portfolio, a portfolio of WOW People & WOW Projects.

Ava (a VC herself!) regularly asks each of her "VCs" in turn to report on how their portfolio is "performing," and they respond with gripping stories about revelatory *demos* conducted by front-line *heroes*.

Did Ava "order" all this to happen? Hardly. Instead, she charged her "direct reports" (VCs) to encourage a thousand flowers to bloom. But when it comes to creating a New Cool Culture, Ava is "merely" fertilizer salesperson for that Georgeous Garden of WOW growing up like topsy around her! That's "*boss* work."

Out of Order: How Not to "Boss"

In an Age of WOW Project Work (or else ... see above), being "the boss" isn't what it used to be. Mostly, that's a Very Good Thing. And a surprisingly easy thing. (See below.) But it can be incredibly hard to give up the old habits of Management by Exhortation and Management by Detailed Plan. Consider the persistent tendency among managers to issue orders ex cathedra—orders like the following:

"Get more entrepreneurial."

"Take risks."

"Implement the zero defects program."

STUPID.

STUPID.

And STUPID.

Why? Regardless of your official rank, "ordering" systematic change is ... a waste of time. Trying to "order a new culture" into being doesn't work.[1] Maybe it worked once upon a time. (Though I doubt even that.) But the boss who operates that way today will find himself going nowhere fast. And maybe even backward. Those "clear" orders will be executed by Frustrated Middle Managers bent on preserving their rapidly disintegrating power base—they will become the worst sort of Innovation Quashers.

The goal of "boss work" must be this: Get people ... *many, many people* ... initiating and then working on WOW Projects! Projects that they put their heart and soul into! Projects that they will want to be remembered by! (And ask yourself: Do you want people working for you who *don't* want to be remembered by what they're doing ... right now?)

One hopes those many, many "powerless" people have read the previous chapter of this book—and are thence busily engaged in Seriously Cool (*and* Seriously Subversive) Projects already.

To take the idea a step further: You, the boss, must turn your company into a place where ... Amazing Stuff ... is *always* percolating. Task One is gathering an awesome array of Incredibly Cool People, people who invest in, and commit to, and execute, an awesome array of Bold Experiments. Bold Experiments and Charismatic Prototypes that turn into ... that Awesome Array of WOW Projects.

Boss Work That Works

"I'm trying to 'lead change' and induce 'risk-taking' at my company. Got any ideas?"

If I've been asked that question once, I've been asked it a hundred times. In fact, after 25 years on the seminar circuit, I've probably heard it a thousand times. The

---

PLAN B—FORGET PLANNING

[1]As with "ordering" enterprise activity, so with "planning" it.

Contention: We don't need—or even want—a "great plan." The days of "seeing around corners" are kaput. The "corners" of the New Economy (and of the New Warfare) are 90-degree bends that come every few breaths and continually reveal the most unexpected places. (Here Be Dragons!)

Instead of old-style planning, we need entirely new definitions of both preparedness and execution.

The new *preparedness*: an adaptable and hyper-energetic talent pool, along with a floating, shifting array of temporary alliances.

The new *execution*: ad-hoc WOW Projects, started on a dime and executed at Warp Speed.

questioner is usually a mid-level boss, running a middle-sized department in a middle-sized division of some Big Company.

She says, "I have a pretty good idea of where we need to go. And I can vaguely sketch the outlines of the new 'culture' that I think we need. I trust my instincts, even though I don't have all the details ironed out. But I'm having trouble getting people to line up behind me. So ...

Got any ideas?"

For years, in response to this question, I waffled. I'd launch a little rant on leadership. Or I'd give a nod to empowerment. Whatever. Not wrong. But not right, either.

Lately, I've changed my tune.

"There is only One Way," I boldly proclaim.

"Find Heroes. Do Demos. Tell Stories."

To elaborate:

We need *heroes*: *Mortal Exemplars* of the Exciting New Way of Doing Things.

We need *demos*: *Palpable Proof* that this Exciting New Way of Doing Things is eminently doable.

We need *stories*: *Riveting Tales* that fire the imagination of ... future-but-as-yet-reluctant heroes-in-waiting.

The "Lead Frog" Strategy

I recently happened upon a phrase, courtesy of the desperately-in-need healthcare industry, which perfectly encapsulates that idea: If you want to "leapfrog" change ... well, then, you need "*Lead* Frogs."

(The Leapfrog Group champions Lead Frogs engaged in improving the pathetic state of healthcare quality in American hospitals.)

Hence, the "Lead Frog" strategy.

It goes like this: Troll through the ranks for would-be revolutionaries—people who have long been itching to make things happen. (Or who are already harboring success stories that they're afraid to go public with ... for fear of the Old Guard's wrath.) Given half a chance, these extant or prospective Lead Frogs will *leap* over the Fortress of Inertia ... and mark out a visible path which others can follow.

The obvious corollary: Don't waste precious time (at least not yet) on the Reluctant Ones—those "frogs" who are too content, or too afraid, to stray from their lily pad.

In any case, you mostly don't need to "hire" revolutionaries.[2] Odds are (very high),

---

KICK-UP-YOUR-HEELS MANAGEMENT?

[2] Here's the best part of this model: You, the boss, don't have to *do* anything!

You've got an idea. Empowerment. Quality. Risk-taking. Innovation. Whatever. To see that idea become something more than an idea, you don't need to "launch an initiative." Because, in any sizable organization, there are bound to be angry, "powerless" people who *are already practicing your "new" idea* ... perhaps at serious risk to their careers.

Your job: Ferret them out. Hold them by the scruff of the neck. Lionize them in front of everyone else.

As in: "Look at *Marilyn*—she's the one! She gets it! She's *done* it! And she's just like you and me!"

you've got 'em already: role models … existing people who actually exemplify a Brash New Way of Doing Things. They are lurking! Waiting to be discovered! Waiting to be listened to! Waiting to be taken seriously!

So what do you do? Seek 'em out. Let 'em loose. Teach these "Lead Frog" heroes a few (but not too many) manners. Make it clear-as-a-bell to one-and-all that … They Are the New Way!

They Could Be Heroes

How do we find these "Lead Frogs," these would-be revolutionaries, these diamonds-in-the-corporate-rough? The obvious—and true—answer: You find them in your "network." But that might not be quite enough.

You might also need to follow what I call the "flypaper" strategy. In other words: Induce these heroes to come out of the woodwork by setting irresistible, sticky traps for them. Here, then, are some ways to add a little "stickiness" to your Systematic Pursuit of Heroes.[3]

Fair Game. Consider the tradition of "event marketing," typically used in the consumer-goods world. Why not do something similar "inside"—that is, within your company? Put on an Idea Fair, a "Bragfest," an internal "trade show." In other words: a public and well-publicized occasion during which the "Lead Frogs" jump out of their pond and demonstrate their Weird Wares. Result: Other freaks are inspired to show their true colors.

To Catch a Freak. Start a monthly "New Economy Seminar Series." But instead of the usual suspects … the gurus du jour (like me!) … invite a Genuine Freak from within your company to lead each seminar. Again: Freaks attract Freaks. (Flypaper, remember!)

Just for Fund. Another powerful approach: Create a play fund, a dedicated bucket-o'-cash that people throughout your company can draw upon in small doses to pursue weird, wild, one-off projects. In short: Show them the money—and see what happens. What usually works best is to define an "area of need" that is specific but not too specific.

Time Off for Weird Behavior. How about setting up a special scholarship fund for … Radical Sabbaticals?[4] People could apply—much as they would for the grant fund

---

BREAK THE QUARANTINE!

[3]Here's another image that gets across the "find heroes" part of leadership: Think "epidemic." Think "infection." Think "germ theory."

That's right. Maybe you should study epidemiology … if you want to become a Master of Culture Change … if you want to start (yes!) an Epidemic of WOW Projects.

The big idea: Help and honor the already-"infected" ones—the ones who are too often shunned as disease carriers … when in fact they are "carriers" of a New and Exciting Culture.

SCARE QUOTE

[4]So how do you know if an idea like "radical sabbatical" is truly radical … and truly right for you?

Answer: Trust your gut.

Alex Trotman didn't get everything right as CEO of Ford, but he did introduce some Very Cool Products. I once read that he wasn't happy unless a new idea "scared me half to death" (or words to that effect).

That's a nice test for the "radical sabbaticals" idea. Or, indeed, for any "radical" idea.

mentioned above—for the opportunity to spend (say) six months with this Cool Customer or that Scintillating Supplier. Or maybe they would work with a Profound Professor on a research project that relates in some way to your company's business. Whatever. Call it "outside-the-company thinking."

ASK THE "EXPERT"

"When he was boss of Travel Related Services at American Express, Lou Gerstner became intrigued by artificial intelligence and, in particular, by "expert systems" technology. He wanted to make something happen. Fast. Even though he was the Big Boss, he didn't issue an order ("Go do expert systems now!"). Instead, he established a smallish expert-systems "fund." Each grant was for a few thousand dollars. Anybody could apply. The grant process was simple—a no-nonsense application, and then quick approval (or disapproval).

Only a couple of years later, according to Ed Feigenbaum (the great pioneer of expert systems and author of *The Rise of the Expert Company*), AmEx had an astonishingly high share of all the world's expert systems then in place! And the company had reaped millions upon millions of dollars as a result. That is, Gerstner hadn't "ordered it." He had, instead, concocted the stickiest of "flypaper."

Bottom line: Gerstner didn't mandate all this from on high. Instead, he induced hidden Weirdos to Come Out of the Woodwork.

My "Children's Crusade"

The "Lead Frog" strategy. Laying out "flypaper." Whatever you call it, I know it works. The mother of all examples (for me): the project at McKinsey & Co. that led directly to my writing *In Search of Excellence*.

When I was handed the reins of a two-bit ("one-bit"?) project on "organization effectiveness," I didn't have much "power." But I did have a few ideas and, more important, a lot of passion. And by dint of that passion, I slowly attracted a posse of "powerless" youngsters to my cause. The ground was ripe for the picking: McKinsey's "strategy-is-everything" emphasis had given rise to a crop of renegade youth. (Young-and-restless types: *Every* sizable firm has 'em. That's the good news. No, that's the ... Great News!) And so I searched high and low for them, using all of my friends' networks.

Hence the origin of what I like to call ... the McKinsey Children's Crusade.[5] I'd like to think that we did make the (management) earth wobble a bit—though "my kids" are all now long of tooth.

My "search for excellence" at McKinsey yielded a slew of excellent insights into the

---

"GUARDIAN" ANGLE

[5] *Just as important as finding "heroes" is protecting them. All freaks need guardians. An inspired youngster (or, for that matter, an inspired oldster!) needs somebody to keep him on the good side—or at least not entirely on the bad side—of the powers-that-currently-be.*

At McKinsey & Co., I had Bob Waterman. During the years we worked together there, Bob probably spent 40 percent of his time protecting me from the Forces of Internal Evil ... the bureaucrats guarding the Conventional Way of Doing Things. Bless him. (And hey, Bob, I do know how much of a pain I was!)

art of "Lead Frog" leadership:

1. "Lead Frogs" ... Upstart Practitioners of Cool ... are always with us.

2. Your job as boss: Find them. Excite them. Acknowledge them. Offer them a Revolutionary Peer Group. (And don't give them too much visibility too soon—or else you'll scare them off.)

3. After you articulate your (contrarian) point of view, your chief role becomes that of Community Organizer, Cheerleader, Provider of Camouflage Gear, and ... Chronicler-in-Chief.

4. "Lead Frogs" tend to be relatively junior ... and formally "powerless." (Which is to say: The "system" hasn't licked 'em yet.)

5. "Powerless" is Cool ... because relative to the "real people" you hope to attract to the cause: "Powerless" = "Pissed Off" = Prepared to Go for It or Go Bust.

The Way of the Demo

Heroes. Demos. Stories.

I don't need to say much here about the second part of that equation. "Demos" is another term for those "WOW Projects for the 'Powerless'" and the Fast "Charismatic" Prototypes I discussed at length in the previous chapter. Demos are what the Heroes you recruit (aka "Lead Frogs") will do (or reveal to you) once you give them the green light. Demos are Exciting Experiments ... under-the-radar, on-a-shoestring efforts that vividly exemplify a New Way. Demos are the true "hard stuff" that sells and compels. Demos are (to repeat): Palpable Proof that Seriously Cool Change is not only possible—it's already under way!

Demos are what you tell stories about.

The *Work* of Stories

"A *key*, perhaps the key, to leadership ... is the effective communication of a story." That's the "story," according to Harvard psychologist Howard Gardner, writing in *Leading Minds: An Anatomy of Leadership*. That's a damn strong statement. ("Single most powerful weapon!") And one I wholeheartedly subscribe to. I'm trained as an engineer, not an anthropologist. (Never the twain shall meet.) But I've spent the last 30 years studying organizational change—which means that I've become a de facto anthropologist. And one thing you learn as a student of human culture ... whether your gig involves

---

STORYTELLER-IN-CHIEF

The ultimate testament to the power of storytelling: presidential speeches.

Presidents who are trying to rally a nation to war ... Franklin D. Roosevelt or George W. Bush ... must have a coherent, noble, and compelling story line. A story that justifies sending American sons and daughters into Harm's Way.

To be sure, our obsessive attention to "spin doctoring" can cheapen the practice of storytelling. But the basic *idea* is right: A leader must be able to tell stories that *cohere*. Stories that *engage*. Or else he won't be able to lead dozens ... or dozens of millions ... into battle against the forces of evil. The forces of bureaucratic evil, in the case of a junior executive leading a corporate training unit; the forces of life-threatening evil, in the case of a president.

primitive tribes or corporate tribes ... is the (often unsung) Power of Storytelling. It was true in the bush. (That's all there was before written language. Try Bruce Chatwin's marvelous *The Songlines*.) It's true in the boardroom. And it's true everywhere in between.

What, after all, do leaders really do? John Seely Brown, head of Xerox's fabled Palo Alto Research Center, puts it very simply: LEADERS ... MAKE ... MEANING. And what does "meaning" consist of? *Compelling* stories! *Coherent* themes! *Soaring* messages!

Those stories and themes and messages are about ... you guessed it ... WOW People (heroes, flesh-and-blood individuals) doing WOW Projects (demos, real projects executed on the front lines.)

As I see it, an effective leader making the rounds asks one ... *and only one* ... question: *GOT ANY GOOD STORIES?*

Stories ... are the "red meat" that animates our "reasoning process."

Stories ... give us "permission" to act.

SLAVE NARRATIVE: "THE BEST STORY WINS"

It took me an hour to find the line again, but it was well worth the effort.

I was watching *Amistad*, the Steven Spielberg movie about a mutiny on a slave ship. The vessel had made it to the United States; now a trial was taking place over the status of the rebellious slaves. Representing the slaves is black abolitionist lawyer Theodore Joadson, played by Morgan Freeman; and advising him is former U.S. President John Quincy Adams, played by Anthony Hopkins. The Hopkins character asks the Freeman character to summarize his case. The summary is brilliant, accurate ... and wholly devoid of emotion.

Old Adams then counsels Joadson: "Early in my career in the law, I learned that he who has the best story wins. *What's your story?*"

I was watching the movie on a pay-TV channel in a hotel room, and I had to replay the whole damn thing to catch that exchange again. I'm glad I did. Mark these words well:

HE WHO HAS THE ... *BEST STORY* ... WINS.

WHAT'S YOUR ... *STORY?*

EVERY PROMOTION TELLS A STORY

A great story has a smash finish. And what's the perfect climax to a successful WOW Project? A promotion!

Whenever you make a promotion, you tell a story, whether you intend to or not. And a Page One story at that.

People watch promotions like hawks: Did the "suck-up" "win"? Or the weirdo? How you, the boss, answer that question will send a message that resonates (to say the least).

Consider doing what the military calls "deep dipping." Take a young hotshot who's stuck her neck way out ... and promote her up three levels ... at one leap. Believe me, that will scare the hell out of the foot draggers and time servers in your group.

The Ultimate Demo: "Guys, meet your new GM, 32-year-old firebrand Sally Martinez!"

Message I: Never waste a single promotion.

Message II: The best measure of your Commitment (or lack thereof) to Radical Change is the Radicals You Promote.

Stories ... are photographs of who we aspire to be.

Stories ... cause emotional responses.

Stories ... connect.

Stories ... are us.

Beyond "Manual" Labor: The Armstrong Story

Back when we were working on *In Search of Excellence*, Bob Waterman and I latched onto a phrase that was popular at Hewlett-Packard. MBWA: Managing By Wandering Around.

A fine phrase. A powerful, useful phrase. But my friend David Armstrong came along and decided to coin a phrase of his own. Armstrong, who runs a middle-sized manufacturing company, attended a seminar of mine, heard the MBWA bit ... and loved it. And then came up with ...

MBSA: *Managing By Story-ing Around.*

Now he runs his company, Armstrong International, according to the principles of MBSA. (And runs it quite successfully, I might add.) Stories, storytelling, and the technology thereof are the guiding forces behind How Things Are Done at David's company.

Armstrong began by actively trolling for stories. He urged and begged others to do the same ... and rewarded them if they did. (Call it "Systematic Story Seeking," a cornerstone idea.) Stories like: the youngster ... working, by herself and unsupervised, on a loading dock at 3 a.m. ... who went the extra mile for a customer. Or: the oldster in accounting who, without guidance, had cleaned up a mess brilliantly ... and salvaged a key client relationship.

Armstrong codified those stories and posted them—along with photos of the heroes—on walls throughout the enterprise. Then he turned the stories into a "policy manual." The *only* such manual that his company has. No baloney: The Armstrong "Policy Manual" is a *storybook*: a chronicle, in effect, of "How Things Are Done When We Are at Our Very Best Serving Our Customers and Communities and Fellow Employees and Suppliers." Fabulous!

The point: David Armstrong took an apparently "soft" idea and turned it into a "hard"—that is, systematic and practical—"management practice." And it worked. Big-time. (Not just at home, either; David has started a movement of sorts, complete with books, training videos, and so on.)

The Ultimate WOW Project? (A Federal Case)

My friend Bob Stone has a ... Great Story. He actually made a dent in the way the federal government performs. Following a career as an obstreperous (that is, loved and hated) change agent in the Department of Defense, he was chosen to be the Big Cheese of then-Vice President Al Gore's "reinventing government" (ReGo) program. No, the sun did not begin to rise in the West; but an amazing amount of unsung—and, truth be known, often profound—change did take place on Bob's watch.

To the point of this chapter: Nobody but nobody played the heroes-demos-stories game better than Bob.

Bob Stone understood, first of all, that you ... obviously ... don't "order culture change" in the federal bureaucracy. But the good news, as he also quickly saw, is that an organization with thousands of units ... and millions of people ... is guaranteed to be

NEW BUSINESS ! NEW WORK

riddled with would-be revolutionaries. The real secret (again): *Find 'em! Unleash 'em! Lionize 'em! Make 'em into the New Hall of Fame! Invite, by their peers' example, others to "sign up"!*

Stone offers a simple mantra that puts a whole new spin on the idea of "corporate" "culture change":

"Some people look for things that went wrong and try to fix them. I look for things that went right and try to build on them."

Which is one reason I'd say he deserves the "job title" that he put on his federal-government "business card": *"Energizer-in-Chief."*

ReGo-a-Go-Go: The 10 Commandments of Stone

In a marvelous book, *Polite Revolutionary: Lessons from an Uncivil Servant*, Bob Stone recounts his adventures as the federal government's top change agent. He asked me to write a foreword to the book, and therein I called it "the best book I've ever read on 'corporate' change." Here are the main messages I took away from Stone's saga[6]:

1. **Talent Scouring.** The primary mission of ReGo staffers was not to create "plans" and "manuals" of their own—but to proactively ferret out heroes, eager change agents who had been hiding in their "dens" on the front lines and performing miracles, despite the inertial or flat-out reactionary forces that surrounded them. Finding those heroes is no walk in the park; chances are they've been working "underground" for years, attempting to avoid scrutiny of their renegade ways. Stone learned to make end runs around recalcitrant insiders and get directly to the Lead Frogs; such a tactic is especially important early on, when the shoots of revolution are tender—and skepticism or outright antagonism is running high.

2. **Field Marshals.** At the Department of Defense, Stone started a revolution among base commanders—real guys (and some gals) out in the field. The farther away one gets from HQ, the greater the frustration. ("Headquarters revolution" is by and large an oxymoron!) Some frustrated commanders had put their tails between their legs and "retired" on the job; but the abiding urge to help real customers (soldiers and airmen and sailors and marines) brought out the renegade best in 10 percent of base commanders. These were Stone's Golden Ones. Their "real world" stories from the boon docks, once surfaced and circulated, packed real punch among their more reluctant peers.

3. **The "Call" of Fame.** Once he found his heroes, Stone was aggressive about putting them out-front—to give not-so-heroic types a sniff of inspiration. To see how this

---

REGO ROLL CALL

[6] *Consider these (largely) unsung heroes: Lynn Gordon, Customs/Miami. Joan Hyatt, OSHA/Colorado. Bill Freeman, OSHA/Maine. Joe Deare, OSHA. Marie Urban, FDA. Ed Esparza, FDA. Sue Bruederle, FDA/Chicago. Bob Wenzel, IRS/Fresno. Joe Thompson, VA/New York City. Gerry Bolden, Ag/Gulfport, Mississippi. Mike Loh, USAF.*

These are some of the Very Cool (and Very Brave) People whom Bob Stone discovered in his ... Search for Heroes. (That is, he "discovered" them after an extraordinary amount of spade work on his and his staff's part.)

These are the sorts of people whose demos he studied ... whose stories he told (and told, and told again). These are the people whose names and faces he put before then Vice President Al Gore, who in turn "certified" their wonderful ways before their peers and fellow citizens.

works on a grand scale, consider the people who get seated in the House Gallery during a presidential State of the Union address. These heroes are the dramatic, living embodiment of issues that are central to the national agenda. Forget the abstract idea of heroism: Here, right next to Laura Bush, is a 9/11 vet from the NYFD; he exemplifies our Way of Life, Our Determination, why we are fighting a War on Terrorism.

4. Awards of State. Positive reinforcement remains the most powerful leadership device known to man. Bob Stone was a badges-and-baubles fanatic in a world where praise is especially sparing—the Federal Service. Mary Kay and the folks at Tupperware had nothing on the ReGo troops when it came to continuous cheerleading ... and a liberal doling-out of commendations of any and every sort. (As a Fed, Stone obviously couldn't toss out gajillion-dollar rewards. This may have been an advantage. His creativity in the arena of recognition provided stimulation and buzz that even a fat check can't match.)

5. Project: Protect. Some of Bob Stone's heroes didn't want publicity, even after he "discovered" them. Many were already at odds with bosses. So ReGo staffers learned to "watch" the bureaucratic "back" of such front-line change-mongers. Instead of a Federal Witness Protection Program, Stone initiated what amounted to a Federal "Heroes" Protection Program. Face-time with Al Gore, for example, kept a few heroes from losing their jobs. (It's difficult to fire someone who just publicly pocketed an Award of Valor from the nation's No. 2!) Another of Stone's tools: support groups. Pioneers need pals—like-minded souls to commiserate with and learn from. ReGo events and various networking practices helped here immensely.

6. See for Yourself. Stone got his first big break when he was appointed Deputy Assistant Secretary of Defense for Installations. In that role, he sought out "practicing radicals." To showcase their brave work, he hit upon (yes!) demos. Or, as he called them at DOD, "Model Installations." These were military bases run by those renegades described before, places where people could go to observe-in-the-raw "best (strange, new) practices." When Stone worked for Gore, "Model Installations" metamorphosed into "ReGo Labs"—Reinventing Government Laboratories. In both cases, the big idea is that we learn by example:

> **"Go. Look. See Cool Concrete Samples of the New Way ... performed by ... People Like Yourself. Go do your own version (only kinkier still). See: It Can Be Done!"**

7. Fast Times at ReGo High. To the quintessential slow-moving organization, the Feds, Stone brought speed. His mantra: Move fast—before the Forces of Evil have a chance to kill you with piles of memos and endless reviews and audits. He cites the dictum of the late John Boyd, an Air Force Colonel who said that whoever has the fastest "OODA Loop" wins. OODA Loop: Observe-Orient-Decide-Act cycle. Confuse and confound the "enemy" by your speed per se. While the Champions of Inertia are busy scheduling the next "planning review," you swiftly get the job done ... and go public with it.[7]

8. Prominent Record. "Storytelling" sounds "soft" ... a far cry from the hard business of government restructuring. Stone demonstrated that stories are anything but soft. He did a masterful job of recording ReGo success through pamphlets, videography, and so forth. Message: If it's not solidly and colorfully chronicled, then it never happened!

9. "Prop" It Up. Stories take on added potency when you deploy leave-behind props that illustrate graphically the Main Point. Example: the piles upon piles of hopelessly bloated federal-regulation books that Stone stacked behind Mr. Gore during ReGo photo-ops ... a classic Stone-ism.

10. Terms of Office. Like any true leader, Stone understood the Power of Language. Some people mocked his insistence on using the word "customer" in the Federal Service—but that one little word made an enormous difference. In general, he changed the Federal Service vocabulary from "procedure first" to "service first." From "HQ boss first" to "field service provider first." From "adversary" (aiming to "score" against, say, a factory owner regarding OSHA regs) to "partner" (aiming to help the owner "get the right things done and create a safer workplace").

Zen and the Art of Culture Change

There's an implicit theme that runs through this chapter: indirection that even a Zen master would admire. We don't "order" change. We "deep dip" (go around the hierarchs) and find the exemplars already lurking within our midst—and anoint them as Carriers-in-Chief of the New Culture.

When Jill Ker Conway became the first woman president of Smith College, she brought a bold agenda of change along with her. But despite her exalted title and the positive publicity that attended her appointment, she was trapped by budget shortfalls and a life-tenured faculty not exactly chomping at the bit for radical change.

Rather than use her "position power," as the sociologists call it, to fight the extant culture, she chose indirection. JKC quietly asked around, found names of faculty and administration renegades, and began inviting them to lunch (thence providing her quiet blessing and building her Fifth Column Rolodex). She also introduced them to one another; and thus the buzz began, and the seeds of a new culture were planted. Reticent radicals began to show their faces on the paths between the ivy-covered halls.

Ms. Conway's outside strategy was equally ingenious ... and again indirect. Despite

---

FROM "REGO" TO RMA

[7]Bob Stone's practices, indeed, are strikingly similar to the tactics developed by Boyd.

Boyd, who has been called the Godfather of RMA (Revolution in Military Affairs), left behind him a generation of disciples who go by the name "maneuverists." Instead of frontal attacks on strong points, they favor seeding confusion in the enemy's mind through agility, speed, and variation of tempo. The goal is to make enemies lose control of their troops and of the battlefield as a whole.

Relevance to the corporate world? Think Microsoft ... the modern-day master of tempo and maneuvering. I.e.: OODA loops to die for!

VC = VOCABULARY CAPITAL

New "Boss Work" requires ... New Boss Words:
Hero. Demo. Story.
Freak. **Skunk.** Lead Frog.
Play. WOW Project.
Experiment. Prototype.
Epidemic. Flypaper.
Portfolio. Venture Capital.
Such words must become part of your lexicon ... if you truly want to Create a New Way. (Fast.)

the fanfare surrounding her selection, even the Board that appointed her was shy about dramatic change. Not true, though, of the many Smith *alumnae*, who had been beside themselves to see a ... woman ... finally in charge of this premier women's college. JKC devoted inordinate amounts of time to visiting with these alums, sharing her audacious plans, and seeking their support. In particular, she solicited "beyond-the-budget" seed money that allowed her to start testing those radical additions (ah, demos again!) to school curricula and programs in general.

(Not so incidentally for would-be leaders, JKC acknowledges that she actually loves this political to-ing and fro-ing. Fact: Effective leaders get off on, not shy away from, organizational politics. More on this in Chapter 25.)

Among this chapter's heroes, David Armstrong, Bob Stone, and Jill Ker Conway co-share the Grand Masters of Indirection Award.

The VC Model; Or: You, Bettor, Believe It!

Lurking beneath the surface of all of the foregoing is a Particularly Big Idea: *Think Portfolio. Think Boss-as-Venture-Capitalist.*

"Portfolio": a roster of "bets" that range from sure things with average payoffs to long shots that will make investors rich ... or poor. All bosses are now, in effect, "portfolio managers." Or, to use a somewhat bolder (and hence more accurate) term: They are Venture Capitalists.

What do Venture Capitalists do? Two things. And only two things: They bet on Cool People. (Heroes!) And they bet on Cool Ideas. (Demos!) The result: Cool Investments. (Stories!) Many of those bets ... most of them, in fact ... don't turn out. But a small number do ... and change the world.

The VC Model goes double if you're a Very Big Deal Senior Manager. You might think that if you run a Big Hunk of Big Co., things would be different. From that lofty height, can't you pretty much have to "order" culture change? Does the Heroes-Demos-Stories approach still hold?

My answer: DAMN RIGHT IT HOLDS!

DICTIONARY MOMENTS

Skunk. Noun. Denizen of a Skunkworks. Idea started in *Li'l Abner* comic strip. Stolen by Lockheed.

Skunkworks. Noun. Out of the way, barebones operation where skunk renegades confound the bureaucracy by rapidly implementing Seriously Cool and Subversive Ideas.

BOSS DANCE

"If I could have chosen not to tackle the IBM culture head-on, I probably wouldn't have," former IBM CEO Lou Gerstner wrote in *Who Says Elephants Can't Dance?* **"My bias coming in was toward strategy, analysis and measurement. In comparison, changing the attitude and behaviors of hundreds of thousands of people is very, very hard."**

Hence this chapter! The old tools come up short time and again when entire new ways of working (a new corporate culture) are required to survive, let alone thrive. I believe that the "heroes-demos-stories" approach is made-to-order for changing attitudes and behaviors in the direction of much greater and much swifter innovation.

Mere "compliance" with plans & policies & edicts (which are outdated before the ink is even dry!) is woefully inadequate—and downright dangerous.

Say there are six vice presidents (or lab directors or department heads or division bosses) who report to you. My advice: Turn each of those half-dozen women or men into ... an avowed Venture Capitalist ... each with a clearly identified ... Portfolio of Investments. You should be able to pull any one of them aside in the hall and ask on the spot, "How's your WOW Portfolio 'performing'?"

(In other words: "Tell me some Cool *Stories*.")

In sum: You, the Big Boss, are a venture capitalist; and each of your direct reports is a VC as well. Evaluate their "portfolios" constantly. And keep an eye on your own "portfolio of portfolios."

In a Disruptive Age, that is the Essence of Boss Work in Pursuit of Excellence.

Boss Tools: Toward a Scintillating WOW Portfolio

Once more from the top: Here are the sorts of steps I think you ought to take if you have a "mandate" to do "culture change." (Or even if you don't.)

1. Chat up people throughout your organization.
2. Develop a list of potential "heroes" ("Lead Frogs").
3. Hang out with those heroes-in-the-making. Find out what they want to change, how they would change it—and what they've already *done* to change it "on the sly."
4. Encourage them to "go for it."
5. Protect them when their bosses seek revenge!
6. Turn the "demos" of the new heroes' best efforts into WOW Stories.
7. Showcase those WOW stories. Incorporate them into your speeches, your newsletters, your weekly emails. Add your public Stamp of Approval.
8. Promote one or two of the most illustrious heroes three levels at one jump. (Now the "Lead Frog" *is* a leapfrog.)
9. Treat that promotion as a Big Story—as a recruitment tool for getting the foot-draggers to "sign up" and "come aboard," or at least get the hell out of the way.
10. Keep the cycle going: more heroes ... more demos ... more stories.

Hint: **It never ends.**

! Contrasts

WAS	IS
Top-down leadership	Tap-the-grassroots leadership
Planing, planning, planning	Projects, projects, projects
Issuing orders	Finding heroes
Micro-managing	Dramatizing demos
Telling people what to do	Telling stories
Promotion by seniority	Promotion as "story"
"Running the show"	Building a portfolio
Working "through channels"	Walking through barriers
Dilbert-ville	WOW-land
Resigned to "life"	Ready to Change the World

NEW BUSINESS ! ● NEW WORK

18 BRINGING WOW WORK TO FRUITION: THE SALES25

! Technicolor Rules ...

● Rules? I've got 25 rules—ready to be harvested.

! RANT

We are not prepared ...

We have depended upon "the hierarchy" to "take care of us" ... as long as we were doing a "decent job." We must understand that in order to survive in this up-ended world, we must all become ... First-Rate Salespeople.

No "sales mentality" = No WOW projects = No Cool Stories = No survival.
Period.

! VISION

I imagine ...

A 26-person project team. Members "belong to" 14 *different* companies in 7 *different* countries on 3 different *continents*. Most have not met more than two or three of their cohorts. Yet to get a sticky job done ... fast ... requires energy and enthusiasm and no boundaries. Which means that every Task Leader's Job No. 1 is "Inclusion, Facilitation, Motivation ... *and* Sales."

The WOW of Sales

There's one part of my 1999 book about WOW Projects (*The Project50*) that I'm quite delighted with: I think I can say with some certainty that it's the only "project management book" with an entire chapter—one of just four!—devoted exclusively to ... SALES.

Getting things done—whether you're a junior staffer in purchasing, a finance director, or POTUS (President of the United States)—is mostly a matter of "sales." That is, getting people ... *inflamed* ... about your ideas. Inducing them to ... *sign on* ... and then to ... *stick with you* ... through thin as well as thick.

Key point: *Every* project has "customers." Imagine that you're trying to bring "radical" change to a mere "business process" in finance. In particular, you have a Seriously Cool Idea for a new financial-reporting method for your division. The "users" in other departments who will benefit from that method—or feel put upon by it!—are your *Customers*.[1]

No matter how "cool" your idea may be, those customers must become ... *Enthusiasts* ... of your project ... *if* you are to make a Significant Impact. (No implementation. No impact. Period.) If you can garner ... Passionate Grassroots "Customer" Supporters ... then you've taken a massive step toward "surrounding the bastards." ("The Bastards" = The Big Bosses = Defenders of the Current Way of Doing Things. Hey, they've been eyeballing that same familiar report, eyes half closed, for 10 years.)

You may well be a technical virtuoso. (That's why you came up with this Seriously Cool Idea in the first place!) But *now* it's time to sharpen your "soft" skills—to master the Rules of Sales and Politics. There are no other rules that matter as much.

All the above is a long-winded way of saying: WELCOME TO THE "AGE OF SALES." (The "Age" that follows the "Age of Hierarchy" and "Order Barking.") I originally prepared the following collection of "rules" for a presentation to the sales leadership team of a several-billion-dollar high-tech company. It draws on 30 years of experience and, I believe, it applies as much to the individual contributor on a six-person WOW Project team in finance as it does to a high-powered "sales" person, officially housed in a sales department.

Here goes:

BUY-IN—OR BUST

[1]It's not just higher-ups and end-users you've got to sell to. No, your "Customers" also include ... fellow project-team members and even people who report to you. Barking orders is "out." Intellectual capital is "in." "Providers" of Intellectual Capital are "volunteers"—by definition.

("Non-voluntary creativity" = Oxymoron.)

Plus, the composition of project teams is ever-shifting. Working again and again with "the same old gang" is history. The members of WOW Project Teams come from hither, thither, and (mostly) yon. Working with them calls for a Full-Court, 24/7 Sales Press.

Bottom line: Leading any part of a WOW Project means selling ... up and down and all around the organizational ladder ... all the time.

1. Know Your Product.

It's an obvious point, but well worth stating (and re-stating): *You've got to be smarter than hell about what you're peddling!* And the "secret" to product knowledge goes beyond attending some classes, beyond reading the literature, beyond training to do demos. True product knowledge is *deep* knowledge. "Straight knowledge" is a necessary jumping-off point, but no more than that.

Deep knowledge comes from finding every known factual—and editorial—comment about your product or service. Everything that's ever been said or written about it in print, on the Internet, wherever—by your competitors! For example, you should know about all "objections" raised in popular reviews of the product or service. (And be able to answer each one, of course.)

Deep knowledge also means developing your internal network: Make friends with (deep) designers and (deep) engineers in your product-development department, and encourage them to share the "real story behind the product"—along with the product's various significant features, and unfeatured shortcomings.

When it comes to product knowledge, remember: More, more, more. And, more important: Deeper, deeper, deeper. In sum: *He or she who has the largest appetite for Deep Knowledge wins.*

2. Know Your Company.

Another truism (which doesn't mean that you can ever afford to forget it): You're selling your company as much or more than you are selling a product or service.

You need to understand—cold and in depth—all the pertinent procedures and functions within your company: finance, logistics, customer support, human resources, manufacturing, engineering. Be prepared to deal with any query on any subject from a customer.

But more than that: Be ready to use that fabulous internal network you've developed! Guides and mentors in every (EVERY!) critical part of your company! Colleagues who will teach you and act as your liaison to those other departments! Which will in turn grease the way to easier customer relations.

3. Know Your Customer.

Here again, you must become a research fanatic. Scour the footnotes in financial analysts' reports. Scour the Web. Fact: As never before, there is an *incredible* amount of Good Stuff available. Beyond that, you ought to be able to find people in your company who worked for the customer's company—or people at one of your vendor's operations who worked for the customer's company. Or call an old college chum who worked there.

The goal: *Get to know the "flavor"/"corporate culture" of the customer's enterprise.* This learning process never stops! *You need to know—cold—the "politics" of the customer's decision-making procedures/structures.*

NEW BUSINESS ! • NEW WORK

PUNCTUATION GUIDE

In this chapter, the word "Client" is always capitalized. It's one (not so small) mark of respect for the person who butters our bread. (Note: I learned this at McKinsey & Co., where failure to do Cap "C" was a sin of the first order.)

Getting to know the customer also means getting to know the individuals you will deal with. Any form of legitimate intelligence—including (especially) personal tidbits—is worthwhile. Advice: Until your "intelligence work" on all of these issues is well advanced, don't even think about making that first customer call!

4. Love the Politics.

Axiom: All sales *is* politics. "Politics" ... meaning "the way people work with one another to get things done."

If you don't like—no, make that "love"—politics, you're going to be a crappy salesperson! To be sure, politics can be frustrating and infuriating. But I've discovered that most people who are "frustrated" and "infuriated" by "politics" just don't cotton to the facts of life of the political game. One person's "mind-melting frustration" with "politics" is another person's "exciting human puzzle."

In short, loving the "fray" per se[2]—all the internal to-ing and fro-ing within your own company, your customer's company, and key vendors' companies—is essential to sales success.

5. Respect Your Competitors.

And when I say "respect" competitors, I mean respect them ... *religiously*. You may hate their guts. Maybe with good reason. (Hey, they screwed you out of a sale! Or so you feel.) No matter.

DON'T BAD-MOUTH COMPETITORS. PERIOD.[3]

Nothing makes you look smaller than dissing a legitimate competitor. The goal—the only goal—is to demonstrate why *your* product or *your* service is *better* for *this* customer than the other guy's ... and why *your* firm is the better firm to deal with.

Deeper truth: There is no greater blessing than an extraordinary competitor. (Every day, the folks at UPS should mentally tip their hat to the folks at FedEx. And vice versa.) Great competitors keep you on your toes! Alas, none of us improves without having somebody who pushes us.

6. Wire Your Customer's Organization.

Develop close, congenial relationships at *all* levels and within *all* functions of your customer's enterprise. A "sale" ... whether it happens in a formal sales transaction or on

---

"POLITICAL" RALLY
[2]A "hard sell" point (I can't say this strongly enough): IF YOU DON'T LOVE POLITICS ... IF "POLITICAL" IS A NASTY WORD IN YOUR BOOK ... THEN DON'T EVEN THINK ABOUT PURSUING "WOW" IN ANYTHING YOU DO. Remember:
No politics, no implementation.
No implementation, no WOW.

TAKE OUT THE TRASH TALK
[3]What goes for competitors also goes for your fellow project-team members. In trying to get things done, you will get "jerked around" by dolts in your own camp. Live with it! Don't belittle yourself or your team by trash-talking your colleagues.
Bottom line: Sales depend on ... respect.

a project team ... is often "made" four levels down[4] from where it *officially* takes place.

Example: Junior staffer Mary Smith is responsible for "researching CRM applications in mortgage banking." Any business that you, as a CRM vendor, do with her company must go through Mary's boss's boss's boss, who will have the "big meeting" with your company and "ink the final deal." But Mary's report is decisive. So is the opinion of Richard, Mary's equally junior colleague, who "knows the real scoop on CRM reliability." Finding and courting the Marys and Richards of the world is not easy. But that's what you must do if you want that sale. Think Mary. Think Richard. Forget "rank."

7. Wire Your Organization.

My premise (again): Your customer is buying not so much a widget as a Widget-Provision-and-Support Experience. So: The more you can bring to bear All of the Multi-Faceted Talent in Your Company upon that Experience ... the better your odds of winning a sale and, better yet, a repeat sale. The same thing goes for all of the ... Talent in your Critical Vendor Companies.

Get to *know* that "talent." (That is: all of the "talent"[5] throughout your supply chain.) *Wire* that talent. Makeit/them *connect* for your customers.

8. Never Over-Promise.

You want to win the sale. Your chief competitor is hungry—indeed, ferocious. You feel an overwhelming temptation to shave a few days off the expected delivery time. A little voice inside you says, "Hey, the factory will figure it out."

Well ... DO NOT LISTEN TO THAT "LITTLE" VOICE.

As a salesperson, you are always "out front" ... *alone* at the battle's edge. Your future is ... *always*... at stake. And it is always totally dependent on your ... Trustworthiness.

My advice: Even if it costs you this sale ... *under*-promise. Add a couple of days here

---

WORK THE STAFF

[4] *During my tour in the White House, I learned a big lesson in "wiring the organization"—the organization being, in this case, the United States Congress. I needed Congressional help to execute my agenda. Lots of people in my position hustled like hell to "get five minutes" with a Representative.*

Those were the fools. The wise ones, my mentor taught me, got to know the junior staffers who did the Representative's leg work on a given issue. The odds of success were directly related to the "hours spent" with those "unimportant" staffers.

THE CUSTOMER WITHIN

[5] One special tip: Spend time with "junior" people in *your* organization. A little attention goes a long way. One special perk that you can offer these "internal constituents": Take them along to meet customers!

These folks in the "bowels" of finance, engineering, logistics, or manufacturing can make miracles occur for you ... *if* they are of a mind to do so. Typically, "salespeople" treat "junior staffers" as poor second cousins or, worse, as roadblocks to "winning the sale." No surprise: Those "lowly" staffers are hardly leaping up to help them.

NEW BUSINESS !

NEW WORK

and there to increase the odds of "making target." (Shit *always* happens!)[6] In the long haul, being the courier of pleasant surprises beats being the constant bearer of ill tidings.

Try this for a personal credo: WINNING SALESPEOPLE ARE ROUTINELY AHEAD OF SCHEDULE!

9. Sell the Solution.

Sell only by ... Solving Specific Problems ... and by creating Identifiable Profit Opportunities. Great salespeople don't sell "widgets" (even "damn-good widgets"). They sell solutions. (*Damn-good* solutions.)

Ask yourself, "Is this a 'product sale' or a 'solution sale' that will get me written up in the trade press?"

Every sales pitch you make should boil down to this: "Our product solves *these* specific problems, creates *these* unimaginably incredible opportunities, and will make you *this* huge amount of money. Here is exactly *how*."

To paraphrase the marketing gurus, one doesn't sell a "Rolex watch." One sells "what it feels like to be a Rolex wearer." That's obvious. Or it should be. And what holds for Rolex holds for every sale ... including the internal "sale" of your "business-process redesign project."

Mantra: Idiots sell ... Rolexes. Geniuses sell ... The Rolex Lifestyle.

10. Ask for Help (and Don't Be "Proud" About It).

As you work to solve a customer's problem, to expand a customer's opportunity, to deepen a customer's experience ... draw on every possible resource. "Resources" means "people." Including mortal enemies.

Example: Once upon a time, you had a lousy experience with Jack Jones, a services vendor. *And you're still pissed off about it, four years later.* But now you have a Client; and Jack Jones is the perfect "consultant" to help you add credibility to your pitch to that Client.

So: GET OVER IT. CALL JACK. BEG HIM TO BE PART OF THE DEAL.

Inspired selling involves bringing to bear the absolute best resources available to create the best outcome imaginable for a Client. And it's your job to muster those resources—even if you are less than charmed by some of the "resource providers."

11. Live the Brand Story.

Your company sells a "story." A story about "the way it is to do business with us." A story about our "vision," the "experience we offer," our "dream." In short, a story about our ... "BRAND."

BE A BAD-NEWS BEARER
[6]A simple formula when the yogurt *does* hit the fan: COMMUNICATE LIKE A MANIAC!

The worst thing you can do is fail to convey bad news that's on the horizon, in the silly hope that it will just go away. (On the other hand, passing on a rumor of bad news that does *not* materialize can work in your favor.)

WORKING THE STAFF—FROM THE DISTAFF SIDE
Research suggests, not so incidentally, that women are frequently better salespeople than men—precisely because they are less rank-conscious, and more willing to invest time in developing relations with "low-level" staffers. (More later.) (See Chapter 21.)

Know that story cold! Tell it! Use it! Make it your own! I'm not urging you to be a mindless suck-up to the company line. I am reminding you that in the best companies, Brand Value amounts to hundreds of billions of dollars; and if you can't "buy into the brand promise," then you probably shouldn't stick around.

Give the brand promise your own twist and your own turn, to be sure. Yes, personalize the hell out of it. But take full advantage of the "goodwill" your company has built up over the decades.

12. Celebrate the "Good Loss."

A "good loss" is a brave and brash effort that ... for whatever reason ... doesn't come to fruition. (Yet.) Particularly in madcap times, and especially over the long haul, a good loss can be far better than a "lousy win" (aka "mediocre success.") (See Chapter 15.)

A lousy win is one that brings in a few more bucks for doing the Same Old Stuff. A good loss comes from repositioning a product or service to create a potentially awesome experience ... one that your Client isn't quite nervy enough for. (Yet.)

Take the "good loss" idea too far, and you'll have nothing to show for it but hubris. Nonetheless, I urge you to err ... ever-so-slightly ... in the direction of celebrating that good loss. Push your Clients beyond their comfort zones; if you don't, you're going to lose them to an upstart, perhaps sooner than you think.

13. Make Every Problem Your Problem.

If anything goes wrong in your dealings with a Client, you're screwed, right? What follows is obvious: *All customer problems are your problems!* For God's sake, don't ever—EVER!—blame a late delivery on the "logistics people."

YOU ARE THE SALESPERSON AND YOU "ALONE" ARE THE LEAD DOG REPRESENTING THE COMPANY TO THE CUSTOMER. YOU ARE THE COMPANY TO THE CUSTOMER. ERGO, IF SOMETHING WENT WRONG, YOU SCREWED UP. NOT THE "LOGISTICS PEOPLE."

Which is not to say that you don't have the right to be pissy with the people in logistics if they did, in fact, screw up. You just can't transmit that ire to the Client. The instant you do, your reputation goes to hell in a hand basket.

Remember: They signed a deal with *you* (Martha Stevens-Schmidt), not with some abstract "company."

14. Take *Full* Responsibility.

You are the customer's "point-person" for your entire enterprise. You make your real money from Repeat Business. And Repeat Business comes somewhat from the product or service that you offer ... but mostly from the Seriously Cool & Continuing Experience that customers have working with you. And that Experience will be absolutely, positively fabulous to the extent that you purposefully *orchestrate* it.

Fact is, if you put calipers on it: Salespeople make their sustaining commissions far more by orchestrating Seriously Cool Client Experiences that emanate from all departments in their company and throughout their supply chain than they do by presenting a "torrid" sales pitch. Think of yourself as an Orchestra Conductor. (Not a diva!)

Repeat after me, then: "*I am fully responsible for making my whole damned organization and its partners respond aggressively and harmoniously to the needs and wishes of my customer.*"

15. Don't Hoard Information.

Some salespeople try to "keep the Client to themselves," to control all contacts between the Client and their company.

Dumb. Dumber. Dumbest.

You do *not* want the Client to be slavishly dependent upon you. You want the Client to have a Scintillating Experience with you—*and* with everyone in your orbit; to feel "at home" with your organization; to have close, usable contacts in your engineering, logistics, and finance departments.

When trouble arises and you're not available, you want the Client to have a fully loaded Rolodex of people within your company who can fix the glitch.

Fact is, if things go well, particularly after a glitch, you *will* get the credit. And things will go well, over the long haul, precisely to the extent that you have created a network of relationships that gives the Client "family" access to every element of your company.

Hoard = Lose.

Share = Win.

16. Walk Away from Bad Business.

Don't be a quitter. Don't give up when the first flies appear on the ointment. On the other hand, don't hang in there ... and in there ... and in there ... and sacrifice your calendar and your soul in perpetuity, in order to make your numbers.

Be clear on this: THERE *IS* SUCH A THING AS "BAD BUSINESS." When you find people in a customer organization to be untrustworthy, when the game-playing involved in making a sale rises far above the normal push-and-pull of politics, when business becomes that painful, you may well need to make a graceful (or not-quite-so-graceful) exit.

I'm not counseling you to become "holier-than-thou." Politics *is* normal. Compromise *is* eternal. Shit *does* happen. But there *are* limits.

For example:

Don't work with people who are dishonest.

Don't work with people who don't keep their word.

Don't work with people who care only about themselves.

Don't work with jerks.

LIFE IS TOO SHORT.[7]

17. Don't Whine About Price.

It's okay to lose business on price. *I've* lost business on price. (Numerous times.) You don't enjoy it, and it's fair to bitch to the controller about the "insane margins" that he's trying to milk from an "ordinary" product or service. And yet ... one of the surest signs of a salesperson-going-nowhere is *continual* complaining about "losing sales on price."

Because, ultimately, what you're selling is no "ordinary" product or service. Once again: You are selling an Opportunity ... a Solution ... an Experience ... a Dream To Be

---

HONOR THY FUTURE

[7]Nobody on his or her death bed says, "I made my numbers 73 quarters in a row." No, when you're on your death bed, you'll talk about Peak Experiences. Sure, most of those "peaks" involve friends and family; but many involve super-cool things that you've done at work. And those things are invariably *honorable*.

Fulfilled. All of which still may not justify a 50 percent premium over an excellent competitor; but it damn well ought to justify some kind of premium!

In a world where "services added" are becoming more and more significant, per our riff in Chapter 6, the only game in town is to "Add an Awesome Armload of Intangibles" that will allow you to charge a healthy premium for what you are offering.

Bottom line: Those who say, "It's all a price issue," suffer from rampant immaturity and a shrunken imagination.

(Period.)

18. Don't Give Away the Store ... to Get a Foot in the Door.

Yes, be flexible! Yes, go the extra mile! But ... be c-a-r-e-f-u-l! I have seen far too many cases of salespeople talking their organization into absurd compromises in order to get the "first sale" with some "big Client." These over-eager, peddle-to-the-metal salespeople always say the same thing: "Let's do it just this once. After that, we'll be able to get our normal margin."

In your dreams!

Remember: The line between "loss leader" and "lead loser" can be ... diaphanously thin. Message: Once (*perceived as*) a sucker, forever a sucker.

19. Respect Upstarts (the *Real* Enemy).

The real enemy these days, over the medium to long term, is rarely your "chief competitor." It's more likely to be the competitor-that-doesn't-make-it-onto-your-radar-screen ... but that really *does* have a Seriously Better Idea that will nail you to the wall over the next several years. That is, if you are not exceedingly alert.

Think Microsoft 20 years ago. Or Wal*Mart 20 years ago.

"Knowing the industry" means having good antennae out for the "little guys"[8] that may not be "little" all that much longer. Toward that end, make sure that your Extended Personal Network includes, perhaps, a few savvy venture capitalists who can feed you the "buzz" on what's coming next. (They may be wrong. But they will be unfailingly interesting. And they will keep you in fighting trim.)

20. Seek Cool Customers.

The "obvious" sales targets are almost always the biggest, most established ones. There is obviously some logic to such an approach. But in a time of dramatic change, it is utterly imperative that your customer portfolio (that P-word again... and more to

---

IF YOU CAN'T BEAT 'EM ...
[8]Here's another option: Give those upstart competitors a break. Work with them. Ask them to become part of the product-service-experience "package" that you offer.

Far better to co-opt an emerging star as an "alliance partner" now than to see that company become a major rival later.

THE LOYAL "WE"
Here's another "trick" I picked up long ago at McKinsey & Co.: Always use the word "we." In talking with customers, say, "*We* will take this approach ..."

Sure, it's a "trick." But the person you end up tricking (in the best sense of that word) is yourself!

come) include a significant share of "leading-edge" companies—folks that are already pursuing *tomorrow's* flavors of excellence today.

You—you, the salesperson, and your company—are as "cool" as your customer portfolio is "cool."[9] And vice versa.

It's that simple!

And that hard!

Message: Be *religious* in the ... QUANTITATIVE ... evaluation of your Customer Portfolio. Ask yourself: Does my list of customers and prospects have a high enough ... Weird Quotient ... to provide me with a genuine bead on the (inevitably) Weird Future?

21. Talk "Partnership."

The word "partnership" is way overused. My advice: Use it anyway. Obsessively. (Hey, if the cliché fits ...)

Why do I insist on using that word? Because what you are selling ... no matter "what" you are selling ... is just that: a partnership. A Seamless, Virtual, Encompassing Web of Colleagues and Vendors who Devote their Herculean Efforts to Creating Opportunities/Experiences/Dream Fulfillment for your Beloved Client.

Your job as a salesperson is to bring to bear—in a seamless fashion—the full power and imagination of your company's entire supply chain.

Sounds like a "partnership" to me.

So I mean it: USE THE DAMN WORD.

"PARTNERSHIP."

22. Send Thank-You Notes!

A half-dozen years ago, I wrote a "summa" on implementation. Some 50 ideas. No. 1 on the list: DON'T FORGET YOUR THANK-YOU NOTES!

Obvious point (all too often honored in the breach): Sales is a ... RELATIONSHIP ... business. And a potent "tool" in the relationship game is a kind word. In other words: a thank-you note.

Thank-you notes.[10] Send them by the truckload.

The note of appreciation to the "Big Guy" who made time on his calendar for you

---

YOU ARE WHO YOU SELL TO

[9]Big, big point: Hanging out with exciting, innovative people automatically makes you more exciting and more innovative—and keeps you ahead of the curve.

The converse is also true: Dull customers = Dull "solutions" and dull "experiences."

Much more later. See Chapter 23.

CAPITAL IDEA

[10]I had a boss in Washington years ago. Insanely busy. But on Day One of working with him, I observed that he closed his office door at about 7 p.m. for a half-hour.

A nip of Chivas Regal? Hardly.

He religiously spent those 30 minutes dictating (that's what we did back then) a dozen or more simple "thank-yous" to people he'd met during the day. People who had "gotten him a meeting" with someone he needed to see, or who had made a supportive comment when he really needed it.

Result (no overstatement): He had a slavish network of devotees throughout D.C. (aka Den of Cynicism).

is one thing. And important. But more important over the long haul: notes to people several rungs down the ladder, people who went a "little bit out of their way" to advance your cause.

Another rule of thumb: At least 50 percent of your thank-you notes should go to people *inside* your company—"unsung" people who help create better *experiences* (remember: that's what you're selling) for your customer.

Oh, and while I'm at it: Remember birthdays. Send birthday cards. And flowers when appropriate. Little touches are *never* little.

23. Make Your Customer a Hero.

When you look across the table at your customer, think religiously and repeatedly to yourself: *"How can I make this dude or dudette rich and famous? How can I get him or her promoted?"*

It's not enough to focus on making the customer's *organization* "successful." Yes, that's clearly the long-term goal. But the practical, near-term imperative is to make a ... Solid Gold Hero ... out of the *Individual* who is responsible for buying (and using) your product or service.

Consider: I am not in the "widget-selling business." I am in the ... "Hero-Making Business."

"Companies" don't buy "things" from other "companies." Rather: *Individuals* buy *Successful Relationships* from other *Individuals*.

(Big deal.)

(BIG DEAL.)

24. Aim to Change-the-Damn-World!

Selling is ... Cool. *Very* Cool. I really do believe, when I hawk my "wares" (present a seminar or write a book), that I'm doing more than buttering the bread and paying the property taxes. While I don't think I routinely change the world for large numbers of people, I know that I give a damn about what I'm up to—and I'm excited about delivering my product-service-experience-dream-impact.

Flash back to that cri de coeur from Apple Computer boss Steve Jobs: *"Let's make a dent in the universe."*

I think the notion that selling can be ... "universe-denting" ... is what keeps us motivated, *and* able to look at ourselves in the mirror.

NEW BUSINESS ▬ ● ▬ NEW WORK

EXIT ... "WORK

"This concludes the four-chapter section called "New Business. New Work." As I worked on the section, I tried to conjure up a "controlling image" for it. That is: WHAT THE HELL POINT DO I REALLY WANT TO MAKE HERE?

My favorite candidate: Work as the ... Theater of Accomplishment.

The Days of Cosseting are done. We are, or soon will be, more or less (mostly "more") on our own.

Hence: The work we do must ... Matter. It must ... Make a Difference.

Hence: Forget the dreary image of the Cubicle Slave in a Tall Tower.

Think: THEATER OF ACCOMPLISHMENT.

Think: This is ... Where I Perform. This is ... How I Make My Mark. This is ... my WOW Project.

(And to hell with Dilbert.)

25. Keep Your Slides Simple.

If you're in sales (and again, if you're in the WOW Project Business, you're in the Full-time Sales Business), sooner or later you drag out Ye Olde PowerPoint presentation.

So: Keep those bloody slides[11] lean and full of meaning!

As noted, this Sales25 discussion derives from a presentation I made to salespeople at a major tech company. I reviewed some of their presentations in the process of doing some of my own prep work. And ... I was appalled. Each of their slides, and they peddle great products, had *way* too much stuff on it.

Is it just my age? Am I just too old to see the fine print? No, damn it! The point of a presentation is to persuade ... not to perplex.

We Are All Salespeople Now

Want to get my dander up? Try saying, "Hey, I'm a finance guy. I don't 'do' sales."

No! No! No!

Success = Sales Success!
Everywhere.
Period.
We're all in sales. All the Time.

! Contrasts

WAS	IS
"The Sales Department is down the hall." –	"The Sales Department is right here!"
"Command and control" –	"All sales, all the time"
The Supreme Leader issues commands –	The team leader develops camaraderie
I was "assigned" to this task –	I *volunteered* for this task
Leader: "I'm in charge here!" –	Leader: "My job is to spread enthusiasm and to sell the project."

---

[11]A few basics on keeping the pith in your pitch:
Cluttered slides = Cluttered thinking.
Keep it clear.
Keep it simple.
Declare your benefits.
State your case.
Tell your (COMPELLING) "story."
Sit down.
Shut up.

**An epoch in which ... "Talent Rules"...
is upon us! Hooray!**

new bus!ness
new people

It's (the New "It") ... ALL ABOUT TALENT!

That should be as obvious "by now" as the ends of our collective noses.

1. Microprocessors supplant rote White-Collar Work ... and More.

2. Value emanates from beyond-the-edge-of-the product; i.e., from the application of Creativity & Intellectual Capital.

3. All survivors' work must therefore and by definition become WOW Projects—starting among the most officially powerless, who are thence the most at risk.

4. Hence: It's ... ALL ABOUT TALENT.

5. Q.E.D.

19 RE-IMAGINING THE INDIVIDUAL: LIFE IN A BRAND YOU WORLD

! Technicolor Rules ...

- "If there is nothing very special about your work, no matter how hard you apply yourself you won't get noticed, and that increasingly means you won't get paid much either."
- "You are the storyteller of your own life, and you can create your own legend or not."
- "I don't think there's anything worse than being ordinary."
- Corporate America is *not* going to cosset you anymore. Think of it this way: You've got a new boss. Buy a mirror: It's *you*.

! RANT

We are not prepared ...

We keep trying (longing?) to veer back to the professional "career path" of old—a model of employment in which Big Companies Ruled and we Genuflected on Command. Dazzled by the still abiding myth of security, we shy away from recognizing that new modes of enterprise require nothing less than the ... Re-imagining of the Individual. Now we must take ... Immediate Charge ... of our new-fangled careers and identities, careers and identities that will consist of a string of WOW Projects that we perform at a series of companies, small and large, over time. That's scary. That's cool. Whichever, it's life in a ... Brand You World.

! VISION

I imagine ...

A truly creative society: Each person moves from project to project, from gig to gig. Global Voluntary Communities of Interest, rather than corporations, provide the bedrock upon which we stand. Learning never ceases. Self-reliance is the norm. The social safety net is not a condescending "corporate benefits package;" it attaches to the individual and promotes flexibility throughout a New (Global) Economy. Each career consists of numerous "mini-careers," with time-outs along the way. The cubicle slave is dead; long live the Free Agent.

Dilbert Unbound!

Work is changing. Irreversibly. (Welcome, again, to WOW Project World.) And now ... the worker[1] (me, you) must change along with the work.

Every several generations, we undergo a massive upheaval in our work lives. We move off the farm, with its never-ending rituals (cows don't take holidays—take it from a Vermonter), and into the factory. Then we move out of the factory, with its Simon Legree–like supervisor, and into white-collar nouveau prisons called—Big City High-rises.

Today, the software robots are taking over the (surprisingly mindless) white-collar jobs of yesteryear. Once again we must find ... Entirely New Ways to Add Value. Yet this time around, the change isn't just a matter of moving by the millions like sheep from Job Slot A in the factory to Job Slot B in the high-rise.

"White-collar *cubicle* slavery," circa 1980, was not all that different from "blue-collar *shop-floor* slavery," circa 1920. Less heavy lifting, sure, but the Conformity Quotient was about the same: "It's 9 a.m., park your uniqueness at the door, please." But the next shift, the one that is accelerating now, promises to be far more dramatic. Everything even vaguely repetitive will soon be automated. Our only recourse: moving beyond any activity that is even remotely "rote," and moving up—WAY UP!—the New Creativity Scale. Along the way, banishing the Conformity Mandate for good.

We must become ... *Independent Contractors* ... at least in spirit, if not immediately in reality. We must exhibit ... *True Distinction*. We must convert ourselves into *Genuine Business people* ... not mere white-collar ciphers. New me/you: Innovative, Risk-taking, Self-sufficient Entrepreneurs—not smooth-functioning organization men (or women).

Sounds scary as hell, right?

You bet.

But here's what I believe ... and I won't mince words. I believe that *Dilbert*-style "cubicle slavery" ... stinks. I believe that the change now under way is ... Cool. I believe that the chance to tear down those wretched cubicle walls, to take a pick-axe to that ergonomically correct but numbingly insipid "cubicle furniture," and to make work for ourselves in the wide-open world beyond is nothing short of ... *Liberation*.

What a challenge! What an opportunity! An opportunity for immense, meaningful value creation! An opportunity for individual reinvention!

LAY OFF "WORKERS"

[1]First order of business: We must change the words that we use to describe ourselves. Take the word "worker." Take it ... and Throw It Away.

We must expunge *that "worker" word from our vocabulary!*

We are not "workers." We are individuals. And the game clock shows one minute to go. The time has come, the time is overdue to ... re-imagine and then unleash the individual.

A HAPPENING THING

The Age of Creation Intensification is no chimera. It's here. In his extraordinary *The Rise of the Creative Class*, Carnegie-Mellon Professor Richard Florida claims that the "creative class" in the U.S. already encompasses 38 million people, or 30 percent of the work force. Impact? "The Creative Class," Florida writes, "derives its identity from its members' roles as purveyors of creativity. Because creativity is the driving force of economic growth, in terms of influence the Creative Class has become the dominant class in society."

THE ROAD TO "RE-IMAGINATION"

Let's look back at the trail we have blazed so far in this book.

I began by discussing the New Context—and the vital need to *destroy* virtually all the ways and means of enterprise, public and private, that have accreted since the beginning of the Industrial Revolution.

I then explored the stunning implications of information technology for our white-collar workforce.

(That is: Me. You.)

That discussion led to an examination of the emergence of a Value Proposition based on "solutions" and "experiences." And conquering New Markets.

The logical next step: All work becomes WOW Project work.

Now we arrive at the completion of an argumentative arc that extends from Context to Core. And the core is ... People ... Talent ... the Human Capital that drives every WOW Project.

In other words: the *Individual* ... primed for Re-imagination.

True Millennial Madness. (Or: OH MY GOD.)

Perhaps this—the changing world of work—is the biggest deal in ... a MILLENNIUM. That's more or less the stunning conclusion of a sober Princeton historian-economist. Philip Bobbitt, author of *The Shield of Achilles: War, Peace, and the Course of History*, calls this one of just a half-dozen turning points in human history.

The issue? Dare I say it, for fear of sounding self-serving: Brand You.

Or at least that's my translation.

Nations for the last several hundred years have treated their territory as a closed system. Their goal was to make the lives of their citizens better, within the confines (keyword) of that territory. Well, that goal is no longer tenable, says Bobbitt. The Global Economy is ... well ... erasing that possibility.

Bobbitt, in an erudite argument I can hardly do justice to here, claims that the mantle of governance is shifting from the mostly autonomous "nation-state" to the globally interdependent "market-state."

Big idea: If I, as President or Prime Minister, can no longer ensure your welfare within our nation state ... then what's left for me to do is to provide you with tools to survive (and, I hope, thrive) in a truly borderless marketplace[2] for skilled providers of services.

Bobbitt offers a summary of his argument that just might make your hair curl: "What strategic motto will dominate this transition from nation-state to market-state?[3] If the slogan that animated the liberal, parliamentary nation-states was 'make the world safe for democracy' ... what will the forthcoming motto be? Perhaps 'making the world

---

"OFFSHORE" PATROL

[2]Headline to February 2003 *BusinessWeek* cover story: "IS YOUR JOB NEXT? A New Round of GLOBALIZATION Is Sending Upscale Jobs Offshore. They Include Chip Design, Engineering, Basic Research—even Financial Analysis."

DEUTSCH (RE)MARK

[3]German Chancellor Gerhard Schroeder: "Either we modernize or we will be modernized by the unremitting force of the market."

available,' which is to say creating new worlds of choice and protecting the autonomy of persons to choose."

President Bill Clinton, who Bobbitt argues understood the coming tectonic economic shift (along with British PM Tony Blair), echoed Bobbitt's conception: "In a global economy, the government cannot give anybody a guaranteed success story, but you can give people the tools to make the most of their own lives."

Bottom line:

1. No nation is an island.

2. Darwin Rules!

3. No Guarantees!

4. The only *quasi-*guarantee is … having (Truly) Great Tools with which to compete in the (Truly) Global Village.

Bottom (bottom) line:

1. Terrifying.
2. Exhilarating.
3. Completely Different.[4]

"Free Agent" Notion

For a precise and dramatic "local" rendition of the shifting nature of "employment," you'll do no better than Dan Pink's masterful book *Free Agent Nation*. Here are some facts from his file (current as of April 2001):

● Fewer than 1 in 10 Americans now work for a Fortune 500 company.

● The No. 1 private employer in the United States, by body count, is no longer GM or AT&T. It's Manpower, Inc., the temporary work mega-agency.

● Between 16 and 25 million of us are freelancers or independent contractors. There are now three million temps—including temp lawyers, temp engineers, temp project managers, and even temp CEOs.

● Microbusinesses, defined as companies that employ four or fewer people, are home to another 12 million to 27 million of us.

In total, then, between 31 million and 55 million Americans are already occupying "nontraditional" job slots. Job slots whose very nature would surprise—indeed, horrify—our fathers' generation. (Certainly, they'd knock my father for a loop!)

Lessons to draw from all this:

1. Lifetime employment is over.
2. Stable employment at large corporations is gone.
3. The average career will likely encompass two or three "occupations" and a half-dozen or more employers.

FAIL …WITH DISTINCTION

[4]A paradox …

Brand You World demands distinction. Distinction demands a constant addition of new skills—sometimes radically new skills. The acquisition of radically new skills requires (many) trials and (many) errors.

Hence: New Excellence = Old-Fashioned Screwing-Up.

Hmmm.

4. Most of us will spend sustained periods of our career in some form of self-employment.[5]

5. Bottom line: We're on our own, folks.

6. It's not theory. It's happening ... NOW.

Broken Premise: The Anxiety of Age

Again: The changes afoot in the world of employment are ... scary as hell. Especially if you're a 47-year-old accountant, and you've worked in the same white-collar office tower ever since you collected your college diploma 25 summers ago.

Something fundamental is going on—beyond the Tidal Wave of Technology, beyond the Great Job Shift. The nature of "who we are" is undergoing a tectonic shift. The transformation affects not just the kind of work we do, but our fundamental relationship to work. And 47-year-old accountants, watching as reengineering and advanced software automation roar into their cubes, are quaking in their loafers: "What the hell am I going to do ... when IBM decides to toss me out of my cubicle?"

They are panicked.[6] And rightfully so.

When I discuss the White-Collar Revolution in my seminars, people respond in one of two very distinct ways. And the breakdown generally runs along what I call the Age 38.5 Divide. If you're less than 38.5 years of age, chances are that you can't wait for dawn to break. If you're more than 38.5 years of age, you're apt to feel seasick ... the victim of broken promises about career certainty.

I don't have any easy answers for those who, chronologically or mentally, find themselves on the wrong side of that Great Divide. Managing our "emigration" to Free Agent Nation won't be easy. It *isn't* easy.

But we *will* get it right!

And it *will* be liberating!

The key ... and there is only one key ... is ... *attitude*. If the security of guaranteed cubicle slavery for life is your cup of tea ... well, you're going to be scared stiff of all that's

---

THE BEST BOSS EVER
[5]Headline to a May 2003 *Forbes* cover story: "JUST GOT LAID OFF? HIRE YOURSELF."

"SPECIAL" WAY
Writing in *Wired* magazine, Michael Goldhaber issued this seminal adult tough-love statement: "If there is nothing very special about your work, no matter how hard you apply yourself you won't get noticed, and that increasingly means you won't get paid much either." Cold, hard truth: Be special—or be spurned.

SAFETY NET LOSS?
[6]Meanwhile, we're not doing enough to equip people—old, young, or perilously in between—for a post-cubicle-slave world.

Our benefits options, public and private, are all wrong: limited or nonexistent healthcare coverage, skimpy funds for retraining, slow-vesting pensions.

Nor, on a related front, is our school system preparing kids for this Weird New World. There is too much emphasis on *obedience* (the main ingredient of "successful" cubicle slavery) and too little on *independence*. (See Chapter 22.)

But, as I say, we *will* (eventually) get it right.

coming down the pike. But if the notion of life as a series of "gigs," in which you learn new tricks and live by your wits, excites you ... well, you'll wake up drooling at the chance to re-imagine yourself... and add yet another memorable-braggable WOW Project to your portfolio.

Can you do it? Of course!

The United States of ... Att-i-tude

The impetus to "re-imagine the individual" is nothing new. It is, in fact, quintessentially American. From its earliest beginnings, America has been a nation that is absolutely *defined* by ... self-reinvention.

People didn't like the way things were in Britain, or Germany, or Russia, or Italy, or wherever. So they made a barely imaginable leap of faith (exactly the right term), uprooted themselves, and sailed on unspeakably unpleasant ships for the United States. They landed at an anthill called Ellis Island, or some such. They scrambled, with great difficulty, to find something to do in Manhattan, or some other great city of the East. Then they moved on. A little bit west. A little further west. And so on.

My paternal grandfather left Germany for the United States in the 1870s. My father stayed put, living and working near Baltimore, where Granddad Peters had landed. And so I was raised in Maryland. But then, courtesy of the U.S. Navy, I winged my way to California in 1966. And there I stayed for 35 years.

The goal ... for my grandfather, for me, for so many others who followed the call of the frontier ... was always the same: to trade in an old identity for a new one. (I was very proud, I tell you, of the persona called ... California Tom. And quite willing to bury Maryland Tom back in Maryland.)

The Pilgrim Fathers understood this point.

Ben Franklin understood it.

Ralph Waldo Emerson understood it.

Horatio Alger understood it.

Dale Carnegie understood it.

And today Stephen Covey, Tony Robbins, and many, many others understand it.

That is, they understand ... the American Impetus and Genius for Wholesale Reinvention.

Imagine great-great-grandfather, scrapping along with great-great-grandmother to

---

HELLO, MR. CHIPS

One group that epitomizes (perhaps surprisingly) the Brand You idea: university professors. People outside academe don't generally realize the degree to which top scholars have become marketing-minded superstars. Yesterday's "absent-minded professor" is today's "entrepreneur of ideas."

Professors' primary loyalty is to their specialty—microbiology, finance, or torts. Their primary community encompasses not their putative employer, but their peers in that specialty—all over the globe. They affiliate themselves with a particular institution for some period, mostly based on its offer of research resources, but everything else about them is portable: their labs, their grants, their book contracts, even their pensions (mostly through TIAA-CREF).

And in fact their career success depends hardly at all on their "employer," and almost exclusively on that global community of peers—right up to the day, for a tiny handful, that they march onto a Swedish stage to accept a Nobel Prize.

sustain a tiny farm on the Kansas prairie. They weren't "workers." They were, in effect, entrepreneurs ... citizens of an earlier Free Agent Nation.

The good news, then: This is in fact a "back to the future" epoch. Our "new world" of WOW Projects and Independent Contracting harkens back to an older "new world" of striking out for the frontier and staking an independent claim.

To say all this about our long and deep heritage of "reinvention" is not to suggest that the current task is easy or painless. Uprooting never was easy. And never will be. But we have done it before ... by the millions ... and will do it again.

YANKEE, COME HOME!

Paul Roberts gets it. Paul has been the prime contractor for the many big projects we've undertaken on our farm in Tinmouth, Vermont. He certainly doesn't *talk* "management theory." No yapping about "new employment paradigms" from him. But he does the Free Agent Nation walk perfectly. Instinctively, in fact. He lives off his incredible reputation—and yet he knows that he is only as good as his last gig.

A few years back, while preparing to do a TV interview, I was thinking about that great Age 38.5 Divide. Suddenly, it dawned on me that all those 38.5-plus-year-olds who live in mortal terror of the world outside their corporate cubicle are actually in a minority. And, in the grand scheme of things, they always have been.

I thought about all the people who had worked on projects at our farm during the previous summer. A stone mason. An electrician. A plumber. A tiler. A cabinetmaker. A building contractor. A blacksmith. A welldriller. A blaster. A sheep shearer. A veterinarian. And probably a dozen more.

Every one of those folks "got it." Got it a lot more thoroughly, and a lot more personally, than the 47-year-old accountant at Kmart or the 39-year-old middle manager at CSX.

Now it's time for cubicle denizens to get it, too. Time to go "back to the future." (Or else.)

Voices from the Frontier

To paraphrase an old saying: Spirit is the mother of reinvention. Here are some quotations that give voice to that spirit. The "westering" spirit. A spirit that is quintessentially American ... but not just American.

WIN SAM, LOSE SAM

No one typified the American heritage of reinvention more exuberantly than Wal*Mart founder Sam Walton.

Walton, for example, had an "absolute fearlessness when it comes to failure." That's what then-CEO of Wal*Mart David Glass told me when I asked him, about a decade ago, to sum up the genius of Sam Moore Walton. Sam was still alive at that time, and I was making preparations to introduce him at a black-tie shindig to be held at the Waldorf-Astoria in New York.

Here's more of what Glass told me: "Sam will make a sorry mess of something, come in to work the next morning with a chuckle, and comment, 'Well, we got that dumb idea out of the way. What's next?' It's not that he tolerates sloppiness or slackards. To the contrary, it's just that he is a champion of the 'brilliant try,' executed right now, with unparalleled vigor. And if it flops, try something else. *Now*. With even more vigor. Don't waste even a minute tut-tutting about what might have been."

Read. Ponder.
Reread ... aloud.
And *listen*.

"No prudent man dared to be too certain of exactly who he was. ... Everyone had to be prepared to become someone else. To be ready for such perilous transmigrations was to become an American."—the great historian Daniel Boorstin

"I am an American, Chicago-born ... and go at things as I have taught myself, free-style, and will make the record in my own way."—Saul Bellow's eponymous hero in *The Adventures of Augie March*

"You are the storyteller of your own life, and you can create your own legend or not."—novelist Isabel Allende

"I don't think there's anything worse than being ordinary."—Angela (played by Mena Suvari), in the movie *American Beauty*

"The time seems appropriate to rethink the notions of self and identity in this rapidly changing age."—Tara Lemmey, Electronic Frontier Foundation

THE *"I work for a company called ME" STREET JOURNAL.*
THE *"rise up and flee your cubicle" STREET JOURNAL.*
—"Adventures in Capitalism" advertisements for the *Wall Street Journal*

"The new organization of society implied by the triumph of individual autonomy and the true equalization of opportunity based upon merit will lead to very great rewards for merit and great individual autonomy. This will leave individuals far more responsible for themselves than they have been accustomed to being during the industrial period. It will also reduce the unearned advantage in living standards that has been enjoyed by residents of advanced industrial societies throughout the 20th century."—James Davidson and William Rees-Mogg, in *The Sovereign Individual*

"BLAME NO ONE! EXPECT NOTHING! DO SOMETHING!"

—sign posted in the New York Jets locker room by then-coach Bill Parcells

"Brand You" ... or Bust

In terms of enterprise—that is, work and business—the upshot of "re-imagining the individual" is a tectonic shift in perspective toward what I call ... Brand You thinking.

I launched this idea as far back as 1997, when I wrote a cover story for *Fast Company* magazine titled "The Brand Called You." Then, in 1999, I wrote a book, *The Brand You50,* that explores the idea in considerable depth. That idea, in brief: Whether or not you are on some firm's payroll, you are well advised to behave as if you were CEO of Me Inc. (Translation of "well advised": Your professional life—or death—is at stake.)

In other words: View yourself as the boss of your own show, even if that show happens to be playing just now at Citigroup or GE or ExxonMobil.

In other words (again): DISTINCT ... OR EXTINCT.

Branding is a perennially "hot" issue in business circles. Reams and reams of stuff have been written about it (including by me—e.g., Chapter 12 of this book), and the emphasis is usually on using "brand image" to sell a product or service. But "branding," at both the individual and the corporate level, is fundamentally *not* a "marketing" issue. It is an *attitude* issue, pure and simple. What I call "brand outside" (that is, what the marketplace "experiences of us") is a function of "brand inside" (what lies within us as an enterprise ... or within our individual soul).

In his marvelous book *Corporate Religion*, Danish marketing expert Jesper Kunde writes: "Only with a strong spirit at its foundation can a company achieve a strong market position."

The same goes for you and your career.[7] (And me and mine.)

Narcissism: No and Yes

Several social commentators have attacked the Brand You idea as an example of '90s-style American self-absorption. In 1998, Jedediah Purdy more or less claimed that Jerry Seinfeld and I symbolized what was wrong with America.

Of course there's an element of self-absorption in the Brand You idea. But the impetus is not ego; it's something much more primal, called "survival." The downside of cubicle slavery notwithstanding, one need not be very self-absorbed if AT&T is taking care of my every need from age 23 (I nearly went to work for them at that age) to, via pensions and coffin allowances, death. But AT&T now has approximately 72,000 employees, down from a peak of 1,009,000 at the time of the Big Bell Breakup on 31 December 1983. And still more professional blood is likely to flow. Call it Brand You or whatever you wish; but don't call it "optional."

I chose Brand You because I think it captures the spirit of offering (selling! period!) one's services in that wide-open, largely unprotected global marketplace Professor Bobbitt describes. Simply put, my "service offering" must be perceived to be of economic value, just like Mr. Purdy's manuscripts. If that's narcissism and self-absorption, then I plead guilty-as-charged.

A "Brand You" Start

In the Brand You training offered by Tom Peters Company, we provide concrete ways for

{ **BRAND U-TURN**
[7]Recall what I wrote in Chapter 12 about "The Heart of Branding." The questions that I said you should apply to your company, or to your "solution" or "experience" offering, apply with special force to ... *you*:

WHO *ARE* YOU?
WHY ARE YOU HERE?
HOW ARE YOU *UNIQUE*?
HOW CAN YOU MAKE A *DRAMATIC DIFFERENCE*?
WHO *CARES*?
(DO *YOU* CARE?)

Clients to renew their Brand You portfolio. They have found one exercise in particular to be of value. We call it the Personal Brand Equity[8] Evaluation. Each participant is asked to complete the following statements:

- *I am known for [2 or 3 items]; next year at this time I will also be known for [1 item].*
- *My current project is challenging me in the following ways [3 items].*
- *New things I've learned in the last 90 days include [2 or 3 items].*
- *My public "recognition program" consists of [2 or 3 items].*
- *Additions to my Rolodex in the last 90 days include [2 to 3 names].*
- *My résumé is Discernibly Different from last year at this time in these [1 or 2] ways.*

There's no magic here. But applying the "brand equity" idea to your career is a clear winner, or so Clients tell us.

10 Degrees of Attitude: The "Brand You" Survival Kit

If you're going to light out for the frontier ... if you're going to reinvent yourself as a Brand You enterprise ... then you'll need to pack some key traits in your old kit bag. (I say "if," but it isn't really an option. Remember: Distinct—or Extinct.) Here are 10 such traits:

1. Think Like an Entrepreneur.

The point of Brand You is not that you should quit your job at, say, JCPenney. It is that you should *re-imagine* yourself as the CEO of Me Inc.—who is currently on loan to Penney's for the "next gig." (Perhaps it's a merchandising project for the spring "junior miss" line.) Now, if Penney's keeps serving up Great Gigs, well, maybe you will stick around for 5 or 25 years. But your point of orientation must always be ... the degree to which the current Great Gig noticeably enhances *your market value.*

In sum: Be the *boss* of your *own show*.[9] Reinvent all Gigs to ensure that they become Brand You Enhancers.

WORD EQUITY
[8]"Personal" ... "Brand" ..."Equity."
Yes: You and I are BRANDS. As much as Coca-Cola is a brand. Thus, you and I have a (high or low) (growing or declining) (solid or fragile) brand equity.
Please: Do not just nod your head when you read that.
Please: Take in the full denotation and connotation of that term.
Words are important. They have value. They have (dare I say?) equity.

UPDATE YOUR ... ANNUAL REPORT
[9]The rule of thumb is that you should "update your résumé" about once a year. I say: Update your *Annual Report* at least once a year. That's what your résumé is, after all—a public announcement that makes the best possible case for your True Commercial Viability and Distinction.

2. Always Be a "Closer."

If you're going to head up an important enterprise, including one called Me Inc., you need to understand the ins and outs of... *making money*. Even if you don't have "line" financial responsibility for your current gig, always acquaint yourself with "the numbers" and keep a close eye on the project P&L and Balance Sheet.

A related point: The track record of Me Inc. derives from only one thing—implemented projects. And implementation is 98 percent a matter of "closing the deal" with a broad array of internal and external stakeholders, many of whom are likely to have conflicting goals. As all true businesspeople know: Life is sales. The rest is details. Or: When it comes to closing the deal, "good try" isn't good enough. (Review Chapter 18.)

3. Embrace Marketing.

No, you don't need to land a spot on *Oprah*. But you do need to master much more of the Marketing Puzzle than you probably did in the past. Brand You World is a long way from the old world in which you hung out for 20 years with the same 17 people in the Credit & Collections Department. Instead, you will be bounding from project to project ... mostly working with strangers. Thus, on *each* gig, you will be selling yourself anew—marketing your point of view, marketing your worth, marketing Me Inc.

4. Pursue Mastery.

Competence (and then some) in baseline business skills like marketing and networking is essential. But it's not enough. To survive the White-Collar Tsunami, you need to be Very Damn Special at something of specific economic value (like those professors discussed above). In a word, you need to exhibit ... True Mastery.

Survival merely as Jack R. Smith, Badge 248, Purchasing Department, is no longer tenable. When I consider Jack for a gig or a full-blown job, I look for as much distinction as I would if I were considering a trade for a left-handed, fadeaway-throwing set-up man to go into the Boston Red Sox bullpen. In Jack's case, the equivalent of that impossible-to-hit screwball means being best-in-industry at, say, Latin American trade-accounting processes.

Mastery goes beyond just having a distinct skill. Think about the top athletes and actors. Those folks are consummate pros who work obsessively at their craft. You should approach your "tradecraft"[10] in the same way.

{
FIRM BELIEF
Recall (from Chapter 5) my reconception of "departments" as Scintillating Professional Service Firms: If you're not close to "best in world" at your "it," then someone else can (and will, and probably should) take "it" away from you.

INTERNATIONAL MAN OF MASTERY
[10]For a profound discussion of the "tradecraft" ethos, go buy George Leonard's slender gem of a book on that topic. The title (what else?): *Mastery*.

5. Thrive on Ambiguity.

Mastery is great. Mastery is essential. Yet in a world where the very categories of thought and action are constantly slipping and sliding, even mastery will not suffice. Just as important as the ability to do one thing extremely well is the ability to do a dozen things at once,[11] and change course without raising a bead of sweat or a shred of remorse.

Remember: All bets are off. Everything is up for grabs. *Nobody knows what the hell he or she is doing.* In such unsettling circumstances, you must be able to not just "deal with," but actually thrive on ambiguity.

6. Laugh Off Vigorous Screw-ups.

The sweet spot of a Brand You attitude is ... a great sense of humor. By sense of humor, I don't mean having a knack for telling off-color after-dinner jokes. No, I mean the ability to *laugh off the fabulous prototype that self-destructs* ... and immediately get on with the next rendition. Reaching and stretching and trying damn near anything is a requisite for survival—let alone some yet-to-be-specified form of New Excellence.

In the current Disruptive Age, we will—by definition—be screwing up far more frequently and far more embarrassingly than ever before. Enterprises that tolerate or even celebrate failure ... that encourage the bold bid[12] for greatness that fizzles or goes down in flames ... will succeed.

The same goes for you and me. For survival's sake, we must always be playing the Re-imagine Game ... which guarantees black eyes aplenty. Remember, this is not your boss's world (he's probably on the next layoff list anyway). This is *your* world, *your* future, *your* responsibility.

7. Nurture Your Network.

Despite numerous reports to the contrary, I do not believe that "loyalty is dead." I believe that loyalty is ... *more important than ever.* But the Axis of Loyalty has shifted a full 90 degrees. "Old loyalty" was *vertical* loyalty. Loyalty to a hierarchy: You grasped one rung after another as you scrambled up a prescribed vertical ladder. Call it "suck-up loyalty," if you will. That's going, going, gone. And good riddance!

MISTRESS OF IMPROVISATION
[11]Juggling a dozen balls at once is a cinch for most women—and a genetic impossibility for most men. The ability to bob and weave through an uncertain world is a distinct "female advantage."

Much more later.

PAINTING ACTION
[12]*Can you imagine seeing these signs plastered in Jackson Pollock's workshop?*
Do It Right the First Time!
Zero Defects!
Spilled Paint Is ... Wasted Paint!
Plan the Work ... Work the Plan!
I think ... not.

"New loyalty" is *horizontal* loyalty. Loyalty to a trade or industry: What matters is what your *peers*[13] think of your work. Which puts a high premium on developing what I call the Rolodex Obsession. You must build—and deliberately manage!—an ever-expanding network of professional contacts throughout your field.

8. Relish Technology.

The brutal truth is that lots of people are simply "past their prime" when it comes to "getting" new technologies.[14] (Talk about self-revelation!) But there's hope: You don't need to be a Certificate-bearing Expert in any particular software package; you don't need to be able to program the stuff yourself. But you must ... *instinctively appreciate* ... the unequivocal fact that the Internet and everything that comes in its wake will turn business upside-down in an astonishingly short period. If that prospect doesn't ... turn you on; if it doesn't ... make you tingle with joy and anticipation ... well, you're going to be in for a very rough ride. And, I suspect, a very short ride.

9. Grovel Before the Young.

Those of us who are a bit north, say, of that Age 38.5 Divide can indeed have that "appetite for technology." But will we ever truly "get it"? Not a chance! So we must surround ourselves with young people.

This is a Young People's Moment—from the astonishingly young men and women who are driving the cyber-warfare paradigm shift at the Department of Defense to the nameless crew of students in a college dorm room somewhere who are dreaming up the next Apple or eBay.

The necessary upshot: Every project team must include at least one youngster—someone well under the age of 38.5 (18.5!?)—who doesn't need to "reinvent" himself, because he was born and bred and genetically certified in the New Economy.

LIGHTS! CAMERA! ... TALENT!
[13]As others have noted, the project-driven, "new loyalty"-oriented New Economy follows the so-called Hollywood Model, in which one goes from one production "company" to another—seeing a few familiar faces at the start of each outing, but mostly working with new people on new stuff.

In that world, success depends on having a good rep among your peers. If you want (say) to be on the lighting crew of the next Oscar-buzz-worthy film, you need people "in the industry" who will say to the chief cinematographer of that project, "If you're going to be doing lots of soft-light shooting, give Joanne Brown a call. I've never seen anyone whose output is as good as hers; she's also a pleasure to work with."

HIRE FOR "NET-ITUDE"
[14]It still happens, even in 2003: I run into an executive whose attitude seems to be, "Why the hell did this Internet thing have to happen on my watch?" For shame.

Much better: "This is cool! I don't fully 'get it.' But I'm going to listen to people who do get it—and then act fearlessly."

10. Cultivate a Passion for Renewal.

Picking up new skills on a catch-as-catch-can, as-needed basis used to be a reasonable career strategy. But these days, a passive approach to professional growth will leave you gathering splinters on the bench, or off the roster entirely. Revolutionizing your Portfolio of Skills ... at least every half-dozen years, if not more often, is now a ... *Minimum Survival Necessity.*

Query: Do you have a formal R.I.P. (Renewal Investment Plan)? And if you do have one, is it as bold as these bold times demand?

Option to Renew (Oneself): Not Optional

Back in the Foreword, ever so many pages ago, I began with a description of the forces breaking loose all around us. My argument there, and throughout the early chapters, was highly analytical (albeit fueled by a certain "mad as hell" impatience.)

This chapter is ... personal.

It goes to ... the root and branch of Who We Are and What We Do. It gets at ... how we contend with those "forces" that are tearing away at White-Collar World. The forces that are turning *Dilbert*-style cubicle slavery into not just a joke, but an anachronism.

Again, my mantra:

DISTINCT ... OR EXTINCT.

Or, to revive a key phrase from the Foreword: Life in a Brand You World is ...

NOT OPTIONAL.

THE "SALLY" ADVANTAGE

Sally Helgesen, author of *The Female Advantage* and several other great books, provides a list of key attitudinal attributes in her most recent book, *Thriving in 24/7.* She and I arrived at our ideas separately, but not surprisingly, her approach to 24/7 World matches my approach to ... Brand You World:

Start at the core. Take regular inventory of where you are. To remain nimble, locate your "inner voice."

Learn to zigzag. Think "gigs." Think lifelong learning. Forget "old loyalty." Work on optimism.

Create your own work. Articulate your value. Integrate your passions. Identify your market. Run your own business.

Weave a strong web of inclusion. Build your own support network. Master the art of "looking people up."

(Note that the two best books about the New Spirit of Independence have been written by women: Sally Helgesen's *Thriving in 24/7* and Harriet Rubin's *Soloing.*)

! Contrasts

WAS	IS
Cubicle slavery	Free Agent Nation
Bland "unit"	Brand You!
Job for life	Gig for now
(Personnel file at Big Company)	(Portfolio of temporary assignments)
Benefits come from the company	Benefits travel with you
Goal: Get through the day	Goal: Get things done
Career strategy: Do what you're told	Career strategy: Do what you excel at
Competence	Mastery
Reference group = The corporation	Reference group = Peers in my craft
Read Fortune	Read Fast Company
The Detroit model: punch in at the factory	The Hollywood model: join a team at a studio
Work with the same old folks, day in and day out	Work with a shifting network of partners
Goal: Become the boss (after 25 years)	Goal: Be the boss (now)
Promotion on seniority	Getting gigs on merit
Work your way up "the ladder"	Leap your way across changing terrain
Vertical loyalty	Horizontal loyalty
Call the tech guy	Be the tech guy
Depend on admin support "back at the ranch"	Carry a wireless "office" wherever you go
Know "the ropes"	Learn to bungee-jump!

NEW BUSINESS ● NEW PEOPLE

BOSS JOB ONE:
THE TALENT25

! Technicolor Rules ...

● Rules? Here are 25 of them. Rules for a world in which ... Talent Rules!

 ! RANT

We are not prepared ...

We pay ever more lip-service to "people power," even as we cling to our longstanding penchant for hiring and cultivating obedient "employees." We say that we take "talent" seriously, while failing to transform our organizations in a way that makes them truly talent-attractants. But now we must become *obsessed* about talent ... as obsessed about finding and developing top-flight, seriously cool men and seriously cool women as the general manager of a professional sports franchise is about recruiting and training top-flight players. We must understand that, in an age when value-added flows from creativity, a quirky, energetic, and (yes) *dis*obedient "talent pool" has become the primary basis for competitive advantage ... perhaps the *only* basis for competitive advantage.

 ! VISION

I imagine ...

A world where "attracting and developing talent" holds as much sway for leaders of a typical Finance Department ... or of any other PSF-like enterprise ... as it does for George Steinbrenner of the New York Yankees. A world where companies focus on creating Awesome Places to Work ... environments that suck in the Best of the Best in every line of endeavor. A world where leaders recognize that talent does not just "support" the brand; it is the brand.

Talent Tale: The Story Thus Far

The Industrial Age is … over. The white-collar paper-processing age is … over. "Great" products are not enough. (Not nearly enough.) *"Great" services are not enough. (Not nearly enough.) New bases for value-added are required—posthaste. And the revolution has only begun.*

You're not going to "make it" in the New Economy solely by pushing TQM (Total Quality Management) or CI (Continuous Improvement) or any of those other New Nostrums that we embraced so vigorously 20 years ago. You're going to "make it" by providing … Solutions! … Experiences! … Beautiful Systems! … Dream Fulfillment! … Design that WOWs! … Brands that Inspire!

And this "new stuff" is (all) about … Creativity! … Imagination! … Intellectual Capital! And *that* stuff is all about … Talent. The new technologies that undergird the White-Collar Revolution may seem like a dehumanizing force; but in fact, they herald the end of "grunge" work and thence a People's Revolution. In other words: a Talent Revolution.

Fundamental premise: We have entered an Age of Talent. "Okay, fine," I can hear you saying. "Put people first. Been there, done that."

No!

No!

No!

My point is *not* that "people are cool," "people are important." It is that … "people" (their talent, their creativity,[1] their intellectual capital, their entrepreneurial drive) is … *all the hell there is.*

Talent Truth: Entertainment, Sports, and Beyond

When I think about "talent," I think first of all about Bill Walsh, former coach, president, and general manager of the San Francisco 49ers franchise in the National Football League. I've known Bill for well over a decade, and he is … *a Talent Freak.* Pro-football GMs like Bill live, sleep, eat, and breathe … Talent. They toil away at the acquisition and development of the best 48-player active-duty roster imaginable, and they do it … *25 hours a day, 8 days a week, 53 weeks a year.*

Talent (if you're serious about it) is a 25-8-53 affair. That's obviously true for the GM of that 48-player pro-football team. So: Why shouldn't it be (equally) true—in (exactly) the same way, and to (exactly) the same degree—if you're the leader of a 48-person finance department?

Why not? (Damn it.)

❗ **COMING TO YOUR LOCAL CINEMA …**
● [1] *Murakami Teruyasu of Nomura Research Institute "gets it": First, he says, we lived through the Age of Agriculture. Next up … the Industrial Age. Now … the Age of Information Intensification. And arriving on the Big Screen … the Age of Creation Intensification.*

❗ **MISSION CRITICAL**
● *Tina Brown, editor extraordinaire: "The first thing is to hire enough talent that a critical mass of excitement starts to grow."*

Alas, the language of "talent"[2] has traditionally been limited to a few rarefied realms. Talk opera. Talk symphony. Talk movies. Talk sports. Talk Stanford's physics department. And the talk inevitably turns to ... this baritone or that soprano, this cellist or that violinist, this actress or that director, this first baseman or that quarterback, this particle physicist or that mathematical physicist. The talk, in other words, turns, almost exclusively, to ... *Talent*.

But the ... Very Same Logic ... applies (must apply) to every other industry and enterprise, public as well as private. Think Microsoft. Think Genentech. Think Fidelity. Think the U.S. Army. Yes, and think Joe and Joan's Chevrolet in God-Knows-Where. Without Great People, each of those organizations would be as worthless as ... Bill Walsh's San Francisco 49ers would have been without ... Great Players.

So let's begin to apply the Logic of Talent throughout the length and breadth of our organizations. And (please!) let's begin to use the "language of talent" as well. As usual (in this book) the words matter ... enormously.

"Talent," the Term

Talent. I love that word!

So different from "employees."

So different from "personnel."

So different from "human resources."

Talent![3] *Just uttering the word makes you puff up and feel good about yourself!*

Talent. I do indeed love that word!

I love it because of the ... images ... that it brings immediately to mind. Yo-Yo Ma playing the cello. Pavarotti at full volume. Gene Hackman or Nicole Kidman in complete command of a scene. Derek Jeter turning a double play. Michelle Kwan doing a triple axel. Michael Jordan "parting the waters" ... and making that famous last shot that won the Chicago Bulls their sixth championship during his tenure with the team.

The fabulous guy at, of all places, the international-arrivals hall at Newark airport who sings—yes, sings—weary travelers towards the baggage-claim area at 6 a.m.

Talent!

What a word!

WORDS (AGAIN)

[2]Think "roster" (sports), or "company" (ballet, theater), and your mind's eye doubtless goes to ... Brilliant Performances. Think "employee" ... and your mind's eye imagines rows of look-alike cubes, with white-collar drones entombed therein.

What's in a word? Everything.

So how would you grade your training department's "roster"?

SAME-SAME

[3]*Basic premise of this chapter/book:*

48-person National Football League "roster" = 48-person IS department/PSF "roster."

E-x-a-c-t-l-y t-h-e s-a-m-e.

P-e-r-i-o-d.

Talent Time: The Ultimate Recession-Proof Market

During the high-roller days of the mid- and late 1990s, there was clearly a ... Major Talent Shortage. Guess what? It still exists!

Indeed, it persisted through the recession of 2001–2002. Unemployment soared, which invariably signals "softness" in the labor market—and that in turn, usually entails a leveling-off of both productivity and wages. But in this instance, productivity continued to rock and roll, and wages remained at a 50-year high.

Something dramatic was happening. Companies were using the recession as temporary cover while they responded to the permanent White-Collar Revolution. In one guise or another, they had been doing so even before the downturn. But the recession provided a matchless opportunity (yes, cover) to accelerate the process of cutting back on their "human resources" burden.

But companies didn't cut back across the board. Nor did they typically lay off the "last hired." Rather, as several analysts noted, this was the first recession in which seniority did not determine who did or didn't get axed. Instead, layoffs were determined by ... Talent!

Then something else happened that contradicted the historical norm. Even after the economy began to rebound, employment numbers didn't bounce back as quickly or as robustly as they had in the past. Companies were accomplishing more than ever before with the smaller numbers of people who remained; that is, with the ... *Superior Talent* ... that remained. (Hence the productivity gains.) And the "Talent" was continuing to command hearty financial rewards. (Hence the durably high wages.)

Talent matters to companies more than ever. Which is to say, there *is* a talent shortage. There *will be* a talent shortage for the foreseeable future ... even when there is a "glut" in the "labor market." Because talent is not about "labor." It's not about "head count." It's not about "bodies in the cubicles." Talent is about ... those who score high on the "distinct" scale. And for those with true distinction ... the world will wait in line to acquire their services.

Talent's Magnet: An Awesome Place to Work

So, on the one hand, Awesome Talent has the freedom to roam the earth—to pick off the best gigs, to pocket the largest financial rewards. In that sense, organizations will increasingly take a back seat. (Compare the way that players have mostly ruled professional sports since the coming of free agency.)

On the other hand, though, enterprises that manage to master the market for talent

---

"LAND" OF THE BRAVE

"When land was the productive asset, nations battled over it," write Stan Davis and Christopher Meyer in *futureWEALTH*. "The same is happening now ... for talented people."

Talent, indeed, has become the productive asset. And the battle for this insufficiently charted "territory" will test the mettle of all organizations, public as well as private. And merely having a couple of intrepid geniuses at the top won't win this battle. We will win this battle ... and the larger war ... only when our talent pool is both ... Deep and Broad. Only when our organizations are chock-a-block with obstreperous people who are determined to bend the rules at every turn ... and to invent something exciting ... before the other guy does. Only when the 48th player on that 48-player roster (NFL) is determined to ... Make a Difference ... during his 4.2 seconds on the field.

will do better than ever. (Compare the way that sports-team honchos shuffle and reshuffle their rosters—relentlessly, constantly, 365 days a year—in order to lock in a winning combination.)

But to attract, retain, and obtain the most from Awesome Talent, organizations will need to offer up an ... Awesome Place to Work. A place where people not only get paid "their due," but also ... Get to Initiate & Execute Great Things. A place where they can add ... "Awesome Entries" ... to their ... WOW Project Portfolio ... and add Equity to their "Brand Called You."

Again, the sports analogy reinforces this notion. Suppose George Steinbrenner lures you to the New York Yankees. The pay is nice. The major-metro endorsement opportunities are nothing to sneeze at, either. Equally important, you'll "work" with the best players in the game, and they'll bring out the best in you. But what cinches the deal is this: The Yanks offer you a chance to cap your career with a World Series Championship Ring ... on every finger of your hand. (Talk about WOW Projects!) The New York Yankees team is an ...

Awesome Place to Work: *A place where people not only get paid "their due," but also ... get to initiate & execute great things.*

The Talent 25

Awesome Places to Work. Just as "individuals," "workers" must re-imagine themselves as "talent," so enterprises that want to draw in enterprising people must re-imagine themselves as ... *talent-magnet organizations*. But how? My solution: The Talent25—a silver jubilee of ideas for vaulting the "people issue" (henceforth to be known as the "talent opportunity") from soaring rhetoric on the first page of an annual report to ... Hard Strategic Reality:

1. Put People First! (For Real.)

phrase has rolled off many a corporate lip: "People are our most important asset." The problem: It's mostly been... BULLSHIT. Subject of lip service, to be sure, and believed at some level, to be sure; but not ... the Essence of What Enterprise Does. Not ... the Essence of... HOW LEADERSHIP SPENDS ITS TIME. (Steinbrenner-standard.)

I don't mean to say that most enterprises ignore the "people thing." Of course they don't. But there is a special meaning to the word "first," as in "putting people first." It

FOLLOW THE MONEY
"Historically, smart people have always turned to where the money was. Today, money is turning to where the smart people are."
From the *Financial Times* (June 2003)

means that "getting the people thing right"[4] is alpha *and* omega ... and every letter, Greek or non-Greek, in between.

2. Be Obsessed!

About twenty years ago, we Americans went after the "quality thing" hammer-and-tong. We made enormous headway. Dr. Deming's Sacred Fourteen Principles had something to do with that success. But the real core of the achievement was this: *We put "quality" at the tip-top of the ... Business Agenda.*

If, in 1975, you had sat down for a two-hour meeting with a cross-section of U.S. managers, "quality" might not have come up at all. Sit down with the same group 10 years later, and half of the discussion would have been on that very topic. Thousands upon thousands of managers had spent 25 percent, and then 50 percent, and then often 75 percent, of their precious time on one thing: quality.

The most important trait associated with ... Mastery (of any damn thing) ... is ... *Attention*. Or: *Time Spent*.

If you're looking to ... Master the Talent Game ... there is a clear first step that you must take: PUT IT AT THE TOP OF THE AGENDA.

And keep it there.

Pursuit of Talent.[5] Either it's an obsession ... or you're not serious about it. Either you spend virtually all your time on it ... or you don't.

Talent obsession. That phrase puts me in mind of a fellow who runs a certain computer-science lab. He's known to be "prickly." Indeed, I've crossed wires with him, and, frankly, I'm none too fond of him. I was venting about this fellow to a friend of mine who knows him well. And my friend interrupted: "I agree, Tom. *I agree.* But you've got to hand him one thing. Nobody, but nobody, is better at attracting—*and keeping!*—extraordinary talent. He doesn't have a bushel full of money. He simply creates an extraordinary working environment—one that's become a magnet to the best of the best from all over the world." What an endorsement! (And my pal is a born cynic.)

PURE REVIEW
[4]When the "business review" occurs, what agenda item comes first? Strategy? Budget?

I believe that the "people stuff" must come first. All too typically, the "HR Stuff" is left until last. That's not what ... Dead Seriousness about Talent ... or ... WINNING THE GREAT WAR FOR TALENT ... is all about.

TALENT IS HIS MOST IMPORTANT PRODUCT
[5]Jack Welch probably spent 70 to 90 percent of his time at GE on talent.

Ed Michaels, McKinsey & Co.'s "talent guru," called GE a ... Talent Machine. And that is largely thanks to Welch, who was arguably the Best Talent Developer in the past century to occupy a corner office in America, or perhaps anywhere in the world.

Shortly before he left GE, Welch announced his post-retirement plans. Run another company? No. Instead, he would become a "coach." And a particular kind of coach: He would work with CEOs of giant companies on ... *developing talent*.

TALENT: YOU KNOW IT WHEN YOU (CAN'T) SEE IT

Below is a list of intangible attributes that mark "talent" as, well, talent. (Believe me, these traits are the real deal: I stole them, shamelessly, from some of the best talent developers around.) A true exemplar of "talent" ...

Displays passion. There are enthusiasts ... those who are visibly energetic and passionate about everything. And there are those who are not. Find the enthusiasts.

Inspires others. Inspirational ability is elusive. It's tough to discover in an interview, for example. To be sure, you can examine leadership experiences. The best test: *Does this candidate inspire me ... the interviewer?*

Loves pressure. One reason former athletes tend to do well in leadership positions: They have been tested in a cauldron of chaos—the last two minutes of a football game or basketball game, when everything is on the line and 70,000 fans are questioning (vocally) your mother's virtue. These are often folks who blather and bumble when things are calm ... and then come into their ... Awesome Own ... when mess and mayhem occur.

Craves action. Former Honeywell boss Larry Bossidy says there are two kinds of people he interviews. Those who talk about "vision and philosophy." And those who talk about the Grubby Details of the Stuff that They've Gotten Done ... and the Barriers They've Smashed to Get It Done ... and the People Who Have Gone to the Mat for Them to Get It Done. Bossidy's advice: Go with the latter—the action fanatics. (That's my advice, too.)

Knows how to finish the job. People who get the "last two percent" done. A lot of folks are great at the "first 98" ... but fail to "tidy up" the "political loose ends" ... or whatever ... that are the Essence of Passion for Implementation with Impact.

Thrives on WOW. Look for the candidate who has a Fat "WOW Projects" Portfolio. He or she *loves* ... to talk about ... Accomplishments that Flew in the Face of Conventional Wisdom. That "took on" the bureaucracy. Jobs that nobody else wanted that were turned into ... Gems.

Exhibits curiosity. One should never say, "There are two kinds of people." But it happens to be true. (More or less.) Particularly on this score. There are those who can't ... *Stop Asking Questions*. And there are those who ... *Don't Ask Questions*. Vote for the former! (And hire them!)

Embodies "weird." I champion the idea of "weird" for only one reason: *These are ... Weird Times*. Therefore (simple logic): We desperately need an Eclectic/Weird/Peculiar Talent Pool. (Not a bunch of clones.)

Exudes a sense of fun. A sense of fun is not quite the same as "energy." It's people with a "twinkle in their eye." People who are performance fanatics—but are able to create a spirited environment. This is as true in the 23-year-old recruit for a front-line job, as it is in the pursuit of the Senior Officer.

Thinks at a high level. Raw smarts is not even close to the top, as I see it. But the challenging nature of today's affairs does indeed require a decent degree of intelligence. Important ... YES. "All-important" ... not compared to the "other stuff" I've talked about.

"Gets" Talent. Amazon CEO Jeff Bezos says that when he's recruiting would-be executives, he spends well over half of his interview time discussing their Track Record as a Recruiter and Developer of People. Nothing is more important!

Bottom line: Real "people" bosses ... even those who are anything but warm-and-fuzzy

"people people" ...
are obsessed with attracting talent.

3. Pursue the Best!

If you are an unrepentant Connoisseur of Talent[6] ... you will not settle for anything less than the best. In finance. In telemarketing. In the First Violinist's chair. You will leave a job open—and indeed, stress out some others in the process—before you will "fill a slot" with mediocrity. A managerial job. Or a telemarketing position.

"Great Talent Pools" are not very kind to those who can't pass muster. (Ask Steinbrenner. Or Welch. Or Wexner.) So do *your* Great Talent Pool a favor: Stress them out a bit—but don't surround them with second-raters chosen to "fill a chair." Give them the best. Period.

It's a big word: BEST. But it's one that can—and should—be used when the issue is the Great War for Talent. Case in point: A few years ago, Home Depot decided to shoot for the moon, to take the then-$20-billion corporation to $100 billion in relatively short order. To make this Great Leap Forward, the company concocted seven significant growth initiatives. Then-CEO Arthur Blank laid down the law: Each of these initiatives would be headed by the ... BEST PERSON IN THE WORLD.

I love *that*!

BEST! WORLD!

For example, one of the seven initiatives was major international expansion. Home Depot pursued the very best, as they saw it, and ended up lassoing the COO of Ikea. Is he the best in the world? Who knows? But he sure is a ... damn good approximation! You're not the Big Boss at Home Depot, but that, I contend ... in no way, shape, or form ... keeps you from going for broke, from pursuing a dogged BIW (Best In World) attitude.

You're the (little) boss. You want to leave a Legacy of Greatness behind. Completed WOW Projects. Transformation of your 62-person IS Department (PSF!), or your 217-person Telemarketing Department, or your 97-person Distribution Center. Your legacy, my friend, is one and only one thing: the TALENT that you beat the

---

SWEATER MAN REFORMS
Shortly after Jack Welch retired from GE, *Fortune* ran an article on a handful of companies that had outperformed GE during the "Welch Years." One was The Limited. Limited founder Les Wexner put their success down to "picking great people" as much as "picking great sweaters."

FOR THE LOVE OF ... TALENT
[6]In *Organizing Genius*, their book on Great Groups (such as the Manhattan Project and Disney's first animation lab), Warren Bennis and Patricia Ward Biederman write that the people in charge of such groups evince one consistent attribute: "Leaders of great groups love talent and know where to find it. They revel in the talent of others."
　NICE.
　Another of Bennis and Biederman's Great Groups was Xerox's famed Palo Alto Research Center. Founding leader Bob Taylor was once described as a ... "connoisseur of talent."
　Nice.

bushes to find and develop to get the job done. Boss of a seven-person unit? You're in the ... Talent Business.[7] FULL TIME. And if you go for less than the Best—in any slot—you are a blooming idiot. (Sorry for the strong language.)

Think "Talent" and you probably think ... Tiger Woods. Sure. But I happen to think that Talent is a ... Pervasive Idea ... in this ... Age of Creation Intensification, as Nomura's Teruyasu labeled it. Thence the "pursuit ofexcellence" is the ... Pursuit of Excellent Talent ... in Every Nook & Every Cranny of the Enterprise.

4. Weed Out the Rest!

When a new head coach is named in the NFL, he rarely holds on to more than one or two of the dozen assistant coaches the team had before. He has a new philosophy. He brings a new air of performance. He brings the promise of freshness of perspective. He needs new talent—in the coaching ranks, as well as in the player ranks—to pull it off.

We think "all this" is as normal as hell if we're talking about the National Football League. (In fact, we fans are irritated if the new broom doesn't sweep vigorously.) Yet we think it's as abnormal as hell when the topic is enterprise. Maybe such "play-it-as-it-lays" strategies were plausible in a more mellow world. But in a world where competition is both new and increasingly brutal ... Only the Best is Good Enough. In other words: Up or out!

Is "up or out" brutal? On one hand, I suppose it is. It is brutal to that 26-year-veteran who has not been held to ... Serious Performance Standards ... for the last 15 years of his career. On the other hand, I've consistently observed that talent likes hanging out with talent. Talented people love to be pressed. The Tiger Woodses of the world love to play against ... The Best. (Mr. Woods wouldn't much enjoy a divot-spattering afternoon on the links with me.) And I happen to think this is just as true for a Flight Crew at Southwest Airlines. They "get off on" the Energy and Vitality and Spirit and Spunk of their Cool Colleagues. They would be "turned off" by the absence of such qualities as evidenced at many of the other "major" airlines.

When a new honcho comes aboard, and a revised "corporate culture" is pursued, must all the old gang be dumped? Of course not. But, often as not, that New Outsider comes into an enterprise that has let things drift ... by allowing seniority or friend-of-a-friend log-rolling to drive promotions. So, while the number of "newbies" a new leader

---

PERFORMANCE (UN)LIMITED
[7] I did a little work, years ago, with Les Wexner's Limited Stores. Not a whole lot of room for merchandising experimentation in one of their small shops. And yet I discovered that the ... Top Limited Managers ... out-performed the center of the herd ... by a factor of ... *three* or *four* or *five*. Time and again.

"NEW GROWTH": MANAGERIAL CLEAR-CUTTING
Just how clean should a new broom sweep? Ed Michaels of McKinsey makes the case for an aggressive talent-turnover strategy. "We believe companies can increase their market capitalization 50 percent in three years," he writes. "Steve Macadam at [the forest-products company] Georgia-Pacific changed 20 of his 40 box plant managers to put more talented, higher paid managers in charge. He increased profitability from $20 million to $80 million in two years."
Wow!

brings in will vary, she should be given a pretty free hand when it comes to picking her "coaching staff."

5. Focus on Intangibles!

When it comes to talent, what are you looking for? The strongest *arm* in a quarterback? The highest *grade-point average* in a would-be pharma lab scientist? Or ... something more?

My discussions with ... Great Leaders ... have led me to conclude that "something more" is always ... something far more. By "something more," I mean those elements of a person that you can't quite put your finger (or a number) on. They matter far more than "raw statistics"—whether you're recruiting for the San Francisco 49ers or for Pfizer.

One of the great tests of leadership maturity, I've come to believe, is the ability to deal with "the intangibles." To get over the pretense that "only the numbers matter." All the great sports coaches I know are of one mind: *Attitude and Heart Rule!* You can compensate for a little bit of slowness ... with a lot of heart and attitude.

6. Change the Profile of "HR!"

I have long believed that human resources people should sit at the Head Table. I'm a fan of "HR." It is ... after all ... an Age of Talent.

Problem: All too often "HR folks" are viewed (all too) correctly as "mechanics." Not as ... Master Architects ... who aim to ... Quarterback the Great War for Talent.

I've devoted my career to the "people thing." I DESPERATELY WANT "HR" TO "WIN."

DESPERATELY.

Why doesn't it happen?

Simple: A FAILURE OF IMAGINATION.[8]

I wasn't born yesterday. I understand there are thousands upon thousands of pages of petty laws and regulations that HR "must administer." But that still does not excuse HR from ... Re-imagining Itself.

As leaders!

As ... *THE*... leaders.

HR ... I ... WANT YOU ... at ... the ... Head Table.

So work to "deserve it."

Please.

7. Forge a Bold HR Strategy!

If you work for a big company, it no doubt has a "strategic plan," a voluminous document that is the offspring of ceaseless deliberation.

NAME THAT DEPARTMENT!

[8]"HR" as a name has one thing going for it: It's better than "Personnel."

I want a new title!

How about: Talent Department?

How about: Seriously Cool People who Recruit & Develop Seriously Cool People?

Words matter!

Question: HOW BIG A "CHAPTER" (AND WHICH CHAPTER?) OF THAT "STRATEGIC PLAN" IS DEVOTED ... EXPLICITLY ... TO THE "HR STRATEGY"?

Maybe I'm out of touch. But most "strategic plans" I've seen don't even *have* an "HR Strategy."

That's criminal.

There needs to be one.

With teeth.

And bravura.

Our "strategic approach" to tackling the "talent thing" is more important than our market analysis. (Or surely as important, eh?) (Forget that: MORE IMPORTANT!)

8. Take Reviews Seriously!

We all do acknowledge that the "people stuff" is important. But do we have a ... FORMAL TALENT REVIEW PROCESS ... that is perceived to be as important as ... say ... the Budget Process?

GE does.

"In most companies, the Talent Review Process is a farce," writes McKinsey's Ed Michaels. "At GE, Jack Welch and his two top HR people visit each division for a day. They review the top 20 to 50 people by name. They talk about Talent Pool strengthening issues. The Talent Review Process is a contact sport at GE. It has the intensity and the importance of the budget process at most companies."

Can you say the same?

If not, why not?

Look at your calendar: If "Talent Review" is not "on the calendar" ... at the tip-top ... then you are ... not serious ... about talent. (Not even faintly serious.)

One successful software executive I worked with had 25 people reporting to him. He told me he devoted fully 100 working days (100!) per year to the evaluation process. Two days per person, twice a year. One of those two days, was spent collecting data; the other was devoted to an intense off-site, one-to-one review with the employee.

I was stunned by the number. And he, in turn, was stunned that I was stunned: "But what do I do that's more important than developing people? I don't do the damn work, Tom. They do." *He added that the lengthy review process went a long, long way toward having people feel as if they were being treated fairly; that he wasn't grabbing a bottle of Scotch at the end of the quarter, sitting down with some "HR forms," and slapping some numbers in blanks that had to be filled out for folks' evaluations.*

TACTIC: LEADERSHIP TRACKING

It happens 100 percent of the time when I visit professional sports franchise "headquarters." It's happened ten times—alas, no more than that—when I have visited corporate headquarters.

That is, a ... WAR ROOM.

And what is ... The Singular Topic ... of that ... War Room: TALENT. That is, there are "institutions" that "track" ... assiduously ... their ... Top Talent.

Nothing is left to chance.

It certainly doesn't mean they get it right 100 percent of the time. (They don't.) But it does suggest that they "worry" about their "roster" (at department, division, and enterprise level) as much as that professional sports franchise does.

9. Pay up!

Do I think that Great Pay will win the Great War for Talent? ABSOLUTELY NOT!

I believe the sine qua non is ... OPPORTUNITY. That is, the chance to shine ... to "Make a Dent in the Universe" ... quickly. To take home a World Series Ring.

On the other hand, if one *is* given a Great Opportunity, and one does respond with Exceptional Vigor, then one should be ... Rewarded Accordingly.

"Technically savvy and innovative people," Peter Drucker told *Business 2.0*, "have become unbelievably expensive." "We value engineers like professional athletes," said Jerry Yang, co-founder of Yahoo! "We value great people at ten times an average person in their function." "Top performing companies," wrote Ed Michaels, "are two to four times more likely than the rest to pay what it takes to prevent losing top performers."

If there's one thing that pisses me off, it's a boss who complains about "high turnover" in the hotel's housekeeping department ... and when I ask what the base pay is ... he or she tells me with pride it's 75¢ above minimum wage. ("Housekeeping's not rocket science, Tom.") Well, housekeeping is "rocket science." (Great housekeeping, that is.) And ... it really does ... *Piss Me Off.*

I'm not arguing that every housekeeper ought to be paid $100,000 a year. I am contending that Housekeepers have more Guest Contact than any other set of human beings in the facility—and are, therefore, invaluable. And if they are "invaluable" ... and if "high turnover" is a problem ... well ... PAY THEM! If not that $100,000 a year, at least start them at $15.50 an hour.

Incidentally (not so incidentally!), when you raise that base pay, something else happens. Something Big. You end up attracting an entirely different pool of applicants. In the case of housekeeping, there is one "applicant pool" for $7.50 jobs. And another, quite different pool for $15.50 jobs. Q.E.D.

There's a famous old saw in management, and I mostly subscribe to it. It goes this way: "What gets measured gets done." But let me add a little something new to that old saw: *What gets measured gets done. What gets paid for gets done more. What gets paid well gets done more ... and better.*

FIT (ONLY) TO PRINT?

Peter Drucker writes, "My ancestors were printers in Amsterdam from 1510 until 1750, when they didn't have to learn anything new."

And now? "Knowledge ... becomes obsolete incredibly fast," Drucker argues. "The continuing professional education of adults is the No. 1 industry in the next 30 years."

THE FLAT-EARTH SOCIETY

Several years ago, Norman Pearlstine became Editor-in-Chief of Time Inc. The company is inward focused. Determined to raise the excellence bar, Pearlstine asked one of his magazine's managing editors who were the 10 top writers he'd like to recruit. The reply, which floored Pearlstine: "I can't think of any."

It's a long way from Arthur Blank at Home Depot. (Best. World.) And the editor's response is downright laughable if you compare it to, say, a movie director or a baseball franchise's General Manager. One simply cannot imagine them limiting their "talent universe" to those already aboard. Alas, I think "can't think of any" is garden-variety normal in most big corporations.

Oops.

10. Set Sky-High Standards!

I remember an old *Fortune* article about the best business-school professors. They had obviously turned their classrooms into ... Great Adventures in Learning.

The poll was based on *student* evaluations. Does that suggest these profs regularly delivered bushels of "A" grades to their grateful minions?

Hardly!

With no exceptions, as I recall, each of these teachers were seen as "tough as nails." (Or some such.) I.e., being a "people place" does not mean running a "warm & fuzzy" place. People places ... Recruit Great People. Urge them to... Sign Up for Great Quests. And then set ... Absurdly High Standards.

It's true in sports!

True in the theater!

True in ballet!

And there's no reason ... WHATSOEVER ... that it should not be ... routinely true ... in the Finance or IS or HR or Purchasing "departments." (Again: "Departments" is put in quotation marks ... because they have now become ... Scintillating Professional Service Firms ... in pursuit of Awesome-or-Else Value Added through Awesome Talent.)

11. Train! Train! Train!

In preparation for a keynote speech to the American Society for Training and Development, I discovered data that pegged the average annual hours in the classroom for the average American worker. The number: 26.3.

THAT IS THE MOST OBSCENE NUMBER I HAVE COME ACROSS EVER.

We live in an age of "intellectual capital"—and 75 percent to 90 percent of what we college-trained white-collarworkers do will be usurped by a $239 microprocessor in the course of the next ten or so years. What are we doing to become ... better and better ... more valuable ... and more valuable still? It sounds to me, based on the ASTD data, that we are spending a ... *full*... six minutes a day working on improvement!

As I prepared for that ASTD speech, I turned lawyerly and kept a record of my own activities for three weeks in May 2001. I performed 41 hours of "work"—seminars

---

TACTIC: LEADERSHIP DEVELOPMENT

My friend Roger Enrico was seen to have been shunted aside at PepsiCo. He left a top "line" operating job to become (mere) head of "Leadership Development."

It turned out differently!

Very!

Roger's next stop was ... CEO & Chairman of the Board. That is, PepsiCo joined the (very stunted) ranks of those who take Leadership Development ... VERY SERIOUSLY. GE, of course, is another. The Leadership Development "process" can be very disorganized. Or it can be the ... Heart of Enterprise Strategy.

So which one of those alternatives describes your joint?

TACTIC: LEADERSHIP CENTER

We need a Bold Leadership Development Process. *And* we need a ... LEADERSHIP CENTER. A ... *PLACE* ... where the "leadership thing" ... WITHIN THE EYE-SPAN OF TOP MANAGEMENT ... is Very Front & Very Center.

(Model: GE Crotonville.)

ranging from an hour-and-a-half to seven hours in length. Life being life, I devoted 17 hours to what can only be classified as "other" (petty bullshit, which dogs us all). And ... my "training"-preparation time ran ... 187 hours.

That is, the ratio of "training" to "work" for the average worker is 0.01. For me it was 4.67. Almost a 500-fold difference.

I'm not bragging. Not at all. To the contrary, I believe that I am increasingly "normal" for a "creation-intensification worker." For a group of people who we typically call "Talent."

Think of "that word." TALENT. Think of its exemplars. Think about ... TRAINING. Can you imagine 26.3 hours ... *per year* ... *for a* ... *diva* ... *violinist* ... *sprinter* ... *golfer* ... *pilot* ... *soldier* ... *surgeon* ... *astronaut?*

OF COURSE YOU CAN'T.

Why is it?

Why is it ... that divas do it, violinists do it, sprinters do it, golfers do it, pilots do it, soldiers do it, surgeons do it, astronauts do it ... and only "businesspersons" don't seem to think it's necessary?

I think it's a disgrace, which is one thing. (ONE BIG THING.) I think it is going to catch up with us—as individuals and enterprises—which is far more important.

12. Cultivate Leadership Aspirations from the Get Go!

Training should not be aimed at simply "increasing skills." Training should be aimed at fostering a ... *"full-fledged entrepreneurial spirit"* ... in each and every employee who works for us.

Remember: The microprocessor will take care of the rest. "Departments" will become exciting Professional Service Firms. Each individual will become, in effect, CEO of Me Inc., the owner-operator of a one-person business ... which may (currently) be embedded in another company's payroll.

And that, I believe, is why we *want* people ... EVERYBODY ... I jest not ... to "own" their piece of the action. Small piece. Big piece. Every piece. Training, therefore, should be training in "business" ... training in "entrepreneurship" ... and, yes, training per se in "disrespect for the way we currently do things."

13. Foster Open Communication!

If the "Talent thing" is all-important ... then ... TALENT ... MUST BE ABLE TO APPLY ITSELF TO THE TASK AT HAND. Which means that Every Iota of Bureaucratic B.S. that keeps "ordinary people" from talking to other "ordinary people" throughout the entire "supply chain" ... TO GET THINGS DONE FAST THROUGHOUT THE SYSTEM-AS-A-WHOLE ... must be eradicated.

Message: If one aims to ... WIN ... the Great War for Talent ... then we must ... UNLEASH THAT TALENT.

Barriers must go! (ALL.)

It goes without saying—though because it seldom happens, it must be said—that INFORMATION IS POWER. If I am ... AN ARMY OF ONE ... then I simply must know ... WHAT THE HELL IS GOING ON. In effect ...Everything That Is Going On.

(Straightforward logic, eh?)

Given the new technologies, and the enhanced pace of competitive change, people close to the action have got to be able to make decisions ... GOOD ONES ... on the fly.

That means that Everybody Must Have Access To Everything.

Message 2003: "Sharing (ALL) information" ... is not an option! (Starting hint: Review Chapter 7.)

14. Lead by "Winning People Over!"

WHAT AN IDIOT!

The "idiot" was quoted in the *New York Times*, as the recession reached its zenith in 2001. He runs a factory, somewhere-or-other, and told the reporter there was some joy to a recession: "Instead of employees being in the driver's seat, now we're in the driver's seat."

WHAT AN IDIOT! (Okay, I repeat myself.)

There's another fellow I know a little bit who's a "boss" ... the boss of a basketball team. He's won nine "world championships" in the last 12 years. Six in Chicago. Three in Los Angeles.

His name is Phil Jackson.

Mr. Jackson said, upon winning his eighth championship in 2001: "Coaching is winning players over."

That's true if those players are Kobe Bryant and Shaquille O'Neal ... making millions. And it's true if those "players" are members of the housekeeping staff in a 300-room hotel.

Only "volunteers" matter! Sure, the pay part's important.

Sure, the person has to make money to support their kids. But World *Hotel* Championships ensue only if "they" ... *bring the attitude of the volunteer* ... to work ... *every morning* ... and thence turn that housekeeping department into a Scintillating Center of Excellence. (And I believe housekeeping departments can be exactly that!)

If that "housekeeping department" is a "Scintillating Center of Excellence" ... it will be because the "coach" (boss) "won players over" ... one at a time.

(And will somebody pull the license from that jerk who was quoted in the *New York Times*?) (Please.)

15. Reward "People Skills!"

There are ... PEOPLE PEOPLE. And then there are those who ... ain't. Institutions that Thrive on Talent ... PROMOTE FOR THE BEST TALENT DEVELOPMENT SKILLS.

PER SE.

I'm into what I do. Thinking about management. Writing about it. Talking about it. The analytics of "the thing." And the presentation thereof. To tell the truth, and I'm loath

NEW BUSINESS ● NEW PEOPLE

THE SEVEN LIVELY "SMARTS"

Diversity isn't just a "good idea." It's a defining attribute of ... the human brain.

Harvard professor Howard Gardner has developed the concept of MI, or Multiple Intelligences. There are, Gardner argues, at least seven formal, measurable varieties of intelligence: logical-mathematical, linguistic, spatial, musical, kinesthetic, interpersonal, and intrapersonal. Each variety has unique value in terms of framing the world.

The problem? Virtually all our educational efforts and company hiring and promotional systems focus on "logical-mathematical" intelligence, perhaps with "linguistic" intelligence sneaking in the side door. We thus end up discarding five out of seven varieties.

The result: multiple stupidities!

to, I'm *not* a ... People Person. I could not call myself, by any stretch of the imagination, a "Connoisseur of Talent." That's not what I do. That's not "my thing." And the only wisdom for which I will congratulate myself is the wisdom of realizing it! And not trying to fake it!

There are People People.

And there are those of us who are not.

Far too often, we promote The Mechanic (best trainer, best salesperson, etc.) into a leadership position becausehe/she is the best mechanic. (Accountant, salesperson, trainer.) Not because he/she is the best "people person." And yet leadership ... in the Great War for Talent ... is all about ... People Who Need People.

LISTEN UP: "People people" are not ... "soft." In fact, the best of them are tough as nails. Performance oriented—to a fault. Determined to collect the Best Damned Group of Talent they can. To persuade that Talent-in-the-Raw to go to and create-from-scratch places they had never imagined they could go.

16. Show Respect!

"The deepest human need," wrote the great American psychologist William James, "is the need to be appreciated." And the most talented humans—because they enjoy such a wide array of choices—will take their talents to places where they feel ... Most Appreciated.

Appreciation means many things. Opportunities. Financial rewards. Corporate awareness of work-family balance. And so on. But at the top of the list (bar none) is ... "SIMPLE" RESPECT.

Some institutions exude ... RESPECT.

Other institutions ... DO NOT.

We've all seen it a dozen times. (A DOZEN DOZEN TIMES.) You're in the presence of the Big Boss. He looks at you ... AND HE DOES NOT SEE YOU. He "sees" the next powerful person, halfway across the room. He does not see ... YOU.

The practical point? I think that we can "pay attention to 'such stuff.'" We can look for it when we hire. We can damn well look for it ... AT THE TOP OF THE LIST ... when we *promote*.

In sum: Institutions that would ... "win" the Great War for Talent are ... Appreciative Institutions.

17. Embrace the Whole Individual!

Some places ... GIVE A DAMN ... about you as a ... Human Being. Some, all too

---

TALENT FOR LUNCH

As a neophyte at McKinsey & Co., I was given a thorny assignment that involved some economic reasoning about cartels, far beyond my training. Befuddled, I called an old friend who was a Ph.D. student in business at Stanford. Before I knew it, I was lunching at Stanford's faculty club with a renowned professor of economics and the head of the Political Science Department. They were bemused by the conundrum, and chatted up a couple of their colleagues. I'm not sure the client ended up with the right advice, but I am sure he benefited from the thinking of some of the Top Talent in the World—all because of my unwillingness to simply "do the best with what was at hand."

obviously, do not. Caring about people as individuals is partly about the details of "programs": maternity/paternity leave, health care benefits, daycare, tuition reimbursement. All those things are important. And one should strive, I think, to be in the Top Quartile on darn near any such measure you can continue.

But it goes beyond that. There are institutions that ... CARE. Institutions that treat you as far more than fodder for the nine-to-five cannon. Institutions where top leaders (AND THENCE LEADERS AT ALL LEVELS!) go the "extra mile" ... to show their concern for their employees' family and community concerns.

I believe it's clear ... CRYSTAL CLEAR ... that people are attracted to ... and retained by ... institutions that ... MAKE THEM FEEL GOOD ABOUT THEMSELVES AS HUMAN BEINGS.

And one of the (BIGGEST) things that makes that happen ... is an institution that gives off "good vibes" on the dimension called ... INTEGRITY. An institution that's "out front" on ethical issues. Family issues. Community issues. Environmental issues. Product safety issues. Quality issues. And so on.

(Even though I'm 60 years old, I have no idea how to define integrity. But ... I KNOW IT WHEN I SEE IT. Some places make me "feel good" ... on the ... INTEGRITY SCALE. Other places make me ... SQUEAMISH.)

18. Measure for Uniqueness!

Who understands Talent? Your kid's third grade teacher! (*If* she/he is one of the good ones.) Teachers are ... in the Talent Business.

Obvious, isn't it?

And when do we *love* that third grade teacher that little Sally or Sammy has? We're especially appreciative when she is not a slave to "teach the test." When she is one of the ... Glorious Ones ... who understands that each of our six billion fellow humans is ... Totally Unique. She treats each of her 19 charges as a ... Totally Unique Human Being ... engaged in a ... Totally Unique Learning & Discovery & Growth Trajectory.

That's a long-winded way of saying that Talent is a "one-at-a-time thing." "Talent" is not easily categorized. (Make that ... NOT CATEGORIZABLE AT ALL.) Sure, we put a stopwatch on players who come to summer training camp in the National Football League, timing them in the 40-yard-dash. But at the end of the week, when we're considering whether they should stay or go, we treat them as ... Totally Unique Individuals. We measure the physical skills ... and then spend the remaining 98 percent of our time on attitude, learning ability, and about 27 other *intangibles*. And then we make a decision about keeping them. Or not.

Measure them by a Standardized HR Instrument? UTTERLY ABSURD! *And* ... if it's absurd for the NFL ... *damn it* ... it's ... *equally absurd* ... for the kindergarten teacher ... or manager of a four-person training department ... or leader of a 68-person telemarketing department.

We are *all* unique!

One size *never* fits all!

One size fits *one*!

Period!

Back to the NFL, where it's ever so obvious: There are 48 guys on an active-duty NFL roster.

NEW BUSINESS ● NEW PEOPLE

Message: *48 Players = 48 Projects = 48 Totally Different Success Measures.*

(I have a moniker for believers in Standardized HR Evaluation Instruments: Jerks!) (We can't print my real moniker.)

19. Honor Youth!

The new technologies are not out of their diapers. In fact, one can see a parade of technology revolutions across the horizon ... for years and years ... and decades and decades ... to come.

And who will lead this parade?

The 50-year-olds? Hardly!

"Why focus on these late teens and twenty somethings?" the *Economist* wrote. "Because they are the first young who are both in a position to change the world, and are actually doing so. ... For the first time in history, children are more comfortable, knowledgeable and literate than their parents about an innovation central to society. The Internet has triggered the first industrial revolution in history to be led by the young." Innovation guru Michael Schrage calls "all this" the Age of Ageism: "The real innovator's dilemma isn't the threat of 'disruptive technologies'; it's the relentless rise of the quasi-adolescents who wield them."

I am 60. Should all 60-year-olds be sent out to sea? For good? Perhaps not. Although I think I should honestly say, "Not clear." I *will* say, and I do routinely: THIS *IS* A YOUNG PERSON'S CRUSADE.

I am curious. But the most curious person I know is 33 years my senior. Namely, my mom, age 94. So I believe that we "old farts" can be curious as the dickens.

But that's not the point. There is something I ... *cannot* ... be. Namely: *Naive!* The great physicist and Nobel Laureate Richard Feynman said it was no coincidence that virtually all major discoveries in physics were made by those under the age of 25. When you're under 25, he concluded, you don't know what you don't know.

I won't let my kids near my computer! The reason: They are too good. They're always trying this. Trying that. Stretching its capability to the utmost. And, of course, in the process ... making it crash.

Which terrifies me.

Which doesn't bother them in the least.

They are members of a ... New Species. In fact, the youngster in Tokyo, born it would seem with a game console in his hand, is sometimes referred to as a member of the "thumb generation." That is, having used their thumbs on the game consoles so much, they now use their thumbs to perform many acts the rest of us use our index finger for ... turning on light switches and the like. A dozen dozen stories like this are

---

"FOREIGN" EXCHANGE

Years ago, a colleague at McKinsey & Co. was working with a Japanese bank. He was in Tokyo when he learned that his father was mortally ill. He returned home immediately, and, alas, his father passed away a few days later. My friend was at home the day before the funeral, when his mother informed him that there was a phone call from some "foreign person." This "foreign person" was the chairman of the giant Japanese bank, who was calling to say that his thoughts were with my friend in this moment of Great Sadness.

I'm sure the "Big (Japanese) Cheese" had an executive assistant who prompted him to make the call. No matter. The Big Cheese did make ... the Big Call.

available. And they all add up to one thing: YOUTH WILL DOMINATE THIS NEW TECHNOLOGY.[9] *(WHICH WILL CHANGE EVERYTHING.)*

THENCE I OFFER YOU MY ...

ACID TEST I: HOW MANY MEMBERS OF YOUR BOARD OF DIRECTORS ARE ... UNDER THE AGE OF ... 35? 30? 25?

That *is* a legitimate question.

Isn't it?

ACID TEST II: WHEN WAS THE LAST TIME YOUR EXECUTIVE COMMITTEE SPENT A ... FULL DAY OFF-SITE ... WITH SOMEONE UNDER THE AGE OF ... 25?

THE SAME IDEA, EH?* (*Stolen from Gary Hamel.)

Among the New Youth entering the World's Work Force, we are discovering—praise be!—a New Attitude. And it's an attitude not likely to be quashed, for more than a whisker of time, by the uncertainties of the current economy. Those uncertainties are, after all, directly driven by the chaos/mess associated with introducing so many ... Truly Transforming Technologies ... at once.

It *is* (redux) the Age of Intellectual Capital. It *is* (redux) the Age of Curiosity Rewarded. (Rather than ... Compliance Demanded.) We need people who ... from the start ... will ... *Talk Back*. Who are ... *Determined* ... to get ahead ... *fast*. Who are ... *Unimpressed* ... by the recalcitrance of the corporate bureaucracies they run up against. Who *are* determined to ... Make a Dent in the Universe. Who are determined ... to stick their shiv between *my* aging & brittle ribs.

Bless them!

May these Youthful Revolutionaries overturn us with great dispatch! (And provide us with coupons to clip in our dotage ... I hope.)

20. Create Opportunities to Lead!

You heard it here first (maybe): THE WAY TO CREATE LEADERS IS TO ... LET THEM LEAD. *New economy. New world. New rate of change. Worst phrase imaginable: "Wait your turn."*

You find somebody great. Terrific. Put them in charge. Of *something*. Right now.

The average complex project has task upon task upon task. Sub-task upon sub-task upon sub-task. Translation: ENORMOUS NUMBERS OF ... LEADERSHIP OPPORTUNITIES.

Use them. Divide the project into a bushel of sub-tasks. Find a "kid" with a bit of energy and spunk and spirit—and a lot more smarts, relative to this New Stuff, than you and I have—and put her or him in charge. So she's 23? SO WHAT?

FRIENDLY USERS

[9]Kids! They take to "all this stuff." Instinctively. Dr. Sugata Mitra, of NIIT in New Delhi, describes a mind-boggling experiment performed in 1999. Personal computers were placed in kiosks in public spaces in Delhi. Because of perpetual dust storms, they were made user-unfriendly courtesy of plastic covers on the keyboard.

Hardly inviting!

Yet the young, computer-illiterate street urchins would approach the computers with glee. (The computers displayed English. The kids spoke Hindi.) The average time that elapsed between a kid's initial confrontation with the computer and his somehow getting onto the Internet and beginning to surf was ... *eight minutes!*

My God!

Get *over* it.

LEADING IS NOT ABOUT AGE.

"Talented people," Ed Michaels of McKinsey & Co. writes, "are less likely to wait their turn. We used to view young people as 'trainees'; now they are authorities. Arguably this is the first time the older generation can—and must—leverage the younger generation very early in their careers." Michaels then presents a list of Gen X "demands," barely dented by the dot.com crash: *Love the challenge. Want responsibility early. Crave freedom, independence, and control. Are obsessed with building their personal human capital. Value more than work. See a very compressed career timeline.*

21. Relish Diversity!

I am a New Economy Fanatic. Thence a Creativity Fanatic. Thence an Intellectual-Capital Fanatic. Thence … a …DIVERSITY FANATIC.

Does that mean I'm an Affirmative Action fanatic? Not necessarily. And in any case, that's beside the point.

What *is* the point? It's really quite simple: Creativity and Great Leaps Forward come from … mix/match/mess. That is, all kinds of people providing all kinds of ideas that crazily bounce against one another … and cause a lot of chaos … and eventually cause a Great Idea to emerge … that … Changes the World.

BusinessWeek, August 2002: "Hiring diverse, even eccentric people, mixing them up in unexpected ways, and asking them to do something unusual can prompt surprising ideas."

"Where do good new ideas come from?" asked highly regarded MIT Media Lab head Nicholas Negroponte. *"That's simple! From differences. Creativity comes from unlikely juxtapositions. The best way to maximize differences is to mix ages, cultures and disciplines."*

Carnegie-Mellon professor Richard Florida writes in a similar vein about the regional accumulation of "creative capital." (Or the lack thereof!) "You cannot get a technologically innovative place," Florida concludes, "unless it's open to weirdness, eccentricity and difference."

So "diversity" means "big deal stuff"—the lifeblood of nations.

BusinessWeek, August 2002: "The coming battle for immigrants: The ability to absorb foreigners could determine whether nations in the industrialized world will grow or stagnate."[10]

Diversity also means, I believe, "a poet in every accounting department." My favorite character in Silicon Valley's long-running drama is Steve Jobs. Steve had … The Vision. And time and again he's turned out incredible products … that change our … View

---

HIP, HIP HYBRID!

[10]Diversity means lots of things. BIG THINGS. Senior Wall Street Journal writer G. Pascal Zachary penned a magnificent book, *The Global Me: New Cosmopolitans and the Competitive Edge*, in 2000. "Diversity defines the health and wealth of nations in the new century," Zachary wrote. "Mighty is the mongrel. … The hybrid is hip. … The impure, the mélange, the adulterated, the blemished, the rough, the black-and-blue, the mix-and-match—these people are inheriting the earth. Mixing is the new norm. … Mixing trumps isolation. It spawns creativity, nourishes the human spirit, spurs economic growth and empowers nations."

Talk about strong language!

of the World. There are many reasons, to be sure, for that extraordinary and consistent record of success. But a significant part of the story is that Steve has always loaded product development teams with all sorts of ... Seriously Cool & Seriously Weird People from Seriously Cool & Seriously Weird Places. "Expose yourself to the best things humans have done," he said at one point, "and then try to bring those things into what you are doing." Such was his explanation for stacking teams with artists, actors, poets, musicians ... and any other Intriguing Kind of "Weirdos"/"Creatives" ... who looked at the world through a different lens.

Diversity, then, is a strategic issue, and an encompassing one, right at the heart of future economic success—for the corporation and the entire nation. Political correctness? Forget it! Diversity's case is about survival—or extinction—in a Brave New World.

Redux: DISTINCT ... OR EXTINCT.

22. Liberate Women!

Often, at a certain point in my seminars, I will queue up this simple slide: DO ANY OF YOU SUFFER FROM TOO MUCH TALENT?

"Of course not!" everyone in the seminar replies. And of course, you don't suffer from too much talent, either. (Do you?) There is, after all, a Great War for Talent going on.

So *where do you look*? All sorts of odd nooks and crannies. But there is one not-so-odd place to look. Namely: the Majority Group of the U.S. (and world) population.

Namely: WOMEN.

(It's such a Big Deal that all of the next chapter is devoted to women's coming surge to the top of corporations.)

23. Celebrate the Weird Ones!

The Northern California psychiatrist's bumper sticker read, *"The Cracked Ones Let in the Light." "Deviance tells the story of every mass market ever created,"* wrote successful tech gurus and entrepreneurs Ryan Matthews and Watts Wacker. *"What starts out weird and dangerous becomes America's next big corporate payday. So are you looking for the next mass-market idea? It's out there ... way out there." "Our business,"* said the great ad man David Ogilvy, *"needs massive transfusions of talent. And talent, I believe, is most likely to be found among nonconformists, dissenters, and rebels."*[11]

COOKIE MONSTER

[11]Years ago I recruited for a Public Policy program at Stanford's business school. I did a quick first pass through several hundred applications, and only one popped out as a "must-under-any-circumstances-have." Don't get me wrong, every kid was bright as blazes. And many had led student governments. But this fellow had also organized a team that ended up making it, as I recall, into the *Guinness Book of World Records*. He and his campus colleagues had baked a *one-ton cookie*—apparently the biggest ever at the time. (Damned hard to imagine, eh?)

I desperately wanted this person ... because he'd done something Weird & Wacky, in a World-Class Way. Yes, his grades were acceptable. (And more.) But he also had demonstrated that ... "Wacky-Weird Factor." And I figured, if you've "done" Wacky-Weird in the past ... well ... then the odds go way-way-way up that you'll do "it" in some form or other in the future.

(My Cookie Man has become my metaphor. I exhort one & all: "Find the One-ton Cookie Freaks!")

Let's stick with Ogilvy. You rebut his assertion, reminding me that he was an "ad man." "He's talking about the 'creatives' in the ad agency," you say. Perhaps he was. But I don't think that makes a bit of difference. In the New World Order—remember our lengthy riff on the value-adding Professional Service Firm idea—we need "radicals" in every nook and cranny and crevice of the enterprise. Radicals ... in training. Radicals ... in purchasing and logistics. Radicals ... in HR. Radicals ... under every bench, radicals clinging like bats to the rafters. Radicals: People who don't buy today's act! People who are disrespectful! People who are bent on inventing a new act!

So what do we do? Embrace (not just "tolerate") their contrarian points of view!

Here's a starting tip: *Quit looking under the lampposts where you've always looked before!* Quit hiring from the same-damn-schools ... even if they are "great" schools.

You want freaks? (YOU DO.) You want weird? (YOU DO.) Answer: Obvious. Look in Weird & Freaky places. Hire from offbeat places. Hire offbeat backgrounds.

Message: *Never hire anyone without an ... aberration in their background. (NO KIDDING.)* If they've been "normal" since birth, even "brilliantly" normal, don't expect them to do something Strange & Cool & Wacky tomorrow morning. Once a toe-er of lines, always a toe-er of lines.

I've often said to seminar audiences: "Never hire anyone with a 4.0 grade-point average." Sounds outrageous. And, of course, it offends a sizeable number of participants—who have invested time and money galore spurring their kids on toward those 4.0s. Of course I'm not against intelligence. But a 4.0 average means: absolutely, positively ... no time ... whatsoever ... for screwing around.

If you have a habit of challenging the rules, it will probably emerge by about age eight. And if you don't have it by age eight, or at least age 18, it probably won't show up by age 88.

Find the aberrant ones!

Embrace them!

Tolerate them!

Reap the rewards of their offbeat behavior!

24. Provide a Setting for Adventure!

"The challenge for IBM, AT&T and other mainstream companies," wrote AT&T HR exec Burke Stinson, "is to re-instill a sense of adventure in recruits."

Great!

But to get from here to there is not easy. Perhaps we should begin by shifting fundamental "management" logic: Perhaps the Main Idea becomes *"What can 'we' do for 'them'?"* rather than "What can 'they' do for 'us'?"

"Firms," writes the ultimate careers guru, Tim Hall, "will not 'manage' employees' careers as they did in the past. They will provide opportunities ... to enable the employee to develop identity and adaptability and thus be in charge of his or her own career."

Bottom line: Talent-obsessed leaders are in the ... Adventure Creation Business.[12] Full time.

25. Revealing the Big Secret!

Labor Day 2000. My mother-in-law's 75th birthday. She said she had but a handful of Big Wishes. One of them: to attend a ballgame at Boston's fabled Fenway Park. So my brother-in-law took her, and my wife and I tagged along. We got lucky. Pedro Martinez was pitching for the Red Sox. He did what Pedro does. He made utter fools out of the nine talented athletes on the other team.

For me, it was a great day. I learned something: PEDRO MARTINEZ IS A BETTER BASEBALL PITCHER THAN I AM.

Not much of an insight, you say.

But I disagree.

FACT: Some people are more talented than other people. FACT: Some people are a *hell* of a lot more talented than other people.

That's what I learned. And that's one of the Big Keys to the Talent Game.

Talent matters. Talent, ultimately, is all there is. The talent in your "pool" constitutes the beginning and end of your *value proposition* ... the beginning and end of your *"solutions"* or *"experiences"* offering ... the beginning and end of your ... *Brand.*

What is a brand? Remember: It's not just a logo. The Boston Red Sox logo looks great on a jersey. It's got lots of tradition ("brand equity") behind it, and so on. But when all is said and done, the essence of the Red Sox brand is ... Pedro Martinez, along with 24 other players who don the Sox jersey 162 games per season (plus the manager, the coaches, trainers, the scouts, and all the other people who make the team go).

What is a "baseball team"? Simple: A baseball team is ... ITS ROSTER. Sports marketing is important. No doubt of it. But all the sports marketing in the world won't make up for a team that loses year after year. In the mid- to long-run, Talent Rules.

In the long run:
TALENT = BRAND. And BRAND = TALENT.
Case closed.

CUTTING PEOPLE "SLACK"? CUT IT OUT!

[12] Could integrity be "more important than ever"? Answer, in a word: YES.

The logic goes something like this: In a "sloppy" world, where competition isn't that intense, where product life cycles stretch out for years, where the enemy and his tactics and weapons are known ... it's possible to cut people a bit of slack. But I've argued that in these (weird) days we need the ... BEST. I've also argued that we need to subject them to an ... UP OR OUT PHILOSOPHY.

To do so puts a special weight on the boss: If we're serious about "up or out," then "cronyism" and other forms of essential dishonesty regarding the "people stuff" are ... OUT. OUT. OUT

Talent!
Now!
Period!
(Period!)

! Contrasts

WAS		IS
People are "important"	–	People are *everything*
"People power" as a slogan	–	"People power" as a strategy
HR pros as paper shufflers	–	HR pros as rock stars
Hire to "fill a position"	–	Hire to position a company for greatness
"Competitive" pay-and-benefits package	–	Excellent pay-and-benefits package
Talent "pays its dues"	–	Talent claims its prize
"Training" is a department	–	Training is an obsession
Filling "diversity" slots	–	Feeling the diversity imperative
Women lag	–	Women lead
A secure job with "potential for advancement"	–	A Great Place to Work!
"Human Resources"	–	Talent!
"Staff"	–	Talent!
"Employees"	–	Talent!
"Associates"	–	Talent!
"Personnel"	–	Talent!

21 MEET THE NEW BOSS: WOMEN RULE!

! Technicolor Rules ...

- "Tomorrow belongs to women."
- Women practice *improvisation* with much greater ease than men.
- Women are more *self-determined* and more *trust-sensitive* than men.
- Women appreciate and depend upon their *intuition* more than men do.
- Women, unlike men, focus naturally on *empowerment* (rather than on hierarchical "power").
- Women understand and develop *relationships* with greater facility than men.
- "Boys are trained in a way that will make them irrelevant."
- "I believe there is a 'secret' to my success. Namely, hiring women."

 ! RANT

We are not prepared ...

We acknowledge that a new, fluid world is emerging. But we retain our male-inspired, male-dominated hierarchies. We "reengineer." But our way of thinking, indeed our very vocabulary ("engineering"), continues to be male-inspired. We recognize women's "rights." But we ignore women's *strengths*. We value "toughness." But we fail to see that women's brand of toughness is far more "steely" than men's. We preach the value of a new kind of enterprise. But we neglect those who are perhaps most fit to lead it. Namely: Women.

 ! VISION

I imagine ...

A woman in the White House.

A new epoch in which we all (men as well as women) honor, reward, and take advantage of women's extraordinary strengths.

An enterprise doctrine that views women as much of the answer not only to the "talent problem," but also to the "leadership problem."

A world in which this damn chapter is ... Totally Unnecessary.

Return to Gender: Where the Talent Is

There is a Great War for Talent. Great Talent *is* in short supply. And the supply will get even shorter ... as the Age of Creativity and Intellectual Capital accelerates. And accelerate it will.

So can we afford to ignore half (or, to be precise, slightly more than half) of our store of potential Great Talent?
Well ... NO.

If we are serious about the pivotal role that talent plays in the New Economy ... then the connection in our minds between "talent" and "leadership" and "women" must become automatic. The kickoff to a *BusinessWeek* Special Report in 2000 says it all: "AS LEADERS, WOMEN RULE: New studies find that female managers outshine their male counterparts in almost every measure."

My core argument[1] here is really quite simple:

1. Talent is ever more important.
2. Our stock of leaders fails to match the needs of the time.
3. Women are a woefully neglected source of talent (especially leadership talent).
4. Women and men are different.
5. Women's strengths match the leadership needs of the New Economy—to a startling (and significant) degree.
6. Ergo, women must play a huge part in solving the "talent problem."
7. Accelerating the movement of women into leadership roles is a ... Strategic Imperative ... of the highest order.

The Helen and Judy Show

Authors Helen Fisher and Judy B. Rosener provide a powerful one-two "punch" on the subject of gender differences and how they relate to the ... New World of Work.

It is a fact (damn it!): Men and women are different (*significantly different!*) when it

---

{ **DEEP END OF THE TALENT POOL**
[1]The extended "rant" that forms this chapter began as but one element of the Talent25. (See Chapter 20.) Then I got, well, pissed off. I decided that tapping the deepest well of talent would require a ... *Revolution*.

Even so, my goals here are fairly modest. The "revolution" that I wish to foment is an *awareness* revolution.

So: Pay attention! Be aware! Listen up! Ponder what follows! Please!

{ **HEAR THEM ROAR**
I never intended to make the "women as leaders" topic a centerpiece of my writing. It snuck up on me ... and then hit me hard at a meeting with women business owners in 1996. (See Chapter 13.)

I listened as one powerful woman after another described her struggle against male-dominated hierarchies that had marked her personal and professional life. Listening to those stories, frankly, made me feel like an idiot or a spoiled brat (at age 54!).

Words like "epiphany" should not be bandied about lightly; but I had an Epiphany of Awareness that day. And it's taken root. And I am determined to ... pass it on.

comes to styles of perceiving and acting in the world. I've been studying this "gender stuff," frantically, for the last half-dozen years. And I am amazed by what I have learned. Books by the score have appeared about this topic, but the work of Fisher and Rosener stands out for its ability to penetrate even a thick male skull like mine.

"TOMORROW BELONGS TO WOMEN." That's the unhedged bet offered by Helen Fisher in *The First Sex: The Natural Talents of Women and How They Are Changing the World*.

Her argument, in summary: "On average, women and men possess a number of different innate skills. And current trends suggest that many sectors of the 21st-century economic community are going to need the natural talents of women. ... Women have many exceptional faculties bred in deep history: a talent with words, a capacity to read non-verbal cues; emotional sensitivity; empathy; patience; an ability to do and think several things simultaneously ... a penchant for long-term planning; a gift for networking and negotiating; and a preference for cooperating, reaching consensus, and leading via egalitarian teams."

(Please stop and reread that. S-L-O-W-L-Y.)

"It's time for U.S. organizations to act," writes Judy Rosener in *America's Competitive Secret: Women Managers*. "No other country in the world has a comparable supply of professional women waiting to be called into action. This is America's competitive secret."

Rosener's list of women's leadership strengths echoes Fisher's list:

- Link rather than rank workers.
- Favor interactive-collaborative leadership styles.
- Sustain fruitful collaborations.
- Comfortable sharing information.
- See redistribution of power as victory, not surrender.
- Readily accept ambiguity.
- Honor intuition as well as pure "rationality."
- Inherently flexible.
- Appreciate cultural diversity.

(Again, please reread. S-L-O-W-L-Y.)

It's a Women's (Work) World

Simply put, then: There is a set of attributes, more commonly found in women than in men, that match the requirements of the new world of ... *Solutions* ... *Experiences* ... *WOW Projects* ... and so forth.

{ **(RE)VIVE LA DIFFÉRENCE**
Recall the material I drew, back in Chapter 13, from *Why Men Don't Listen and Women Can't Read Maps*, by Barbara Pease and Allan Pease. Among the items that I took from their often humorous, but always very serious book:
"Women love to talk. *Men talk silently to themselves.*"
"Women multitrack."
"Women are indirect. *Men are direct.*"
"Women talk emotively, *men are literal. Men listen like statues.*"
"*Boys like things*, girls like people."
"*Boys compete*, girls cooperate."
"*Men hate to be wrong. Men hide their emotions.*"
Again, see Chapter 13 for more on all this.

NEW BUSINESS ● ! NEW PEOPLE

Here's my own short list of such attributes:

- Women practice *improvisation skills* with much greater ease than men.
- Women are more *self-determined* and more *trust-sensitive* than men.
- Women appreciate and depend upon their *intuition* more than men do.
- Women, unlike men, focus naturally on *empowerment* (rather than on "power").
- Women understand and develop *relationships* with greater facility than men.

One difference in particular throws a spotlight on why the New Economy favors women. Namely: Women are far less "rank-conscious" than men.[2]

The Bedrock Rules of the New Economy:

1. Shout good-bye to "command & control!"
2. Shout good-bye to "knowing one's place!"
3. Shout good-bye to hierarchy!

Guys like rules. They like commanding and controlling. They like "knowing their place." They like hierarchical structures and the certainties associated therewith. (Hey, you can trace this instinct directly back to the cave.) Such structures exist not just because of "organizational needs," but rather because hierarchy and male thinking go hand-in-glove—and because men have always (until now) dominated organizations. But all of that is changing. The "organizational needs" of new enterprise are increasingly consonant with the female side of the "male-female difference" divide.

COURTESY CHECK

Women are relationship junkies. Men are not. A truism, right? But is it true? To find out, I conducted what might seek like a trivial experiment.

Over the space of three busy weeks, I took 21 commercial-airline flights. In each case, I had but one seatmate; among my 21 companions were 17 men and 4 women. I kept score of the frequency with which these seatmates uttered a simple "Thank you" whenever a flight attendant performed some small bit of service for them (handing them a hot towel, serving them dinner, refilling a drink, and so on).

Here are the results: Among the 17 men, the total number of thank-yous was ... 11. (That's 0.65 thank-yous per guy.) Among the 4 women, the total came to ... 23. (Or 5.75 thank-yous per gal.)

So what does this "trivial" experiment amount to? You decide. I wouldn't touch a conclusive "finding" with a 10-foot pole. My "sample" was not statistically significant. (And I won't guarantee that I didn't miss a stray thank-you along the way.) But to me, the results of this little survey are ... Pretty Damn Suggestive. And, actually, not at all trivial.

WHAT'S IT ALL ABOUT, ALPHA?

[2]The male pack-animal mind-set is something that even a few men will admit to. "Guys want to put everybody in their hierarchical place," says Paul Biondi, of Mercer Management Consulting, with perhaps far too much frankness. "Like, 'Should I have more respect for you, or are you somebody that's south of me?'"

Hey, guys: Is there any possibility—any possibility whatsoever—that a woman could ask such a question ... and cop such an attitude?

Think about it. Please.

Male Trouble

Message to guys: It gets worse. Consider the following analysis, from a cover story in the *Atlantic Monthly*:

In 1996, there were 8.4 million women and 6.7 million men in American colleges; by 2007, that disparity will have grown to 9.2 million women versus 6.9 million men. Moreover, more of the women stick around and finish. (FYI: M-F wage gaps reverse as education level increases.) As one surprising (to men?) result of this extraordinary gap, we actually have more women than men these days in high-level math and science courses.

Almost everywhere you look, the numbers tell a compelling tale. (Yes, guys, the numbers. This isn't touchy-feely, wishy-washy stuff you can brush aside with your "just the facts, ma'am" attitude.) For example:

- There are far more girls in student government than boys.
- There are far more girls in honor societies than boys.
- Girls read far more books.
- Girls outperform boys in tests of artistic and musical ability.
- Girls study abroad at a higher rate.

Yikes![3] But don't despair, fellas. We still rule in some areas. Namely: Crime and violence of all varieties. Alcohol abuse. Drug use. Learning disabilities.

Selling Point: All Men Out?

Okay, enough Sociological Big Think. What's the practical, actionable upshot of all these gender differences for your enterprise? How about this one:

FIRE ALL MALE SALESPEOPLE.

I'm only kidding. More or less.

Consider: "TAKE THIS QUICK QUIZ. Who manages more things at once? Who puts more effort into their appearance? Who usually takes care of the details? Who finds it easier to meet new people? Who asks more questions in a conversation? Who's a better listener? Who has more interest in communication skills? Who is more inclined to get involved? Who encourages harmony and agreement? Who has better intuition? Who works with longer 'to do' lists? Who enjoys a recap of the day's events? Who's better at keeping in touch with others?"

That "quick quiz" appears on the back cover of the book *Selling Is a Woman's Game: Fifteen Powerful Reasons Why Women Can Outsell Men*, by Nicki Joy and Susan

---

TO A DEGREE: WOMEN SURPASS MEN

Headline to a May 2003 *BusinessWeek* cover story: "THE NEW GENDER GAP. From kindergarten to grad school, boys are becoming the second sex."

Telling statistics: In 2010, the female-to-male ratio of bachelor's-degree recipients will be 1.42:1; for master's degrees, the ratio will be 1.51:1.

And note well: Degrees are the best overall indicator of future financial success.

BOYS WILL BE BOYS (UH-OH!)

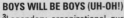
[3]Legendary organizational guru Phil Slater says, with tongue nowhere near cheek, "Boys are trained in a way that will make them irrelevant."

Kane-Benson. And, as you will not be surprised to learn, the answer to each of those questions is ... WOMEN.

Now, obviously I don't counsel firing all male salespeople. But I do advise you to think about what makes for a great sales force. What qualities go into ... not just making "the sale," but making and maintaining the kind of ongoing relationships that yield ongoing business?[4]

Several years ago, a senior executive at a travel-services company (he now has a much bigger job at a much bigger corporation) approached me after one of my seminars. This guy, who had made his "bones" by selling systems at AT&T, got to musing about the "women factor." "Tom," he said, "I believe there is a 'secret' to my success. Namely, hiring women." You can imagine my surprise. This was prior to my effort to understand the implications of gender differences in enterprise.

"My guys," he continued, "only wanted to call on 'Mr. Big.' But the women I worked with were willing to invest extraordinary amounts of time in 'wiring the organization.' They would routinely develop relationships several layers 'down' the org chart. By the time they were ready to call on the top executive, the deal was essentially already closed. It was eerie, really. Women 'did it.' Guys *couldn't* do it, to save themselves. I never really looked into the root causes of all this, but I sure as hell made a ton of money out of it."

The Reich Stuff: How One Guy "Got" It

From one conversion narrative to another ...

For some men, the path to recognizing the unique leadership talents of women travels along "the bottom line." For others, the pilgrimage is more personal. Put it this way: If a conservative is a liberal who's been "mugged by reality," then maybe a male feminist is ... a guy who's watched his wife get the short end of the professional stick.

Bob Reich is a former U.S. Secretary of Labor (1993–1997). He is also, according to one extensive recent survey, the third most important management thinker of our time. As part of his (ultimately unsuccessful) run for the governor's job in Massachusetts, Bob penned a book that outlined his views. The following excerpt, from a chapter titled "The Day I Became a Feminist," is one that I found absolutely riveting. It concerns the day that Reich's wife, a renowned legal scholar, was denied tenure at Harvard:

"RELATIONSHIP" TALK
[4]Hardwick Simmons, former CEO of Prudential Securities: "Investors are looking more and more for a relationship with their financial advisers. They want someone they can trust, someone who listens. ... In my experience, in general, women may be better at these relationship-building skills than are men."

He says, "women may be better ..." I say women "most assuredly are" better ...

RATIO AD ABSURDUM

In early 2001, I addressed three of the world's largest financial advisory services companies. Operations at such companies fall into two big categories: service and sales. On the service side at all three of those firms, about 80 percent of the employees were female, and 20 percent men. On the sales side, the proportion was rigidly reversed: about 80 percent male, and 20 percent female.

If you believe, as I and many others do, that women are better "relationship sellers" than men, then that distribution of talent is ... Truly Stupid.

"A string of white males had been voted tenure just before her. Most had not written as much as she, nor inspired the same praise from specialists around the nation as had her work. None of their writings had been subjected to the detailed scrutiny—footnote by footnote—to which her colleagues had subjected her latest manuscript. Not one of the male candidates had roused the degree of anger and bitterness that characterized her tenure decision.

"Why? At first I was bewildered. I knew most of the men who had voted against her. A few I knew to be narrow-minded, one or two I might have suspected of misogyny. But most were thoughtful, intelligent men. They had traveled widely, read widely, had held positions of responsibility and trust. I was sure that they felt they had been fair and impartial in judging her work. They would be appalled at any suggestion of sexual bias.

"Gradually, I came to understand. They were applying their standard of scholarship as impartially as they knew how. Yet their standard assumed that the person to whom they applied it had gone through the same training and had the same formative intellectual experiences as they. It assumed further that the person had gained along the way the same understandings of academic discipline, and the same approaches to core problems, as they had gained. In short, their standard was premised on the belief that the people they judged had come to view the modes and purposes of scholarship—of the life of the mind—in the same way they had come to view it.

"Through the years my wife has helped me to see the gender biases of these assumptions. Her experiences and understandings, and those of other women scholars, have been shaped by the irrefutable reality of gender. The values and perspectives she brings to bear on the world—and in particular, the world of ideas—are different from theirs, because she has experienced the world differently. In fact, it is the very uniqueness of her female perspective that animates her scholarship, that gives it its originality and intellectual bite. They had applied their standard as impartially as they knew how, but it was a male standard."

Reich goes on to explain how he has integrated an awareness of gender differences into his own teaching:

"In my class I present a complex management problem. An organization is rife with

NEW BUSINESS ● **NEW PEOPLE**

A "LONG WAY"? GO FIGURE (I)

Women, to quote the old slogan, "have come a long way, baby." But ... they have an even longer way to go.

At the turn of the millennium, Susan Estrich reports in *Sex and Power*, just 63 of the top 2,500 earners at Fortune 500 companies were women. Only 8 percent of partners at Big Five accounting firms were women. A scant 14 percent of partners in the top 250 law firms in America were women. In medical schools, 43 percent of new students are women; 26 percent of faculty are women; but only 7 percent of deans are women.

PATHETIC!

OPPORTUNITY KNOCK-OUT

Sometimes opportunity knocks. And sometimes it's a battering ram, and you just have to get out of its way.

My beat is business performance, not social justice. So I look at the issue of women and talent through a business-performance lens. And what I see, quite simply, is a strategic opportunity of the first order.

That opportunity is knocking ... and it won't wait very long for you to open the door.

dissension. I ask, what steps should the manager take to improve the situation? The answers of my male students are filled with words like 'strategy,' 'conflict,' interests,' 'claims,' 'trade-offs,' and 'rights.' My female students use words like 'resolution,' 'relationship,' cooperation,' and 'loyalty.' Have their vocabularies and approaches to problems always been somewhat different, or am I listening as never before?

"The vice president of a corporation that I advise tells me he can't implement one of my recommendations, although he agrees with it. 'I have no authority,' he explains. 'It's not my turf.' Later the same day, his assistant vice president tells me that the recommendation can be implemented easily. 'It's not formally within our responsibility,' she says, off-handedly. 'But we'll just make some suggestions here and there, at the right time, to the right folks, and it'll get done.' Is the male vice president especially mindful of formal lines of authority and his female assistant especially casual, or do they exemplify differences in how men and women in general approach questions of leadership?

"If being a 'feminist' means noticing these sorts of things, then I became a feminist the day my wife was denied tenure. But what is my responsibility, as a male feminist, beyond merely noticing? At the least: to remind corporate recruiters that they shouldn't be asking about whether prospective female employees want to have a family; to warn male colleagues about subtle possibilities of sexual bias in their evaluations of female colleagues; to help ensure that women are listened to within otherwise all-male meetings; to support my women students in the classroom, and to give explicit legitimacy to differences in the perceptions and leadership styles of men and women. In other words, just as I seek to educate myself, I must also help educate other men.

"This is no small task. The day after the vote on my wife's tenure, I phoned one of her opponents—an old curmudgeon, as arrogant as he is smart. Without the slightest sense of the irony lying in the epithet I chose to hurl at him, I called him a son of a bitch."

Bravo, Bob!

Gender Mercies: Toward a Talent Revolution

Elevating women into the positions where they deserve to be ... and where they will add real bottom-line value ... isn't easy. One organization that has made big strides in this direction is Deloitte & Touche. Douglas McCracken, Deloitte's former big boss, brilliantly described his firm's "epiphany" in a *Harvard Business Review* article titled

---

A "LONG WAY"? GO FIGURE (II)

Another entry from the "long, long way" file: Women occupy 4 percent of top management jobs at U.S. companies. The comparable figure in Britain is 3 percent; in the European Union as a whole, 2 percent; and in Japan, less than 1 percent.

Again: PATHETIC!

HOW *YOU* CAN DO IT: READ THIS BOOK

Allison Pearson's extraordinary novel *I Don't Know How She Does It* is not a "must read." It's a "MUST DAMN WELL READ ... NOW." It's a great read but also a profound one—especially when it comes to subtle stuff.

Example: When a *woman* skips a meeting to go to a kid's soccer game, she gets points *off* for doing "the Softie Mom Thing." When a guy takes time off to do the same, he scores a bushel of points for "having the guts to do the family thing."

It *is* that bad!

"Winning the Talent War for Women: Sometimes It Takes a Revolution."

Deloitte was doing pretty well in that "war." It was working hard to hire Great Women. It was giving them very high marks—higher than men!—in their early years. (No surprise: They deserved it.) *And then ... the women left.*

Ah, you say: The Great Baby Problem strikes!

Not so fast, amigo.

"Deloitte was doing a great job of hiring high-performing women," McCracken writes. "In fact, women often earned higher performance ratings than men in their first years with the firm. Yet the percentage of women decreased with each step up the career ladder.

"Most women weren't leaving to raise families; they had weighed their options in Deloitte's male-dominated culture and found them wanting. Many, dissatisfied with the culture they perceived as endemic to professional service firms, switched professions."

Deloitte then did a "Deloitte" on Deloitte. It carefully examined what was driving women to leave the firm. And it found assumption after assumption that inadvertently blocked women's progress within Deloitte. For example, writes McCracken: "The process of assigning plum accounts was largely unexamined. Male partners made assumptions: 'I wouldn't put her on that kind of company because it's a tough manufacturing environment.' 'That client is difficult to deal with.' 'Travel puts too much pressure on women.'"

So Deloitte went to work on banishing those assumptions. The firm has not transformed itself overnight, but it has made a decade-long *strategic* commitment[5] to move women—in much higher numbers than before—into its top leadership ranks.

And that, indeed, amounts to ... *A REVOLUTION.*

McCracken's word. And mine!

DOWN TO THE WIAR

[5]WIAR stands for Women's Initiative Annual Report. I can't "command" you to read this invaluable document ... but I desperately wish that I could. So please ... race to the Deloitte & Touche Web site (www.public.deloitte.com/wiar/home.htm), download the report, and read it.

This is *exactly* what a serious "strategic" approach to this issue looks like!

NEW BUSINESS ! • NEW PEOPLE

! Contrasts

WAS	IS
Competition –	Cooperation
Rules –	Relationships
Unitasking –	Multitasking
Issuing orders –	Asking questions
Rigid claims –	Subtle cues
"Yes, sir" –	"Thank you"
Conquest –	Communication
"Management" –	"Empowerment"
Command & control –	Connect & cajole
Information: "need to know" –	Information: "want to share"
Women in "support" functions –	Women in sales positions

NEW BUSINESS ❗ ● NEW PEOPLE

22 GETTING IT RIGHT AT THE START: EDUCATION FOR A CREATIVE & SELF-RELIANT AGE

! Technicolor Rules ...

- Our school system is a thinly disguised conspiracy to quash creativity.
- We are at an inflection point. We seem to be reinventing everything—except the school system, which should (in theory) underpin, even lead, the rest.
- "The main crisis in schools today is irrelevance."
- "Our education system is a second-rate, factory-style organization pumping out obsolete information in obsolete ways."
- "Our educational thinking is concerned with: 'what is.' " It is not good at designing: 'What can be.' "
- "Every time I pass a jailhouse or a school, I feel sorry for the people inside."

! RANT

We are not prepared ...

We attempt to "reform" an educational system that was designed for the Industrial Age—for a Fordist era in which employees needed to "know their place" and in which employers needed uniformly "trained," interchangeable "parts" ("workers" in collars both blue and white). Yet now we must prepare for a world in which value emerges from individual initiative and creativity. And we must reject all notions of "reform" that merely serve up more of the same: more testing, more "standards," more uniformity, more conformity, more bureaucracy.

! VISION

I imagine ...

A school *system* that recognizes that learning is *natural*, that a love of learning is *normal*, and that real learning is *passionate* learning.

A school *curriculum* that values questions above answers ... creativity above fact regurgitation ... individuality above uniformity ... and excellence above standardized performance.

A *society* that respects its teachers and principals, pays them well, and (most important) grants them the autonomy to do their job ... as the creative individuals they are, and for the creative individuals in their charge.

"Unsatisfactory!": Raising or Hazing?

Gordon MacKenzie spent a three-decade career in the creative department at Hallmark. Left because he felt the company was getting a bit stodgy. And wrote a brilliant book on the topic of keeping an enterprise energetic: *Orbiting the Giant Hairball: A Corporate Fool's Guide to Surviving with Grace.*

Following his "retirement," Gordon devoted a lot of time to the school system, coaching and commenting. He recalled a typical visit to an American elementary school at the turn of the century/millennium:

"'How many artists are there in the room? Would you please raise your hands.' FIRST GRADE: En masse, the children leapt from their chairs, arms waving. ... Every child was an artist! SECOND GRADE: About half the kids raised their hands, shoulder high, no higher. [Their] hands were still. THIRD GRADE: At best, 10 kids out of 30 would raise a hand. Tentatively. Self-consciously. By the time I reached SIXTH GRADE, no more than one or two kids raised their hands, and then ever-so-slightly ... betraying a fear of being identified by the group as a 'closet artist.' The point is: Every school I visited was participating in the systematic suppression of creative genius."

Strong language.

Sad language.

Tragic language.

Now, another story. (I'm not making this up ...)

"My wife and I went to a [kindergarten] parent-teacher conference," writes Jordan Ayan in his brilliant book on creativity, *Aha!,* "and were informed that our budding refrigerator artist [Christopher] would be receiving a grade of "Unsatisfactory" in art.[1] We were shocked. How could any child—let alone our child—receive a poor grade in art at such a young age? His teacher informed us that

he had refused to color within the lines...

which was a state requirement for demonstrating 'grade-level motor skills.'"

Like Gordon MacKenzie, I believe our school system is a thinly disguised conspiracy (his term: "systematic suppression") to quash creativity. That would bother me at any point in history. But this is not "any point in history." We are at an inflection point. A short period of time during which we're re-imagining everything. Economics and commerce. Organizations in general. Politics. Healthcare. War-making. That is: We seem to be re-imagining everything —except the school system, which should (in theory) underpin, even lead, the rest.

THE UN-COOLEST CUT

[1] Steve Jobs has done more Cool Stuff than anybody else in Silicon Valley. As mentioned previously, one of his success "secrets" is loading every development team with artists ... and historians ... and poets ... and musicians ... and dramatists. He says he wants to bring to bear, on each project, the best of human cultural accomplishment.

So how come the schools don't get it? Budget crunch? First programs to be cut? Art and Music. I say ... the hell with the math budget. (I really don't mean that.) Let's *enhance* the art budget and *inflate* the music budget. Training in Creativity is important, in general. But it is absolutely essential in this Age of Intangibles & Intellectual Capital.

"Irrelevant": Learning and Earning in the New Economy

I've devoted two-thirds of this book to urging ... a Total Renovation of Enterprise. We are in the midst of a White-Collar Revolution. Rote work is being ripped out of the White-Collar Economy—which employs about 90 percent of us in the developed nations. It amounts to an impact on "bureaucrats" who inhabit "cost centers" that's at least as big as the impact of containerization at the dock, forklifts, and other forms of "factory automation" in the distribution center.

THE ENTIRE NATURE OF WORK WILL CHANGE. DRAMATICALLY. QUICKLY. ARE WE READY FOR THAT? ARE OUR CHILDREN READY? NO!

And much of the problem starts at the moment we send our kids off to school.

Richard Rosecrance, author of *The Rise of the Virtual State*, writes, "At the ultimate stage competition among nations will be competition among educational systems, for the most productive and richest countries will be those with the best education and training."

The private sector doesn't operate in a vacuum. TALENT IS EVERYTHING. And the "production" of "talent" is significantly dependent upon ... schools.

As I see it, our school system is getting it all wrong ... for an age in which creativity and intellectual capital drive the economy. The school "system" abhors creativity. Obstreperousness. Entrepreneurial instincts.

To this day, our schools are driven by rigid and perhaps effective rituals created well over a century ago—for another age, for another economy. Moreover, the modern "school reform" movement amounts to ... a Giant Step Backward.

"Teach to test." "Standardization." Ye gads. Not in my Silicon Valley!

New World of Work = Age of Creativity. The Rare & Best School Stuff fits the New World Order to a T. The "normal" way of doing things—"Reformers' Rote Rules" (the *wrong* "3 Rs")—fits the "Old World of Work" to a T.

"The main crisis in schools today is irrelevance," writes Dan Pink in *Free Agent Nation*. Dan's book is among the very best so far written about the New World of Work. A world which virtually all of us are becoming, for survival's sake, independent-minded Brand Yous ... CEOs of Me Inc. (See Chapter 19.) We're effectively on our own, aiming to forge our way in a more-chaotic-than-in-several-hundred-years context. Fending off the imminent possibility of the computer's surpassing us in usefulness.

Irrelevance. The school system is irrelevant ... relative to our New Needs.

This is not the rant of an "education expert." It is the rant of a business analyst.[2] Of someone who is looking as intensely as I can at the new world of enterprise—public and private—and the new world of careers. Mustn't some form of "new education" by definition be at the epicenter of this new world?

NEW BUSINESS ● NEW PEOPLE

ACT YOUR RAGE

[2] *I apologize. I get very emotional about this topic. This chapter—in the spirit of another Tom, Tom Paine—is written in a rage. A rage against the knowing malevolence of the designers of our school system. How could so many people be so collectively stupid?*

"Perfect Docility": How Rules Overtook Schools

Blame the whole damn thing[3] on John D. Rockefeller. He was interested in education. (Hooray!) Created the General Education Board. (Hooray!) And this was the goal of those "educators," circa 1906: *"In our dreams, people yield themselves with perfect docility to our molding hands. ... The task is simple. We will organize children and teach them in a perfect way the things their fathers and mothers are doing in an imperfect way."*

There's only one response to that one: GOOD GOD!

(Read it again. Please. "PERFECT DOCILITY." GOOD GOD! And, a century later, has ... anything ... changed?)

Listen up to John Taylor Gatto's telling of this now-tragic tale. Gatto is a man who lives to color outside the lines, to scratch out all the existing lines. Yet somehow he was named New York City Teacher of the Year three times in a row and once named New York State Teacher of the Year. In his amazing book *A Different Kind of Teacher*, Gatto traces the history of the tragically narrow views that HAVE DOMINATED American education to this day:

"Schools were designed by Horace Mann, E. I. Thorndike, and others to be instruments of the scientific management of a mass population. Schools are intended to produce, through the application of formulas, formulaic human beings whose behavior can be predicted and controlled. To a very great extent, schools succeed in doing this. But in a society that is increasingly fragmented, in which the only genuinely successful people are independent, self-reliant, confident, and individualistic, the products of school ... are irrelevant."

There we go again!

"IRRELEVANT."

Also to blame is Frederick Taylor, damn his eyes. He gave us the "one best way" of doing things. For a world where there was, perhaps, one best way of swinging a pick at a coal face, that made some sense. But it's been a long journey from the coal pits of Pennsylvania to the Project Studios in Redmond, Washington, where Bill Gates' programmers and designers ceaselessly work to invent a new "best way" every single day that supersedes the prior day's "best way."

> ### GLOBAL CLASSROOM
> A word on the world at large: I acknowledge that school systems are peculiar to individual national cultures. And, yes, the observations in this chapter relate most directly to the United States. Yet the fundamental problems are the same everywhere: We are moving into a New World of Work. A new world where "creation intensification," as a Japanese analyst from Nomura Research Institute called it, is the sine qua non of success. And schools around the world are simply not designed to prepare kids—French kids, British kids, German kids, Japanese kids, Korean kids, Singaporean kids—for that kind of creative work.

> ### NONE OF YOUR ... BISMARCK
> [3]Two other villains in the piece: Bismarck and Ford.
> The leading lights of what has become today's American education system were mesmerized, over a century ago, by the hyper-disciplined educational approach taken by the Germans under Chancellor Otto von Bismarck. Henry Ford, among (many) prominent others, became a devotee. And you and I paid—and continue to pay—the price.

A frightening addendum: Those who achieve the most are invariably those who don't buy into the educational act. Even at our "best" schools. "The boys who were the best 'Grotties,'" wrote FDR biographer John Gunther, "usually turned out to be nonentities later; boys who hated Groton did much better."

Or consider Thomas Stanley, our foremost student of the backgrounds of those who go on to achieve significant financial success. In *Whoever Makes the Most Mistakes Wins*, management gurus Richard Farson and Ralph Keyes summarize Mr. Stanley's argument: "Thomas Stanley has not only found no correlation between success in school and an ability to accumulate wealth, he's actually found a negative correlation. 'It seems that school-related evaluations are poor predictors of economic success,' Stanley concluded. What did predict economic success was a willingness to take risks. [Yet] the success-failure standards of most schools penalized risk takers. Most educational systems honor those who play it safe ... . As a result, those who do well in school find it hard to take risks later on."

"Our education system is a second-rate, factory-style organization," writes futurist Alvin Toffler, "pumping out obsolete information in obsolete ways. [The schools] are simply not connected to the future of the kids they're responsible for." "Our traditional thinking," adds the creativity guru, Edward de Bono, "is concerned with: 'What is.' It is not good at all at designing: 'What can be.'"

Let's review, then, the key terms of our indictment: "Irrelevant." "Penalize risk takers." "Second rate." "Obsolete."

I'm pissed off. *So pissed off.*[4] So incredibly annoyed that we have made "education" so damn bloody difficult. So "rote." So divorced from ... true learning ... which in fact is joy not agony, and all about ... Re-imaginings.

JUST DO IT

John Merrow, in *USA Today*: "What actually correlates with success are not grades, but 'engagement'—genuine involvement in courses and campus activities. Engagement leads to 'deep learning.' ... That's very different from just memorizing stuff for an exam. ... As Russ Edgerton of the Pew Forum on Undergraduate Learning notes, 'What counts most is what students *do* in college, not who they are, or where they go to college, or what their grades are.'"

CONFESSIONS OF AN IDLE MIND

[4]*Again: I know I'm ranting. I've been annoying people at cocktail parties and dinner parties. Damn near terrifying people I collar on the street. I'm so mad I can't see straight. The school system stinks. It is a conspiracy. An anti-education conspiracy. At exactly ... the wrong moment.*

BLAME "IT" (THIS RANT) ALL ON "FREE TIME." I was supposed to be on vacation. Summer. Martha's Vineyard. 2001. And then I read John Taylor Gatto—at the urging of my 19-year-old stepson. I kept on reading. And I became furious. Furious that we do know how to educate kids. And that we don't do it.

"IRRELEVANT."
"Penalize risk takers."
"Second rate."
"Obsolete."

"Brutally Simple": Testing Versus Questing

For more than 100 years, we've been doing the education thing wrong. Perversely so. By design. And now we have yet another "school reform" movement ... doing it wrong ... all wrong ... all over again.

George W. Bush, conservative Republican ... *embraces*... Edward M. Kennedy, liberal Democrat. They pass (another) school-reform bill! Another 20 years of going in the wrong direction! I do not at all question the positive intent of those leaders. I must, however, upon reflection, acknowledge bewilderment about the processes chosen.

Of course our kids must "know the basics" of reading, 'riting, and 'rithmetic; and, alas, those basics are often neglected. But they are but a starting point, not the end point, of education. Moreover, even the basics, in the hands of inspired teachers— allowed to teach and to get to know their charges—can be infused with excitement. As one wag put it, math comes easily in the after-school clerking job; it's just that math in the jailhouse-called-school, with all eyes on yet another standard-and-dehumanizing test, is devoid of the motivational heat that leads to true learning.

The Most Obscene Phrase in the English language ... TEACH TO TEST. (IT MAKES ME REACH FOR AN AIRLINE BARF BAG.)

"I discovered the brutally simple motivation behind the development and imposition of all systematic instructional programs and tests—a lack of trust that teachers can teach and that students can learn," writes educational-thought leader Frank Smith in his superb book *Insult to Intelligence.*

"What [standardized tests] actually measure," writes John Taylor Gatto, "is the tractability of the student, and this they do quite accurately. Is it of value to know who is docile and who may not be? You tell me." Gatto continues: "School teachers aren't allowed to do what they think best for each student. Harnessed to a collectivized regimen, they soon give up thinking seriously about students as one-of-a-kind individuals, regardless of what they may wish were true."

"Learning-for-tests" is the ultimate oxymoron. Tests test stuff that goes on tests. "Learning," on the other hand, is about stuff that actually matters. Of course tests "matter" to students. But that, too, is revelatory. "Testing" is not an "end product"[5] ... except in school. Tests do *not* lead to mastery. They mostly lead to (a) fear of the subject matter, and (b) an understanding of the subject matter that accords with constrained test "answers," rather than with a deep appreciation of the topic.

John Taylor Gatto: "Schooling takes place in an environment controlled by others. ... Education describes efforts largely self-initiated for the purpose of taking charge of your life wisely and living in a world you understand. The educated state is a complex tapestry woven out of broad experience, grueling commitments, and substantial risk taking."

Please understand: When I rail against "standardized testing," I do not at all mean to rail against performance evaluation or accountability. In fact, I am a ... Performance

---

SWEDISH MESSAGE

[5]The obsession with Testing also runs smack into another school-reform nostrum: Hours-per-Year-in-Class. Test scores in Sweden, for example, are near the top in almost every category. Yet Swedish kids don't start school until age *seven.* Nor do they spend very many hours in the classroom thereafter. Meanwhile, our "reformers" think that if we lengthen the school day ... and the school year, too ... we'll catch up with the Swedes and the Koreans and whoever else on (yes) test scores. (Again: Aaargh ...)

Fanatic. I am an ... Accountability Fanatic. I'M NO SOFTY. Not in my business practices. Nor in my life. I demand performance and accountability ... from myself, first and foremost, and from others as well. But real-world performance and "test-taking performance" are two entirely different things. Standardized tests are but one form of evaluation—and a highly abnormal one at that.

> ## STUFFING AND PUFFING
>
> Mark Edmundson, who teaches English at the University of Virginia, wrote this in the *New York Times Magazine* as the 2002 school year began: "Genuinely great teaching—the sort of thing that Socrates and his spiritual descendants have delivered—is exactly what the American education establishment is now working to discourage. Many of us are being told that our primary task is to prepare students for fact-based tests, to stuff our charges with information, like Christmas birds. We are also being pressured to act as uncritical supporters, sometimes even cheerleaders, for our students. We are encouraged to inflate our grades, pushed to turn our recommendations into exercises in Madison Ave. puffery, urged never to say or even imply a critical word about students."

"Absurd and Anti-Life": Classes for "the Masses"

Classrooms are abnormal places, unless you dream of a career as a prison guard. They have nothing whatsoever to do with the Real World. Nothing to do with the Real World ... at the age of two months ... at the age of 72 years. Classrooms stunt learning. Tragedy: Millions never recover from the experience!

"The best evidence that our schools are set up to 'school' and not be useful educationally lies in the look of the rooms where we confine kids," writes John Taylor Gatto. "Rooms with no clocks or mirrors, no telephones, no fax machines, no stamps, no envelopes, no maps, no directories, no private space in which to think, no conference tables on which to confer. Rooms in which there isn't any real way to contact the outside world where life is going on."

"It is absurd and anti-life to be compelled to sit in confinement with people of exactly the same age and social class," Gatto continues acerbically. "This ... cuts children off from the immense diversity of life and the synergy of variety. ...

It is absurd and anti-life to move from cell to cell[6] at the sound of a gong every day of your natural youth in an institution that allows you no privacy. ... In centuries past, children and adolescents would spend their time in real work, real charity, real adventures, and in the search for mentors who might teach them what they really wanted to learn."

Schools, John Taylor Gatto observes, "create Kafka-like rituals." They ...

- "Enforce sensory deprivation on classes of children held in featureless rooms."
- "Sort children into rigid categories by the use of fantastic measures like age grading, or standardized test scores."

"JAILHOUSE" RANT
[6]"Every time I pass a jailhouse or a school," writes Jimmy Breslin, the prickly *Newsday* columnist, "I feel sorry for the people inside." The context: Breslin was critiquing "summer school" in New York. He continues: "If they haven't learned in the winter, what are they going to remember from days when they should be swimming?"

- "Train children to drop whatever they are occupied with and move as a body from room to room at the sound of a bell, buzzer, horn or klaxon."
- "Keep children under constant surveillance, depriving them of private time and space."
- "Assign children numbers constantly, feigning the ability to discriminate qualities quantitatively."
- "Insist that every moment of time be filled with low-level abstraction."
- "Forbid children their own discoveries, pretending to possess some vital secret which children must surrender their active learning time to acquire."

"The time bomb in every classroom," laments Frank Smith in *Insult to Intelligence*, "is that students learn exactly what they're taught." And schools spend most of their time contriving contexts in which kids learn *not to like* particular subjects. Research shows that such brilliant anti-learning sticks! Standardized testing mostly teaches kids that they are not competent. And so they drop out of science ... they drop out of math. The school system really does accomplish something, after all: It *discourages* large numbers of competent human beings from exploring things they might actually care about.[7]

"Pre-Fabricated": Teaching Means *Reaching*

In a class of 25, there are 25 totally different learning trajectories ... 25 totally different journeys-in-progress. Each kid is a ... Totally Unique Case ... proceeding from a Different Place ... to a Different Place ... at a Different Pace. Learning is idiosyncratic. All cognitive research is in agreement: Different people learn at very different rates and in very different ways. Some people learn pictorially. Some people learn abstractly. Whatever. Sadly, the school system doesn't get that. At all. Isn't designed for it. At all. Ignores it. Dismisses it. Dismisses those who don't "learn at the same rate" as everybody else."

It is an inescapable reality," argues Ted Sizer, brilliant educator and creator of the Coalition of Essential Schools, "that students learn at different rates in often differing ways. That creates the need for a schedule of sensitivity that only the teachers close to the students can devise—not some theory-driven central-office, computer-managed schedule."

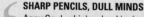

SHARP PENCILS, DULL MINDS
Anny Gaul, a high school junior from Charlotte, North Carolina, wrote the following in the *Charlotte Observer*: "While it is true that some sort of evaluative measure must be implemented to gauge the progress of our students and the effectiveness of our teachers, as a student I've found that if we aren't careful, a classroom can be transformed from a haven for the education of young minds to a factory for producing automaton test-takers (complete with two well-sharpened No. 2 pencils and a sheet of blank paper for scratch work). Education is a privilege; we live in a society in which learning should be held as sacred, not something that is considered to be ultimately quantifiable or reduced to a selection of multiple-choice responses."

THAT'S ALL SHE ROTE
[7]Let me revise what I wrote at the start of this section. Maybe classrooms *are* like the Real World—that is, the old Real World. Rote tasks in the standardized factory. (Blue-collar Real World.) Rote tasks in the standardized cubicles of the office tower. (White-collar Real World.) The problem, of course: Robots will soon do all that. But for humans, doing rote work will (mostly) not be an option.

We get it wrong.
All wrong.
Backwards.
Completely backwards. Tragically ... perversely ...
ass-backwards.

Teachers need enough time and flexibility to get to know kids as individuals. Teaching is about one and only one thing: Getting to *know* the child. Getting inside his or her psyche. Getting close enough to learn something about his or her learning trajectory, learning style. *Partnering* (BIG WORD) with him or her in a unique learning-exploration-growth experience. This is not done in bitty chunks. This is de facto psychotherapy. WHY DON'T WE GET IT RELATIVE TO THE DESIGN OF THE SCHOOL SYSTEM?

One factor contributing to widespread teacher dissatisfaction, Gatto writes, "is the extremely shallow nature of intellectual enterprise in schools. Ideas are broken into fragments called subjects, subjects into units, units into sequences, sequences into lessons, lessons into homework, and all these pre-fabricated pieces make a classroom teacherproof."

The logic is clear. Frightening. (I use that word ... "frightening" ... with extreme care.) Ted Sizer captures it: "If we spend more than a day on the Bill of Rights, we can't get to Grover Cleveland by Valentine's Day."

Learning in 40-minute blocks is ... Utter Bullshit. You don't learn in 40-minute blocks.[8] The research is clear. Common sense is clear. Every damned idiot understands it. Except for the idiots who run the school "system."

Ted Sizer comments: "We parade adolescents in groups before teachers for snippets of time. Any one teacher will usually see more than 100 students and often more than 160 in a day. Such a system denies teachers the chance to know many students well ... to know how a particular student's mind works."

In *Insult to Intelligence*, Frank Smith echoes Sizer: "The myth is that learning can be guaranteed if instruction is delivered systematically, one small piece at a time, with frequent tests to insure that students and teachers stay on task."

Question Time: Learning to Learn

Management guru Karl Weick says the most important thing a leader can say in these turbulent times is "I DON'T KNOW." He explains the point thus: "'I don't know' is the ultimate license to one's followers to explore, to ask open-ended questions ... create novel frameworks for viewing the world ... take risks ... and figure it out for themselves."

THE "REST" OF THE STORY

[8]And hey, if you're going to cut up the school day into tiny, rigidly defined periods, at least give kids a break between chunks-o'-learning. Here, believe it or not, American educators can learn a lot from the Japanese. The Japanese school system is way too rote in its design. But it gets one thing right: Japanese kids have recesses ... *after every class*. That makes sense. It is not normal for a growing child ... in particular, a growing boy (it's a gene thing) ... to be strapped into a chair for five or six hours straight.

Recess after every period!

Amen.

TO "TEACH HIS OWN"

Every kid is different. So is every teacher. And that's a good thing. Parker Palmer frames that point superbly in his book *The Courage to Teach*:

"It [is] impossible to claim that all good teachers use similar techniques: some lecture nonstop and others speak very little; some stay close to their material and others loose the imagination; some teach with the carrot and others with the stick. *But in every story I have heard, good teachers share one trait: a strong sense of personal identity infuses their work. 'Dr. A. is really there when she teaches.' 'Mr. B. has such enthusiasm for his subject.' 'You can tell that this is really Prof. C's life.'* ... One student said she could not describe her good teachers because they differed so greatly, one from another. But she could describe her bad teachers because they were all the same: 'Their words float somewhere in front of their faces, like the balloon speech in cartoons.'"

Stability is dead. Education must therefore prepare young people for an unknowable, ambiguous, rapidly changing future. Which means that "learning to learn" is far more important than mastering a static body of "facts."

Alas, the classroom rarely works according to that principle. The traditional logic: Teachers are "experts" who "have the answers"—and aim to ensure that students mimic those answers. Posthaste. And especially on Test Day.

Frank Smith quotes Richard Paul, director of the Center for Critical Thinking and Moral Critique, on this point: "We need to shift the focus of learning from simply teaching students to have the right answer to teaching them the process by which educated people pursue right answers."

Great teachers are great learners, not great "fact-imparters." They are, in effect, "co-learners" with their students. That's what great teachers tell me. The incompetent, fearful, hesitant ones are "fact-imparting machines." They play it by the Ford Model: Hammering Facts Down The Constricted Throats of Innocents. (Preparing for the "Teach To Test" moment ... no doubt!)

Roger Schank, in *The Connoisseur's Guide to the Mind*, writes, "Actual content may not be the issue at all, since we are really trying to impart the idea that one can deal with new areas of knowledge if one knows how to learn, how to find out about what is known, and how to abandon old ideas when they are worn out. This means teaching ways of developing *good questions* rather than memorizing known answers, an idea that traditional school systems simply don't cotton to at all, and that traditional testing methods are unprepared to handle."

If "learning" is more about "good questions" than "correct answers," consider this from Christopher Phillips's *Socrates Café*: "Questions, questions, questions. They

---

SIZE MATTERS (SORT OF)

Yet another nostrum of the "school reform" movement: smaller classes. In fact, though, class size doesn't really correlate to educational efficacy. Some teachers can't handle seven kids. Some handle 27 brilliantly. Some can handle 37.

But there is something to say about size. Namely: school size. Small schools—those with around 100 students—are "intimate communities" where learning tends to flourish. Giant schools are impersonal. And impersonality begets problems. Discipline problems. Attendance problems. Learning problems.

Big classes are slightly problematic. (Perhaps.) But big schools stink. (Totally.)

disturb. They provoke. They exhilarate. They intimidate. They make you feel a little bit like you've at least temporarily lost your marbles. So much so that at times I'm positive that the ground is shaking and shifting under our feet ... . *Welcome to Socrates Café."*

("Socrates Café" refers to gatherings in which, following the rules of Socratic dialogue, people examine the trivial and the grand, with extraordinary learning and growth experiences the outcome for many of the participants. It hinges on one thing: Questions, questions, and more questions.)

Phillips's book is not about school; or, rather, it is about *real* school: life. About exploration. About learning. About learning forever. Which is all about ... that thing which is, alas, anathema in the classroom ... *QUESTIONS!*

Easy as ABC: Learning Is Natural

As I began writing this chapter, my wife and I had just added a "child" to our family. The human kids are ages 18 and 22. The rest of our family are dogs. Rosie, age 8. Hummer, age 5. And now ... Wally, age 10 weeks. I have seldom had so much fun as I did watching Wally ... "educate himself." Watching Wally "learn." Wally has found his way to the front door. Wally has learned how to deal with Hummer, his fellow Australian shepherd, who accepts him ... and with Rosie, a Collie who doesn't accept him at all. He learns by the minute. (He learns *by the second.*) Learning is all-important to him. His "survival" in our "family" depends on it.

The way God's creatures learn their way around is ... amazing ... *IF YOU OPEN YOUR EYES.*

I'm naïve. I'm not a "professional" educator. But I know this as much as anyone knows anything: We do not ever need to "teach" children how to ... *learn*. Children *know* how to learn! It's in the genes! Learning *is* natural! Learning *is* normal! For Wally. And for little boy George. And for little girl Jane. Learning is "what we do." It's both our avocation and vocation. We do it ... at age 7. We do it ... at age 77. The only folks who've made learning hard are ... the Proprietors of the School System.

"Education," George Leonard writes in *Education and Ecstasy,* "at best, is ... ECSTATIC. AT ITS BEST, ITS MOST UNFETTERED, THE MOMENT OF LEARNING IS A MOMENT OF ... DELIGHT.[9] This essential and obvious truth is demonstrated for us every day by the baby and the preschool child. ... When joy is absent, the effectiveness of the learning process falls and falls until the human being is operating hesitatingly, grudgingly, fearfully." (I am deeply enamored of George Leonard. Read his stuff. Please.)

I'm 60. I recently read every damn single word of David McCullough's 736-page,

NEW BUSINESS ● NEW PEOPLE

CHAPIN'S MARCH

[9]My 10th-grade history teacher, Mr. Chapin, was a Civil War fanatic. He spent almost a full year on that conflict. Much of the rest of American history was dumped in service to his passion. Did I miss out on learning "facts" about other periods in U.S. history? Surely. Would that gap in knowledge have hurt me on a standardized test? No doubt. But ... I was exposed to in-depth, passionate analysis of a topic for the first time in my life. No, it didn't make me a Civil War buff. It did much more: It made me a "deep analysis" buff, and a history buff.

I'm intensely interested in the 15 years following the Revolutionary War. I've probably read 75 books on the topic. I still don't know half, or a tenth, of what I'd like to know about. But I'm working ... like the dickens ... on that 15-year period. That's what real learning is all about.

best-selling work *John Adams*. I loved it! Loved it because my education in history is not what it ought to be. Loved it because ... *I LOVE LEARNING!*

And as I've studied education (education at its best), I've learned ... that I'm not as cool or as different as I thought I was. Because: *EVERYBODY LOVES LEARNING*.

Harvard education professor Howard Gardner, in *The Unschooled Mind*, says, "During the first years of life,[10] youngsters all over the world master a breathtaking array of competencies with little formal tutelage." Hmmm.

"We underrate our brains and our intelligence"[11] writes Frank Smith in *Insult to Intelligence*. "Formal education has become such a complicated, self-conscious and over-regulated activity that learning is widely regarded as something difficult that the brain would rather not do. ... Such a belief is probably well-founded if the teachers are referring to their efforts to keep children moving through the instructional sequences that are prescribed as learning activities in schools. ... *We are all capable of huge and unsuspected learning accomplishments without effort.*"

"Care" Curriculum: Learning Stuff That Matters

Learning. It's so damn simple. We learn ... like hell ... when we *want* to learn. And don't learn a damn thing ... no matter what the "consequences" might be ... if it isn't interesting, exciting, fun, and relevant.

Do you doubt that the appetite for learning is insatiable? Well, you've got a point—if your focus is on *classroom* learning. But learning is as normal as can be, even for the most apathetic adolescent. Consider a typical 16-year-old who also happens to be on the junior-varsity football squad. He has a tough time staying awake during English and Math. But he can learn a dozen new and intricate plays in an hour and a half ... when he trots onto the practice field at 2:45 p.m. each day. Why: It matters! It's salient! He's engaged!

"Children learn what makes sense to them," Frank Smith continues. "They learn through the sense of things they want to understand." Smith adds that young children who are, like my new dog Wally, essentially *on the make* (they must learn in order to make their way in the world) ... are "informavores" who "eat up new knowledge."

LEARN, BABY, LEARN

[10]Our most amazing, and most important, "learning achievement"—the mastery of our native language—does not require any schooling whatsoever. Indeed, it doesn't even require "teachers" who are particularly competent. Most parents are lousy linguistics teachers. And yet most kids pick up their native language with incredible speed, with awesome skill, and without much in the way of "instruction." How do they do it? They do it because they are built to learn, and because they have a ... *desperate need to know*.

Language acquisition by children at nine months of age is the best example of why the school system (as we have configured it) is silly.

HOME TRUTH

[11]"I want to give you a yardstick," writes John Taylor Gatto, "a gold standard, by which to measure good schooling. The Shelter Institute in Bath, Maine will teach you how to build a 3,000-square-foot multi-level Cape Cod home in three weeks' time, whatever your age. If you stay another week, it will show you how to make your own posts and beams; you'll actually cut them out and set them up. You'll learn wiring, plumbing, insulation, the works. Twenty thousand people have learned how to build a house there for about the cost of one month's tuition in public school."

I love that: "Informavores." "Eat up New Knowledge." Learning happens fast. It happens insanely fast ... WHEN IT MATTERS.

"Learning," says Smith, "is never divorced from feelings." Smith goes on to provide us with what he labels "The Learners' Manifesto":

The brain is always learning.
Learning does not require coercion.
Learning must be meaningful.
Learning is incidental.
Learning is collaborative.
The consequences of worthwhile learning are obvious.
Learning always involves feelings.
Learning must be free of risk.

As James Coleman put it in 1974, Education must "develop in youth the capabilities for engaging in intensive, concentrated involvement in an activity."

Stop. Reread that phrase: "*... capabilities for engaging in intensive, concentrated involvement in an activity.*" That's how you become a chess champion! Or a medalist sprinter! Or a great operatic performer! Or a great heart surgeon! Whatever!

Mihaly Csikszentmihalyi and Barbara Schneider expand on that point in their extraordinary book *Becoming Adult*: "Without the enthusiasm that leads to intense, concentrated activity, a child will likely lack the perseverance ... needed to face the future successfully. We may not know what jobs will be available to young people ten years from now. ... But to the extent that teenagers have had experiences that demand discipline, require skillful use of mind and body, and give them a sense of responsibility and involvement with useful goals, we might expect the youth of today to be ready to face the challenges of tomorrow."

Stop. Reread that entire passage. Every word in that quote rings clear and true. The essence of a genuine education is the ability to learn continuously ... and enthusiastically. Perhaps that quality wasn't so critical in the era dominated by Bismarck and Ford and Rockefeller, by Big Companies and Jobs-For-Life. But it *is* critical now.

There is nothing "lightweight" about this idea. It is not about "doing your own thing" or "letting it all hang out." It is about focus and commitment. The message: *Become purposeful! Do the stuff that makes a difference to you! Get an (independent) life!*

School Play—or School *Versus* Play

Hubert B. Herring wrote, in an essay called "Sometimes, Second Place for Homework":

"There are, last I heard, still only 24 hours in a high school student's day. Into those hours must be crammed school, homework, chilling with friends, piano lessons, talking on the phone, tennis practice, a bare minimum of sleep and perhaps a few minutes of

LEARNING AS PLAY
Psychologist Edward de Bono: "Children should be taught in an active way by doing things and playing games. It's very different than what is taught in schools, which involves sitting back and absorbing information."

NEW BUSINESS ! NEW PEOPLE

ADULT (RE)EDUCATION

> Csikszentmihalyi and Schneider go on: "Growing up to be a happy adult gets more difficult as occupational roles become more vague and ephemeral. ... Young people can no longer count on a predictable future and cannot expect that a set of skills learned in school will be sufficient to ensure a comfortable career. For this reason we need to take a long look at the conditions that prepare youth for a changing, uncertain future."

quality time grudgingly bestowed on parents.

"It is all a bit like an overstuffed school backpack, and all pretty routine. The schoolwork grinds on, igniting a spark here, a spark there—but usually not much more.

"But what happens when some huge passion smacks into this tightly interlocked schedule like a fireball? (And no, I'm not talking about boy-girl matters; that fireball, from a planet of its own, is something else entirely.)

"It might be a love of dance or ancient Greek, a devotion to soccer, even a mania for chess, that ultimate mental Stairmaster. But whatever it is, how can it be allowed to burn brightly without devouring much in its path, like essential homework time or sleep?

"Let it devour, I say. ...

"How often are today's overscheduled, under-stimulated students swept away by something they can truly sink their teeth into—not to mention their hearts and souls?

"Just such a fireball made a direct hit on our house not too long ago, when our daughter had the great good fortune to land a leading role in the high school production of 'Camelot,' causing an exuberant disruption in our household for a good many exhausting weeks. ...

"I can think of nothing ... that matches the intensity, the sheer number of hours, of rehearsing for a lead role in a musical. ... When she was in her room, supposedly studying biology or history, we would suddenly hear strains of 'Lusty Month of May' or 'I Loved You Once in Silence' wafting through the door. Some homework did not get done as well as it should have been. Some exam grades left a bit to be desired. She even started missing her beloved 'Gilmore Girls.' (Now that's a sacrifice for art.) As the rehearsal pace picked up, dance classes were missed and piano lessons were stuffed into odd corners of the week. ...

"But the triumph of the performance weekend made it all worth it. Even if her grades had suffered greatly—which in the end, miraculously, they didn't—the soaring experience she got would have been more important. ...

"If she sticks to her passion for performing, she will be choosing a frighteningly

---

LEARN ONE FOR THE GIPPER

I recollect tuning in to an interview with a former Notre Dame football coach. He was asked, "How do you motivate your players?" His response: "I don't 'motivate' my players. What I work hard to do is not *de*-motivate them. They come with 'motivation.' I try like the dickens not to switch it off."

I probably butchered the quote, but I haven't butchered the idea. The man was right. My dog Wally is motivated as hell to learn ... at an incredible speed. And so is a five-year-old. And so is the 78-year-old. What we must work like hell to do is not to de-motivate people from learning.

tough career, and we have told her that. But there is no way we will be like those parents who struggle to fit a round peg in a square hole, insisting that a born dancer go to medical or law school (or stuffing a born lawyer into toe shoes).

"We may nudge a bit here, sand the peg a bit there, make sure college is in the mix. But beyond that, the passion's the thing."

The Apprentice's Source: WOW Projects (Redux)

On the topic of salience, Howard Gardner touts the importance of "apprenticeships and projects" in effective education. They are the meat and potatoes in "real" life, especially in the New Economy. Whether it's an aspiration to go to the Olympics, or to be elected to the local school board, or to do something extraordinary with an IS project that confronts us in the Finance Department.

Apprenticeships. Projects. Those experiences define what we have learned ... and how we have applied it to something we care about. They mark us. And they form the essence of ... Brand You. That is, after all, Life 101. Especially ... life in these new, extraordinary, uncertain, and ambiguous days.

"If we were to configure an education ... for the world of tomorrow," Prof. Gardner adds, "we need to take the lessons of the museum and the relationship of the apprenticeship extremely seriously ... to think of the ways in which the strengths of a museum atmosphere, of apprenticeship learning, and of engaging projects can pervade all educational environments."

Why not?

Obvious answer: It's hard. It requires ... *Imaginative* Teachers. It requires ... *trust in* teachers. It requires a "hands-off" policy by armies of nit-picking central ed staffers.

Gardner also notes how science, in particular, really makes sense only in the context of hands-on project work. In *The Unschooled Mind*, he cites studies done at MIT and Johns Hopkins University and concludes: "Students who receive honor grades in college-level physics courses are frequently unable to solve basic problems encountered in a form slightly different from that on which they have been formally instructed and tested."

In other words, the scientific-discovery process and the teaching of science are utterly at odds. Scientific discovery is about ... open-ended exploration. Scientific "teaching," alas, is all too often about spoon-fed "facts." John Taylor Gatto echoes that critique: "A substantial amount of testimony exists from highly regarded scientists like [Nobel laureate] Richard Feynman that scientific discovery is negatively related to the procedures of school science classes."[12]

HOOPER'S LAW

[12]My 11th-grade physics teacher, Mr. Hooper, taught me that science is not a slew of facts, but a way of life. He had come to education from industry, and was (as I recall) a co-inventor of one of the first workable automatic-transmission systems, the revolutionary Buick Dynaflow.

I don't think he ever gave us a "textbook" assignment. Instead, he had us do our own projects—and then he'd guide us back toward "inventing" the math that would explain what we'd just done.

Short Answer: Educational Models That Work

In the spirit of true education, my focus here has mostly been on questions, not answers. Still, it is fair to ask: What specific examples of great educational initiatives can one point to? A couple of cases come to mind.

First, there is John Taylor Gatto, who called his classroom the Lab School. In one chapter of his book *A Different Kind of Teacher*, he hands the authorial reins over to a former student of his, 13-year-old Jamahl Watson. Here's how Jamahl delineated the five parts of the Lab School curriculum:

1. **Independent study. One day a week out of the school building, chasing one "big idea."**
2. **An apprenticeship. To somebody. Somewhere.**
3. **Community service. One day a week.**
4. **Teaming up with parents, yours or somebody else's. (Gatto calls this the Family Teamwork Curriculum.)**
5. **A smidgen of "standard" class work.**

Second, there is my friend Dennis Littky, one of America's most brilliant educators. He has brought forth miracles of educational excellence a half-dozen times in his career. Today his bailiwick is the Met School, in Providence, Rhode Island. Two principles define how the school operates: EBI (Education by Interest) and LTI (Learning through Internship). Both are in sharp contrast to standard-issue "EBF"—"Education by Fiat."

The Met School emerged from the transformation of what had been a typically decrepit inner-city school. Students at "the Met" work on Big Projects of their own concoction. They describe and report on those projects to their peers and to highly demanding outsiders as well. They are evaluated on their projects' success. And they find those projects through internships that they must hustle up on their own. The first graduates of this intense internship program finished in 2000. The best measure of how those kids (most of whom were "disadvantaged" by any standard definition): *One hundred percent of them were accepted to college.* "When they tell the stories of their projects," Littky says, "they're irresistible to [college] admissions officers."

Being a student at the Met is not for the faint of heart. Projects and self-developed apprenticeships are demanding. As are the frequent reports thereon. In Dennis Littky's world, accountability is sky-high. Accountability? *Damn right!* Littky's kids must

---

SCHOOL BORED

In his novel *Thinks*, David Lodge offers this wonderful exchange between a scientist ("Messenger") and an English professor ("Helen"):

Messenger: "The mind is a machine, but a *virtual* machine. A system of systems."

Helen: "Perhaps it isn't a system at all."

Messenger: "Oh, but it is. If you're a scientist you have to start from that assumption."

Helen: "I expect that's why I dropped science at school as soon as they let me."

Messenger: "No, you dropped it, I would guess, because it was doled out to you in spoonfuls of distilled boredom."

explain—often and ably—what they've been up to, why they've been up to it, what they've learned, and why it matters. I've had the privilege of spending a bit of time with some of those kids. They are engaged, articulate, and self-assured in ways that I'm not used to seeing among traditionally "educated" high-school students.

My Stubborn Hope: The (Beneficial) Limits of Education

There are thousands upon thousands of inspired teachers ... working like hell ... with little appreciation ... and, often, with little in their every-other-Friday paycheck.

There are hundreds of fabulous schools. Some are our public schools ... in wealthy communities. Some are public schools ... in poverty-stricken communities. Some are charter schools. Some are Waldorf schools. Some are Montessori schools. In fact, there *is* a *lot* of Very Cool Stuff going on in education.

The problem is drift, and the apparent drive of the Educational Establishment ... which focuses on ... Uniformity ... Testing ... Standardization ... and thence ... "schooling" kids into submission.

So is there any hope?

To be honest, I despair. I despair of the education system more than any other part of our society. I can imagine the CIA and FBI and U.S. Army changing to deal with new threats long before I can imagine education changing to deal with the ... New Context.

The great horror in all this, as I've come to see it:

WE KNOW EXACTLY WHAT TO DO.

It's just that we don't do it. Governors want to be able to brag to other governors about percentage increases in test scores, as opposed to kids who actually got educated, kids who went on to become entrepreneurs, kids who went on to become be-medaled sergeants in the Air Force.

Recall the Richard Rosecrance quote from early in this chapter: "Competition among nations will be competition among educational systems." The only "good news", I suppose (and it's perverse), is that no country seems to be doing it right.

An editorial I once read said the only saving grace in U.S. schooling was the fact that throughout history our kids have never shown much respect for their teachers. That's an odd thing to be proud of. But the writer has a point. German kids and Japanese kids practically stand at attention and salute when the teacher walks into the room. Ours don't. We are a nation whose history is based on obstreperousness. This is an Age of

NEW BUSINESS ● NEW PEOPLE

WHO TEACHES THE TEACHERS?

Teacher training programs, a friend of mine deeply involved in them says, attract people who "typically color inside the lines." Sad. (Hey, such institutions used to be called "normal schools"—not, I guess, without reason.) Yes, there are Great Teachers and Great Principals. But they fail to have much sustained impact on the entire system. Therein lies the problem. It isn't so in the private sector. When a "revolutionary" comes along ... a Dell, a Schwab, a Wal*Mart ... the rest of the world stands up and takes notice ... or gets beaned. In the school system, it's the "revolutionary" who gets beaned.

Constant and Revolutionary Change. We need ... more obstreperousness ... than ever. Either we need to drastically change the school system ... or we need to pray that our kids will continue to "disrespect their teachers."

Now, there's a Hobson's choice.[13]

NEW BUSINESS ▮ ● NEW PEOPLE

! Contrasts

WAS	IS
Teach-to-test	Teach to *quest*
Devouring "facts"	Developing talent
SAT prep (Think "multiple choice")	WOW Project (Think individual choice)
Fetishing generic "standards"	Honoring individual creativity
Quiet classrooms	Noisy classrooms
School as factory, with focus on "units"	School as studio, with focus on uniqueness
Turning out docile workers	Building up creative "talent"
Obedience as key virtue	Initiative as key virtue
Teach to a standard "norm" (lowest common denominator)	Teach to a standard of excellence (highest possible achievement)
Focus on similarities	Focus on differences
Test for "intelligence" (singular)	Teach to "intelligences" (multiple)
Math and English dominate	Art and music thrive

SINGLE CHOICE

[13]My choice, though, would definitely be Option A: Let's change the school system. Drastically. And let's start by putting the radicals in charge. If I were king, I would appoint Dennis Littky and John Taylor Gatto and Ted Sizer as co-secretaries of education. Then I'd charge them with attracting as many Radicals and Freaks as possible to the teaching profession.

Freaks change the world! Freaky principals! Freaky teachers! We need freaks! Desperately!

IF YOU HAVE TO ASK ...

I love studying. The harder I study, the more confused I get. The more confused I get, the deeper I want to dig. The deeper I dig ... the better questions I ask.

I've been doing my "thing"—worrying in one way or another about business and management—for 35 years. Fact is, I'm more confused now than I was when I began. And yet I hope, and believe, that I'm asking better questions now than when I started out. Maybe somebody will put that on my tombstone, come to think of it:

Thomas J. Peters
1942–????
He Kept Asking Better
and More
Annoying Questions

"Out of the box?" Burn the box!
Re-imagine! Call it: Leaders' Job One!

new bus!ness
new mandate

New times call for ... a New Mandate. Shake free of the past—including past successes—and re-imagine your entire way of doing business. The point is not to "push the envelope" or to "think outside the box." The point is ... to *rip* up the envelope and to *burn* the box.

My problem with both traditional phrases (other than their overuse): They suggest that there is an intact envelope or sturdy box from whose known borders we can simply step out. But the envelope is torn and crumpled, and the box has been run over by a careening 16-wheel truck.

Our task in this concluding section: Think "weird." (Re)think "excellence." Re-imagine "leadership."

Good luck ...

THINK WEIRD: THE HIGH VALUE-ADDED BEDROCK

! Technicolor Rules ...

- Hang out with dull ... and you will become dull. Hang out with weird ... and you will become weird.
- We are in an Age of High Standard Deviation. All kinds of Strange Stuff is going on. All kinds of Strange Competitors are popping up. All kinds of Strange Alliances are being formed. How do we deal with such strangeness? Get strange!
- Innovation Source No. 1 is Pissed-Off People—people who are unable to deal with the silliness they see around them.
- Fire the planners. Hire the freaks.

! RANT

We are not prepared ...

We champion innovation. Then we genuflect when a giant customer "urges" us to cancel a risky new product that would upset the status quo. We beg for "more risk taking." Then we videotape the "be daring" speech featuring the boss in a Brooks Brothers suit, sitting stiffly behind an old oaken desk. We exhort people to "get with the new technologies." Then we require them to work with only "safe" vendors. (No wonder the "innovative organization" remains a chimera!)

! VISION

I imagine ...

A sales team that exerts as much energy to land "the Strange Account" as it does to land "the Big Account."

A hiring manager who says to interviewees, "Describe the weirdest project you've ever undertaken, and how you managed to live to tell the tale."

A purchasing boss who looks for suppliers who will not just fill Ongoing By-the-Book Needs, but also present Emerging Off-the-Wall Opportunities.

A CEO who insists that his board of directors include, along with the usual aging-white-male yes-men, a goodly allotment of freaks—men and women of every stripe who can't say "yes" without also saying "but ..."

With a Little Help from My (Freaky) Friends

Along about 1984, I was stuck in a rut. My thinking was mired in the giant-company theory and practice that I'd acquired at McKinsey & Co.

Then I got lucky. I met Frank Perdue, of Perdue Farms. And Roger Milliken, of Milliken & Co. And Bill and Vieve Gore, of W. L. Gore. And Tom Monaghan, of Domino's Pizza. And Les Wexner, of The Limited. And Don Burr, of People Express. And Anita Roddick, of The Body Shop.

I began to hang out with those and other feisty, we-can-change-the-world-and-damn-well-are-changing-it-and-isn't-that-a-kick characters. And guess what? Their spirit rubbed off on me. I was dragged into their quirky world.

And I've never looked back!

Along the way, I picked up a hard lesson: INNOVATION IS EASY.

Call me insane. I can handle that. But kindly hear me out. "Innovation"—the sine qua non of achieving excellence in a disruptive age—is easy. Not hard.

Fundamental proposition: Hang out with weird ... *and you will become more weird.* Hang out with dull *... and you will become more dull.*

Could it really be that simple? I think so.

Though I have often been called an "organizational change consultant," I don't much believe in change. I don't much believe that launching a "strategic initiative" or creating a "brilliant training program" will suddenly cause people to lose their fear of failure, to become entrepreneurial, or whatever.

What I do believe is that if I can force myself into contact with "strange things"[1] ... then those strange things will drag me, willingly or not, toward something new and thrilling, something weird and wonderful. I will change because of one and only one thing: I've been forced to!

The "Big" Problem: Poor Little Rich Company

In 2002, *Advertising Age* claimed that domestic sales are declining in 20 of Procter & Gamble's 26 major product categories—including 7 of the top 10 categories.

Staggering!

What's the reason? Some analysts point in particular to what they call the "billion-dollar problem": Given P&G's enormous size, the company rarely looks at a new

---

{ **BACK TO THE (FREAKY) FUTURE**
[1]Recall the basic formula for starting a WOW Projects epidemic (Chapter 17): You, the boss, don't have to do anything. You just need to find those who are already doing Cool Things, mostly on the sly—and then publicly label them as the Wave of the Future.

Same idea here: Right now, in 2003, there are people who are, in effect, already living 2013. You don't have to do a damn thing. You don't have to "launch a strategic initiative." You just need to find those people, and then allow them to drag you—kicking and screaming if necessary—into the Brilliant & Bizarre Future.

product opportunity unless it has humongous potential. And in this case, "humongous" means ... about a billion bucks.

But therein lies a problem. Anything with "demonstrated" billion-dollar potential is, almost by definition, "more of the same"—more of the same kind of product, sold in mostly the same way to the same kind of people whom P&G has sold to in the past. In times of change, big companies—enamored of "me-too" focus groups, and devoted to over-sized products aimed at over-sized customers—are doomed to a future of waddling after slow growth.

Simple and oft demonstrated fact from the world of world-flipping innovation: Things that alter the world invariably enter by the side door. A small group of pioneering customers ("early adopters"),[2] paired with a pioneering vendor, act as flag bearers for the rest of the world.

Disruptive Criticism: Being Safe *and* Sorry

The most articulate spokesman for the perils of "playing it safe" is TBWA/Chiat/Day CEO Jean-Marie Dru. He summarized his views in a magnificent book called *Disruption* ... which he followed up with another magnificent book called *Beyond Disruption*. Dru claims there are three primary obstacles that keep companies from adopting "disruptive" strategies:

1. *Fear of "cannibalism."* Companies worry that introducing a Cool Product might "confuse" the marketplace and impinge on sales of their current market leaders. (Presumably, as in the case of P&G, even if those "leaders" are declining in sales.)

2. An *"excessive cult of the consumer."* Too great an emphasis on a "customer driven" approach results in "slavery to demographics, market research and focus groups." Could that old stand-by, "listening to customers,"[3] really be the No. 1 sin in marketing? Well, that's more or less what Dru says, and I think he's more or less right. Account planning at ad agencies, says TBWA/Chiat/Day creative director Lee Clow, "has become 'focus group balloting.'"

3. The *"sustainable advantage"* seduction. Sustainable advantage, Dru contends, is a snare, a myth, a delusion. Instead companies should focus on achieving a Current Advantage—and then pray they can hold onto it long enough to invent something new.

The Next Weird Thing

The statistical term "standard deviation" stands for, approximately, *the average difference from the average among a given set of observations.* A "low" standard

---

SMALL IS BANKABLE
[2]Seth Godin, writing in a February 2003 *Fast Company* article: "Think small. One vestige of the TV-industrial complex is a need to think mass. If it doesn't appeal to everyone, the thinking goes, it's not worth it. ... Think of the smallest conceivable market and describe a product that overwhelms it with its remarkability. Go from there."

THE CUSTOMER IS ALWAYS LATE
[3]Who wanted Post-it notes? Nobody, for a dozen years. Then they became inevitable. Who wanted fax machines? Nobody, for the longest time. Then a critical mass of "pioneering users" came along—and traffic began to soar. Who wanted CDs? Nobody, or at least none of us who had just been through the transformation from phonograph records to tapes. Then our kids started using CDs—and we noticed that the quality of the sound was awesome. Ka-boom.

deviation signals a very "tight" distribution: All the observations are close together. A "high" standard deviation," on the other hand, connotes a very "loose" distribution: The observations are all over the map.

Using this language, I would argue that we are in an Age of High Standard Deviation. All kinds of weird stuff is going on. All kinds of weird competitors are popping up—terrorists, in the realm of national defense; upstarts like Dell and Wal*Mart and eBay, in the realm of commerce.

How do we deal with weirdness? Get weird! We need to introduce ... Weirdness in Our Midst. Weird employees. Weird customers. Weird vendors. Weird alliance partners. Weird members on Boards of Directors. And so on.

The main idea, then, is incredibly simple (and, I am quite sure, incredibly powerful): Hang with the dull ... and you become dull. Dreadfully dull. Hang with the weird ... and you become weird. Wonderfully weird.

I will go way out, to the end of the limb, and argue that this is the *only* surefire strategy for ... Continual Personal Renewal and Radical Organizational Innovation.

Weird Customers: Always Check the Sell-By Date

"Future-defining customers may account for only 2 percent to 3 percent of your total, "concedes Adrian Slywotzky of Mercer Management Consulting. But, he adds, "They represent a crucial window on the future." In sum, Slywotzky writes: "The future has already happened. It's just not evenly distributed." (Sounds like a fellow statistician!)

So what ... EXACTLY ... have you done to insure that your Portfolio of Customers includes "four-sigma weirdos?" I am encouraging you, actually begging you, to measure ... quantitatively ... each customer in that portfolio. ARE THERE ENOUGH FREAKS ON BOARD? (Warning: If you find yourself unable to sign up freakish customers, then your product or service portfolio really *is* in trouble!)

DULL CUSTOMERS = DULL YOU.

COOL CUSTOMERS = COOL YOU.

Weird Competitors: Don't Fence Yourself In

I'm not a fan of "benchmarking." To be sure, I believe in "learning"—from anybody and everybody. I readily admit that's the useful idea behind benchmarking. But here is my (BIG) problem: In nine cases out of ten, benchmarking is done against the "industry leader." A GM, say, measures its supply-chain management practices against Toyota. Or some such. While I'll acknowledge that Toyota still probably has the drop on GM in

---

CONSUMER RETORTS

Joseph Morone, President of Bentley College and former dean of the RPI business school: "If you worship at the throne of the voice of the customer, you'll get only incremental advances."

Doug Atkin, a partner at Merkley Newman Harty: "These days, you can't succeed as a company if you're consumer-led—because, in a world so full of so much constant change, consumers can't anticipate the next big thing. Companies should be *idea*-led and consumer-*informed*."

supply-chain practices, they aren't the right "benchmark." "Benchmarking" is cool—but only if that benchmark is a truly cool,[4] far-out, four-sigma (six-sigma!?) organization ... doing something wild and wacky and oh-so-2013.

The first member of the Loyal Opposition to Benchmarking was arguably none other than Mark Twain. "The best swordsman in the world doesn't need to fear the second-best swordsman in the world," Twain wrote. "No, the person for him to be afraid of is some ignorant antagonist who has never had a sword in his hand before; he doesn't do the thing he ought to do, and so the expert isn't prepared for him; he does the thing he ought not to do, and often it catches the expert out and ends him on the spot."

I came across the Twain quotation shortly after the tragedy of 9/11; it gave me the cold shivers.

Our military managed itself around defending us against the Soviet Union. And yet we have begun the new century/millennium with one of the most supreme challenges in our nation's history—from, in effect, "some ignorant antagonist who has never had a sword in his hand before ... [who] doesn't do the thing he ought to do, and so the expert isn't prepared for him."

That *does* give one cause for the shakes, no?

On a more mundane note, Twain's description is also the best analysis I've come across of the problems that beset formerly invincible IBM during the 1980s. Many say IBM was arrogant and complacent. My contact with them would support the arrogant idea, but I don't buy the complacent bit for a minute. IBM always ... by design ... quaked in its boots. The problem (not unlike the military's problem): IBM was quaking over the wrong enemy.

The "invincible" firm had watched "invincible" Detroit humbled by brilliant competitors from Japan and Germany. Hence, as I hung about IBM in the early 1980s, the Giant was mortified by the threats from Germany's Siemens and Japan's Fujitsu.

THE GOAL STANDARD

[4]When Jacques Nasser was CEO at Ford, he "benchmarked." And I applauded. Why? His "benchmark" was Dell! That is, a company *outside* his rather screwed-up industry.

Likewise, the U.S. Marine Corps is benchmarking its supply-chain activities against ... Wal*Mart. Again, I applaud.

(DON'T) FOLLOW THE LEADER

Seth Godin, in *Fast Company*: "You can't be remarkable by following someone else who's remarkable. One way to figure out a great theory is to look at what's working in the real world and determine what the successes have in common. ... But what could the Four Seasons and Motel 6 possibly have in common? Or Neiman Marcus and Wal*Mart? Or Nokia (bringing out new hardware every 30 days or so) and Nintendo (marketing the same Game Boy for 14 years in a row)? It's like trying to drive looking in the rearview mirror. The thing that all those companies have in common is that they have nothing in common. They are outliers. They're on the fringes. Superfast or superslow. Very exclusive or very cheap. Extremely big or extremely small. The reason it's so hard to follow the leader is this: The leader is the leader precisely because he did something remarkable. And that remarkable thing is now taken—so it's no longer remarkable when you decide to do it."

Meanwhile, a bunch of geeky kids—with names like Gates and Jobs and with hair and sideburns ever-so-long—reinvented the industry right out from under IBM's feet. To be sure, IBM made a remarkable recovery during the 1990s, but it was touch and go prior to Lou Gerstner's makeover.

Message Twain: Do you have the truly weird, upstart competitors in the center of your radar screen? The next generation of Bill Gates, Steve Jobs, Charles Schwabs, Ned Johnsons, Michael Dells, Les Wexners ... and, yes, Osama bin Ladens? Benchmark? Sure! But first, identify the fringe players worthy of benchmarking against. Then track them, engage them in joint ventures; perhaps even follow the Cisco-Microsoft-Omnicom Model ... and buy them!

DULL COMPETITORS = DULL YOU.
COOL COMPETITORS = COOL YOU.

Weird People: Hire for Latitude

While I've never met him, I'm told that Craig Venter is a bit of a pain. (Some colleagues of his have told me that "a bit" is understatement.) Venter was CEO of Celera Genomics, the upstart that successfully mapped the human genome—and in the process embarrassed the much better-funded Human Genome Project.

I had the opportunity to address the leadership of a giant pharmaceutical company's laboratories. At one point, I asked, "Do you think that Craig Venter would have come to work for you?" Few questions, I would contend, are more important: Can you—especially those of you in "established" companies—attract the prickly likes of Craig Venter?

At a business leadership roundtable in London a few years ago, I witnessed an extraordinary exchange. Among those present was an old friend who was a senior professor of business strategy in Sweden; also in attendance, the top management of a large, revered Swedish technology company. (Incidentally ... now showing signs of age.) Perhaps an extra glass of wine or two, or something stronger, was inhaled. At one point, my friend the professor approached the CEO of the "revered" company and said (*I remember every word*): "I've got about 20 of the sharpest kids in Sweden in my advanced business-strategy seminar. Every one of them tells me he'd sooner die than come to work for you. They're not willing to 'wait their turn' before taking charge of something interesting." There were perhaps 40 of us in the room; my friend hardly boomed his comment. But a hush swept the room and you could have heard that proverbial pin drop.

You know what: MY PAL WAS ON TO SOMETHING! (BIG.)

Established enterprises tend to reject mavericks. Far worse, mavericks[5] wouldn't consider joining them to begin with. Sure, Big Co. has the benefit of "vast resources" and a "vast distribution network." But who the hell cares, if you have to expend 98.6 percent of your youthful energy fighting city hall ... day after day ... week after week ...

LAB TEST

[5]I recall another encounter with a leader from the pharmaceutical industry. This woman, the head of a giant lab, pulled me aside after one of my seminars. "As I was leaving our recent board meeting," she said, "I was accosted by our vice chairman, who once ran R&D. He asked me if I had 'enough weird people' in the labs these days."

It's a "weird time" in the world of pharmaceuticals in general and drug discovery in particular. And: Weird Times call for ... Weird People.

month after month ... year after year?

One of my hobbies is reading about the history of innovation. While I acknowledge that the issue is complex, I also think it offers a rather simple lesson:

Innovation Source No. 1 is Pissed-Off People.

Irritation. Anger. That's *the* source of serious innovation. Which must, of course, be coupled with spine—a willingness to take on the powers that be. And risk it all.

Question: Would Craig Venter come to work for you? Are you able to attract freaks and weirdos and world flippers? Are you Totally Determined to keep jogging after Baby Travis comes into your hectic life?

ANGER MANAGEMENT

Walt Disney created Disneyland—because (as rumor has it) he couldn't find the kind of place he wanted to entertain his grandchildren. Mickey Drexler started Gap Kids—because he couldn't find any place to buy decent clothes for his own kid.

And Phil Baechler invented the baby jogger—because he wanted to be able to continue to jog after a baby, Travis, came into his life. Phil told us the story: "When Travis was born, I was working a night shift as an editor at the local newspaper. The only way I could get out for my runs during the day was to figure out a way to take him with me. Baby packs sucked, because all they did was bounce him around. Since I was also a former bicycle racer and mechanic, I remembered the early bike trailers and thought it would be great to be able to push him around in some sort of chariot. I got an old stroller, welded a piece of pipe on the back to hold a couple of bike wheels, stuck a Schwinn fork on the front to make it a three wheeler, and we hit the road. I took him in a race when he was six months old and blew everybody's mind. 'Great idea' turned into 'What if?' so I made some prototypes, stuck a mail-order ad in *Runner's World* and it was off to the entrepreneurial (rat) races."

In Big Co.? In your 28-person HR unit?

DULL EMPLOYEES = DULL YOU.

COOL EMPLOYEES = COOL YOU.

Measurement is once again called for: Do you have enough Freaks and Weirdos on the payroll?

Weird Suppliers: Hey, Big Vendor ... Go Away

"Strategic suppliers" has been one of the hottest topics in management over the last decade. Idea: Prune your supplier base from an unwieldy number to a handful with whom you can reliably "partner." Efficiency follows, it is said. And that's usually true.

So what's the problem? Here's the problem, and it is ... ENORMOUS. Strategic suppliers have a principal goal in life relative to you. Namely ... SUCKING UP.

I recently spoke to an association of equipment producers supplying a single industry. The good news: They were shedding the "strategic supplier" dogma. Big customers had decided they wanted to simplify life by getting all their equipment from one or two producers. BIG ONES ... of course ... who could offer ... ECONOMIES OF SCALE. Problem: The industry is loaded with dozens of smallish and middle-sized suppliers that are doing seriously innovative things. Since the smallish and middle-sized (COOLEST) suppliers were effectively shut out of the big customers' business, those rejected suitors turned to middle-sized and smallish customers. Thence, within the supply chain, it was the middle-sized customers, paired with the middle-sized (or smaller) producers, who were introducing the innovative stuff! It took a half-dozen years, but the "big customers" woke up to the fact that they had unintentionally cut themselves off from interesting equipment innovations. As I addressed the group, the tide was reversing. "Strategic supplier" had almost become a contemptuous phrase.[6]

Message: Do you have enough … Weird Suppliers … in your portfolio? (Measure. Please. Again.) Or are you too dependent on a small number of Suck-up (Big) Suppliers?

DULL SUPPLIERS = DULL YOU.
COOL SUPPLIERS = COOL YOU.

Weird Acquisitions: Buy the Company, Keep the "Change"

I am well known as a Noisy Public Enemy of giant acquisitions. (See Chapter 2.) Mating dinosaurs, I have said again and again, is utterly out of step with the times. But my aversion to dinosaur-duos does not make me an enemy of acquisitions per se.

One of the biggest problems at the giant pharmaceutical companies, for example, is the hopelessly complicated drug-discovery processes they've inflicted upon themselves—partly in response to the hopelessly complicated government-approval process, partly in response to the increasingly complicated scientific and administrative processes that obtain within the companies. In any event, the thoughtful pharma companies have invested significant resources into partnering with, and sometimes acquiring, smaller start-ups. (Pfizer alone is said to have 1,000 such alliances.) This, I believe, is wise.

Wise … but not easy to execute. Anything but automatic. Most acquiring giants end up quickly running off the leaders of the acquired start-ups, even if those renegades have very sweet compensation packages. They're left with only a shell of their purchase. Cisco Systems (at least when its stock was soaring), the ad giant Omnicom, and damn few others have beaten that rap—by creating post-acquisition environments that give leaders of the acquired firm access to big markets without quashing the entrepreneurial fervor that made a start-up worth buying in the first place.

WEIRD, "WIDE" STUFF

I considered my "weird" thesis to be wholly original—that is, until I stumbled across Wayne Burkan's marvelous book *Wide Angle Vision: Beat Your Competition by Focusing on Fringe Competitors, Lost Customers, and Rogue Employees.* In a messy world, Burkan argues, those who lead us to salvation (or at least save us from extinction) will be precisely the kinds of people and enterprises that big companies are wont to dismiss or ignore.

"Corporate consciousness," Burkan writes, "is predictably centered around the mainstream. The *best* customers, *biggest* competitors, and *model* employees are almost exclusively the focus of attention."

This chapter, I gleefully admit, piggybacks off Mr. Burkan's ideas.

THEY SUPPLY, YOU DEMAND

[6]"There is an ominous downside to strategic supplier relationships," Wayne Burkan writes in *Wide Angle Vision.* A strategic supplier "is not likely to function as any more than a mirror to your organization. Fringe suppliers that offer innovative business practices need not apply."

DULL ACQUISITIONS = DULL YOU.
COOL ACQUISITIONS = COOL YOU.

Weird Directors: Get "Board" Out of Your Skull

All you have to do is look! LOOK AT A DAMN PICTURE OF THE BOARD OF DIRECTORS IN THE ANNUAL REPORT. Old. Old. Old. Tired. Tired. Tired. Unweird. Unweird. Unweird. *And* frighteningly, hopelessly unrepresentative of the market being served.

Boards matter. (A lot.) So ... appoint weird outsiders to your board![7]

Ask yourself: Does your Board of Directors include ...

- At least 30 percent women?
- At least one Hispanic?
- At least an African-American duo?
- A couple of members under the age of 35?
- About as many non-U.S. members as your share of non-U.S. sales?

I am *not* championing "quotas," even if the above reeks thereof. I *am* championing a board whose composition mirrors the market (diversity) and technologies (youth) that represent our biggest challenges.

DULL BOARD = DULL YOU.
COOL BOARD = COOL YOU.

Weird Projects: Measure for Madness

WOW Projects. Weird projects.[8] Same idea, in essence: Your department (that is: your PSF!) defines itself by its portfolio of projects. So: *Is that project portfolio as weird as the times demand?*

I examined the "portfolio idea" at some length in Chapter 17. I wish to cap it here. All of life is ... *portfolios*. You have a Roster I (people) ... and a Roster II (projects):

1. ARE THERE ENOUGH "WEIRD PEOPLE" IN YOUR 26-PERSON TRAINING DEPARTMENT? (ROSTER = PORTFOLIO.)
2. ARE THERE ENOUGH "WEIRD PROJECTS" IN YOUR DEPARTMENT'S PORTFOLIO? (DEPARTMENT = PORTFOLIO OF PROJECTS.)

Departments (PSFs) *have* people. Departments (PSFs) *do* Projects.

So: Measure (DAMN IT!) your department for ... weirdness.

Idea in detail: You've got 14 active projects. Four of them are major. On a

---

BOARDROOM BRAWL?

[7]Yale School of Management prof Jeffrey Sonnenfeld has done research on boards of directors. The upshot: "Weird" wins! Top-performing companies, he concludes, are marked by "extremely contentious boards that regard dissent as an obligation and that treat no subject as undiscussable."

OVERSIGHT OVERKILL

[8]A Hollywood producer let me in on a not-so-little secret about the movie biz: "Giant projects often contain within them the almost certain seeds of mediocrity. The very fact of their size causes constant, microscopic scrutiny and hence constant 'political' interference. Such oversight saps the passion of champions, and risks—to the point of certainty—fatal 'dumbing down' and loss of the very distinction and quirkiness sought in the first place."

strangeness scale (1 = Polishing current apples. 10 = Far out, dude.), how many of the 14 score 7 or above? Of the four major projects, how many score 6 or above?

DULL PROJECTS = DULL YOU.

COOL PROJECTS = COOL YOU.

Weird Encounters: Let's Re-Do "Lunch"

Who did you go to lunch with today? Same-old, same-old? Or some weird new somebody?

Fred Smith, founder and CEO of FedEx, sat with me on an economic-forecasting panel a few years ago. We chatted a bit before we got going, and at one point he turned on me with a look of determination in his eyes: "Tom, who's the most interesting person you've met in the last 90 days? And how do I get in touch with him or her?" Honestly, that's exactly what he said. Fred was a ... Collector of "Weirdos." He wanted to make sure that his business remained years ahead of its vigorous rivals. To have even a chance of doing so, he needed to perpetually put himself in contact with people who were (at least) a half-dozen years ahead of the norm.

How do you do that?

HANG WITH THEM. Measure (again!): Carefully examine your last 10 business lunches. (Check your calendar. No fudging.) Exactly how many of those lunches have been with newbies (to you) who would score 8 or higher, out of 10, on a "Strangeness Scale"? (Granted, strangeness is never easy. "Comfortable" is far easier. And well-nigh ... USELESS.)

These *are* strange times. Strange times call for strange companions.

DULL ENCOUNTERS = DULL YOU.

COOL ENCOUNTERS = COOL YOU.

Weird Ideas: How to Achieve "Sutton" Impact

For a matchless exposition of the Power of Weird, inhale Bob Sutton's book *Weird Ideas That Work: 11½ Practices for Promoting, Managing, and Sustaining Innovation.*

Here, in summary, are his 11-plus strange practices:

1. Hire slow learners (of the organizational code).

1½. Hire people who make you uncomfortable, even those you dislike.

2. Hire people you (probably) don't need.

3. Use job interviews to get ideas, not to screen candidates.

4. Encourage people to ignore and defy superiors and peers.

5. Find some happy people and get them to fight.

6. Reward success and failure, punish inaction.

7. Decide to do something that will probably fail, then convince yourself and everyone else that success is certain.

8. Think of some ridiculous, impractical things to do, then do them.

9. Avoid, distract, and bore customers, critics, and anyone else who just wants to talk about money.

10. Don't try to learn anything from people who seem to have solved the problems that you now face.

11. Forget the past, particularly your company's success.

DULL PRACTICES = DULL YOU.

COOL PRACTICES = COOL YOU.

FROM "GOOD" TO ... CRAZY

Hajime Mitarai, CEO of Canon: "We should do something when people say it is 'crazy.' If people say something is 'good,' it means that someone else is already doing it."

That is the secret to renewal. Think about it. Ponder it. Sleep on it. Talk with friends about it. Try to dismiss it. Come back to it. Again: This is the secret to the innovative, force-fed, self-renewing life.

The Obsolescence of "Planning"

Those 11½ Weird Ideas, I think, could almost be reduced to one:

Fire the planners. Hire the freaks.

We don't need elaborate plans! There is no time to plan! WE NEED ACTION! WE NEED NEW HEROES!

Heroes ... aka freaks ... aka exemplars ... aka people who have the nerve to stand up, stick out, and fight conventional wisdom.

Recall my friend Bob Stone, who went a long way toward reinventing government. No "plans." No "processes." Instead: a host of extant ... New Exemplars ... ferreted out of the boondocks and paraded before their peers as ... New Culture Carriers.

These are "weird times." Therefore, we must think "weird."

Again: Innovation is easy.

DULL MATES = DULL YOU.

COOL MATES = COOL YOU.

Of Ships and Fools: Brute Force and Brave Freaks

Real innovation is all about ... FORCE. Forcing yourself into contact with those who will pull you in directions that are significantly different from your prior path.

The ultimate exemplar of that approach was an explorer. Hernando Cortéz. As the story goes, Cortéz landed with his hearty band of soldiers in Veracruz, Mexico. They headed inland. They faced disease, brutal living conditions, and a resolute enemy. Fearing that the soldiers might flag in their determination to keep going, Cortéz resorted to a brutal, beautifully simple remedy: BURN THE SHIPS.

SUTTON DEPTH

I love Bob Sutton's *Weird Ideas That Work*. But even more, I am head-over-heels in love with the fact that such a book even exists, and that it was written by a Tenured Professor of Industrial Engineering at no less an institution than Stanford University. Are we finally reaching a point where "strange ideas" are deemed ... not so strange?

WE HAVE IGNITION

Jack Kerouac, writing in *On the Road*: "The only people for me are the mad ones, the ones who are mad to live, mad to talk, mad to be saved, desirous of everything at the same time, the ones who never yawn or say a commonplace thing, but burn, burn, burn like fabulous yellow roman candles exploding like spiders across the stars."

NEW BUSINESS ● NEW MANDATE

Now, *that* is a Bold Strategy.[9]

Question: HAVE YOU "BURNED YOUR SHIPS"? HAVE YOU DUMPED ANY OF THE ONES WHO BRUNG YOU?

In practical terms, "burning your ships" means ... cleansing your portfolio of its "successful" yesterdays. There are companies out there—even Big Companies—that "get it."

- *HP* sold off several divisions that were the founding pillars of the company.
- *3M* sold off several divisions that were the founding pillars of the company.
- *Corning* sold off several divisions that were the founding pillars of the company.
- *Nokia* sold off virtually all the literally founding pillars of the company. (E.g., trees.)
- *Perkin Elmer* sold off everything—including its name—and went after the biotech revolution as the newly reborn PE Biosystems. (In the new guise, they attracted ... yes ... Craig Venter ... and thence mapped the human genome.)

How do you put yourself in a "ship-burning" state of mind? Simple:

FIND THE FREAKS!
SIGN 'EM UP!
LISTEN TO 'EM!
TAKE 'EM INTO YOUR CONFIDENCE!
MAKE 'EM YOUR PARTNERS!
LET 'EM HELP YOU MAKE REVOLUTION!
Q.E.D.

! Contrasts

WAS		IS
"Be ahead of the pack"	–	"Be ahead of the curve"
Get big fast:	–	"Size will defend us"
Get a clue:	–	"Size is no defense"
Sales: the "usual suspects"	–	Sales: unusual prospects
Maximize revenue by focusing on a few big customers	–	Maximize innovation by seeking out "strange" small customers
Benchmark against "industry leaders"	–	Benchmark against leading-edge firms
"Strategic" suppliers	–	Fringe suppliers
Reliable employees	–	Rambunctious employees
Hire the guy (gal) from a prestigious school	–	Hire the guy (gal) with a freaky portfolio
Passive board of directors	–	Pushy board of directors
Acquisitions: buying bulk	–	Acquisitions: buying innovation
"Safety-first" partners	–	"Risk-ready" partners
Playing it safe: "Cover all the bases"	–	Playing it "weird":"Burn all the ships"

GRAVEYARD SHIFT

[9]There is a wretched old saying in the world of science: "If you want a paradigm shift, it's not good enough for the old professors to retire. They must die."

That's a little strong for me. However: I BELIEVE IT.

24 IN SEARCH OF EXCELLENCE: A THREE-GENERATION REPORT CARD

! Technicolor Rules ...

- The absence of a bias for action remains the biggest problem for Large Organizations. They simply think too much. Plan too much. Meet too much. And accomplish too little.
- It is an Age of Perpetual and Accelerating Transience. "Permanence" is dead.
- Why does "lifetime employment" sound so much like "life sentence" to me?
- All "basic principles," including those that graced *In Search of Excellence*, are up for grabs. We've got to "play it as it lays." We've got to "make it up as we go along."

! RANT

We are not prepared ...

We assume that enterprise excellence is something that we can define, analyze, plan for, and then maintain in perpetuity. With each turn of the Business Wheel, we fancy that we now understand the One True & Lasting Thing that will distinguish a good idea from a bad one, a winning strategy from a dud. Indeed, we labor still under the delusion that the key to winning is ... the right strategy. But we must learn that excellence is not something that we can "envision." We create it as we go along. Then blow it up, and start anew. Simply put: The search for excellence is ... never-ending, ever-shifting.

! VISION

I imagine ...

A young guy—no, let's say it's a young gal—who is afire with the need to know How Things Work in the world of enterprise. Like me at McKinsey 20-odd years ago, she tackles the Big Subject. She picks up where I left off, offering answers to questions about "the search for excellence, circa 2022" that I can only begin to raise here. What happens when the microchips really start calling the shots, as well as taking away the jobs? How do we "stick to our knitting" when one form of "knitting" after another unravels? She publishes a book that profiles and analyzes people and organizations that are redefining excellence for a new age. She offers ideas and lessons that, well, I can scarcely begin to imagine.

In Search of ... a Calling

I know exactly when and where I acquired my fascination with management. It was 1966. Danang. I Corps. Vietnam. I was a 24-year-old commander of a U.S. Navy construction detachment, a member of the fabled Seabees. I did "well." I re-upped for a second tour. In time, I was "promoted" to a staff position at the Pentagon.

In short, I saw a lot of management, up-close and (literally) under fire. I did a fair amount of "managing" myself. And ... I wasn't turned off by it. I was turned on by it. I became deeply intrigued by organizations. Why, I wondered, did some groups do incredibly well, while others—faced with apparently similar circumstances and staffed by apparently similar people—didn't do well at all?

I went West. To Stanford, where I got an MBA. Morph again. Starting in 1973, I worked in the White House ... focusing on drug-abuse issues. After the boss (Richard Nixon) lost his job, I went back West. To San Francisco and McKinsey & Co. Amid all this, I finished up a Ph.D. in Organizational Behavior from the Stanford Graduate School of Business. Then along came a "little" project, commissioned by the Big Bosses in New York, that would change my life.

In Search of ... "Effectiveness"

At McKinsey, "strategy" was the flavor of the decade. The main idea: Get the plan right, and everything else will fall brilliantly and profitably into place. The same idea held sway at the Boston Consulting Group. And at every other name consultancy.

Yet the new McKinsey chief, Ron Daniel, imagined that there might be more to life than just getting "the strategy" right. So, around 1977, Ron asked me, ink still damp on my Ph.D., to "look into organizational effectiveness issues." I did, gradually turning my pursuit of "effectiveness" into ... a search for "excellence."

I wandered around. Talked to experts all over the world. Sweden, Norway, England, Germany, The United States, too, and was fascinated by what I learned. Because virtually all of it contravened conventional wisdom. My take: What separates the Winners from the Losers is not ... the Brilliance of the Strategic Plan. It is ... the way a company organizes and motivates its people. In 1976, that was a Very Strange and Very Wild Idea.

My colleague and putative boss, Bob Waterman, bought that idea and became, like me, an avid student of "excellence." Together, we pursued "excellent companies"—those few U.S. firms that, despite daunting competition, seemed to be "getting it right." From 1977 to 1982, we visited people at those companies, talked to them about what worked and what didn't, and presented our findings to the folks at McKinsey; then we sat down and wrote *In Search of Excellence*. And then ...

But that gets us a little ahead of our story. Let's shift for a moment from personal history to ... History.

I IMAGINE ...

I imagine ... Rip Van Winkle. Falling asleep in 1962. Waking up in 2002. *When RVW entered the Big Snooze:* George Babbitt ruled. Certainty was King. Jobs lasted a lifetime. Ozzie & Harriet provided comfort. Wars were between clumsy behemoths. *When RVW awoke:* Speed was King. Certainty was Dead. The fast lane was the only lane. Kids were in charge. Armies of millions had become ... ARMIES OF ONE.

1950: Excellence Unbound

American management had, in effect, won World War II. The United States didn't sacrifice the most bodies. The Russians did. And Churchill gave more stirring speeches than Roosevelt. But the U.S. war machine took the Allies over the top. We produced more guns than the Bad Guys did. *More* planes. *More* tanks. *More* trucks. *More* amphibious landing craft. We overran them with ... Industrial Might. Much more so, truth be told, than we did with the well-celebrated spirit and spunk of our rifle-toting Iowa farm boys. (Not to take anything away from those Iowa farm boys.) And after World War II, our Masterful Industrial Enterprises went back to peacetime concerns ... and ruled the world. In the early 1950s, we produced almost half the world's GDP. Our companies were invincible. Ergo, our *management practices* were invincible.

American management: the alpha *and* the omega of Economic Excellence, circa 1950.

Gradually, cracks began to appear in that mighty edifice. For example: Sputnik, 1957. The Russians vaulted into space before we did. That sparked a national crisis. And, perversely, it sent exactly the wrong message: Central Planning (Soviet-style) is Very Cool.

Enter Sovietus Americanus. It was ... an age of Central Planning! ... an age of Mechanical Organizations! ... an age of Technocrats!

1980: Excellence Lost

More and bigger cracks appeared within the structure of American business hegemony. The biggest "crack" of all: Japan got its house in order during the years after World War II—and with withering tenacity it reconstructed its industrial economy. As the 1960s yielded to the 1970s, Japanese industry began to embarrass its U.S. counterparts. First in shipbuilding. Then in steel. Then in automobile manufacturing. Then in semiconductors.

By 1980, America was in a funk. Unemployment hit double digits for the first time since the Great Depression. Inflation was well over 10 percent. Interest rates topped 20 percent. So much for invincibility!

When awakened, Americans learn quickly. This time around, we learned that the right way to manage was ... the *Japanese Way*. In 1980, if you didn't "get" that—well, you didn't get anything.

The new critique of Pax Business Americana took hold even at that citadel of American management, the Harvard Business School. Two senior HBS professors,

NOT SO RANDOM A WALK

All in all, the companies featured in our "search" have done surprisingly well, according to a meticulously researched article that appeared in Forbes.com in 2002:

"One remarkable fact ... remains: [The book's] list of companies have held up quite well over time. ... Over a 5-, 10- or 20-year period, the *Excellence* index—an unweighted basket of the 32 public companies among Peters' and Waterman's [set]—substantially outperformed the Dow Jones Industrial Average and the broader S&P 500. ... If you invested $10,000 in the *Excellence* index 20 years ago and then did nothing at all, you would have $140,050. An equal investment in the Dow would have fielded just $85,500. ... Some might assume it easy to pick 30 or 40 companies that would outperform the Dow. But precious few mutual fund managers do it—even though that's their job and they can change their mix of companies at will."

manufacturing experts Bill Abernathy and Bob Hayes, wrote an article titled "Managing Our Way to Economic Decline" for the *Harvard Business Review*. They argued that American business leaders had become obsessed with numbers. With abstractions. With plans. They had lost touch with the essence of enterprise: people, quality, customers. That was the Shot Heard Around the Land—the death knell, it seemed to many of us, of American management supremacy.

Bob Waterman and I ended up firing the next shot.

1982: Excellence Regained?

When Bob and I wrote *In Search of Excellence*, "firing a shot" was hardly our intent. We (and I, in particular) were simply pissed off. The mantra of U.S. business had long been "The plan is all." And I thought that "The Plan" was (mostly) ... bullshit.

In any event, the book struck a chord. Our timing, though accidental (isn't that always the case?), was positively brilliant. Amid intimations of American economic "decline," we demonstrated that not all American businesspeople were idiots. We found some American Islands of Hope ... at exactly the right moment. We sold a ton of books. (Only our Moms were not surprised!) And the world—the world of management, at least—wobbled on its axis ever so slightly.

Meanwhile, the forces of economic change remained at least as ferocious as they had been from the 1960s (when I started out) to the 1980s (when I started to make a name for myself as a management "guru").

A number of companies that we featured ran into very rough sledding. Very quickly. Only three years after our book appeared, *BusinessWeek* ran a nasty cover story (titled "Oops") that took us to task because three of our star companies in particular—Hewlett-Packard, Digital Equipment, and Disney—had been taken to task in the marketplace.

Yes, some portion of our original Golden 43 have performed at levels short of "excellence." Still, by my estimate, about 30 of them have done reasonably well—especially given the inherent clumsiness associated with their size and the extraordinary quantity of yogurt that whipped through the fan in the years after 1982.

Eight Basics: The Axis of Excellence

What's more, even if some of our exemplars of excellence have staggered, our Big Ideas have proven their staying power. In fact, some of those ideas ("people are cool," "customers are cool") have become routine elements of the business vocabulary. Eight notions in particular—eight "basics" as we called them—were the heart of *In Search of Excellence*. And while some of them now require serious revision, all serve as salient points of reference as we gauge the New Mandate of our disruptive age.

What follows is a review of those "eight basics" from a three-generation

---

ANALYZE THIS!

Let me re-emphasize: I don't dismiss any of this. We tried to run the biggest of enterprises, in effect, out of cigar boxes. We needed some analytics. (Desperately.) We needed some metrics. (Desperately.) We needed to understand the power of data. (Desperately.) But ... like All Good Things ... the "analytics" and "abstractions" came to subsume the Real World of the living, breathing, emotional, *complaining* customer.

perspective. Taking 1982 (the book's birthday) as a baseline, I'll go backward 20 years and forward 20 years, yielding a series of snapshots of what has defined management "excellence" over the years—in 1962, in 1982, in 2002. Also, to demonstrate sheer foolhardiness on my part, I'll offer a brief word (no more!) on what may lie in wait for us in 2022.

Basic 1: Bias for Action

1962. Bias for Planning.

In the early decades of the last century, management had been a rather "seat of the pants" affair. Then World War II came along. Robert McNamara left the Harvard Business School, where he'd been an accounting professor, and started counting planes for the Army Air Corps, instead of counting "beans" for companies. (No kidding, the Air Corps didn't know how many planes it had.) Our enterprises, both private and public, had grown large—yet our systems were still quite small. McNamara counted the planes. We won the war. McNamara went to Ford. He counted the cars. We "won" the peace.

And so, over time, we came to worship ... *The Plan* ... to the exclusion of almost everything else. Business management became a playground for abstractions. The numbers ruled. Analysis ruled. All right-thinking dudes wanted to be "strategic planners." *Think* your way to success. *Out-think* the competition. Forget the folks with dirty fingernails. Forget the folks on the front line. *The best plan wins!* I overstate—but not by much.

1982. Bias for Action.

Bob Waterman and I believed in planning. Both of us were engineers—and McKinsey consultants. Both of us grooved on analysis. But both of us also saw the limits thereto. We wandered around. We talked to people at 3M and Hewlett-Packard. And we discovered that ... *they* wandered around. They weren't glued to their offices. They weren't defended by secretaries and executive assistants. They wandered around their own companies ... and when they met people on the front lines who might have a weird new idea, they said the damnedest things. Such as: "Try it."

We hadn't expected that. We encountered company leaders who didn't just think and think and think ... and meet and meet and meet. Instead, they got an idea—and then they went for it. Meanwhile, the absence of a bias for action remains the biggest problem for Large Organizations. They simply think too much. Plan too much. Meet too much. And accomplish too little. And adjust too slowly.

ARTICLE OF FAITH

Forty years into my professional career, I believe one thing with absolute certainty: Those who win are those who ... try stuff (quickly) ... watch what happens ... adjust (quickly) ... and then try something else (quickly). All with little fuss or muss.

In the BusinessWeek article (July 1978) that laid the groundwork for In Search of Excellence, I labeled that approach "Do it. Fix it. Try it." Which later became "a bias for action."

Bias for action. I'll stake my life on it. Gladly.

NEW BUSINESS ! • NEW MANDATE

2002. Bias for Madness.

Call it "Life at Internet Speed." Call it "the Age of Instant Obsolescence." Call it what you will, but business today operates at a maddening pace. There is no rest ... even for the succesful. As media theorist Marshall McLuhan presciently observed many years ago, "If it works, it's obsolete."

I began to worry about the new business "metabolism" almost a decade ago. In *Liberation Management* (1992), I conjured up a dawning Age of Fashion. Today, as never before, fickleness controls the fate of computer companies and semiconductor makers and financial-service providers ... as well as lipstick and automobile producers.

Incidentally, don't let the pricked dot-com balloon throw you off. "Dell speed," "Wal*Mart speed," and "Amazon satisfaction" represent a Wholly New Phenomenon. One that is here to stay. One that calls for nothing less than ... a Total Restructuring of the Enterprise (along with its extended family of suppliers and customers).

2022. Bias for ... Who the Hell Knows?

All hell is already breaking loose. Computer experts insist that we are fast approaching infinite-speed change. Computers and computer networks will think for themselves, and the man-machine boundary will get very, very fuzzy.

The role for humans, then? NOT CLEAR.

Basic 2: Close to the Customer

1962. Research the Customer.

The "analytical paradigm" came to rule all with amazing swiftness. "Marketing" was a classic example.

Consider: Before industrialization and mass consumption took hold, the connection between enterprises and their customers was inherently close. Sheep shearers, blacksmiths, pub and brothel owners—presumably, they didn't need to be told to "cozy up" to their customers.

But that era passed. And "marketing" arrived. Close on its heels came "market research." Which was a swell idea, a necessary idea, an idea worth billions of dollars. Get beyond "seat-of-the-pants" piloting? That's a no-brainer.

But a funny thing happened on the way to the future. A very appropriate orientation toward analysis became ... a "bias for abstraction" ... a "bias for inaction." (Think first, act never.) Customers? ("Who the hell's the customer?") Data ruled. Flesh and blood decayed.

1982. Close to the Customer.

Bob Waterman and I studied IBM. We studied Carl Sewell's car dealerships. We found what others would come to call "customer intimacy." We called it "Stay Close to the Customer." There's plenty of room for those marketing abstractions! You damn well better know your market stats *cold*!

But there's also room for ... the human being ... aka the breathing, bleeding customer. And there's especially room for the service dimension on the front pew; after all, the "service bit" is the principal determinant of loyalty and repeat business.

2002. One with the Customer.

I well know how jargony the phrase sounds: "Become One with the Customer." The thing is, it's exactly … right.

The "close to the customer" idea was "right," circa 1982. The "marketing analytics" developed by Ted Levitt, Phil Kotler, and their colleagues at Harvard and Northwestern were "right," circa 1962.

But now, thanks largely to the magic of Internet technology and advanced telecommunications, you can have your cake and eat it, too. That's the story I recounted earlier in my discussion of "solutions." Company after company after company has plied that trail—from Omnicom ("integrated marketing services") to UPS ("integrated logistics management") to Otis ("integrated building systems") to the Farmers Group (with its "dream fulfillment" approach to financial services). Jargony or not, the idea is as powerful as it is simple: *Get beyond*[1] *the "product." Get beyond the "service." Become One With the Customer*.

Once companies like Dell and Amazon show us what they can do, we'll accept nothing less from *anyone*.

2022. Inseparable from the Customer.

Dell Computer, I think, offers a premonition of what's to come. A premonition about what it means when everyone throughout the supply and demand chain is seamlessly entwined with everyone else, forming automatically guided, ever-changing Web connections to get stuff done.

One tosses off terms like "symbiosis" or "synergy" rather lightly. But what the new technologies allow is exactly that—synergy, symbiosis—the precise look and feel of which is hard to imagine. (Unless you're Michael Dell or Ray Kurzweil.) But we know that the scale and scope of networked computer "intelligence" will be staggering. I wouldn't be surprised if the term "customer" or "vendor" ceased to exist by 2022. Or, for that matter, perhaps by 2012.

ONE-TO-ONE = WIN-WIN
[1]Two authors provide language that cuts to the core of what marketing smarts, customer smarts, and new technology combined make possible. (And inevitable.) Don Peppers and Martha Rogers tell us this is (to cite the title of their book) *The Age of One-to-One Marketing*.

　Nice.

DENNIS TURNED MENACE
Alas, we never tire of exalting the consolidators with Big Dreams. Soon after taking over from Jack Welch at GE in 2002, Jeff Immelt gave an interview with *BusinessWeek*. Asked which companies' approach he admired, Immelt offered Dennis Kozlowski's Tyco and Jean-Marie Messier's Vivendi as favorites.

　Sorry, Jeff.

Basic 3: Autonomy and Entrepreneurship

1962. Conglomeration and "Management."

The 1960s saw the advent of … the "Ultimate Celebration and Certification of Bigness." Namely: THE OMNIPOTENT CONGLOMERATE. Put everything under one roof! Why not? Just apply those Guaranteed American Management Principles and—voilà—you were home free. (Hey, maybe there would be only one hyper-mega-conglomerate by 1982.)

The "big idea" was that a "good manager" could manage *anything*. You didn't need to understand healthcare in order to manage healthcare. You didn't need to understand forest products in order to manage forest products. The classic exemplar of this model was Harold Geneen, Supreme Ruler of ITT. The firm owned timberlands and telephone companies, insurance companies and hotel companies and bakeries. And much else. And Geneen, in his own mind and in the minds of many stalwart observers, was fully capable of … managing it all. Until it came unglued.

The conglomeration movement marked … the Apex of Hubris. That is: the point right before Japan and Germany taught us some harsh lessons about actually understanding the product and pursuing quality.

1982. Autonomy and Entrepreneurship.

I fell in love with three of the 43 principal companies we researched for the book: 3M. Johnson & Johnson. Hewlett-Packard. They performed brilliantly. One (big) reason why: their almost religious devotion to promoting entrepreneurship within a highly decentralized structure.

A 3M division was a little company … that frequently told corporate headquarters staffers where and when to get off. A Johnson & Johnson division was a little company … that prided itself on telling off the headquarters flunkies. A Hewlett-Packard division was a little company … that typically refused to acknowledge that there even was a corporate headquarters. (Indeed, there barely was at the time.) These three enterprises— and a few others—"proved," to my mind, that it was possible to maintain energetic-small-within-big.

HP and 3M subsequently had problems. (HP has become an entirely different company, far more centralized in attitude and practice than the HP of 1982.) But I never lost a shred of my passion for small-within-big, though I did gain a far better appreciation of how difficult it is to sustain.

2002. Outsourcing and Network Management.

Remember Forrest Gump: "Don't own nothin' if you can help it. If you can, even rent your shoes." That Gumpian Pronouncement was prophetic. The new model: Outsource, outsource, outsource …

Outsource IT to EDS.
Outsource HR to Forum.
Outsource facilities management to Accenture.
Outsource R&D to small start-ups.
And so on.

The old mantra: Unless you owned it, you couldn't control it. Today, that kind of commitment to "vertical integration" is mostly seen as lunacy. Why deny yourself access to the World's Best Partners? And why not shift partners as new opportunities arise? (New mantra? *If* you own it, you'll probably screw it up.)[2] Our Job One becomes: Create, manage, destroy, and Re-imagine the overall network that assembles value.

In fact, the "autonomy and entrepreneurship" model has become problematic. In times of madness (like our own), the very notion of a stable, lasting company structure—small-within-big, whatever—may be a trap. Perhaps the better model is this: A company comes onto the scene, changes the world, spends a couple of years (or a couple of decades) at the top, and then passes on.

Even the kind of anti-complacency tools that I was mesmerized by at 3M, HP, and J&J (small "independent" divisions and such) are rarely a match for the collective force of … Next Generation Rivals. The upshot: We must develop entirely new ideas about "organization" and "control" and "sustainability."

2022. Transience and More Transience.

Permanence (the assumption of 1962, even 1982) is giving way to transience (the emerging assumption of 2002). Which is giving way to … more and more transience.

In days gone by, we had entrepreneurial bursts, followed by periods of consolidation. Such waves lasted perhaps 30 or 40 years. But technological change is accelerating at a merry clip. Global financial markets continue to pour money into new ideas. It is … an Age of Perpetual and Accelerating Transience. New ideas will follow upon new ideas— with reckless abandon, total disregard and disrespect for today's regnant geniuses, and at unprecedented speed. "Permanence" is dead.

Basic 4: *Productivity Through People*

1962. Employees as Interchangeable Parts.

A century ago, enterprise was disorganized. Totally Disorganized. It *did* need to be organized. Frederick Winslow Taylor organized it. Peter Drucker organized it more. By 1962, people like Robert McNamara had organized the hell out of it. No, I don't deny the importance of "getting organized."

On the other hand: Enterprises got so … DAMN, BLOODY ORGANIZED … that they purposefully drove the intelligence and passion out of almost every employee.

Previously, the "employee" had been self-reliant. A self-employed blacksmith, or farmer, or printer. Then, when he went to work for Bethlehem Steel (or some such), he

---

SALIENT PARTNERS

[2]Years ago, I closely studied MCI. It was a small company then, audaciously going nose to nose against AT&T. It manufactured nothing. Many observers saw that as a huge handicap in the company's battle against the owner of Western Electric and Bell Labs.

But one of MCI's top officers told me that the company's lack of manufacturing capacity was its most striking advantage. MCI, he said, had necessarily developed a towering "core competence" in creating and managing what we would now call "strategic alliances." Thus, MCI could pick and choose among the Globe's Coolest Partners, including numerous upstarts that were quietly redefining the telecom industry.

had to park his brains at the door. He was an "interesting guy" before 9 a.m. ... and an "interesting guy" after 5 p.m. But from 9 to 5, he and his peers were ... Interchangeable Parts. Pieces of a Machine.[3]

And such a construct applied not just to the blue-collar heavies working for Beth Steel or in the Model T factory ... but also to the white-collar "suits" occupying tall, taller, tallest office towers. The guys with the ties and the briefcases had to park *their* imaginations at the door, too—and process those forms created by the white-collar Taylorists.

1982. Productivity Through People.

Bob Waterman and I learned this "basic" idea at the knee of Ren McPherson. Later a member of *Fortune's* Business Hall of Fame, he was the Big Boss at Dana, an old-line autoparts manufacturer. There, he made a transformation—nay, a revolution. He said: Workers have brains! Workers have ideas! Ren created an extraordinary company in a merciless industry. All we did was listen to him and take notes, and then write it up. (We all but worshipped him.)

Bob and I didn't use the word "empower." (That came a few years later. And quickly became overused.) Instead, we followed in McPherson's footsteps, and basically said: WORKERS HAVE BRAINS! WORKERS HAVE IDEAS! We were a long way from the world of today. But we were also a long way from the conventional wisdom of 1962.

2002. Employees as ... Talent!

Ah, so much has happened since 1982. Jobs for life? *Forget it.* We're heading "back to the future"—back to the days when self-reliant "independent contractors" rule.

You and I are ... In Charge of Our Lives. (Again.) CEO of Me Inc. To be sure, Me Inc. may be temporarily in association with GE or Fidelity. But it's still Me Inc.—with no expectation that Big Company will cosset the "CEO"/me for 40 years.

Back in Henry Ford's day, the idea was to bring individuals aboard and mold them to a predefined task. To trample on their individuality. To discipline any sign of aberrant behavior. Now the idea is to ... win the Great War for Talent. Almost all economic value emerges from the accumulation of intellectual capital. From creativity. From enthusiasm. From individuality. Yes, from aberrant behavior.

2022. Productivity Without People.

Humans and computers will converge. Rote jobs were dying in 2002, and they will be dead—dead and gone—by 2022. Bold prediction for 2022: Computers will be as smart as we are. They will learn faster than we do. They will exhibit creativity in every measurable "human" sense of the word. They may even display "emotions" that are indiscernible from the real thing. (If I'm premature in these prognostications, I suspect it's only by a few years.) What will be the role of the "ordinary human" in all this? Frankly, I haven't the slightest idea.

HARD TIMES
[3] *Why does "lifetime employment" sound so much like "life sentence" to me? Well, anyway, it does. (Am I nuts?) (Don't answer.)*

Basic 5: Hands-On, Value-Driven

1962. By the Numbers, By the Book.

Business ain't for wimps! Business ain't warm and fuzzy! Learn your business at Harvard Business School! Forget that people crap! (That is, forget the soft stuff.) Measure! Measure! Measure! Numbers rule!

That was the deal. And we did pretty damn well by it ... for a while. The iconic figure here (again) is Robert McNamara. He was the ultimate representative of the Age of Analytics-Are-Us. For the Army Air Corps during World War II and then at Ford, as mentioned. But he truly took it over the top as Secretary of Defense under Kennedy and Johnson. In each incarnation, he brought order to disorder. His way of doing things—the Harvard Business School[4] way—ruled both the marketplace and the battlefield. The analytic model ruled war as well as peace. Both were treated as abstractions. Anybody could manage anything ... if you were a "good manager." (If you "had the numbers right.") That was the dictum of the time.

Bless the Toyotas and Hondas and Sonys for exposing the shabbiness of the emperor's not-so-new clothes!

1982. Hands-On, Value-Driven.

Of all the notions surfaced in *Excellence*, Bob Waterman and I both loved one idea most. Namely: MBWA. Managing by Wandering Around. The phrase, mentioned earlier, that we collected from the folks at HP, may well appear trite—but the idea was anything but. Especially in 1982. The people at HP understood that a "winning enterprise" is *not* an abstraction. Of course they tallied the numbers, but they also managed to stay in intimate touch with their employees and their customers, even as they became a gigantic firm.

MBWA: an excellent bit of shorthand for ... *Intimate Involvement with the People Who Actually Do the Damn Work, and the People Who Actually Buy the Damn Product.*

2002. "Soft" Stuff, Intellectual Capital.

It is an Age of Ideas. All Economic Value Creation comes from Talent ... from "Solutions" and "Experiences" and "Branding" ... from Intellectual Capital. "Soft" stuff rules.[5]

NEW BUSINESS ● **NEW MANDATE**

DOMINANT THEORY

[4]Enron was not our worst accounting scandal in modern times. My nominee is McNamara's bankrupt "Body Count" approach to "war management." "Bring in those enemy ears, boys," the lieutenant intoned. War by misleading measurement = Humiliating defeat. And 58,000 dead Americans. Mostly thanks to that paragon of analytics—Body Count Bob McNamara.

Do I sound bitter? I am. If you think positively about the forces that *In Search of Excellence* unleashed, don't thank me. Thank my anti-mentor. Robert Strange McNamara.

CHART THE BILLBOARDS

[5]Next time you're racing through an airport, notice how two out of every three billboard ads seem to be for ... consulting firms. Yikes. Just a few years ago, these folks were economic "parasites." Now they are: "The Main Game." The lesson: Companies are desperate to reinvent their way of doing business ... and they rely increasingly on a new group of "intellectual capital" specialists to make that happen.

Welcome to: Schwab World. Dell World. Microsoft World. Celera Genomics World. Amazon World. And, yes, IBM (aka International Business "Machines") World.

Back in 1982, the notion that the "service economy" could be a Big Deal was revolutionary (no kidding). In fact many leading policy makers worried about the undue and growing influence of service firms, wholeheartedly believing that Stuff is the only True Basis for Economic Prowess. Now we don't even talk about the "service economy." Why? The service economy is ubiquitous.[6] *Everything* is a service, even in "manufacturing." Everything derives from the "soft" stuff ... from that intellectual capital.

2022. By the Skin of Our Teeth?

If you listen to people like Ray Kurzweil and Stephen Hawking, then you will suspect (as I do) that we are entering the "last phase of human dominance." The computer will in some form or other take over within about 40 years. Thus, by 2022 ... we'll be halfway there.

From the vantage point of 1982, the world of today would appear "far out." Meanwhile, the pace of change is accelerating. Madly. I don't know what's coming, but only a fool would dismiss "far out" scenarios.

Basic 6: Stick to the Knitting

1962. The God Complex.

In the first decades after World War II, the U.S. share of the world's GDP was enormous. American business faced no real competition. And that was reflected in its business practices. We're good managers! We can scarf up any company we want—and turn it into gold! I call this attitude ... "The God Complex."

1982. Stick to the Knitting.

The height of corporate arrogance ... of the God Complex, of Pax Business Americana ... was Conglomeration Nation. But well before 1982, the conglomeration movement hit the skids. And companies began to focus anew on "core competencies."

In Search of Excellence picked up on that notion. But we didn't advocate a play-it-safe, take-no-risks strategy. We relied on research by UCLA professor Richard Rumelt—who most certainly did not argue that companies should keep doing what they had always done. In fact, Rumelt said that narrow-minded "stick-to-it-ive-ness" was disastrous. But winners, he argued, generally do follow a strategy of "related diversification." They "branch out"—but their "branches" grow organically from their trunk and roots. The models here were companies like 3M and Johnson & Johnson ... companies that did *lots* of "new" stuff, albeit new stuff that always related to a Coherent Business Proposition.

{ **SERVICE CHARGE (BIG-TIME)**
[6]Recall that in 2000, Hewlett-Packard—makers-of-stuff par excellence—offered $18 billion for the services of 31,000 Pricewaterhouse-Coopers consultants. Note well: *consultants.*

HO-HUM.

2002. What Is Your Knitting?

Perhaps there are a small number of things that you are really good at. The obvious strategy (in 1982 terms): Focus on those. Subcontract the rest.

The problem: It's not that easy. Not nearly. The thing-that-you're-really-good-at (your "knitting") might cease to be relevant, and hence profitable, the day after tomorrow. Or some start-up might swoop down from out of nowhere with a plan for being not just "really good" but "really great" and "dramatically different" at your "thing."

What do you "stick to"? I don't know. Who the hell knows what you're supposed to do? I don't. Sorry. (Refunds available upon request.)

2022. The "Ye Gads" Complex.

If I'm confused about 2002, then I'm *beyond* confused about 2022. Indeed, I haven't a clue! What is "core"? What is a "competency"?[7] What the hell is "the knitting"? It's all a ... GREAT MYSTERY.

Basic 7: Simple Form, Lean Staff

1962. Headquarters Knows Best.

The message: Hire a bunch of "college boys." Pay them a bunch of money. Put them in staff jobs. Install them in ... Headquarters. Have them tell the "others" what to do. The others: the wretches, the dirty-fingernails types, the ones without the college degrees, the ones who (horror of horrors!) work in the plants.

Superstructure was Cool. (Very.) MBAs were on the verge of Cool. (Very.) Those assumptions characterized the Morally Certain Spirit of the era. Analysis. Abstraction. Control from the Center. Those ideals defined the New and Perfect World of ... *Technocratic Management.*

Again, this monster superstructure was a necessary corrective to the "manage-out-of-a-cigar-box" mentality of the previous era. But it went too far. Way, way too far.

1982. Simple Form, Lean Staff.

Bob Waterman and I absolutely blew this one.

We do get points. We said, "Line Officers Must Rule." We argued that those dirty-fingernails types were in fact ... finger-on-the-pulse-of-the-company types. After all, they were closest to both the employees and the customers. We were right about all of that.

But when we argued on behalf of a "simple form, lean staff," we had no idea how "simple" or how "lean" organizations could become. Or needed to become. We didn't realize just how bulky—how grotesquely flabby—the old superstructures were, even at our so-called "excellent companies."

"CORE" CASUALTIES

[7]In the past few years, we've seen many intelligent (and honest!) CEOs—Mike Armstrong at AT&T, Chris Galvin at Motorola, George Fisher at Kodak—get into extraordinary amounts of trouble, all while trying to do the smart thing. They try to figure out what their "core competencies" are. But they can't. The ground beneath their feet is quicksand, and the quicksand is shifting ever more quickly.

More to the point: We hadn't anticipated the likes of Dell. And we surely hadn't anticipated the Internet.

2002. Friction-Free World.

"Simple form, lean staff" made sense in 1982—even if we missed the magnitude of the flab waiting for competitive liposuction. But it was so, so far from where we were about to go.

"Staff functions" as we knew them are dead or dying. All rote work will be outsourced—or automated. The result: a "friction-free" organization (and family of organizations) in which documents no longer sit on people's desks, often for days or weeks (or more), waiting to be "initialed."

What does this new organization look like? *Weird. Very, very weird.* Think of an instantly, seamlessly linked supply chain. Think Dell. Think Oracle. Think Schwab. Think the emergent military model. These are the icons of new, friction-free enterprise.

2022. People-Free World?

Computers that think and learn. Computers that do *all* the work. Will there be any room left for people? NOT CLEAR. If there is anything left for people to do, it will center on producing Incredible Creative Value Added. (Yikes! Hooray! Scary! Cool! Or something.)

Basic 8: Simultaneous Loose-Tight Properties

1962. Read the Policy Manual. Follow the rules.

Way back when, we knew with great certainty "how to manage." Frederick ("Stop-watch Freddy") Taylor fervently pursued that … One Best Way. Via Peter Drucker and Michael Porter and others, we parlayed Taylor's initial ideas into the theory and practice of "modern management." In short: There were "ways" to "manage," and those ways were "right." There were "Principles of Management,"[8] and if you followed them, Good Things Would Follow. And good things did follow … for a while.

1982. Simultaneous Loose-Tight Properties.

Bob Waterman and I did not completely abandon the principle of "Principles." We believed in "tight." We believed in shared "values" and a unified company "culture." We believed that every great enterprise (even one as enormous as GE) must bear the mark of certain "core philosophies."

But we also believed that "excellent enterprises" were excellent to the extent that they simultaneously allowed people enormous latitude to Invent & Do Their Own Thing … in general accord with those Core Values. (That's the "loose" bit.) We prescribed, in other words, a *massive* dose of autonomy—at both the individual and the unit level—guided by a small, only somewhat constraining set of useful truths.

Little did we know what was coming …

ONE BEST PLAN
[8]Management expert Henry Mintzberg claims that the "strategy era" was, in effect, Taylorism carried up to the boardroom.

2002. Business Models Come. Business Models Go.

Here today, Enron tomorrow. All "basic principles," including those that graced *In Search of Excellence*, are up for grabs. We've got to ... "play it as it lays." We've got to ... "make it up as we go along."

Over the next 10 to 20 years, we will be reinventing every aspect of life ... business and government, culture and warfare, and the meaning of what it is to be human itself. If that's true—and I very much believe that it is—then there is Only One Strategy to follow.

Namely: Screw Around Vigorously. SAV, for short.

Hint: I'm dead serious.

2022. Business Models Mostly "Go."

SA(EM)V: Screw Around (Ever More) Vigorously?

Reflections

Eight "Basics." Three generations (and counting). Along those coordinates, we have charted an incredible journey that shows no signs of reaching a "destination." From *1962* ... when I was halfway through college, getting ready for my first job as an Ensign in the U.S. Navy. To *1982* ... when Bob Waterman and I put forth alternatives to the Proven Way Things Are Done. To *2002* ... when the Internet and other new technologies were in the process of rewriting all eight of our "basic" ideas. (Control Alt Delete.) To *2022* ... when profound changes will have occurred in something as "basic" as what it means to be human.

A strange world awaits. A world in which defining "excellence"—let alone "searching" for it (let alone achieving it!)—will be more and more elusive. And more and more exciting.

How frightening! How COOL!

ARE YOU UP FOR IT?

How
frightening!

How
COOL!

ARE YOU
UP FOR IT?

NEW BUSINESS ! ● NEW MANDATE

! Contrasts

WAS	IS
Planning	Acting
Analyze the customer	Ally with the customer
"Workers" (interchangeable parts)	Talent (indispensable partners)
Stop at nothing (The God complex)	Stick to the knitting (The goal, completed)
Vertical integration	Vertigo + innovation
Organization-centric	Network-centric
White-collar world	No-collar world
Tangibles (lumps of stuff)	Intangibles (bits of data)
Real (property)	Virtual (possibility)
Slow and steady	Fast and faster
Certainty	Ambiguity
Leadership mantra: "In the know"	Leadership mantra: "I don't know"
Management "by the numbers"	Management by the nimble
Structure: noose-tight	Structure: loose-tight
Fashion cycles: years, decades	Fashion cycles: days, weeks
GM. Ford. Bethlehem Steel.	Dell. eBay. Wal*Mart.
Cleveland. Detroit.	San Jose. Bangalore.

PURSUING EXCELLENCE IN A DISRUPTIVE AGE: THE LEADERSHIP50

! Technicolour Rules ...

● **Rules? Will 50 of them suffice?**

 ! RANT

We are not prepared ...

We fall back, in these crazy and chaotic times, on the command-and-control model of leadership—a model that no longer accords with how dynamic leaders actually operate.

We seek shelter in the fantasy of a leader who has The Answers ... who promises "change" or "success" or "profits" in exchange for patient "followership" (aka "obedience"). But in an age when all value flows from creativity and initiative, we must imagine and embrace a model of leadership that is loose, open, and perpetually innovative.

We ask leaders to be "good stewards" of the assets they inherit. But in an age when permanence is a dangerous delusion, we must instead ask leaders to challenge the legacies that they have inherited, to create entirely new value propositions—and then to get out before they get stale.

◉ ! VISION

I imagine ...

A young woman, aged 27, who espies a Wondrous Opportunity to reinvent her company's chronically creaky customer-service operation. She tells everyone she meets about this exciting inkling, and everyone says, "Great idea, but good luck!" Even so, she works (and works) (and works) the problem ... and eventually cobbles together a six-person project team. Fanatics all. The team includes a Talent Developer and a Profit Mechanic; our SuperWoman is Visionary and Head Cheerleader. Leading her team on a Voyage of Mutual Discovery, she finds out that her original notion wasn't close to right ... but the Unbounded Quest ultimately results in something ... far, far better ... and far, far more strange.

Lead-Off Matter (A Muscular Definition)

Leadership is ... *Joyous!* It's a matchless opportunity to Make a Difference by marshaling the talents of others to a ... Seriously Cool Cause.

Leadership is ... *Horrible!* It's an exercise in sorting through the mess of human relations, in all their gory detail, day after day. (After day.)

Leadership is ... *Cool!* It's a Glorious Adventure that enables us to magnify our impact on the world.

Leadership is ... *Lonely!* It's a battle against doubt and dread in which you have only your own judgment about human nature to fall back on.

Leadership is ... *Different!* It's a matter not of "doing" excellence but of "inspiring" excellence in others.

Leadership is ... *The Ultimate Responsibility!* It's an assumption of accountability ... for people you cannot control, for actions that you do not perform, for institutions that may not share your sense of accountability.

Leadership is ... *Not what you think!* It's not about "command and control" or kingly charisma. It's about living in the depths (flourishing in the chess game of egos and institutions) and soaring to the heights (rallying others to invent and then pursue seemingly impossible dreams).

New Leadership is ... *The Ultimate New Mandate!* It's an apt prism through which to summarize this long journey that we have taken through our Disruptive Age. It's a never-ending project with a breathtakingly simple (and breathtakingly difficult) core objective: Re-imagine!

Leadership is ... *50 ideas.*

PREMISE: A LEADER'S LIMITS

1. Leaders Create Opportunities.

I was reading a newsletter from an educational organization (one that I support, incidentally). The title of the lead article sent me into a ... Big Rage. It suggested that excellent (educational) institutions "transform people."

Nonsense!

Nobody "transforms" anybody else!

Instead, we create *opportunities* for people ... and then encourage them to apply their latent talents to grasp the opportunities. The difference between the two notions is as subtle as ... A TRAIN GRAND VITESSE COMING TOWARD YOU AT 115 MILES AN HOUR.

Leaders do NOT ... "transform people."[1] Leaders instead construct a context in which ... *Voyages of Mutual Discovery* ... can take place. Leaders provide access to a

---

! TERMS LIMIT

[1] I hate the terms "organizational change," "empowerment," and "motivation." We don't "change" people (or organizations). We don't "empower" people (or organizations). We don't "motivate" people (or organizations).

Scrap those terms. Stomp on them. Every one of them.

At the risk of sounding too much like Tony Robbins, I say: We awaken the latent talent already within those who work with (or for) us ... by providing opportunities that justify their choosing to invest in us their most precious resources: their time and their *emotional commitment*.

luxuriant portfolio of WOW Projects that challenge people to express their Innate Curiosity and to visit (or, indeed, to create) places that they (*and* their leaders) had never dreamed of. And when the voyage bears fruit, leaders applaud like hell, stage "photo ops," and ring the church bells 100 times to commemorate the bravery of their "followers" explorations!

"Places Never Dreamed Of." That is the heart of the matter: NO ONE HAS A CLUE! BOSS = DOESN'T HAVE A CLUE. FOLLOWER = DOESN'T HAVE A CLUE. We must ... THE VERY DEFINITION OF THIS WILD & WOOLLY AGE ... discover-invent places that have not heretofore existed. (THAT'S THE WHOLE DAMN POINT!) And as a leader ... if you don't have the ... NERVE ... to Encourage People ... to Redraw the Map/Create a New Map ... well ... then ... YOU SHOULD NOT BE LEADING. ANYONE. ANYWHERE.

In other words: HERE BE DRAGONS!

2. Leaders Say "I Don't Know."

For a leader, three words matter above all others. Those words, according to management guru-to-gurus Karl Weick, and mentioned before in another context: *"I DON'T KNOW."* "I don't know" is the ... ALL-TIME PERMISSION SLIP.

"I don't know" means: "Hey, you figure it out."

Karl explains: "The leader who says 'I don't know' essentially says that the group is facing a new ballgame where the old tools of logic may be its undoing rather than its salvation. To drop these tools is not to give up on finding a workable answer. It is only to give up on one means of answering that is ill-suited to the unstable, the unknowable, the unpredictable. To drop the heavy tools of rationality is to gain access to lightness in the form of intuitions, feelings, stories, experience, active listening, shared humanity, awareness in the moment, capability for fascination, awe, novel words, and empathy."

The "textbook" idea of leadership: Leader knows all! Leader gives orders! Followers follow! But in weird, wild, textbook-defiant times like these, the model of leader as "all-knowing commander and order-giver extraordinaire" is fatally and fundamentally flawed.

Leaders resort to the Command and Control model when they are ... *scared.* That is: *scared as hell that followers will figure out that they (the leaders) don't have a clue as to what-the-hell-is-going-on.*

The Big Trick is turning "I don't know" into a show of strength, rather than an acknowledgment of weakness. Leaders *do* have a "weakness": They really *don't* "know." But what leaders offer isn't knowledge—it's a smidgen of wisdom and (above all) spirit. The spirit that goes into having the raw nerve to unleash the passion and unleash the talent of others. In fact, that's the ultimate "toughness" of leadership.[2]

3. Leaders Are Rarely the Best Performers.

A symphony conductor is usually a good musician, but seldom a world-class performer. The most effective university deans are often not the best professors. The ability to lead

---

"HARD" TIME

[2]Note well: This is *not* a "soft" idea. This is a quintessentially *hard* business idea. The subtext of "I don't know" is: "We are Venturing into the Unknown. I hired you for a reason, and it wasn't to 'follow orders.' So figure *something* out. Make it up as you go along. And ... damn well don't come home empty-handed."

NEW BUSINESS ● NEW MANDATE

... to Engage Others and to Turn Them On ... rarely coincides with being at the tip-top of the ... Individual Performance Heap.

Which is not to say that leaders shouldn't have a fingertip familiarity with their particular line of business. But the factors that make you good at the "people stuff" and the "inspiration stuff" and the "profit-making stuff" are quite distinct from the factors that vault you to the Pinnacle of Individual Mastery.

In business, alas, it's all too common to promote the "best" practitioner to the job of leading other practitioners. The best trainer becomes head of the training department. The best account manager becomes head of the sales department. And so on. Tellingly, that's not how things work in ... True Talent Enterprises. (A symphony orchestra. A baseball team.) So why do we go that route in business? Beats me. Gross stupidity? Maybe. But more likely: a refusal to see that leadership is ... a *discrete, limited, special* quality.

4. Leaders Are Talent Developers (Type I Leadership).

Great leaders on snorting steeds are important—but great talent developers are the bedrock of organizations that perform over the long haul.

Talent Development ... worthy of the name ... is a 25/8/53 activity. (See Chapter 20.) And ... THE OBSESSION... for those who would Truly Create a Legacy of Greatness. Jack Welch ... *didn't* ... have a vision ... in my book. Jack *was*... the Premier Talent Developer of our times. Some people (leaders) get their Ultimate Jollies out of ... Developing Extraordinary Talent. (Their Hall of Fame hires are their Ultimate Bragging Rights.) Alas, some (most?) don't. Even though we may call this group (majority?) "leaders," they are fearful of hiring people who are better than they are, fearful of true diversity, fearful of odd ducks and rabble rousers.

5. Leaders Are Visionaries (Type II Leadership).

Two pieces of "art" hang on my writing-room wall in Vermont. Both are covers from *Life* magazine. Franklin Delano Roosevelt, 1933, in the pits of the Great Depression. Winston Churchill, 1940, in the midst of the Battle of Britain.

The experts say Roosevelt was not much of an economist. And that Churchill was a questionable talent as military strategist. Yet they kept hope alive. "A leader," Napoleon famously said, "is a dealer in hope."[3]

Over the long haul, we honor most those leaders who are matchless talent developers. But there are indeed times when a "dealer in hope" is essential. Think FDR.

HOPE DIALOGUE

[3]John Gardner, a former senior government official and a brilliant student of leadership, made the same point: "The first task of a leader is to keep hope alive."
Amen.

EXULTANT CONSULTANT

Leaders create projects. Great Leaders create ... Quests.
Personal story: I reported to work as a McKinsey consultant in December 1974. Arrived at 8:30 a.m. Had keys and credit cards by 10 a.m. A project assignment by 11a.m. A plane ticket by noon. Off to Calgary by 2 p.m.—to scope out demand and supply in the Canadian agrichemical business (by myself).
Within 5.5 hours, that is, I was pursuing my first of many ... Quests. I was scared to death. I was exultant.

Think Churchill. Indeed, think Gerald Ford after the Nixon debacle. In business, think Lee Iacocca at Chrysler in the late 1970s. Or Howard Lutnick at Cantor Fitzgerald after 9/11.

6. Leaders Are "Profit Mechanics" (Type III Leadership).

A colleague runs a $200 million business. He's thoughtful as hell, a real people guy. And his presence, if not charismatic, is certainly energetic and reassuring. But that's not the vital secret to his stunning success as CEO over a 15-year period.

My pal majored in mathematics. He *loves* the *New York Times* Sunday Crossword. And ... more to the point ... he loves the Puzzle-Called-Business.

The hair stands up on the back of his neck (I expect) when he examines a P&L or a Balance Sheet. He loves to tease the most extraordinary conclusions from the most obscure, gigantic data sets. It makes him chortle. He hums ... no baloney ... when he plays with numbers. (I've observed it.)

I've come to call this type of leader the IPM: Inspired Profit Mechanic.

An IPM, by himself, would be ... a total disaster. On the other hand, the other two—the Talent Developer and the Fearless Visionary—might also end up being total disasters unless our friend the IPM is on duty ... humming over those numbers.

7. Leaders Understand That ... It All Depends!

I read Summer 2001's "hot read," David McCullough's brilliant *John Adams*. One of the author's avowed goals was to resurrect the importance of the dour Adams in the panoply of "Rushmorian candidates who led America at its most precipitous stage of development." Adams is now ascendant. Jefferson is in decline. However, I came away from the book with an entirely different take: First, it led me to do a lot more Jeffersonian reading. And second, it led me to believe we were ... damn lucky. We needed ... Adams ... and Jefferson ... and Washington ... and Tom Paine ... and Alexander Hamilton ... and James Madison. Remove a single strut from that structure ... and we're still a colony of Britain. (Perhaps.) Each of those "Rushmorian" individuals had astonishing flaws. Astonishing short-sightedness. As much as they had long-sightedness ... and astonishing strengths.

Message: Leadership is a complex affair! The "Renaissance man (or woman)" is a snare, a myth, and a dangerous delusion.

And what's true for the Founding Fathers (*plural!*) is equally true for the start-up restaurant. You need that visionary chef! You need that "people person" who can deal with minimum-wage busboys! You need the IPM who dreams in balance sheets—and who can talk her way through a skeptical banker's objections! In short, you need strengths at various times.

HIRE HIGHER
There's an old saw in business management: You will be great exactly to the extent that you are willing and eager to hire people who are better than you. (An old, old saw indeed. But no less sharp for being so.)

TRILATERAL CONVICTION
Three types of leadership. One big idea: We need all three! We need the Talent Fanatic and Mentor. We need the Visionary and Cheerleader. We need the Profit Mechanic and Operational Genius. The Golden Leadership Triangle is as essential for a six-person project team as for a 60,000-person corporation.

PROFILE: THE DANCE OF LEADERSHIP

8. Leaders Thrive on Paradox.

Forget what they taught you at the Harvard business school. The Illinois business school. The Stanford business school. The Wharton business school. Management ain't science! It is ... 100 PERCENT OF THE TIME ... ART.

MANAGEMENT IS AN ... ART. An art of paradox.

The Ultimate Paradox of ... LEADERSHIP: In order to be "excellent" you must be ... CONSISTENT. *(By most definitions: Excellence = Consistency of Superior Performance.) But the very moment you become excellently "consistent" ... you become ... TOTALLY VULNERABLE ... to attack from the outside.*

We must be constantly vigilant. Vigilant about ... OPPOSITES.

For example: Are we organized "enough"? If so ... *WORRY.* Are we disorganized "enough"? If so ... *WORRY.*

Worry ... constantly ... about the balance ... the wobble ... the swing of the pendulum.

Well ... this idea is actually not about ... *balance.* It's about going one way ... for a while ... & TOO FAR ... and then going back for a while ... & TOO FAR. My view: Relatively extreme, wild oscillation between[4] ... too much control ... and too little control ... is probably the secret to long-term effectiveness.

9. Leaders Love the Mess.

Consider these words from the late advertising genius, Jay Chiat: *"I'm not comfortable unless I'm uncomfortable."*

Definition of crappy leadership? The leader who needs to be "comfortably" "in control."

Definition of Truly Great Leadership? Leaders who get most energized ... when the Shit Hits The Fan.

Leading is ... dealing with issues that couldn't be "dealt with" "below you" in the organization. The issues that are laden with ambiguity. A senior exec at AT&T told me, 20 years ago, that if a "problem" arrived in his in-basket that he was capable of deciding on the spot ... then something was wrong with the "organization"/"system." That particular problem should have been solved a level or two below. He earned his hefty paycheck solely by prowling among the intractable issues.

The boss of a 6,000-person systems-engineering company told me that, oddly (his word—"oddly"), the top Project Managers were typically not from the ranks of his highly degreed engineers; instead, they were "the sort who'd been 'AV guys' in high

---

OUT OF ALIGNMENT

[4]The great General Motors CEO Alfred Sloan said that management consisted of ... steering back and forth between (a) centralizing-the-hell-out-of-things, which saps creativity and thus leads to (b) decentralizing-the-hell-out-of-things, which encourages reckless risk-taking and thus leads to ...

(You get the idea.)

My only problem (big) with Sloan's insight: Over the long haul, most organizations (including his) net out in the direction of too much centralization. The Control Freaks prevail ... and run their organizations into a ditch. (Or off a cliff.)

school or college, the ones who are used to facing crisis after crisis after crisis, then grabbing a roll of Duct Tape and fixing The Damn Thing—on the fly and on the spot."

Interesting, eh? One possible message: *Never hire somebody who doesn't bring Duct Tape with him or her to an interview!* (That's certainly what we Vermonters think.) And if not the real thing, at least metaphorical duct tape. (Hmmm.) Maybe one should plan a crisis in the midst of an interview—a fire alarm or a feigned heart attack. And watch the candidate's reaction. Flustered or calm? Engaged or withdrawn? Maybe not so silly? (Hmmm.)

The "bottom line" here: In selecting leaders, we must be assiduously on the lookout for those who get their jollies in the face of madness[5] ... where others waffle or fold.

10. Leaders Do!

If you don't know what the hell is going on ... if you don't know the shape or even the location of the playing field ... if you don't know the nature of the rule book or even if there is one ... then, in the immortal words of My Old Man, *"Thomas, don't just stand there. Do something."*

It's a cute phrase. But it's far more profound than that. If you don't know what's going on ... Stop Thinking. (It won't do you much good.) Try ... *Something*. See what happens. That is, until you let fly the new system ... or new product ... or new procedure ... or whatever ... you have ... Utterly No Idea What the Hell Is Going On.

11. Leaders Re-Do.

If something goes awry, the typical Big Company ... shoots the messenger. Appoints a ... Special Investigator. Aims to make sure that ... this aberration ... Never Occurs Again. In the process, the possibility of ... Rapid Progress ... is severely diminished. In short: "*Do it right* the first time" is ... stupid. A Snare. A Delusion. (An Abomination.)

Consider two superstars that don't give a second thought to what happens the "first time." (Or the 21st.) Namely: Sony and Microsoft. They "do" ... fast. *And then they ... re-do ... even faster!*

"Sony Electronics," *BusinessWeek* reported, "has a well-earned reputation for persistence. The company's first entry into a new field often isn't very good. But, as it has shown with laptops, Sony will keep trying until it gets it right."

"If Microsoft is good at anything," writes Internet marketing guru Seth Godin, "it's avoiding the trap of worrying about criticism. Microsoft fails constantly. They're eviscerated in public for lousy products. Yet they persist, through version after version, until they get something good enough. Then they leverage the power they've gained in other markets to enforce their standard."

The Sony-Microsoft approach is remarkable—*and an all-too-rare trait*. Most either flog the tepid First Version ... until they look like idiots. Or retreat ... deciding that the failure means they weren't supposed to be in the market in the first place.

CHECK YOUR "MESS" KIT

[5]A Penchant for Chaos is particularly necessary in wartime. In peacetime, the military will tend to promote the "desk jockey." But at the first whiff of grapeshot, you want to invest command in ... those who can shine amid the "fog of war," as Clausewitz called it.

NEW BUSINESS ●! NEW MANDATE

12. Leaders Know When to Wait.

Leaders act. And … ah, the paradoxes of leadership … leaders wait.[6]

Years ago, I spent an afternoon with Dallas Cowboys (America's Team) President Tex Schramm. He told me he had a third, very special "in box" … in addition to "In" and "Out."

The extra one … *Too Hard*.

The truly troublesome stuff, Schramm told me, he tossed into a third box. Often as not (more often than not!), in a few days or a couple of weeks, there would be some natural motion on somebody's part that would provide the key to sorting things out. Axioms:

1. Pick your battles … carefully. (Know when to raise and when to fold.)
2. Sometimes inaction promotes sorting out and the preservation of options.

13. Leaders Are Angry.

Jack Welch, GE's masterful CEO for 20 years, is … an angry man. So, too, Steve Jobs. Both imagine Better Universes—and are irritated (mostly at themselves) because those New and Better Universes continue to elude full realization.

Yes, *angry*. Completely unhinged by the status quo. Completely and perpetually pissed off by the failure of the sun to rise in the West … and determined to do something about it.

Right now.

Axiom: Don't … ever … promote "unangry" people into leadership positions. In fact, don't *hire* unangry people[7] in the first place. The ideal job candidate walks in, looks you in the eye, and says, *"I can't believe this place is so screwed up. But I'm willing to take a chance—as long as I think I've got a decent shot at changing it."* You don't get those very often. But if you ever do … hire her on the spot. And pay her whatever the hell she wants.

One reader of my original *Fast Company* article on leadership, a senior exec at a financial services firm, offered this: "Leaders don't 'want to' win. Effective leaders *need* to win."

Around the time that Tiger Woods won his fifth consecutive "major" tournament title, I heard a radio commentator ask an expert, "Don't you suppose Tiger feels at least a little bit bad that the runner up, Phil Mickelson, still hasn't chalked up a Major?" (Or words to that effect.) The expert replied, "You're joking. Tiger is vicious on the course.

DELAY OF THE LAND

[6]Patience is *still* a virtue. Consider 9/12/01. The day after 9/11. Probably 279 million out of 280 million Americans wanted President George W. Bush to "bomb somebody" that very day. But he didn't. He bided his time. He did some planning. And then—not quite a month later—he acted.

DARK SIDE OF THE MOOD

[7]Is there a Dark Side to this necessary anger? Of course! All good things are products of excess. And all good things therefore breed their extreme opposite. In this case, an anger-fueled "need to win" can produce anti-social behavior. Hence my emphasis on framing leadership as … a Dance of Opposites.

He wants to win every tournament. He wants to crush the competition."

Craig Venter, scientist and former CEO of Celera Genomics ... *Needed to Win* ... the race to be the first to map the human genome. Not "desire" (a great starting point) but ... "need." This is a deep psychological issue ... that's certainly somewhere near the epicenter of effective-project-leadership-in-messy-and-totally-ambiguous-times.

14. Leaders Are Optimists.

Leaders must have not only "fire in the belly" but also ... a smile on their face. Yes, life *is* tough. Some of us absorb that reality—and then exude the resulting fear and anxiety through our pores. But effective leaders exude a sense of confidence and determination that inspires others. Inspires them to quit licking their wounds ... and get on with the (sometimes outrageous) task at hand.

Reporter Lou Cannon observed Ronald Reagan up-close for many years. His take on what made the 40th President so effective: Ronald Reagan "radiated an almost transcendent happiness."

There's also a more elementary way of phrasing this point: *Leaders show up.* Leaders are there. They keep on "keeping on." By their very presence, they inspire others to ... stay the course.

Think Rudy Giuliani. Rudy "showed up"—when it really mattered, on 9/11. As one wag put it, he went from lame-duck, philandering husband to *Time* magazine's Man of the Year ... in 117 days. How? Not through his "strategy." But by showing his face. By standing as the embodiment of Manhattan's Indomitable Spirit.

Woody Allen said it best: "Eighty percent of success[8] is showing up."

15. Leaders Convey a Grand Design.

A leader "sets the tone."[9] That's obvious. The leader is also ... Chief Architect. Not necessarily chief strategic planner.

The "architect model" suits me better: i.e., she/he sets out the ... General Design Parameters. Lets us know what she/he thinks about ... quality. About ... tolerating well-intended and energetically pursued failures. About ... innovation. About ... logistics performed to perfection.

Call it ... Core Values. Call it ... Essential Philosophy. Or our ... Charter. Or ...

"SUCCESS" CHANGE
[8]Friends tell me that Woody Allen originally said, "Eighty percent of *sex* is showing up." Whatever. For my *current* purposes, I'll stick with the Official Authorized Version.

A MAN OF QUALITY
[9]One of the all-time greats at "setting the tone" and then sending a message is Roger Milliken, the CEO of Milliken & Co. When Roger undertook his Incredible Quality Quest, he developed a fascinating habit. Whenever a factory manager came for a visit, Roger would ride out and meet that person at the airport.

Milliken would ask: "What have you done to *dramatically* improve quality in the past 90 days?" And for that factory manager, it was a "good career move" to have a compelling 30-minute spiel at the ready.

Quality was Roger' passion! He wore it on his sleeve! It wasn't that he knew the answers. But at the level of "Grand Design," he knew precisely the nature of the Quest he wanted the leadership team to be engaged in.

Constitution. I call it ... THE DESIGN SPECS. The essential ... "stuff" we care about, the way we intend to ... Live & Make Our Mark. And the stuff we ... won't ... compromise on. The stuff that is the Essence of our Organizational Character.

Conglomerates (of loosely related enterprises) are out of fashion. For good reason—most have proven unmanageable. But there's one I know that seems to work. That's the Virgin Group. Founder-CEO Richard Branson fits the ChiefArchitect model to a T. He says he won't launch a new product unless it's "cheeky." (It also has to be of high quality ... and very affordable.)

Branson ... SETS THE DESIGN SPECS. He ... EMBODIES ... LIVES ... THE DESIGN SPECS. So, too, Welch's ... Performance Fanaticism and Talent Obsession ... at GE. Iacocca's ... Pugnaciousness, in a time of great darkness at Chrysler. Churchill's ... Determination. Gandhi's ... Persistence and Unshakable Philosophy of Non-violence.

16. Leaders Attend to Logistical Details.

I love great design! I love scintillating business concepts! But I will be the first—and I hope among the loudest—to acknowledge the basic "blocking and tackling" that lies behind the historically brilliant execution of, say, marketing campaigns at Coca-Cola. Or PepsiCo.

Fact: Much, if not most, of the dot-com implosion of 2000 was a logistics-driven implosion. The sexy stuff—the websites per se—was in place. But the ability to "deliver the goods," or the toys, at Christmas 1999 was more at issue.

For want of a nail, the shoe was lost. For want of a shoe ... (And the next thing you know, you're toast.) Sure it's an old homily. But it's as true in 2003 as it was hundreds of years ago. Wars ... commercial as well as military ... are won and lost as much ... if not more ... as a result of the absence of shoes and food and bullets and nails and gasoline ... as of faulty strategy or tactics.

Gus Pagonis is the 1991 Gulf War general who got an early battlefield promotion—his third star—from General Norman Schwarzkopf. Why? In astonishingly short order, General P. got the "stuff" (they call it logistics!) to the desert needed to support an American force of well over 500,000 people.

True of George Washington. (Who regularly exited the battlefield at critical moments for Philadelphia, to beg the Continental Congress for soldiers' pay and supplies.) True of George Patton. (Whose amazing feats in the Battle of the Bulge would have been even more amazing with a little more fuel for his tanks.) True of Norman Schwarzkopf and Gus Pagonis.[10]

"ALL KINDS" BULLETIN
[10] Along about now, I worry that you are ... pulling your hair out.

"Too much. Too much. Too much. How can I do all 50 of these things?" you might say (or scream).

Well, of course you can't do all of these things. But you don't have to. Remember: In leadership, it takes all kinds. Or rather, it takes at least three kinds. (See above on "three leadership types.") Norman Schwarzkopf didn't need to *be* Gus Pagonis. He just *needed* to know that he needed Gus Pagonis. The best leaders recognize and recruit other (different) (extraordinary) leaders

17. Leaders Side With the "Action Faction."

Bill Creech, the retired four-star general who conducted an extraordinary turnaround at the U.S. Air Force Tactical Air Command, framed the leadership challenge this way: "*There's a war on ... between the people who are trying to do something and the people who are trying to keep them from doing something wrong.*"

Bill makes a fascinating point. The "bad guys" ("the people who are trying to keep them from doing something wrong") are rarely representatives of the ... Forces of Evil. They are "simply" trying to keep the "action fanatics" from "doing something wrong" ... from breaking the rules. In the process, they use "due process" and "compliance" to hopelessly gum up the works, slow things down, and stifle innovation. *(All innovation = Breaking today's rules.)* (Right?)

In fact, there must always be Total War (right term!) between the Vital Forces of Action and the Necessary Forces of Control. (Enron defines the opposite case of the "smart," "entrepreneurial" "action fanatics" run amok.) The problem: The Victors in this Eternal Tug of War ... in nine cases out of ten ... are the "Sanctioned" Enforcers of Bureaucratic Rules. Thus, on balance, one attempts to pursue ... IMBALANCE ... in favor of the Action Faction[11] ...especially in these Traumatically Turbulent Times. (The price: a few Enrons.)

PROVOCATION: IF IT AIN'T BROKE, BREAK IT

18. Leaders Honor Rebels.

It's fairly common for companies to pay close attention to their most disgruntled customers. After all, the customers who are roughest on us may potentially lead us to critical reforms.

Unfortunately, we rarely extend the idea of listening to dissidents to a group that's even more important: *pissed-off employees.*

Recent Gallup research shows that 55 percent of employees are effectively "tuned out." Of the remainder, 19 percent are actively at work sabotaging their company, and 26 percent support their company's current goals and practices.

Conventional wisdom says: Focus on getting more productivity out of the 26 percent. However, I'd contend that the 55 percent typically have damn good reasons for

---

"FIRE," EVERY TIME

Phil Kotler posits three management eras:

1965–1980: Era of Strategic Planning. Motto of those times: *Ready. Aim. Fire.*

1980–1995: Era of Global Competitive Warming. New motto: *Ready. Fire! Aim.*

1995 to ????: Era of the Discontinuous Change. Motto of this age: *Fire! Fire! Fire!*

THE HIGH COST OF "DOING"

[11]If I were Secretary of the Treasury, I'd gladly accept the occasional Enron or WorldCom as the price of a truly entrepreneurial economy. Likewise: If I were the leader of an eight-person project team, I'd gladly take the heat for a renegade member ... in return for her turning a humdrum project into a ... Show-stopper.

being tuned out. And the group that interests *me* the most is the 19 percent who are ... active saboteurs.[12] At least they give enough of a damn to do ... *something*. They are your ... saviors-in-waiting. The rebels in your midst! What if we took their ire ... *seriously*? What if we said it was a ... *fabulous reflection of reality*? What if we ... *listened to them*? What if we altered our ... strategy ... as a result?

19. Leaders Hang Out With Freaks.

As I wrote earlier: *Innovation is ... easy*. To wit: Want to "get more interesting"? Hang out with "more interesting" people. I call it the ... *putting-yourself-in-harm's-way approach*.

BECOME A COLLECTOR!

The collections: Weird consultants! Weird employees! Weird suppliers! Weird customers! Weird hobbies! Weird vacations! Weird any-damn-thing! As long as it's ... WEIRD.

Innovation is *"easy."* Spend your time with innovators! Surround yourself with freaks![13] That's *my* secret. And I think it'll work for any ... leader.

Message: WE BECOME WHO WE HANG OUT WITH!

20. Leaders Promote (Weird) Demos.

Recall Chapter 17: The leader is determined to start a supply chain revolution. Should he/she bark, "Thou Shalt Overhaul the Supply Chain?"

Maybe. But probably not.

Instead the leader makes it clear that this is the priority, makes some seed money available, and asks for quick (and a little dirty) demos—Demonstration Projects that quickly test and dramatically alter and greatly improve the idea.

To enhance-cement his/her case, the leader needs: (1) Hard evidence, (2) Cool-Weird-Imaginative Evidence, (3) A Cadre of Zealous Test Pilot-Pioneers (of any rank!). (4) And the leader needs all this ... Fast.

AN AGING OF "CHANGE"?

[12]Recently, when an Irish journalist asked me to state my view of the current state of (corporate) play, I replied: *"Twenty years ago we honored those who didn't 'rock the boat.' Ten years ago we started begging everyone to become a 'change agent.' And, now, in the midst of full-blown madness, I'm asking ... begging ... 'everyone' to become no less than ... patently disrespectful."*

I think he thought I was nuts. But, then, these are nuts-y times.

NEW WEIRD ORDER

[13]A very large corporation once brought me in to introduce its leadership team to "radical" points of view. So I rolled out the old projector and regaled members of the team with a scintillating PowerPoint presentation, right?

No!

Instead, I introduced them to ... WEIRD. They wanted to "get serious about branding." So I introduced them to the best branding freaks I know: Jean-Marie Dru of TBWA/Chiat/Day. Mickey Drexler, formerly of Gap. Rich Teerlink of Harley-Davidson. And so on.

For every opportunity, there is ... Someone(s) Weird.

Weird rules. (In weird times.) (Duh.)

The key idea is ... Heroes. Demos. Stories.

"Ordering" the thing done "across the board" usually backfires. It usually results in premature, top down, staff-run, conservative, cookie-cutter approaches—often dominated by the biggest (and thence most conservative) units. But putting out the call for *"something, anything, cool, fast"* sets in motion a competition, engaging a ... Widespread Band of Sanctioned Pirates ... from anywhere and at any rank in the corporation.

Bottom line: *Leaders aiming to change their world ... fast ... identify ... Palpable Heroes ... who executed palpable "New Look Projects"; then the leaders point to these pioneers and say to the masses: "Look. Here. It looks like this, and it was done by ... one of your own."*

21. Leaders Make Mistakes.

And they make no bones about it. Another thing that hangs on the wall of my Vermont writing studio is a quote by David Kelley, founder of IDEO Product Design: "Fail faster. Succeed sooner." Next to it hangs a saying by the extraordinary photographer Diane Arbus, who told her students: *"Learn not to be careful."*

In placid times, leaders may well have ... The Answers. In turbulent times, leaders have the ... Best Questions. Questions that encourage (note the root word: "courage") others to undertake those ... Voyages of Mutual Discovery.

And the essence of process: allowing people to ... screw up. Screwing up is the Essence of ... Trying New Stuff. If you try new stuff ... you screw up. If you try ... a lot of new stuff ... you screw up a lot.

22. Leaders Make Big Mistakes.

MISTAKES ARE NOT ENOUGH. IN DISCONTINUOUS TIMES. BIG MISTAKES[14] ARE CALLED FOR. NAY ... DEMANDED.

Recall my nomination for favorite PowerPoint slide, among the thousands in my portfolio: "REWARD EXCELLENT FAILURES. PUNISH MEDIOCRE SUCCESSES."

These tumultuous times beg for ... Bold Initiatives ... to up the odds ... of even staying afloat.

While thoughtless recklessness is not to be applauded, the word "reckless" must be examined ... carefully. Most who change the world—King, Galileo, Picasso—were indeed "reckless." But not thoughtless. They were certainly doing more than "thinking outside the box." (A tepid term that I loathe!) The Kings and Galileos and Picassos (and Churchills and de Gaulles) ... attempted ... Against Hyper-long Odds ... to ... Re-imagine an Entirely New Box. If that ain't "reckless" ... I don't know what the word means.

FAIL, FAIL AGAIN

[14]At first, you *rarely* succeed. Hence, you need to ... fail, fail again. Consider my mantra:

> No failures ... no successes.
> No fast failures ... no fast successes.
> No big failures ... no big successes.
> No big, fast failures ... no big, fast successes.

NEW BUSINESS ● **NEW MANDATE**

23. Leaders Create Blame-Free Cultures.

Just making mistakes (even big mistakes) isn't enough. Creating an error-friendly culture is the final, all-important step.

Jorma Ollila has a secret. Ollila transformed a hodgepodge "conglomerate" into a focused, ferocious global power. Ollila is CEO of an ... Invention Machine ... called ... Nokia. And in *Cold Calling: Business the Nokia Way*, author Trevor Merriden attributes much of Nokia's extraordinary success to a purposefully blame-free, go-ahead-and-try-it corporate culture.

BIG POINT: Honoring "mistakes" and creating a "blame-free" culture does *NOT* mean ... tolerating sloppy work. Or reneging on accountability. To the contrary. The essence of accountability: PEOPLE WHO CARE ... *SO DAMN MUCH* ... THAT THEY WILL RISK EVERYTHING ... AND SCREW UP BIG TIME ... IN ORDER TO ACHIEVE THEIR ENDS.

Clear?

24. Leaders Break Down Barriers.

We are Re-imagining the World! We are adding value in totally new fashions which require ... Bringing to Bear the Entire Resource Set of the Enterprise ... and its Full Supply and Distribution Chain. Which means: *NO #!@&*X&* STOVEPIPES!* No barriers ... Whatsoever ... to communication!

WE HAVE TO LEARN TO TALK TO ONE ANOTHER! SEAMLESSLY! INSTANTLY! DEMOLISH STOVEPIPES!

So doing *is* the Exacting & Detailed ... Work of Top Management. Again: Dirty fingernails. Dive into the details. Do not rest ... until ... ALL THE BULLSHIT ... has been eradicated.

MEASURE YOURSELF! WHAT ... EXACTLY ... HAVE YOU DONE ... TODAY (!!) ... IN THE LAST TWO HOURS (!!) ... IN THE LAST MEETING (!!) ... TO "REMOVE THE BULLSHIT" ... "DEMOLISH THE FUNCTIONAL STOVEPIPES"?

25. Leaders Forget.

How about this? Leader Job One: *Forgetting!*

The extraordinary inventor and Polaroid founder Edwin Land said that innovation was "not so much having a new idea as stopping having an old idea." And Visa founder Dee Hock says: "The problem is never how to get new, innovative thoughts into your mind, but how to get the old ones out."

Forgetting! (Destroying!)

This issue obsesses me!

Bottom line: What if we said ... THE ESSENCE OF LEADERSHIP2004 IS THE ... WILL TO FORGET?

PEOPLE: A RELATIONSHIP TO TALENT

26. Leaders Are Talent Fanatics.

I'm aware of the problems of "hype." (I've caused some of those problems.) Nonetheless: *"Talent"* may be the most potent word I know in the businessperson's language.

Use the word ... "Talent" ... and a certain type of image comes to mind. An image that's about as far away from either "employee" or *Dilbert's* "cubicle slave" as one can imagine.

I think "talent" ... and I conjure up a winning football team. Or the production of "The Lion King" I saw in New York a few years ago.

I'm not naïve. Yet I think there's no reason we can't ... *imagine* ... each and every ... "employee" as ... TALENT. In fact, I think that's precisely what leaders of the future will ... and must! ... do.

Talent: *Attract it. Nurture it. Mentor it. Reward it. Create the context in which it can thrive.*

So: Are you a ... Certified Talent FANATIC?[15] As the head of a six-person project team, at age 24? As the head of the public works department for the City of Long Beach? (Age 42.) Think about it. Call it the "NFL General Manager Standard." How do you measure up?

27. Leaders Nurture Other Leaders.

The honors here go to leader-iconoclast-political-activist Ralph Nader. *"I start with the premise,"* he said, *"that the function of leadership is to produce more leaders, not more followers."*

The first image that comes to mind when I think about "leadership" is the fabled 1945 picture of Roosevelt, Churchill, and Stalin sitting together on the fantail of the good ship U.S.S. Quincy. Hitler's sagging. Twenty million Russians are dead. London's been flattened by bombs. And earth's three most potent human beings are quite calmly divvying up the earth, preparing for a post-war environment.

Message: The Leader as ... Strong Man.

But I suspect those times are past. That the technology is changing ... too fast. As I mentioned before, I talked to Bill McGowan, de facto founder of the telecom upstart MCI. "The 'chump-to-champ-to-chump' cycle," he lectured me, "used to be three generations. Now it's about five years." Staying power ... historically mostly fantasy ... is now ... Total Fantasy. Therefore, I will offer a new guideline for leaders.

Namely: LEADERS DON'T CREATE "FOLLOWERS"! THEY CREATE ENERGIZED, AUTONOMOUS LEADERS. "LEADERS" THROUGHOUT THE ORGANIZATION, STARTING WITH INSPIRED YOUTH AT THE "BOTTOM," HELP OTHERS DISCOVER NEW WORLDS. ENCOURAGE "LEADERS" WHO INVENT NEW WORLDS. LEADERS WHO OUTSTRIP—AND DETHRONE—THEIR PUTATIVE LEADERS.

I am not suggesting that everyone is ... Albert Einstein. Or ... Winston Churchill. I *do* mean that everyone is responsible for ... Making-Defining Her Own Way. EVERYONE IS CHARGED WITH OVERTURNING TODAY'S BELIEFS.

One can no longer depend on the Big Corporate Fuzz Ball to nurture them ... for 30 or 40 years. Or even 10 or 20 years. Or even ... 5 or 10 years.

NEW BUSINESS

NEW MANDATE

NO STRATEGY, PLEASE—WE'RE MCKINSEY

[15]For 7 years, I worked at McKinsey & Co. The firm has its flaws. (Big flaws.) But for 70 years, it's been successful. (Astonishingly successful.) And one big reason for that success, I contend, is that while this renowned strategic consultancy has *never* had anything approaching a strategy (!) ... it has been absolutely *obsessed* with ... Talent ... from Day One. As the saying goes: Watch what "they" do, not what "they" say.

Everyone a ... Renegade.
Everyone an ... Innovator.
Everyone a ... Leader.

28. Leaders Engender Trust.

My colleague and Chairman Emeritus of Tom Peters Company, Jim Kouzes, co-wrote with Barry Posner a book with a one-word title ... *CREDIBILITY*. Jim and Barry insisted ... based on 20 years of data collection ... that at the end of the day ... what gave the Leader ("powerful" or "powerless") the ability to ... Ask for Great Contributions ... in the nation or on a seven-person project team ... was the degree to which he or she was ... Credible.

Call it ... Credibility.
Call it ... Trust.

Superficially, it's the "softest" of ... Leadership Attributes. And not exactly what they teach you at Harvard Business School. (Even in 2003.) And yet ... over the long haul ... Credibility is the Absolute "Hardest" of Leadership Traits.

I'd not go so far as to say that "Good Leaders" ... "never tell a lie." Roosevelt lied like hell as he evaded the Constitution and more or less edged us into World War II. To make it through the maze on the way to the top, leaders ... of anything ... must exhibit ... shrewdness.

And yet ... without sounding corny about it ... the best of them understand that ... Leadership ... in the end ... is a ... Sacred Trust. The responsibilities are enormous. Whether it's Hilda Stewart's Cub Scout Troop that I belonged to in Severna Park, Maryland, in 1949 ... or the one-person counseling sessions between a mentor-professor and her Ph.D. student ... or working with a team of 2,500.

"Trustworthy" is about the biggest and most sacred word in the English language.

29. Leaders Are Relationship Mavens.

It may well be the Age of the Internet, but premier sports agent Mark McCormack insisted that there are times ... and not all that infrequently ... when one should fly 5,000 miles for a five-minute meeting. I've taken his advice. It's as obvious as the end of your nose. Or at least it should be: LEADERSHIP IS ... IN THE END ... PURELY PERSONAL ... THE ULTIMATE RELATIONSHIP GAME.

When Lou Gerstner took over at IBM, many scoffed (yours truly included), because he lacked a technical background. And though IBM was touted for providing "great customer service" ... the company had become a bully and forgotten the ... Art of

---

"ONE" TRICK PLANNER

Once, after I spoke to the leaders of a financial advisory-service company, the CEO said something to me about leadership that has stuck with me ever since. The company's field forces consist entirely of independent contractors, many of whom were then nearing retirement age. The CEO commented that many of these guys would have no one to sell their businesses to. "They understand, better than I do, how to be truly great financial advisors," he said. "What they don't understand is that the 'trick' to creating a legacy is *mentoring*. I keep telling them: Spend time—lots of time—developing *just one* person to follow in your footsteps."

I love that idea: "Just one."

Intimate Listening. Gerstner hit the road ... visiting customers of all sizes and shapes ... and asking them ... point blank ... what the hell the IBM problem was. They told him. Point blank. He fixed it. And IBM turned around. Obviously, the story is not that simple, but the impact of Mr. G.'s Magical Intimate Listening Tour is hard to overestimate.

It's (Intimate) Relationships, Stupid!

30. Leaders Are Networking Fiends.
Some people are ... Instinctive Networkers. Women are better at it than men. Much better. Bill Clinton ran around Oxford in the '60s taking detailed notes on damn near everybody he met. I once saw Senator Bob Graham of Florida working a room. WOW! Same deal. Two or three minutes with each person. Sometimes a little less. Rarely more. And as he turned to meet the next person, almost surreptitiously, but without fail, he reached into the breast pocket of his suit, pulled out a note card, and jotted something down.

Even if a large share of "all this" is born rather than made, and training can take us only so far, awareness of ... The Wiring Proclivity ... means paying very explicit attention to it in the leadership development process. (Especially in an Age of Instability ... where changing arrays of project partners is the New Norm.)

Mantra: LEADERS WEAVE DENSE WEBS OF INCLUSION AT ALL LEVELS. LOSERS ARE SLAVES TO HIERARCHY & RANK & FORMAL COMMUNICATION PROCESSES.

31. Leaders Connect.
Great Leaders really are ... THERE. They really are ... INTENSELY CONCENTRATED ON YOU. They really are ... *REAL*. They really do ... CONNECT.

There's nothing I'd rather do than meet the most extraordinary human being alive today: Nelson Mandela. And I bet twice the price of this book that if I met him, I'd come away from the 2.5-minute meeting thinking that Mandela had thought that I was ... THE MOST INTERESTING PERSON ON EARTH. Yes, that's exactly what ... Great Leaders ... "do."

There's an intriguing story that goes more or less like this: Ms. X had sat at dinner between Mr. Y and Mr. Z. Mssrs. Y and Z were renowned individuals. Z in particular. Said Ms. X about Mr. Y, "When you sat at dinner with him, you came away believing that he was perhaps the smartest individual you'd ever met." About Mr. Z (the truly successful one), she said, "When you sat at dinner with Mr. Z, you came away thinking that *you* were the smartest person on earth."

I've been somewhat misleading in making this point, and a few others. I imply that there are some tried and true "techniques" ... that will allow you to master the "relationship thing." I do believe we *can* get better at the "relationship thing." (I have a

NEW BUSINESS **!** NEW MANDATE

{ **WOMEN SOAR**
This chapter leaves out an essential factor in the leadership equation. Namely: the 51 percent chunk of the population who constitute the "mother lode" of leadership potential. The reason for that omission: I covered that (big) story in Chapter 21. For a brief sample of my argument there, recall this headline to a *BusinessWeek* Special Report: "As Leaders, Women Rule: New Studies Find that Female Managers Outshine Their Male Counterparts in Almost Every Measure."

no-nonsense friend I bludgeoned into doing "thank you notes"; he openly calls it "life-transforming.") But I think, in the end, unless you are a "relationship sort"—and I'm not sure how much of this can be learned or taught—you're going to have the devil's own time with these ideas. Because Investing In Relationships means two big things: (1) SINCERITY. (2) TIME. Neither can be faked. Frankly, if you don't "get off" on people ... there's not much hope in terms of Leadership Effectiveness. For those who are choosing leaders ... beware.

PROFESSION: THE "JOB" OF LEADING

32. Leaders Push Their Organizations into the Value-added Stratosphere.

In particular, they push their organizations to move up, up, up the Value-Added Ladder. Making "good stuff" is no longer enough. Not by a long shot. "Good stuff" has become but the ... Starting Point. In fact, even "Great Stuff" has assumed near-commodity status.

Remember Chapter 6: "These days," said Ann Livermore, head of Hewlett-Packard's services division, "building the best server isn't enough. That's the price of entry." This remark was made on the heels of an $18 *billion* offer that Hewlett-Packard made in 2000 for 31,000 PricewaterhouseCoopers consultants. The idea: Services Added ... Intellectual Capital Added.

Lots of both!

The story is ... *the story* ... amongst many of the best-of-the-best. UPS. (Brown!) Home Depot. FedEx. GE. Hewlett-Packard. Yellow. (Formerly Yellow Freight.) United Technologies/Carrier. United Technologies/Pratt & Whitney. United Technologies/Otis Elevator. And on. And on.

Question: What about *your* flavor of "turnkey-services-added"?

33. Leaders Create New Markets.

I posit: NO ONE EVER MADE IT INTO THE ... BUSINESS HALL OF FAME ... ON A RECORD OF LINE EXTENSIONS.

Think Gates. (Microsoft.) McNealy. (Sun.) Ellison. (Oracle.) Dell. Jobs. (Apple.) Bezos. (Amazon.) Welch. (GE) Walton. (Wal*Mart.) Blank & Marcus. (Home Depot.) Carnegie. Rockefeller. Sloan. Ford.

Does "line extension" come to mind?

Hardly.

The short list above is not marked by champions of look-alikes. Some (Jobs, Ellison, McNealy) were brilliant ... Product Innovators. Some (Dell, Gates, Bezos, Welch, Ford, Sloan) were brilliant ... Business Systems Innovators. But all were ... Market Creators.

There's another (huge) problem with the "line extension" mentality at Huge Co.

ALL SALES, *ALL THE TIME.* ♥ **Politics =** Getting Things Done *Through People.*

Most Huge Co. "hurdle rates" demand ... Big Bucks ... fast ... from those "line extensions." What's wrong with that? Plenty, it turns out. Fact: Most re-defining products start out as little niche ideas, that take off ... and only years later ... change the world.

34. Leaders Love New Technology.

The technology ... *is*... changing ... *everything*. I'm not insisting that the leader, of whatever, also be the Chief Technology Officer. That's too much to ask, especially from 52-year-old Big Boss of Enormous Corp.

But I am asking something ... specific. Something ... verifiable. Something ... BIG. That 52-year-old CEO need not be able to hack her firm's computer network. But she does need to be ... DESPERATELY ... IN LOVE... WITH THE NEW TECHNOLOGY.

I'm hardly a dewy-eyed technologist. To be honest, the last programming language I learned was ... FORTRAN. My kids "get" the Web far better than I. (Understatement.) But I am a ... PASSIONATE APPRECIATOR.

My strong belief: Effective Leaders ... circa 2003 ... must be ... IN LOVE WITH/ DEEPLY APPRECIATE (in the truest sense of that word "appreciate") ... the New Technologies ... and instinctively "get" their power to topple all regnant industry wisdom.

35. Leaders Are Salespeople Extraordinaire.

Leaders Know It's ... ALL SALES, ALL THE TIME.

Leadership = Sales.

PERIOD.

Don't agree? Don't ask me.

Ask George W. Bush. Ask William J. Clinton. And ask ... the successful "chief" of a six-person project team who was able to induce Significant Change in the way her 600-person division handles logistics. Doubtless she had a good idea. Doubtless she has good technical skills. Beyond doubtless: *She is ... a Great Salesperson.*

Axiom: If you don't LOVE SALES ... find another life. And don't pretend to be a "leader." (Harsh ... but true.)

36. Leaders Love "Politics."

POLITICS. I've observed that most "staffers" hate it. They consider it ... "slimy" ... "demeaning" ... "wasteful."

They're wrong.

They're stupid. (Sorry.)

LOVE POLITICS ... OR DON'T EXPECT TO GET ANYTHING DONE DURING YOUR TENURE.

Politics = *Getting Things Done Through People.*

Compromising. (True!)

Listening. (All the time!)

Standing your ground upon occasion. (Even if it costs you.)

Giving in ... upon occasion. (Even if it costs you.)

There's literally nothing that gets my goat more than the "scientist" or "engineer" or "administrator" who says to me, "It's all shit ... it's just damned politics. I don't have the stomach for it."

People who govern in times of war ... *do politics.*

People who get scientific papers accepted at prestigious journals ... *do politics.*

People who win Nobel prizes ... *do politics.*

The project manager of Boston's Big Dig ... *does politics.*

People who lead the effort to get a community center built ... *do politics.*

Sure it's sometimes downright dirty. (Sometimes you put your mirror away.) Yet ... politics ... is all about human beings coping and succeeding (or failing) ... in marriage ... or in a business setting.

So: IF YOU DON'T *LOVE* POLITICS[16] ... YOU'LL NEVER GET *ANYTHING* DONE. YOU ARE *NOT* A LEADER.

37. Leaders Master Their Organizations.

In Chapter 17, we discussed Smith College President Jill Ker Conway's efforts to find and use dissidents to implement her audacious goals for reinvention. She ferreted out reticent sympathizers and gave them her blessing ... and was particularly successful at soliciting "discretionary" funds from alums charged up at the appointment of Smith's first woman president.

Ms. Conway's strategy, I believe, has universal applicability: (1) Effective Leaders (even "Presidents") Are Masters of the End Run. (2) Effective leaders mostly avoid—rather than fight—the "Old Culture." (Be polite. But don't expend most of your precious hours trying to change 'em.) (At least until you've "won"—in which instance they will be among the first to rush aboard and tell you how they've always secretly supported you.) (3) Effective leaders know that while you can't change "people," you can change "cultures"—by unearthing ... New Species ... that demonstrate "The New Way." (4) As was said in "All the President's Men" ... follow the money; find ... NEW $$$ ... to evade the budget & launch the novel & discretionary programs that will define your tenure.

38. Leaders Are Great Learners.

The best (and brightest) consultant I worked with in seven years at McKinsey had, I thought, one True Secret: He fearlessly and invariably asked ... "WHY?"

"Why?" is ... *sooooo* ... powerful! Tool No. 1 of the Intrepid Explorer! And not nearly so innocent as it sounds.

It's damn tough for a ... Leader ... who some contend is supposed to "know the answers" ... to humbly and repeatedly ask, concerning the "simplest" of issues ... WHY? And yet it is the unasked "Why?" in those so-called "simple" settings that's usually the key to the mint. Nobody asks, "Why?" about this or that procedure. For

---

years. "Hey ...it's the way we do things around here." Oops!

Hence: Effective Leading = Invariably Asking "WHY?"

At least a dozen times a day.

Count 'em!

39. Leaders Are Great Performers.

FDR claimed, *"It is necessary for the President to be the nation's No. 1 actor."* Amen.

Is this a plug for disingenuous behavior?

No. (Or mostly not.)

If a leader attempts to induce risk taking ... she or he must *embody* risk taking, even if she or he is a naturally reticent person.

As one of my friends put it, bluntly, "Look, Tom, leaders aren't allowed to have bad days, especially on bad days. From the retail battlefield to the real thing, leaders must exude the energy and confidence that will embolden others to act in the face of peril. It's that simple. And that hard."

Every move by the 24-year-old supervisor, as well as the President of the United States, is scrutinized and dissected as to what it portends to the organization's (and individual's) future.

Hence: *Act* ... accordingly!

40. Leaders Are Great Storytellers.

A scintillating story makes an (abstract) strategy real. Brings it to life. Ronald Reagan had a handful of beliefs that were truly dear to him. And he held onto them ... despite the insane pressures of the presidency. Above all, Ronald Reagan was ... a Great Storyteller. (You can love him or hate him. But you can't deny his splendid storytelling ability, or the degree to which it changed the overall dialogue in America—for the better!)

It's simple. Profound. (And mostly not understandable to scientists, engineers, and their ilk.) (I'm only half kidding.)

So: What's your (compelling) story?[17]

PASSION: THE "INSIDE" GAME

41. Leaders Enjoy Leading.

At the end of a Dublin seminar in December 2001, the head of a marketing services company approached me, made some very complimentary remarks about my leadership commentary ... and proceeded to say that I'd missed the most important point. (Oops.) "Leaders," he insisted, "must get a kick out of leading."

He has a (brilliant) point.

Why?

Why?

Why?

{ **THE "LEAD" STORY**
[17]Recall the words of leadership guru Howard Gardner: "A key—perhaps *the* key—to leadership is the effective communication of a story."

So ... with thanks ... here it is.

An historian claimed that Franklin Roosevelt, crippled though he was, couldn't wait to get to his desk in the morning—he loved *the game* so much. On the other hand, Warren Bennis, the leadership guru and my great friend, did a stint as president of the University of Cincinnati, and was often unhappy. He said an old friend spotted the source of his problem with frightening acuity: "Warren," he told me, "you want to '*be*' president, but do you want to '*do*' president?"

Leading isn't for everyone! Me, for one! I love what I do—the researching and writing and presenting bits. I do not get an "unmitigated kick," as one of my leader pals put it, out of the issues that occupy a true leader's day. And that's that. At least I award myself a few points for having had the good sense to recognize this—and thence, within my own company, "delegate" the CEO job to someone else, who does get his kicks out of coming to the office in the morning and finding a host of intractable "people problems" awaiting.

Message: If you don't *love* leading, look ... quickly ... for the nearest Exit. Do *not* try to fake it.[18]

42. Leaders Know Themselves.

Leadership is ... personal.

Leaders must first and foremost: *Know Themselves. Be aware of their impact on others. Have an Honest Coach who can Shoot Straight with them.*

LEADERS—AT ANY LEVEL!—HAVE AN ENORMOUS RESPONSIBILITY. (They are responsible for the Development & Future of Others!)

The frightening fact is that leaders ... *do* make a difference.

For good.

Or for ill.

And they make that difference as a result of ... the way they present themselves.

Inspired Leadership (in the Telemarketing Center, or with a single Ph.D. student) is a ... MUTUAL DISCOVERY PROCESS. (See above.) My experience is clear:

Individuals (call them Leaders) cannot engage in a "liberating mutual discovery process" unless they are comfortable with themselves.

MUTUAL DISCOVERY ... means ... by definition ... confronting the unknown, head on, fearlessly taking the ambiguous path. "Leaders" who are not comfortable with themselves tend to be or to become control freaks. They need to constantly remind you of "Who's in charge." (I AM.) Of course, what they are really doing is trying to convince *themselves* that *they* are in charge!

Back to that marvelous Weickian term: "I DON'T KNOW." The Bald Fact is that

---

There's a thing called
"LEADERSHIP."
If you don't revel in it ...
EXIT, STAGE LEFT,
NOW!

GOOD HUMOR MANAGER
[18]People (LEADERS) who are comfortable with themselves also laugh a lot. That's my experience. Thus, here are two of my rules:
1. Never work in a place where laughter is rare.
2. Never work for a leader who doesn't laugh.

"I DON'T KNOW" is an act of the Utmost Bravery ... on the part of the Leader. It suggests a willingness to ... Cede Control.

So maybe leadership is the opposite of what it seems: LEADING IS GRANTING "EXPLORATION RIGHTS" TO ONE'S "FOLLOWERS." Remember that the idea of "followership" is really about ... Creating More Leaders.

I think all this makes sense. Common sense. (Probably, alas, *un*common sense.) If "excellence," for example, is the goal, especially amidst today's madness, then we (leaders) ... must have ... the ... Full Emotional Engagement ... of "followers"/"explorers."

Catch 22+: People are only 100 percent engaged if they are ... *in perceived charge of the/their Personal Quests.*

(And again, one more time, you-the-leader will only permit that level of growth, and thence experimentation & subsequent failures, if you are secure with ... YOU. I.e., if you get an Unmitigated Kick Out of the Mess.)

43. Leaders Accept Responsibility.

It's simple: *Leaders take responsibility—visibly!—for the decisions they make and the outcomes that ensue.*

(The spectacle of senior officers from giant, formerly high-flying companies "Taking the Fifth" on national TV has not been inspiring.)

At any level, at any age, in any position of responsibility: To play the "Blame Game"[19] destroys the ... CREDIBILITY ... of the blamer-"leader" faster than any other single act.

Does this mean that retrospective analysis of things that go awry is inappropriate? Of course not. On the other hand, I've argued for 20 years that "a bias for action" is the single most significant positive attribute a successful enterprise—public or private—can have. A "bias for action" does not suggest thoughtlessness about the past. But it does suggest that there is a limit (relatively low) to the amount of introspection that might go on. Recall my hearty endorsement of "quick prototyping"; the best response to a screw-up is to do a dab of retrospective assessment—and then, hastily, get on with the next try/trial/demo/pilot/prototype.

Simple fact: Huge bureaucracies think too much ... and act too little. "Scapegoating" is a big part of this debilitating, paralytic process.

44. Leaders Focus.

The just retired chairman of CVS/pharmacy chairs the advisory board of an educational foundation. The very creative educational leader was about to embark on a program to expand his extraordinary school to a nationwide system of schools embodying his

GAME BLAME

[19]In 2001, the Texas Rangers signed Alex Rodriguez (A-Rod) to a quarter-*billion*-dollar contract. The Rangers began the next season slowly. *Very* slowly. The "axe" clearly had to fall. So who to fire? A-Rod or the manager? The manager ... *of course*. Likewise, when a symphony starts losing its way, it's the music director or the conductor who has to go—not the first violinist.

The point: In a talent-based enterprise (and what enterprise today is not based on talent?), failure is ... *the leader's fault.*

Message: You recruited 'em. You hired 'em. You trained 'em. You evaluated 'em. You managed 'em. They didn't perform. *Your* fault.

philosophy. My pal is at one of those "inflection points" ... where the emphasis shifts from "making one great school" to "making a great *system*." "Your number-one priority," this chap said, "is creating a 'to-don't' list."

Nice. A "TO-DON'T" LIST!

Fact: There's nothing ... NOTHING! ... easier than speed-typing a 50-item "TO-DO" list.[20] In which ... EACH ONE OF THE 50 ... is ... truly ... of the ... Utmost Importance.

Fact: During a six-year tour as Housekeeping Chief ... Finance Chief ... whatever ... GETTING ONE[21] SERIOUSLY COOL THING DONE ... IS A ... V-E-R-Y BIG DEAL.

Our sage advisor then went on to add that my insanely talented colleague should sit down once a week, or at least once a month, with a friendly-but-formal "To-Don't Advisor" to review his calendar ... and consider what might have been *eliminated* during the last few days or weeks, and what ought to be eliminated during the coming days and weeks.

Nice. A formal "system" to "manage" the "To Don't" list.

45. Leaders Take Breaks.

The demands of leadership at any level could fill our waking hours thrice over, especially these days. And at times, 18-hour days are a must. But ... beware of burnout. Beware, in particular, of your *unawareness* of burnout ... and the unwillingness of those around you to point out that you are a ... Zombie.

This is not a homily about "work-life balance." I leave that to your spouse or preacher-priest-rabbi-shrink. This is a warning: Stress may kill. Literally. (The bodily version thereof.) And it surely kills effectiveness!

Antidote? That's up to you. A few deep-breathing breaks, or two-minute-eyes-closed meditative stints, can be invaluable during the course of the day. So, too, a *long* holiday—and the occasional+ four-day weekend. Such breaks are essential, and you probably need some active coaching-intervention to pull them off.

OVERLOAD EXPRESS
[20]In any organization, there are always 100 Big Things that need doing. But in my experience as an observer, the leaders who flounder are those who to try do them all at once.

I call this ... SIO: Strategic Initiative Overload. It invariably confuses and pisses off everyone in an organization.

ORDER OF BATTLE
[21]When James Schlesinger was preparing to become U.S. Secretary of Defense under Jimmy Carter, he got some shrewd advice from Col. Richard Hallock: "You must understand that if you want to leave a legacy it is vital for you to make a quick decision about what you want that legacy to be ... because after several months you become so caught up in the business of the Pentagon ... so overwhelmed ... that it will be too late. Pick a few projects and put the full weight of your office behind them. Guide the projects. Nurture them. Know from the very beginning that they will be your legacy. Force them through the bureaucracy."

One more thing: The tougher the circumstances, when breaks are "impossible", the more you need a break! Mr.Bush says that he has relied more, since 9/11, on his daily workouts. That makes sense to me. For crippled FDR, it was regular time with his stamp collection.

Message I: *Zombies are rotten leaders!*[22]

Message II: *Zombies are the very last to realize that they are ... Zombies!*

Message III: *It's up to you to ensure that those workaholics in your stable take breaks—at gunpoint if necessary.*

Do a friend a favor: Drag her/him out of the office ... at the end of yet another 16-hour-day.

46. Leaders Express Their Passion.

In their book *The Leader's Voice*, my colleagues Boyd Clarke and Ron Crossland argue that: *"Vision is a love affair with an idea."*

"Vision" is not something created by a ... *committee.*

"Vision" is not something generated by ... *analysis.*

"Vision" is not the byproduct of a ... *consultant's report.*

"Vision" *is* about ... wild, passionate, intemperate ... *LOVE.*

When I started writing about leadership, I created a PowerPoint slide that surprised me. I said leadership was ... "all about love."

Love as defined by Tom P.: *Passion. Appetite for life. Engagement. Commitment. Great causes and the determination to make a difference. Shared adventures. Bizarre failures. Growth. Insatiable appetite for change.*

I took a real shine to Tracy Kidder's 1981 book, *The Soul of a New Machine*, the saga of building a very risky—and eventually very successful—mini-computer at Data General. I particularly recall the process the project leaders went through to "sign up" team members.(*"Sign-up"*—their term.) Remember, these were the days when taking risks was unusual. But DG's pirate-leaders asked the best-and-the-brightest to eschew the mainstream company project and "sign up" ... join them in a low-odds ... Quest to Change the World.

47. Leaders Are the Brand.

Brand is a "character issue." Hence "branding" is ... personal. A Pure Leadership Issue. The leader—Welch at GE, Goizueta at Coca-Cola, Gates at Microsoft, Jobs at Apple, Branson at Virgin Group—is the brand.

While a dozen dozen programs may *support* the brand, it is the moment-to-moment

---

TAKE TIME—OR DO TIME

[22]People who rise to the top of an enterprise generally have more energy than the rest of us. But not as much energy as they think. When I see CEOs carted off to court in handcuffs before national TV, I wonder a little whether they might have averted that fate ... *if* they had taken a few more weeks' vacation.

"*LEADERS* need to be the Rock of Gibraltar on Rollerblades!"

actions of Nike's Knight or Oracle's Ellison or America's Bush that define the brand for a host of publics.

Fact: There is *no* "minutiae" for leaders. Whether you are that 24-year-old, fresh-caught Project Team Leader ... or POTUS ... all of the people who work "for" you are Inveterate Readers of Tea Leaves. (YOUR ... Tea Leaves.)

That is, they are looking (metaphorically, at least) at the way you spend your time, for instance.

The way you spend your time: a ... BIG ... "for instance." The way you spend your time ... in detail ... Illustrates *Exactly* What You Care About.

Manage yourself! (*Truly!*) Watch yourself! (*Truly!*) You will live ... or die ... as Leader ... by the degree to which ... Your Calendar ... *Precisely and Minutely* ... Reflects Your Brand Priorities.

Summary:

1. You = Your Calendar.
2. You = The Brand.
3. The Brand = Your Calendar.
4. Q.E.D.

POSTSCRIPT: TOWARD A LEGACY

48. Leaders Know When to Leave.

There's a time to come. And ... a time to go.

People who are great at "roiling the waters and stirring up change" are, typically, woefully inept at "keeping the damn thing afloat" once it's been launched within "the system."

None of us, it turns out, are "men [or women!] for all seasons." We are men and women for a *particular* season ... that is, at our best for a short period of time.

Think about it.

49. Leaders ...

In an earlier (and considerably different) version of this list that I wrote for *Fast Company* magazine, I asked readers to submit their definitions of "leadership." Of the 287 replies I received, a great many were at least as "on point" as my own preliminary observations. Here are my favorites:

"Hire smart. Go bonkers. Have grace. Make mistakes. Love technology. Start all over again."

"Leadership is the process of engaging people in Creating a Legacy of Excellence."

"Leaders are living individuals whom employees can smell, feel, touch their presence."

"Leaders love their work. That passion is infectious."
"Leaders have a kid alive in them."

"'It's only business, not personal': IT ALWAYS IS PERSONAL."

"Leaders love their work. That passion is infectious."

"Leaders have a kid alive in them."

"Leaders ooze integrity." [This one came up at least two dozen times amongst the 287 responses. And this was before Enron, WorldCom, Adelphia, et al.]

"Leaders are never afraid to walk away from [bad] business."

"Leaders communicate relentlessly."

"Leaders select their battles carefully."

"Real leaders don't always get their way."

"Leaders care."

"Leaders serve."

And my favorite ...

"Leaders Need to be the Rock of Gibraltar on Rollerblades."

50. Leaders Do Stuff That Matters.

Sometimes I think that all "leadership literature" stinks—including much of the stuff I've written. Too much of the focus is on tactics and motivation (and, frankly, manipulation). All of that misses the point: *Leadership for what?* From King and Gandhi and Jefferson ... to Bill Gates and Steve Jobs and Richard Branson ... leaders lead because they want to get Some Particular Thing ... done. They want to ... Do Stuff That Matters.[23]

Steve Jobs aimed to change the world ... with an "Insanely Great" (his term) idea about what a computer could be. Staying with the tech industry, you could say the same about Michael Dell. So, too, Larry Ellison (Oracle). Or, in the world of financial services, you could point to Charles Schwab and Ned Johnson (Fidelity).

Those and other Great Leaders are not (merely) great at "leading." They are great at inducing others to take novel journeys to ... Places of Surpassing Importance.[24]

PROUD RICHARD
[23]"I never, ever thought of myself as a businessman," says Branson. "I was interested in creating things I would be proud of."
(Also see Chapter 12.)
It doesn't get any better than that!

(JET) SET IN STONE
[24]New York Jets Head Coach Herman Edwards, after his team unexpectedly made the NFL playoffs in 2002. "I picked up one of those [NewYork] Jets books and I told them, 'What you do as a football team is your legacy. When you're 80 years old, what you've done will be in this book and no one can take that away from you. Your kids, your grand kids after that, they will know what you did. It's about leaving your name in stone.'"

! Contrasts

WAS		IS
"Changing" people	–	Charging people up
Command and control	–	Creation of "context"
Think big thoughts	–	Do bold deeds
Plan, plan, plan	–	Play, play, play
Serenely aloof	–	Stubbornly angry
Purity	–	Paradox
"I don't care" ("... what you think")	–	"I don't know" ("... all the answers")
"Transforming" people	–	Transferring opportunity
Doing it all	–	Delegating
Smoke & mirrors (leadership as mystique)	–	Nuts & bolts (leadership as mastery)
The "plan clan"	–	The "action faction"
Worrying about one's image	–	Working one's imagination
Pure logic	–	Prosaic logistics
"Correcting" people	–	Connecting people
Leader as "wise man" (forget women)	–	Leader as "whys man" (or "woman"!)
Presiding	–	Pushing
Leading for ... the long haul	–	Leading with ... a long shot
Making a "killing"	–	Making a mark

NEW BUSINESS ❗ ● NEW MANDATE

DREAM AS IF YOU'LL LIVE FOREVER. LIVE AS IF YOU'LL DIE TODAY.

—JAMES DEAN

NEW BUSINESS **!** NEW MANDATE

Index

Acknowledgments

This 2009 edition of *Re-imagine!* was created by:
Editor Philip Morgan
Designer Edward Kinsey

The 2003 edition of *Re-imagine!* was created by:
Project Editor Nicky Munro
Editors Corinne Asghar, May Corfield, Antonia Cunningham, Jude Garlick, Cathy Rubinstein
Managing Art Editor Karen Self
Designers Sarah Cowley, Michael Duffy, Jackie Plant
Indexer Janet Shuter
Proofreader Amy Corzine

PERMISSIONS Grateful acknowledgment is made to the following:
The Assoicated Press: Excerpts from "Forever Young," by Colleen Long. Reprinted with permission of The Associated Press.

The Economist: Excerpts from "Over 60 and Overlooked" © The Economist Newspapers Limited, London, 10 August 2002.

The New York Times Co.: Excerpts from "One Woman's Account of Two Hotel Experiences," by Joe Sharkey, copyright © 2002 by The New York Times Co. Reprinted with permission.

The New York Times Co.: Excerpts from "Sometimes, Second Place for Homework," by Hubert B. Herring, copyright © 2002 by The New York Times Co. Reprinted with permission.

Robert Reich: Excerpts from *I'll Be Short: Essentials for a Decent Working Society*, by Robert Reich. Copyright ©2002 by Robert B. Reich. Reprinted by permission of the author and Beacon Press, Boston.

Rodale Inc.: Synonyms for 'experience' reprinted from *THE SYNONYM FINDER* © 1978 by Rodale, Inc. Permission granted by Rodale, Inc., Emmaus, PA 18098. Available wherever books are sold, or visit www.rodalestore.com or call the Publisher at (800) 848-4735.

Thanks also to Stewart Clifford at www.enterprisemedia.com for providing the video tapes.

Author's Acknowledgments

If you've been involved in a project like this, you well know there's no such thing as a "small" contribution. The most "minor" contribution is life or death for the outcome. Hence, at one level, everyone, including the "author," deserves exactly equal billing. No more. No less.

Nonetheless, I shall acknowledge differences in contribution. First and foremost, Erik and Mike. Erik Hansen is "project manager" for all this. It's the sixth book we've worked on together. In short, if Erik quit project managing, I'd quit writing. For those not of our (strange) world, you've no inkling of the thousands upon (literally) thousands of balls that must be juggled with vigor and aplomb. Erik is the best there is.

Mike Slind is labeled "editor." Try silent (except to me) co-author. His awesome authorial and editorial talent shines from every paragraph and page of this book. Not since my collaboration with Bob Waterman on *In Search of Excellence* have I had such a true partnership with a wordsmith and ideasmith.

Stephanie Jackson is Erik's counterpart at Dorling Kindersley. I'm used to standoff-ish publishers. Not Steph. Her passion for this book—and incredible follow through—also shines from every page.

Susan. The dedication is to my wife Susan Sargent. An artist and businesswoman, she essentially demanded that I re-form my message in an energetic way. As I despaired of ever doing another "big book," she insisted that I seek out Dorling Kindersley, a one-of-a-kind publisher. In the seminal meeting with Marjorie Scardino, CEO of DK's owner, Pearson, it was effectively Susan who made "the pitch," not me.

DK has turned out to be a marvelous partner. In addition to Marjorie and Stephanie, let me single out Publisher Chris Davis. Chris believed from the start, and pushed us to keep pushing until we'd done something grand. (We hope we have.)

PeterLuff is uber-design-guru at DK. And since DK is design ... well you get the picture. We have been blessed to have Peter's clear attention to every aspect of what's contained herein. Peter has worked with project editor Nicky Munro, editor Jude Garlick, and the day-to-day maestro of this book's design, Jason Godfrey of Godfrey Design. Like Mike Slind, Jason got "in the zone" and did much more than design around our words; his energetic approach brought to life the spirit and character of this book.

On our "print team," Cathy Mosca gets special billing. She's been quarterback of literally a dozen drafts of a 1,000 page manuscript, Mistress of facts, and, mostly, queen of "no detail is too small to be sweated." I sleep at night because Cathy doesn't! Cathy has hardly been alone; the grueling task of fact checking, the apex of my concerns, has been brilliantly and assiduously handled by Sue Bencuya, Tara Calishain, and Martha Condry. There was a "once upon a time," about 15 months ago, when all this started. I initially dictated about 37 tapes— and Connie Procaccini, Je'Nise Goss, Susan Wegzyn, Roszi Moser, and the late Kevin Clarke at Mulberry Studio turned my hems and haws into a first (rough!) draft.

Susan and I and Marjorie Scardino and Penguin publisher John Makinson hit it off from the start. But then came the time to translate our lofty aspirations into business reality. Namely: Esther Time! Esther Newberg has been my agent for almost 20 years. Ha! I have been her author for 20 years is more like it. She has guided me through every kind of swamp and thicket with care and firmness. Assisting her this time around was John DeLaney, my favorite lawyer.

My "book stuff" comes from my "speaking stuff." And my speaking stuff comes courtesy of my matchless partners at the Washington Speakers Bureau. Founders Harry (Rhoads) and Bernie (Swain) revolutionized an industry—and gave me an incredible opportunity to Jabber-around-the-Globe. Harry's probably my best pal (certainly the most empathetic) and his longtime partners—among them Georgene Savickas, Tony D'Amelio, Bob Thomas, Michael Menchel, Shayna Stillman, Bob Parsons, Christine Farrell, Theresa Brown—are All-Star members of Team Tom. (No jaw-jaw, no book-book.)

Coordinating my life in the midst of a year of book creation is not exactly a walk in the park. If you don't believe me, just ask Shelley. Shelley Dolley is my Life Manager. She's performed a million "admin" tasks—and as the most literary of our team she's added a host of editorial suggestions as well. With classic Downeast (Maine) softness: "That's awful." In the midst of our travails Shelley had the temerity to produce Baby Ava. I'm not entirely sure of Ava's contribution to the book, but I am sure this will be Ava's first formal book acknowledgment! Virtual Shelley is ably assisted by Abbey Bishop in Vermont; and my frenetic to-ing and fro-ing is in turn made plausible by travel agent and life coach Jen Kruger and Washington Speakers Bureau Event Coordinator Andrea Chlebek. Not to mention John Stauss, big boss of the amazing-stupendous Four Seasons hotel in London, which became de facto home as the book neared completion.

Also thanks to Charlie Macomber, able and dedicated business partner for my part of Tom Peters Company; Gary Gras, who helps me in Vermont with every task known to humankind; Boyd Clarke, CEO of Tom Peters Company; and Geoff Thatcher who oversees, among other things, our extremely important Web activities.

Two more special mentions. Julie Anixter is Official Muse. Now with the branding company LAGA, she is more an embodiment of me than I am most of the time. Her passion for these ideas is boundless—and often makes me feel I'm not as nuts as I sometimes think. I've been blessed with four or five stupendous mentors in the last 40 years. None more important than Warren Bennis. I'll make this short: He's a wise and caring person who took my quest seriously when others didn't. To say more would be superfluous.

And two truly special mentions. My stepsons Max Cooper and Ben Cooper. Age 22 and 18 respectively, they are the enormously talented free spirits who define tomorrow for me—and influence me far more than they imagine.

My silent partners are the many practitioners of my craft whose work I rely upon. E.g.: Faith Popcorn, Marti Barletta, Sally Helgesen, and Judy Rosener ... whose writing and research on Women's Issues has influenced my thinking so forcefully.

A special nod also to Donna and Ken. Donna Carpenter and Ken Silvia were my "book partners" from 1993 to 1999. They nudged me out of my clunky print comfort zone into a world now culminated by my DK alliance.

Last, but hardly least, honors go to Rosie, Wally, and Hummer. Writing is a nasty business. One eventually alienates all one's friends. Enter the Terrific Trio—the Collie and two Aussies who shared my writing room for a year. Their world view can cure almost any ill and unblock almost any writer's block.

And ... one more time. Thanks, Susan.

London 4 July 2003

Tom Peters

Tom Peters has been called the "father of the post-modern corporation" by the *Los Angeles Times*. "In no small part," according to the *New Yorker*, "what American corporations have become is what Peters has encouraged them to be." *Fortune* adds, "We live in a Tom Peters world."

Peters arrived on the public scene with the 1982 publication of *In Search of Excellence*, co-authored with Bob Waterman, which topped bestseller lists for over two years. As 2000 approached, National Public Radio tagged *Search* as one of the "top three business books of the century;" a 2002 Bloomsbury poll ranked it as the "greatest business book of all time."

Peters followed Search with *A Passion for Excellence* (1985, with Nancy Austin); *Thriving on Chaos* (1987); *Liberation Management* (1992, acclaimed in one poll as the "management book of the decade" for the 90s); *The Tom Peters Seminar* (1993); *The Pursuit of Wow* (1994); *The Circle of Innovation* (1997); *The Project50* (1999); *The Brand You50* (1999); and *The Professional Service Firm50* (1999). Two recent biographies of Peters have also appeared: *Corporate Man to Corporate Skunk: The Tom Peters Phenomenon*, by Stuart Crainer; and *Tom Peters: The Best-selling Prophet of the Management Revolution*, by Robert Heller.

In addition to writing, Peters presents about 80 seminars a year and serves as Chairman of Tom Peters Company. His background includes two engineering degrees, two business degrees and various honorary degrees; four years on active duty in the U.S. Navy (including tours in Vietnam); a stint on the White House staff working on drug abuse issues; and seven years at McKinsey & Co., where he became a partner.

Tom and his family live on a farm in Vermont. He can be reached at: tom@tompeters.com.